International Management

As the economies of many countries become more interrelated, international managers are facing huge challenges and unique opportunities associated with their roles. Now in its fifth edition, Sweeney and McFarlin's *International Management* embodies a balanced and integrated approach to the subject, emphasizing the strategic opportunities available to firms on a global playing field, as well as exploring the challenges of managing an international workforce.

Integrating theory and practice across all chapter topics, this book helps students to learn, grasp, and apply the underlying principles of successful international management:

- Understanding the broad context of international business, including the critical trends impacting international management, the legal and political forces driving international business, and the ethical and cultural dilemmas that can arise
- Mastering the essential elements of effective interaction in the international arena, from cross-cultural understanding and communication to cross-border negotiation
- Recognizing and taking advantage of strategic opportunities, such as entering and operating in foreign markets
- Building and leading effective international teams, including personal and behavioral motivation, as well as taking an international perspective on the hiring, training, and development of employees

These principles are emphasized in the text with current examples and practical applications, establishing a foundation for students to apply their understanding in the current global business environment. With a companion website featuring an instructor's manual, powerpoint slides, and a testbank, *International Management* is a superb resource for instructors and students of international management.

Paul D. Sweeney is a Professor of Management and Associate Dean at the University of Dayton, USA. He is also a member of the Academy of Management (International & Organizational Behavior Division).

Dean B. McFarlin is the Dean of the Palumbo-Donahue School of Business at Duquesne University, USA. He also serves as an Associate Editor for *Academy of Management Perspectives* and is a member of the editorial board for *Journal of Management*.

D1225849

International Management

Strategic Opportunities and Cultural Challenges

Fifth Edition

Paul D. Sweeney and
Dean B. McFarlin

Routledge
Taylor & Francis Group

NEW YORK AND LONDON

Fifth edition published 2015
by Routledge
711 Third Avenue, New York, NY 10017

and by Routledge
2 Park Square, Milton Park, Abingdon, Oxon OX14 4RN

*Routledge is an imprint of the Taylor & Francis Group,
an informa business*

© 2015 Taylor & Francis

Fourth edition published 2011 by Routledge

Library of Congress Cataloging-in-Publication Data

McFarlin, Dean B., author.
International management : strategic opportunities and cultural
    challenges. — Fifth edition / Paul D. Sweeney & Dean B. McFarlin.
        pages cm
    Includes bibliographical references and index.
    1. International business enterprises—Management. I. Sweeney,
Paul D., 1955– author. II. Title.
    HD62.4.M395 2015
    658′.049—dc23

ISBN: 978-0-415-82527-6 (hbk)
ISBN: 978-0-415-82528-3 (pbk)
ISBN: 978-0-203-40649-6 (ebk)

Typeset in Sabon
by Apex CoVantage, LLC
Printed and bound by CPI Group (UK) Ltd, Croydon, CR0 4YY

To three Hohmans that I adore—Emma, Farrell, and Mary

Paul D. Sweeney

To Laurie, Andrew, Elizabeth and Nathaniel . . . no one could ask for a better family!

Dean B. McFarlin

Contents

3 Doing Things Right: International Ethics and Social Responsibility — 85

8   Taking Stock: Developing International Strategy   305

9   Jumping In: Foreign Market Entry and Ownership Options   347

Preface

The field of international management continues to evolve rapidly. The "half-life" of principles, problems, and proscriptions about how to manage globally is getting shorter and shorter by the year. But, this also makes the field lively and, as the Chinese say, "may we all live in interesting times." Yet for authors like us, it is a big challenge to stay on top of the field. Of course, our problems pale in comparison to those who are actually doing international management. We can only imagine how difficult it must be for them to operate effectively when the ground is always shifting under their feet. As a result, as educators, we admire the skills of international managers and hope that bringing together their collective responses to these challenges in our book will help benefit current and future global leaders.

Indeed, the fifth edition is designed to help students grasp the complexities of international management. Our revised chapters emphasize adaptability and flexibility more than ever given the current environment, a theme that we weave throughout the book. Because the field is both relatively new and subject to rapid change, there are no precise sets of topics that must be covered in an international management text. Consequently, this offers a lot of flexibility in both our choice of topics and how we treat them. To make this latest edition even more accessible, we have retained most topics from the previous edition, but have streamlined our coverage. In doing so, we have worked to update each chapter with newer and more pointed examples of both challenges and opportunities in the field of international management.

Strategic Opportunities and Cultural Challenges

The fifth edition will continue to balance our two themes of strategic opportunities for firms and the challenges of managing an international workforce against the backdrop of rapidly evolving global markets. Clearly, the economies of many countries are becoming more interrelated and integrated. This presents huge challenges and unique opportunities that underscore the importance of our balanced approach. There are some very good textbooks that strongly emphasize a strategic orientation to international management whereas others emphasize a people-oriented focus, primarily centering on employee behavior.

Our view, however, is that *both* should add to the effective practice of international management. For that reason, in every chapter we discuss state-of-the-art practices made by companies and managers as well as offer advice from experts in the field. This guidance includes an emphasis on flexibility and adaptability—attributes critical for today's volatile international markets. Managers need to think creatively but also analytically about potential international opportunities, weighing firm strengths and weaknesses as well as possible competitive threats in the process. Ultimately, that process should culminate in the formation of strategies and tactics designed to take advantage of those opportunities while side-stepping threats. But actually capitalizing on them is another matter entirely—that is where skills such as executing and implementing come into play. That takes time, and these days events can overtake a well-laid plan in a heartbeat (or a Tweet). As a result, managers need to stay alert and nimble so they can alter course quickly in the face of change.

The best-laid plans or strategy will not work if they are not implemented correctly. This is where the human side of the international management equation comes into play. Many plans derail because they fail to include and anticipate people-related complexities and complications. Indeed, in the international environment cultural challenges probably trip up companies just as much as misguided business strategies do—and can trump even the best-laid plans. Either way, it is fair to say that strategy development *and* cross-cultural management skills are both critically important. Ideally, they should be inter-related. Possible cross-cultural challenges should inform strategy creation. Strategic needs should help shape management approaches and human resource policies around the world. Neither is more important than the other. We will continue to present this balanced perspective in a lively fashion. Generally speaking, we will take an applications-oriented approach that is solidly grounded in the latest research. We will briefly describe this approach next with reference to specific elements of each chapter

Overview of the Fifth Edition

International Management has been revised and updated in the fifth edition in order to reflect the latest trends and changes in the field of international management. In doing so, we combine theory and practice across chapter topics with plenty of current examples.

To underscore the principles, we include a number of features that highlight important themes while providing students and instructors alike accessible ways to put those principles into practice:

Combining Theory and Practice: Integrative and Chapter-Specific Cases This edition offers both integrative cases and chapter-specific cases in one volume for the convenience of instructors and students. The fifth edition includes four of the most highly rated integrative cases from some of the best providers available (e.g., Harvard Business School). Three of these cases are popular carryovers from the fourth edition with one new case that focuses on bribery issues in an international joint venture.

These integrative cases are placed at the end of the appropriate set of chapters. As was true in previous editions, these integrative cases are placed where they coordinate with topics across several chapters.

In addition, each chapter includes a new feature, *Global Innovations*, which directly aligns with the content of that chapter. These features focus on unique or controversial approaches being used by firms and/or managers to tackle chapter-specific international management issues. Some professors have reported that they and students like having both shorter, chapter-specific cases in addition to longer, integrative cases for each section. This is an effort to be responsive to those needs. Overall, each case in the fifth edition will reflect contemporary international management concerns and provide comprehensive background information for analysis. Cases are selected or written by us to provide an overview of management challenges faced by organizations of all sizes in a cross-section of industries.

Opening and Closing Chapter Challenges We have kept the well-received "bookend" feature from previous editions. The opening (*International Challenge*) and closing (*Up to the Challenge?*) chapter vignettes remain in this new edition. These short vignettes kick off each chapter by framing issues written specifically for that chapter's content, posing direct questions and enabling students to have meaningful analysis and discussion of important chapter concepts. Many of these vignettes have been replaced or updated for this edition.

International Insights The popular boxed section feature within each chapter carries over to this edition. These are brief stories focused on companies or leaders of those firms and some of the challenges and opportunities faced in various parts of the world. We updated and streamlined this material, eliminating some and adding new ones in the process. Our goal in doing so was to better integrate these interesting examples of international management in practice with relevant material in the main text. Overall, this helps improve the flow and readability of the main text while still capturing the best of what this boxed section feature has to offer.

Updated with Quality Sources As suggested already, each chapter has been updated to ensure relevancy and timeliness. We have updated each chapter with new research and thinking about international management issues, and new illustrations and examples are provided in each chapter as well. This does not mean that we have abandoned perennial issues in international management—pernicious ones that seem to remain a challenge, whether it is 1975 or 2015. We continue to discuss such issues in nearly every chapter (e.g., communication problems, culture and perception, leadership style across cultures, stages of international firm development, to name just a few).

Our chapters rely on the most recent and most prestigious publications available. All of the chapters were updated with the latest articles from *The Wall Street Journal*, *The Economist*, the *Financial Times*, and the *Harvard Business Review*, among other sources. Consequently, we will capture some of the most contemporary thinking about issues and opportunities in international management. Likewise, the fifth edition continues to include many updated references to top academic journals such as the *Journal of International Business Studies*, *Academy of Management Journal*, and *Strategic Management Journal*, among others.

Two Experiential End-of-Chapter Features As we have done in earlier editions, we present two hands-on exercises at the end of each chapter and sketch out projects that students can complete outside of class on chapter topics. *From Theory to International Practice* focuses on application-oriented projects that require students to conduct research and/or other outside-of-class work about a variety of chapter-relevant issues. Students are sometimes asked to analyze mini-cases, assess international competitive issues, or evaluate how specific companies are dealing with particular international management issues (e.g., how do you get an export license?). We provide students with suggested resources for research and direction to help them get started. The other experiential feature carrying over from the fourth edition, *International Development*, has been tweaked and improved. You will see that it asks students to focus on an activity designed to enhance their skills in areas that are important for success in international management roles. These include assessing where a student stands on key international dimensions.

Concise, Engaging, and Action-Oriented Presentation Finally, the fifth edition is shorter than the previous edition, yet written in a style that does not skimp on content. We believe this concise yet engaging approach will connect with both students and faculty alike. Our audiences have regularly provided feedback that they want a "get to the point" approach in a package that focuses on key issues in depth without getting bogged down in too much minutiae. This edition better meets this need and permits instructors to augment the course with their favorite cases or readings. Moreover, international management is ultimately about *application* and figuring out what works. Consequently, each chapter will have plenty of examples and illustrations from corporations around the world. We also include concrete guidelines and action recommendations in most every chapter. We aim to make students as excited about international management as we are—whether we are describing a piece of research or pitching action "takeaways."

We believe that all these experiential features make for more interesting reading and better learning of this important material. Ultimately, we hope this approach can help students translate the learning into more effective action when they "get out there" in the international management arena.

Intended Audience

Students with limited exposure to international issues will appreciate the basic foundations and concepts that are laid out in each chapter. Students with some international coursework or work experience, however, will be attracted by the book's scope and concise, to-the-point coverage of critical issues. From a pedagogical perspective, the book will work well as a primary text in a course on international management. It can also be used to cover the management side of an introductory international business course.

The strong focus on applications, with a variety of applications-oriented features, appeals to both students and instructors who wish to take a concise, hands-on approach to the study of international management.

Organizing the Challenge of International Management

The fifth edition focuses on the four underlying principles of effective international management that have been used in earlier editions.

First, managers need to understand the broad context of international business. Specifically, that includes critical trends impacting international management, the legal and political forces driving international business, and the ethical and cultural dilemmas that can pop up when business crosses borders.

Second, managers need to master the essential elements of effective interaction in the global arena. That means understanding how different cultures perceive and process information, developing skills in cross-cultural communication, and figuring out how to negotiate successful cross-border deals.

Third, effective international management requires the ability to recognize and take advantage of strategic opportunities. That often means deciding how best to enter foreign markets and then figuring out how to operate successfully once there.

And finally, international managers must motivate and lead people from a variety of cultures and be able to build effective international teams. It also means taking an international perspective on the hiring, training, and development of employees—if for no other reason than the rules of the game on factors such as compensation and labor relations are very different when borders are crossed.

Preview of Chapters

To emphasize these four principles, this edition will include plenty of contemporary examples, an active writing style and approach, and a heavy dose of the theory-to-practice approach detailed above.

Chapters 1–3 cover the essential foundations for successful international management. *Chapter 1* discusses the basics of international competition, trends impacting international management, and developments in countries and regions around the world. We wrote this chapter last to ensure these trends and developments are as fresh as possible for the reader. Next, *Chapter 2* focuses on legal and political issues that managers need to take into account in their international operations. We discuss the different legal and political systems that exist around the world and their effects on international business. The chapter also tackles various types of political risk that managers may face in foreign markets and what they can do about them. Much of international business is set within the legal context of trade and transactions and is why we include this chapter here. *Chapter 3* examines ethical values and corporate social responsibility in an international environment. We consider in detail current and enduring ethical issues such as bribery, human rights abuses and successes and how global firms have risen to the social responsibility challenge. We conclude this first major section with a new integrative Harvard case that cuts across this chapter content.

The second part of the book includes Chapters 4–6. The effect of culture on interpersonal interactions is a strong theme throughout this section. *Chapter 4* begins this section by examining culture in more detail. There has been a lot of thinking about how culture operates, and we present several basic cultural dimensions and their implications for managing people around the world. *Chapter 5* shows how these culture dimensions can affect employees' perceptions of their work environment, their jobs, and the people around them. We also explain how to manage perception problems—such as stereotyping—in a culturally diverse business environment. *Chapter 6* shows how cultural differences can impede communication and offers advice for improving verbal, nonverbal, and written communication in an international environment. Again, we conclude with an integrative case in international management that addresses the core themes of the section.

The third part of the book includes Chapters 7–9 and addresses the broad strategic and operational decisions faced by international managers. *Chapter 7* examines how to manage international conflicts and conduct successful cross-border business negotiations. Clearly, effective negotiation requires outstanding preparation and an appreciation of how strategies vary across cultures. *Chapter 8* focuses on defining and developing international business strategy. First, we distinguish among common international strategies and explain when they might be pursued. This includes detailed coverage of the process involved in developing winning international strategies. We conclude by discussing how companies need to ensure that their internal systems are aligned to support their international strategy to increase chances of success. In *Chapter 9*, we take things a step further by considering implementation issues that companies face in executing their international strategies. We present the various options available for entering foreign markets, including the pros and cons of each. In essence, each option can work under the right conditions, whether exporting, licensing, or foreign acquisitions, just to name a few possibilities. Finally, a third integrative Harvard case that was well received in the previous edition is included at the end of this section—one that addresses whether and under what conditions a firm should step into international markets for the first time.

The final part of the book includes Chapters 10–13 and focuses squarely on the people side of the international management equation. Mishandling people-related issues can jeopardize even the best strategy, if not the best intentions, of management. *Chapter 10* tackles the challenge of how best to motivate and lead employees across cultures. We show that cultural values can affect how employees behave and that managers may have to alter their style accordingly. *Chapter 11* explains how managers can build an effective international workforce. That process starts by taking a strategic approach to international human resource management—one that aligns human resource needs with the firm's international business strategy. Next, we discuss the staffing options available to firms for their foreign operations (e.g., hire locals or send expatriates?) and methods for developing their international talent. We conclude with a presentation of strategies that firms can use to help expatriates succeed through appropriate selection mechanisms, training practices, and support systems. *Chapter 12* continues this theme by discussing how to ensure the effectiveness of a firm's international workforce. That means figuring out how to best appraise performance and design compensation systems that work for employees around the world. This can be complex, but tools are available to help. *Chapter 13* is the last chapter of the book and examines some of the most vexing "people problems" facing international managers. In particular, we discuss how managers can develop effective international teams, especially in an environment of increasing diversity. We also suggest ways to strategically manage union issues and labor relations around the world. These are no small challenges since the scope, purpose, and historical roles of unions vary dramatically across countries. A fourth Harvard case concludes this last section—one that deals with the often vexing challenges facing expatriates posted abroad.

Supplementary Materials

Accompanying this book is a set of supplements:

- *Instructor's Resource Manual with Test Items* includes chapter outlines, plenty of supplementary lecture materials, including a set of *Reality Checks* (interviews with practicing international managers), comments on special text features, teaching notes for the cases, and recommended videos.
- *PowerPoint Presentations* for each chapter that outline chapter material and present key chapter exhibits as well as some supplementary material. Some website supplements are imbedded within the PowerPoint slides.
- *Test Bank* offers both multiple-choice and essay questions for every chapter.
- *Sample Syllabi* and related materials will help new instructors get up and running with their courses and which provide experienced instructors a way to organize their treatment of material in this book as well as gauge their presentation of material with others
- *Student-centered activities* on the book's website that will provide forums for student discussions, additional exercises, links to various websites of interest to international managers, and a discussion board for hosting debates and information exchanges about the issues raised in the text (and act as a repository for all the above resources as well).

Acknowledgements

Behind every successful book project is a set of professionals who provide the support, guidance, and advice so vital to making everything click. We are extremely grateful for the outstanding reviewers who contributed their time, energy, and academic expertise toward the development of this project across several editions including: Lawrence A. Beer, Arizona State University; Kristinia Bourne, University of Wisconsin–Eau Claire; Charles Byles, Virginia Commonwealth University; John E. Call, New Mexico State University; Mason A. Carpenter, University of Wisconsin–Madison; Norma Carr-Ruffino, San Francisco State University; Xiao-Ping Chen, University of Washington; Amon Chizema, Loughborough University; Simon Collinson, Warwick Business School; Arthur Cyr, Carthage College; Mark Fenton, University of Wisconsin–Stout; Joseph Fontana, George Mason University; Bob Goddard, Appalachian State University; Farhad Hossain, The University of Manchester; Donald Hsu, Dominican College; Selim Ilter, St John Fisher College; Robert Isaak, Pace University; Daniel James, University of Northern Colorado; Dong I. Jung, San Diego State University; Marios Katsioloudes, West Chester University of Pennsylvania; Lauryn McManus, University of Central Florida; Amy McMillan, Louisiana Tech University; Jeanne McNett, Assumption College; Marin A. Marinov, University of Gloucestershire; Mark Mendenhall, University of Tennessee; Behnam Nakhai, Millersville University of Pennsylvania; Lynn Neeley, Northern Illinois University; John O'Del, Rhode Island College; John P. Orr, Webster University; Tara Radin, Hofstra University; Roy W. Reeber, Hawaii Pacific University; Kathleen Rehbein, Marquette University; Daniel James Rowley, University of Northern Colorado; Deepak Sethi, University of Texas at Dallas; Arnold Sherman, University of Montana; John Stanbury, Frostburg State University; Richard Steers, University of Oregon; Barb Stuart, University of Denver; and Kara Swanson, Boise State University.

Likewise, we owe an enormous debt of gratitude to our editor, John Szilagyi, and his staff at Routledge. John has recently retired and we will greatly miss him—he is a true professional and we have gained many new insights about the publishing business from him over the years and across several projects. We wish him all the best in his retirement. We also wish to thank a very patient Lauren Athmer of LEAP Publishing, Inc., for her talent at using a variety of "motivational" techniques to move us/drag us along in the writing and editing process. As a result, we have a greater understanding of the challenges of procrastination faced by students than we did before!

Paul D. Sweeney
Dean B. McFarlin

part I

on a global stage

the context of international management

chapter 1

on a global stage

the world of international management

Learning Objectives

After reading this chapter, you should be able to:

- describe today's competitive environment in international business;
- identify major trends, both positive and negative, in international business;
- describe how managers can respond to international business challenges;
- identify key foundation concepts in international management.

International Challenge

New Balance: Still Running with Production in the United States

Athletic shoes are everywhere, as are brand names such as Nike. The industry's largest firms have all of their shoes made in low-wage locations such as China, Vietnam, and Indonesia, usually in factories owned and run by foreign subcontractors. Started in 1906 by an immigrant from England, New Balance Athletic Shoe, Inc., is a major player in the athletic shoe industry worldwide. New Balance also has foreign subcontractors. Stroll down the aisle of a subcontractor's plant in China and you will see young women performing repetitive sewing tasks to produce New Balance shoes and earning very little, at least by American and European standards.

Of course, the idea is that by reaping big labor savings companies can earn much higher profits. Plus, some argue that developed economies are better off when low-skill, low-wage jobs can migrate to countries where labor is cheap and plentiful. But New Balance really is different. Unlike its main competitors, New Balance has 1,300 employees making 7 million pairs of shoes annually in its five U.S. factories. A few years ago, New Balance opened a new state-of-the-art research facility at its Lawrence, Massachusetts, manufacturing site to develop innovations and new products. Overall, New Balance makes about 25 percent of its shoes sold in America at its U.S. factories.

But what is interesting is that, the enormous gap in labor costs notwithstanding, the difference in *total* costs between the Chinese and American plants is not that great. In China, the total cost of producing a pair of shoes is about $3 less than in the U.S., only around 4 percent of the price for the average shoe. And that 4 percent is manageable, especially since American production means New Balance can fill orders and change styles more quickly than its competitors in the U.S.

New Balance narrows the costs of producing in the United States enough to compete effectively by being extraordinarily efficient. Its American employees produce a shoe from scratch in less than 25 minutes compared to three hours in China. So, what accounts for the American plants' productivity and efficiency? And what role does management play in all of this? As you read through this introductory chapter, you will notice that change is a constant theme in international management. Adapting to change often means coming up with new paradigms, even if they go against what passes for conventional wisdom. After you have read the chapter, take a look at our closing Up to the Challenge? feature for an overview of New Balance's approach.[1]

International Business: A World of Constant Change

Even if you're on the right track, you'll get run over if you just sit there.
—Will Rogers, American social commentator and humorist

Will Rogers' words are from the early twentieth century. Yet, his observation perfectly captures the challenge of international business in the twenty-first century. Indeed, Rogers' words underscore that today's international managers must be nimble, innovative, and adaptable. They must bridge cultural boundaries and cope with extraordinary global competition that changes and evolves at a pace that is faster than ever. Competitors can pop up quickly from anywhere, including emerging countries (such as China or India), while new technologies appear overnight.[2]

Other factors that contribute to this "new normal" of international business include global trends toward increased outsourcing of components, flexible manufacturing, and greater reliance on logistics systems that can deliver parts as needed (i.e., on a "just-in-time" basis).[3] These trends have helped China and other emerging nations with cost advantages, such as labor and materials, attract investment, develop home-grown technologies, and build competitiveness. Of course, astounding innovations in information technologies have made it possible for firms to manage inventories, interact with employees, collect customer data, and track shipments around the world 24 hours a day, seven days a week.

The ubiquitous availability of information technology also allows companies to scour the planet for the best talent at the best price. Wireless technologies, along with clever local partnerships, are allowing companies to reach hundreds of millions of new customers in poor economic areas of India and Africa with cell phone and other wireless services, despite the weak technological infrastructures within those locations. Overall, technology enables companies to stitch together far-flung outposts as well as reach new customers, both of which will help grow international business over the long haul.[4]

Globalization and the World Trade Organization

In essence, technology facilitates the interconnections between national economies. This ongoing connecting process, known as globalization, has increased international growth, particularly in emerging economies. In the past 20 years, the value of international trade has surged over 400 percent to more than $18 trillion annually. As tariffs and trade barriers slowly fade, the growth in international business should continue. Indeed, just a 1 percent reduction in the cost of international trade could boost income globally by $40 billion.[5]

Of course, plenty of concerns remain in the meantime. For instance, consider the World Trade Organization (WTO). This governing body is made up of 159 member countries (as of 2014), and sets the global rules for trade. Determining those rules typically requires protracted negotiations, the latest series of which is known as the Doha Round (begun in 2001 and still used today). The WTO also has elaborate mechanisms to enforce its rulings on trade disputes between members. A key goal for the WTO is to reduce barriers and stimulate trade worldwide.[6]

The WTO, however, is also a battleground for national interests and a lightning rod for criticism about globalization. For example, in responding to the charge that globalization destroys jobs and increases the gap between rich and poor, the WTO argues that freer trade promotes job creation and wealth building over the long haul. Naturally, the WTO's critics are unlikely to be persuaded. Regardless, what is not in dispute is that the trade issues the WTO wrestles with are very complex. For instance, a single dispute between the United States and the European Union (EU) over banana tariffs (a government-imposed tax on imports) took several years to resolve. Of course, the WTO is not the only body that governs international trade. The growth of regional and bilateral free trade agreements in recent years has been enormous. While these agreements have many advantages and are generally positive, they also can make managing broader economic issues more difficult and complex, especially as new powerhouses such as Brazil, China, and India continue to flex their economic muscle.[7]

Our Plan for This Chapter

Trade agreements and the WTO notwithstanding, international managers should expect downturns and setbacks to occur, sometimes in the blink of an eye. Overall, grappling with the speed of change and the increasing complexity of international business makes the role of management—and the stakes—more important than ever. If you are wondering how international business leaders view the threats and challenges facing them, look at Figure 1.1. It summarizes the threat perceptions of roughly 1,400 international CEOs. As you can see, international executives have plenty of things to worry about.[8]

Yet, all companies face challenges and there are many good reasons to be fundamentally optimistic about the long-term prospects for international business. Consequently, the goal of this chapter is to give you a sense of the trends, opportunities, and challenges facing international managers today. It is also important to sketch out how firms approach international competition as well as provide a snapshot of the major players in the global economy. The chapter begins by describing how international business has grown in recent years, as well as profiling the countries and regions playing important roles in that growth.

Threat Issue	Overall Rank	% Mentioning
Over-regulation	1st	18%
Increased international competition	2nd	17%
Currency fluctuations	3rd	15%
Price deflation	4th	11%
Loss of critical talent	5th	11%
Global terrorism	6th	10%
Risk to reputation (i.e., anything that might hurt the firm's image or reputation)	7th	10%
Cost of capital	8th	8%
Emerging technologies	9th	6%
Corporate governance issues	10th	5%

Figure 1.1 What Keeps Them Up at Night: International CEOs List Their Top Ten Threats.
Source: Adapted from Champion, M. (2004). CEOs' worst nightmares. *The Wall Street Journal,* January 21, A13. Note that the total percentage exceeds 100 since CEOs could mention multiple threats.

Globalization and the Growth of International Business

Today, many companies look for ideas, workers, materials, and customers everywhere. Tough competitors can appear from anywhere. As one European manager put it, "The scope of every manager is the world." Needless to say, managing that way is not easy. Among other things, it requires worldwide information networks, a supportive corporate culture, and the ability to tap into local needs and initiatives when they exist. For instance, Electrolux, the Sweden-based appliance maker, routinely rotates hundreds of appliance designers through the eight design centers it has scattered around the world. The idea is to expose people to different ways of thinking and the often divergent appliance needs people have in different parts of the world. By doing so, Electrolux hopes to speed up product development and be more innovative—something it must do to thrive in the face of tough competition from America's Whirlpool and China's Haier brands. But there is no single answer. For some companies, just letting local managers pursue their own ideas is a big step forward.[9]

The Hottest Areas for Growth and Investment

So, where is all the growth in international business occurring? One way to measure things is by the flow of foreign direct investment (FDI) into a particular country over several years. More than just capital, FDI also means that managerial knowledge and technical know-how is flowing into a country from outside its borders. As such, FDI is a good measure of a country's prospects on the international business stage, either as

Country	FDI Inflow (in $ billions)	
	2010	**2012**
U.S.	198	168
China	114	121
Hong Kong	83	75
Brazil	49	65
United Kingdom	51	64
Australia	36	57
Singapore	54	57
Russia	43	52
Canada	29	46
Spain	40	28
India	21	26
France	34	25
Sweden	6	14
Mexico	21	13
Turkey	9	13
Developed Countries	696	561
Developing Countries	637	704
Total World FDI	1400	1300

Figure 1.2 Top Foreign Direct Investment Magnets in 2010 and 2012.

Source: Adapted from United Nations Conference on Trade Development (2013). *World Investment Report: FDI Flows by Region and Economy: 2007–2012*, available from: http://unctad.org/en/PublicationsLibrary/wir2013_en.pdf (retrieved November 20, 2013).

an established market or an emerging one. Figure 1.2 lists the top FDI magnets in 2010 and 2012.

The total worldwide inflow of FDI was roughly $1.3 trillion in 2012, with 52 percent of that total being invested in developing countries—the first time developed countries as a group saw less investment. As you can see from Figure 1.2, the U.S. was the single biggest recipient of FDI in 2012 among developed countries. Yet, China and Hong Kong (combined) raked in $191 billion in 2012 to lead the pack among developing countries. On a percentage basis, Africa was the region with the biggest recent increases in FDI inflows. Overall, experts predict FDI inflows worldwide will grow in the years ahead, perhaps reaching as high as $2.0 trillion by 2017. Interestingly, developing countries are also investors that, collectively, represent an increasing share of where FDI comes from. What are now commonly referred to as the BRICS countries (Brazil, Russia, India, China, and South Africa) collectively accounted for 10 percent of the total FDI outflow in 2012. Indeed, China alone was the third largest investor country in the world in 2012 after the U.S. and Japan. Clearly, China is an emerging economic power—one that both attracts significant FDI and has increasing clout as an investor nation.[10]

In essence, much of the growth in international business continues to occur *outside* the traditional economic powerhouses such as the U.S., Germany, and Japan. For instance,

China's economy has expanded by a factor of ten over the past 30 years. Granted, the U.S. may not be growing fast, but it remains the biggest economy in the world. At $16.2 trillion worth of gross domestic product, the U.S. eclipses second-place China's $9 trillion. Yet, statistics underscore that trade among the U.S., Japan, and the EU is becoming less important over time while trade with developing nations and trade within regions is growing. For instance, U.S. trade with Japan shrank after passage of the North American Free Trade Agreement (NAFTA), with regional partners Mexico and Canada making up the difference.[11]

Clearly, the total value of economic activity in a country, or gross domestic product (GDP), has generally been growing at a much faster rate in developing rather than developed nations. Consumer demand in developing markets is rising as citizens become more affluent and have more disposable income. Consequently, many American, European, and Japanese firms consider developing countries as markets where they can reach out to populations eager for new products and services as their income rises. Indeed, companies everywhere are increasingly creating products squarely aimed at developing markets, where incomes, albeit rising, are still lower than those in the developed world. This helps explain why Indian firms have designed $23 stoves and $70 battery-powered refrigerators for their local market. Foreign giants such as General Electric are taking notice, creating cheap, innovative products for developing markets.[12]

While we tend to think of large firms when international trade comes to mind, do not forget about small companies. Starting in 1995, firms with fewer than 500 employees accounted for a bigger share of total manufactured exports than large firms for the first time. Exports by small U.S. businesses have grown every year since that time, many facilitated by government agencies such as the Office of U.S. Trade Representative and the Small Business Administration. In 2010 small U.S. businesses exported nearly $270 billion, up nearly 70 percent since 1995. Overall, small businesses now account for *98 percent* of known U.S. exporting companies (although they account for a smaller percent, 31 percent, of the overall value of U.S. goods exports). Even small start-up companies are in the mix, often thanks to the Internet—technology that puts customers and outsourced help (e.g., for marketing, customer support) in easy reach.[13]

A Snapshot of Regional Trends

This section offers brief snapshots of important trends in specific countries and regions. Special attention is paid to key developed nations as well as to their developing brethren.

The Americas

United States

Steady, if unspectacular, economic growth seems to be the watchword for the U.S. in the near term. In 2014, while low interest rates continued and energy production soared, corporate investment generally remained weak, as did job and income growth. Throw in government gridlock and China inching closer to seize the mantle of the world's

Top Five Trading Partners*		Top Five Deficit Countries		Top Five Surplus Countries	
2013	1998	2013	1998	2013	1998
Canada (617)	Canada (329)	China (–315)	Japan (–64)	Hong Kong (+32)	Netherlands (+12)
China (536)	Japan (180)	Japan (–76)	China (–57)	Australia (+22)	Australia (+7)
Mexico (494)	Mexico (174)	Mexico (–61)	Germany (–23)	UAE (+20)	Belgium (+6)
Japan (216)	China (85)	Germany (–60)	Canada (–21)	Netherlands (+19)	Brazil (+5)
Germany (157)	Germany (77)	Saudi Arabia (–38)	Mexico (–16)	Belgium (+12)	S. Arabia (+4)

Figure 1.3 A 15-Year Snapshot of America's Trade: Goods Deficits and Surpluses with Top Five Partners.
* Value of imports + exports; all values in $ billions.
Source: Adapted from www.census.gov/indicator/www/ustrade.html.

biggest economy and it is easy to see why many Americans are concerned about the future going forward. In particular, some feel angst about the increasing presence of Chinese companies buying American businesses (for example, Lenovo's purchase of IBM's personal computing unit) or investing in commercial property (such as a restaurant complex in Toledo, Ohio).[14]

Others point to the trade deficits that the U.S. has been running for many years. For instance, thanks to stronger exports, the U.S. trade deficit in 2013 was just over $470 billion—a sizeable drop from the $535 billion deficit in 2012. Of course, these are still large gaps regardless, with the U.S. continuing to import more goods from other nations than it exports. China is one of the U.S.'s top trading partners and accounts for a large chunk of annual U.S. trade deficits. That said, the United States does have trade surpluses with a variety of countries. Figure 1.3 lists countries producing the top five deficits and top five surpluses with the United States in recent years.[15]

But the United States remains a huge target for foreign investment and, over the past 20 years, has accounted for roughly a third of global economic growth. While some of its advantages are eroding, the U.S. still leads in knowledge creation, innovation, entrepreneurship, higher education, and information technology. In essence, the United States has the most creative economic environment in the world.[16]

Today, prominent American multinational corporations enjoy considerable success worldwide. For instance, consumer products giant Colgate operates in over 200 countries, with foreign sales accounting for 75 percent of the firm's revenues. In 2012, 132 of the 500 largest companies in the world were American. Yet, back in 2002, over 185 of the biggest firms were U.S.-based. Figure 1.4 presents the world's ten largest companies in both 2002 and 2012. Even in this abbreviated list, it is clear that large energy companies are more dominant now than they were in 2002. Moreover, Sinopec, a Chinese energy firm, was not listed in 2002, but was among the top ten largest companies in 2012. This underscores the rapid growth of multinational corporations from developing countries over the past 15 to 20 years. In 1997, there was only one firm from a developing

2012 Rank/Firm	2012 Revenues ($ billions)	Home Country	Industry	2002 Rank/Firm	2002 Revenues ($ billions)	Home Country	Industry
1. Royal Dutch/ Shell	485.5	Nether-lands	Energy	1. Wal-Mart	240.53	U.S.	Retail
2. Exxon Mobil	452.9	U.S.	Energy	2. GM	186.76	U.S.	Auto
3. Wal-Mart	446.9	U.S.	Retail	3. Exxon Mobil	182.47	U.S.	Energy
4. BP	386.5	Britain	Energy	4. Royal Dutch/ Shell	179.43	Nether-lands	Energy
5. Sinopec	375.2	China	Energy	5. BP	178.72	Britain	Energy
6. China National Petroleum	352.3	China	Energy	6. Ford	163.87	U.S.	Auto
7. State Grid	259.1	China	Energy	7. Daimler-Chrysler	141.42	Germany	Auto
8. Chevron	245.6	U.S.	Energy	8. Toyota	131.75	Japan	Auto
9. Conoco Phillips	237.3	U.S.	Energy	9. GE	131.69	U.S.	Diversified
10. Toyota	235.4	Japan	Auto	10. Mitsubishi	109.39	Japan	Trading-diversified

Figure 1.4 World's Largest Companies by Revenue: Comparing the Top Ten in 2012 and 2002. *Source:* Adapted from *Fortune*. (2003). Global 500: The world's largest corporations. *Fortune*, July 21, 106; and http://money.cnn.com/magazines/fortune/global500/2012/full_list/index.html.

nation large enough to be among the 500 largest companies in the world. In 2012, however, China alone had 73 companies on the top 500 list.[17] NAFTA has dramatically increased trade and investment among the three signatory countries by gradually eliminating tariffs, import quotas, and barriers to foreign ownership.[18]

Canada

America's northern neighbor emerged from the 2008–2009 financial crisis in reasonably good shape, though it will likely trail U.S. growth rates over the near term. Canada has low corporate tax rates at the federal level that promote business investment and it embraces cultural diversity. Yet, it remains joined at the hip to the U.S., with roughly 75 percent of Canadian goods exported to American customers. Indeed, Canada's relationship with the U.S. is fraught with awkward comparisons. Canada and the United States are each other's largest trading partner. But Canada's smaller economy (less than 10 percent the size of the U.S.'s) is much more dependent on foreign trade. Canada frets about keeping up with its giant neighbor, at least in certain respects. Put simply, Canadians are taxed more and paid less than their American neighbors. Nevertheless, Canada's situation is enviable, both as a place to live and a place to invest.[19]

Mexico

Predating NAFTA was the maquiladora sector. Established by the government, maquiladoras are foreign factories that can import parts and materials into Mexico duty free, as long as they are used to make products for export. Most maquiladoras are in Mexico's northern states, adjacent to the primary destination for their exports—the United States. NAFTA's implementation was a huge boost to the maquiladora sector. In less than ten years, maquiladoras created some 800,000 new jobs as foreign companies, including American household names such as Ford and General Motors, came in to set up shop. Today, while Mexico still faces significant challenges, including crime and corruption, it also has a large and open economy where nearly 70 percent of the national GDP comes from international trade.[20]

Like Canada, Mexico is inextricably tied to its American neighbor. Indeed, Mexico sends 90 percent of its exports to the U.S. Because wages have been rising in China, labor cost differences between Mexico and Asia's manufacturing powerhouse are now minimal. Combine that with cheaper and faster access to American customers and it is no wonder that having Mexico as an export platform is more compelling than ever for foreign companies such as Honda. Mexico also has some impressive multinationals in its own right, including Grupo Bimbo, a Mexican food company that recently bought part of U.S.-based Sara Lee and is planning to invest some $1 billion north of the border in the next few years.[21]

South America

Experts now estimate that 30–50 percent of the population of this important region is now middle class with significant disposable income. Regardless of the precise definition of "middle class," the current situation represents a dramatic improvement from 10 to 15 years ago and is largely the result of faster economic growth in the region. The causes of that growth are multifaceted to say the least, but include a variety of economic and educational reforms that most expect will continue. Granted, the pace of reforms is likely to be uneven. Generally speaking, countries enacting the most significant reforms, such as Chile, have done better than countries that made fewer changes, such as Ecuador. The region has also been prone to instability because of its dependence on foreign capital. In short, capital can move in or out of the region quickly, depending on the whims of foreign investors and external events. Plus, poverty, corruption, and business infrastructure issues remain regionwide concerns.[22]

Argentina, Chile, and Brazil are the region's three largest economies. Brazil and Chile have arguably been the most successful in recent years. For instance, American and Indian information technology firms poured into Chile to take advantage of outstanding computer engineers, low wages, and a modern business infrastructure. Of course, with over 200 million people and a $2.3 trillion GDP, Brazil is by far the biggest economy in South America, and the eighth largest in the world (as of 2012). Brazil has some positives going for it, including better fiscal policies, demand for commodities and other exports, and growing offshore oil revenues. Winning the summer 2016 Olympics was also a coup for Brazil, providing impetus to improve the infrastructure, tackle persistently high crime, and reduce poverty in Rio de Janeiro. Overall, there is reason to be cautiously optimistic about the long-term future for South America. Many South American countries are looking beyond the region for trading partners. For instance, over 40 percent of Mercosur (a trading block including Argentina, Brazil, Paraguay, and Uruguay) exports go to the European Union and the U.S.[23]

The Asia–Pacific Region

Excluding Japan, the Asia-Pacific region is the world's fastest growing with a rising share of global GDP. For instance, growth was expected to average 5.7 percent for 2014, with 15 of 17 countries in the region predicted to exceed the world average. Generally speaking, the developing economies in Asia have been the most dynamic and fastest growing in the world for some time—expanding over 7 percent annually in the past 10 to 15 years, a rate more than twice that of the rest of the globe. That said, while Asian countries have some similarities, they also have many differences. Countries that have structural problems such as high government debt, weak corporate governance, and poor legal protections, and are also highly dependent on key overseas markets tend to be most vulnerable to economic shocks.[24]

China

Over the past 30 years, China's ascendance has been astounding, with billions of foreign direct investment pouring in annually. For much of this period, foreign firms coveted China's cheap labor and low costs while salivating at the prospect of serving over a billion increasingly affluent consumers. Yet, the bloom may be off the proverbial rose for foreign multinationals. Chinese labor costs have risen dramatically, top talent is tough to find, and the government is trying to steer the nation toward developing more sophisticated products while it encourages more local innovation. These and other factors are making it harder for foreign firms to do business, much less make money, in China. For instance, home-grown Chinese firms are now formidable global competitors in their own right, increasing the pressure on foreign firms (e.g., Alibaba in e-commerce, Huawei in smartphones and Haier in appliances). Moreover, foreign companies that approach China as one big market are likely in for trouble. China is a huge and diverse nation with a variety of regional differences, tastes, and languages (some 400 million Chinese speak a language other than Mandarin). As General Electric's CEO Jeffrey Immelt simply put it, "China is big, but it is hard."[25]

Indeed, there are the formidable obstacles that China puts in front of foreign businesses, including a weak legal system and opaque government policies. China also effectively limits foreign competition in strategic industries, a list that includes financial services and telecommunications. Business in China is also guided by *guanxi* (relationships or connections built on mutual dispensing of favors) as much as by rules and laws. This can mean a long courtship for foreigners who want to "get down to business" quickly—perhaps six to twelve months of relationship building, if not more, to build personal trust and friendships before business issues can be addressed in depth.[26]

Overall, China's competitive intensity is extremely high. Competitors are legion and the pace of business activity is frenetic. In 2000, there were over 360,000 foreign firms in China. In less than ten years, the number had soared to more than 660,000. No other country has experienced this kind of corporate influx in such a short period. Plus, millions of small, privately owned firms offer plenty of formidable competition in China. When we visited China, a manager at a U.S. consumer products firm said besides competing against other world-class multinationals such as Unilever, the company faced thousands of local competitors (mostly small, family-run enterprises) just in Shanghai alone![27]

India

Inevitably compared to China, India has a $4.7 trillion economy and a population of 1.2 billion. But within a few decades, India's population is expected to eclipse China's. While India is getting ready, it is getting a late start compared to China, with much less foreign direct investment, a lower literacy rate, and a larger percentage of its population in poverty. But the gap with China is closing, especially in India's southern states. Indeed, more than 50 percent of the population in these states, where much of India's booming technology industry is based, should achieve middle-class status by 2025. Experts urge the Indian government to keep moving forward and to focus on reforms in key areas:

- Accelerate the sell-off of state-owned enterprises and remove restrictive barriers to foreign ownership of companies.
- Reform India's complex and restrictive labor laws.
- Deregulate various industries and continue reducing tariffs.
- Encourage private banking and relax currency restrictions.
- Keep improving the business infrastructure (e.g., roads, ports, sanitation, power).[28]

India's most significant impact on the global economic scene is probably in information technology (IT) services. In 1999, India's IT industry had roughly $4 billion in revenues—a figure that soared to nearly $60 billion over the next ten years. India is an excellent source of cheap, well-educated, English-speaking high-tech labor for U.S. firms. For instance, General Electric, IBM, Microsoft, and Intel are among the American companies with R&D facilities in India. Moreover, leading Indian IT firms such as Infosys, Tata Consultancy Services, and Wipro Technologies are now world-class competitors.[29]

Japan

With a 2012 GDP of nearly $4.7 trillion, Japan is among the top five economies in the world. Yet, Japan has endured years of weak growth. Recently, the government has taken more aggressive steps to enact structural reforms that would place the country on an upward track. That said, the failing value of the yen in recent years has boosted exports of the complex goods that many Japanese firms make efficiently at home (e.g., Japan's Hitachi Construction saw Chinese demand for its power shovels soar while Toyota enjoyed big profits on cars exported to the U.S.). Nevertheless, some critics say that Japanese firms still have too much expensive factory capacity at home for things like domestic car production when much cheaper labor can be had in places such as Vietnam. Other challenges for Japan include high government debt, weak support for entrepreneurship, and an inflexible labor force—especially compared with many developed countries. In part, problems with Japan's debt and its financial system reflect the government's efforts to simultaneously protect weak domestic industries (e.g., chemicals, financial services, retailing) and maintain a thriving export machine. Weak industries hurt the economy, driving up both the cost of living and the cost of doing business in Japan.[30]

It would be a mistake, however, to underestimate Japan. Indeed, Japanese companies are surprisingly dominant in some unexpected global markets not visible to most consumers. For instance, a number of strong, mid-size electronics firms (called *chuken kigyo*) have carved out leadership positions in important areas such as semiconductor substrate and capacitors for electronic devices. These successes play to traditional Japanese strengths, including strong cultural values of continuous improvement (*kaizen*) and making things (*monozukuri*). But other Japanese values, including distrust of foreigners, inhibit *chuken kigyo* from partnering with, and learning from, foreign companies. Overcoming this may become particularly important in the years ahead if Japan's dominant specialists in electronics want to stay ahead of foreign competitors. Overall, Japan is a formidable international competitor, its problems notwithstanding. As a nation, Japan has impressive strengths, including a highly educated workforce, many world-class firms, and excellent capabilities in technology.[31]

South Korea

A key player in the region with a $1.6 trillion economy, South Korea has a highly skilled workforce, an improved banking system, and a burgeoning information technology industry. It has incredible export strength in a variety of areas—and not just in cars (e.g., Hyundai) and electronics (e.g., LG, Samsung), but in heavy industries such as shipbuilding. South Korea faces plenty of challenges too, including an education system that is extremely rigid, foreign investment restrictions, government bureaucracy, a relatively inflexible labor market, and a need to continue reforming the chaebol (huge diversified conglomerates such as Samsung that still account for a big slice of the economy). Although transparency and accountability have improved, some problems remain in chaebol firms. On the positive side, the South Korean government has made it easier for foreigners to own pieces of the chaebol (e.g., roughly 50 percent of Samsung stock is owned by foreigners today), although critics charge that, too often, transgressions by the chaebol continue to be overlooked or treated lightly.[32]

This may reflect official concern that South Korea must protect firms in strategic sectors such as electronics and automobiles, especially because they provide jobs and help support thousands of vendors and suppliers. Others counter that South Korea would be better off in the long run if the chaebol sold off or shut down losing businesses. In fact, many chaebol have disappeared over the past several years, crushed by their mountains of debt. A good example is Daewoo, which made everything from fertilizers to cars around the world, before collapsing. Interestingly, South Koreans are more interested in entrepreneurship these days and willing to embrace greater risk than ever before. Indeed, the percentage of South Korean adults working in firms less than four years old is far higher than in other industrialized countries.[33]

Europe

Over the past 25 years, staggering political and economic changes have occurred in Europe, especially in Russia and its former satellites. Since the Berlin Wall fell in 1989, the people of the region have seen more change in a shorter period of time than just about anywhere else in the world.

The European Union

Today, the European Union (EU) has grown to a nearly $16 trillion economic colossus with 28 member countries (thanks, in part, to the EU's currency, the Euro). Where future expansion will come from is hard to predict. For instance, while Turkey's application for membership continues to be controversial, eastern EU members such as Poland advocate bringing in other eastern nations like Belarus, Moscow's objections notwithstanding. Figure 1.5 provides a snapshot of all EU nations.[34]

Yet, the EU is also facing stern tests about its future. With the exception of a few member countries (including Germany), unemployment, particularly among younger workers, is incredibly high. For instance, unemployment among younger workers is pushing 30 percent in Portugal and 50 percent in Spain. Indeed, a broader north–south divide has emerged, with deeply indebted members such as Greece and Italy clashing with creditor nations like Germany. Then there are conflicts between the 17 member countries that use the Euro, such as France, and those that do not, such as the United Kingdom. Indeed, economic growth has been uneven across the EU in recent years. Some members, such as Poland, have done well by embracing free markets and transforming their management talent to match. Others, such as Croatia, still have a long way to go.[35]

Nevertheless, the EU has come far from its roots in the 1950s as a regional economic partnership among six nations. Indeed, the EU as we know it today was launched in the early 1990s with the signing of the Maastricht Treaty. The treaty expanded the boundaries of monetary and economic integration and laid the foundation for the current EU model. Therein lies both the opportunity and the challenge for international companies. On one hand, manufacturing in the EU allows firms to move their products to any member country without duties or currency hassles—an attractive prospect, to say the least, and something that has prompted billions in foreign investment in recent years. A unified market, however, does not mean that Europe's diverse cultures have disappeared. So, companies doing business in Europe often need to be highly responsive to local preferences to do well, the EU notwithstanding.[36]

As Figure 1.5 suggests, many of the newer Eastern European members of the EU are considerably poorer than their Western counterparts in terms of per capita GDP (the numbers are adjusted for price differences across nations) and are more vulnerable to economic shocks (Poland being an exception). On the other hand, the EU's newer Eastern members generally have cheaper skilled labor and faster growing productivity than their Western EU counterparts. These factors suggest that the EU's newer members will continue to be an attractive target for foreign direct investment and, as a consequence, put pressure on the more established economies of the EU (e.g., Germany, France) to reform their more costly tax, welfare, and labor systems. Indeed, cost-cutting pressures in

Country	2012 GDP Per Capita (relative to EU average of 100; purchase power parity)	2012 GDP Per Capita in US $ (purchasing power parity)	2012 GDP Growth (% change over 2011)	Year Joined the EU	Using Euro, 2012?
All 28 EU members	100.0	$33,700	−0.4	—	some yes
All 17 EU members using the Euro	108.4	$36,530	−0.7	—	yes
Belgium	120	$38,500	−0.1	1958	yes
Bulgaria	47	$14,500	0.8	2007	no
Czech Republic	81	$27,600	−1.0	2004	no
Denmark	126	$38,300	−0.4	1973	no
Germany	123	$39,700	0.7	1958	yes
Estonia	71	$22,100	3.9	2004	no
Ireland	129	$42,600	0.2	1973	yes
Greece	75	$24,900	−6.4	1981	yes
Spain	96	$31,100	−1.6	1986	yes
France	109	$36,100	0.0	1958	yes
Croatia	62	$18,100	−2.0	2013	no
Italy	101	$30,600	−2.5	1958	yes
Cyprus	92	$27,500	−2.4	2004	yes
Latvia	64	$18,600	5.2	2004	yes
Lithuania	72	$22,000	3.7	2004	no
Luxembourg	263	$81,100	−0.2	1958	yes
Hungary	67	$20,000	−1.7	2004	no
Malta	86	$27,500	0.9	2004	yes
Netherlands	128	$42,900	−1.2	1958	yes
Austria	130	$43,100	0.9	1995	yes
Poland	67	$20,900	1.9	2004	no
Portugal	76	$23,800	−3.2	1986	yes
Romania	50	$13,000	0.7	2007	no
Slovenia	84	$28,700	−2.5	2004	yes
Slovakia	76	$24,600	1.8	2004	yes
Finland	115	$37,100	−1.0	1995	yes
Sweden	126	$41,900	−0.2	1995	no
United Kingdom	106	$37,500	0.3	1973	no

Figure 1.5 The European Union: 28 Countries and Counting.

Sources: Adapted from: Europa. *GDP Per Capita in PPS—GDP Per Capita in Purchasing Power Standards*, available from: epp.eurostat.ec.europa.eu/ (retrieved January 18, 2014); The Central Intelligence Agency. (2014). *The World Factbook*, available from: https://www.cia.gov/library/publications/the-world-factbook/index.html www.cia.gov/library/publications/the-world-factbook/ (retrieved January 18, 2014).

Western EU nations may lead companies there to another round of outsourcing to cheaper Eastern EU locations, or what one expert called "the China next door."[37]

Overall, the EU markets are less efficient and less flexible than America's for reasons including onerous taxes, red tape, and rigid labor laws. Such factors could limit the EU's GDP growth over time, everything else being equal. In fact, high labor costs and rigid employment rules are among the reasons that German engineering giant Siemens has been shifting jobs and production capacity from Germany to lower-cost locations such as Hungary, Brazil, and China. This underscores the fact that EU firms, especially those in Western Europe, have been looking outward for places to invest for some time.[38]

Russia

Turning back to the east, Russia's GDP was $2.5 trillion in 2012. With a population of over 140 million, Russia seems to punch below its weight as a market. Despite joining the WTO in 2012, the country has been weighed down in recent years by low levels of foreign investment, weak growth, capital flight, and its dependence on oil and gas mining for revenues. Critics blame the government for not doing more to curb corruption, strengthen the legal system, streamline regulations, and reform banking rules—all things that would make doing business in Russia easier. Yet, Russia is too large and has too many attractive assets (such as huge oil deposits, well-educated professionals, and higher disposal income than many developing countries) to ignore. This explains why companies such as U.S. chip maker Intel have been there for years—Intel has sunk $800 million into its Russian operations since 1999. The firm employs over 1,000 highly skilled, but inexpensive, Russian engineers who tackle complex problems for the company.[39]

Nevertheless, Russia faces other challenges. Infrastructure improvements are sorely needed and Russian firms must become more innovative. The country is plagued by bad roads, toxic waste dumps, inadequate electric power, and leaking gas pipelines. Finding the money, much less actually repairing and modernizing Russian infrastructure, will take years. Finally, as already noted, corruption is a persistent thorn in the side of Russia and its foreign investors. The following International Insights feature provides a closer look at corruption in Russia.[40]

International Insights

Russia: Corruption in the Wild, Wild East

When your own president describes the country's economy as "primitive" and beset with "systemic corruption," you know that there is a problem. Vladimir Putin, president of Russia, made similar public statements about corruption, noting at one point that in Russia, "anywhere you go, you have to go with a bribe." A Russian think tank estimated that corruption cost Russia 20 percent of its GDP and that 80 percent of Russian firms paid bribes averaging $130,000 annually.

The roots of this are deep, driven by an old psychology in which government officials see their role as protecting the state (and enriching themselves in some cases) instead of helping people. As one Russian business owner put it, "You go to the local administration to get permission for something and they send you to a private firm that will sort out the paperwork for you, which happens to be owned by their relatives." Many businesspeople in Russia often pay bribes just to be left alone rather than to get something done (what Russians refer to as the "bribe of survival").

What is the foreign business perspective on Russia, given the environment of corruption there? Clearly, many foreign multinationals are in Russia to stay—the corruption challenges notwithstanding. Moreover, multinationals tend to be less exposed to blackmail and extortion attempts from officials (other than occasional requirements to make "voluntary donations to the community," perhaps in the form of new police cars or fire trucks for the local government). Of course, that does not mean that multinationals do not get hassled. Motorola, for instance, once had a shipment of over 160,000 cell phones impounded when they arrived in Moscow. Government officials at different points alleged that the phones violated Russian patents, were counterfeit, and were "smuggled" into the country. In the end, Motorola got most of its phones back—except the 50,000 or so that may have ended up on the black market (government officials claimed the missing phones were "destroyed").

So, how should multinationals navigate Russia's murky and often corrupt waters? Here is some commonly offered advice:

- Avoid "strategic" industries (e.g., aerospace, oil, telecommunications) where foreign ownership is limited and partnerships with unsavory local firms may be required.
- Avoid "oligarchs"—rich, powerful businesspeople who amassed vast fortunes through dubious means and whose political fortunes can shift quickly.
- Focus on locations with the best local government reputations (e.g., St. Petersburg has attracted considerable foreign investment from U.S. multinationals such as Ford, thanks to local officials who cut red tape and offered tax incentives).
- Be prepared to pay bribes for small, routine tasks—such as getting parts through customs (one U.S. executive noted his company used customs brokers who "build bribes into the invoice").
- Be prepared for delays if your company refuses to pay bribes (one pharmaceutical firm noted building facilities in Russia took two to three additional years than it would elsewhere because of the company's refusal to pay bribes).

The good news in all of this is two-fold—many multinationals are sticking with Russia and senior Russian leaders seem to be talking about reining in corruption more than ever. But whether this translates into significant action that makes a difference remains to be seen. Experts argue that political competition, combined with independent media and courts, is what is needed to really make a major dent in Russian corruption. That may be a tall order indeed.[41]

The Middle East and Africa

The Middle East and Africa represent regions that come with plenty of risk, uncertainty, and unrealized potential.

The Shadows on the Middle East

Despite the region having many highly sought-after assets, including oil, political unrest casts a shadow on investment and economic growth in the Middle East. Civil war in Syria, ongoing Palestinian–Israeli discord, and political turmoil in Egypt are cause for great concern. Regional nervousness is a continuing boon for American (e.g., Raytheon) and British (e.g., BAE Systems PLC) defense contractors looking for business. Yet, when violence occurs in the region, nearby economies and their peoples often suffer. That includes Israel, a prosperous and stable nation in many ways—one with an open economy, impressive support for entrepreneurship, and technologically sophisticated companies. Economic hardship, however, is more pervasive in the Palestinian territories, which have many unemployed people, fewer assets, and must cope with Israeli restrictions. Economic hope, however, springs eternal. For example, a cell phone service operator, Wataniya Mobile, opened in the West Bank. Wataniya's majority owner, Qatar Telecommunications, announced that it would invest some $700 million and create thousands of new jobs in its new venture over the next decade.[42]

Overall, long-term prospects for regional GDP growth are hard to predict. The Middle East faces major hurdles to becoming an integrated economic power. Israel is the only country in the region to resemble a dynamic, modern economy—with a true middle class and some globally competitive companies. There are also some successes, such as greater foreign direct investments and more government encouragement of entrepreneurship, in places as diverse as Dubai, the United Arab Emirates, and Jordan. Outsourcing is on the rise in the Middle East, led by Indian firms such as Satyam Computer Services and Wipro. These companies are putting tech support and service centers in the region because of multilingual populations, growing local markets, cheap labor, and time zones that fall between the big economies in Asia, Europe, and North America. Nevertheless, countries in the region generally need to do more to spur foreign investment and create jobs.[43]

Africa Ascending

Much of sub-Saharan Africa has emerged from years of slow growth, high inflation, and untapped potential onto stronger footing. Indeed, some of the fastest growing economies in the world in 2014 were in Africa. The region ranked second in the world overall, placing behind Asia.

China, India, and several Middle Eastern nations have become big investors in Africa in the past decade. For instance, Chinese companies have built power plants, roads, and mining operations across Africa in recent years and continue to invest. All that said, many African countries are still beset with heavy government intervention in their economies, official corruption, tribal conflicts, and weak business infrastructures. Indeed, there are still horror stories in Africa, such as in Zimbabwe, which has suffered under President Robert Mugabe and can no longer feed itself. But there seems to be optimism across the continent, especially in sub-Saharan Africa. As one Nigerian investment manager put it, sub-Saharan Africa is "where China was 15 years ago."[44]

Speaking with one economic voice could help Africa obtain even more foreign direct investment and better access to overseas markets, especially for its quality textile and agricultural products. To improve regional cooperation and self-reliance, the presidents of several sub-Saharan countries have been working to create "sustainable economic development" across the continent by improving African infrastructure (roads, telecommunications, and air service), sharing resources, eliminating internal trade restrictions, and lobbying for easier access to developed markets.[45]

Of course, the star of the continent is South Africa. Its peaceful transformation from a racist, white minority government to an elected majority-rule democracy, led by Nelson Mandela, inspired the world in 1994. Today, challenges for South Africa include high unemployment (officially around 25 percent), persistent poverty, and insufficient electric power. In essence, South Africa is both a rich and a poor country, one with extreme income gaps. But as an emerging market, South Africa has much to admire, including excellent legal and financial systems, plenty of natural resources, a growing high-tech industry, and modern roads, ports, and telecommunications. In fact, foreign investment has been rising in South Africa since 1994. The world's car companies are a good example of that investment. BMW, Ford, GM, Toyota, and Volkswagen all operate in South Africa. They see South Africa as both an existing market and a jumping off point to the rest of Africa and beyond.[46]

Key Challenges Facing International Business

This discussion of regional trends underscores the fact that growth and prosperity are not guaranteed. Optimism has to be tempered by an awareness that a variety of factors, including political uncertainty, corruption, disputes over trade issues, tough new competitors, and fiscal mismanagement, just to name a few, can derail the best-laid plans very quickly and at any time.

Technological Sophistication and International Volatility

Advances in communications, information technology, and manufacturing processes have created new foreign markets and helped firms internationalize. Indeed, innovations in information technology have made innovating itself quicker and cheaper. Firms can put new pricing models, products, and services on their websites, quickly giving them detailed information about how customers react. Being able to respond quickly to customers' needs is a boon in highly competitive international markets. As a P&G executive put it, "we do the vast majority of our concept testing online, which has created truly substantial savings in money and time." So, instead of long, complex R&D processes, companies use technology to quickly run many small experiments constantly with immediate impact. Fortunately, the cost of installing a digital infrastructure is falling, making it easier for companies in poorer countries to catch up and tap technology to innovate more quickly. Of course, realizing the benefits of technology requires an educated population as well as affordable access. As you might expect, that is a tall order in some cases.[47]

Technological advances, however, do little to eliminate international business problems that are driven by cultural differences, political upheavals, corruption, and mismanagement. While technology can make life easier for international business in certain respects, it also can increase complexity in other areas and help accelerate how quickly new crises hit companies—challenges that management must grapple with. The key for international management is take advantage of technology while creating operational resilience and agility in the company to respond to rapid changes in the environment.[48]

Currency Volatility

Another challenging area of volatility for international management is currency fluctuation. National currencies can move up or down in ways that dramatically impact businesses—and often very quickly. For instance, the Euro plunged in value against the U.S. dollar from its introduction in 1999 to mid-2001, only to reverse course, rising 50 percent against the dollar through early 2004. Currency volatility can also escalate dramatically during economic downturns—for example, from mid-2008 to mid-2009, the dollar moved up or down against the Euro by at least 1 percent in a single day over 70 times, compared with just 16 times in the preceding year. And in late 2009, countries such as South Korea began buying dollars to slow its fall, fearful that their own exports would become too expensive too quickly as their own currencies rose.[49]

Volatile currency fluctuations underscore the impact of rapidly shifting business conditions as well as the use of technology by sophisticated investors. Virtually anywhere, anytime, an investor can electronically move in or out of international currency markets. Billions of dollars can flow in and out of a country in *minutes*, whether sparked by a real crisis or not. Plus, the sheer size of the currency markets (over $5.3 trillion is traded daily) makes stabilizing currencies difficult.[50]

Sudden currency updrafts can make a firm's exports more expensive overnight, increasing the pressure to reduce costs. For example, such was the case for Toyota in 2008 when the yen rose 19 percent against the dollar. When you consider that every 1 yen increase in value against the dollar meant a $450 million hit to operating profits, the point (and pain) is clear and so is the impact on the bottom line for currency anomalies like these. The reverse is true as well—falling currencies help exporters. For instance, by 2013 the situation had flipped for Toyota, with the yen down considerably against the dollar. As a result, Toyota was making an additional $1,500 on each car exported to the U.S. because of the currency swing. Likewise, the dollar's slide in recent years against the Euro made American companies exporting to Europe gleeful. Farm equipment giant Deere & Company was a good example—its exports surged, at least in part, owing to the weaker dollar.[51]

Overall, currency volatility clearly increases the risks inherent in international business. So, what can international firms do to combat wild currency fluctuations? Currency hedging is an option. Companies can buy currency options that fix exchange rates for a period of time. For instance, during periods when the U.S. dollar was falling, many large European firms bought hedges to protect dollar-based revenues earned in the United States. Indeed, both BMW and Volkswagen stepped up their currency hedging in 2012 because of worries about currency fluctuations, including in top markets such as the U.S. But hedging is basically pricey, complex guesswork. Imagine that a company wants to protect $500 million in earnings against a drop in the dollar against the Euro. If the dollar's value slipped 10 percent, then that $500 million would be worth only $450 million. But the cost of that protection could run a steep $26 million. Another way to minimize the risks associated with exchange rate swings is to use local suppliers and make more products in the places where you sell them. This is referred to as natural hedging. Honda, for instance, manufactures three out of every four cars that it sells in the United States in American factories, isolating U.S. sales against a rising yen. Some companies use both options. Dow Chemical, for example, uses financial hedges and scatters its production facilities around the world.[52]

Of course, currency volatility often hits small firms the hardest. While currency fluctuations may slice a sizeable chunk off a big multinational's earnings, it is often just a nibble in the overall scheme of things. Such firms typically have more experience with currency problems and thus have more options available for dealing with them than their smaller brethren. Consequently, more small firms are copying bigger firms by shopping for materials at cheaper locations, opening overseas operations in major markets, looking for foreign partners, and dabbling in currency hedging. Nevertheless, many of these steps are beyond the reach of small firms that want to sell abroad.[53]

While technology helps stitch national economies together, it also makes international business a volatile proposition. One way that firms try to minimize that volatility is by scattering facilities and suppliers across many countries. Granted, this is hardly foolproof—creating supply chain complexities and raising transportation costs in many cases. Moreover, such moves lead to another set of challenges, including managing people from diverse cultures. These workforce challenges are examined next.

International Workforce Challenges

Also driving the increasing complexity of international management is the need to have innovative and productive employees in order to compete. In essence, a global talent race is underway, one that has profound implications for companies, employees, and countries alike. Today, companies scour the globe to find the most talented employees at the most reasonable overall cost, with the jobs involved following the talent overseas.[54]

Offshoring, Reshoring, and Global Job Dispersion

This process of sending jobs overseas, sometimes referred to as offshoring, is not limited to big multinationals. Indeed, according to some American venture capital firms, up to 75 percent of the small companies that they invest in disperse jobs abroad. For instance, a number of small American software companies have offshored jobs such as customer support and software testing to places as diverse as Greece, India, and the Ukraine.[55]

This example also begs to question what kind of work firms offshore and why. Clearly, the reasons vary. The stereotype is that firms are merely chasing cheaper labor for back-office tasks (for example, the prototypical service center overseas fielding calls from disgruntled credit card holders). While cheaper labor is a motivation, especially for smaller companies with limited resources, it may not be the only or even the primary reason. Instead, education quality and location factors (e.g., political stability) may also be important. When firms are looking to innovate and create new products, labor savings may be a secondary motivation. Indeed, offshoring jobs for the purpose of innovation, product development, and other knowledge-generating activity has soared in recent years. When U.S. firms offshore such jobs, their main motivation is often that better employees, particularly in technical fields, can be found elsewhere. Because fewer Americans are earning degrees in technical fields and because the U.S. government restricts the number of foreigners who can be brought into the country, the local talent supply is limited. As a result, U.S. firms needing technical employees with science or engineering backgrounds may move those jobs overseas, especially if innovating in particular locations provides quicker access to foreign markets.[56]

This is not to say that potential labor savings from offshoring are trivial, but labor savings in places such as China and India are evaporating thanks to rapidly rising wages. Indeed, firms' expectations regarding labor cost savings can be unrealistic. Take call centers, for example, which are often located in low-wage locations with well-educated English-speakers. The Philippines is a top two call center location meeting these criteria. First, the costs of running call centers tend to be underestimated. Turnover is high and annual pay increases are often automatic, meaning that costs can rise quickly. In recent years, companies such as Delta Airlines and insurer AXA SA either closed call centers or turned them over to outside firms to run to save money.[57]

Likewise, some firms that offshored skilled manufacturing jobs or knowledge workers (such as software designers and programmers) have pulled back the jobs to their home countries, sometimes referred to as "reshoring." Their reasons included underestimated costs (thanks to rising wages overseas and transportation expenses), cultural challenges, and better quality and intellectual property control. For instance, companies as diverse as Google, Ford, GE, Apple, and Caterpillar have pulled manufacturing back to the U.S. in recent years. In particular, NCR pulled production for complex ATMs back to the U.S. after it realized company engineers were spending too much time flying around the world to fix production problems and design glitches.[58]

Successful offshoring starts with good management—including analyzing the costs and benefits, hiring the right people overseas, laying out expectations clearly, providing support to offshored employees, and effectively dealing with cultural differences. Without this, cost savings are unlikely regardless of the circumstances. For instance, one California-based security software firm found this out when it started offshoring software development to India. Its Indian software engineers did not understand how the firm's software was used (because they were not told) and, as a consequence, they left out features that customers wanted in new products. When customers balked, attempting to solve the problem quickly across a dozen time zones turned into an expensive nightmare that hurt relationships on both sides until things were turned around. Offshoring requires careful thought about what jobs should be sent abroad and how to establish effective foreign operations.[59]

Besides these management challenges, offshoring is controversial, particularly in the United States. Companies respond that offshoring is part of a worldwide competition for jobs and talent. Of course, the realities associated with offshoring are complex. For instance, some argue that thanks to foreign companies that come to the U.S., the number of imported jobs (which tend to be high paying, skilled jobs) far exceed the number of exported jobs (which are more likely to be lower paying). Others argue that offshoring allows American companies to save money, thereby allowing more high-skilled hiring at home as well as cheaper goods and services for customers. Yet, these arguments are likely to be cold comfort to American employees whose jobs have been lost to offshoring. For instance, American software application developers and database engineers are, as one executive put it, "competing with everyone else in the world who has a PC."[60]

Nevertheless, controversy is not likely to slow, much less reverse, offshoring. In fact, in certain parts of the world, offshoring continues to grow. The call center business in the Philippines is one such example, thanks to Filipinos' good English skills, an excellent communications infrastructure, cheap facilities, and low wage costs. Cincinnati's Convergys Corporation has 12 centers in the Philippines—the company's Filipino employees do sales-related work and perform debt collection calls. Convergys is hardly alone. India's Wipro Ltd recently opened a call center in the Philippines.[61]

Granted, many of these offshored jobs provide basic customer and service support functions. As we have already suggested, however, professional jobs, such as scientific research and pharmaceutical development, are increasingly moving to "centers of excellence" worldwide. In the meantime, developed nations should embrace the idea that workforces will more than likely continue to disperse around the world in the years ahead. In terms of high-tech innovation, product development, and manufacturing, American skills need to be upgraded to keep up. For example, over 20 years of offshoring have undercut the U.S.'s technology base as work shifted overseas—and increasingly, the skilled jobs that went with it.[62]

Workforce Quality and Competitiveness

The common bottom line for international firms everywhere is that they need employees who can handle increasingly complex work. The best workforce usually wins (and keeps) their jobs in the process. All of this raises a question: what makes for a highly qualified workforce? Education, on-the-job training, motivation, and computer literacy all matter. Having a sophisticated industrial base where new technologies can be developed, commercialized, and manufactured helps create and retain demand for technical workers and professionals.[63]

Plus, there is little doubt that workforce quality is an important factor for determining how competitive a country is—or at least how competitive a country's companies are in a particular industry. India's increasingly competitive IT service companies (including Infosys and Wipro) are a case in point and are increasingly a force to be reckoned with. Part of their success is due to India's well-educated, high-skilled, and experienced workforce of inexpensive IT professionals. Figure 1.6 ranks the world's 25 most competitive countries in 2013, 2009, and 2005. You will notice that India is not on the list. While there is little doubt that India's IT workforce is superb in many respects, the country as a whole still faces enormous challenges with respect to raising the incomes and educating a large swath of its population.[64]

Indeed, although they have many differences, a common thread among the top countries in Figure 1.6 is the *overall* quality of their workforces. But harbor no illusions about what can be done *anywhere* given good worker training and the right infrastructure. After touring several award-winning Mexican plants, one American union official put it this way: "The workers at those plants make a fraction of what American workers

Country	2013 Rank	2009 Rank	2005 Rank
U.S.	1	1	1
Switzerland	2	4	14
Hong Kong	3	2	6
Sweden	4	6	11
Singapore	5	3	2
Norway	6	11	17
Canada	7	8	3
UAE	8	*	*
Germany	9	13	21
Qatar	10	14	*
Taiwan	11	23	12
Denmark	12	5	7
Luxembourg	13	12	9
Netherlands	14	10	15
Malaysia	15	18	16
Australia	16	7	4
Ireland	17	19	10
U.K.	18	21	22
Israel	19	24	*
Finland	20	9	8
China (mainland)	21	20	24
Korea	22	28	30
Austria	23	16	13
Japan	24	17	23
New Zealand	25	15	18

Figure 1.6 Rankings of the World's 25 Most Competitive Countries over Three Timeframes.
* indicates not in top 25 rankings.

Source: Adapted from The International Institute for Management Development's (IMD) 2013, 2009 and 2005 *World Competitiveness Scoreboards,* available from: www.imd.ch/research/publications/wcy/index.cfm.

make, but there's no drop in quality. Most Third World countries are turning out world-class products."[65]

While the U.S. is at the top of the competitiveness heap at this point, there is reason for concern, particularly in certain industries. Experts suggest that the U.S. industrial infrastructure is challenged to produce sophisticated new products in some areas because the knowledge, skills, and people required have largely been lost (owing to offshoring, for example). Consider the Kindle e-reader. This innovative electronic reader was designed by Amazon in California but its parts are largely made in Asia (Taiwan, South Korea, and China) and it is assembled in China. Asian firms have the necessary skills to produce these parts thanks to their experience making flat-panel displays and other electronic components, an outgrowth of the migration of semi-conductor and consumer electronics production to Asia—where a large supplier network is now concentrated.[66]

Moreover, the U.S.'s ability to develop world-class products in some areas is eroding as sophisticated design work is increasingly done overseas. For instance, besides Apple, no American computer firm even designs laptops in the U.S. anymore. One response to this concern is that rising wealth, innovation, and workforce competitiveness in certain nations does not necessarily mean long-term declines in developed countries such as the U.S. Regardless, complacency is not likely to do the U.S., or other countries, much good when it comes to maintaining a top-notch workforce and a rising standard of living for citizens.[67]

Increasing Workforce Diversity

Workforce competitiveness aside, globalization is also bringing people from diverse cultures and backgrounds together. Many American and European companies aggressively recruit foreign immigrants, especially for jobs requiring specific technical skills. Demographic shifts within nations are having a similar impact. In the United States, for example, people of Hispanic descent will represent almost 25 percent of the population by 2050, up from 10 percent in 1995. At the same time, the share for non-Hispanic whites will drop to around 50 percent from over 70 percent in 1995.[68]

A diverse workforce can help firms better serve their increasingly diverse customer base. Targeting these and other groups in recruiting brings in employees who can help connect firms with important segments of their customer base. Indeed, P&G had greater success penetrating the Hispanic population in the United States after it set up a bilingual team of employees to do so. Today, according to one P&G executive, "Hispanics are a cornerstone of our growth in North America." So, companies cannot afford to let antiquated attitudes permeate the workforce. For instance, key corporate decisions are increasingly made in cross-functional groups that bring together people from diverse backgrounds. In fact, experts recommend introducing cultural diversity into decision-making groups and teams, putting a premium on managers' abilities to overcome the difficulties of making it all work. But few companies have created an atmosphere where diversity is taken seriously. In one survey, less than 10 percent of firms felt they did a very good job of supporting diversity.[69]

Managing in a Challenging International Environment

All of this raises a larger question about the impact of today's challenging international environment on management. Clearly, the goal of international management is to achieve the firm's international objectives by effectively procuring, distributing, and using company resources (e.g., people, capital, know-how, physical assets) across countries.[70]

So, what happens if management decides that China (for example) is a place to develop, manufacture, or sell a product? What then? How should managers *manage* in the environment they find themselves in? These questions defy easy answers. Just imagine all of the contextual challenges facing managers in firms that operate in dozens of countries. How do they find the best talent worldwide, much less deploy, train, and reward them properly? After all, business practices, laws, languages, cultural values, and market structures may all vary across countries, globalization notwithstanding. These factors can effect every aspect of management, including communication, motivation, compensation, employee development, business strategy, and ethics.[71]

Executives are feeling the pressure, especially those charged with running complex global empires. For instance, some two decades ago, P&G was already big, with $7 billion in sales, 50,000 employees, and facilities in 23 countries. But as of 2014, the firm was downright gargantuan, with over $84 billion in annual revenues, over 120,000 employees, and facilities in several dozen nations. As one executive put it, P&G today is "a much more diverse, much more culturally different, much more global company." Senior leaders worry about how to manage their vast operations when information and capital fly around the world in a heartbeat, economies bounce around rapidly, and customer preferences are fickle. Many want to improve communications and somehow knit together company outposts to be more responsive to, if not anticipate, changes in international business.[72]

Overall, this book will provide some guidelines for responding to these challenges. Today, successful international firms will be led by managers who:

- value ethnic diversity and have multicultural experience;
- embrace teamwork and information sharing;
- act globally where possible while fine-tuning things for local markets where necessary;
- look to local managers abroad for ideas and give them control;
- embrace and encourage adaptation to help the firm thrive in a world where change is constant and sometimes unpredictable;
- offer employees around the world an implicit contract where good work is rewarded with decent wages, continuous learning, and recognition.[73]

Embracing these ideas, however, may require new assumptions about how to run a business. For example, many managers still see their roles in control terms, with corporate headquarters making decisions for foreign subsidiaries. Unfortunately, this does not take full advantage of local expertise, nor permit a quick response to rapidly changing local conditions. In fact, international corporations with a rigid control mentality are fading from the scene. Wholly owned subsidiaries are giving way to networks of alliances between organizations. Managing companies this way, however, requires flexible managers who are willing to accept the ambiguity inherent in relationships not based on control.[74]

Basic Conceptual Foundations

Some of the points in this chapter rest on several management concepts. These are introduced now to help you with the rest of the book.

Defining Culture

Culture plays a big role in determining success or failure in international management, impacting how managers lead, hire, and compete in various countries. But what exactly is culture? We agree with international management expert Geert Hofstede, who defined culture as "the collective programming of the mind which distinguishes one group or category of people from another." This "programming" cannot be observed directly. Rather, it can only be inferred from behavior. Likewise, people are often unaware of the pervasive impact of culture on their own attitudes, beliefs, and behaviors.[75]

Culture is a concept that is only useful if it can accurately predict behavior. While cultural values can change dramatically when borders are crossed, this is not always the case. Furthermore, many distinct cultural groups can coexist within individual countries. On the other hand, knowing someone's national or group culture may reveal very little about them as individuals. Consequently, international managers must resist automatically seeing people as fitting into some kind of cultural stereotype. Despite these complexities, it is nevertheless important to understand country- or group-specific differences in cultural values that exist and to consider their potential implications for managerial behavior.[76]

International Corporations and Their Evolution

Firms tackle international business in many different ways. Some export products from a home base while others have sales facilities in foreign countries to handle their exported products. Other firms build or buy facilities abroad to manufacture products or deliver services. The various approaches to international business are discussed in later chapters, but for now, a basic understanding of how firms approach the international business arena might be very helpful.

In particular, you have already been reading about multinational enterprises—companies that operate in many overseas locations (referred to as *multinationals* throughout the rest of the book). Multinationals are large, well-developed international firms that operate facilities to produce products or deliver services in a variety of overseas locations and have considerable resources invested abroad. The number of multinationals in 1970 was around 7,000—since then, that number has soared by more than ten times. As of 2013, there were 1,000 multinationals with sales of $1 billion or more just in emerging market nations alone (e.g., from Mexico to South Africa to Indonesia). Many of the biggest "economies" in the world are actually gigantic multinationals such as Wal-Mart that have annual sales that surpass the total GDP of about 90 percent of the countries in the world. Moreover, the world's 1,000 biggest multinationals are responsible for about 80 percent of industrial production worldwide. Interestingly, multinationals, regardless of their nationality, tend to use management techniques more effectively than local firms. Indeed, an important role that multinationals play is the dissemination of best practices when it comes to management—something that their international experiences have helped shape.[77]

This does not mean, however, that multinationals all compete in some identical "global" fashion. As discussed later in this book, some multinationals (such as those in the semiconductor industry) compete in global industries where few, if any, location-specific preferences exist. Other multinationals, however, operate in industries where a high degree of local tailoring has to be done. Even within industries, multinationals may operate quite differently. This variation results from many factors, including culture, firm values, and the moves of competitors. For some multinationals, the home country is where the head-quarters resides and where decisions about firm culture, policies, and practices are made. In others, local operations have more freedom to make their own decisions. Such multi-nationals tend to be more diverse internally in terms of both culture and structure. Business practices, technologies, and cultural values may all vary depending on the needs of particular locations where the firm operates. In short, headquarters may offer suggestions and guidance, but it is up to local managers to make operational choices. This emphasis is often reflected in multinationals that rely on local managers to run foreign operations, as opposed to sending an expatriate from the home country to run operations abroad.

Some multinationals, usually referred to as transnational firms, take diversity one step further. Their firm cultures have evolved to the point where organizational diversity is a core value. This value is part of the glue that both holds the firm together and allows enormous flexibility. Such multinationals tend to be run by teams of managers from several countries. In fact, other than a few practices that are not subject to negotiation, such as indoctrinating employees in the firm's core values, these multinationals operate on a diverse basis.[78]

Multinationals have changed greatly in the last 100-odd years. As shown in Figure 1.7, multinationals have gradually changed both their geographic scope and their orientation toward foreign subsidiaries. But while not all multinationals develop in the same way or at the same rate, they are generally expected to continue moving toward the more liberal model in the years ahead.

Era	Time Frame	Description of Multinational Operations
Paternalism	1900–1960s	• Firms innovate in the home country, moving products out to the rest of the world from there. • As foreign subsidiaries evolved, however, it became clear that the home office did not have a monopoly on good ideas. • IBM and Procter & Gamble are prominent examples during this period.
Expansionism	1970s–1980s	• Some firms set up R&D or other units abroad in an effort to capture ideas in key markets. • But these outposts had difficulty integrating ideas across the company and holding headquarters' attention. • Plus, establishing outposts signaled to other foreign facilities that their ideas weren't needed (e.g., because they weren't in a big enough market or important enough to warrant an R&D operation).
Liberalism	1990s–today	• The emerging approach takes a more democratic twist to the pursuit of new ideas. • It assumes that great ideas can come from anywhere, especially in parts of the firm directly connected to customers/ other constituencies. It also assumes that the farther a foreign outpost is from the home office, the less constrained it is by corporate traditions and beliefs. • Foreign subsidiaries are better viewed as peninsulas than as islands. With that in mind, firms can expect some of their most innovative ideas to come from the edges rather than center of the organization. Leveraging those ideas is a key challenge for management.

Figure 1.7 The Evolution of Multinationals and Their Approach to Innovation: Three Eras.
Source: Adapted from Birkinshaw, J., and Hood, N. (2001). Unleash innovation in foreign subsidiaries. *Harvard Business Review* (March), 131–138.

Chapter Summary

The purpose of this chapter is to describe the basic landscape of international business and the competitive environment that it represents. The strongest growth in globalization will most likely be in emerging markets. An important way to assess such prospects is by examining the flows of foreign direct investment. To do so, examine trends in specific regions of the world, including the Americas, Asia-Pacific, Europe, the Middle East and Africa.

Challenges in international business include sweeping technological changes and the volatility of international business. Rapid currency fluctuations can impact business and what management can do in response. Small firms are particularly vulnerable to such fluctuations, especially because their resources are often more limited than those of larger firms. Another set of challenges involves offshoring, reshoring, and the increasing internationalization of workforces around the world. Companies are willing to look anywhere in the world to find employees with the right set of skills, at the right price, for just about any job—including innovative work and new product development. So, jobs are dispersing throughout the world as never before and countries are more formidable competitors when they can offer firms a hardworking and skilled pool of employees.

For international executives, maintaining workforce quality and managing diversity are important challenges. To meet these challenges, international managers must, among other things, value ethnic diversity, have multicultural experience, embrace teamwork, and be open to ideas from anywhere. The chapter concludes with a discussion of the role of culture in international management and how multinational enterprises have evolved over the last 100 years.

Discussion Questions

1. What are the most important trends in international business?

2. Which are the biggest management challenges for international firms? Why? What can firms do in response?

3. Which markets represent the biggest opportunities for international firms? Which markets represent the biggest risks? Why?

4. What is culture? Why is it important for international management?

5. In your view, what are the pros and cons about the influence of multinationals on the global economic scene?

6. How have multinationals evolved over the years? What are the implications of this for management?

Up to the Challenge?

New Balance Makes "Made in the U.S.A." Lean and High-Tech

At the beginning of this chapter it was stated that New Balance was unique among athletic shoe companies in that it manufactures 25 percent of its shoes in the United States. New Balance has minimized the cost gap with Asian subcontractors to the point where it can remain competitive while producing in high-wage locations such as the U.S., where it feels obligated to keep a foothold in manufacturing. Plus, being close to customers in a major market offers speed and quality control advantages in terms of fulfilling orders and changing styles.

But making this philosophy work essentially meant shifting from low-tech to high-tech, both in terms of equipment and employee skills. Borrowing a page from manufacturing methods in higher-tech industries, New Balance had employees take classes on computerized manufacturing and sophisticated teamwork so that they could operate in small, flexible teams. Employees master many skills, switch jobs continuously, help each other out, and take responsibility for production activities, while employee training is constant and ever-evolving.

New Balance also took a creative approach in adapting high-tech equipment from other industries to its needs. For instance, the company bought computerized sewing machines that came with templates designed for other products, then ripped out the templates and set up facilities to make their own. With the right templates in place, the result was a technology-intensive manufacturing operation. With a highly skilled workforce to run the equipment, New Balance factories in the United States need only one employee for every six that overseas plants using ordinary sewing machines require.

The New Balance story raises some interesting questions. On the one hand, it suggests that firms in developed countries can avoid shifting production to low-wage locations abroad by upgrading the skill levels of work at home. Indeed, the reality is that while the overall manufacturing workforce in the U.S. has been shrinking, productivity has actually been rising, with the result that American manufacturing output has soared 100 percent over the last several years. But what are the limits to this? Should we be concerned about them? Moreover, what are the costs and risks associated with New Balance's approach? What might happen if demand spikes up sharply or drops precipitously? Is New Balance at a disadvantage because it owns and operates some factories, whereas competitors such as Nike do not? Only time will tell if New Balance's approach represents a long-term competitive advantage for the company.[79]

International Development

International Management: Living at 35,000 Feet?

Purpose

To give a snapshot of what life is like as an international manager, to discuss the implications of that life, and to present some of the execution challenges companies face in running their international operations.

Instructions

Read the following short case. Then have a class discussion around the questions raised at the end of the case. Alternatively, your instructor will divide the class into groups of three to six students and ask each group to consider the discussion questions and develop a list of their three most important reactions or ideas (20 minutes). If time allows, your group could then make brief presentations about its findings to the class (20 minutes). You may conclude with a general discussion about life as an international manager and what implications that may have for corporations (15 minutes).

Have Manager, Should Travel?

Accounting powerhouse PricewaterhouseCoopers (PWC) is a bona fide global empire, with some $32 billion in revenues in 2013. Driving that revenue is more than 180,000 employees serving clients in over 150 countries from almost 800 offices. Ellen Knapp was one of the executives who helped build that PWC empire. During her tenure as PWC's chief knowledge and information officer, Knapp's role was to expand PWC and keep its empire running well. As such, she spent much of her time traveling overseas.

Knapp's was hardly a unique situation. She once survived three international red-eye flights crammed into less than a week. In the process, she ran into a colleague in London who was about to endure two such flights in two days. On another occasion, she ran into an acquaintance from consulting giant McKinsey at the Philadelphia airport. He was bound for New Delhi while Knapp was in transit to London and Frankfurt.

These days, international travel is not confined to CEOs who hop on corporate jets for two-week-long business trips spanning a dozen time zones. The growth of international business means that managers such as Knapp slog through airports as they crisscross the globe on their firm's behalf. But at least Knapp could fly business class. Lower-ranking employees in most companies endure international travel wedged into economy seats.

Nevertheless, how did Knapp survive such grueling travel burdens? Being extremely organized, dedicated, and optimistic certainly helped, as did being amazingly immune to jet lag. On the home front, Knapp had few complications because her two children were grown. Her two administrative assistants also kept Knapp plugged in at the home office. PWC helps its traveling executives by holding meetings near big airports and providing office support when they arrive at a company outpost.

If you are wondering why executives such as Knapp have to travel overseas so much, the answer can be summed up in one word: bonding. Most travel is aimed at building relationships and trust between employees scattered around the world. The idea, at least in theory, is that over time better relationships encourage more cross-border information sharing and greater collaboration. That said, some question whether direct, face-to-face contact is the best, if not only, way to encourage international sharing and collaboration. Clearly, many believe that relationship building requires plenty of informal face time (e.g., over lunch). Nevertheless, whether traveling really pays off or not is debatable. But one thing is certain—it makes airlines happy.

Discussion Questions to Address

1. How does the work life of an executive such as Knapp sound to you? Attractive? Tiring? Why or why not?

2. How can executives manage this kind of travel if they have younger kids at home? What if they also have spouses with demanding careers?

3. Is all this flitting around the world really necessary? How might technology be used to eliminate some of this travel? What are the potential costs and benefits? To whom? The limitations? Can technology really substitute for relationship building, especially in far-flung corporate empires?

Source: Adapted from *The Economist*. (1999). On a wing and a hotel room, January 9, 64; see also: www.pwc.com/gx/en/about-pwc/facts-and-figures.jhtml.

From Theory to International Practice

Hitting Home: Understanding Your Local "China Syndrome"

Purpose

To conduct an analysis of companies that import from and export to China in your local environment.

Instructions

Your instructor will place you into small groups to do research, outside of class, in order to answer the following questions:

• Which companies are major importers from and exporters to China in the local environment (city, state, province, region, etc.)? What industries do they represent?

• What efforts, if any, are being made to encourage or help local companies to export to China (or to discourage imports)?

For some general background information about China as well as tips for exporting into the Chinese market, visit one or more of the following links:

- U.S. Commercial Service: www.buyusa.gov/china/en/.

- Canadian government's Foreign Affairs International Trade: http://infoexport.gc.ca/eng/home.jsp.

- European Commission's Trade homepage: http://ec.europa.eu/trade.

Many national, state, and local government agencies provide help to local firms wanting to do business abroad. For instance, as part of the U.S. Department of Commerce, the Commercial Service is a government agency that helps American firms do business in China and other countries. The U.S. Commercial Service has been in existence for over two decades and has thousands of trade experts in more than 100 American cities and 150 government offices outside the United States (e.g., in American trade centers and embassies). If the class is small enough, your instructor may have your groups make brief presentations (10 minutes) about your findings to the class. This may be followed by a discussion about the level of involvement with China by local firms. Alternatively, your instructor may make this an individual assignment and have you write a report and ask you to take part in a general class discussion on the issues raised.

Notes

1. www.newbalance.com/Made-in-the-USA/made_in_usa,default,pg.html; Lamppa, R. (2009). New Balance celebrates its shoemaking heritage, June 18, available at: www.coolrunning.com; Martin, E. (2012). New Balance wants its tariffs. Nike doesn't. *Bloomberg Businessweek*, May 7–12, 14–15.
2. *The Economist*. (2009). The long climb, October 3, 3–5; Guillen, M. F., and Garcia-Canal, E. (2009). The American model of the multinational firm and the "new" multinationals from emerging economies. *Academy of Management Perspectives*, 23(2), 23–35.
3. Engardio, P. (2000). The barons of outsourcing. *Business Week*, August 28, 177–178.
4. Anderson, J., Kupp, M., and Moaligou, R. (2009). Lessons from the developing world. *The Wall Street Journal*, August 17, R6; Baker, S. (2004). Jobs go overseas—under water. *Business Week*, April 5, 13; Friedman, T. (2004). The incredible shrinking world. *Dayton Daily News*, March 6, A8.
5. Avent, R. (2013). Trade's triple chance. In *The Economist: The World in 2014*, 129–130. London: The Economist.
6. See www.wto.org.
7. *The Economist*. (2013). The World Trade Organization: Unaccustomed victory, December 14, 78–79; *The Economist*. (2009). Trade agreements: Doing Doha down, September 15, 15–16; *The Economist*. (2000). A different, new world order, November 11, 83–85; King, N., Samor, G., and Miller, S. (2004). WTO rules against U.S. cotton aid. *The Wall Street Journal*, April 27, A2; See also: www.wto.org.
8. Champion, M. (2004). CEOs' worst nightmares. *The Wall Street Journal,* January 21, A13; Carpenter, M. A., and Fredrickson, J. W. (2001). Top management teams, global strategic posture, and the moderating role of uncertainty. *Academy of Management Journal*, 44, 533–545.
9. *The Economist*. (2013). Electrolux's holy trinity, November 4–10, 55–56.

10. See http://unctad.org/en/publicationslibrary/wir2013_en.pdf; see also Economy Watch. (2013). Economic statistics and indicators, available at: www.economywatch.com/economic-statistics.

11. *The Economist.* (2001). Trade in the Americas: All in the familia, April 21, 19–22, available at: www.economywatch.com/economies-in-top/; see also http://money.cnn.com/news/economy/world_economies_gdp/.

12. Bellman, E. (2009). Indian firms shift focus to the poor. *The Wall Street Journal*, October 20, A1, A18; Cooper, J. C., and Madigan, K. (2004). The economy is showing real muscle. *Business Week*, May 3, 33–34; Engardio, P. (2001). America's future: Smart globalization. *Business Week*, August 27, 132–137; www.economywatch.com/world_economy/world-economic-indicators/world-gdp.html; www.nationmaster.com.

13. Masserman, M., and Zuelke, A. (2013). America's small businesses find competitive edge with creativity. *Tradeology*. International Trade Administration, Department of Commerce; http://blogtrade.gov; Bruto, D. (2010). Small business, big world. *Forbes*, available at: www.forbes.com; Barrett, A. (1995). It's a small (business) world. *Business Week*, April 17, 96–101; Engardio, P. (2008). Mom-and-pop multinationals. *Business Week*, July 14 and 21, 77–78; see also: www.ustr.gov/trade-topics/small-business and www.sba.gov/.

14. *The Economist.* (2013). Working partners, August 25, 23–24; Freedland, J. (2013). The China question. In *The Economist: The World in 2014*, 40; Ip, G. (2013). The wind changes. In *The Economist: The World in 2014*, 42–43.

15. *Fortune.* (2003). Global 500: The world's largest corporations, July 21, 106, available at: https://www.cia.gov/library/publications/the-world-factbook/geos/us.html; http://latino.foxnews.com/latino/news/2014/02/06/us-trade-deficit-narrows-by-nearly-12-pct-in-2013/.

16. *The Economist.* (2009). Output, prices, and jobs, September 26, 113; Dougherty, C. (2009). Economy snaps long slump. *The Wall Street Journal*, October 30, A1, A2; Miller, R. (2004). Business burns rubber. *Business Week*, February 2, 34–35; Porter, M. E. (2008). Why America needs an economic strategy. *Business Week*, November 10, 39–42.

17. Mero, J. (2008). Power shift. *Fortune*, July 21, 161–182; http://investor.colgate.com/colgate World/colgate_world-glance.cfm?; http://money.cnn.com/magazines/fortune/global500/2012/full_list/index.html

18. Kalwarski, T., and Foster, D. (2009). Numbers: Tipping the global scales. *Business Week*, November 16, 25; Whalen, C. J., Magnusson, P., and Smith, G. (2001). NAFTA's scorecard: So far, so good. *Business Week*, July 9, 54–56.

19. *The Economist*, Output, prices, and jobs; Drohan, M. (2013). Uncool Canada. In *The Economist: The World in 2014*, 53; www.statcan.gc.ca/tables-tableaux/sum-som/l01/cst01/gblec02a-eng.htm.

20. *The Economist.* (2012). Special report Mexico: Going up in the world, November 24, 1–16; *The Economist.* (2012). The global Mexican, October 27, 70.

21. *The Economist*, Special report Mexico: Going up in the world; *The Economist*, The global Mexican; www.tradingeconomics.com/Economics/GDP-Growth.aspx?Symbol=MXN.

22. Joyce, H. (2013). Let the games begin. In *The Economist: The World in 2014*, 49; *The Economist.* (2012). The expanding middle, November 10, 39–40; *The Economist*, Output, prices, and jobs; *The Economist.* (2009). Latin America's economies: Pain but no panic, May 2, 37–38.

23. Joyce, H., Let the games begin; *The Economist*, The expanding middle; *The Economist.* (2009). Rio's expensive new rings, October 10, 41; *The Economist*, Output, prices, and jobs; *The Economist.* (2001). Another blow to Mercosur, March 31, 33–34; Jana, R. (2009). South America's new IT hub. *Business Week*, August 24 and 31, 73; Reid, M. (2008). Latin drift. In *The World in 2009*, 49–50. London: The Economist Newspaper; https://www.cia.gov/library/publications/the-world-factbook/geos/br.html.

24. *The Economist.* (2013). The world in figures: Countries. In *The Economist: The World in 2014*, 4101–4109; *The Economist*, Output, prices, and jobs; Beinhocker, E., Davis, I., and Mendonca, L. (2009). The 10 trends you have to watch. *Harvard Business Review*, July–August, 55–60; Kalwarski and Foster, Numbers: Tipping the global scales; Woodall, P. (2008). Riders on the storm. In *The World in 2009*, 55–56.

25. *The Economist*. (2014). China loses its allure, January 25, 9: *The Economist*, The world in figures: Countries, 101–109; https://www.cia.gov/library/publications/the-world-factbook/geos/ch.html.

26. *The Economist*. (2009). Time to change the act, February 21, 69–71; Gimpel, L. (2008). Global hot spots. *Entrepreneur*, June, 62–70; Roberts, D., and Engardio, P. (2009). The China hype. *BusinessWeek*, November 2, 36 and 42.

27. Higgins, A. (2004). As China surges, it also proves a buttress to American strength. *The Wall Street Journal*, January 30, A1, A8; Powell, B. (2009). China's hard landing. *Fortune*, March 16, 114–120; Schlevogt, K. A. (2000). The business environment in China: Getting to know the next century's superpower. *Thunderbird International Business Review, 42* (January–February), 85–111.

28. *The Economist*, The world in figures: Countries, 101–109; *The Economist*. (2008). An elephant, not a tiger, December 13, 1–18; Wessel, D. (2003). India could narrow its economic gap with China. *The Wall Street Journal*, July 24, A2; Wonacott, P., Bellman, E., and Sabharwal, B. (2007). Foreign firms find rough passage to India. *The Wall Street Journal*, February 1, A6; https://www.cia.gov/library/publications/the-world-factbook/geos/in.html.

29. *The Economist*, The world in figures: Countries, 101–109; *The Economist*. (2008). The world is rocky, December 13, 9; Einhorn, B., Kripalani, M., and Engardio, P. (2001). India 3.0. *BusinessWeek,* February 26, 44–46; Sharma, A., and Worthe, B. (2009). Indian tech outsourcers aim to widen contracts. *The Wall Street Journal,* October 5, B1, B7.

30. *The Economist*, The world in figures: Countries, 101–109; *The Economist*, Output, prices, and jobs; *The Economist*. (2009). Unplugged, February 7, 55–56; *The Economist*. (2007). Going hybrid: A special report on business in Japan, December 1, 1–18; *The Economist*. (2004). (Still) made in Japan, April 10, 57–59; https://www.cia.gov/library/publications/the-world-factbook/geos/ja.html.

31. *The Economist*. (2009). Invisible but indispensable, November 7, 64–66; *The Economist*. (2007). Gaijin at the gates, August 18, 53–54; Naughton, K., and Trudell, C. (2013). Toyota's awesome yen advantage. *Bloomberg Businessweek*, March 25–31, 21–22.

32. *The Economist*, The world in figures: Countries, 101–109; *The Economist*. (2008). The odd couple: A special report on the Koreas, September 27, 1–18; Ihlwan, M. (2009). Korean exporters' won advantage. *BusinessWeek*, October 26, 22; https://www.cia.gov/library/publications/the-world-factbook/geos/ks.html.

33. *The Economist*, The odd couple: A special report on the Koreas; https://www.cia.gov/library/publications/the-world-factbook/geos/ks.html.

34. *The Economist*. (2008). In the nick of time: A special report on EU enlargement, May 31, 1–16; Kalwarski and Foster, Numbers: Tipping the global scales; La Guardia, A. (2013). The anti-European question; https://www.cia.gov/library/publications/the-world-factbook/geos/ee.html.

35. *The Economist*, Insider aiding; *The Economist*, Walls in the mind; *The Economist*, In the nick of time: A special report on EU enlargement; La Guardia, The anti-European question.

36. *The Economist*, In the nick of time: A special report on EU enlargement; https://www.cia.gov/library/publications/the-world-factbook/geos/ee.html.

37. *The Economist*, Down in the dumps; *The Economist*, Walls in the mind; *The Economist*, In the nick of time: A special report on EU enlargement; Kalwarski and Foster, Numbers: Tipping the global scales; https://www.cia.gov/library/publications/the-world-factbook/geos/ee.html.

38. *The Economist*. (2001). A survey of European enlargement: Europe's magnetic attraction, May 19, 1–16; Ewing, J. (2004). Is Siemens still German? *BusinessWeek*, May 17, 50–51; Hofheinz, P. (2002). One currency, many voices: Issues that still divide Europe. *The Wall Street Journal,* January 2, A6; Mehring, J. (2004). The newbies will set the pace. *BusinessWeek*, May 3, 34.

39. Ostrovsky, A. (2013). Putin's pause. *The Economist: The World in 2014*, 94; Bush, J. (2009). The krisis in Russia's industrial heartland. *BusinessWeek*, March 23 and 30, 74–76; Matlack, C. (2009). The peril and promise of investing in Russia. *BusinessWeek*, October 5, 48–52; https://www.cia.gov/library/publications/the-world-factbook/geos/rs.html.

40. *The Economist*. (2012). Lurching into the fast lane, July 52; *The Economist*. (2012). Vladimir the victor, November 3, 51, 58, available at: www.economist.com/news/europe/21565643-russian-president-firmly-charge-and-he-not-inclined-pursue-any-big-political-or (retrieved May 17, 2014); *The Economist*. (2008). Enigma variations: A special report on Russia, November 29, 1–18; Champion, M. (2009). Medvedev blasts Russian system. *The Wall Street Journal*, September 16, A19; Matlack, C. (2009). The peril and promise of investing in Russia. *Business Week*, October 5, 48–52; Starobin, P., and Belton, C. (2002). Russia: Cleanup time. *Business Week*, January 14, 46–47.

41. *The Economist*, Enigma variations: A special report on Russia; *The Economist*. (2007). Dancing with the bear, February 3, 63–64; Champion, Medvedev blasts Russian system; Matlack, The peril and promise of investing in Russia; Pipes, R. (2009). Pride and power. *The Wall Street Journal*, August 22–23, W1, W2.

42. *The Economist*. (2008). The next generation: A special report on Israel, April 5, 1–16; *The Economist*. (2007). The revolution strikes back: A special report on Iran, July 21, 1–16; Bianchi, S. (2009). Defense firms see growth in Mideast. *The Wall Street Journal*, November 12, B2; Levinson, C. (2009). Mobile venture lifts hope in West Bank. *The Wall Street Journal*, November 11, B1; Smiley, K. (2013). The people still want a bigger say. In *The Economist: The World in 2014*, 71–72; https://www.cia.gov/library/publications/the-world-factbook/wfbExt/region_mde.html.

43. *The Economist*, The world in figures: Countries; Fam, M. (2007). Middle East beckons as outsourcing hot spot. *The Wall Street Journal*, August 21, A6; https://www.cia.gov/library/publications/the-world-factbook/wfbExt/region_mde.html.

44. *The Economist*. (2013). More than minerals, March 23, 53–54; Campbell, M., Kirchfeld, A., and Nicholson, C. V. (2013). Dealmakers dream of African riches. *Bloomberg Businessweek*, January 21–27, 42–43; Gazzar, S. (2009). China to lend Africa $10 billion. *The Wall Street Journal*, November 9, A15; O'Sullivan, J. (2013). Digging deeper. In *The Economist: The World in 2014*, 73; Thurow, R. (2003). Once a breadbasket, Zimbabwe today can't feed itself. *The Wall Street Journal*, December 24, A1, A2.

45. *The Economist*. (2013). Special report: Emerging Africa—A hopeful continent, March 2, 1–16; *The Economist*. (2004). Trade and Africa: Emerging deals, February 21, 73; Halfa, W. (2013). Transport in Africa: Get a move on. *The Economist*, February 16, 50–51.

46. *The Economist*, Special report: Emerging Africa—A hopeful continent; *The Economist*, Output, prices, and jobs; *The Economist*. (2006). South African business: Going global, July 15, 59–60; Ewing, J. (2008). South Africa emerges from the shadows. *Business Week*, December 15, 52–56; https://www.cia.gov/library/publications/the-world-factbook/geos/sf.html; www.southafrica.info/business/economy/sectors/automotive-overview.htm.

47. Brynjolfsson, E., and Schrage, M. (2009). The new, faster face of innovation. *The Wall Street Journal*, August 17, R3; Jana, R. (2009). Inspiration from emerging economies. *Business Week*, March 23 and 30, 38–42.

48. Cavusgil, S. T., Knight, G., and Riesenberger, J. R. (2008). *International Business: Strategy, Management, and the New Realities*. Upper Saddle River, NJ: Prentice-Hall; Prahalad, C. K. (2009). In volatile times, agility rules. *Business Week*, September 21, 80.

49. *The Economist*. (2009). When a flow becomes a flood, January 24, 74–76; *The Economist*. (2004). Competitive sport in Boca Raton, February 7, 65–68; Levisohn, B. (2009). Dollar strategies. *Business Week*, April 13, 56–57; Slater, J., Mallard, W., and Davis, B. (2009). World tries to buck up dollar. *The Wall Street Journal*, November 12, A1, A22.

50. Phillips, M. M. (2001). Financial contagion knows no borders. *The Wall Street Journal*, July 13, A2; www.reuters.com/article/2013/09/05/bis-survey-volumes-idUSL6N0GZ34R20130905.

51. *The Wall Street Journal*. (2009). Currencies, November 12, C4; *The Economist*. (2004). Tested by the mighty Euro, March 20, 61–62; Levisohn, B. (2009). Dollar strategies. *Business Week*, April 13, 56–57; Miller, R., Arndt, M., Capell, K., and Fairlamb, D. (2003). The incredible falling dollar. *Business Week*, December 22, 36–38; Naughton, K., and Trudell, C. (2013). Toyota's awesome yen advantage. *Bloomberg Businessweek*, March 25–31, 21–22.

52. *The Economist*. (2004). Currency hedging: Holding back the flood, February 21, 72; *The Economist*, Tested by the mighty Euro; Zaun, T. (2001). As the yen weakens, Japan's car makers smile. *The Wall Street Journal*, April 10, A15, A19; www.bloomberg.com/news/2013-04-12/bmw-adds-currency-hedges-with-volkswagen-to-mitigate-volatility.html.

53. Aeppel, T. (2002). The dollar's strength tests the ingenuity of U.S. manufacturers. *The Wall Street Journal*, January 22, A1, A10; Cooper, C. (2000). Euro's drop is hardest for the smallest. *The Wall Street Journal*, October 2, A21, A24.

54. Lewin, A. Y., Massini, S., and Peeters, C. (2009), Why are companies offshoring innovation? The emerging global race for talent. *Journal of International Business Studies*, 40, 901–925.

55. *The Economist*. (2013). Special report: Outsourcing and offshoring—Here, there and everywhere, January 19, 1–20; Ante, S. E., and Hof, R. D. (2004). Look who's going offshore. *BusinessWeek*, May 17, 64–65.

56. *The Economist*, Special report: Outsourcing and offshoring—Here, there and everywhere; Doh, J. P., Bunyaratavej, K., and Hahn, E. D. (2009). Separable but not equal: The location determinants of discrete services offshoring activities. *Journal of International Business Studies*, 40, 926–943.

57. *The Economist*, Special report: Outsourcing and offshoring—Here, there and everywhere; Hookway, J., and Cunneta, J. (2009). Philippine call centers ring up business. *The Wall Street Journal*, May 30–31, A14; Worther, B. (2009). Firms close back offices in India to cut costs. *The Wall Street Journal*, June 8, B1, B2.

58. *The Economist*, Special report: Outsourcing and offshoring—Here, there and everywhere; Aeppel, T. (2009). Coming home: Appliance maker drops China to produce in Texas. *The Wall Street Journal*, August 24, B1, B2; Engardio, P. (2009). Why NCR said, "let's go back home." *BusinessWeek*, August 24 and 31, 19.

59. *The Economist*, (2013). Special report: Outsourcing and offshoring—Here, there and everywhere; Ante, S. E. (2004). Shifting work offshore? Outsourcer beware. *BusinessWeek*, January 12, 36–37; Thurm, S. (2004). Lesson in India: Some jobs don't translate overseas. *The Wall Street Journal*, March 3, A1, A10.

60. *The Economist*, Special report: Outsourcing and offshoring—Here, there and everywhere; *The Economist*. (2004). The great hollowing out myth, February 21, 27–29; Haberman, S. (2004). Software: Will outsourcing hurt America's supremacy? *BusinessWeek*. March 1, 84–94; Mandel, M. (2007). The real cost of offshoring. *BusinessWeek*. June 18, 29–34; Schlender, B. (2004). Peter Drucker sets us straight. *Fortune*, January 12, 115–118; Schroeder, M. (2004). Outsourcing may create U.S. jobs. *The Wall Street Journal*, March 30, A2.

61. *The Economist*, Special report: Outsourcing and offshoring—Here, there and everywhere; Hookway, J., and Cunneta, J. (2009). Philippine call centers ring up business. *The Wall Street Journal*, May 30–31, A14; Kripalani, M., and Engardio, P. (2003). The rise of India. *BusinessWeek*. December 8, 66–78; Teves, O. (2003). Philippines latest to feel jobs surge. *Dayton Daily News*, December 6, D1, D4.

62. *The Economist*, Special report: Outsourcing and offshoring—Here, there and everywhere; Engardio, P. (2009). Can the future be built in America? *BusinessWeek*, September 21, 46–51.

63. Pisano, G. P., and Shih, W. C. (2009). Restoring American competitiveness. *Harvard Business Review*, July–August, 114–125.

64. Kripalani, M., Hamm, S., and Ante, S. (2004). Scrambling to stem India's onslaught. *BusinessWeek*. January 26, 81–81; www.imd.ch/research/publications/wcy/index.cfm.

65. Kripalani, M., Hamm, S., and Ante, S. (2004). Scrambling to stem India's onslaught. *Business Week*. January 26, 81–81; Montgomery, C. (2002). Chief: No delivery from labor pains. *Dayton Daily News*, March 2, 1E, 8E; www.imd.ch/research/publications/wcy/index.cfm.

66. Pisano and Shih, Restoring American competitiveness.

67. *BusinessWeek*. (2009). Why the statistics point toward progress, August 24 and 31, 64–66; Pisano and Shih, Restoring American competitiveness.

68. Coy, P. (2000). The creative economy. *BusinessWeek,* August 28, 76–82; Ewing, J., Carlisle, K., and Capell, K. (2001). Help wanted: Germany starts wooing skilled workers. *BusinessWeek*,

September 17, 52–53; Valbrun, M. (2000). Immigrants find economic boom brings more than higher pay. *The Wall Street Journal,* August 16, B1, B4.

69. Eisenberg, J., Lee, H., Bruck, F., Brenner, B., Claes, M., Mironski, J., and Bell, R. (2013). Can business schools make students more cross-culturally competent? Effects of cross-cultural management courses on cultural intelligence. *Academy of Management Learning & Education,* 12(4), 603–621; Grow, B. (2004). Hispanic nation. *Business Week,* March 15, 59–67; Joplin, J. R. W., and Daus, C. S. (1997). Challenges of leading a diverse workforce. *Academy of Management Executive,* 11, 32–47; Robinson, G., and Dechant, K. (1997). Building a business case for diversity. *Academy of Management Executive,* 11, 21–31.

70. Phatak, A. V. (1997). *International Management: Concepts and Cases.* Cincinnati, OH: South-Western College Publishing.

71. Stanek, M. B. (2000). The need for global managers: A business necessity. *Management Decision,* 38, 232–242; Roberts, K., Kossek, E. E., and Ozeki, C. (1998). Managing the global workforce: Challenges and strategies. *Academy of Management Executive,* 12, 93–106.

72. Murray, M. (2001). As huge companies keep growing, CEOs struggle to keep pace. *The Wall Street Journal,* February 8, A1, A6; www.marketwatch.com/investing/stock/pg/profile.

73. Dwyer, P., Engardio, P., Schiller, Z., and Reed, S. (1994). Tearing up today's organization chart. *Business Week,* November 18, 80–90; Heifetz, R., Grashow, A., and Linsky, M. (2009). Leadership in a (permanent) crisis. *Harvard Business Review,* July–August, 62–69; Kossek, E. E., and Ozeki, C. (1998). Managing the global workforce: Challenges and strategies. *Academy of Management Executive,* 12, 93–106; Stanek, M. B. (2000). The need for global managers: A business necessity. *Management Decision,* 38, 232–242.

74. Birkinshaw, J., and Hood, N. (2001). Unleash innovation in foreign subsidiaries. *Harvard Business Review* (March), 79, 131–138; Shrader, R. C. (2001). Collaboration and performance in foreign markets: The case of young high-technology manufacturing firms. *Academy of Management Journal,* 44, 45–60; Harris, T. G. (1993). The post-capitalist executive: An interview with Peter Drucker. *Harvard Business Review* (May–June), 71, 115–122.

75. Hofstede, G. (1993). Cultural constraints in management theories. *Academy of Management Executive,* 7, 81–94; Triandis, H. C. (1996). The psychological measurement of cultural syndromes. *American Psychologist,* 51, 407–415.

76. Peterson, D. B. (2007). Executive coaching in a cross-cultural context. *Consulting Psychology Journal: Practice and Research,* 59, 261–271.

77. *The Economist.* (2013). The best thing since sliced bread, January 19, 68; Progressive Policy Institute. (2008). The number of transnational companies grows by 2,500 a year, December 3, available at: www.ppionline.org; Melloan, G. (2004). Feeling the muscles of the multinationals. *The Wall Street Journal,* January 6, A19; Thrum, S. (2008). The "same ol" is actually good enough for many. *The Wall Street Journal,* September 8, B4.

78. Hordes, M. W., Clancy, J. A., and Baddaley, J. (1995). A primer for global start-ups. *Academy of Management Executive,* 9, 7–11.

79. Lamppa, New Balance celebrates its shoemaking heritage; Pope, J. (2004). Athletic shoemaker creates new path. *Dayton Daily News,* February 23, D1, D4; Martin, New Balance wants its tariffs. Nike doesn't; see also www.newbalance.com.

chapter 2

legal and political foundations of international management

Learning Objectives

After reading this chapter, you should be able to

- identify the major legal systems in use around the world today and understand how they impact business done within (as well as outside of) a nation's borders;
- link together the elements of the major legal systems with the effect that they have on international business;
- understand political risk and pinpoint its key elements, as well as its effect on global commerce;
- determine risk management methods that can reduce, or even avoid, problems in doing business across borders.

International Challenge

Crouching Tiger, Hidden Knockoffs: Making It and Faking It in China

Even if you have not had the pleasure of traveling abroad yet, you probably know people who have. They may have told tales of designer goods being sold on the streets and in back alleys of Rio, Moscow, Istanbul, and Jakarta—all for pennies on the dollar. Yet, surely everyone knows that the $20 Rolex watch sold on Silom Road in Bangkok, the $2 *Windows* 8 disc bought in the Ziyuangang market in Guangzhou, and the $30 Louis Vuitton purse acquired on Canal Street in New York City are not the real deal. From Vietnam to Venice, Chile to Chicago, there is a thriving world market in knockoffs. Yet, the epicenter of this phenomenon remains in China.

China's role in this business has been recognized for some time, but what is remarkable is that, increasingly, counterfeit goods look just as good as the real thing. And this stretches beyond just material goods to truly important and possibly life-threatening items such as medications. Pfizer, Inc., received a call from a woman complaining that its cholesterol-lowering Lipitor tasted bitter. Lab staff in Connecticut could not determine from the look of the pill, but chemical analysis confirmed that what the woman, and many others, had bought were fake, causing the removal of 17 million tablets from pharmacy shelves in the U.S. Whether it is millions of bogus HP inkjet cartridges seized in Brazil, Turkish police impounding knockoff Buick windshields or fake Viagra, the confiscation of bogus Nokia phones in France, or Korean authorities uncovering phony Honda motorcycles, a common denominator is that all were "knocked off" in China.

To be sure, there are clever counterfeiters everywhere, but none take a back seat to China—a back seat that may have an American GM stamp on it, but which was made illegally in Guangzhou. The Organisation for Economic Co-operation and Development (OECD) and the World Customs Organization estimate that up to two-thirds of all pirated goods world-wide come from China. In 2011, over 25,000 seizures of counterfeit goods were made by U.S. Customs, nearly 65 percent of which were Chinese (only a fraction of what slips through undetected). Indeed, according to some estimates, upwards of 8 percent of China's GDP comes from the sales of counterfeits.[1] The scale of the activity means that virtually every industry has been affected by knockoffs: from clothing, to electronics, to luxury goods, and increasingly auto and motorcycle parts, memory chips, cigarettes, shoes, and (alarmingly) medications. The World Health Organization (WHO) recently estimated that up to 10 percent of medicines worldwide are counterfeited at an annual cost of $46 billion to the pharma industry.

Counterfeiting today combines skilled labor and product knowledge with good distribution networks. The results can be impressive and attractive to "consumers." Factories in Shenzhen, China, for instance, can copy a new Callaway golf club in less than a week. Yimu is a city about five hours away from Shanghai and could well be called "Counterfeit Central." Global buyers can visit some 40,000 shops to buy products in bulk—90 percent of which are well-done imitations. Sony PlayStation controllers or Cisco routers take only a little longer than the Callaway drivers to replicate. As one expert said, "If you can make it, they can fake it"—even extending to a Mitsubishi elevator that was discovered to be an imitation when the building owner called the firm for service.[2]

The trouble is that counterfeiters are getting really good at faking it, leading some company execs to say that it "takes a forensic scientist to figure it out." GM has had to cut apart brakes and batteries and do chemical analysis to determine whether products were real, while Coach has had to cut apart luxury handbags to confirm a set of imitations. This speaks to the skill of the counterfeiter, but also to the fact that some licensees keep the designs and blueprints of former Western partners. New Balance recently sued a contract manufacturer in Guangzhou for selling knockoffs that looked exactly like their shoes as far away as Europe. And, it is not just exports. Chinese consumers can shop at a store that looks amazing like Ikea (down to the blue and yellow colors and the navigation arrows on the floor), then go eat at stores that are identical to Subway (including the logo and sandwich sizes, despite the fact that China uses the metric system!) and then have dessert at "Dairy Fairy," which features colors and products just like Dairy Queen. A store identifying itself as an Apple Store in Kunming has the same layout as a true Apple store and their *identical* logo—selling real iPads and iPhones, although Apple had no affiliation with them. These may be as, or more, alarming for domestic firms since retail spending in China will rise by two-thirds from 2011 to 2015, reaching the $4.3 trillion level.

So, what can be done about this epidemic? As you read this chapter, consider options, both legal and political, that can be used to stem the rising tide of counterfeiting and piracy. Then, take a look at our Up to the Challenge? feature at the end of the chapter for some suggestions.[3]

The Legal Environment of International Management

In Chapter 1, we looked at both developing and longer-term trends in international management that together provide background for your reading of the remaining chapters. We will apply that background here in Chapter 2, where we will examine the features of the many political and legal systems in use around the world, as well as the role these systems play. Laws are the written codes of conduct that guide and restrict the actions of companies and individuals and there are three main systems used by the majority of countries in the world today. Information about these legal systems and the differences and implications of each approach is critical for those doing business across borders, as non-compliance could result in monetary losses and other negative impacts. The second half of the chapter looks at political issues that emerge in international business. These issues may be even more important for global managers to know as laws may be constrained, altered, or ignored altogether because of global politics. What is more, if political power changes hands, the legal framework may also be altered. For these reasons, multinationals should closely monitor the political situation occurring at home and abroad and may also engage themselves in political activity in order to better operate their business.

Legal Systems Across the Globe

Several systems have been devised for categorizing the different types of legal systems within countries. Although no one approach covers every legal system in operation, an approach that helps familiarize us with cultural variations among laws is presented in Figure 2.1.[4] The figure shows that the number and types of laws are varied and complex. Yet, most prevalent systems are civil law and common law.

Civil Law

Civil law is the most common legal system, used in over 80 countries.[5] Also referred to as *code law*, this approach is based on an elaborate and detailed set of rules. At its core, the civil law system operates on a detailed set of regulations about what is right and wrong. In Western culture, this legal system can be traced back to Roman times (around the fifth century B.C.). Major developments have included the Napoleonic Code and its spread throughout French colonial possessions during the nineteenth and twentieth centuries. It was a major advancement from previous feudal laws and was established to outline that laws could only be applied if they had been published and communicated to all citizens, as well as to prevent judges from refusing justice. In addition, the impact of German civil code on Germany's colonial possessions also advanced the role of the civil law system. Most European Union states, as well as Greece, Indonesia, Japan, Mexico, Turkey, and many South American and African countries, are examples of those that use the civil law system. Because of the detailed code of legal regulations, there is consistency among countries in the conduct of legal proceedings, especially in contrast

Type of Legal System	Characteristics of the System
Civil law	• codified • based on abstract principles • predictable because of elaborate code
Common law	• based on precedent • emphasis on procedures • flexible
Islamic law	• religious/faith-based code • codified and predictable • applicable to daily life
Communist/socialist law	• based on ideology • based on bureaucracy • minimal private rights
Sub-Saharan African law	• community oriented • based on custom • group-based outcomes
Asian law	• social order/harmony stressed • low use of legal mechanisms • bureaucratized

Figure 2.1 International Legal Systems.

Source: Adapted from Richards, F. L. (1994). *Law for Global Business*. Boston, MA: Irwin.

to the common law system. Code law typically involves less interpretation than other legal systems, including common law, because stipulations are concise and codified and more directive.

Common Law

Common law is practiced in over 30 countries, including the United Kingdom and most of its former colonies, such as the United States (except Louisiana), Canada, Australia, Ireland, Pakistan, and Malaysia.[6] Instead of relying on elaborate preexisting codes, common law uses the balance of previous cases (or precedent) to resolve legal disputes. Because of the focus on the case at hand and its similarity to previous cases—instead of an application of general principles or codes—there is great emphasis on procedural issues in common law. A judge in a common law system is less active than those in civil law systems, typically controlling the courtroom by functioning as a neutral referee. Yet, judges do exercise the power to interpret the law and its application to the case at hand, whereas in civil law, there is little room for judicial interpretation. In common law approaches, the lawyers for the plaintiff and defendant are expected to present evidence and develop the legal case in order to resolve the dispute. In the civil law system, however, a judge takes a much more directive role in the proceedings, including the decisions about what evidence will be presented to the court.

To those unfamiliar with the common law system, rulings seem widely discrepant, often changing from year to year and even case to case. The effects of previous rulings, court interpretations, and legal modifications lend themselves to some inconsistency. Because of the elaborate specifications featured in civil law, there is considerable stability in statutes. Being influenced by precedent is a plus for common law in that it is a more flexible system than code law. But, this also means that common law can be more adversarial and that parties work hard to detail elements of their cases based on a large body of sometimes contradictory rulings. A good contrast between civil and common law is provided by comparing legal proceedings in Japan and the U.S., as we show in the accompanying International Insights feature.

International Insights

Courting Trouble: American-Style Litigation and Lawyers in Japan

Before 2005, foreign law firms in Japan were required to follow rules that did not apply to Japanese firms. For instance, foreign firms had to first list the name of their resident partner in Japan, followed by a phrase meaning "foreign business lawyer," and only then display their trademark firm name. So, on their office doors, business cards, stationery, and even in the directory of the American Chamber of Commerce, the Tokyo office of the well-known U.S. firm of Coudert Brothers was called "Stevens *gaikokuho-jimu-bengoshi* Coudert Brothers."

Yet, foreign law firms (*gai-ben*) say that these naming rules were only a minor irritant compared to other restrictions. For example, they were not permitted to advise on Japanese law or even to employ Japanese lawyers who could give advice. Foreigners were not allowed to join with national firms to get around the restriction and were barred from lucrative arbitration proceedings. For years, the Japan Federation of Bar Associations opposed the opening of the nation's legal market by supporting the above restrictions. In 1990 there were fewer than 50 *gai-ben* (mostly Americans) registered in Japan and only about 350 there 20 years later.

Additionally, the bar exam in Japan restricted all but a very few Japanese college graduates from becoming lawyers. The passage rates fluctuated between 2 percent and 3 percent for most of the post–World War II era. (Consider that about 65 percent of those who sit for the bar exam in the state of Ohio, U.S.A., pass the exam.) This meant that only about 500 lawyers each year were admitted to the bar in all of Japan. Many believed that the 20 to 1 ratio of lawyers in the U.S. vs. Japan reflected values steeped in years of social norms and business practice. Japanese businesses were often organized into a close network of relations (*keiretsu*) and disputes could be handled informally or through agreed-upon third parties.

The head-on, aggressive legal style of American lawyers was also anathema to the Japanese, while formal litigation is viewed as a last resort in Japan. Consider some of the American behavior that Japanese would find offensive: Within 24 hours of a major accident at a Union Carbide plant in India, American lawyers were on the ground soliciting clients, and in four days they were back home having already filed lawsuits in U.S. courts (where judgments would be of higher authority than in India). The Japanese react very differently to these situations. After a Japan Airlines (JAL) flight crashed near Tokyo, the airline's president, Yasumoto Takagi, humbly bowed to families of the victims and apologized "from the bottom of our hearts." He vowed to resign once the investigation was complete. Next of kin received condolence payments and settlements with the airline; only one lawsuit was filed and it was quickly resolved.

This all seemed to change as the 1990s came to an end. Perhaps as a result of a period of economic stagnation and national deregulation, more and more legal disputes occurred. In part because of this, Japan began undertaking a series of steps to transform the nation's education system in order to meet the need for more attorneys. In 2004, for the first time, the Japanese government allowed universities to begin graduate law programs. In the decade since, 74 new law schools have opened. The first graduating classes (of more than 3,000) began to take a less restrictive bar exam in 2006. Now, a graduate degree is required to sit for the bar exam, whereas before, anyone over the age of 18 could take the test. More lawyers also began to enter private practice in lieu of government or business. And, more American-style court outcomes also started to emerge. For example, Sumitomo Bank and Mitsubishi Financial squared off in court after a desired purchase fell apart.

Despite this shift, however, we are certainly not predicting that Japan will be just like the litigious U.S. Indeed, as of 2006 there was still only one lawyer per every 5,800 Japanese, a tiny fraction compared to the 1 to 270 U.S. figure. As of 2009, there are already signs of oversupply, especially because accountants complete a fair amount of legal work. Prior to 2006, the proportion of associates who made partner was very high (35 percent) by U.S. standards, but it appears that this number may be tracking downward. The Japanese economy apparently has just not needed the number of attorneys being minted at law schools, resulting in an oversupply. The Mishimura law firm, for example, has doubled in size since 2004 and is now the largest law firm in Japan (with 450 lawyers). No layoffs are planned, but some employees are wary. Others, however, are optimistic and point to Japanese experience with down markets and generally predict that the "legalization" of Japanese society will continue.[7]

Impact of Code and Common Law Systems

If common law emphasizes the active role of attorneys making their case, then there should be a greater need for attorneys and litigation than in civil law countries.[8] Figure 2.2 presents some data that support this claim. The left side of this figure shows the per capita number of lawyers in a variety of civil and common law countries. In general, there is a tendency for countries with civil law (such as South Korea, Japan, and France) to have relatively few lawyers, whereas common law countries (such as the U.S., Canada, and Pakistan) have a relatively high number of lawyers. In fact, the U.S. alone has nearly 40 percent of the world's lawyers, whereas Japan seems to have only a small fraction of this percentage. Figure 2.2 also provides further data on this point; it shows the tort costs as a portion of GDP across different countries. This measure refers to the costs (legal and damage awards) associated with lawsuits involving products (such as

Country	Number of Lawyers per 100,000 People	Country	Tort Costs (as % of GDP)
Pakistan	508.4	United States	2.20
Singapore	396.0	Italy	1.70
United States	312.0	Germany	1.1
Belgium	214.0	Spain	1.0
Germany	190.1	Belgium	1.0
Canada	168.5	Japan	0.8
Australia	145.7	Switzerland	0.8
United Kingdom	133.8	U.K.	0.7
Japan	101.6	France	0.7
Italy	81.2	Denmark	0.6
Brazil	69.1	Poland	0.6
France	49.1		
India	34.4		
South Korea	7.7		
China	4.2		

Figure 2.2 Number of Lawyers and Tort Costs in Various Countries.

Sources: Cherry, T. R. (2006). U.S. tort costs and cross-border perspectives: 2005 update. New York: Tillinghast-Towers Perrin; *The Economist*. (1994) Frequency of lawyers across the globe, March 5, 36.

automobiles and cigarettes) and services (such as malpractice). The U.S. (at 2.2 percent) has a very high proportion relative to a set of other industrialized nations (about three times as much as Japan, which is a civil law country).[9] These costs are significant. To put the U.S. figure into context, consider that tort judgments cost $260 billion in 2005, which translates to about $880 per person.

We should note that the tort costs are not driven solely by the form of the legal system. A number of factors that are responsible for the differences are presented in Figure 2.2, including health care systems across those countries. Many countries have national health care that mitigates lawsuits, whereas malpractice judgments against doctors alone cost about $30 billion in 2009. Even within countries with a stable legal system, tort activity can vary, as it did in the U.S. when the relative growth of tort costs tripled from 1970 to 1990.[10] Furthermore, managers should be aware of important differences even among similar systems. The U.S. and the U.K. are common law countries, yet the discovery process in the U.S. is extensive and open. A defendant's counsel is well aware of the witnesses that will be called by the prosecution and they may also depose those witnesses to find out exactly what they will testify. In the U.K., however, no extensive discovery process exists. Often, a defendant will simply be provided with a list of potential witnesses and a brief summary of why they were called. Likewise, contingency fee arrangements (whereby an attorney might take 40 percent of the trial judgment) are common in the U.S. but are considered unethical in the U.K., where clients pay hourly rates. It is common in the U.K. for the losing party to pay trial costs and attorney's fees of the opposition.[11]

Islamic Law

Islamic law relies upon religious stipulations in the Koran—the holy book of Islam. Islamic law is also known as *sharia* (or God's rules) and functions as both a moral and legal code. While the Koran is not, strictly speaking, a code of law, it includes covenants of relevance to business, including admonitions to honor agreements and to observe good faith in business transactions. This legal system considers that God's law was given to the prophet Mohammed. Some experts go so far as to claim that by the end of the tenth century, religious scholars had determined that divine law had been translated and clarified sufficiently and that no more substantial interpretation (*ijtihad*) was necessary.[12] In practice, however, there is a good deal of debate about the application of Islamic law to more contemporary issues, and thus it is typically practiced as a hybrid mixed with civil and common law components.

As with the other legal systems, there are differences across the approximately 30 countries that embrace Islamic law (or parts of it). Yet, the fact that much of the code was developed centuries ago and that some of it endures today with relatively few changes can create challenges for multinationals, particularly Western ones. Consider the basic principle in many Western countries of interest earned on an investment. Islamic law requires obedience to the principle of *riba*, which prohibits the collection of interest on loans in deference and respect to the poor. Speculation is also taboo under *sharia*, yet risk and speculation are an essential part of many financial systems. Money provided as capital must be backed by collateral. And, if financial instruments are traded, they have to sell for face value. An advantage of this approach is that this has prevented many banks from repackaging debt. As a result, many Islamic banks avoided the trouble associated with collateralized debt obligations and other toxic investments that so many others experienced in the late 2000s.[13]

Islamic courts have acted consistently with such principles. A federal court in Pakistan, for example, ruled that interest earned on an investment was non-Islamic and thus illegal. The Pakistani Supreme Court subsequently sided with that court, and even went further by ruling that over 20 laws dealing with financial and banking issues were in violation of Islamic law.[14] A government commission formed in response to the Court's ruling recommended that a banking system without interest be instituted. Several banks challenged the rulings, as did the finance minister, Sardar Asif Ahmed Ali, who said that the ruling would negatively affect foreign investment and the treatment received by Pakistan from international agencies such as the World Bank.[15]

To overcome some of the practice problems that occur in international commerce, Muslim businesses have devised some unique approaches. In Kuwait, Saudi Arabia, and Malaysia, for example, banks have charged up-front fees for a loan in lieu of interest payments or have created leasing arrangements that comply with Islamic law.[16] Some U.S. banks have developed similar creative financing arrangements to address the Koran's prescriptions. For example, when Dr. Ala-ud-Din, a dentist in San Jose, California, wanted to buy a house in the most expensive U.S. real estate market, he faced problems. Fortunately, a small Islamic financing company actually bought the house for Dr. Din and leased it to him over a 15-year period that eventually made him the owner.[17] Banks in some countries, eager to be seen as respectful of *sharia* principles but also eager to do business, try to uphold the spirit of the law by doing the same thing. Many times they will engage in *ijara*—they will acquire a capital item for a firm and then lease it to them or sell it at a mark-up to reflect the risk taken by the bank. Some firms have used this approach and variants to handle foreclosures and defaults.[18]

Many people who live in Islamic law countries have seen newfound wealth and are seeking ways to put that to use. Despite its current financial challenges, Iran has the largest amount of *sharia*-compliant assets under management as of 2007 ($154 billion), three times as much as Saudi Arabia. What has resulted is a huge rise in Islamic equity funds and bond issues. Aggressive banks will also issue interest-free bonds at a discount to par.[19] In its 2008 Islamic Funds Report, leading professional services organization Ernst & Young estimated that monies in Islamic bond funds (*sukuks*) rose from just over $1 billion when first issued in 2002 to nearly $50 billion in 2007.

In 1999, there were just about a dozen such funds but this figure grew to about 200 in 2006. To be *sharia*-compliant, however, there can be no investment in firms that sell alcohol, tobacco, pork-related products, conventional financial services, entertainment, and more.[20] Experts estimate that this still leaves more than half of the Standard and Poor's (S&P) 500 companies (e.g., Microsoft, SWA, and Nike) in compliance. They also estimate that in 2008, the amount of Islamic assets under management was about $800 billion, although some believe this figure was closer to $4 trillion.

Sharia compliance can be tricky. Consider that investment in a manufacturer of women's clothing could be a violation because the company may make clothes that do not cover the whole body. To many, whether or not the eventual user is Muslim is irrelevant. Even firms included on the Dow Jones Islamic Market Index are not immune to such analysis, as was the case for Malaysia, which solved these interpretation problems by creating a national *sharia* board. Groups such as the Accounting and Auditing Organization for Islamic Financial Institutions and the Institute of Islamic Banking and Finance are having increasing influence. This process is driven by scholars, not financiers, who act as a spiritual rating agency in conjunction with banks and funds.[21] It is easy to see why Islamic entrepreneurs are thinking broadly about Muslim-specific ventures, including such ideas as social networking platforms, as illustrated in the following Global Innovations feature.

Global Innovations

Social Networking: Islam Style

With nearly 1 billion users globally, it seems as though everyone has a Facebook account. Growth in older users (women and men over 55) has been tremendous. These social networking sites provide a way to connect with nearly anyone in the globe and to cut across many social (and physical, ethnic, racial, gender, etc.) boundaries. Further, no one is turned away (as long as you are over the age of 13) and there are few, but reasonable, restrictions on use (no spamming, nudity, etc.). Is there room for another social networking site—one that is more specific in scope, as well as more defined for a group than for individuals, than Facebook?

Some investors from Turkey, Russia, and Kazakhstan think so and are on the verge of launching what they hope is the next big hit in the social networking world–Salamworld. The company's directors believe that there is a huge market for a Facebook-like site for Muslims—one based on Islamic values and law. The founders believe that a platform that promotes an Islamic community (rather than Western-style individualism) will be a hit in the market. Existing products contain content that is not appropriate, says the chairman of Salamworld, as "there are 250 million Muslim Facebook users because there is no *halal* alternative." (*Halal* is Arabic for "lawful" or "permitted.") "We've created a *halal* alternative that addresses the needs of the modern Muslim."

That alternative includes a positive view of Islam, something the developers believe is of value today. But, more than that, they want to connect Muslims to other Muslims and, because they are businesspeople, they want to make money. A beta version of the site was recently released and is to be followed by launches in 17 other countries in short order. In addition to pages of photos, videos, and posts that characterize other social media products, Salamworld will provide an e-library of books on Islamic history and heritage, city guides for Muslim attractions (such as mosques, centers, restaurants, etc.), and counseling from certified *imams*. Funding has been secured for the first three years of operation and Salamworld already has offices in 12 different countries. Their goal is to have 50 million users within five years—an attractive number to advertisers. There are over 300 million Muslim Internet users and the research firm Halafire estimates that the value of *halal*-type products and services is near $1 trillion.

But, the going is not likely to be easy. You cannot just "like" an advertiser. Ziad Mokhtar, for example, a partner at a Cairo-based venture firm, says, "Facebook doesn't contradict Islam, so there's nothing wrong with the current product." He says that the Salamworld group would be better off developing applications (apps), and points to the failure of Muslim-based predecessors. Muxlim.com launched in 2006 (when Facebook had only 10 million users and $52 million in revenue) and recently failed. At least two other platforms with the same business proposition have also failed. And, obviously, Facebook now presents a much bigger challenge. Another challenge results from an ambiguous definition of what is *halal* and what is *haram* (unlawful or prohibited). The firm does tout that it will have a strict filtering process based on what is acceptable content in various countries (e.g., Indonesia, Malaysia). Salamworld also points to the fact that Facebook uses filters and other constraints and that this is a "dynamic" process too.

It remains to be seen if Salamworld will be able to stake out its position with Muslim users. It will probably be decided on good old-fashioned and relatively universal business lines, as Sultan Sooud Al-Qassemi, a Dubai-based investor, stated that "the social networking area is already overpopulated . . . if they don't give customers what they want, they simply won't migrate from Facebook or Twitter."[22]

Other Legal Systems

There are other legal systems in operation today, including socialist and communist or bureaucratic law and sub-Saharan African law, as well as combinations of systems.[23] In China, for example, the legal system is a complex and dynamic combination of several systems, leaning toward civil law. Chinese law now represents an interesting case, one that should be watched closely by firms eager to enter and capture that market. In 2004, at the National Congress of the Communist Party of China, Hu Jintao introduced a far-reaching plan to overhaul laws dealing with the nation's burgeoning market economy, which some consider the biggest economic change since Deng Xiaoping's introduction of the "socialist market economy." Many believe that this reform will yield internal benefits, such as reduction in bureaucratic corruption. Experts such as Professor Li Shuguang at the China University of Science and Law voice this view: "China has been operating under a market economy for 20 years, but it doesn't even have such basic laws as a bankruptcy law or a monopoly law to ensure fair competition."[24]

This gap in bankruptcy laws rose to prominence during the worldwide economic recession that also slammed China. In 2008, over 300,000 factories closed (many small ones). If this had happened within the U.S., owners could file for bankruptcy protection from creditors and even external funding to continue operating. Reforms enacted after Hu's speech were supposed to provide similar protections in China, but they were complex and few judges understood the laws. As a result, many business owners shut their factories down, sometimes in the middle of the night, leaving behind the mess for workers, suppliers, and others. In Dongguan alone, for example, there were 673 cases of owners abandoning their factories (affecting over 100,000 workers owed $44 million). Nevertheless, these reforms and a very robust economy will continue to help China over time.[25]

Differences aside, many feel that legal systems around the world share more and more in common as decades pass. It remains to be seen if this is actually the case and opinions vary, as we illustrate with one example in Figure 2.3. There, data collected from over

Highest-Ranked Countries			Lowest-Ranked Countries		
Rank	Country	Rating	Rank	Country	Rating
1	Denmark	9.21	52	Bulgaria	3.00
2	Austria	8.94	53	Portugal	2.85
3	Iceland	8.93	54	Indonesia	2.75
4	Finland	8.91	55	Romania	2.58
5	Hong Kong	8.78	56	Mexico	2.46
6	Norway	8.78	57	Croatia	2.42
7	Australia	8.71	58	Russia	2.39
8	Netherlands	8.66	59	Poland	2.11
9	New Zealand	8.61	60	Argentina	2.03
10	Canada	8.57	61	Venezuela	.55

Figure 2.3 Ratings of the Fair Administration of Justice in Various Countries.
Source: Adapted from IMD (2006) *The World Competitiveness Yearbook, 2006*, Lausanne, Switzerland: IMD.

10,000 executives in over 60 countries is presented on views about whether justice is administered fairly. More developing economies fall at the bottom of these. The U.S. ranks at #23 (rating = 6.87, with higher ratings equating to better justice), a drop of seven places since 2002. China is ranked #37 (rating = 5.45). Things can change quickly and the next such survey may show considerable change. All this suggests that one additional source of regulation that multinationals need to pay attention to is international law.

International Law

While no single body of law or code applies across borders, some sets of rules or guidelines do exist. Moreover, some important agreements have been reached over the years that can serve as relatively clear and important guidelines for international law. These are important because: (a) they have resulted in a number of standing organizations that seek to promote international commerce law, and (b) each has a big impact on the conduct of international business.

GATT/WTO

The General Agreement on Tariffs and Trade (GATT) is one such agreement that affects international commerce. GATT resulted from a 1948 conference of 53 nations concerned with the effect of protectionism and high tariffs on the world economy. The purpose was to extend fair and similar trade policies to all other GATT members, a so-called "most-favored-nation" status that provided a stable set of preferential tariffs. Currently, 153 nations are members of the World Trade Organization (WTO), which was the 1995 successor to GATT, and others are in the process of seeking membership (e.g., Algeria, Belarus, Iran, Serbia). Member nations are responsible for 95 percent of all world trade. The membership process can prove long and contentious, averaging about five years if the process goes well. China's 1986 application for entry into the WTO was initially delayed by a public fight between the United States and the EU over insurance. One complicating factor was whether AIG, the largest insurance company in the United States, should continue to receive preferential treatment by China at the expense of its EU competitors.[26] China finally became a WTO member in 2002. Russia waited the longest to hear about its application, some 19 years.

Once it becomes a member, however, a nation is required to make its tariff and other business laws consistent ("harmonize") with guidelines or it is liable to face rebuke and sanctions from the WTO. Membership requires compliance with the more than 60 major agreements that are part of the WTO and many specific stipulations which were negotiated in lengthy sessions or "rounds." For example, the Uruguay Round lasted 87 months and the still-running Doha round began in 2001, with several major impasses occurring since then.[27]

While the WTO has resulted in several positive outcomes (such as stiffer guidelines regarding intellectual property), it has also been criticized. For one, the organization is often seen as too slow—perhaps because over 150 countries are involved in the negotiation process and because of the periodic process involved.[28] Additionally, there are some escape clauses in the WTO structure that allow countries to have disparity, not harmony, in their tariffs on a selected few products (as the U.S. has done in the past for textiles, steel, and motorcycles).

Countries have become increasing aggressive in filing complaints with the WTO in recent years. For example, the EU complained that subsidies provided to Boeing presented an unfair advantage to Airbus in 2002, and complaints by Brazil and Canada moved the WTO to open an investigation into U.S. farm subsidies in early 2008. Complaints come from all quarters—some feel that the WTO has a reputation as a bully, whereas others (such as *The Wall Street Journal*) say it is indecisive and powerless.[29] There is also a trend for countries to act on their own to strike deals with a few others, possibly undercutting WTO influence.[30]

Resolving International Disputes

The mere presence of an agreement to oversee trade does not ensure a lack of conflict between countries. Instead, there is considerable trade and legal disagreement among countries. Resolving any disputes across borders can be and is very complex. This is partly because the trade conflict may be viewed or treated differently by international and domestic laws. The U.S., for example, has been castigated by some countries for trying to restrict U.S. and foreign exports to nations it is in conflict with, such as Cuba or Iraq. They claim that the U.S. action violates WTO stipulations, whereas U.S. officials point to domestic laws and constraints that force their hand. An important question in situations like this is: where should the issue be resolved? Which court or country has or should have jurisdiction in situations like this?

Source of Jurisdiction

One of the most important examples of this issue happened in 1984, when one of the deadliest industrial accidents in history occurred near Bhopal, India. Union Carbide India, Limited (UCIL), an Indian corporation, operated a chemical plant near Bhopal. An accident, allegedly resulting from negligence of the operators, was catastrophic. Winds blew a lethal gas into the densely populated city and the death toll was staggering. Over 2,100 people lost their lives and nearly 200,000 others suffered injuries, some of which were debilitating. It is important to note that UCIL was incorporated under Indian laws and its stock was traded publicly on the Bombay Exchange (Bombay is now Mumbai). A majority of its stock (50.9 percent) was owned by Union Carbide Corporation (UCC), a U.S. company; 22 percent of the stock was owned by the Indian government; and the remaining 27 percent by private Indian investors.

Immediately after the accident, American lawyers traveled to India and signed up many Indian clients (most all of those affected were Indian). Within four days of the accident, the first of over 100 legal actions was filed in the U.S. District Court. To justify the filings in U.S. courts, the argument was made that the American parent corporation (UCC) controlled the subsidiary (UCIL). Union Carbide countered by claiming that they no longer had operational control over this or the other seven UCIL plants in India; plant operation was terminated at least a year before the accident. They claimed, therefore, that Indian courts were the correct forum to hear the case. All parties (UCC, the U.S. lawyers, and the victims' families) were of course, aware that any damage awards would probably be substantially higher in U.S. courts. The U.S. Circuit Court of Appeals ruled in 1987 that India was in fact the appropriate forum to hear the case, provided that UCC submit to the jurisdiction of Indian courts and agree to satisfy any judgment reached against them. Eventually, Union Carbide (U.S.) reached an agreement with the Indian Supreme Court to pay $480 million to the victims, a relatively small amount by U.S. standards.

In a more far-reaching case, an Australian court ruled in early 2003 that a flamboyant Australian mining mogul (and rabbi), Joseph Gutnick, could sue New York-based Dow Jones & Co. (owners of *The Wall Street Journal Online*) in Australian courts. Rabbi Gutnick claims that an article published in the U.S., and distributed via the Internet, defamed his reputation. The ruling let Gutnick avoid U.S. courts where free speech traditions would likely have been a dead end and enter Australian courts where defamation laws gave him a good chance of winning. This left *The Wall Street Journal Online* to defend itself in this distant venue; they settled the case in late 2004. Many companies paid close attention to the case as it raised troubling issues for cross-border commerce. For example, what if an Englishman sues an American publisher for defamation and the American firm must defend itself under the British legal code? Libel laws in the U.S. place the burden on the plaintiff to show intent to defame, whereas the burden falls on the defendant in British courts. Or, what might happen to an American firm that made a movie with nude scenes? Could they be prosecuted in those countries that ban such scenes, such as Kazakhstan?

The Wall Street Journal is read online in hundreds of countries and one implication is that it would have to heed laws in those countries. Another case was brought forward by a Saudi businessman, Yousef Jameel, in Britain against *The Wall Street Journal* for defamation. He claimed that the article incorrectly linked him to a list of contributors of money to al-Qaeda. The case, however, was dismissed by a high court in the U.K. in 2005 without ruling on the jurisdiction or location issues, because it was read by only a few people. While many companies are watching these cases closely, some others have already acted. Intuit, the database software maker, has pulled its products from countries such as France as a protective reaction to avoid libel, product liability, and other legal actions.[31]

These cases raise issues about whether foreign companies are responsible for the effects of their products and alliances in foreign markets and illustrate that it is difficult to decide which country's courts and laws apply to Internet and other such situations. Several legal principles apply. One of these is the principle of sovereign immunity, or the general protection of a country or leader from civil suit or criminal prosecution. An interesting example recently occurred when a deep-sea treasure-hunting company in Tampa, Florida (U.S.), found over $500 million in coins, silver, and gold on a Spanish galleon sunk by the British off the coast of Portugal in 1804. The firm spent millions locating and salvaging the find. Spain disagreed that the U.S. firm had the right to keep the treasure and filed suit in the U.S. to claim the booty as theirs, according to maritime law. U.S. courts ruled in Spain's favor and dismissed suits against the country based on sovereign immunity. Spain flew two C-130 cargo planes to Tampa to recover the massive treasure. Likewise, a law passed in 1789 by the first U.S. Congress, called the Alien Tort claims law, although inactive for centuries, has recently been used by non-U.S. citizens to sue in U.S. courts over what are claimed to be violations of international law committed overseas. For example, a recent suit was filed in the U.S. on behalf of Nigerian refugees against Royal Dutch Shell (an Anglo-Dutch firm). It alleges that the country aided the oppressive Nigerian regime in abusing workers and other serious violations. The case has reached the Supreme Court and justices have raised questions about why the case belongs in a U.S. court, since it has nothing to do with the U.S. other than that a subsidiary of Royal Dutch Shell is in the U.S. A ruling was expected in July of 2014 that will have far-reaching effects for this little-used law from the late 1700s.[32]

As illustrated by these cases involving governments and cross-border issues, problems may be the result of political issues surrounding the legal ones.

Political Issues and Risks in International Management

We have shown that it is important to be aware of the prevailing legal system operating in any one country, but legal systems can be impacted or changed altogether by the prevailing political situation. This can have far-reaching consequences on the conduct of business in that country. Many multinationals are experienced at evaluating the political environment of their home country. They may have less experience, however, with making such judgments about other countries. It is easy to understand that it is tough for a multinational to run smoothly in times of great political strife, revolution, or war. Less obvious, however, is the fact that there are many other sources of risk for international managers to consider. In this part of the chapter, we will first define political risk, give examples of various forms of business risk, discuss predictors of risk used by firms, and then talk about ways to manage or reduce that risk.

What Is Political Risk?

Political risks are the actions by groups of people or governments that have the potential to affect the immediate or long-term viability of a firm. This definition encompasses a large number of events—all the way from a revolution that results in confiscation of a firm's operations and assets, down to small changes in the tax code. Some of these directly involve legal issues (such as a law that does not permit exports to a certain country). Although they may be based on legal code, their enforcement or existence itself represents a form of political risk for a multinational.

Many of the factors involved in determining political risk are difficult to predict or anticipate, even for an expert in international politics. For example, many experts believed that Iraq would not invade Kuwait in 1990 and therefore did not consider the potential negative effects on operations in that country. Conversely, many thought that the Chinese economy was bound to cool off after several years of remarkable growth, but growth did not abate. While there is no doubt that the Middle East is generally viewed as risky, there are forms of risk inherent in most areas of the world. For example, the EU severely restricts Japanese auto imports and the United States has a history of tight control over foreign investment in the banking industry and strong government support of agriculture, both of which are due to internal political reasons.

Because even experts have difficulty with political predictions, it would be difficult for business leaders to anticipate all of the political risks affecting global business. Nevertheless, because of the potentially calamitous effects of political events, management needs to investigate political risk before entering a new market, and continually monitor political events that may affect ongoing operations. To accomplish this, some firms maintain and consult up-to-date descriptions of the political environment in an effort to predict the effects on their operations.

Types of Political Risk

What is the nature of the many political risks involved in international operations? Some feel that there are too many to account for, and this may be true. Nevertheless, there have been some efforts to help companies respond by classifying political risks into manageable categories. One system divides types of threats or risks into three main categories. These include risks resulting from (1) the political environment, (2) prevailing domestic economic conditions, and (3) external economic relations.[33]

Figure 2.4 presents examples of each of these three main categories, and we will talk about each of these in turn. Please note that in this figure numbers are assigned to each risk variable. This effort to quantify many different threats to doing business in a particular country has two main purposes. If you sum up the total scores for each country, you can get a relatively accurate way to compare the risks of doing business internationally. By quantifying specific types of risk, a company can target and work on specific threats. For example, if there are severe restrictions on money transfers from a country that a firm otherwise finds attractive, the system can focus its entry efforts on dealing with that threat. Perhaps the company could strike a deal with the government that would reduce such restrictions for a reasonable period of time.

Political Environment Risk

First, there are many types of political variables that could present a risk to conducting business. For instance, the stability of a country's government and political system are important sources of uncertainty. In recent years, we have seen the effects of dramatic and sometimes violent changes in political systems, and these changes have had major negative effects on the multinationals operating in those countries.

Perhaps the most important risk faced by firms in such situations is *nationalization*. This occurs when a government forces the transfer of ownership from private to state control. The height of this activity occurred from the 1960s through the 1970s, during which time over 1,500 firms were nationalized by about 70 different countries. Industries that were capital-intensive and based on indigenous resources such as crude oil production, mining, and steel were most susceptible to nationalization. The reasons for government takeover of an industry are many. For one, a new government may wish to show that it is tough—tough enough to face up to foreign powers and businesses. A government may

Type of Risk	Examples	Minimum Score	Maximum Score
Political/ economic environment	Stability of political system	3	14
	Possibility of internal conflicts	0	14
	External threats to stability	0	12
	Degree of economic control	5	9
	Dependability as trading partner	4	12
	Provides constitutional guarantees	2	12
	Effectiveness of public administration	3	12
	Quality of labor relations/social peace	3	15
Domestic economic conditions	Size of population	4	8
	Per capita income	2	10
	Economic growth, last 5 years	2	7
	Potential growth, next 3 years	3	10
	Inflation, last 2 years	2	10
	Openness of cap market to foreigners	3	7
	Availability of high-quality labor force	2	8
	Ability to hire foreign nationals	2	8
	Availability of energy resources	2	14
	Regulations on environment/pollution	4	8
	Degree of infrastructure development	2	14
External economic relations	Import restrictions	2	10
	Export restrictions	2	10
	Foreign investment restrictions	3	9
	Ability to enter into partnerships	3	9
	Protection for brands, trademarks	3	9
	Restrictions on money transfers	2	8
	Currency revaluation previous 5 years	2	7
	Balance of payments condition	2	9
	Amount of oil/energy imports	3	14
	International financial standing	3	8
	Currency exchange restrictions	2	8

Figure 2.4 A Method for Rating Political Risk across Countries.

Source: Adapted from Dichtl, E., and Koeglmayr, H. G. (1986). Country risk ratings. *Management International Review*, 26, 4–11.

also nationalize a company because of its value to national defense or because of the power that industry may wield globally. The crude oil industry is an excellent example of this goal. At the beginning of the century, most crude oil operations were foreign owned. Through the decades, especially during the 1970s, oil operations were nationalized—so much so that most oil production facilities are now domestically owned.[34] Recently, Bolivia, Venezuela, and Ecuador have all engaged in this process. In 2006, for example, Bolivia's President Evo Morales nationalized the oil and gas industry by sending in troops. As the largest investor in Bolivian energy, Brazil was the biggest loser in that action.[35]

If a government nationalizes an industry or company *and* then compensates the multinational that is affected, then that action is called *expropriation*. Many countries (including the U.S.) recognize the right of a country to expropriate assets via the sovereign immunity principle we discussed earlier. Here, this principle means that no nation has the right to judge or challenge the internal actions of another state, provided that state has proceeded justly.[36] Of course, the meaning of just action is complex and open to interpretation. Nevertheless, it appears that a government cannot expropriate property or other assets unless three requirements are met:

1. The expropriation must be for a public purpose.
2. The action must be performed in a nondiscriminatory way—foreign investors must be treated the same way as domestic investors.
3. Investors must be provided prompt and adequate compensation for their equity holdings.

Courts have typically ruled that if a sovereign government acts consistently toward domestic and foreign firms, then full compensation may not even be necessary.[37] The mass nationalization of the crude oil industries by many countries in the Middle East and North Africa in the 1970s is an example of expropriation since foreign and domestic firms were typically offered compensation for their losses. Although there may be long-term negative effects when a country expropriates (such as future reluctance to invest by foreigners), usually an agreement is reached that both parties find at least acceptable.

When nationalization discriminates against foreign firms by offering little or no compensation for loss of property, however, this action is called *confiscation*. In this case, courts have typically ruled that property owners are entitled to full compensation. Regardless of a favorable court ruling, confiscation can be devastating and there are many recent examples. For instance, in the years following World War II, governments in China and Eastern Europe confiscated a great deal of private property with little or no compensation to foreign investors. Cuba did the same following the communist takeover in 1959, and more recent examples include Venezuela, Chile, Peru, and Zimbabwe. Although expropriation and confiscation have been relatively rare since the early to mid-2000s, firms should be mindful of the risk. When it does occur, the effect is substantial. Consider BP's experience in Russia in 2008, where it was forced to cede control over its Sakhalin oilfield to Russian companies.[38] One tactic used by some big Russian firms was to pay public officials to raid offices of BP (or other foreign business competitors) and make them subject to criminal investigations.[39]

Figure 2.4 shows that many other political events can happen. Internal strife and violence may result in disruption of production and productivity as well as more important things such as threats of injury and possibly even death to employees or their families. Likewise, radical political activity such as terrorism and other forms of violence have created great hardship and problems in many different countries,[40] including the U.S., India, Indonesia, and many more.[41] Unfortunately, one such example is the dramatic increase in crimes such as kidnapping. While Mexico may not be the first example that comes to mind, kidnapping has skyrocketed there over the last six years. Latin American countries in general have some of the highest kidnapping rates in the world. There are about 3,000 kidnappings each year in Colombia,[42] resulting in millions of dollars of payout money. Up to one-third of executive time is spent on security issues and coordination while in Colombia.[43] See the following International Insights feature for more detail on this serious topic and what firms can do about it.

International Insights

In Harm's Way: The Danger of Doing Business Abroad

Among all of the business success stories over the last decade, one is not particularly well known—the explosive (and growing) "industry" of kidnapping. While no international agency keeps precise records, a non-governmental organization (NGO) that is headquartered in the Netherlands estimates that there were 25,000 confirmed kidnappings in 2007. Because of mistrust of government officials in many countries, resolutions of kidnapping are often done without their involvement. So, this figure may be closer to 75,000. Nearly half of these crimes occur in Latin America, with Mexico leading the way, although kidnapping is becoming more prevalent globally. Some kidnappings are politically motivated and make the news, such as kidnapping, and subsequent rescue, of Colombian presidential candidate Ingrid Betancourt, 3 American (Northrop Grumman) contractors, and 11 Colombian police in 2008. They were held by rebels in the jungle for over six-and-a-half years.

But, experts believe that this case is the exception. Most kidnappings involve the old-fashioned profit motive and this is why the abduction of wealthy individuals and executives has metastasized into a worldwide business. In fact, U.S. businesspeople are victims of nearly 100 violent attacks each year while doing business in foreign countries, recently affecting firms such as Adobe, Chevron, Halliburton, and Schlumberger. Criminals target tech executives and their children in India, oil company workers in Nigeria, ship operators off Somalia, and affluent businessmen in Asia. *Forbes* reports that the frequency of kidnapping, robberies, and other crimes rose steadily throughout the 1990s into late 2008. Between 2005 and 2007, nearly 500 non-Iraqi workers (44 Americans) were kidnapped. A third of the Americans and one in seven others were killed outright, even though ransoms of nearly $100 million were paid.

Africa has its share of problems too. In the Niger Delta, 150 oil industry workers were kidnapped for ransom. Shell, Chevron, and Transocean have all grappled with this problem. An oil engineering firm, Willbros Group, left Nigeria after nine of its employees were kidnapped by militants. In Haiti, 150 Americans have been kidnapped since 2004. Most victims were taken while visiting family during holidays and involve relatively small ransoms.

But, nowhere has the rise been as steady as in Mexico. Powerful drug cartels have "diversified" their portfolio by expanding into kidnapping, with a focus on businesspeople. A particularly brazen event occurred recently when armed members of the Zeta cartel abducted two Americans in Austin, Texas. They were moved in a car trunk to Dallas before Dallas police rescued them thanks to a tip from a third American who had been kidnapped but who escaped. Even Mexicans were shocked recently when the 14-year-old son of Alejandro Marti, the wealthy owner of a Mexican sporting goods chain, was kidnapped. A $500,000 ransom that was paid to the La Flor gang did no good. Sadly, the boy was killed and his body later recovered in a car trunk. Demonstrators took to the street after the arrest of the ringleader, a former Mexico City police detective. Still, about two people a day are kidnapped in Mexico, leading the U.S. State Department to issue travel alerts for visitors to Mexico.

Oddly, all of this has given rise to a cottage industry surrounding this increasingly popular crime—that of private security companies that provide information as well as personal security and negotiation skills. Kidnappings and ransom insurance are an example of this growth: 60 percent of Fortune 500 firms carry this insurance for their employees. Firms such as Chubb Insurance have seen their global premium revenue jump 15 percent each year since 2000, generating $370 million in 2010. Insurers, in turn, contract with consultants who size up the kidnappers, deal with their demands, negotiate the ransoms, and determine when to pay. Data show that this is effective: victims are four times more likely to survive if they are insured. In total, the kidnapping industry racks up about $1 billion a year, not counting the $500 million portion for the perpetrators.

So, what are businesspeople to do? Experts say that terrorists often target high-profile executives before they even set foot in a country. Increasingly, the lower and mid-level employee is also feeling the negative effects of crime, yet they are the ones least likely to be protected by a security service. How can they—or anyone, for that matter—travel and do business more safely? One way is to follow the advice of Chuck Vance, a former Secret Service agent who worked for three presidents and now has clients in over 1,500 companies in more than 50 countries (www. vancesecurityusa.com). He suggests to "learn how to blend in with the scenery." You may become a target simply because you look very foreign and wealthy. Leave your Rolex watch and your Armani suits at home. Rent a mid-sized Ford rather than a Mercedes. Fly commercial, as opposed to the corporate jet. Criminals monitor the airports and use this as a marker for a good target. Fly non-stop, as take-offs and landings are the most dangerous times. If you are one of Vance's famous clients and are willing to spend the money, he will eliminate trouble ahead of time. Agents will travel to the country in advance of your visit to scout the airport, your proposed routes, and your hotel. If you cannot afford these services, Vance recommends that you do your own homework by investigating the country that you will visit and contact the U.S. embassy and State Department before you go. One final piece of advice from Vance is to "think like the terrorist. If I were going to knock me on the head, where would I do it? When would I strike?" More than 85 percent of all kidnappings occur on a weekday morning, on a public highway while the victim is on the way to or from work. This means that you have to stay alert and vary your daily routine. Do not eat every night at the same bistro at the same time, or go jogging every morning at 7 a.m. Swap cars with other employees unpredictably and avoid cabs. Do not share any personal information, including your hotel name or room number, cell phone number, or the like. Give out your work address and office phone number at most. After all, history shows that wherever international business goes, bandits are sure to follow![44]

Figure 2.4 also presents other forms of political risk. Although less sensational in their effects, they are probably more common. For example, the climate surrounding a country's labor relations is something to consider in every region where a multinational might do business. As Chapter 13 discusses, labor regulations vary dramatically, and some are not favorable to business. It is important to review those relations periodically in the countries in which the company already has a presence. Regardless, like the other specific examples of political threats or risks, each can be evaluated and scored by the concerned company.

Domestic Economic Conditions as Risk Factors

Figure 2.4 also presents a number of domestic economic criteria that could make a foreign investment more or less risky. Domestic conditions such as per capita income and growth rate and the presence of roads, airports, and communication systems can add or reduce the amount of risk a company may face. Ordinarily, good infrastructure support reduces risk and thereby facilitates entry and expansion of business. At the same time, however, risk can present opportunity. Take, for example, the telephone infrastructure in Hungary, where in the early 1990s there were only 96 phone lines per 1,000 people (the U.S. rate was 545 phone lines per 1,000 people), and the installation of a new home land line required a five-year wait. A U.S. firm, Qwest, viewed this as an opportunity and entered the Hungarian market with their cellular division. Business boomed; they immediately received over 10,000 requests for service.[45] While Hungary is widely viewed as one of the most stable and risk-free economies around, this example highlights the fact that risk evaluation systems should not be applied thoughtlessly or without creativity.[46]

Other domestic risk factors include the passage of legal regulations on environmental pollution. The enforcement of such laws could restrict how a multinational may operate in a foreign country. In turn, these restrictions almost always increase operation costs to the company. For example, in Germany, companies must abide by rigid packaging laws when selling and shipping their products. This "green dot" law requires businesses to do two things:

1. accept back from consumers all excess packing materials;
2. encourage recycling of the materials by alerting customers about this option with a green dot on the material and with prominent recycling facilities at the point of purchase.

Many experts suggest that such laws will continue to spread across the globe and that "green" is the new watchword in business today—not necessarily resulting in cost or risk, but instead in opportunity. Chapter 3 discusses Nike's "green" changes that save the firm some $800 million a year.

In Germany, as in the U.S., there are many similar restrictive environmental laws that affect the production and disposal of industrial wastes. In some countries, however, environmental laws are lax or, in some cases, almost nonexistent. This absence of regulation may be due partially to the struggles of developing countries to improve economic conditions. Environmental issues may be lower on the priority list, or a country might wish to do as little as possible to discourage foreign investment. As a result, these countries may become places for waste-producing countries to dump this material. For example, "e-waste" such as old computer monitors, keyboards, printers, and TVs, contains dangerous amounts of lead, cadmium, and mercury.

This is a huge problem today in the U.S., where the electronics market is massive and product turnover cycles are getting shorter.[47] Nearly 1,200 mostly smaller companies have emerged that "recycle" this waste. Some, even those who extol green practices, are breaking the law with illegal shipments of such waste overseas. These dealers may set up trucks in suburban mall parking lots and advertise that they will recycle equipment for free or a small charge, so many environmentally conscious and well-minded people head to these to recycle old TVs and computer monitors. Yet, some of these firms have been accused of shipping this waste to places such as Guiyu, China, a notorious e-waste site where local children have lead levels twice that of EPA limits. This is especially problematic for China because it already faces an environmental crisis due to its quest for (and use of) resources to fuel its burgeoning economy.[48] To deal with this problem, over 50 countries became signatories to the Basel Convention, an agreement on the international transport of hazardous wastes. A key element of the agreement is that informed consent about the movement of the toxic waste must be given and permission received from all countries through which it passes.

Many countries are increasingly concerned with the effect of industry on their environment. In addition to the direct costs to firms doing business, there are also indirect effects of concern for the environment. Because of several major environmental disasters, awareness of these important issues has intensified. Some countries like Germany even have major political parties organized around environmental issues. Thus, there are direct and indirect forms of risk associated with this factor. Clearly, these affect the business decisions of multinationals. A consumer products company may build its plant in Mexico rather than in the U.S. (its intended market) because American pollution control regulations require expensive equipment. Similarly, a chemical company may manufacture in Indonesia rather than in Germany because of the extensive industry restrictions. These examples raise ethical and other issues, such as whether a multinational should capitalize on weaker restrictions in another country, a topic discussed in the next chapter. For now, we note that the relative presence or absence of legal restrictions in any one country is often considered in an overall risk rating system like that presented in Figure 2.4.

External Economic Relations as Risk Factors

Figure 2.4 shows that the manner in which a country relates economically to another country can also be a source of risk. Whereas some of the earlier factors we considered were rare (e.g., civil war), virtually every country restricts its external economic relations in several ways. This makes this final risk category all the more important. For example, many countries have restrictions on imports, usually in the form of *tariffs*. A tariff is a fee paid by an exporter to the country of import and, therefore, is something that increases the price of that foreign product or service relative to the domestic counterpart. Through the use of taxes such as these, a country can restrict imports and provide protection for domestic industry (even if unwittingly).

Tariffs, however, are not the only way that imports can be restricted. One country may wish to limit imports. This might be done in order to force another country to accept more of its goods or because of internal politics that impact imports (e.g., a weak motorcycle industry). Until 2000, when it was prohibited by the WTO, the EU limited the import of Japanese autos to a percentage of the total autos sold in the EU. The U.S. did the same at one point in order to pressure Japan into purchasing more American-made components because it was believed that Japan had informally restricted the import of those parts. Finally, a country may restrict imports when they are perceived as a threat to the health or safety of its citizens. In 2003, "mad cow disease" was discovered in U.S. livestock. While the U.S. argued (similar to the British before them) that the disease did not affect the harvesting of the beef, 65 countries placed restrictions on the import of U.S. beef products. Exports of U.S. beef declined from 1,300,000 metric tons in 2003, before the first mad cow was detected in the U.S., to only 322,000 metric tons in 2004. It has since risen to its earlier levels.

Export controls, or restrictions, are important concerns for international managers and there are many different forms. *Sanctions*, *embargoes*, and *boycotts* are three terms that refer to actions by a country that constrain trade for political rather than economic reasons, but they differ in their intended magnitude. Sanctions are sets of specific restraints involving trade and can take many different forms. For example, a country may cancel its preferential tariff fees for another country, restrict access to computers or other high technology, or prohibit the export of certain weapons systems. Some of these sanctions were used by the U.S. against China after that government's violence against the pro-democracy movement in 1989, and again in Haiti in 1994 in an effort to restore a democratically elected government. The U.S. also maintains sanctions against Iran, Sudan, Cuba, Syria, Burma, North Korea, Venezuela, and the Democratic Republic of Congo, among others.

An *embargo* is an all-out prohibition of trade with another country—not just commerce in several specific service industries or of critical goods. Typically these are imposed in order to protect national security or to promote a certain foreign policy, and they have been used by the United States since the late 1700s. Often embargoes are instituted during times of war, but they are imposed during peacetime as well. The President of the United States has considerable discretion to enact an embargo. He or she can direct the Department of Commerce's Bureau of Export Administration to add a country to an embargo list because it impacts national security or is not in compliance with world agreements on weapons.[49]

Based on these criteria, the United States currently has designated Cuba, Iran, Libya, North Korea, Sudan, and Syria as countries for which this broad set of controls currently applies.[50] The embargo against Cuba, for example, has been in place since 1961, when the attempted invasion of U.S.-backed forces was crushed. An extremely strong lobby in the U.S. has kept this embargo in place despite some efforts to remove the trade ban and some signs from the Obama administration of a willingness to open relations.

Critics have pointed out that the use of embargoes (and sanctions) is not effective. For example, an analysis of the nearly 50 different uses of sanctions and embargoes to achieve political goals from 1970 to 1983 showed that few were successful.[51] Partly, this lack of success resulted from the diffuse focus of the sanctions, some dealing with improvement of human rights and others as protests against terrorism. But mainly the restrictions were ineffective because other countries filled the void left by the sanctioning country. This is one of the major complaints from the business community about such restrictions. American businesspeople sometimes object by asking, "Why should we be penalized by our government from doing business in Burma because their human rights record is not up to our standards?" They maintain that U.S. multinationals are unfairly punished because American sanctions are often not observed by other countries that may continue to do business, and even take advantage of opportunities created by American sanctions.

The relevant U.S. government agencies (such as the Departments of Treasury, Commerce, and State) that are responsible for developing and implementing sanctions and embargoes are familiar with these complaints. The Commerce Department (via its Bureau of Export Administration) is in fact charged with issuing licenses for exports, some of which may override existing sanctions. A business must file an application for an export license, the first step of which is to properly classify for the government the commodity that you want to export. This is a complex process that involves classifying a product, detailing where it is going, and learning the nature of the restrictions that are in place. An application for the export of scuba gear and outboard engines to a Gulf country, for example, might not be permitted because of fears of attacks on oil tankers in the Gulf.[52] After receiving an application, the Department of Commerce then has 90 days to issue or to deny a license to export the product(s), although approval recently has averaged only about five days.

The application for license, like a tax return, is a self-report of one's behavior. As is the case with a tax return, there are some applicants who do not tell the truth. One example is those who provide misleading information about the nature of their product or where it is going. An infamous example of this occurred in 1986, when the U.S. Navy determined that Soviet submarines were somehow able to move without any detectable noise. Over the next several months, it was revealed that the Soviets had acquired advanced equipment from Toshiba, in violation of Japanese and U.S. export laws. It was discovered that Toshiba received permission to export because they had deceived the Japanese government by changing the description of the exported equipment. Because of this threat to security, the U.S. reacted strongly: government contracts totaling over $200 million with Toshiba were canceled, and Congress banned the company from doing business with the government for three years. The Japanese reacted lightly to the infractions, suspending the sentences given to Toshiba executives and imposing only a $16,000 fine.[53]

Violations can also occur via the problem of *diversion*. This term refers to the use of an export license to provide materials to a third party not included on the license. A U.S. oil company might legitimately seek a license to export oilfield equipment to one country, but that recipient could in turn send the equipment on to Tripoli, which would be in violation of the U.S. export embargo on Libya. This situation is not uncommon and has led courts to rule that the burden is on the exporter. That is, it is the exporter's responsibility to screen and proceed diligently with foreign buyers regarding their intended uses of the product. There are very extensive civil and criminal penalties in place for those found in violation of export laws.

Even if a company proceeded with good faith, filed a legitimate application for a license, and then went to great lengths to investigate a customer, they still may be denied a license. Most likely this will be because of the national importance of the export controls that have been implemented (such as weapons technology). Nevertheless, they still have an avenue of appeal. A firm could request that the Secretary of Commerce determine the foreign availability of their product. If there is a non-U.S. source of the product that is comparable in quality, they may still be granted a license to export despite the controls that are in place. Almost certainly, however, an application and appeal will be denied if the business involves exporting controlled weaponry (such as missile technology or nuclear equipment and materials). Supercomputers are also highly controlled because of their strategic significance. There are many global agreements on the trade in these items, and several important governing organizations, such as COCOM (Coordinating Committee for Multilateral Export Control), are devoted to the control of such exports. COCOM, in particular, was originally formed in 1949 to prevent the Soviets from acquiring technology that could lead to a military advantage (now superseded by the Wassenaar Agreement and involving over 40 countries).

Export controls such as sanctions, embargoes and control lists can often be ineffective because the products can be provided by companies in other countries who are not so constrained. If the issue is important enough, a set of countries may wish to go one step further to restrict trade by enacting a *boycott*. If sanctions and embargoes represent a unilateral unwillingness to engage in trade (such as the U.S. against Cuba), a boycott is a multilateral or collaborative effort to do the same thing. Examples of the collaboration of many countries to try to restrict trade include the Wassenaar Agreement, mentioned previously, and the international coalition formed to confront Iraq's invasion of Kuwait in 1990. Thus, boycotts have the same purpose as sanctions, embargoes, and other controls. They are simply more extreme in their scope. Because of the collaborative nature of boycotts, they tend to be more effective than export controls established by only one country. As you might guess, boycotts are much more difficult to organize and implement, as illustrated by the incredible effort of getting traditional enemies (such as Israel and Jordan or Saudi Arabia) on the same side against Iraq in the Gulf War.

One additional problem with boycotts is that unless the organization is very complete, it can polarize sides against one another. An example of this situation is the boycott instituted against Israel in December 1954 by the League of Arab States. The League (currently composed of 22 nations) agreed that companies that traded with Israel could be blacklisted and would not be permitted to do business with League members. Because of its close political ties with Israel, the U.S. enacted anti-boycott laws that prohibit American firms from complying with, or otherwise supporting, the boycott by refusing to do business with Israel or a blacklisted firm. Courts have ruled that by merely returning an Arab League questionnaire that sought information about business relations with Israel, Briggs and Stratton Corporation was in violation of the law.[54] Given the volatile situation in the Middle East, it remains to be seen what will happen regarding business risk for firms via the boycott. After the Gulf War, some Arab countries (such as Kuwait) resumed doing business with Israel, but events that occurred since the beginning of the Intifada in 2000, the Gulf War, and the U.S. military presence there, have deflated hopes that the nearly 50-year boycott may be coming to an end. While the boycott has lost considerable steam since its peak in the 1970s, it still presents a risk to U.S. business that some other countries do not face.[55] U.S. firms are required by law to report efforts by companies around the globe to force them to obey the boycott and this number is tracking upward. An example might be when ship entry documents for entry into the United Arab Emirates (U.A.E.) ask if any of the cargo is of Israeli origin.[56]

Exports are significant parts of the economy of every country; they provide much-needed foreign exchange and are the source of many jobs. But they are only one important example of external economic risk factors. In Figure 2.4, we presented many other types of risk involved, including restrictions on the extent of foreign investment allowed in a particular country. Some EU countries, for example, restrict the ownership of television and radio stations to nationals. Germany gives preference to companies that are majority owned by its nationals when awarding licenses to broadcast. The U.S. also has some detailed restrictions on the percent of foreign ownership of radio and TV stations. Typically, restrictions like these are imposed to prevent foreign control of critical industries (e.g., finance, communications, etc.). And, these restrictions increase the risk of doing business since they prevent the foreign multinational from having key operational control of the firm.[57]

Protection for Trademarks and Other Intellectual Property

One of the biggest external risks that companies face is the lack of legal protection of their products and trademarks in a foreign country. The most common legal protections are the use of patents, trademarks, and copyrights. Several international agreements are in place to provide such protection. The Paris Convention, for example, is a set of international guidelines recognized by nearly 80 countries. Ultimately, however, a multinational must rely on law enforcement within a country to protect its products and intellectual property rights. To comply with WTO requirements, India again began to honor international pharmaceutical patents in 2005—something that it had not done since the early 1970s. In 2009, the Swiss firm Novartis had its patent on the cancer drug Gleevec rejected by India's Intellectual Property Board. Novartis has filed a lawsuit in Indian courts seeking to change an element of that country's patent law.[58] Market share of foreign drug firms in India has dropped considerably. Hopes were raised with a new patent law passed to fulfill its WTO obligations, but the patent rules in India are a major source of frustration to the large pharma companies.[59]

Yet, if the reward is great enough, a firm may wish to take the risk of operating in a country where the enforcement is lax at best. Such is the case in Spain, where unlicensed generics create a major headache for U.S. drug firms. Spain has a complex court system, one with no special courts or judges with expertise in patent law or the complex pharmaceutical industry. So, when U.S.-based Merck sued the Spanish generic maker Chemo-Iberica for violating its patent on the anti-cholesterol drug Zocor, the case was mired in Spanish courts for years. At one point, Chemo-Iberica even claimed that they had developed a new fungus fermentation process (*aspergillus obscurus*) to produce Zocor, and in doing so bypassed Merck's patent (the generic price was about $11 vs. Zocor's price of $24). This procedure was "obscurus" all right—in fact, mycology experts finally convinced the court that this procedure just did not exist. Finally, Spanish courts ruled for Merck, but they awarded no damages and the process went on so long that the patent expired two days after the case concluded anyway.[60]

Firms that enter China are worried about critical design features or recipes of their products.[61] Professor Kenneth DeWoskin, a Chinese expert at the University of Michigan School of Business, believes that "Chinese research and design institutes look for the best technology in the country and spread it around. They also examine plans and [the] specifications of new ventures, so [there is] bound to be some leakage."[62] Clearly, there is a good deal of "leakage," and the losses extend beyond the entertainment and computer industry. For example, after DuPont introduced its Londax herbicide in China, it decided to build a $25 million plant in Shanghai to produce the chemical. By then, however, a state-owned company jumped into the market with a much cheaper knock-off of Londax. Likewise, shortly after Pilkington opened a plant in China to make glass, a state glass factory sent an order for production equipment to Germany—complete with detailed and obviously pirated plans that were emblazoned with Pilkington's name. And, in plain sight of police on main streets in Guangzhou and Shanghai, Chinese music fans can pick up the latest popular music CDs or Microsoft Office computer software for only $1.50. The U.S. Trade Representative's office states that "anyone can walk into a store in Beijing and buy a pirated copy of Microsoft software. The store simply copies it while you wait." Toymakers such as Mattel and Hasbro are especially concerned, as it is common for their new toys on display at the international Hong Kong Toy Fair to also be displayed by a Chinese competitor that had advance information about them. Because China makes about 70 percent of the world's toys, including those of many American companies, the designs can easily and quickly be copied. After Mattel decided to prototype its new designs in-house and then bring them to the Hong Kong fair, their staff had to chase away would-be copiers who were using cameras, copiers, and iPads to spy on and to copy the designs. Mattel no longer attends the fair.[63]

It's not just products, either—protecting a brand name in the China market is difficult at best. A bogus Chinese breakfast cereal product called "Kongalu Cornstrips" has a trademark and packaging identical to that of Kellogg's cornflakes. A small Chinese computer manufacturer, called "Mr. Sun," has used Sun Microsystem's trademark for all its machines.[64] And, Shanghai consumers can now enjoy coffee at a series of Xing Ba Ke stores. The loose translation of this is "Shanghai Starbucks," although you do not have to read closely as their logo appears identical to that of Starbucks. The general manager of Xing Ba Ke states that "we have a totally different operation" and cites waiters and higher prices as examples of this "new" business model. Starbucks is hardly convinced and had gone to the mat before to protect its brand and logo by suing companies called "Mr. Charbucks" and "Sambucks," among others. In 2006, a Shanghai court ruled in Starbucks' favor, saying that Xing Ba Ke's use of the name and logo from Starbucks was "clearly malicious and improper," and ordered the company to pay a fine as well as to stop using those marketing materials.[65]

Despite this danger of product piracy, once its critical features are revealed, many companies move into the Chinese market anyway. Coca-Cola is one firm, however, that steadfastly refuses such revelations and thus has been careful in China. Because of a similar restriction in India, they have left that country altogether. Coca-Cola quit India after the government demanded that it reveal its secret recipe and transfer other technical information to local management.[66] Many companies, such as Pilkington, are now wary of seeing their partners become their rivals. New Balance Shoes is aggressive in this regard. At a shoe factory in southern China, a man named George Arnold closely inspected the stitching and workmanship of a run of nearly 7,000 New Balance shoes. Arnold pronounced the lot as authentic and promised Horace Chang, the plant owner, that he would wire the $120,000 payment soon. But, in fact, this was a sting orchestrated by New Balance using private detectives. It and other companies such as Rolex, Reebok, Gucci, and Cartier are making these interdiction efforts to stem the tide of counterfeiting. Interestingly, Chang was a licensed supplier and manufacturer for New Balance since 1995. But after a disagreement about shoe quality and brand name, and armed with evidence that his factory was producing "on the side" shoes, New Balance began its crackdown. It was galling to see its $60 shoe being sold for around $20 (from Chang's factory) and it severed any relation with Chang. This reflects an increasing trend for authentic products, not knockoffs, to be in competition in the marketplace. Procter & Gamble recently fired a supplier that sold its empty shampoo bottles to a counterfeiter who then filled them with different product, and Unilever recently found its partner was producing extra soap and selling it directly to stores.[67]

Stopping this illegal activity is difficult, especially at the company level. In general, however, research indicates that the presence of laws protecting intellectual property rights has a positive impact on foreign direct investment and that this is especially the case among developing countries.[68] Software piracy, for instance, seems to happen in many places, not just China. Several years ago *The Wall Street Journal* reported a raid by the Spanish police at a Madrid monastery where Jesuit priests trained their students on computers using mostly pirated software.[69] Figure 2.5 shows the impact of piracy in a number of markets. This figure presents the percentage of software that is pirated in use for a particular country, a figure estimated each year by the non-governmental organization Business Software Alliance (BSA). BSA estimates that over 90 percent of all software in use in Georgia is pirated. Several countries have dramatically reduced their percentage of pirating in recent years. Since 2004, Russia has had the greatest reduction (19 percent) and China the third largest decrease since that time (10 percent). Japan and the U.S. have among the lowest software piracy rates in the world. Still, about one in five software

Country	Piracy Rate	Losses Due to Piracy (in $m)
Georgia	91	52
Bangladesh	90	147
Libya	90	60
Pakistan	86	278
Indonesia	86	1,467
Nigeria	82	251
Vietnam	81	395
China	77	8.902
Russia	63	3,227
India	63	2,930
Mexico	57	1,249
Saudi Arabia	51	449
Canada	27	1,141
Germany	26	2,265
Sweden	24	461
Japan	21	1,875
U.S.	19	9,773

Figure 2.5 Piracy Rates and Losses in Selected Countries.

Source: Adapted from Business Software Alliance (BSA). (2012). BSA website, available at: www.bsa.org/globalstudy.

systems are pirated. Plus, the total losses in the U.S. are the highest in the world because of the number of computer users in the U.S. relative to other countries.[70]

Many of these knockoffs and originals alike are targeted to the U.S. market. Some of the more commonly fake products are a "who's who" list of brands: Nintendo, Nike, Louis Vuitton, and Nokia, among others. While some shipments are intercepted before reaching the U.S., many items get through. A few years ago, we witnessed knockoffs of $250 Oakley sunglasses going for $15 near the Pike Street Market in Seattle. Students at our own university (the University of Dayton) were even a source of some leakage. On a summer exchange program in Thailand, students brought home DVD copies of the hit Disney movie *Finding Nemo*, before it had even been released to video stores in the U.S. The price on Bangkok streets was $1.[71] Given the importance that knowledge plays in the economy, some analysts have targeted intellectual property as one of the main competitive advantages for a country into the next century.[72] The ability to preserve those property rights may become an even more important risk factor for the U.S. economy in the near future. In 2006, all WTO members were to have implemented basic rules for protection and enforcement of counterfeiting and intellectual property protection. Yet, a number of high-profile cases have been brought before the WTO in this regard. In 2007, for example, the U.S. brought several actions against China. These sought to force China to improve legal protections and to increase enforcement of those laws. The case ruled in favor of the U.S. in early 2009. As Chinese law is tightened and more Chinese firms file patents, those of other countries are more likely to be honored.[73]

Summary of Risk Factors

As this chapter has shown, there are a large number of legal and political risk factors associated with doing business in a foreign country. A plus of using a category system like the one presented in Figure 2.4 is that this large number can be itemized and evaluated. A firm considering a big investment in a foreign country may wish to systematically weight all of these factors themselves or use information provided by companies specializing in risk assessment. Many such providers exist in the marketplace and for a fee will provide a detailed analysis of the risks of market entry. Political Risk Services and the Economist Intelligence Unit are two firms with widely circulated lists of annual risk ratings for countries around the globe. If the overall score is too high, a multinational might be advised to drop that country from consideration unless the risk can be managed or reduced in some way. For example, Burma, Nigeria, Russia, Sudan, and Yemen often make the top ten of riskiest countries, whereas Norway, the Netherlands, and Canada are examples of countries often rated as the least risky. China recently broke the top 30 in the world (among about 150 countries rated), and the U.S. is often within or near the top 15 the least risky countries.

The details provided by these firms can often surprise you, as in the case of India. In late 2008, a widely publicized terrorist attack and siege on the Taj Mahal luxury hotel in Mumbai brought attention to political violence in India. Over 160 people were killed and many more were injured during a 60-hour attack captured on television—one that featured great heroism among hotel employees and security forces alike. But, many outsiders (including investors) are now aware of how dangerous India can be. In fact, there were nearly 2,500 deaths in 2008 in India from acts of terrorism. From 1993 to 2008, over 29,000 people have died in terrorist attacks in India. This figure excludes about 5,000 who have died since 2002 in the Maoist rebellion in the Chattisgarh region, as well as the thousands who have died in anti-Muslim riots in the country.[74] This does not mean that firms should not enter India—in fact, the opposite is true, even though some foreign firms are rightfully concerned. Experts believe the tipping point for such decisions is an investor's assessment of whether the government will make changes to correct these and other related problems. Of course, there is plenty of room for optimism. Consider the strong governance and education systems in southern India (especially Bangalore). These are features that have helped this region build a $60 billion outsourcing industry from scratch.[75] The same can be said about Russia and elsewhere, where investors must weigh the risk and rewards of doing business there.[76]

Managing or Dealing with Political Risk

One advantage of quantifying risk is the ability to make better decisions about entering a country or whether to scale back existing operations in a particularly risky country. Leaving the country completely or scaling back within the country are only two options that firms can use to manage risk. Another advantage of using a rating scheme such as the one discussed earlier is that serious sources of risk can be isolated, and then concentration on those factors can help manage risk. Take, for example, a situation in which labor relations are shaky at best. If this is a critical risk factor, then the multinational might be able to deal with poor labor relations by making some concessions or other proactive steps.

Categorizing Risk Reduction

There are many ways in which a multinational could potentially stave off risk—probably as many methods to reduce risk as there are actual sources of risk. For our purposes, however, we can classify all of these techniques into a more manageable set of categories. For example, there are defensive/reactive strategies that a multinational could use to deal with risk.[77] These types of methods try to keep company operations or other assets out of the reach of the risk factor, such as a hostile government. There are also linking/merging strategies. These entail methods by which a firm tries to get closer to the risky country, perhaps even making itself indispensable to the local economy. Each of these strategies can also be direct, in that efforts to take on the problem in a head-on manner are used (such as by legal action). But, a strategy could also be indirect in that it is approached in a roundabout way, with hopes that in the long run risk will be reduced. Figure 2.6 presents some examples of each of the four types of risk management.

Examples of Risk Reduction

A type of direct/defensive risk reduction is to make operations in the target country dependent upon your work in one or more other countries that are less risky. This dependency allows firms to preserve control over key supplies, components, and critical

Type of Strategy	Direct	Indirect
Defensive/ reactive	• Legal action • Make operations dependent on parent company • Control makeup of management	• Risk insurance • Contingency planning methods • Home country government pressure
Linking/ merging	• Long-term agreements (e.g., NAFTA) • Joint ventures • Promoting host goals	• Lobbying of foreign governments • Becoming good corporate citizen to host country

Figure 2.6 A Classification of Approaches to Managing Risk.

technology that are necessary to run the subsidiary, and it can have a number of positive effects on the firm's exposure to risk. For example, operation dependency would make a subsidiary less attractive for expropriation by a host government X. This is because the plant could not operate without supplies that are provided via a plant in country Y. This approach would also leave your firm less open to risks of trademark or copyright theft if critical technology was deployed in another country. In this way, a multinational can reap multiple benefits from one action, a characteristic typical of many of the risk management strategies listed in Figure 2.6.

It is not uncommon for companies to use several different risk management techniques simultaneously in an effort to hedge risk. Another type of risk management that could be used is a direct/linking strategy. A multinational may wish to enter into long-term agreements with a foreign country that specifies treatment of its subsidiary, and the home country may do the same. The North American Free Trade Agreement (NAFTA) is one example of this method. The option to enter into joint ventures (discussed in Chapters 8 and 9) may be available; in this case, the subsidiary is already jointly owned by either the host government or a firm headquartered in the host country. In those situations, a company has less equity at risk and other national firms also share a fair amount of the risk. But, there are also significant barriers to overcome in order to have successful links.[78] Another common example is when a government itself invests in a venture in another country, as Thailand has done with its strategic plan to open over 3,000 Thai restaurants in the U.S. and to partner with Starwood Hotels.[79]

A multinational may also wish to use a set of indirect methods to manage risk. It may purchase political risk insurance as an indirect/defensive strategy. Political risk insurance is an indirect strategy because it does nothing to deal with or alter the actual potential risk; it simply serves to protect the firm if and when the risk materializes. Several private firms provide insurance to cover various risks that are inherent to doing international business, including many of the risks reviewed previously (e.g., political violence and nationalization). These private firms have increased their presence in recent years and have offered new products. A Bermuda-based insurer, Sovereign Risk Insurance, is in over 100 emerging markets. One of its contracts is for a seven-year, $95 million policy for a bank's structured finance deal in Brazil. Banks increasingly seek this type of insurance against foreign governments that abrogate contracts for political reasons (e.g., an infrastructure loan which a government subsequently expropriates).

In the U.S., the federal agency Overseas Private Investment Corporation (OPIC) also provides similar coverage. Started in 1971 in order to promote private American business investment in developing countries, OPIC is self-sustaining, has recorded a positive net income every year of operation, and runs at no net cost to U.S. taxpayers. Currently, the insurance programs are available for new and expanding business in over 140 countries, although they now specialize in emerging markets that fit U.S. policy priorities.[80]

Risk insurance covers some but not all of the risks, though. A company can purchase protection against expropriation and confiscation of its foreign enterprise or coverage for property and income losses caused by political violence (e.g., declared or undeclared wars, civil war, revolutions, terrorism, sabotage and more) are covered. OPIC compensates the investor's share of income loss resulting from the political violence and other risk factors. Riders to the policy can be added that compensate for losses resulting from damage outside a firm's plant or facility that affects business (such as railways, power stations, and suppliers). OPIC also protects the multinational against currency inconvertibility. This is not insurance against currency devaluation; the company has to assume this risk itself. Instead, investors are compensated if they suffer new currency restrictions that prevent the conversion and transfer of profits from their foreign investment. In general, this insurance is very comprehensive and can help overcome a firm's reluctance to deal with risk factors in a foreign operation or investment.[81] The From Theory to International Practice exercise at the end of the chapter will provide additional information about OPIC.

Other examples of indirect/defensive strategies are presented in Figure 2.6. These can be used as contingencies that help manage events after the decision is made to take on the risk. This "scenario planning" approach, proven in military applications, is becoming an increasingly popular method for balancing risk in international business.[82] Or, a firm could gradually increase its investment in a foreign operation while appealing to its own government to pressure the foreign (host) government. This was a common practice in Japan a decade ago when American automakers felt that the risks of closed markets and opportunities could be altered by pressuring the U.S. government to seek concessions from the Japanese.

Finally, a multinational can use indirect/linking strategies to remove or reduce some forms of risk. One way it can do this is by making itself into a "good corporate citizen" by contributing to local charities and supporting public projects. This strategy involves linking with the local community as opposed to pulling away, and is indirect because it is hoped that the goodwill generated by the donations will eventually spread to the company itself. Starbucks' approach is a good example of a market acting locally while thinking or doing business globally. In addition to seeking to protect its trademark in China (a direct approach), the company has also made an effort to position its stores as members of the local community. In Beijing, for example, Starbucks supports many local groups and it feels that these indirect approaches have paid off. When the mistaken U.S. bombing of the Chinese embassy in Belgrade happened in 1999, protestors cut through Starbucks, buying coffee on their way to (violent) protests at the U.S. embassy. Sales actually rose at Starbucks that day, whereas other prominent American businesses suffered some damage.[83]

Indirect/linking strategies are used by firms in many nations. Japanese efforts to increase U.S. philanthropic activity in the late 1980s and early 1990s is yet another example. Lobbying is another method of this type of risk reduction, although it is difficult to classify in practice. It can be a form of linking in that lobbying could be done to directly increase relationships with other countries (e.g., to jointly form trade associations). Lobbying could be a defensive strategy as well, as when U.S. special interest groups (such as steel, automobiles, and textiles) seek import restrictions that reduce the risk in their businesses.[84] Foreign firms long ago recognized the important role that lobbying plays in the operation of the U.S. federal government. The Foreign Agents Registration Act (FARA) was passed in 1938 out of fear that German firms were exercising too much influence in the U.S. The FARA still requires that every agent lobbying on behalf of a foreign client register and detail what he or she is working on, which government officials he or she visits, and any donations provided.[85] Records indicate that Belarus, sometimes referred to as the last dictatorship in Europe (because of a terrible human rights record), has hired AG Consulting to "urge for a more favorable attitude toward" the country. Indeed, the number of registered lobbyists to the U.S. government has grown from about 7,000 in 1991 to nearly 15,000 in 2012.

Chapter Summary

We reviewed several of the most important legal systems in operation around the world today, including *civil law*, *common law*, and *Islamic law* systems. Each has unique implications for commerce that take place under its jurisdiction. Other systems have their own characteristics and constraints.

Laws operate—or sometimes fail to operate—within a particular political system, and a new regime can dramatically change the legal system. The importance of political issues above and beyond the rule of law are highlighted within the chapter. We also showed that the amount of *political risk* incurred by a multinational can have major negative effects. Political risk can result from many different events or actions taken by governments or groups of people. A variety of domestic and external economic conditions can also increase risk.

The chapter concludes on one of the most important points of all—what a multinational can (and should) do after it senses or encounters a risk. The options include strategies of direct risk reduction and/or indirect efforts to stave off potentially catastrophic effects if the risk materializes. Finally, we recognize that while some multinational actions might be both legally consistent and politically astute or expedient, the action might still be inconsistent with company or society values—this last point provides a bridge to our next chapter on international ethics and social responsibility.

Discussion Questions

1. Describe the differences among the three main legal systems that exist today. How might each affect the commerce that is conducted within its jurisdiction?

2. How might the specifics associated with a civil or Islamic legal system present problems for U.S. business? What behaviors might you see, and which ones could you tie to their respective legal systems?

3. What are the key forms of political risk and why might Nigeria, Peru, or Burma be considered relatively risky places to do business? Why might the U.S. be not as highly ranked as you might think and what steps would you recommend to deal with this risk?

4. What steps would you recommend to deal with other forms of risk in the above and other countries?

Up to the Challenge?

Combatting Counterfeiting in the Middle Kingdom

At the beginning of the chapter we presented a challenging problem for manufacturers around the globe—the ability of Chinese companies to quickly develop, manufacture, and distribute counterfeit products of some of the world's most famous brands. These bogus products are often tough to distinguish from the authentic ones, whether those are Callaway golf clubs, Winston cigarettes, or Louis Vuitton handbags. We asked you to consider what can be done to combat this issue.

This is a tough problem that needs to be tackled in multiple legal and political ways. For one, multinationals are going to have to spend money. Louis Vuitton spent more than $16 million in 2007 on investigations and legal fees into knockoffs of their products. GM added seven full-time staff members to scour the globe for counterfeit parts, and Pfizer has five such staff members in Asia alone. This money and personnel on the ground can be helpful in designing anti-counterfeit measures. Nokia, for example, learned that making their phone batteries with holographic images and 20-digit identification codes that must be authenticated online would help. Cigarette maker JT International has spent millions of dollars over the last half decade developing a network of investigators and informants within factories that they suspect of counterfeiting. Pfizer introduced RFID tags on all Viagra pills sold within the U.S., allowing them to track drugs from the lab to the consumer. Callaway scans websites looking for low-priced golf clubs bearing their name. But, many complain that once they shut one illegal manufacturer down, another opens quickly. So, some clever companies have tried to beat the knockoffs in the market with overt and covert tracking methods.[86] Anheuser-Busch has taken big hits from knockoffs in China. In some cases, counterfeiters were simply refilling discarded Bud bottles. The firm started to use more expensive, imported foil on the bottle tops and added a temperature-sensitive label that changed colors when cold; this kept knockoffs at a low level.

A bigger challenge has been getting the Chinese authorities on board with enforcing the anti-piracy laws within the country. A small Danish furniture franchise shows that this can be done if you persist. Bo Concepts makes attractive modern furniture and its outlet in Shanghai did well. But, within its first two years of operation, 12 companies opened nearby that made furniture whose resemblance to Bo Concepts' design was uncanny. These competitors had the Bo Concepts catalog and bragged that they would make exact replicas for one-sixth of the price. Bo Concepts petitioned the State Administration for Industry and Commerce (SAIC) for help. It hired private detectives to present evidence before SAIC judges, but this was a dead end. It persisted, however, using old-fashioned Chinese connections (*guanxi*). Through contacts in the SAIC, it repeatedly petitioned the judges and the local Chinese patent bureau. After months of constant badgering, Bo Concepts got the board to confront the copycats and force them to stop making fakes. While the "war" continues in China for Bo Concepts, it at least won a battle.

Increasingly, however, Chinese officials have gotten more aggressive about this illegal activity, in part because knockoffs are now starting to hurt Chinese firms in their potent domestic market. Some recent cases have also changed the view that counterfeiting is a victimless crime. In 2005, for example, 15 infants died from phony milk powder; the perpetrators were sentenced to eight years in prison. Recently, Li-Ning Co., China's market leader in athletic apparel, reported that many of its products were being counterfeited. Now, it too employs a staff to ferret out counterfeiters. U.S. firms who distribute products made by Chinese suppliers can also run into trouble, especially when safety shortcuts occur. U.S. product recalls of space heaters, table lamps, wooden toys, and tires have all impacted American distributors. Efforts to seek compensation from those Chinese suppliers go unaddressed and have brought down the U.S. firm.[87]

Under political pressure from the OECD, the U.S., EU, and the WTO, China has begun to toughen laws regarding knockoffs. The value of goods that a counterfeiter was required to have on hand upon arrest in order to be prosecuted was lowered from $12,000 to $3,600. And, a high-profile trial of two Americans charged with selling nearly $1 million of DVDs via the Internet emphasized the point. Having stricter laws is one thing, but enforcement often depends on local officials, who may themselves be involved. Raids conducted on behalf of Titleist and Nike Golf in the Fujian province turned up a "plant," hidden by a dirt-covered hatch and protected by a dark empty cave. The occupants had apparently left earlier with their products, having been tipped off by local officials.

Microsoft has tried the "carrot" in addition to the legal and political "stick" to fight piracy in China. It agreed to build a new cloud computer center in Hangzhou; a $1 billion investment. The purpose was to establish a model city where property rights have greater protection than elsewhere in China. Hangzhou has promised to "robustly" clamp down on pirated software and officials have set enforcement targets, including shutting down knockoff shops and encouraging local businesses to use authentic software. Yet, the deal has been criticized by many because even if the Hangzhou/Zhejiang government enforcement is effective, it is but one city or province within a large country.

Either way, this particular strategy is unusual, even for Microsoft, which in the past has used its muscle to lobby the central government to increase enforcement. The Hangzhou deal comes on the heels of a 2009 case pushed by Microsoft in which 11 people were convicted in a Chinese court of making and distributing counterfeit software. Likewise, in late 2008, Microsoft started sending out software updates that turned computer screens black if they had a pirated version of Windows—a move that angered a large number of Chinese. In the meantime, the U.S. is aggressively moving to protect American firms, including initiating direct talks with China (and other countries) and putting added pressure on the WTO to enforce its piracy guidelines. There are some initial promising signs—the Business Software Alliance reports that piracy has dropped 10 percentage points since 2005.[88]

International Development

Culture Knowledge Quiz

Purpose

To promote an awareness of cultural differences.

Instructions

The following questions are intended to provide insights into your awareness of other cultures. Please indicate your best answers to the questions listed below—there is no right or wrong answer. Use the following scale, recording it in the space before each question. When you have finished, add up your score and compare it with those of others in your group. Generally, higher scores are associated with greater knowledge and awareness of cross-cultural features. Your instructor may place you in small groups and ask you to look at differences in more detail. One way to approach this is to discuss *sets* of questions in more detail (see categories below). Talk about the general strengths and challenges your group might have (what area might be the biggest challenge to your group? What subarea is a real strength?) Compare these strengths and weaknesses with those of other groups. Are there consistencies among students as a whole in terms of possible strengths and challenges?

(Note: This brief instrument has not been scientifically validated and is to be used for classroom discussion purposes only.)

1	2	3	4	5
Definitely no	Not likely	Not sure	Likely	Definitely yes

1. ___ I can conduct business effectively in a language other than my native language.
2. ___ I can read and write in a language other than my native language with great ease.

3. ___ I can understand the proper protocol for conducting a business card exchange in at least two countries other than my own.

4. ___ I can understand the role of the *keiretsu* in Japan or the *chaebol* in Korea.

5. ___ I understand the differences in manager–subordinate relationships in two countries other than my own.

6. ___ I understand the differences in negotiation styles in at least two countries other than my own.

7. ___ I understand the proper protocols for gift-giving in at least three countries.

8. ___ I understand how a country's characteristic preference for individualism versus collectivism can influence business practice.

9. ___ I understand the nature and importance of demographic diversity in at least three countries.

10. ___ I understand my own country's laws regarding giving gifts or favors while on international assignments.

11. ___ I understand how cultural factors influence the sales, marketing, and distribution systems of different countries.

12. ___ I understand how differences in male–female relationships can influence business practices in at least three countries.

13. ___ I have studied and understood the history of a country other than my native country.

14. ___ I can identify the countries of the European Union without looking them up.

15. ___ I know which gestures to avoid using overseas because of their obscene meanings.

16. ___ I understand how the communication styles practiced in specific countries can influence business practices.

17. ___ I know in which countries I can use my first name with recent business acquaintances.

18. ___ I understand the culture and business trends in major countries in which my organization conducts business.

19. ___ I regularly receive and review news and information from and about overseas locations.

20. ___ I have access to and utilize a cultural informant before conducting business at an overseas location.

Scoring: Sum up the scores you assigned to each item in the categories below to create these subscores. Then, add together your five subscores for your total scale score.

1	Language/communication (sum of items # 1, 2, 15, 16)
2	Interpersonal protocol (#s 3, 7, 12, 17)
3	Business practices/approaches (#s 4, 5, 6, 11)
4	Basic county features, such as laws, history, news (#s 10, 13, 14, 19)
5	Key cultural values (8, 9, 18, 20)
Total	(Sum all subscores above)

From Theory to International Practice

Calibrating International Business Risk

Purpose

To provide hands-on understanding of the risks present in an international environment. You will be asked to apply this knowledge to one or more specific countries.

Instructions

The Overseas Private Investment Corporation (OPIC) is a U.S. federal agency whose purpose is to provide services, including insurance, to companies that invest overseas. One service that it offers is political risk insurance to protect firms against the risks of expropriation, war, and other negative economic events (e.g., inconvertibility of local currency). OPIC is well organized and service oriented. Its website (www.opic.gov) is detailed and informative about a number of OPIC programs.

For this exercise, we want you to choose one or two countries in conjunction with your instructor. Research these countries with a special eye toward legal, political, and economic risk factors. Many sources are helpful here (e.g., the CIA Factbook is an excellent example: https://www.cia.gov/library/publications/the-world-factbook/; the U.S. government supersite can also be helpful here: www.export.gov; as can the Export–Import Bank of the U.S., which has country-specific features: www.exim.gov/). Additionally, you may also be able to obtain a political risk rating for your chosen countries. To get this number and an interpretation, you could refer to several sources: (1) The Economist Intelligence Unit's analysis of risk (registering allows you access to sample country reports), or (2) a more widely available source, such as the annual risk ratings that appear in *The Wall Street Journal*.

Then, scour the OPIC website, especially the pages dealing with its insurance programs. Its "Doing Business with Us" page is a good overview of the organization's history and activities, and its "Publications and Resources" page has lots of detail on its insurance programs. Look through this latter page with an eye toward information you would find useful for investigating the countries you have chosen. After reading those materials, prepare a brief (one page or less) report on your countries of choice. Some of the questions you may wish to address in this report are:

- In general, what is the OPIC and what is its purpose?

- Are your countries eligible for OPIC support?

- In particular, what kind of support is available?

- How would you or an interested company request support?

- What exactly is insured by your participation in the program?

- What is the approximate cost to a company of such insurance?

- What aspects of risk in your countries would be covered by OPIC?

Notes

1. Homeland Security News Wire. (2011). China overwhelms U.S. with counterfeit goods, available at: www.homelandsecuritynewswire.com/ (retrieved May 31, 2013); ABC News. (2013) China big in counterfeit goods, available at: ABC News.com (retrieved May 30, 2013).
2. Rocks, D., and Halperin, A., (2008). Stalking the wild copycats. *Business Week*, August 18, 62–63; Yatsko, P. (2000). Knocking out the knockoffs. *Fortune*, October 2, 216.
3. This opening box is based lar Endnote Text gely on: Burkitt, L., and Chao, L. (2011). Made in China: fake stores. *The Wall Street Journal*, August 3, B1–B2; Balfour, F. (2005). FAKES! The global counterfeit business is out of control, targeting everything from computer chips to life-saving medicines. It's so bad that even China may need to crack down. *Business Week*, February 7, 54–64; Behar, R. (2000). Beijing's phony war on fakes. *Fortune*, October 30, 189–208.
4. Richards, E. L. (1994). *Law for Global Business*. Boston, MA: Irwin.
5. Czinkota, M. R., Ronkainen, I. A., Moffett, M. H., and Moynihan, E. O. (1995). *Global Business*. New York: Dryden Press.
6. Czinkota, Ronkainen, Moffett, and Moynihan, *Global Business*.
7. Lin, A. (2009). Glut of lawyers in Japan, but no layoffs. *Law.com International News*, March 4, 1, available at: www.law.com; Rowley, I., and Hall, K. (2006). Lawyers wanted. No, really. Once litigation-averse, Japan is rushing to fill a shortage of attorneys. *Business Week*, April 3, 46; Reutter, M. (2003). Japanese legal education system undergoing radical transformation. News Bureau: University of Illinois, November 13, 1–3, available at: http://news.illinois/edu; Darlin, D. (1989). Foreign lawyers in Japan chafe under restrictions. *The Wall Street Journal*, February 7, B1.
8. Richards, *Law for Global Business*.
9. Tillinghast, E. (1992). A survey of the legal profession. *The Economist*, July 18, 1–18.
10. Ball, D. A., McCulloch, W. H., Frantz, P. L., Geringer, J. M., and Minor, M. S. (2004). *International Business: The Challenge of Global Competition*. New York: McGraw-Hill/Irwin.
11. Cullison, A. E. (1991). Product-liability claims hard to win in Japan. *Journal of Commerce*, August 9, 2A.
12. Schaffer, R., Earle, B., and Agusti, F. (1993). *International Business Law and Its Environment*. Minneapolis, MN: West.
13. Balfour, F. (2008). Islamic finance may be on to something. *Business Week*, November 24, 88.
14. *The Economist*. (1992). Islam's interest., January 18, 33–34; see also www.Islamic-banking.com for information about this topic.
15. Rao, N. V. (1992). Islamic interest rule threatens Pakistan's bid for aid. *The Journal of Commerce*, January 29, 2A.
16. Balfour, Islamic finance may be on to something; Ginsburg, J. (2005). Koran-friendly lenders. *Business Week*, February 14, 20.
17. Mohieldin, M. (2012). Realizing the potential of Islamic finance. *World Economics*, 13, 127–141; *The Economist*. (1996). Islamic finance: Turning the Prophet's profits, August 24, 58–59.
18. Fidler, S. (2009). Defaults pose latest snag in Islamic-bond market. *The Wall Street Journal*, June 16, C1, C2; Frangos, A. (2007). How Islamic finance handles foreclosures. *The Wall Street Journal*, December 12, B6.
19. Al-Salem, F. (2008). The size and scope of the Islamic finance industry: An analysis. *International Journal of Management*, 25, 124–130; Batchelor, C., and Roberts, A. (2003). Sharia-compliant financing starts to take off. *Financial Times*, August 13, 27.
20. Pope, H, (2005). Islamic banking grows, with all sorts of rules. *The Wall Street Journal*, May 3, C1, C4; Batchelor, C. (2004). Investors unsure about sharia. *Financial Times*, May 12, 29.
21. *The Economist*. (2008). Savings and souls, September 6, 81–83; Albrecht, K. (1998). Turning the Prophet's words into profits. *Business Week*, March 16, 46.
22. Bohn, L. E. (2012). Uniting the Muslim world, one cat photo at a time. *Bloomberg Businessweek*, September 24–30, 37–38; Brunwasser, M. (2012). Salamworld, the Facebook

for Muslims? April 12, available at: www.theworld.org (retrieved May 27, 2013); Flock, E. (2012). Salamworld to be Facebook for Muslims—but much cleaner. *The Washington Post*, February 28, available at: www.washingtonpost.com (retrieved May 25, 2013); Ungerleider, N. (2012). Pan-Islamic Facebook competitor Salamworld to launch in November, September 4, available at: www.fastcompany.com (retrieved May 20, 2013).

23. Richards, *Law for Global Business*.

24. Chen, K. (2003). A see-through China? Leaders aim at transparency. *The Wall Street Journal*, August 13, A8.

25. Roberts, D. (2009). As factories fail, so does business law. *Business Week*, April 13, 46–48; see also: *The Economist*. (2009). Hard to swallow: China indicates that the real targets of its anti-monopoly law: outsiders, March 21, 68–69.

26. *The Economist*. (2001). Unprofitable policies: Insurance in Asia, August 11, 57–58.

27. Miller, J. W. (2009). Economic downturn makes trade talks a priority: WTO chief says rest of world is waiting for U.S. to make its position clear. *The Wall Street Journal*, July 7, A5; *The Economist*. (2006). In the twilight of Doha, July 29, 63–64.

28. Roberts, D. (2002). Clear sailing for pirates. For now, the WTO can't stop mainland counterfeiters. *Business Week*, July 15, 53; Roberts, D., and Magnusson, P. (2002). The tricks of trade: WTO neophyte China is learning fast. *Business Week*, July 15, 52–53.

29. De Jonquieres, G. (2003). Modest goals in Cancun: Trying to achieve liberalization in a group of 146 countries is well-nigh impossible. *Financial Times*, September 4, 11.

30. King, N., and Miller, S. (2003). Post Iraq influence of U.S. faces test as new trade talks. *The Wall Street Journal*, September 9, A1, A10; Newman, M. (2003). So many countries, so many laws: The internet may not have borders, but the legal system certainly does. *The Wall Street Journal*, April 28, R8.

31. Newman, So many countries, so many laws.

32. Berfield, S. (2012). Odyssey and the lost Spanish treasure. *BloombergBusinessweek*, June 7, 70–75; *The Wall Street Journal*. (2012). Alien tort invasion, October 1, A14; Bravin, J. (2012). Justices probe "alien tort" law. *The Wall Street Journal*, October 2, A4.

33. Dichtl, E., and Koeglmayr, H. G. (1986). Country risk ratings. *Management International Review*, 26, 4–11.

34. Kobrin, S. J., and Punnett, B. J. (1984). The nationalization of oil production. In D. W. Pearce, J. Siebert, and I. Walter (eds). *Risk in the Political Economy of Resource Development*. London: Macmillan.

35. Luchow, D., and de Cordoba, J. (2006). Bolivia's President Morales orders nationalization of natural gas. *The Wall Street Journal*, May 2, A1, A12.

36. Richards, *Law for Global Business*.

37. Richards, *Law for Global Business*.

38. Powell, B. (2008). How the KGB (and friends) took over Russia's economy. *Fortune*, September 15, 85–94.

39. Bush, J. (2008). Russia's raiders: companies are paying public official to raid the offices of business rivals. *Business Week*, June 16, 67–71; Bush, J. (2008) Roughed up in Russia. *Business Week*, June 16, 69.

40. Cohen, L. P. (2007). Chiquita under the gun. *The Wall Street Journal*, August 2, A1, A9; Timmons, S. (2000). Doing business among the body snatchers. *Business Week*, July 31, 22–23.

41. *The Wall Street Journal*. (2008). Companies caught in India drama, November 28, A3.

42. Bray, R. (1997). Busy execs can be easy targets. *Financial Times*, February 6, 12.

43. *The Economist*. (2009). Kidnapped: Bosses are taken hostage in France, March 21, 68; Fifield, A. (2003). War on terror creates unlikely allies. *Financial Times*, August 18, 4.

44. *The Economist*. (2012). Buying safety, June 9, 65; Vardi, N. (2008). Kidnap, Inc. *Forbes*, October 13, available at: www.forbes.com; Booth, W. (2008). Kidnap consultant taken in Mexico. *The Washington Post*, December 16, (www.washingtonpost.com); Conley, J. (2009). Kidnapped: Protecting executives abroad. *Risk Management*, available at: www.rmmag.com

(retrieved July 15, 2009); Yu, R. (2010). Companies try efforts to protect workers in world's danger zones. *USA Today*, August 24, A1.

45. Griffin, R. W., and Pustay, M. W. (2000). *International Business: A Managerial Perspective*. Reading, MA: Addison Wesley.

46. *The Economist*. (2003). Political and economic stability, May 17, 90; *The Economist*. (2003). Political and economic stability, August 16, 82.

47. Grow, B., and Elgin, B. (2008). The dirty secret of recycling electronics. *Business Week*, October 27, 41–44; Kollar, M. (2005). Cops of the global village: How standards of conduct set half a world away are shaping big companies' behavior. *Fortune*, June 27, 158–166.

48. *The Economist*. (2008). A ravenous dragon: A special report on China's quest for resources, March 15, 1–22; *The Economist*. (2008). Melting Asia: China and India are increasingly keen to be seen tackling climate change, June 7, 29–32; Engardio, P., Roberts, D., Balfour, F., and Einhorn, B. (2007). Broken China. *Business Week*, July 23, 39–45.

49. Richards, *Law for Global Business*.

50. U.S. Department of Treasury, Office of Foreign Asset Control. (2009). List of country sanction programs, available at: www.treas.gov/offices/enforcement/ofac/programs/; U.S. Department of State. (1995). U.S. exports: Non-proliferation and foreign policy controls. *U.S. Department of State Fact Sheet*, December 6, 1–2.

51. Hufbauer, G. C., and Schott, J. J. (1984). Economic sanctions: An often used and occasionally effective tool of foreign policy. In M. R. Czinkota (ed.) *Export Controls*. New York: Praeger.

52. Schaffer, Earle, and Agusti, *International Business Law and its Environment*.

53. Domain-b.com (2007). "I didn't sell aircraft parts to Iran," says Dutch businessman, September 21, 1–2; available at: www.domain-b.com/economy/trade/20070921_businessman.html; Bandler, J. (2006). Ports in a storm: U.S. probes whether shipper acted to bust trade embargoes. *The Wall Street Journal*, May 20, A1, A14.

54. Richards, *Law for Global Business*, 325.

55. U.S. Bureau of Industry and Security. (2009). BIS Annual Report, Office of Anti-Boycott Compliance, Bureau of Industry and Security, U.S. Department of Commerce, available at: www.bis.doc.gov/news/2008/annreport07/fy2007_oac.htm.

56. www.bis.doc.gov/antiboycottcompliance/oacantiboycottrequestexamples.html.

57. Sharma, A., Bahree, M., and Beckett, P. (2012). Rising risk: Foreign firms sense hostility in India. *The Wall Street Journal*, March 30, B1–B2.

58. Whalen, J., and Greil, A. (2009). Novartis patent rejected in India. *The Wall Street Journal*, July 7, B3; Ahmed, R., and Guha, R. (2012). *The Wall Street Journal*, October 2, B1.

59. *The Economist*. (2012). Taking pains: Indian drug patents, September 8, 62; Pesta, J. (2001). India braces for brave new drug world. *The Wall Street Journal*, March 7, A17.

60. Johnson, K., and Fuhrmans, V. (2002). Spain's generics are a headache for drug firms. *The Wall Street Journal*, December 11, B1, B2.

61. Kraar, L. (1995). The risks are rising in China. *Fortune*, March 6, 179–180.

62. Kraar, The risks are rising in China.

63. Fowler, G. A. (2003). Pirates in China move fast to pilfer toy makers' ideas, turning to stealth marketing. *The Wall Street Journal*, January 31, B1, B4; *The Economist*. (2003). Imitating property is theft, May 17, 51–54.

64. *The Economist*. (1996). Chinese piracy: A case for copying, November 23, 73; Faison, S. (1996). Copyright pirates prosper in China despite promises. *The New York Times*, February 20, 1996; Kraar, The risks are rising in China.

65. Mickie, M. (2006). Starbucks wins case against Chinese copycat. *Financial Times*, January 3, 1; Adler, C. (2003). Copied coffee? *Fortune*, September 29, 48.

66. Spaeth, A., and Naj, A. K. (1988). PepsiCo accepts tough conditions for the right to sell cola in India. *The Wall Street Journal*, September 20, 44.

67. Kahn, G. (2002). A sneaker maker says China partner became its rival: New Balance, other brands claim suppliers flood market with extra goods. *The Wall Street Journal*, December 19, A1, A8.

68. Lemper, T. A., (2012). The critical role of timing in managing intellectual property. *Business Horizons*, 55, 339–347; Seyoum, B. (1996). The impact of intellectual property rights on foreign direct investment. *Columbia Journal of World Business*, 31, 51–59.

69. The Associated Press. (2007). U.S. puts 12 nations on copyright piracy list, April 30; Greenberger, R. S. (1996). Software theft extends well beyond China. *The Wall Street Journal,* May 20, A1.

70. The Business Software Alliance. (2009). Sixth Annual BSA/IDC Global Software Piracy Study, available at: www.bas.org/globalstudy.

71. Barnes, W. (2003). Thai TV group battles pirates. *Financial Times*, August 20, 17; see also: Schuman, M., and Ressner, J. (2005). Disney's great leap into China. *Time*, July 18, 52–54.

72. *The Economist*. (2009). Hard to swallow: China indicated the real targets of its anti-monopoly law: Outsiders, March 21, 68.

73. Sherr, I., and Robinson, F. (2012). EU probes Motorola patents, April 4, B4; *The Economist*. (2009). Battle of ideas: Chinese companies are enforcing patents against foreign firms, April 25, 68; Murphy, J. (2009). Toyota builds thicket of patents around hybrid to block competitors. *The Wall Street Journal*, July 1, B1, B2.

74. Czinkota, M. R., Knight, G., Liesch, P. W., and Steen, J. (2010). Terrorism and international business. *Journal of International Business Studies*, 41, 826–843; Srivastava, M., and Lakshman, N. (2008). How risky is India? In the wake of the Mumbai siege, business must weigh the persistence of political violence against the strength and promise of the Indian miracle. *Business Week*, December 15, 24–26.

75. Srivastava and Lakshman, How risky is India?

76. Bush, J. (2008). Russia: It's scarier than you think. Risk and reward in Russia. *Business Week*, October 20, 44–49; Powell, B. (2008). Just how scary is Russia? *Fortune*, September 15, 80–83.

77. Gregory, A. (1989). Political risk management. In A. Rugman (ed.) *International Business in Canada*. Scarborough, ON: Prentice-Hall.

78. Kunreuther, H. (2003). The pitfalls of an interdependent world: Businesses can reduce their exposure to the risk of catastrophic events by co-operating with others. *Financial Times*, August 28, 9.

79. *The Economist*. (2007). Of coups and coverage: Political risk insurance, April 7, 71–72.

80. Bennett, J. (2001). Small businesses abroad get a big hand from OPIC. *The Wall Street Journal*, May 14, B10.

81. Federgruen, A., and Van Ryzin, G. (2003). New risks put scenario planning in favour. *Financial Times*, August 19, 7.

82. Gadiesh, O., and Pean, J. M. (2003). Think globally, market locally. *The Wall Street Journal*, September 9, B2.

83. Rugman, A. M., and Verbeke, A. (1990). *Global Corporate Strategy and Trade Policy*. New York: Routledge; Yoffie, D. B. (1988). How an industry builds political advantage. *Harvard Business Review*, May–June, 82–89.

84. Frank, R. (2001). Thai food for the world: Government of Thailand plans to open 3,000 restaurants to promote nation abroad. *The Wall Street Journal*, February 6, B1, B4.

85. Barron, A. (2011). Exploring national culture's consequences on international business lobbying. *Journal of World Business*, 46, 320–327; Please see the home page of FARA: www.fara.gov/

86. Li, L. (2013). Technology designed to combat fakes in the global supply chain. *Business Horizons*, 56, 167–177; Sudler, H. (2013). Effectiveness of anti-piracy technology: Finding appropriate solutions for evolving online piracy. *Business Horizons*, 56, 149–157.

87. Berman, B., and Swani, K. (2010) Managing product safety of imported Chinese goods. *Business Horizons*, 53, 39–48; Welch, D. (2007). Importer's worst nightmare: A Chinese supplier, safety shortcuts, and an American middleman under siege. *Business Week*, July 23, 46–48.

88. This closing box is based in large part on Balfour, FAKES; Back, A. (2009). Microsoft tried carrot to fight China piracy. *The Wall Street Journal*, May 16–17, B5; Yatsko, Knocking out the knockoffs, 213–218; Zimmerman, A. (2013). Contending with Chinese counterfeits: culture, growth, and management responsibility. *Business Horizons*, 56, 141–148; Stumpf, S. A., and Chaudhry, P. (2010). Country matters: executives weigh in on the causes and countermeasures of counterfeit trade. *Business Horizons*, 53, 305–314.

chapter 3

doing things right

international ethics and social responsibility

Learning Objectives

After reading this chapter, you should be able to:

- identify the two major approaches to ethics in international management and appreciate their complexity and overlap;
- understand cross-national differences in ethical views and practices and corporate codes, as well as enforcement of those codes;
- recognize how multinationals deal with issues of questionable payments and bribery;
- describe the Foreign Corrupt Practices Act and its implications for U.S. and non-U.S. firms.

International Challenge

Competitive Intelligence: Dumpster Diving for That Extra Edge

Global business is a high stakes competition. Many firms want an edge on the competition, and for some firms this comes via *competitive intelligence* (CI). CI does not refer to blatantly illegal acts such as stealing another firm's proprietary documents. Instead, CI is often a fuzzy set of activities that involve the acquisition of useful information about one's competition. That is not to say that (in practice) this activity does not skate close to, and sometimes over, the line when it comes to ethics and legality—it does. When practiced in a devious way, as it is sometimes, CI becomes a genteel term for what we know as spying. When Oracle, a hardware and software engineering company, went dumpster diving in Microsoft's trashcans in search for documents and clues as to its most recent moves, the whole concept of CI received much attention. But most companies have more panache than Oracle did in that one case. Indeed, that dumpster operation "was the sort of thing that gives legitimate business intelligence a bad name," stated Alden Taylor of Kroll Associates, a large CI firm in New York.

But what exactly is CI? Part strategic planning, CI is designed to anticipate the moves of a firm's competitors via a range of data collection techniques. CI involves sifting through vast amounts of information for emerging trends and information about what competitors might be doing about them. Who conducts CI? Analysts range from librarians to ex-spies and from in-house experts to outside consulting firms. These analysts prowl web pages and trade shows, traipse through the patent office, and keep their eyes and ears open in airports. Companies such as Real World Intelligence, for instance, offer customized versions of software created for the CIA. The software scans through voluminous Internet data, such as new product information on firms' web pages.

How effective is all of this CI effort? It seems to work well, according to insiders. Former bosses of Monsanto's CI unit estimated returns to the tune of $50 million annually. Motorola's former chair, Robert Galvin, hired former government intelligence officers to set up a CI unit for the firm back in the 1970s. Since then, Motorola has never been blindsided in the way Xerox was in the 1980s when their market share in copiers was cut down to size by Japanese firms.

The real issue for business ethicists is not whether CI helps the bottom line, but whether it is morally defensible. For example, a food company wanted to win market share from a competitor with a surprise price cut. First, its CI agents interviewed former employees of the competitor. The idea was to find out exactly when the competitor's sales reps and managers had to get approval from senior management before offering retailers a discount. Next, the actual next-door neighbors of the competitors' senior executives were telephoned under various (false) pretexts in an effort to learn about their schedules. That is when it was discovered that the executives were on a European plant tour. An unwitting, but cooperative, travel agent even handed over their entire itinerary. As a result, the food company's price cuts were launched immediately because they knew that the competitor's executives could not respond quickly. The competitor lost business as a result.

CI and related activity is on the rise. The number of countries spying on U.S. industry has actually increased—not declined—since the end of the Cold War. A 2011 report produced by several U.S. government agencies suggests that the cost to U.S. business, governments, and universities from espionage is in the billions annually, and points fingers at other countries. Some of this activity is blatant, such as when former Russian President Boris Yeltsin chided domestic business leaders for not effectively using stolen technological secrets. And being an ally to a company (or nation) is no assurance that you will be free from CI. The former head of French intelligence publicly admitted that he organized a unit to spy on U.S. firms and that Air France flight attendants eavesdropped and taped the conversations of U.S. businesspeople flying on that airline.

Thefts of U.S. industrial secrets from firms involving Chinese citizens in particular have significantly raised the profile of CI. Yan Ming Shan, an employee of PetroChina, a state-owned oil company in China, was recently charged with stealing the source code for one of the world's most powerful programs for locating oil and gas deposits. Mr. Shan was training on the software at 3DGeoDevelopment Inc. in San Francisco and transferred that code from its network to his computer. A week after 3D officials confronted him, Mr. Shan was arrested at the San Francisco airport as he was about to board a flight to Shanghai. Officials found the source code on his laptop as well as several programs used to break passwords and gain illegal access (one was called "Crack"). The indictment since then shows that prior to Shan's arrest, officials from his company (PetroChina) had visited the U.S. and gave him a large-capacity storage drive. The CEO of 3DGeo admits "it could have killed the company" but yet expressed hopes to continue working with PetroChina. This is only the tip of the iceberg according to a U.S. Inter-Agency report—a large number of cases involving China have come to light recently.[1]

It is easy to see unethical qualities when someone is arrested and charged with a felony. But what about more subtle CI activity? Is that unethical? For example, think about whether the following information-gathering activities are unethical:

- Digging through a company's trash on public property.
- Deliberately eavesdropping on private company conversations.
- Sending phony job-seekers in response to a competitor's want ads.

- ■ Hiring a competitor's former employees.
- ■ Sending phony visitors to tour a competitor's facilities.
- ■ Attending trade shows where a competitor's wares are displayed.

The Up to the Challenge? feature at end of this chapter provides some surprising answers to these questions.[2]

Ethics and Social Responsibility in International Management

As shown in Chapter 2, it is important to have an understanding of the legal and political framework of the countries in which you do business. But, just because business actions are legal or politically expedient does not mean that the action should be taken. There are cases in which those steps might raise a larger personal, organizational, or societal concern. As a result, firms might be better served in the long run by acting within a broad set of value-based guidelines. Yet, practical, useful guidelines are difficult to develop and to implement. Experience has also shown, however, that exacting such rules may increase customer goodwill, help avoid litigation, and possibly even benefit the culture and country in which firms conduct business.[3]

It is important to start by discussing ethical values—an individual's moral judgment about what is right or wrong. Once this is discussed, it is important to move from the personal realm to the corporate one, taking a look at corporate guidelines and how they help companies in various communities and nations in which they do business. For decades now, multinationals have been urged to build such corporate social responsibility (CSR) clearly into their business strategies. Several frameworks exist to help multinational corporations (MNCs) move in this direction by spelling out various types of ethical and socially responsible corporate behavior.[4] Yet, this is a complicated issue—one that becomes even more intricate and tangled when we move from country to country.

Philosophies and Perspectives on Ethics

How should we act and how should others behave? These are major, and enduring, philosophical questions that have been debated for centuries. Ongoing debate reveals many answers to these questions, as well as strong feelings associated with each. Because these philosophies are not our direct concern here, we will boil them down to two main positions: universalism and relativism. These two perspectives suggest sharply different behavior for international managers.[5]

Universalism

Universalism is the belief that there are widespread and objective sets of guidelines for behavior that cut across countries and cultures. Advocates of this position agree that there is a set of moral rules that everyone should follow. For example, universalists point to the fact that there are certain behaviors that most every culture considers wrong, such as harming others or the property of others, and that even seemingly disparate religions share some basic values such as these.

Likewise, advocates also point out that there is wide acceptance of some basic principles for doing business. For example, virtually every country in the world has some sort of law that prohibits bribery, lying, and stealing in business.[6] Such laws may be enforced differently across nations, but the underlying moral code exists, and thus they are widely applicable "rules" for doing business that everyone should obey. Universalists are typically not content to sit back passively with the hope that people will discover these basic principles on their own and then act accordingly. Instead, a common strategy has been to actively develop a set of acceptable behaviors that constitute universal guidelines. Several transnational or global codes of ethics for businesspeople currently exist.[7] For example, universalists have developed a set of minimal rights for international workers. Among other things, these include the right to physical security, free speech, subsistence, and nondiscriminatory treatment.[8] A large-scale study of over 30,000 respondents from 29 countries shows that those from Middle Eastern countries (such as Egypt and Saudi Arabia) are more likely to endorse a universalist position on ethics than are those from over 20 other Western and Eastern countries.[9] This can have important implications for business dealings such as negotiation and conflict resolution across these cultures.

Figure 3.1 outlines several of the more well-known global guidelines.[10] These codes deal with topics as diverse as basic human rights, product safety, environmental concerns, and illegal payments. Figure 3.2 provides a more in-depth look by examining the United Nations Global Compact (UNGC) code. This code consists of a number of principles that multinationals should follow, but it also provides some specificity in areas such as human rights, the environment, and corruption, all of which should be taken into account

---

UN Universal Declaration of Human Rights

Organization for Economic Cooperation and Development Guidelines for Multinational Enterprises

European Convention on Human Rights

Helsinki Final Act

International Labor Organization's Declaration of Principles Concerning Multinational Enterprises and Social Policy

International Covenant on Economic, Social, and Cultural Rights

International Covenant on Civil and Political Rights

UN Code of Conduct on Transnational Corporations

European Economic Community Code of Conduct for Companies with Interests in South Africa

Sullivan Principles: *A set of seven rules, set forth by Rev. Leon Sullivan of the U.S., for companies doing business in South Africa during the apartheid-era (pre-1994). They advocate equal treatment for all in pay, advancement, and other employment practices*

Figure 3.1 Sets of Ethical Obligations for Firms Conducting International Business.

Human Rights—*Businesses should:*

Principle 1	Support and respect the protection of internationally proclaimed human rights
Principle 2	Make sure that they are not complicit in human rights abuses

Labor Standards—*Businesses should:*

Principle 3	Uphold freedom of association and the recognition of the right to collective bargaining
Principle 4	Work to eliminate all forms of forced and compulsory behavior
Principle 5	Eliminate child labor
Principle 6	Eliminate discrimination due to employment and occupation

Environment—*Businesses should:*

Principle 7	Support appropriate cautions to protect the environment
Principle 8	Undertake initiatives to improve environmental responsibility
Principle 9	Encourage the development and diffusion of environmentally friendly technologies

Anti-Corruption—*Businesses should:*

Principle 10	Work against corruption in all its forms, including extortion and bribery

---

Figure 3.2 The United Nations Global Compact.

Source: United Nations Global Compact (2000) *The Ten Principles*, available at: www.unglobalcompact.org/AboutTheGC/TheTenPrinciples/index.html.

if firms wish to operate with integrity. This initiative, launched in 2000, is a partnership among companies, labor, academics, and governments. Over 3,000 companies from 100 countries have endorsed the principles. U.S. firms, such as Nike and Cisco, exemplify the willingness of the private sector to promote corporate citizenship and for business to be part of UNGC's goal of a better and more inclusive global economy.

In practice, however, at least two problems emerge with the implementation of universal principles. First, because the codes attempt to be broad and universal, there is plenty of ambiguity about how they should be interpreted. This has led to inconsistency in the way that different multinationals view (and use) principles such as "favorable working conditions" and "cooperation with local government." Are favorable conditions defined by a 10-hour work day, by regular breaks, and a minimum wage? Some codes, such as the UNGC, have made efforts to provide specific definitions. They have elaborated on the ten basic principles, providing website tools, resources, and implementation details that can help firms better deploy the principles.

A second issue is that many countries and companies have not officially adopted all (or even some) of these ethical obligations. For example, although the U.S. is often seen as being highly concerned with ethical issues, it was slow to sign on to several sets of these global principles presented in Figure 3.1.[11] This is partly because the U.S. disagrees with certain aspects of the guidelines. In addition, it is due to internal political pressures. At times, the U.S. has endorsed various international agreements dealing with ethical issues, but has had trouble getting other countries to cooperate. The enforceability of agreements *after* getting parties to sign on is a related problem. The UNGC, for example, has little regulatory or enforcement "teeth" to it; indeed, it does not police or measure the actions of companies that have signed on. Members are required to report annually on their progress, while the U.N. takes complaints of egregious or systematic abuse of the principles. If there is some evidence of abuse, companies will be asked to respond. If no response is received or if it is inadequate, companies are removed from the Compact.

Relativism

A popular alternative viewpoint is that of cultural relativism.[12] Proponents of relativism believe that ethical behavior in any one country is determined by its own unique culture, laws, and business practices. Therefore, if it is common to provide a public official with a nominal payment to process paperwork for imports, this may be the thing to do—even though it may be illegal in your own country. This perspective of "when in Rome" is often justified on several counts. Perhaps the most important argument is that to do otherwise is to disrespect the culture in which you are a guest. The obvious implication of this argument is that international managers should follow the accepted practices of the country in which they are doing business.

An example of this situation occurred some time ago when American actress Michelle Pfeiffer was in Moscow filming the movie *The Russia House*. She left the set after a few weeks of filming to protest the fact that Russian extras were not allowed to eat the lavishly catered food provided to foreign actors. She was embarrassed by this because the movie was being made at a time and in a place where it was often difficult or very expensive to get quality food, soap, and other necessities. As it turns out, however, there was a law forbidding Western film companies from feeding the Russian extras that they employed. Local officials were called to explain this to Ms. Pfeiffer, as well as convince her to return to the set, stating that this was just the way things were done in Russia. Pfeiffer was eventually convinced, stating, "I didn't sleep that night. Then I realized, this is so typically American of you. Whether I was right or wrong wasn't the issue. The issue was, do I have the right as an outsider to come in and force my sensibilities on this culture?"[13] Ms. Pfeiffer's reaction here is a good example of cultural relativism in practice.

Research shows that there may be differences in adherence to the universalist vs. the relativist position. For example, one study compared views about marketing ethics and found that a U.S. sample was significantly higher in what they called idealism (universalism) and lower in relativism than was a Chinese sample. In this study, U.S. marketers were more likely to believe that actions are moral if they conform to some absolutes (e.g., the appropriateness of a successful ad campaign that may have been offensive to certain groups). The Chinese relied on a combination of relative and absolute values to make their ethical decisions. Moderation of behavior in concrete situations rather than absolute rules has a bigger impact in guiding their decisions.[14]

Corporate Social Responsibility

Becoming a relativist—even if only temporarily—does not give a manager or a firm a "get out of an ethics issue free" card. Unfamiliar, and perhaps distasteful, customs are not immune from analysis or judgment. For example, most people would not agree that suppressing political freedom, using slave or prison labor, or other violations of human rights are morally acceptable because these happen in Rangoon rather than Santiago, Jakarta, or Miami.[15] Likewise, being a universalist does not always translate into the need for action, such as the enforcement of those codes for the good of others. In fact, the belief that corporations are responsible for the impact of their activities on various stakeholders (such as their shareholders, their local and foreign communities in which they operate, and the environment) is the relatively recent notion of corporate social responsibility (CSR). CSR is the deliberate inclusion of public interest into corporate decision making, including attention to the so-called triple bottom line: people, planet, and profit. Critics of this approach argue that CSR detracts from the fundamental role of business—which is business! It's not personal. Others are skeptical of efforts made by organizations in order to engage in CSR, calling it "window dressing" and an effort to keep watchdog groups and government off their back.[16]

Likewise, devotion to a relative or a universal belief set does not always lead to clear choices, nor does it always satisfy critics. Consider that firms sometimes provide responses and justifications for continuing their business activity in countries where indisputably immoral actions are taking place. In apartheid-era South Africa, for example, many multinationals argued that if they divested their business interests in the country, greater harm would result to those for whom sanctions were intended to help. In particular, many thought that divestiture would cause many black employees to lose their jobs. Some firms also argue that they would be better able to push for government reforms by, for example, remaining a player in the South African economy.[17]

Is a corporation being socially responsible by "staying in the game" or taking their capital and going home? "Stay in the game" arguments continue to be made by firms doing business in countries with problematic records in human rights, the environment, and more. PepsiCo continued its business in Burma for years after a coup d'état in 1962 that brought a repressive military regime to power. Under increasing pressure from consumers, government and human rights organizations, PepsiCo decided in 1997 to end its presence there.[18] This is the same year that international economic sanctions were imposed on Burma by the U.S. Many other firms have since left. The Burma military government has also cut deals with foreign companies to commercialize its vast natural gas reserves, including U.S. firms such as Unocal (now Chevron). In the accompanying International Insights feature, we provide background on the social responsibility issues raised by this business arrangement—some of which might conflict with the UNGC's basic principles for multinationals, presented in Figure 3.2.

International Insights

Beyond Rangoon: Chevron and Human Rights in Burma

The behavior of the repressive military government in Burma has been well known since at least 1988, when it initiated a crackdown on pro-democracy demonstrators, killing thousands. Free elections in 1990 resulted in a new prime minister, Aung San Suu Kyi, but the military refused to recognize the election and placed her under house arrest. Although the outside world did recognize her contributions (she won a Nobel Prize in 1991 as well as a U.S. Congressional Gold Medal), she has remained confined for 14 of the last 20 years, only having been released in 2011.

After the 1988 crackdown, some U.S. companies pulled out of Burma because of what they saw as a hostile investment climate, disappointing returns, and an active anti-Burma movement within the U.S. Sanctions have prevented U.S. investment there since 1997, and an import ban on Burmese goods to the U.S. has been in place since 2002. Prior to these actions, Burma signed a contract in 1992 with a French firm giving them the right to develop their massive Yadana gas field, enough gas for 40 years of heavy production. The French invited other companies to buy in as partners, with the military government netting an estimated $400 million a year.

Unocal (purchased by Chevron 2005) decided to invest in the project, despite the known risks, including a U.S. State Department report indicating that the Burmese military maintained order via "arrests, harassment, and [the] torture of activists. Torture, arbitrary detentions, and compulsory labor existed." Unocal felt that the benefits to shareholders and the Burmese people outweighed these problems, and in late 1992 it bought a stake in the venture. A pipeline was built for the gas (under the sea) across Burma and crossed a region inhabited by the Karen, a minority group hostile to the government. Between 1993 and 1998, the pipeline was completed, but at huge costs to the Karen. Human rights groups and the U.S. State Department reported that the military forced hundreds of thousands of Burmese to labor on the project, under very harsh conditions, and that many thousands were subject to forced resettlement. Unocal's own consultant, hired in 1995 to investigate the situation, concurred with earlier reports of human rights violations and added that imprisonment and executions of those opposing to forced labor occurred.

Unocal asserted that engagement rather than an isolation strategy was the best course of action in order to move toward a more open Burma. By 2004, the pipeline was delivering 600 million cubic feet of gas per day. During construction, Unocal had begun programs to benefit the Burmese living along the pipeline, including paid jobs to over 7,000 construction workers and continued employment of about 500 afterward. New medical programs were developed, schools and roads were built, and Unocal provided opportunities for small Burmese businesses. Those negatively affected by Unocal's engagement strategy, however, did not feel that the benefits outweighed the downsides. Fifteen Karen Burmese minority individuals filed suit in U.S. courts, seeking millions in retributions for injuries inflicted by the military along Unocal's pipeline via a law allowing foreign litigants to seek damages in U.S. courts. They claimed that Unocal was a partner with a repressive government and thus complicit. The case was first dismissed, then appealed, and finally settled quietly by Unocal in early 2005. The Burmese litigants received $30 million and Unocal also agreed to create a new fund to improve living conditions there (beyond the programs above they already initiated).

Some observers were shocked that Unocal settled, especially those who were defendants in similar cases (e.g., ExxonMobil, Coca-Cola, and Del Monte Foods). Weeks after the settlement, Unocal merged with Chevron. This case is important because, as one law professor observed, "[t]raditionally, international human rights law is applied only to countries and not individuals or companies." Yet, even human rights groups are divided around the question of whether the pluses outweigh the downsides. EarthRights International said "whether Chevron is there or not, those dollars are still going to flow to the generals as long as someone is paying the gas bills." Others, however, maintain that there would be great symbolic and moral value if the American firm had refused to profit from an alliance with a repressive military regime. Importantly, in 2011 the military took steps to relinquish control in what they say will return Burma to the family of nations, including the release of Aung San Suu Kyi. The EU and the U.S. have in turn eased sanctions on Burma.[19]

Pressure on Firms to Engage in CSR

Corporations that seek to act as relativists are not always given a free pass, as suggested by the governmental pressure put on PepsiCo and by Unocal's (Chevron) out-of-court settlement with Burmese citizens. Likewise, special interest groups and non-governmental organizations (NGOs) also press their cases for CSR. For example, well before Unocal settled its lawsuit, protestors showed up at Unocal gas stations in the U.S. to draw attention to the indirect support provided to the authoritarian regime in Burma. Other companies, such as Heineken and Carlsberg, terminated their investments in Burma after similar protests. In 2007, Apple came under fire from Greenpeace and Computer TakeBack Campaign for the use of toxic chemicals in manufacturing, as well as the production of e-waste, a great deal of which is disposed of overseas. Steve Jobs responded to criticism with an open letter reinforcing Apple's commitment to the environment and outlining new steps that the company would take to demonstrate this, including the phasing out of the most toxic chemicals used in its product production. The Rainforest Action Network pressured Citigroup with full-page ads in national publications, lobbying by actors shown cutting up their credit cards, and more. Citigroup agreed to no longer finance projects in emerging markets that would damage the environment.[20] This reactive stance of many firms has led to criticism of high-profile CSR efforts of some firms as mere public relations. Yet, there are several signs that this criticism might be misplaced, including research on CSR.

Firm Performance and CSR

A review of 167 studies conducted over the past 35 years indicates that there is a link, albeit small, between firm performance and social responsibility actions. A more recent study of 200 companies found that the firms most engaged in social and environmental sustainability in developing countries were also the most profitable.[21] This goes hand in hand again with a global survey of executives (see the Global Innovations feature), which reported that over 50 percent of surveyed executives felt that CSR provided a better brand reputation, made a firm more attractive to employees, and provided better decision making in the long term. Figure 3.3 takes a peek into the future. The figure shows the issues that executives from different countries feel will be important five years down the road. The continued attention given to this topic, as well as pressure from NGOs,

Issue (global rank)	U.S.	Germany	China	Brazil
Environment (1)	2	2	2	1
Safe products (2)	5	6	3	2
Retirement benefits (3)	4	1	4	7
Health care benefits (4)	1	8	1	8
Affordable products (5)	6	3	5	3
Human rights standards (6)	8	9	9	4
Workplace conditions (7)	9	4	7	6
Outsourcing job losses (8)	3	5	13	13
Privacy/data security (9)	7	7	6	10
Ethically produced products (10)	10	10	8	9
Investment in developing countries (11)	16	14	12	5
Ethical marketing (12)	12	16	11	11
Political influence of firms (13)	11	12	14	14
Executive pay (14)	15	11	10	15
Other (15)	13	15	16	12
Opposition to freer trade (16)	14	13	15	16

Figure 3.3 What Corporate Social Responsibility Issues Will Matter Most in Five Years?

Source: Adapted from *The Economist*. (2008). Just good business: A special report on corporate social responsibility, January 19, 20.

has changed the minds (if not hearts) of some multinationals. This could be, in part, due to a changing perspective on CSR, one that also makes good business sense. In the accompanying Global Innovations feature, please read about the proactive efforts that firms take in order to do good for the global community as well as to profit from their CSR efforts.[22]

Global Innovations

Doing Good to Do Well: The Changing Value Proposition for Corporate Social Responsibility

Recent views of corporate social responsibility (CSR) suggest it is no longer a "do-good sideshow," but instead is more mainstream and a source of value to a firm. According to *The Economist* magazine, CSR business is booming. Many firms have preferred to call their efforts "corporate responsibility," dropping the *social* part of the title because it is too narrow or confining. Some even refer to it as "building sustainable business." Nike was ahead of this curve, releasing a twenty-fifth anniversary edition of the Pegasus running shoe that was designed around the concept of green principles and techniques in 2008. Nike now rates each sneaker that it makes according to a sustainability index, a software tool that scores each product on its environmental impact.[23] Importantly, Nike has also used this method as an impetus for saving the company a lot of money. The Eco-index was developed by a consortium of over 100 apparel companies who ultimately want a common index for rating the effects of their products along environmental/human rights line—similar to the energy rating tags on home appliances.

While the group is comprised of large players in the apparel industry (such as Levi Strauss, Nike, and Target), the message is being widely heard. A survey of over 1,000 global executives conducted in 2011 by *The Economist* showed that nearly 67 percent of executives believe the degree of priority that their company has given to CSR to be high or very high, rising from 35 percent (shown in a 2005 survey).[24] More and more of those executives believe that CSR actually works and is not just for public relations, which has been hinted at in the past. In this same survey, only 4 percent of executives reported that corporate responsibility activity was a "waste of time." Nearly 60 percent did say that it is a necessary cost of doing business, but about the same percentage said that it gave their firm a distinctive position in the market. If anything, experts suggest that firms may be too defensive about their contribution to society.

Consider the apparel industry and its major impact on the environment. Tanning leather for shoes requires toxic chemicals and synthetic fabrics need lots of crude oil and other materials that release volatile compounds. A staple of the apparel industry (cotton) requires huge amounts of water in order to grow. The cotton is then shipped from the U.S. to Asia, where it is turned into thread and fabric. It is then shipped to the Dominican Republic for cutting, then to Haiti for sewing, then back to the U.S. to be distributed to outlets. Some clothes circle the globe multiple times before then ending up on the shelves of Old Navy or the Gap in your town. And Americans tossed out nearly 13 million tons of textiles last year, after they were finished with these products (such as jeans)—it is a figure that has risen much faster than any other source of trash.

The Eco-index can be used here to rate a product such as jeans. Questions covering the various stages of product creation and the processes involved in producing the products feed into a product grade. For example, Levi's can gain "points" by developing a recycling program for donating worn jeans to Goodwill, and Timberline's shoe score will rise if its tannery suppliers have water purifying systems. Points are lost for the inclusion of, or use of, too many packing materials or a lengthy supply chain. The index also factors in estimates of how many times the product will be washed. They know, for example, that the 3,480 liters of water used in a pair of jean's lifetime can be reduced by using a cold water wash and more points are gained via line drying. Critics say that the estimates are just that—estimates—and that the self-report nature of the measure leaves too much open to the manufacturer. The index has yet to be officially released as members have not yet agreed on various index elements.

Nevertheless, Levi's has also done well with the current index, thus illustrating the new, truly dual purpose of CSR. It has improved operations by changing its transportation routes for increased efficiency and reduced carbon emissions by 700 million tons. It also saved money by cutting back on packaging costs and materials and now only permits three labels to be attached to jeans (before, there were up to eleven tags!). The business benefits of CSR extend well beyond the apparel industry. Firms as varied as PepsiCo, FedEx, Intel, and Pfizer are supporting small teams of their employees to go to developing countries such as India, Ghana and Nigeria to provide free consulting services to non-profits. IBM, for example, gets more volunteers than it can handle—those chosen continue to receive their salary while on the two- to four-week assignment, representing a significant firm investment per employee. The program has received great publicity, but there is also great value to IBM. For one, the firm credits millions of dollars of new business to the program, such as a contract it received to manage a public service program in Nigeria. Moreover, the firm gains local name recognition in markets that it seeks to enter. IBM employees report that the experience is personally valuable and "gives meaning" to their career. Data also show that these IBM employees remain on the job longer and rise further in the organization. Doing *good* can mean doing *well*![25]

Cross-National Differences in Ethical Perspectives

The universalism–relativism debate and the CSR movement raise the question of whether countries diverge in how they view and act on ethical principles in business. Many studies have been conducted on this topic and they generally confirm that there are different approaches taken to ethical issues across countries. One study, for instance, found that American managers were more likely to view personnel issues (such as employee theft and misuse of company information) in ethical terms than were their counterparts from Austria and Germany, who were more likely to view these from a legal lens. On the other hand, Austrian and German managers were more likely to view involvement in local politics in ethical terms, whereas Americans thought this to be a personal choice not of ethical significance. These differences may reflect cultural values. Americans tend to be highly individualistic and, as a result, may feel that the individual is the main source of ethical values. Germans and Austrians, while also generally individualistic, tend to be more community oriented. In fact, business ethics in these countries has been described in terms of the relationship between businesses and their local environments.[26]

Another interesting study compared the reactions of managers in the U.S., France, and Germany to several ethical topics, including illegal payments, coercion, conflicts of interest, and environmental concerns. These issues were presented to the managers in the form of short stories that provided background. The following is an example of one of the stories that managers read:

> *Rollfast Bicycle Company has been barred from entering the market in a large Asian country by collusive efforts of the local bicycle manufacturers. Rollfast could expect to net $5 million per year from sales if it could penetrate the market. Last week, a businessperson from the country contacted the management of Rollfast and stated that he could smooth the way for the company to sell in his country for the price of $500,000.*

The managers were then asked whether they would pay the bribe. In most cases, U.S. managers were less likely to pay the bribe than either of the European managers, who in turn did not differ much from one another. Managers were also asked about the *reasons* for their behavioral reactions. Not surprisingly, the reasons varied across countries. For example, nearly 50 percent of the U.S. managers said that they would not pay a bribe because they thought it was unethical, illegal, or against company policy. Only 15 percent of the French and 9 percent of the Germans mentioned these reasons. Instead, the Europeans were much more likely to pinpoint competitive forces as the reason why they might consider paying the bribe (e.g., "It is the price to be paid to do business in that country" or "Competition forces us to take the offer"). Overall, the U.S. managers were more concerned about ethical issues, while the Europeans were more concerned about maintaining a competitive business presence in the market.[27]

Studies using different research methods in several other countries have reached similar conclusions. Remarkably, this research shows that even when attitudes about ethical issues are similar across countries, they may be the result of *different* moral reasoning processes. These different perspectives may result from the legal frameworks of each country, their economic environments, or their unique cultural values. As a result, cross-national differences in ethics may also be fairly resistant to change in the short term, even if the political, social, and economic conditions in a country are shifting dramatically.[28]

For instance, despite the incredible changes that have occurred in South Africa over the past decades, attitudes toward ethical business practices in the country have remained stable. Another recent study underscored this cultural "persistence" effect on ethical attitudes. These researchers wanted to separate the impact of country and culture on ethical behavior patterns. They compared the responses of Chinese, Americans, and Chinese-Americans (living in the U.S.) from a questionnaire that included items measuring general and ethical values. The results showed that cultural background and beliefs were more important than national background in predicting similarity in values and ethics.[29] More research shows that these ethical postures have an effect on business interactions across culture. Chinese negotiators, for example, are more likely to rate cultivating relations and friendships through gifts, entertainment, or personal favors as more appropriate than are U.S. or British negotiators. Chapter 7 will show that personal gifts are a more common relationship-building method in Asian cultures.[30]

Codes of Ethics

Another example of the different emphasis that nations place on ethics can be found by looking at the presence (or absence) of corporate codes of conduct across countries. One important study looked at this issue by comparing 600 European firms (British, French, and German) with a similar sample of American companies and several interesting findings were presented. First, U.S. firms were more likely to have ethical codes in the first place. Only about 30 percent of French firms, 51 percent of German firms, and 41 percent of British firms had codes of ethics in place—all less than a corresponding figure of 75 percent for American companies. Further, most European firms that *did* have codes had instituted them after 1985. The Zeiss Company of Germany introduced a code for its employees as early as 1896, but this is the exception rather than the rule. Those

European firms with corporate codes were also more likely to have a stronger U.S. connection than those without codes: 25 percent of European firms with codes were U.S. subsidiaries, whereas only 2 percent without such codes were U.S. subsidiaries.[31]

In addition to looking at whether a company had a code of ethics in place, research has also looked at differences in the content of the codes.[32] Although there are some differences among European companies, when considered as a whole they differ sharply from the codes of U.S. firms. For example, 100 percent of European firms mentioned employee conduct somewhere in their corporate codes. Only 55 percent of U.S. firms dealt with this issue. In keeping with the traditional American focus on marketing, however, U.S. firms (80 percent) were more likely to mention customers than European companies (67 percent). And, U.S. firms (86 percent) referred to government relations much more frequently than did their European counterparts (20 percent).

What the codes said about political issues also reveals important things about their outlook. Many U.S. firms state that their commitment to abiding by the law is strong, but they appear to mistrust the role of government in business. For example, the corporate code of Dow Chemical (at the time) stated that "[we] pay our taxes *gladly*, yes, but we do not pay them *blindly* [emphasis added]. We have the right to question the wisdom of regulatory zeal."[33] In contrast, the few times that European firms mention political issues, they do so in general, positive ways. Bertelsmann (Germany) states that it "supports a free, democratic and socially responsible society" and Wella Corp. (Germany) says that it "welcomes political, social, and cultural activities of employees."

Impact and Enforcement of Codes

Although there has been a good deal of attention placed on the presence and content of ethical codes, this does not mean that corporate actions always align well with those prescriptions. In fact, one expert suggests that claims made about the impact that these codes have on employees and stakeholders—especially on those in developing countries— are exaggerated. Many companies freely admit this problem, including Levi Strauss, J. C. Penney, Target, and Walmart. They say that with operations located around the world, the real issue is enforcement.[34] Code enforcement, auditing of foreign partners to assure they comply with code elements (e.g., no child labor), and applying sanctions are all easier said than done.

In highly publicized cases in the 1990s, Nike was slow to act on allegations of violations of its code in areas such as treatment of workers and child labor among its subcontractors in Pakistan and elsewhere. Nike's policy at the time suggested that it would be sufficient if contractors adhered to local labor laws, but the company eventually toughened its ethical code after critics demonstrated that local laws did little to protect workers in some countries.[35] Boycotts conducted on college campuses and protests held at NikeTown stores helped change Nike's ethical stance, so much so that in 1998 CEO Phil Knight acknowledged that the Nike product "had become synonymous with slave wages, forced overtime, and arbitrary abuse."

Nike responded to this view by increasing the presence of monitoring programs, the use of auditors, and adding more external observers at suppliers' plants. In 2005, Nike became among the first companies to release the names and location of its factories—both to increase transparency and to pressure those overseas suppliers to hold to ethical codes. Yet, this is a tall task to fulfill, as Nike has nearly 700 contract factories, which employ thousands of workers across multiple countries in its global supply chain, many with weak local regulations. This leaves Nike and other companies like it to police their suppliers. With over 95 percent of its shoes produced in China, Vietnam, Indonesia, and Thailand, the challenges are huge—success is far from complete. To its credit, Nike turned over its audit data to an independent evaluator (MIT). The findings released in late 2006 were stark: "despite significant efforts and investment by Nike . . . workplace conditions in almost 80 percent of its suppliers have remained the same or worsened over time."[36] For its part, Nike continues to make changes and to work to respond to criticisms, as well as to report actions taken to improve these conditions and criticisms. At least one observer has stated that Nike now has a "well-developed focus for improving conditions in contracted factories, aiming for carbon neutrality, and making sports available to young people across the world." Overall, critics charge that without enforcement, codes are nothing more than public relations efforts designed to assuage customers about poor working conditions in developing countries.[37]

The solution is not easy, as Nike found when it severed a contract with Saga Sports, its chief supplier in Pakistan, over a child labor dispute. About 4,000 workers lost their jobs, which in turn impacted thousands more who lost their family income as a result. In addition, while government officials admit Saga did wrong, they worry about the void left behind and the potential impact of extremists who may now have more appeal there.[38] Also in the 1990s, in Bangladesh, clothing makers tried to head off criticism of child labor practices in that country by removing children from the workplace, only to see them end up in worse situations, such as prostitution.[39] As shown by these examples and the International Insights feature, doing the "right thing" is not always an easy or obvious decision.

International Insights

Is Doing the Right Thing Wrong?—An American Faces an Ethical Dilemma in South America

Several years ago, we spoke to a global purchasing executive of a medium-sized multinational about the challenges of doing business in some international markets. John Williams (a pseudonym) had been with his firm for over 25 years and had a variety of challenging assignments. One of those assignments was in a South American country where he encountered a very thorny ethical issue—one that he said still bothers him today. His firm had just purchased an operation from a large local company. This allowed his company to move its equipment to a new building and to start operations back up in record time. The company hired new line employees, but used the existing staff line already located in the South American country, as well as some divisional support from the U.S.

The problem started when Mr. Williams, as the country manager, requested the purchasing unit and others to cut costs and improve quality. He asked the managers of these units to tour factories of their suppliers in some small rural towns to address these issues. In one factory, suppliers noticed that about a half dozen of the workers were very young, maybe 13 years old at most. Recalling the company's ethical code (that had been drummed into them), the suppliers were deeply concerned. One of the managers raised this child labor issue, making the supplier very embarrassed. The suppliers began a frantic discussion in their native language with one of the firm's managers in the visiting party. After several minutes of emotional discussion, an explanation was offered by the suppliers (in English) to all. The firms' managers from that country supported the explanation, and underscored to Mr. Williams later that it was normal, acceptable, and legal—generally not a problem.

The explanation that had convinced the managers that this practice was acceptable was not obvious when it was considered from afar in the U.S., especially because it so clearly violated corporate code. The argument was that, even in this small town, children are left homeless and parentless. The only alternative for these children is to live off the street, thus they end up begging and stealing. If they do, the townfolks pressure the police to "run the delinquents off." Strangers may victimize the children or recruit them for criminal activities in the big cities. So, the courts have required local large businesses to provide room, board, and other services (medical care, education, an allowance) to these homeless children. In return, the businesses can have them do some tasks similar to household chores (run errands, wash cars, etc.). The suppliers stated that this was a successful program designed to help abandoned children, unlike what they had heard is done in the U.S. Interestingly, every one of the company's local managers in South America thought that it was okay. They also pointed out that the firm's headquarters in-country has office boys that run errands and the like, and that the law there allows 12-year-olds to work in some jobs. Yet, Mr. Williams was strongly opposed to this practice and also suspicious of the suppliers who had explained the situation to him.

Given the seriousness of this issue, you might understand Mr. Williams's suspiciousness. Child labor not only violates corporate code, but if this practice became public, it could have serious consequences for the firm. Mr. Williams demanded copies of documents that sanctioned the relationship between the courts and the children/company. Representatives told Mr. Williams that it would be insulting to ask for this and a sign that they were not trusted. He replied that he understood this cultural issue, but that he needed his American cultural values met, too—which meant some form of proof that this was acceptable. But, he did not yet press that course of action.

Instead, Mr. Williams followed up with visits in smaller, informal groups where he asked a trusted local national, with lots of U.S. experience, to make the request yet again, in private, to the supplier's management. The result of this was a promise that they would provide some documentation. Feeling satisfied, Mr. Williams returned to his office. But the documentation never arrived. Over time, the issue was always in the background and never quite resolved—no paperwork was ever presented. He finally resolved this lingering situation by not giving that supplier any new business and as the "legacy" business was completed, they dropped them from their bidders list.

Upon reflecting on the situation, Mr. Williams told us that he did not know whether the children were exploited by the company any more than they would be by an orphanage, foster parents, or by begging on the streets. He also said that "I do know, though, that I still have a very uncomfortable feeling about the whole affair."

Ethics Associated with Bribery and Other Questionable Payments

Concerns about whether multinationals are responsible for protecting the rights of workers—even employees of their foreign contractors— form a big ethical question, to be sure. There are many other issues, however, around which ethical concerns swirl. The treatment of women in the workplace, for example, is highly uneven. In some countries, it is illegal to hire female managers for many jobs, whereas other countries have legal protection for gender discrimination in employment.[40] Is it unethical to do business in, or with, those countries that do not hire female managers? Similarly, is it unethical for firms to avoid strict domestic environmental laws by locating facilities offshore? Is it right for a multinational to market a drug in India that has yet to pass very stringent trials in the U.K. or the U.S.? In some of these situations, multinationals have argued that their actions are justified and even morally correct, occasionally using relativist arguments.

One international business practice that intersects with ethical relativism is the use of questionable payments. Practices such as bribery, extortion, and "grease" payments made to bureaucrats and business leaders, both foreign and domestic, still hold a dubious place in international business.[41] In addition to direct monetary payments, suspicious practices such as giving expensive gifts (e.g., jewelry and art), providing lavish entertainment (e.g., exclusive dinners, tickets to sporting events, or concert seats), and offering free trips to foreign or domestic dignitaries also occur in business around the globe.

In fact, the use of illegal or questionable payments has been common practice in many societies throughout recorded history—including Africa, Asia, the Middle East, Europe, and the Americas. Research done on many early civilizations show that careful records were sometimes kept for such payments, a practice still replicated today. Bribery is so much a part of nearly every culture that most languages have a word for it. For example, the payment of *baksheesh* in some Arab and Turkish-speaking countries may reflect centuries of rule by an all-powerful state (such as the Ottoman Empire). In these countries, *baksheesh* could provide the protection for businesses that an imperfect and sometimes abusive legal system could not. Likewise, in Mexico the term *la mordida* (literally, "the bite") might reflect a similar sense of powerlessness with the government bureaucracy. Similar terms in other languages—such as the Italian *bustarella* ("little envelope") and the French *pot au vin* ("jug of wine")—carry vivid and evocative images. In Nigeria, a foreign firm that does not *dash* local bureaucrats may not be able to compete well within that country. Countless other countries from all continents also have terms for such payments.[42]

Interestingly, almost every country in the world explicitly outlaws bribery of its own officials.[43] So, if an illegal payment is made to a foreign official, that person or corporation risks prosecution. Despite this near universal view of bribery, countries vary dramatically in terms of how much they tolerate the practice. In some countries, there is actually little or no risk of prosecution because bribery is so commonplace, if not *expected*. A recent survey of Indonesian businesspeople showed that over 65 percent of households said that they had been asked for "unofficial" payments by public officials. Likewise, over 50 percent of respondents also said that, in some locations, teachers ask for payments in order to ensure a child's continued enrollment in school. Even public officials themselves acknowledged their role in bribery—nearly 50 percent admitted that they received "under the table" payments.

In other cases, however, the magnitude of bribery and other forms of corruption (e.g., embezzlement of company or government funds) may be just too great to ignore, even if bribery is an accepted practice within a given country. In 2003, nearly two-thirds of Indonesian businesspeople polled stated that they would willingly pay up to 5 percent of their annual revenue in additional taxes if it would be used to battle corruption.[44] The situation has changed dramatically for the better since then, however, beginning with the election of President Susilo Bambang Yudhoyono in 2004—the nation's first directly elected leader. Mr. Yudhoyono is a retired four-star general who rose through the ranks during Indonesia's era of dictatorship. But, beginning with his handling of a tsunami and its aftereffects during his first year in office, he has proven to be a strong leader. Plus, his image as a dedicated corruption fighter with high moral integrity has ushered in a time of financial and political stability for Indonesia. He was re-elected to another five-year term in 2009.

Bribery Across Countries

In Figure 3.4, we present the results of a survey conducted annually by Transparency International (TI), a nonprofit organization that tracks corruption worldwide. The 2013 survey interviewed over 114,000 people across 107 countries regarding corruption-related activity in their respective country. Corruption was defined as the percentage of people who have reported paying a bribe within the last year to one or more service agencies (e.g., a government office, to police/law enforcement, to an educational agency, etc.). In the figure, bribery rates are shown for the ten most corrupt nations, as well as the ten least corrupt nations. As you will see, bribery is rare in Australia and in several of the Nordic countries. The U.S. rate of 7 percent compared well, but it is not in the top ten. You will also note that some African countries (such as Sierra Leone and Liberia) bring up the rear as the most corrupt nations, according to TI. In Sierra Leone, for example, 84 percent of people surveyed reported paying a bribe in the previous year. Overall, nearly one in four people around the world reported paying a bribe last year—a shockingly high number, but relatively consistent across survey years.[45]

Some countries that have ranked relatively high in previous survey years have experienced well-publicized corruption scandals or crackdowns. French magistrates became fed up with a system of cozy relationships between business and government, especially

Least Corrupt		Most Corrupt	
Nation	**% reporting**	**Nation**	**% reporting**
Australia	1	India	54
Denmark	1	Uganda	61
Finland	1	Zimbabwe	62
Japan	1	Mozambique	62
Spain	2	Libya	62
Canada	3	Cameroon	62
Korea (S)	3	Kenya	70
Malaysia	3	Yemen	74
New Zealand	3	Liberia	75
Norway, Portugal, Uruguay	3	Sierra Leone	84

Figure 3.4 Rankings of the Most Corrupt and Least Corrupt Nations.

Note: Corruption is defined as the percentage of respondents in each country who report having paid bribes in the past year (to any of eight service areas such as law enforcement, police, education, etc.).

Source: Adapted from Transparency International, *Global Corruption Barometer* (2013), available at: www.transparency.org/gcb. About 1,000 people in each of 107 countries responded to this survey.

at a time when an anemic economy and high unemployment rate plagued the country. Since 1995, dozens of top executives and politicians have been targeted for investigation, if not already convicted and jailed, and these include leaders of some of France's most well-known companies.[46] *The New York Times* reported (at the time) that French and Swiss investigators researched claims that the French engineering firm Alstom had paid hundreds of millions of dollars in bribes in order to obtain contracts in Asia and South America from 1995 to 2008.[47] France, and some other European countries, have immunity laws that protect those with high government roles from prosecution. This law helped Jacques Chirac, the former president of France, avoid facing charges of financial impropriety that allegedly occurred while he was in a position of authority in Paris. During Mr. Chirac's 2003 re-election campaign, opponents carried pictures of him that read "Vote for me or I go to jail."[48] To their credit, however, Transparency International ranked France (and Germany) as countries that made among the most progress in investigating and prosecuting corporate bribery since that time. A case in point is presented in the accompanying International Insights feature involving a massive bribery scheme by the giant German firm, Siemens AG.

International Insights

Bribery as a Business Model—Bavarian Baksheesh at Siemens AG

What do the following have in common: transit companies in Venezuela; medical equipment firms in China, Vietnam, and Russia; power companies in Iraq and Israel; oil firms in Mexico; IT firms in Argentina; and telecom companies in Nigeria and Bangladesh? They have all been bribed by Siemens AG, the giant German engineering firm that makes everything from wind turbines to high-speed trains. The Department of Justice and the SEC presented evidence that the firm's level of corruption was widespread and systemic. Between 2001 and 2007, Siemens made at least 4,283 bribery payments totaling $1.4 billion to company and government officials around the globe in order to win business.

These crimes involved employees at all levels of the firm, including senior management. In early 2007, Munich police raided Siemens' headquarters and carted away mounds of bank records and other data. Shortly thereafter, CEO Klaus Kleinfeld abruptly resigned. More evidence was then uncovered showing a pattern of bribery unprecedented in magnitude and geographic scope.

The SEC showed that Siemens used "slush funds," unreported accounts, and a system of intermediaries to facilitate payments to government officers. For example, the firm paid $40 million to Argentine officials, including the president who received $2.6 million. Payments were made via sham consulting contracts in which officials were paid for "professional services." Siemens used removable "post-it notes" with affixed signatures to obscure audit trails. They also set up "cash desks" where employees filled up empty suitcases with as much as $1.3 million at a time to pay the bribes. Ironically, the cash desks used an "honor" system: no questions asked, no documents required, with managers "approving" their own requests. Between 2001 and 2004, roughly $70 million traveled in those suitcases. The SEC charged the Siemens board with malfeasance because it ignored and suppressed red flags. The SEC also accused Siemens' former CFO of ignoring suspicious Nigerian payments, payments flagged by auditors, and of misleading the board on compliance matters. About 300 other suspects were investigated, and the German courts handed out suspended prison terms to three former Siemens' managers.

Although Siemens is a German company, the U.S. claimed Foreign Corrupt Practices Act (FCPA) jurisdiction because the company was listed on the NYSE. For its part, Siemens vowed to clean up its operations as part of a settlement agreement. In fact, the Department of Justice described cooperative steps taken by Siemens after the corruption was uncovered as "extraordinary." It cited efforts made by Siemens to replace board members and the action of hiring hundreds of new compliance officers since that Munich police raid in 2006. The Department of Justice went on to state that Siemens took "aggressive steps" in order to preserve evidence after that raid, sharing over 100,000 pages of relevant documents. As a result, U.S. prosecutors argued for leniency for Siemens and factored this into their decision not to press for the maximum fine of $2.7 billion.

Siemens was not formally charged with bribery, but instead admitted to inadequate internal controls and doctoring of its books. Keeping charges of bribery out of the case allowed Siemens to keep bidding for public sector projects within the U.S. Instead, it paid an $800 million U.S. fine and $830 million in German fines. Plus, there is an additional $1 billion in internal costs and reforms to be made, including hundreds of millions of dollars paid to a U.S. law firm to conduct an investigation of Siemens in order to show that it was coming clean. Coming clean is going to be a hard process for Siemens, because bribery has played such a big role in business development since 1946. Plus, until 1999, bribes were deductible as a business expense under German tax code and paying off foreign officials was not a crime. But, Siemens found it hard to part with the old ways and created only a shell of a compliance program. Even after 1999, other countries complained of suspicious payments flowing offshore. In 2008, the new CEO announced the fines and agreement and vowed to make Siemens a model for best practice in anti-corruption. Skeptics, however, say that old habits are hard to break and that Siemens only got unlucky and broke the eleventh commandment—"thou shall not get caught"—with many others continuing the practice.[49]

France is hardly the only country where concerns about bribery and other corrupt practices have prompted crackdowns.[50] There have been plenty of examples over the last decade. Consider the following sample roster of incidents that have either resulted in criminal convictions or have prompted various investigations:

- The Japanese construction firm JCF Corp. recently agreed to pay over $200 million in fines for its part in a long-running case involving bribery to obtain contracts for a natural gas business in Nigeria. JCF admitted guilt in the case brought forward by the U.S. involving a project worth $6 billion. Other firms were also involved in this venture, including French, Dutch, and U.S. companies. This and other such cases came on the heels of a loan scandal involving the Japanese Ministry of Finance and organized criminal gangs (collectively known as the *yakuza*). Questionable loans were allegedly made to *yakuza* front companies even as *yakuza* members were attending fundraisers for Japanese politicians.[51]

- A grand jury recently indicted a handful of executives from Kolon Industries, Inc., a South Korean firm. The action, filed in a U.S. court, accuses employees of a multi-year espionage conspiracy to steal trade secrets from DuPont. They are also charged with paying DuPont employees for trade secrets on production, production data, and sales figures for the Kevlar body armor product of DuPont's. This comes on the heels of a $920 million judgment against Kolon the previous year (a claim made by DuPont). This was preceded by several previous wages of graft and corruption where, for example, the Chairman of Korean's SK Corporation (the son-in-law of the former president of Korea) was released from prison after serving only three months for a multi-billion dollar tax fraud. Koreans reacted with outcry and suspicion.[52]

- Corruption in China is a major issue for the government. Thousands of cases of graft and corruption have been investigated since 2003. A survey conducted by KPMG found that 43 percent of businesses that had operations in China claimed to have suffered from fraud. This often involves government officials themselves. Convictions in the last few years included a 16-year sentence for the Beijing mayor and Communist Party secretary, a suspended death sentence for the mayor of Shenyang for corruption and ties to gangsters, another suspended death sentence for the Vice-Minister of Public Security, and a completed death sentence for the vice chairman of the Chinese parliament.[53]

- Opposition party leaders in Moscow threatened investigations in addition to legislative changes in order to curb emerging Russian conglomerates that seem to have "uncles" (*dyadyas*) within the government to watch out for them. They provide the conglomerates with breaks on taxes, import duties, and legislation involving foreign competitors, allegedly in return for payoffs. Some 32 of these Russian industrial giants run 500 factories and 72 banks, and have 2.5 million employees.[54]

■ DaimlerChrysler, BMW, and Volkswagen have been raided just as German police raided Siemens, as well as put under investigation and had employees arrested. Recently, investigations initiated by an online whistleblower have been opened into Deutsche Post's DHL unit for alleged payments to Kazakh officials.[55]

The U.S. is hardly the perfect bastion of proper business practices. A recent case involving charges that U.S.-based multinational corporation Halliburton bribed Nigerian officials during the construction of a gas plant is a case in point. The company agreed to pay $559 million to settle those charges brought by the Department of Justice. This judgment far exceeds the previous record of $44 million in 2007 paid by U.S. oil services firm Baker Hughes for improper payments made to Kazakhstan officials.[56] Recent examples also include Wal-Mart's admission of paying millions of dollars in bribes to Mexican officials in order to sidestep regulations; Pfizer and Johnson&Johnson's settlement fines based on a federal investigation into bribery overseas; Avon's internal investigation of millions of dollars of questionable payments to officials in China, Brazil, India and Japan; and HP's recent indictment by German officials for kickbacks paid to obtain business.[57]

Still worse, people from other nations often think Americans fail to acknowledge their own ethical foibles. As a result, the U.S. is sometimes seen as being pious or hypocritical, especially considering that Americans have had their fair share of scandals and ethical problems, even before the first wave of well-known scandals involving Enron, Worldcom, and Tyco in 2000, and the second major wave in 2008 involving fraud and financial Ponzi schemes. Europeans, for instance, think that the United States needs to "lighten up a little" and be less naive about separating business and personal ethics.[58]

Perhaps the major reason why this corrupt activity continues across countries and across the ages is that "you get who you pay for." That is to say, bribery may be less pernicious if it did not end up being a pretty good investment. *The Economist* reported on research conducted at Cambridge University regarding a study of 166 prominent cases of bribery since the mid-1970s. The sample spanned over 50 countries and involved firms listed on 20 different world equity exchanges. The research showed that the average return on bribery payments was nearly 11 times the value of the payments made to obtain the business. The U.S. Department of Justice found similar levels of "return" for firms that it has prosecuted. It is no wonder that over 15 percent of respondents to an Ernst & Young survey stated that bribery to win business can be justified if it helps a firm survive hard times (a figure that has nearly doubled since a survey conducted the previous year). A whopping 39 percent of businesspeople report that bribery is common in regions where they do business.[59]

The Foreign Corrupt Practices Act

Many of the provided examples involve corruption in which the political or business leaders of foreign countries may somehow be "on the take." Few countries, however, outlaw bribes by their own citizens to those foreign public officials. Most countries act as though the "when in Rome" perspective applies and that common practice should be followed when operating in a foreign nation. Until 1999 in Germany and 2000 in France and Switzerland, tax laws allowed bribes to be deducted from corporate taxes.[60] It could be argued that, at minimum, this is a tacit endorsement of corruption.

Until a few decades ago, payoffs made by U.S. firms to foreign representatives were also more common. In the mid-1970s, however, several high-level cases of corporate corruption became widely publicized, perhaps because sensitivities were heightened because of the Watergate scandal that occurred at the time. For instance, the then-president of Lockheed, Carl Kotchian, made payments to Japanese government officials to secure a large contract from Nippon Air to buy Lockheed airliners. Japanese officials told Lockheed that if it wanted the contract, payments were needed to close the sale. Kotchian was approached several more times for further payments, in the end totaling $12.5 million.[61] When the press uncovered the Lockheed payments, the firm was charged with many tax code violations as well as with falsifying records. In Japan, the public disclosure of the Lockheed payments created quite a furor in that country too. Officials involved in this incident were criminally charged and one even committed suicide.[62]

The Lockheed case received wide attention, including an article detailing the events by Mr. Kotchian himself ;[63] other articles also revealed a corporate pattern of bribery.[64] Lockheed, however, was hardly alone. Nearly 450 U.S. corporations made inappropriate payments to foreign officials or companies between 1974 and 1976 when the Lockheed situation occurred. The reaction of an already outraged American public pushed Congress to pass the Foreign Corrupt Practices Act (FCPA) in 1977, making it the first such bribery law enacted by a country. The FCPA made it illegal to pay or to offer to pay officials of foreign governments to gain or increase business. Penalties for violators included fines of millions for companies, as well as fines and up to five years of imprisonment for the individuals involved.

The current version of the FCPA does *not* prohibit all "questionable" payments to foreign officials or governments. A distinction is made between bribes and facilitating payments. The latter are often called "grease payments" because they are made to "grease the wheels" of business. It is *not* illegal to make payments to low- and middle-level officials to get them to perform functions that they perform and are needed in the ordinary course of business. For example, in some countries it is necessary to provide small payments to customs officials in order to get them to do what they legally *should* do, such as inspect and pass shipment or validate a passport. A customs official might impede or backlog a shipment until he or she receives the grease payments. Other examples of grease payments that are not illegal under the FCPA include: (1) providing "gifts" that help overcome bureaucratic technicalities that impede business; (2) "gifts" given to supplement an environment of low wages, with the gifts acting as gratuities for services performed; and (3) the facilitation of permits and equipment that are allotted via the extra payments. The difference between a bribe and a grease payment is that the latter are small and they are not offered to get anything more than a business is entitled to anyway (the import license, passport stamp, etc.).

Effects of the FCPA

Although the FCPA was enacted with some fanfare, a number of U.S. multinationals complained about it. The complaints centered on the law's effect on the competitiveness of American business. Several prominent business leaders pointed out that they had lost contracts with foreign governments in the past because they had refused to pay requested bribes. In fact, they noted that companies with inferior products and services—who in a fair environment would not receive a contract—often ended up getting the business.

Opponents argued that the FCPA would dramatically exaggerate this effect. In order to compete effectively, U.S. businesses must also be allowed to use methods of competition—including bribery—that foreign multinationals are able to use.[65] Furthermore, the critics noted that many other governments do not outlaw bribes and indeed sometimes sanction them (e.g., by making them tax deductible). This situation changed in 1999 with the passage of European anti-bribery statutes, laws that have many elements similar to the U.S. FCPA, and other countries have developed their own statutes with mixed success. Nevertheless, executives still wonder how U.S. business can compete in world markets with such one-sided restrictions.[66]

Research has been done to address the question of whether or not the FCPA had a negative effect on the competitiveness of U.S. business. One study looked at the market share of U.S. business since the passage of the FCPA. This involved surveying U.S. Embassy and Department of Commerce officials about business practices in over 50 different countries. The goal of this part of the study was to identify countries in which the prevalence of improper payments was very high and countries in which this practice was rare. Researchers then examined whether the passage of the FCPA was more likely to be an export disincentive in countries where illegal payments are common. A key measure was the change in market share before the passage of the FCPA (1971–1976) and after passage (1977–1980). Interestingly, the FCPA did not decrease the overall competitiveness of American multinationals overseas. In fact, there were no differences in market shares between the two types of countries either before or after the passage of the FCPA.[67]

This study, however, does have some limitations. For one, the researchers studied the effects over a relatively short time interval after passage of the FCPA. Competitiveness could decline slowly as a result of the act. Second, the market share data itself is quite variable. For example, in the airline industry it was common to observe market share changes of nearly 100 percent over one year. Although this was not consistently associated with countries in which bribery is common, it does show that the data can jump around dramatically. Boeing, for example, may sign a contract with Saudi Arabia one year and be shut out entirely the next year when Airbus Industries wins the next Saudi contract.[68]

Nevertheless, although the data are far from perfect, an initial conclusion would be that the FCPA does not significantly affect American international competitiveness overall. This does not mean, however, that U.S. multinationals do not lose out on specific contracts because they will not provide a cut to a foreign partner. Indeed, American telecom firms complained about being shut out of contracts awarded by Ecuador as it privatized the state-run phone company. Some 90 percent of the nearly 200 contracts awarded went to non-U.S. firms, allegedly because American firms would not pay 10 percent of a contract's value to government officials. Other firms, such as Ford, Johnson&Johnson and others, feel the same way.

Summing Up Questionable Payments

At this point, we can only speculate about the level of corrupt activities currently being carried out by American firms—FCPA or not. Yet, there is also little doubt that the FCPA has worked to reduce corruption in international business.

One response of many U.S. firms is to develop clear corporate guidelines about illegal payments and to communicate them directly to their managers. In fact, it is estimated that almost 80 percent of U.S. multinationals have incorporated such guidelines into their operations. As we pointed out earlier, the percentage for U.S. multinationals with such guidelines is larger than for multinationals of several other nations. Some of these codes, such as Caterpillar's, provide detailed guidelines about what payments are and are not permitted. In fact, some corporate codes, such as that of IBM, take a very strong ethical position by not allowing managers to even use legally permitted grease payments. In general, however, these codes are not very precise, and they usually tell managers what they should not do as opposed to what they should.[69]

As a result, some experts actually recommend that multinationals set up ethics hotlines that employees can call anonymously.[70] Although there are many hurdles to overcome, including how to deal with false allegations, at least some firms are starting such hotlines and other reporting mechanisms. Another proactive step is to make efforts to convince foreign multinationals and their governments—mostly through U.S. government channels—to implement stronger laws against bribery and other corrupt practices.[71] In general, however, such efforts have not been very successful. And those that have passed such laws or signed on to international agreements have few or no prosecutions under their belt. The following International Insights provides more details on these and other obstructions that U.S. managers face in conducting international business.

International Insights

Making Friends and Influencing People: The Long Arm of the FCPA Got Longer

Some aggressive foreign companies use payoffs to gain access to markets and some U.S. firms are doing the same thing. Unlike their European and Asian counterparts, however, American firms are subject to the big teeth of the FCPA. Lockheed-Martin was convicted in 1995 of paying $1.5 million to an Egyptian official and paid $24 million in fines—more than twice the profits from the contract itself. GE paid a $69 million fine after one of its employees bribed an Israeli general. In 2008, Baker Hughes paid $44 million in a settlement with the Department of Justice. Other companies subject to FCPA review include Sun Microsystems, Royal Dutch Shell, Titan Corp., and Lucent Technologies.

Until recently, FCPA prosecutions were not common. Fewer than 50 cases were filed between 1977 and 2003, partly because cases often required cooperation from the countries in which the violation occurred. In addition, some firms paid settlement fines despite not admitting guilt. Yet, when U.S. officials were tipped off about payments made by Exxon-Mobil to the tune of $78 million, routed through the Swiss accounts of Kazak officials (including their president), this resulted in indictments of a Mobil executive. Likewise, cooperation with German officials was key to the settlement of charges against Siemens.[72]

The U.S. government, however, has become much more aggressive lately. By 2007, the Department of Justice had open investigations into 84 companies, which was a dramatic jump since 2002, when only four cases were open. Experts, such as those at Sherman & Sterling LLP, a law firm that tracks corruption, say that in the more than 30 years of the FCPA's existence, they have never seen this degree of activity. Justice department officials believe that anti-corruption cases have become a "significant priority" and have added additional lawyers and an FBI team. The severity of the penalties given has risen too. By 2010, $1.5 billion in penalties were because of violations of the FCPA. The recent judgment of over $500 million against Halliburton in the Nigerian bribery case is another example. Plus, a Halliburton officer who masterminded the bribery scheme received a seven-year prison sentence—and he had even cooperated with prosecutors. This was the longest term ever handed out under the FCPA.[73]

Interestingly, the costs associated with uncovering aspects of the corruption and all that is involved can often be more expensive for firms than the FCPA fines themselves. In what has now become widespread practice, firms often spend millions of dollars investigating themselves, hoping that this show of good faith will reduce sentences and fines. The Siemens case illustrates this effect all too well. Siemens engaged more than 300 lawyers, forensic accountants, and other professionals from law firms and Deloitte LLP to conduct a two-year internal investigation. Siemens estimated that it was charged for over 1.5 million billable hours during that investigation—one that involved 34 countries, nearly 2,000 interviews, and over 100 million documents. About 24,000 of those documents were given to the Department of Justice, which cost Siemens $100 million alone.[74]

All of these costs aside, it is clear that, relative to other countries, the U.S. appears vigilant. The Organisation for Economic Co-operation and Development (OECD), a group of 34 industrialized nations, has required its members (since 1999) to promise to enact and enforce tougher bribery laws. Yet, a 2007 OECD report suggests that members have a long way to go, as some have yet to launch a single prosecution. The U.K., Denmark, Japan, and Canada were not spared in the report—it said that one-third of member states have yet to take any significant action to enforce corruption laws. Dozens of nations, such as China and Russia, have laws that prohibit overseas bribery, but adoption does not equal enforcement. The U.S. has brought more cases than anyone else. An exception might be the new U.K. anti-bribery law passed in 2010, which is wide in coverage and tough on penalties. Nevertheless, OECD countries may still have reason to fear the U.S. FCPA law. Foreign firms listed on U.S. exchanges must obey the law, as illustrated by the Siemens experience. Likewise, a Norwegian company paid a bribe in Norway, but the money was wired through a U.S. bank and it was caught.[75]

A more common strategy for U.S. firms is to make friends via donations and other "philanthropic" activity—something acceptable under the FCPA. When IBM chairman Louis Gerstner visited Beijing in 1995, for instance, the company donated $25 million in hardware and software to 20 Chinese universities. A related strategy is to spend hundreds of thousands of dollars to bring foreign officials to the U.S. to court their business. Officials spend at least part of their time visiting factories and the like, but side trips to Walt Disney World, Las Vegas, and Atlantic City are common. But, even this may be a thing of the past. Lucient recently settled charges that it failed to record millions spent in travel for about 1,000 Chinese Telecom officials to Las Vegas, Los Angeles, and Orlando. The company had characterized the trips as "factory tours." They admitted guilt and paid $2.5 million in fines in 2007. As the Department of Justice cracks down further, perhaps these "creative" approaches, and good old-fashioned direct payments, will decline in popularity.[76]

Chapter Summary

This chapter reviews various writings and research done on ethical values and corporate social responsibility in international business. It reviews two major perspectives on ethics. Universalism argues that there are sets of ethical values that should apply everywhere. Many international and corporate codes of conduct have been developed based on this perspective. Relativism is a perspective that embraces the idea that countries often have different sets of ethical values that are shaped by their own unique laws and practices. In practice, each is difficult to enact.

Most research suggests that Americans tend to be more concerned with ethical issues than their counterparts in Europe, Asia, and other parts of the world although that gap is narrowing. U.S. multinationals, for example, are more likely to have written codes of conduct in place that spell out what is considered unethical behavior than are European or Asian multinationals.

Most nations have laws that prohibit the bribery of officials. Few, however, actually outlaw bribes that their citizens may pay to foreigners—some view bribery as simply a part of doing international business. Bribing foreigners to get business for U.S. firms came to a head with several high-profile cases in the 1970s and led to the passage of the Foreign Corrupt Practices Act (FCPA), which made it illegal to pay foreigners bribes in an effort to win business. Other countries have since followed suit.

Discussion Questions

1. What role do universalism and relativism play in international management? What are the practical constraints involved in each perspective?

2. How should multinationals deal with human rights abuses made by foreign governments? Should they involve themselves in social issues that follow from their businesses? Why or why not?

3. How should multinationals handle bribery attempts? How should they address other questionable practices? Should they involve themselves in social issues that follow from their businesses? Why or why not?

4. What is your assessment of the Foreign Corrupt Practices Act (FCPA)? Is it likely to be a major hindrance for U.S. multinationals? What position should the U.S. government take regarding the tactics used by foreign multinationals in international competition?

Up to the Challenge?

Competitive Intelligence: Lots of Gray Areas, No Easy Answers

At the beginning of this chapter we challenged you to make some judgments about the ethics and legality of some specific behaviors associated with information gathering about other firms. While the field of competitive intelligence (CI) has grown as a legitimate business discipline, some firms take short cuts and do not follow legal or ethical guidelines in this increasingly popular practice of competitive information gathering. The following exhibit summarizes the behavioral incidents mentioned earlier, as well as, according to experts, whether or not they are legal, illegal, or in an ethically gray area. Deliberate theft of company materials or secrets from company property is illegal, at least in the U.S. Several of the examples of competitive intelligence that we have cited, however, would be considered unethical by many Americans.

U.S. Legal Behavioral Example	Ethical Status
1. Calling neighbors under false pretenses to assess managers' whereabouts	Ethically gray area
2. Securing a copy of a competitor's travel itinerary from a travel agent	Ethically gray area
3. Digging through a company's trash on public property	Legal
4. Deliberately eavesdropping on private company conversations	Illegal
5. Sending phony job-seekers in response to competitor's want ads	Ethically gray area
6. Hiring competitor's former employees	Legal
7. Sending phony visitors to tour competitor's facilities	Ethically gray area
8. Attending trade shows where competitor's wares are displayed	Legal

Many of these situations have involved U.S. companies. For example, a crayon company employee posed as a potential customer and easily gained access to the firm's production processes. While this is unethical, what about standing outside a plant to count employees who leave various shifts? What about the Japanese firm that sent employees to measure the thickness of rust on train tracks leaving a U.S. plant and then used that data to estimate plant output?[77] Raytheon Co., a defense contractor, agreed to pay a multimillion settlement not long ago to resolve charges that it hired private detectives to eavesdrop in a failed attempt to outrun Ages Group's bid for a U.S. Air Force service contract. Even universities are getting into the act. At the University of Missouri classes are taught in how to do "pipeline" analysis in the drug industry. This involves using public sources to ferret out what products are in the competition's research pipeline.

The early 2000s was a down market, but some companies still found the funds to engage in CI. John Pepper, then CEO of Proctor and Gamble (P&G), for example, was surprised to find out that CI had gotten out of hand in that firm. Michael Mace, the CEO at Palm, did not give a second thought to commissioning a $70,000 "scouting report" on the Japanese PDA market. As times got tougher in the late 2000s, more firms got involved in the process. A major survey conducted in 2008 showed that corporate interest in CI was on the rise. One finding was that firms in countries such as Israel, Sweden, India, and Brazil rank as the most sophisticated technology users for corporate intelligence programs. The U.S. and most European companies fall into the middle or the bottom rankings. John Nolan, a former intelligence officer now running a CI training business, said it best: "Nothing changes table manners faster than a smaller pie." Data showed that among firms *without* an organized CI capability, 45 percent said that they planned to start one the following year. A major survey conducted in 2008 showed that corporate interest in CI is on the rise. One finding was that firms in countries such as Israel, Sweden, India, and Brazil rank as the most sophisticated technology users for corporate intelligence programs, with the United States and most European companies falling into the middle or the bottom of the rankings.[78]

If CI is on the rise and is getting more competitive itself, what should a firm do? In our opening scenario we asked about recommendations that you might give multinationals that are interested in protecting their secrets from prying. Here are some tips:

- Have all joint venture partners and consultants sign nondisclosure agreements.

- Be sure to tightly control access to all facilities and electronic mail systems.

- Use written policies to make all employees more aware of the risks of security lapses.

- Test areas within the firm itself that might be vulnerable to information leaks.

- Establish a centralized electronic reporting system that will allow employees to report any suspicious incidents.

Plus, the firm might consider what P&G did in 2001. CEO John Pepper was informed that a competitive intelligence effort toward competitor Unilever had spun out of control. After hearing the details he was shocked and put an end to the "operation" immediately. When Pepper found that three of his managers had hired others to gather Unilever information via dumpster diving, misrepresentation and more, they were fired immediately. P&G had obtained dozens of documents that spelled out Unilever's plans for its U.S. hair care business (including prices, launch plans, and margins). None of these actions violated U.S. law, but they did violate P&G's internal guidelines and CEO Pepper took more action. He confessed to Unilever, calling its CEO personally and following this with a memo outlining the transgressions. P&G also agreed to pay Unilever $10 million, to take actions so that the information would not be used, and to toughen up internal enforcement of its code. It also agreed not to employ the "consultants" who conducted the above activity (the Phoenix Group, headed by John Nolan, quoted above).

While this was a sad chapter for P&G, its actions after uncovering the events are laudable. One expert has observed that firms with formal competitive intelligence systems tend to have fewer legal and ethical problems, probably because the guidelines make it clear what is and what is not acceptable.

Finally, the Society for Competitive Intelligence Professionals maintains an ethical code that can help guide business in this important area (www.scip.org/). Competitive intelligence properly done is a legal activity, indeed one that is needed in today's environment. Yet, this is all the more reason to be concerned with how you do CI so that it becomes an asset to the firm rather than an ethics problem.[79]

International Development

Bribery in International Business

Purpose

To discuss ethical issues associated with bribery and corrupt practices that may be encountered in international business dealings.

Instructions

To accomplish this, 12 short mini-cases are presented. These are designed to get you thinking about ethical issues associated with bribery. Your instructor may review the Foreign Corrupt Practices Act (FCPA) and other background material before getting started. These brief mini-cases deal with issues including bribes versus grease payments, whistleblowing, the black market, and interaction with government officials.

Your instructor will divide the class into groups of four to six members. Depending on the time available and the number of groups, your group may be assigned to all 12 or a smaller number of the mini-cases. Discuss the cases with your group and decide what course of action should be taken. (Try to spend 20–30 minutes on each case, depending on the number of cases that your group must tackle.)

Your instructor will then lead a discussion about the ethical issues raised by the mini-cases. An instructor may choose to ask your group to briefly present its recommended courses of action.

Mini-cases

1. You are driving to a nearby country from your job as a manager of a foreign subsidiary. In your car are a number of rather expensive gifts for family and friends in the country that you are visiting. When you cross the border, the custom official tells you that the duty owed on these items will be equivalent to $200. Then he smiles, hands back your passport, and quietly suggests that you put a smaller sum, equivalent to $20, in the passport and hand it back to him. What do you do?

2. You have been hired as an independent consultant on a U.S. development grant. Part of your job involves working with the Ministry of Health in a developing country. Your assignment is to help standardize some procedures to test for various diseases in the population. After two weeks on the job, a higher-level manager complains to you that money donated by the World Health Organization to the ministry for purchasing vaccines has actually been used to buy expensive computers for top-ranking officials. What do you do?

3. You have been trying for several months to privatize what was formerly a state-owned business. The company has been doing well and will likely do better in private hands. Unfortunately, the paperwork is slow and it may take many more months to finish. An official who can help suggests that if you pay expenses for him and his family to visit the parent company in the United States (plus a two-week vacation at Walt Disney World in Orlando and time in New York City), the paperwork can be complete within one week. What do you do?

4. One of your top managers in a Middle Eastern country has been kidnapped by a terrorist group that has demanded a ransom of $2 million, plus food assistance for refugees in a specified camp. If the ransom is not paid, they threaten to kill him. What do you do?

5. On a business trip to a developing country, you see a leather briefcase (which you badly need) for a reasonable price in the local currency (the equivalent of $200 at the standard exchange rate). In this country, however, it is difficult for the locals to get U.S. dollars or other hard currency. The shop clerk offers you the briefcase for $100 if you pay in U.S. dollars. What do you do?

6. You are the manager of a foreign subsidiary and have brought your car with you from the U.S. Because it is a foreign-purchased car, you must go through a complicated web of lines and bureaucracy (and as the owner of the car, you yourself must do it—no one can do it for you), which takes anywhere from 20 to 40 hours during business hours. One official tells you, however, that he can "help" if you "loan" him $100 and buy him some good U.S. bourbon. What do you do?

7. Your company has been trying to get foreign contracts in this developing country for several months. Yesterday, the brother-in-law of the finance minister offered to work as

a consultant to help you secure contracts. He charges one and one-half times more than anyone else in a similar situation. What do you do?

8. You have been working as the director of the foreign subsidiary for several months. This week, you learned that several valued employees have part-time businesses that they run while on the job. One of them exchanges foreign currency for employees and visitors. Another rents a few cars to visitors. You are told that this has been acceptable behavior for years. What do you do?

9. As manager of a foreign subsidiary, you recently discovered that your chief of operations has authorized a very convoluted accounting system, most likely to hide many costs that go to his pocket. Right now, you have no real proof, but rumors are circulating to the effect as well. This chief, however, has close ties to officials in the government who can make or break your company in this country. What do you do?

10. You have been hired to do some management training in a developing country. The costs of the program are almost entirely covered by a U.S. government agency. The people responsible for setting up one of the programs in a large company tells you they want the program to be held in a resort hotel (which is not much more expensive than any other) in a beautiful part of the country. Further, because they are so busy with all the changes in their country, they cannot come to a five-day program, which is what has been funded. Could you please make it a little longer each day and shorten it to three days? You would get paid the same. What do you do?

11. You have been hired by an investment firm funded by U.S. dollars. Your job is to finance companies in several former communist countries. If you do not meet your quota for each of three months, you will lose your job, or at least have your salary severely cut back. One of the countries is still run by communists, though they have changed the name of their political party. They want you to finance three companies that would still be tightly controlled by the state. You know that they would hire their relatives to run those companies. Yet if you do not support them, no other opportunities will exist for you in this country. What do you do?

12. Your new job is to secure contracts with foreign governments in several developing countries. One of your colleagues takes you aside one day to give you "tips" on how to make sure you get the contracts you are after. He tells you what each nationality likes to hear, to soothe their egos or other psychological needs. For example, people in one country like to be told they will have a better image with the U.S. government if they contract with your company (of course, this is not true). If you tell them these things, he says, they will most definitely give you the contracts. If not, someone in another company will tell them similar things and they will get the contracts. What do you do?

Source: This exercise was prepared by Dorothy Marcic. Copyright © 1993 by Dorothy Marcic. All rights reserved. As appeared in *Management International: Cases, Exercises, and Readings* by Dorothy Marcic and Sheila Puffer. Copyright © 1994 by West Publishing Company, Minneapolis/St. Paul, MN, a division of International Thomson Publishing Inc.

From Theory to International Practice

Analyzing Corporate Codes

Purpose

This activity seeks to understand important elements of corporate codes, the complexities involved in constructing such guidelines for behavior, as well as to examine differences and similarities across countries/cultures.

Instructions

In this chapter, we talked a good deal about corporate codes of ethics and the ways they are both similar and different. For this exercise, do some research to find codes of conduct for three multinational corporations. Using websites or library information, compare the codes and evaluate them. After getting this information, please do the following:

1. Answer these questions about the codes that you have chosen and those of others discussed in class.
   - What topics are covered in the codes?
   - Which topics are *not* covered?
   - How are these issues communicated in the codes?

   The instructor may wish to keep a tally of the common themes across the various companies. Compile a list by industry and jot down what you think the reasons are for possible differences across those industries.

2. Put together *your* version of a generic corporate code of ethics. Many international accords exist that provide a good base for your work (and for corporations), and a variety of websites are useful for this purpose and for answering the questions raised above:
   - **www.ethicsweb.ca/resources/** This site includes a discussion of many business ethics issues and links and discussion of corporate codes of ethics.
   - **http://commfaculty.fullerton.edu/lester/ethics/codes.html**. A set of links dealing with issues involved in corporate codes of ethics.
   - **http://managementhelp.org/businessethics/ethics-guide.htm**. A tool kit on business ethics with many available resources and links.
   - **www.transparency.de/English.1222.0.html**. The site on international corruption mentioned earlier in this chapter.

Notes

1. Riley, M. A., and Vance, A. (2012). Inside the Chinese boom in corporate espionage: It's not paranoia if they're stealing your secrets. *Bloomberg Businessweek*, March 19–25, 76–83; Fialka, J. (2010). Hugger-mugger in the executive suite. *The Wall Street Journal*, February 5, A10; Gorman, S. (2011). China singled out for cyberspying. *The Wall Street Journal*, November 4, A8; Wilke, J. R. (2003). Two silicon valley cases raise fears of Chinese espionage: Authorities

try to tie alleged thefts of secrets to government-controlled companies. *The Wall Street Journal*, January 15, A4.

2. Drab, D. (2004). Economic espionage and trade secret theft. Defending against the pickpockets of the new millennium. A White Paper: Xerox Global Services, available at: www.xerox.com/downloads/wpaper/x/xgs_business_insight_economic_espionage.pdf (retrieved 17 July 2013); King, N, and Bravin, J. (2000). Call it Mission Impossible Inc.: Corporate-spying firms thrive. *The Wall Street Journal*, July 3, B1, B4.

3. Wood, D. J. (1991). Corporate social performance revisited. *Academy of Management Journal*, 16, 691–718; Gottlieb, J. Z., and Sanzgiri, J. (1996). Towards an ethical dimension of decision making in organizations. *Journal of Business Ethics*, 15, 1275–1285.

4. L'Etang, J. (1995). Ethical corporate social responsibility: A framework for managers. *Journal of Business Ethics*, 14, 125–132; Schlegelmilch, B. B. and Robertson, D. C. (1995). The influence of country and industry on ethical perceptions of senior executives in the US and Europe. *Journal of International Business Studies*, 26, 859–879.

5. *The Economist*. (2000). Business ethics: Doing well by doing good, April 22, 65–67.

6. DeGeorge, R. T. (1993). *Competing with Integrity in International Business*. New York: Oxford University Press.

7. Buller, P. F., Kohls, J. J., and Anderson, K. S. (1991). The challenge of global ethics. *Journal of Business Ethics*, 10, 767–775; Frederick, W. C. (1991). The moral authority of transnational corporate codes. *Journal of Business Ethics*, 10, 165–177.

8. Donaldson, T. (1989). *The Ethics of International Business*. New York: Oxford University Press.

9. Forsyth, D. R., O'Boyle, E. H., and McDanile, M. A. (2008). East meets West: A meta-analytic investigation of cultural variations in idealism and relativism. *Journal of Business Ethics*, 83, 813–833.

10. Jackson, K. T. (1994). Jurisprudence and the interpretation of precepts for international business. *Business Ethics Quarterly*, 4, 291–320.

11. Jackson, K. T. (1994). Jurisprudence and the interpretation of precepts for international business.

12. Baron, D. P. (1996). *Business and Its Environment*. Upper Saddle River, NJ: Prentice-Hall.

13. Hinson, H. (1990). Movie stars. *Esquire*, December, 120–126.

14. Singh, J. J., Vitell, S. J., Al-Khatib, J., and Clark, I. (2007). The role of moral intensity and personal moral philosophies in the ethical decision making of marketers: A cross-cultural comparison of China and the United States. *Journal of International Marketing*, 15, 86–112.

15. Kaltenheuser, S. (1995). China: Doing business under an immoral government. *Business Ethics*, May/June, 20–23; Kelly, M. (1996). Is Pizza Hut Burma's keeper? *Business Ethics*, July/August, 73–75.

16. *The Economist*. (2010). Companies aren't charities, October 23, 82; *The Economist*. (2012). Good business; nice beaches, May 19, 76.

17. Sethi, S. P. (1993). Operational modes for multinational corporations in post-Apartheid South Africa: A proposal for a code of Affirmative Action in the marketplace. *Journal of Business Ethics*, 12, 1–12.

18. Kazmin, A. (2003). Burma's timber may blunt impact of sanctions. *Financial Times*, October 5, 3. Kaltenheuser, China: Doing business under an immoral government; Kelly, Is Pizza Hut Burma's keeper?

19. *USA Today* (2012). *Obama Administration Eases Burma Sanctions Before Trip*, USAToday.com, November 16, available at: www.usatoday.com/story/theoval/2012/11/16/obama-lifts-sanctions-burma-visit/1710253/ (retrieved July 12, 2013); Magnusson, P. (2005). A milestone for human rights. *BusinessWeek*, January 24, 63; Coile, Z. (2008). *Chevron's Dilemma Over its Stake in Burma*, San Francisco Chronicle Online, July 5, available at: www.sfgatge.com; Goldstein, J. (2008). *Feinstein Fights McCain on Burma Tax Break for Big Oil*, The New York Sun Online, June 6, available at: www.nysun.com.

20. Jobs, S. (2007). *A Greener Apple*, Apple.com, available at: www.apple.com (retrieved May 3, 2013); *Los Angeles Times*. (2003). WTO to allow access to cheap drug treatments, August 31, A4.

21. Kaufmann, L., Reimann, F., Ehrgott, M., and Rauer, J. (2009). Sustainable success: For companies operating in developing countries, it pays to commit to improving social and environmental conditions. *The Wall Street Journal*, June 22, R6.

22. Data cited in this whole paragraph was taken from: *The Economist*. (2008). Just good business: A special report on corporate social responsibility, January 19, 3–24; Also see: Gunther, M. (2006). The green machine. *Fortune*, August 7, 42–57; Egri, C. P., and Ralston, D. A. (2008). Corporate responsibility: A review of international management research from 1998 to 2007. *Journal of International Management*, 14, 319–339.

23. Levenson, E. (2008). Citizen Nike: A decade ago the shoe giant was slammed as a sweatshop operator. Today it's taking responsibility to heart. *Fortune*, November 24, 166.

24. *The Economist*, Good business; nice beaches.

25. This box relies heavily on material presented in Binkley, C. (2010). How green is my sneaker? *The Wall Street Journal*, July 22, D1, D6; also see: Tergesen, A. (2012). Doing good to do well: Corporate employees help and score out opportunities in developing countries. *The Wall Street Journal*, January 9, B7.

26. Schlegelmilch and Robertson, The influence of country and industry on ethical perceptions of senior executives in the US and Europe.

27. Becker, H., and Fritzsche, D. J. (1987). A comparison of the ethical behavior of American, French, and German managers. *Columbia Journal of World Business*, 22, 87–95.

28. Dubinsky, A. J., Jolson, M. A., Kotabe, M., and Lim, C. U. (1991). A cross-national investigation of industrial salespeople's ethical perceptions. *Journal of International Business Studies*, 22, 651–670; Kennedy, E. J., and Lawton, L. (1996). The effects of social and moral integration on ethical standards: A comparison of American and Ukrainian business students. *Journal of Business Ethics*, 15, 901–911; McCabe, D. L., Dukerich, J. M., and Dutton, J. (1993). Values and moral dilemmas: A cross-cultural comparison. *Business Ethics Quarterly*, 3, 117–130; Husted, B. W., Dozier, J. B., McMahon, J. T., and Kattan, M. W. (1996). The impact of cross-national carriers of business ethics on attitudes about questionable practices and form of moral reasoning. *Journal of International Business Studies*, 27, 391–411.

29. Tan, J., and Chow, I. H. (2009). Isolating cultural and national influence on value and ethics: A test of competing hypotheses. *Journal of Business Ethics*, 88, 197–210; Li, S., Triandis, H. C., and Yu, Y. (2006). Cultural orientation and corruption. *Ethics & Behavior*, 16, 199–215.

30. Rivers, C., and Lytle, A. L. (2007). Lying, cheating foreigners! Negotiation ethics across cultures. *International Negotiation*, 12, 1–28; Al-Khatib, J. A., Malshe, A., and AbdulKader, M. (2008). Perception of unethical negotiation tactics: A comparative study of US and Saudi managers. *International Business Review*, 17, 78–102.

31. *The Economist*, Business ethics: doing well by doing good; Langlois, C. C., and Schlegelmilch, B. B. (1990). Do corporate codes of ethics reflect national character? Evidence from Europe and the United States. *Journal of International Business Studies*, Fourth Quarter, 519–539.

32. Schlegelmilch, B. (1989). The ethics gap between Britain and the United States: A comparison of the state of business ethics in both countries. *European Management Journal*, 7, 57–64.

33. The most recent Dow code is detailed and complete and part of the reason they received the highest rating possible for corporate governance practices from Governance Metrics International (GMI), an independent research and ratings agency. Over 4,200 firms were rated, with only 1 percent receiving this highest rating. The firm, however, remains a target of criticism from various groups.

34. Holmes, S. (2003). Free speech or false advertising: Nike's sweatshop statement case hits Supreme Court. *BusinessWeek*, April 28, 69–70.

35. Montero, D. (2006). Nike's dilemma: Is doing the right thing wrong? *Christian Science Monitor*, December 22, 1–2.

36. See www.nikeresponsibility.com; Levenson, E. (2008). Citizen Nike: A decade ago the shoe giant was slammed as a sweatshop operator. Today it's taking responsibility to heart. Will it work? *Fortune*, November 24, 165–170; see Nike's map and list of all suppliers: http://nikeinc.com/pages/manufacturing-map.

37. Baker, M. (2013). Corporate social responsibility: Nike in the news, available at: www.mallenbaker.net (retrieved July 15, 2013); but see Oxfam's differing viewpoint on Nike: https://www.oxfam.org.au/explore/workers-rights/nike/

38. Montero, Nike's dilemma, 1–2.

39. Lund-Thomsen, P. (2008). The global sourcing and codes of conduct debate: Five myths and five recommendations. *Development and Change*, 39, 1005–1018.

40. Buller, P. F., Kohls, J. J., and Anderson, K. S. (2000). When ethics collide: Managing conflict across cultures. *Organizational Dynamics*, 28, 52–66.

41. Noonan, J. (1984). *Bribes*. New York: Macmillan.

42. Jacoby, N. H., Nehemkis, P., and Eells, R. (1977). *Bribery and Extortion in World Business: A Study of Corporate Political Payments Abroad*. New York: Macmillan.

43. Schaffer, R., Earle, F., and Agusti, B. (1993). *International Business Law and its Environment*. Minneapolis, MN: West.

44. Borsuk, R. (2003). In Indonesia, a new twist on spreading the wealth: Decentralization of power multiplies opportunities for bribery, corruption. *The Wall Street Journal*, January 29, A16.

45. Transparency International. (2013). *Global Corruption Barometer*, available at: www.transparency.org/gcb (retrieved July 20, 2012).

46. *The Economist*. (2000). Shenanigans in France, November 4, 53; Toy, S. (1996). Under suspicion: Le tout business elite. *Business Week*, January 22, 58.

47. Clark, N., Saltmarsh, M., and Brothers, C. (2008). In Europe, sharper scrutiny of ethical standards. *The New York Times*, May 7, 8.

48. *The Economist*. (2003). Comparative corruption: Different standards of probity across the continent pose a problem for the European Union, May 17, 47.

49. Esterl, M., and Crawford, D. (2008). Siemens to pay huge fine in bribery inquiry. *The Wall Street Journal*, December 15, B1, B5; Lichtblau, E., and Dougherty, C. (2008). Bribery case will cost Siemens $1.6 billion. *The New York Times*, December 16, 8; *The Economist* (2008). Bavarian baksheesh: The Siemens scandal, December 20, 5–6; Schubert, S., and Miller, T. C. (2008). Where bribery was just a line item. *The New York Times*, December 21, 1.

50. Clark, Saltmarsh, and Brothers, In Europe, sharper scrutiny of ethical standards.

51. *PBS News Hour*. (2009). Corruption case exposes the degree of bribery in Nigeria, originally aired April 4, available at: http://www.pbs.org/newshour/bb/africa/jan-june09/nigeria_04-24.html (retrieved July 3, 2013); *The Economist*. (2001). Another bad apple in Japan, January 27, 39.

52. Barrett, D. (2012). Korean executives indicated in case over DuPont Kevlar. *The Wall Street Journal*, October 19, B3; Ward, A. (2003). South Korea's mixed messages over corruption clampdown. *Financial Times*, October 1, 20; Ward, A. (2003). Transparency should by now be a given in Korea: The fraud at one of the country's most powerful industrial groups raises doubts about how far reform has really advanced. *Financial Times*, July 9, 11.

53. Mavin, D. (2013). Caterpillar's wayward path in China. *The Wall Street Journal*, January 29, B1; Peel, M. (2008). Cost of turning a blind eye to graft. *Financial Times*, April 10, 16; Nihalani, S. (2007). Cracking down on corporate cheats: Companies in the region could find themselves in hot water if they are not aware of strict U.S. anti-corruption laws. *South China Morning Post*, July 14, 28; Bandsuch, M. R. (2009). Understanding integrity across generations in China. *Journal of International Business Ethics*, 2, 21–37.

54. Pope, H. (2000). Corruption stunts growth in ex-Soviet states. *The Wall Street Journal*, July 5, A17.

55. Matthews, C. M., and Palazzolo, J. (2012). Oil giants launch bribe probes. *The Wall Street Journal*, June 7, B1, B2; Dougherty, C. (2007). Germany battling rising tide of corporate corruption. *The New York Times*, February 15, C1, C10.

56. Gold, R. (2009). Halliburton to pay $559 million to settle bribery investigation. *The Wall Street Journal*, January 27, B3; Gold, R. (2008). Halliburton ex-official pleads guilty in bribe case. *The Wall Street Journal*, September 4, A1, A15.

57. Crawford, D. (2012). H-P is named in bribery indictment. *The Wall Street Journal*, September 20, B3; Foroohar, R. (2012). Walmart's discounted ethics. *Time*, May 7, 19; Byron, E. (2011). Avon bribe investigation widens. *The Wall Street Journal*, May 5, B1, B2; Rockoff, J. D., and Matthews, C. M. (2012). Pfizer settles federal bribery investigation. *The Wall Street Journal*, August 8, B7.

58. *The Economist*. (1990). Hey, America, lighten up a little, July 28, A5.

59. *The Economist*. (2012). The economic case for bribery: You get who you pay for, June 2, 89.

60. Gold, R., and Crawford, D. (2008). U.S., other national step up bribery battle. *The Wall Street Journal*, September 12, B1, B6.

61. Singer, A. W. (1991). Ethics: Are standards lower overseas? *Across the Board*, 28, 31–34.

62. DeGeorge, *Competing with Integrity in International Business*; Cohen, J. A. (1976). Japan's Watergate. *The New York Times Magazine*, November 21, 104–119.

63. Kotchian, C. A. (1977). The payoff: Lockheed's 70-day mission to Tokyo. *Saturday Review*, July 9, 7–16.

64. Boulton, D. (1978). *The Grease Machine*. New York: Harper & Row.

65. Palazzolo, J., and Matthews, C. M. (2012). Bribery law dos and don'ts. *The Wall Street Journal*, November 15, B1, B2; Kim, S. H., and Barone, S. (1981). Is the Foreign Corrupt Practices Act of 1977 a success or failure? A survey of members of the Academy of International Business. *Journal of International Business Studies*, 12, 123–126.

66. Fadiman, J. A. (1986). A traveler's guide to gifts and bribes. *Harvard Business Review*, July/August, 122–136; Singer, Ethics: Are standards lower overseas?

67. Graham, J. L. (1984). The Foreign Corrupt Practices Act: A new perspective. *Journal of International Business Studies*, 15, 107–121.

68. Graham, The Foreign Corrupt Practices Act.

69. Donaldson, T. (1994). Global business must mind its morals. *The New York Times*, February 13, 11.5 ; Schlegelmilch, B. (1989). The ethics gap between Britain and the United States: A comparison of the state of business ethics in both countries; Calderon, R., Alvarez-Arce, J. L., and Mayoral, S. (2009). Corporation as crucial ally against corruption. *Journal of Business Ethics*, 87, 319–332.

70. *Ethikos*. (1996). Operating an ethics hotline: Some practical advice, March/April, 11–13.

71. Keatley, R. (1994). U.S. campaign against bribery faces resistance from foreign governments. *The Wall Street Journal*, February 4, A6.

72. *The Economist*. (2012). Walmart's Mexican morass, April 28, 71; Searcey, D. (2009). U.S. cracks down on corporate bribes. *The Wall Street Journal*, May 26, A1, A4.

73. Gold, R., and Crawford, D. (2008). U.S., other nations step up bribery battle. *The Wall Street Journal*, September 12, B1, B6; Peel, M. (2008). Cost of turning a blind eye to graft. *Financial Times*, April 10, 16.

74. Palazzolo, J. (2012). The business of bribery. *The Wall Street Journal*, October 2, B1, B4; Jones, A. (2012). The costs of compliance grow. *The Wall Street Journal*, October 2, B4.

75. *The Economist*. (2011). Bribery abroad: A tale of two laws, September 17, 68; Searcey, D. (2010). U.K. law on bribes has firms in a sweat. *The Wall Street Journal*, January 2, B1; Peel, M. (2006). Hurdles in countering cross-border corruption. *Financial Times*, August 14, 10.

76. Palazzolo, J. (2011). Critics target bribery law. *The Wall Street Journal*, November 28, B1, B8; Dunne, N. (2000). Bribery helps win contracts in developing world. *Financial Times*, January 21, 6; Milbank, D., and Brauchli, M. W. (1995). How U.S. concerns compete in countries where bribes flourish. *The Wall Street Journal*, September 29, A1, A14; Greenberger, R. S. (1995). Foreigners use bribes to beat U.S. rivals in many deals. *The Wall Street Journal*, October 12, 3.

77. Ball, D. A., and McCulloch, W. H. (1999). *International Business: The Challenge of Global Competition*. Burr Ridge, IL: Irwin McGraw-Hill.

78. Fuld. (2008). Asian, Latin American corporate intelligence technology users claimed to be "more sophisticated" than those in US, Europe, sweeping global survey of almost 500 companies finds, available at http://www.fuld.com (retrieved August 21); Girard, K. (2003). Snooping on a shoestring: Competitive intelligence doesn't go away during a down market—it just gets that much more competitive. *Business 2.0*, May, 64–66.

79. Sawka, K. A. (2008). The ethics of competitive intelligence. Kiplinger Business Resource Center, March, www.kiplinger.com; see also: www.fuld.com/News/PressReleases/pr080821.html.The room was already packed when Liu Peijin walked in. His flight from Shanghai to Chongqing had been delayed, and he had fretted about missing the training. But fortunately he'd gotten there in time. Liu knew his presence was important. As the president of Almond China, he wanted to show his Chongqing colleagues how much he cared about the topic under discussion: ethical business practices.

Case 1: Culture Clash in the Boardroom

The room was already packed when Liu Peijin walked in. His flight from Shanghai to Chongqing had been delayed, and he had fretted about missing the training. But fortunately he'd gotten there in time. Liu knew his presence was important. As the president of Almond China, he wanted to show his Chongqing colleagues how much he cared about the topic under discussion: ethical business practices.

Taking his seat, Liu nodded at the head of HR, who was running the training. The two went way back: Both had been with their German parent company, Almond Chemical, since 1999, when it first established operations in China. Since then Almond China had set up two joint ventures with local partners—the only way foreigners could do business in chemicals in the country. Almond controlled 70% of the stock in one of them. The other was a venture with Chongqing No. 2 Chemical Company, in which Almond had a 51% stake and the Chinese directors were very active.

Liu sat next to Wang Zhibao, the vice president in charge of sales for the Chongqing joint venture. Wang looked skeptical. He was good at his job, having closed several key deals that had kept the business afloat during its early years. But he was also at the center of a conflict between the venture partners: The Chongqing executives were increasingly vocal about how difficult it was to operate according to European standards, particularly the rules against gifts and commissions. Such incentives were commonly accepted in China and routinely

employed by Almond's competitors. Trying to do business without them, Wang argued, was foolhardy. "This is China, not Europe," was his refrain.

But the line between these practices and breaking the law was a fine one. Almond was headquartered in Munich and listed on the New York Stock Exchange as well as the Frankfurt Stock Exchange, meaning it was required to adhere to the U.S. government's Foreign Corrupt Practices Act, which specifically forbade the bribing of foreign government officials by U.S.-listed companies.

Liu kept an eye on Wang as the HR director explained Almond's ethics regulations and the legal consequences of business bribery. Liu knew the rules made sales more difficult, but Almond's policy was clear, and he wanted to make sure that every member of the sales team understood it.

He had taken the same hard line on safety and environmental practices. The production facilities in Chongqing had been built according to German national standards, and all the safety equipment—helmets, shoes, and protective clothing—had come from Europe. The Chinese partners had called these investments "wasteful" and "frivolous"—"luxurious expenditures" that the young venture couldn't, and shouldn't, afford. But, with backing from the head office, Liu had stood firm. Similarly, he'd insisted that the factory's MDI (methylene diphenyl diisocyanate) waste be treated as a dangerous substance and processed with a special cleaning agent, in accordance with European standards, even though Chinese law didn't mandate it. His partners had been dismayed at the millions of yuan this would cost. But Liu refused to compromise, because he had witnessed the consequences of lesser standards firsthand. Years before, when he was working for another Chinese chemical company, an affiliate's chlor-alkali plant had suffered an explosion, injuring 200 staff members and residents of the surrounding area and halting production for more than a month.

The training was reaching its end, and the HR director signaled to Liu that it was his turn to speak. Liu hesitated slightly as he looked at his Chongqing colleagues. "At Almond, ethics are non-negotiable," he said. "We need to remember these laws as we go about our business. We are not just a Chinese company; we're a global one." Solemn, blank faces stared back at him.

As he left the room, he couldn't help feeling that his remarks had fallen on deaf ears.

"We Cannot Concede"

Two weeks later, Liu was back in Chongqing for the second-quarter board meeting. As he walked into the lobby of the Hilton, he ran into George Ho, the finance director for the joint venture. Ho looked flustered.

"Are you all right?" Liu asked in English. Ho was from Hong Kong and didn't speak fluent Chinese. He held a unique position: He reported to the general manager of the joint venture but also to the finance director at Shanghai headquarters.

"I'm worried about this meeting, Liu," Ho said. "I had a disturbing conversation with Wang last week."

Liu nodded, not surprised.

Ho continued. "Wang is close to making a huge sale—30 million yuan—but the customer's purchasing manager is insisting on a 1% commission. He says that's what he's being offered by other companies."

"We can't do that," Liu said.

"That's what I said. But Wang was insistent. He said that if we can't do that, we should at least be able to offer the manager a trip to Europe, a visit to Almond headquarters."

"What did you say to that?" Liu asked.

"No—of course," Ho replied. "But he accused me of jeopardizing the venture. He said that we 'foreigners' have so much money, we don't care about the performance of the business."

"You did the only thing you could do," Liu said.

"I can't believe Wang thought that suggestion would fly, especially after the training," Ho said. He walked down the hall toward the boardroom. Liu followed.

The meeting had barely begun when Chen Dong, the chairman of the joint venture and a Chongqing No. 2 Chemical executive, raised the commission issue. (His leadership position was one of the many concessions Almond had made to lure his company into the joint venture.)

That was fast, Liu thought. He sat quietly while Dolf Schulman, the vice chairman of the venture and Almond Chemical's senior vice president of business development, fielded the question.

"Chen, we cannot concede on these issues," Schulman said. "There are no exceptions to be made. Almond must be a law-abiding corporate citizen—as should every Almond employee."

Ho looked up and nodded at Liu. But Chen was not ready to end the discussion. "To the best of my knowledge," he said, "many foreign-owned companies reward Chinese customers for their business. Some companies organize overseas visits, some provide management training, some arrange golf outings. This is good business practice in China. We need to be flexible in order to compete. If we can't provide the commission, let's at least consider a visit to Munich headquarters."

This was typical behavior for Chen. He had a tendency to develop very strong opinions but keep them to himself until the board met. Schulman waited for the translator to finish; then he hesitated, trying to come up with a suitable response. Liu knew he needed help.

"Commission or trips, it's all the same thing: business bribery," Liu said. "We can get orders without these tactics."

Chen picked up the Q2 financial statement that had been distributed at the beginning of the meeting and said, "Orders? What orders? We made only 60% of our target for this quarter. When we set up this joint venture, we assigned our very best people to it—our best technicians, best salespeople, best managers. Why? Because we believed we could manufacture some of the best chemical products in the world and, in turn, get more orders. But look at this." He threw the statement down on the table. "Our performance is sinking fast. This joint venture has done nothing but hurt us. We have yet to see any return at all."

Chen paused to let the translator catch up but then thought better of it.

"All you do is make us spend, spend, spend—on German goggles, unnecessary waste processing, and ridiculously high salaries." He turned to Ho, who looked bewildered. "And now I hear rumors that you are planning to launch SAP's ERP software to synchronize with headquarters. When will the spending stop?"

Chen continued, his voice rising. "We need a tighter control on costs. We can't possibly meet our profitability target when our expenses are so high. We want to choose the finance director going forward, so we can give this venture a real chance at succeeding. We see no other option."

He sat back in his chair and crossed his arms. Schulman was squirming in his seat. Ho was pale with shock. Liu wasn't sure what to say. He was astonished that Chen had brought up the safety standards—he'd thought that issue was settled long ago—and astounded by the slap at Ho. But he needed backup if he was going to oppose the joint venture's chairman.

Finally Schulman spoke. "Chen, thank you for being honest about your concerns," he said. "At this point I think all these issues are still open for discussion."

Liu almost choked. What was Schulman thinking? Seeing Liu's expression, Schulman looked at his watch and said, "Should we take a 15-minute break?" With that, he stood up.

"This Venture Is Critical"

As Liu walked out of the room, Schulman grabbed his elbow and steered him toward a smaller meeting room down the hall. Once the door was closed, Schulman's shoulders slumped.

"Liu, what should we do?" he asked. "Do you think we should concede to these demands? This venture is critical for us—you know that."

Liu did understand how high the stakes were. China accounted for only 3% of Almond's current business, but the company was depending on the country for future growth. The Chongqing operation was supposed to prove that Almond could expand further in China, and the company was already planning additional acquisitions. But Liu was shocked that Schulman would even consider bending the company's standards regarding ethics and safety.

"We need to stand strong," Liu said, "not give in." He was thinking about Almond's reputation as well as the future in China. He had joined the century-old German company not only because it boasted the world's leading chemical-production technology, but also because of its values, management approach, and safety ethic, which he'd hoped would serve as a model for Chinese industry.

"But we shouldn't annoy them," Schulman said. "We need Chen. And he's right about the numbers. We could be in trouble without Wang's sale. Besides, where do we draw the line? Is a golf game bribery? We do that in Germany all the time."

Liu realized that Schulman wasn't asking for his opinion. He was asking for permission to give in. Suddenly Liu felt like a kid stuck between two warring parents. The break time was almost up. They needed to get back to the meeting and respond to Chen's demands.

Assignment Questions

1. Outline the dilemma facing Liu Pei-jin (and the firm). Be sure to explain all the contributing elements to this 'culture clash'.

2. What should Liu do? He has only minutes to determine how he can juggle these competing demands and how he should approach these issues.

3. Be sure to fully explain the options and potential consequences he faces as he struggles to deal with these issues. Provide some specific and tangible recommendations for how Liu should react when the meeting resumes.

part II

interacting effectively in an international environment

chapter 4

making distinctions across cultures

implications for international management

Learning Objectives

After reading this chapter, you should be able to

- categorize cultures and countries based on their key, overall value sets;
- identify the impact of embracing particular underlying values on work behaviors and practices;
- identify differences and customize management practices to specific cultures.

International Challenge

Hidden Strengths: Is India the Proverbial "Elephant" in the Global Room?

India is a complex, messy, and chaotic place with hundreds of millions of poor citizens and a ramshackle infrastructure. This is accentuated particularly when compared to the gleaming new ports, highways, and airports that China has been installing across the country in recent years. Moreover, India has long been plagued by a notoriously inefficient, albeit democratic, government. As a result, China has more than made up economic ground on India (and the rest of the world too). On most measures of development, the "Dragon" (China) beats the "Elephant" (India) hands down. On indicants ranging from life expectancy, to literacy rates, to Internet use and GDP per person, China enjoys a healthy lead over India. For example, a child's odds of surviving past their fifth birthday are as bad in India today as they were in China in the late 1970s.[1] Interestingly, these and other challenges and barriers may have uncovered a latent but remarkable set of assets among the Indian people. All these challenges may have inculcated a problem-solving mentality that provides crucial help to many Indians to quickly, cheaply, and cleverly invent new products and new ways of doing things.

Indeed, this way of thinking has caused multinationals the world over to flock to India, not just for backroom outsourcing in Bangalore, but to tap some of the most innovative minds around. As a result, optimists are saying that India today is booming in many respects, and that while growth rates lag behind those of China, the steady progress in India is more manageable and better for the economy in the long run. India also has a variety of world-class firms such as Tata Motors and mobile phone provider Bharti Airtel. Not surprisingly, some of those same experts who believe in India's booming economy predict that India's GDP growth may pass China's in a few years. By 2016, estimates are that another 200 million Indians will join the ranks of the middle class, bringing their spending power to bear on the Indian and world economy.

Interestingly, while China's approach to growth has been, for the most part, government driven, India's successes are more connected to the collective efforts of its nearly 50 million entrepreneurs. The unleashing of India's entrepreneurial culture has been driven by several factors, including reforms that started 20 years ago, such as lower tariffs on imported goods, friendlier rules for foreign investment, and less red tape for businesses. Another factor is the domestic market. While many Indian companies do a brisk export business in services, the local market is large and demanding, with customers wanting cheap products that work well from the get go. India's "frugal innovators" give them what they want. In fact, some of what they have come up with is nothing short of mind-boggling. For instance, Tata Chemicals has developed a water filter that costs less than $1, needs no power, and provides 30 days of pure drinking water for a five-person family. Indian scientists have also developed a new laptop that they hope to bring to market—one that costs just $35.

All of this is consistent with recent research about cultural values that seem to encourage people striking out on their own and becoming entrepreneurs. The real question, however, is whether this problem-solving mentality that is embedded within the culture can continue to help lift the country up faster and farther than its challenges and weaknesses will hold it back. Think about this as you read about the various distinctions made among cultures in this chapter. Do you think that India is well positioned (culturally and otherwise) to move its economy forward? What specific elements of its culture might contribute to this advancement? Which features might provide strong support for continued success at various entrepreneurial ventures? Taking this a step further, how might you, as an international manager on assignment in India, adapt to the business and culture milieu and possibly capitalize on India's expertise in "frugal innovation"? After reading this chapter, take a look at the Up to the Challenge? closing box for some insights into India's cultural values.[2]

Defining and Understanding Culture

Chapter 1 describes culture as "the collective programming of the mind which distinguishes one group or category of people from another." Given this very abstract description, it is believed that people are not fully aware of the pervasive impact of culture on their own attitudes and actions.[3] Yet, there is plenty of evidence that culture has an impact on the management of international business, often in some very unexpected ways. Cultural differences can impact everything from the treatment that employees expect from their companies, to how expatriates adapt to foreign environments, to overseas investment strategies and patterns. The influence itself may cut both ways—cultural differences have the potential to produce friction and disruption as well as enormous benefits. On the one hand, lack of appreciation of "indigenous" methods of motivation and leadership can lead to very bad outcomes. On the other hand, when managers work to understand and use the best of what various cultures offer, this can lead to very good performance.[4] The chapters that follow explain how culture plays a role in many different facets of international business.

The stakes for management have never been higher. The ongoing growth of international business has helped raise questions about the impact of cultural values. So, expatriate managers need to know which motivation strategies work best in their operations across the globe—and that is just the beginning. Human resource practices, organization structure, strategy formation and implementation, conflict management approaches, negotiation tactics, and leadership styles can also vary across cultures.[5] Even the reasons that entrepreneurs *start* companies can be driven in part by culture. For instance, in East Asian countries (such as Indonesia and Thailand), the level of interest in entrepreneurship may be more strongly connected to concerns about social status, such as gaining status from success or losing it from a business failure, than it is in Anglo countries such as Australia and the U.S.[6] Research has even examined whether varying beliefs in the importance of hard work and thrift may help explain different economic growth rates among nations.[7]

The management challenge is not only to be aware of the role that culture can play within business, but to turn that awareness into action where possible. For example, research shows that foreign subsidiaries perform better financially, as indexed by a higher return on assets and return on sales, when they use management practices that are consistent with the local culture.[8] Good opportunities may pop up anywhere in today's rapidly evolving global environment, sometimes in parts of the world that are poorly understood. So, those firms that are culturally aware, and can more quickly size up and intelligently interpret local business practices, will be in the best position to succeed.[9]

There are not many businesspeople these days who would disagree with the conclusion that understanding culture is an asset. But, there are many more who underestimate the difficulty and time needed to do this well. Not surprisingly, managing "smart" from a cultural perspective is not easy. Part of the problem is the complexity of culture itself. Yet, managers sometimes feel in desperate need of tools to help sort out the culture of their latest assignment in Jakarta, Guangzhou, or Santiago, even at the risk of oversimplifying matters. This state of affairs explains why so many cultural frameworks have popped up over the past few decades trying to explain the pattern of norms, behaviors, and customs that are common in a given society. Yet cultural frameworks are seductive in that they can reinforce management tendencies to rely on the time-saving analytical shortcuts they offer. In turn, this can actually inhibit managers' ability to be effective as they oversimplify culture and paint employees around the world in a series of broad-brush generalizations.

Nevertheless, when they are used thoughtfully, cultural frameworks can prove helpful. This means that managers should treat these frameworks not as one-size-fits-all labeling devices, but instead as a guide and a starting point for helping them understand different work environments. Managers also need to remember that all cultural frameworks have inherent limitations. For instance, we will review four influential frameworks that each try to capture cultural differences through sets of bipolar dimensions (e.g., individualism–collectivism). Typically, nations are located somewhere on each cultural dimension. But this reductionism cannot fully capture the complexities and paradoxes we see in specific cultures. For instance, if Americans are so self-focused, then why are they also so generous with charities and willing to help when natural disasters such as hurricanes and floods strike? If Central American countries are so well known for displaying interpersonal warmth, then why do service workers in those countries often seem indifferent to customers? Indeed, in one survey, bank customers in Costa Rica preferred to interact with "polite" machines (ATMs) instead of human tellers.[10]

With these limitations in mind, we will next present four major cultural frameworks that have attracted considerable attention from international managers. Along the way, we will also point out their benefits and limitations. We will wrap up the chapter by suggesting ways in which managers and multinationals can better combat cultural stereotypes and bridge cultural differences.

Classifying Cultures around the Globe

Ronen and Shenkar's Country Clusters

The Clustering Approach   Trying to make sense of cross-cultural differences among nearly 200 countries, which are then each comprised of many subcultures, is an extremely difficult task. One way to make things easier is to identify a core set of values that are shared by a specific set of countries. In 1985, Ronen and Shenkar did just that—they created a set of clusters based on their exhaustive and comprehensive review of previous research.[11] They also conducted a comprehensive survey of thousands of employees in nearly 50 countries to help improve the classifications. The survey included questions about:

- **Various work goals/what employees want from work** (e.g., interesting work, job security, or promotion opportunities)
- **The extent to which work satisfies certain needs** (e.g., personal accomplishment, job satisfaction)
- **Preferences for various management styles** (e.g., preferences for autocratic versus democratic leadership)
- **General questions about work roles and relationships** (e.g., how well managers relate to subordinates).

Ronen and Shenkar's goal was to cluster countries based on the patterns of similarity among all these attitudes toward work. The result of their classifications is presented in Figure 4.1. There are several features about this figure that are noteworthy. First, eight country clusters were identified. Four separate and independent countries were also identified. This did not fit well with the attitude patterns of the other clusters; you will see those placed outside of the circle of clustered countries. Second, countries within a particular cluster were said to share some basic cultural values. Third, within each cluster you will see that the richer, more developed countries are positioned closer to the center. For example, the Nordic cluster shows that Sweden is the most highly developed, whereas in the Latin European cluster this distinction belongs to France.

According to these researchers, the level of development and technological advancement within a country is one of the factors driving the clustering of countries. It stands to reason, therefore, that as development proceeds, cultural values may also change. Another thing to note about Figure 4.1 is that the clusters generally include countries that are close to each other geographically. This reflects the idea that cultural values should develop first in those areas nearest to a particular culture's point of origin. At

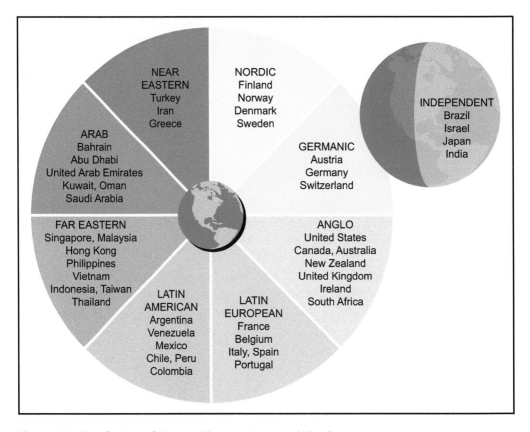

Figure 4.1 Classification of Country Clusters: Ronen and Shenkar.

Source: Ronen, S., and Shenkar, O (1985). Clustering countries on attitudinal dimensions: A review and synthesis. *Academy of Management Review*, 10, 449.

the same time, however, you might see that great geographic distances exist between some countries in the Anglo-American cluster. This certainly reflects the immigration patterns and reach of the British Empire, which took Anglo cultural values to many different parts of the globe.

Another similarity within clusters is language. For example, the Latin American cluster contains Spanish-speaking countries and the Anglo cluster English-speaking countries. While the countries in the Latin European cluster have different languages, they are considered Romance, or Latin-derived, languages. Many work values, goals, and attitudes can be shaped by linguistic meanings and interpretations.

Work values and goals may also reflect religious attitudes and beliefs. Catholicism is the major religion in both of the Latin clusters. Buddhist and Confucian values tie the countries together in the Far Eastern cluster; these values emphasize the obligations people have to their families and the shame that is associated with failing to live up to those obligations. Finally, the countries labeled as independent (Brazil, Japan, India, and Israel) have unique religions, languages, and histories. In the case of Japan, this also includes a level of geographic isolation that further contributed to a distinctive culture.[12]

Overall, Ronen and Shenkar's clusters provide a useful snapshot for international managers interested in knowing where broad similarities and differences may exist between countries in terms of the business practices and approaches used in various countries. Consequently, those armed with such knowledge are likely to operate more effectively in foreign environments.[13]

Limitations of Ronen and Shenkar's Approach

While providing great value for thinking about cultural/country differences, there are also some limitations associated with this approach. For instance, the clusters are missing many countries (e.g., none of the countries in the former Soviet Union are included). Likewise, few developing countries are represented, nor are those countries that are now economic powerhouses (such as China). Where would these countries fit today? We do not know for sure, and the answer to this question is more complex than it might seem. For example, it is easy to imagine a new Asian cluster consisting of Japan, China, and South Korea. All three countries are well known for emphasizing harmony in interpersonal relations, an emphasis traceable to some common Confucian values. But, "harmony" takes on a different meaning in each country. In Japan, harmony is often defined in terms of group activities and membership, whereas in China and Korea harmony is often defined in terms of relationships between individuals (Figure 4.2 presents a summary of these differences).

Feature	Country Term for Harmony		
	Japan *Wa*	China *Guanxi*	Korea *Inhwa*
Definition	Stress on group harmony, mutual cooperation to reach group goals	Stress on friendly relationships that are based on the exchange of favors	Stress on harmony between unequals; workers are loyal, bosses are obligated
Employees' commitment	To company	To boss, family	To boss, family
Role of the individual	Be an effective group member	Maintain favorable exchange relations	Be loyal to boss
Decision-making	Participative, consensus-based, illusion of agreement key	Based on personal loyalties and favors owed	Based on family ties, hierarchy
Performance feedback	Indirect, often done via third parties to preserve group harmony	Indirect, often done via third parties to maintain equity in relationships	Indirect, often done via third parties to preserve harmony among unequals
Management style	Group facilitation	Benevolent paternalism	Clan management

Figure 4.2 Defining "Harmony" Differently in Japan, China, and Korea.

Source: Adapted from Alston, J. P. (1989). Wa, guanxi, and inhwa: Managerial principles in Japan, China, and Korea. *Business Horizons*, March–April, 26–31.

The Japanese may value *wa*, group cohesion and group loyalty, above individual needs. This means that they may work for the group's benefit and identify strongly with their company. Since harmonious group relations are so important, interpersonal conflict tends to be minimized. For example, achieving a consensus in decision making is critical, even if it requires maintaining an illusion of agreement among everyone during the decision-making process. Open disagreements tend to be avoided. While American managers often feel free to disagree (sometimes in very frank terms), some Japanese managers avoid conflicting views to a great extent. For Americans, the word *sincerity* means telling the truth. The closest Japanese equivalent, *makoto*, means promoting harmony and showing support for colleagues.[14] As mentioned, however, cultural values are always evolving, even if slowly and incrementally— something that may be the case with Japan, a society that's faced tough economic times in recent decades.

In China, however, harmony is expressed by *guanxi*, the special relationship that Chinese have when they are mutually obligated to each other. This obligation includes the exchange of favors and can take precedence over firm procedures and sometimes even law. A failure to return favors results in a loss of face and may lead to the end of the relationship. Employees tend to be loyal to their individual *guanxi* relationships, rather than to the company. *Guanxi* can exist between two people of unequal status, like a manager and a subordinate. In this case, the subordinate will be loyal in exchange for being taken care of by the manager. This unequal exchange honors the more powerful member of the relationship and is linked to Confucian expectations that powerful family members help weaker members.

The result in China is a benevolent paternalism where managers may act as kindly father figures who provide for their "children" (subordinates). These complex but informal relationships affect how business gets done: laws, procedures, and regulations are routinely circumvented because of *guanxi*. Developing *guanxi*-based "connections" can help foreign companies succeed in China.[15] But, just like those in Japan, traditional Chinese values may also be evolving. See the accompanying International Insights feature for a look at the case of one of those traditional values, *guanxi*.

International Insights

Old-Fashioned Chinese Guanxi Gets a Decidedly Yiddish Edge . . . and Begins to Look More Like Schmoozing All the Time

The Chinese term *guanxi* means connections (loosely translated) and anyone with a passing familiarity with the country will tell you that it is necessary to have *guanxi* in order to get anything done. Having it and getting it are key to setting up important meetings, getting vital approvals, and cutting a business deal. In fact, the sky's the limit sometimes if you have good *guanxi*, an appetite for banquets, and enjoy XO brandy![16]

Like many things in Asia, and China in particular, times are changing. Increasingly, *guanxi* seems to be evolving and has now taken on a more Western feel, where lots of schmoozing is done. The word "schmooze" is of Yiddish origin and means to converse casually, especially in order to gain a business advantage or make a social connection. One Chinese MBA graduate talked about the new *guanxi* in this same way: "it used to mean access . . . now it's about relationships that inform and educate you." Even the likes of Yang Yuanqing, chairman of Lenovo Group (the Chinese giant that bought IBM's laptop business several years ago) had come to value more Western-style schmoozing: "more and more Chinese who studied or worked overseas need to understand how to build these networks." One networking source consists of Chinese who meet in an American or European MBA program, such as Gary Wang, who earned an MBA from INSEAD, a top-ranked business school in France. Mr. Wang now runs a YouTube-type firm called Tudou that he built largely based on his business school connections. His business partner is a Dutch MBA classmate, who in turn married another one of their fellow classmates. Another alum helped with public relations work. Yet another is a partner at a global ventures firm and helped raise $9 million after yet another friend heard him speak at a conference.

This general ring of information, education, and relationships seems to be on the rise as Chinese businesspeople become more globally savvy. Some business schools have systematically fostered this "schmoozing." They encourage alumni networks and provide the foundation for continuing smaller, more intense circles of relations. Multinationals are also getting into the act. Proctor and Gamble (P&G) China "graduates" of a "class" of over 80 college recruits 1997 were all asked to reflect on their personal bonding experiences within the company. The group now has its own website, where members share information with each other, from golf lessons to job opportunities. Of course, playing the game is still paramount—knowing the party boss (or his kids) probably cannot hurt in any country or in any business—especially in China. Plus, working the room for 30 minutes is neither good *guanxi* nor good schmoozing; that only goes so far and does not build relations of lasting value. That said, increasingly it seems that East is meeting West in China.[17]

Similar to China, the South Korean version of harmony (*inhwa*) is defined by relationships between individuals. In South Korea, however, the relationship commonly involves people of unequal status and power. The guiding principle is the Confucian norm that individuals are to be loyal to parents and to authority figures. Thus, harmony is a function of observing hierarchical ranking. At work, managers sometimes expect the same loyalty and obedience that a person would give to a parent. In fact, in many large Korean firms *real* parent–child relationships exist in executive ranks. Traditionally, a company's founder brings members of his family or clan into top positions.[18] Nevertheless, all parties are expected to be emotionally supportive of each other, regardless of their rank or family status. One consequence is a strong reluctance to engage in direct criticism or provide negative performance feedback.[19]

Overall, the differences among Japan, China, and South Korea illustrate the limitations of clustering countries that appear to have very similar cultural values. Similarly, in the Anglo cluster, British managers tend to be more formal, more class-conscious, and more autocratic than their American counterparts.[20] It would be a mistake to assume a high degree of cultural homogeneity in a region.[21] The same point is true for "within-country" differences. Immigrant migration to the U.S., Germany, and other countries has put managers in the position of having to motivate employees from diverse cultural backgrounds. Doing a better job of managing this diversity can enhance the competitiveness of American companies.[22] Likewise, in South Africa, approximately 10 percent of the 45 million population are white descendants of Dutch and British settlers. South Africa's black citizens come from several ethnic groups (such as Zulus and Xhosas).[23] In the presence of such diversity, it is not surprising that cultural differences affect work in South Africa in complex ways.[24]

In summary, Ronen and Shenkar's approach to clustering countries has important limitations—ones shared by *all* frameworks that seek to cluster countries and cultures. Hofstede's effort to distinguish countries is no exception.

Hofstede: Clustering Countries on Work-Related Value Dimensions

Geert Hofstede's work represents the largest and most influential effort to cluster countries by cultural values.[25] Hofstede's conclusions are based on a survey that asked over 116,000 employees in more than 70 countries about their values and beliefs. From these data, Hofstede extracted four basic cultural dimensions: individualism–collectivism, masculinity–femininity, power distance, and uncertainty avoidance. He created scores, ranging from 1 to 100, for each dimension and then used these scores to compare countries. In addition, to help interpret his results, Hofstede also created cultural "maps" that position each country in terms of pairs of culture dimensions. Since countries also tend to cluster, similarities and differences between groups of countries were assessed. Overall, Hofstede's work, especially around these four dimensions, has important implications for managing employees around the world.[26]

Individualism–collectivism

This dimension describes whether people in a culture tend to view themselves primarily as individuals or as members of a group. In individualistic cultures, people are expected to take care of themselves, and a high value is placed on autonomy, individual achievement, and privacy. In collectivist cultures, however, people are more likely to view themselves as part of a group that protects and takes care of them in exchange for loyalty and devotion. The group may be the family, a clan or tribe, or an organization. It is believed that these values are deeply embedded in a culture and have been communicated among members throughout their lives—including very early on in life and children's school years. Some research confirmed this belief by studying grade school textbooks. As you might expect, even in the process of conveying knowledge, authors regularly impact key values to their readers and this is exactly what one author recently found. Nearly 100 grade school textbooks from both Japan and the U.S. were coded for the number of references and stories that related to individual (self-direction, personal achievement) or collective (group harmony, fitting in) themes. The results confirmed that individualistic values are much more common in U.S. textbooks and collective themes more common in Japanese books. This same effect even extended to pictures (single individuals vs. group interaction), narrators, and more.[27]

Individualism–collectivism is the most widely studied of Hofstede's dimensions, and it also may be the most complex. Recent research suggests that collectivism and individualism are actually multifaceted.[28] For instance, individualism may include both economic (e.g., "I achieve things by competing") and expressive (e.g., "I want to be seen as a unique person") elements. Likewise, collectivism may also contain economic (e.g., "members of the group should share resources") as well as expressive (e.g., "group members should be emotionally involved with each other") components. On top of that, cultures may vary considerably when it comes to how they view a particular component of individualism or collectivism. For example, while cultures that share Confucian and Latin roots tend toward collectivism, at least compared to the U.S., they may view expressiveness quite differently. In many Latin American countries, open displays of emotion and warmth are expected and encouraged. On the other hand, such displays are much less likely to be found in Japan. In short, what constitutes "collectivism" (or "individualism," for that matter) may vary from place to place and it is important to dig deep to understand that.[29]

Masculinity–femininity

This describes whether success and the assertive acquisition of money and power (at the expense of others, if necessary) is highly valued—or whether people, the quality of life, and good relationships with co-workers should take precedence. Hofstede noted that in most cultures men were more likely to endorse the assertive (or "masculine") view. Masculine cultures are achievement oriented, tend to view the ambitious pursuit of high performance as the ideal, and feel that men are better suited for positions of power. School systems in such cultures tend to identify and develop "high performers." Likewise, an important social value is having a "successful career." Workplaces tend to be competitive, stressful, and prone to conflict.

Feminine cultures, on the other hand, emphasize the equality of men and women, place a high value on taking care of the disadvantaged, and desire harmony in the workplace. Consequently, there is a stronger emphasis on job security and creating stress-free work environments. Career pressures also tend to be lower and labor–management discord less likely.

Power distance

Power distance (PD) reflects the extent to which people accept large differences in authority and power between individuals or groups in an organization. Put simply, how acceptable is it to have power distributed in an unequal manner? In *high* PD cultures, people are more likely to accept their station in life and follow the direction of those with greater authority. The view is that some people either deserve or are destined to be in command and others are not. So, a company hierarchy that spreads powers unequally is acceptable because managers and employees are seen as different types of people. Overall, leadership discretion and managerial authority tends to be more concentrated in high PD cultures.

People in low PD cultures, in contrast, are more likely to be wary of concentration of authority. Power is more likely to be used in a decentralized way, with companies having fewer layers of management. In these low PD cultures, managers tend to develop close, trusting relationships with their subordinates and use their power with care. Free wielding of power is frowned upon and is often subject to a variety of laws, procedures, and standards, which, if violated, can create a backlash as well as other problems for managers. Research shows that empowerment methods (e.g., giving employees discretion on decisions) are more effective in low PD cultures than high PD ones.[30] But, a recent study suggests that it is important to be careful about how empowerment is defined. Depending on its definition, using empowerment methods can be successful in both Canada (low PD) and China (high PD). When the empowerment is defined as the degree of management trust and support (leadership empowerment), it can have positive effects in high and low PD cultures.[31]

Uncertainty avoidance

How people react to uncertain or ambiguous events defines Hofstede's uncertainty avoidance (UA). People in cultures that are low in UA embrace the idea that life is unpredictable by definition. As a result, there is less concern with or adherence to rules, procedures, or organizational hierarchies. Risk taking, especially in the pursuit of individual achievement, is desirable. Competition and conflict are both viewed as inevitable parts of life in an organization.

Individuals in countries or cultures where UA is high, however, tend to feel threatened by ambiguity and will go to great lengths to create stable and predictable work environments. In such cultures, there is an emphasis on 'absolute' truths and unusual behavior or ideas tend to be rejected. As a result, rules and procedures designed to keep uncertainty at bay, such as employee treatment, tend to be more common. Likewise, there tends to be less risk taking in decision making and reduced personal initiative in regard to career moves in high UA cultures.

Cultural maps

Hofstede created cultural maps by crossing pairs of cultural dimensions and plotting the corresponding scores for each country. Each map is divided into quadrants representing different combinations of the cultural dimensions. Countries whose pairs of scores tend to cluster together are also identified. The basic idea is that countries may possess certain combinations of cultural values that have unique managerial implications. We will look at managerial implications of this in more detail later. For now, we will focus on understanding

ARA	Arab countries (Egypt, Lebanon, Libya, Kuwait, Iraq, Saudi Arabia, UAE)	JPN	Japan
ARG	Argentina	KOR	South Korea
AUL	Australia	MAL	Malaysia
AUT	Austria	MEX	Mexico
BEL	Belgium	NET	Netherlands
BRA	Brazil	NOR	Norway
CAN	Canada	NZL	New Zealand
CHL	Chile	PAK	Pakistan
COL	Colombia	PAN	Panama
COS	Costa Rica	PER	Peru
DEN	Denmark	PHI	Philippines
EAF	East Africa (Kenya, Ethiopia, Zambia)	POR	Portugal
EQA	Ecuador	SAF	South Africa
FIN	Finland	SAL	Salvador
FRA	France	SIN	Singapore
GBR	Great Britain	SPA	Spain
GER	Germany	SWE	Sweden
GRE	Greece	SWI	Switzerland
GUA	Guatemala	TAI	Taiwan
HOK	Hong Kong	THA	Thailand
IDO	Indonesia	TUR	Turkey
IND	India	URU	Uruguay
IRA	Iran	USA	United States
IRE	Ireland	VEN	Venezuela
ISR	Israel	WAF	West Africa (Nigeria, Ghana, Sierra Leone)
ITA	Italy	YUG	Former Yugoslavia
JAM	Jamaica		

Figure 4.3 Abbreviations for Countries and Regions Used in Hofstede's Culture Maps.

Hofstede's culture maps. Figure 4.3 shows the abbreviations for the countries used in Hofstede's research.

We will start with the positions of countries on the individualism–collectivism crossed by the power distance dimensions. As Figure 4.4 shows, only Costa Rica combines collectivism and small power distance. Instead, large power distance and collectivism more commonly occur together, with most countries in this quadrant being either Asian or Latin American. Similarly, small power distance and individualism go together, with northern European and Anglo countries such as Sweden and Great Britain populating this quadrant.

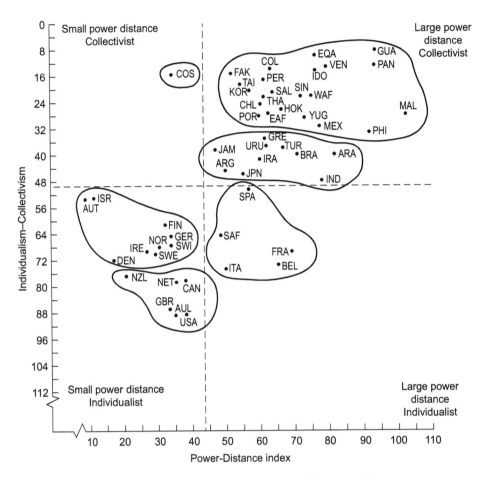

Figure 4.4 Culture Map for Individualism–Collectivism Crossed by Power Distance.

Source: Hofstede, G. (1991). *Cultures and Organizations: Software of the Mind*, 54. London: McGraw-Hill U.K. Used with permission.

Figure 4.5 displays the map crossing the uncertainty avoidance and masculinity–femininity dimensions. Hofstede suggested that cultures with weak uncertainty avoidance and masculine values will be *achievement-oriented*. These tend to be Anglo countries or their former colonies (such as India, Hong Kong, and the Philippines). The second quadrant, combining strong uncertainty avoidance and masculinity, produces *security motivation*. For countries in this quadrant, both performance and job security are valued. In contrast, the combination of feminine values and strong uncertainty avoidance produces *social motivation*. Here job security, positive relationships, and a good quality of life are prized. Scandinavian countries dominate the fourth quadrant, which combines feminine values and weak uncertainty avoidance. In these countries, risk and performance are acceptable, but social relationships and a high quality of work life are valued more than individual achievement. We might expect to see a larger number of paid holidays in these countries as opposed to countries exemplifying achievement motivation, and research typically finds this to be true.

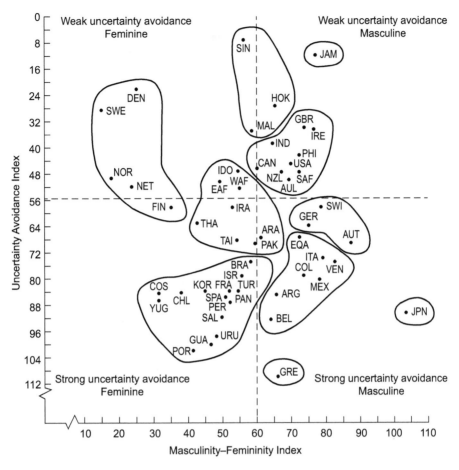

Figure 4.5 Culture Map for Uncertainty Avoidance Crossed by Masculinity–Femininity.
Source: Hofstede, G. (1991). *Cultures and Organizations: Software of the Mind*, 123. London: McGraw-Hill U.K. Used with permission.

Figure 4.6 displays the final map that crosses uncertainty avoidance and power distance. Asian countries dominate the *family quadrant* (large power distance and weak uncertainty avoidance). In these countries, there is often somewhat less concern about laws and procedures than on being loyal to strong, paternalistic leaders. In contrast, the *pyramid of people quadrant* (large power distance and strong uncertainty avoidance) produces cultures accepting of powerful leaders, but in a context that is fairly hierarchical and rule-bound. We count 14 Latin American countries within this quadrant. Organizations in these countries often have vertical and clear lines of communication—they know who reports to whom. Of course, by clarifying these features, organizations become more predictable. This diverse quadrant contains Mediterranean, Latin, and some Asian countries.

Germanic countries dominate the *well-oiled machine quadrant* (small power distance and strong uncertainty avoidance). In this environment, leaders are less important than having clear rules and procedures that promote efficiency. Finally, the *village market quadrant* contains Anglo and Scandinavian countries. Here the combination of small power

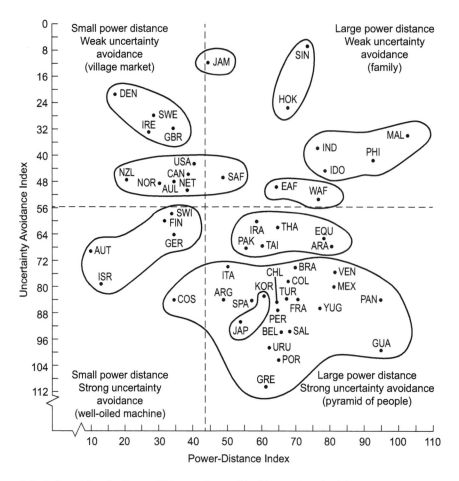

Figure 4.6 Culture Map for Power Distance Crossed by Uncertainty Avoidance.

Source: Hofstede, G. (1991). *Cultures and Organizations: Software of the Mind*, 141. London: McGraw-Hill U.K. Used with permission.

distance and weak uncertainty avoidance allows for a great deal of experimentation and risk taking that's not automatically limited by powerful leaders. In such cultures, good negotiation and conflict management skills may be critical for getting things done since elaborate procedures are replaced by fewer management layers and less formal controls.

Long- versus short-term orientation

More recently, Hofstede proposed this fifth cultural dimension, which evolved from his work on Asian cultures with colleague Michael Bond. This helps distinguish between cultures that have a forward-looking perspective on life (long-term) and those that are more concerned with the past and present (short-term). Specifically, cultures that are long-term oriented feel that values focusing on the future (e.g., frugality, hard work, adaptability, persistence) are most important. Indeed, many Asian societies are long-term oriented, something that may help explain the economic success enjoyed by some

More Long-Term Oriented
China
Taiwan
Japan
South Korea
Brazil
India
Thailand
Netherlands
Sweden
Germany
Australia
United States
Great Britain
Canada
Philippines
Nigeria
Pakistan
More Short-Term Oriented

Figure 4.7 Long- Versus Short-Term Orientation: Where Do Various Countries Stack Up?
Source: Adapted from Hofstede, G. (2001). *Culture's Consequences* (2nd ed.), 356. Thousand Oaks, CA: Sage.

Asian countries (e.g., South Korea, China, Japan) over the last decades, despite some major bumps in the road (e.g., Asian financial crisis of 1997). On the other hand, cultures that are short-term oriented feel that values focusing on the past and present (e.g., respect for tradition, stability, fulfillment of social obligations) are most important (e.g., Pakistan, Philippines, Canada, U.S.). In general, Asian countries tend to have the strongest long-term orientation, while those with more short-term orientation include both some "Eastern" and "Western" countries (see Figure 4.7). If you are wondering about how long- versus short-term orientation relates to Hofstede's other four dimensions, the answer is fairly complex. That said, there is some evidence that wealthier countries that strongly embrace a long-term orientation also tend to be high on power distance and low on individualism (South Korea being a good example).[32]

Limitations of Hofstede's Cultural Dimensions

Like Ronen and Shenkar, the Hofstede model misses some key countries in its clustering effort. For example, countries in Eastern Europe are missing, as are developing Asian nations such as Vietnam. To help rectify this, Hofstede's more recent work includes cultural value estimates for emerging economic powers such as China and Russia. For instance, he views China as a country that is long-term oriented, low on individualism, and moderate on uncertainty avoidance and masculinity. Russia, on the other hand, is seen as short-term oriented, high on power distance, strong on uncertainty avoidance, moderate on individualism, and low on masculinity. Nevertheless, certain regions of the world remain underrepresented even in the most recent efforts to cluster countries by culture.[33]

Another limitation of Hofstede's work is that it ignores differences that exist between countries within a specific cluster or quadrant. Research suggests, for example, that cultural differences exist between the U.S. and Australia despite their similar scores on Hofstede's cultural dimensions. For example, Americans tend to be more interested in intrinsic rewards like responsibility and recognition, while Australians tend to be more interested in having job security and a good income.[34] Hofstede's approach has a hard time explaining these results. Finally, some have been concerned that the wide generalizations made of Hofstede's work are not tempered or qualified enough. Those critics note that the results were based on employees of *one* large multinational (IBM) at *one* point in time (most in mid to late 1970s). One study recently reviewed nearly 500 separate studies, conducted among 50 different countries and comprising nearly 500,000 participants across decades on Hofstede's dimensions and found support for their validity. But, they also noted that the support degraded over the last three decades, suggesting that cultures may be converging more toward one another as the world becomes "flatter."[35] Finally, others have noted that Hofstede's approach doesn't consider major subcultures within a country.[36]

Despite these limitations, however, Hofstede's work continues to have tremendous impact on the field of international management and remains a valuable guide for interpreting the effects of culture.[37] Plus, some recent research has reinforced both the value and applicability of Hofstede's cultural dimensions.[38] One study, for instance, found that business leaders were seen as prioritizing their goals in ways that reflected their national cultures. Specifically, business leaders in countries with high power distance are perceived to value personal honor, family interests, and power more than business leaders in countries with low power distance.[39] Take a look at the following International Insights feature which shows how the Walt Disney Company developed practical solutions, in part based on an appreciation of some of these cultural values.

International Insights

It's a Small Park After All: Queuing Up at the House of the Mouse

Anyone who has ever been to a Walt Disney theme park has learned how to maximize time for the next visit—and there is a next time for many, many people! Rookies learn about which rides to avoid, what time is best for the most popular attractions, and how the "fast pass" system (the Disney "reservation" approach to avoid waiting in lines at popular attractions) works.

Whether you are an experienced visitor or not, you are bound to spend some time waiting in lines. How you line up at the "House of the Mouse" can have some cultural underpinnings. In addition to the U.S. theme parks, Walt Disney has locations in Europe,

Japan, and Hong Kong. Like they had done elsewhere, Disney put the new Hong Kong theme park through its paces in several weeks of trial runs prior to its official opening. Disney felt that they had a good handle on operations, partially because it was a far smaller park (only 300 acres) than others that had already been established. Yet, Disney was smart to prototype as a number of "flaws" were found, several of which could be traced to cultural differences.

The long waits for rides were problematic. The wait time was so bad that Hong Kong officials (and social media participants) lobbied Disney to reduce the daily guest limit of 30,000, citing the two-hour waits at some rides, unclear traffic patterns, and more. Interestingly, research on cueing behavior found that Asians and other guests from collective cultures tend to compare their situations with others around them. This makes it more likely that they will stay in really long lines more readily than a Westerner would. The study found that it is the people behind a person in line—rather than the number of guests waiting in front of a person—that determines an individual's staying power in the line for a collective society. The chance of a Chinese visitor leaving an attraction line is lower when they see more people *after* them. Researchers said that, in Hong Kong, this could make lines grow even bigger: "the longer the line, the more people think it's worth it." This view contrasts with Americans and other individualistic cultures that are likely to focus on who's in front of them in line— the longer the line, the less likely an individualistic guest is to join in.

This does not necessarily mean, however, that the Chinese or other cultures are completely patient. Mr. Jay Rasulo, chairman of Disney Parks and Resorts, said that the (mainland) Chinese are "not as impulsive" as some customers in Europe, but that the more experienced Hong Kong Chinese "seem a little more respectful" than most. Yet, according to Rasulo, neither are as patient as the Japanese. Europeans have yet a different view about how long they will wait. At Disneyland Paris, the British visitors are orderly and know how to properly cue, whereas the French and Italians "never saw a line they couldn't be in front of", says Rasulo. They then improvised at their Paris theme park by making lines narrower by moving handrails closer together to prevent cutting ahead. This was not necessary at Tokyo Disney, where mats spread out by people along parade routes to reserve space (unattended) were respected for hours before the parade.

Disney, however, is ever the innovator and their designers ("Imagineers") have put their renowned attention to customers into play, such as with the handrail solution at Disneyland Paris. In China, they discovered that wait times were increased by the Chinese penchant for taking photos of the characters just before entering the rides, which in turn slowed "traffic" to a standstill. To adjust, they installed other life-size figures, such as stationary Mad Hatter tea cups from Alice in Wonderland throughout the wait line for this ride in order to help speed loading of the ride—guests can take pictures while waiting for the ride, as opposed to only having one opportunity for pictures just before boarding the ride itself. Park additions were assisted by a feng shui master out of cultural respect, despite keeping the strong American Walt Disney themes, because these are features that Chinese visitors say they want to see. There will be more problems, especially as a new Shanghai theme park begins construction in 2015. But, as Disney officials say, other parks where people do not have to wait in lines are the failures. Nobody has to wait at Walibi Schtroumpf (a Smurf-themed French park)—"you don't wait because nobody's there."[40]

Trompenaars's Alternative: Another Look at Cultural Dimensions

Fons Trompenaars's recent work represents a unique and ambitious attempt to identify cultural dimensions. Focusing on values and relationships, Trompenaars surveyed more than 15,000 managers over a ten-year span. These managers represented 28 countries, and Trompenaars was able to identify a variety of bipolar cultural dimensions as a result.[41]

Outer vs. Inner Directed

Outer-directed employees tend to accommodate their behavior to their situation in life. Why? Because they feel that life's outcomes are not under their control. Such employees may desire stability as well as have a strong need for harmonious relationships. In contrast, *inner-directed* employees tend to believe that they control their own destinies. Consequently, they are likely to be more willing to change their environment. According to Trompenaars, Americans tend to be inner-directed, while at the other extreme, Chinese tend to be outer-directed. Similarly, research comparing managers from the U.S. and four Arab countries found that inner-directed values were endorsed most by the Americans, while outer-directed values were more dominant on the Arab side. Because of outer-directed concerns, business in Arab countries often functions on a more relationship-oriented basis than it does in Western nations.[42] Several of the most important cultural dimensions identified by Trompenaars focus on relationships with others. A brief discussion of some of these additional dimensions along with examples of countries most representative of each polar extreme follows.

Universalism–particularism

This refers to the extent to which people usually believe that one set of rules and practices should apply to everyone (*universalism*) or whether the rules should be adjusted depending on the person or situation (*particularism*). Many countries stress good relations with family and friends (particularism) rather than focusing just on the performance-based considerations (universalism) that are more common in the U.S. Countries as diverse as Venezuela, Indonesia, and China, however, tend toward particularism. Overall, managers from cultures that embrace particularism are more likely to take an employee's personal family troubles and job demands into account when deciding on rewards than are managers from cultures that embrace universalism.

Neutral–emotional

Cultures in which emotions are suppressed and stoicism is important are the neutral end of this dimension. The Japanese are well known for their reserve and composure. The flip side is an emotional culture, where feelings are expressed with gusto, such as in Mexico. You can imagine some of the challenges that might occur if employees from neutral cultures find themselves in an emotional culture or vice versa. Adapting to the "rules of the game" that you are in is probably a safe guide for behavior (e.g., by being more expressive in an emotional culture or more reserved in a neutral culture).

Specific–diffuse

In specific cultures, such as within the U.S., life tends to be compartmentalized. Work and family roles, for instance, are kept relatively separate—behavior that you see, titles that are used, and the level of formality displayed will all vary depending on what role an individual happens to be in (for example: boss, personal friend, co-worker, husband, mother, etc.). Thus, having a relationship with someone carries little risk because that relationship is limited to a specific role (e.g., you can be very friendly with people on the job but never see them outside of the workplace). But in diffuse cultures, such as in China, the lines between roles are fuzzy. A person's job title might affect the way that person is treated and viewed outside of the office and in many other spheres of life. The Chinese therefore tend to be somewhat cautious in dealing with others for the first time, especially since access to one area of life may mean access to all.

Achievement–ascription

In achievement cultures, your status depends on how you have performed and the goals that you have been able to reach (e.g., a degree from a top university or landing a prestigious promotion). "Being the best" at whatever it is that you do carries a lot of weight. In ascription cultures, by contrast, status depends on things such as age, social connections, class, or gender. For instance, social connections are likely to have a larger impact on hiring and other business decisions in ascription cultures such as in China or Indonesia than in achievement cultures such as the U.S.

Individualism–communitarianism

This dimension is similar to the distinction that Hofstede draws between individualism (thinking of yourself as an individual first) and collectivism (thinking of yourself as part of a group first). A comparison of the two frameworks, however, reveals some differences. For instance, Argentina and Mexico are described as relatively group-oriented by Hofstede but as individualistic by Trompenaars. Why this is the case is not completely clear. One possibility is that each researcher has defined his terms somewhat differently. Another possibility could be that Trompenaars's newer data may be revealing shifts in cultural values that have occurred over the years. As stated earlier, cultures are constantly evolving and changing. Trompenaars's work may help underscore that point, as might the last classification system to be discussed.

Spanning the GLOBE: One Final Classification System

One of the most recent attempts to classify countries based on their cultural orientation is the Global Leadership and Organizational Behavior Effectiveness study—GLOBE.[43] Over 200 social scientists from over 60 countries/cultures around the globe are involved in this cooperative effort to collect data. This team of researchers studied roughly 20,000 middle managers from nearly 1,000 companies in the financial, food service, and telecom industries. Researchers worked to select countries so that every major region of the globe was represented. Note that these study features represent efforts to deal with the problems raised by critics of the Hofstede and to a degree Trompenaars's research. That is, many different companies were studied (in contrast to just one in Hofstede's research), various industry sectors were sampled (only IBM was sampled in Hofstede's research), and many researchers around the world weighed in. The study was originally designed in order to measure cross-cultural views of leadership (discussed further in Chapter 10). But, the results have since been extended to general differences across countries and, again, clusters of countries.

Researchers began by developing a questionnaire with items that would measure nine different cultural dimensions. They derived these dimensions from their reading of the existing research (including that of Hofstede and others), and through interviews and focus groups in various countries. In Figure 4.8, we present these GLOBE dimensions, their similarity to Hofstede's research, and some sample countries that rank high and low on these dimensions.

Six of the dimensions either overlap with the Hofstede dimensions directly or were improvements on those.[44] Even though there is overlap, the GLOBE researchers believe

Dimension and Definition	Countries Ranked High	Countries Ranked Low
1. **Uncertainty avoidance** (Hofstede)	Switzerland, Sweden, Singapore	Guatemala, Hungary, Russia
2. **Power distance** (Hofstede)	Morocco, Nigeria, El Salvador	Denmark, Netherlands, Israel
3. **Collectivism I, Societal** (Hofstede)	Sweden, South Korea, Japan	Argentina, Germany, Hungary
4. **Collectivism II, In-group**—the degree to which people are loyal and close to families or organizations	Philippines, Iran, India	New Zealand, Sweden, Denmark
5. **Gender egalitarianism**—does society minimize gender role difference and promote gender equality? (Hofstede's Mas–Fem)	Russia, Poland, Denmark	Egypt, Kuwait, South Korea
6. **Future orientation** (Hofstede's LTO)	Singapore, Switzerland, Netherlands	Poland, Argentina, Russia
7. **Assertiveness**—are people generally assertive in their relations with others?	Albania, Germany, Hong Kong	Switzerland, New Zealand, Sweden
8. **Performance orientation**—degree to which society encourages and provides rewards for performance and excellence	Switzerland, Singapore, Hong Kong	Russia, Venezuela, Greece
9. **Humane orientation**—does society encourage and reward for being fair, altruistic generous, and caring, and kindness to others?	Philippines, Ireland, Thailand	Germany, Singapore, Greece

Figure 4.8 GLOBE Cultural Dimensions.

Note: US ranking: 1 (middle), 2 (low), 3 (middle), 4 (low), 5 (middle), 6 (high), 7 (middle), 8 (high), 9 (middle).
Source: Adapted from House, R. J., Hanges, P. J., Javidan, M., Dorfman, P. W., and Gupta, V. (eds) *Culture, Leadership, and Organizations: The GLOBE Study of 62 Societies.* Thousand Oaks, CA: Sage.

that their study improvements, as well as their sharper way to measure all the dimensions, are great benefits—not to mention that a few additional distinctions across cultures were found. Figure 4.8 shows the first three dimensions in detail under Hofstede, and readers should be familiar with these. The fourth dimension is a separate type of collectivism dealing with pride in, loyalty to, and closeness of family and work groups, not necessarily society as a whole (see Globe dimension #3/Hofstede). So, for example, ties of this sort are very important in business dealing in countries such as the Philippines, India, and South Korea. South Korea in particular is known for major companies tied to families.[45]

In Figure 4.8, Dimensions 5 and 6 are also derived from Hofstede. The final three dimensions in the figure are new and offer measurement and conceptual clarity over the other existing models discussed. For example, the *performance orientation* dimension could be a particularly useful way to understand motivation across culture. This refers to the importance of improving performance, the value of good performance, and the degree to which people in a society are encouraged to strive to be better (similar to Trompenaars's achievement–ascription dimension and related to Hofstede's masculinity–femininity dimension). Singapore, Hong Kong, and Switzerland scored the highest among the 62 countries on this behavioral dimension. The U.S. scored in the middle third of countries on this dimension in the GLOBE study. Russia, Venezuela, and Greece scored the lowest in the sample on this dimension. This does not mean that these countries are not, or cannot be, great economic successes (indeed, Russia is doing quite well as of this writing); instead it suggests that other factors such as background, loyalty, family are more important.

The final dimension listed in the table is called *humane orientation* and refers to the degree to which society encourages and rewards its members for being fair and considerate of others. Figure 4.8 shows that countries such as the Philippines, Ireland, and Thailand all score very highly relative to other countries around the world. The GLOBE researchers suggest that people in these countries have a greater focus on the less privileged and powerless in their societies. Taking care of others, including at work, and friendly relations and tolerance are very important. Contrast this with the countries of Germany and Singapore, where more importance is attributed to obtaining power and material possessions, as well as improving the individual self.

Summary of GLOBE

Overall, the GLOBE study is the most contemporary approach and offers the best measurement features and study scope. This bodes well for future uses of these dimensions, scales that measure those dimensions well, and their findings. All of this suggests that the GLOBE clustering approach may overtake Hofstede's model as the most cited and researched. For our purposes in this book, however, findings across models might be helpful to managers as they stand right now. For example, those in or about to enter the international arena can be made aware of these general differences and can potentially capitalize on them. At the minimum, classification approaches allow for one to be sensitive to behavior that is appropriate to local societal norms and expectations. This is something that the social media website Facebook did recently, as it tried to expand the global use of its platform. See the following Global Innovations feature for more information.

Global Innovations

Sharing Is Caring (about Market Penetration): Facebook in Unfamiliar Places

With over 900 million members worldwide, Facebook is a social networking giant. While the U.S. has the most users (estimated at over 160 million as of this writing), international growth of users has been phenomenal. In 2008, there were only about 35 million users outside the U.S., but this figure ballooned to over 400 million by 2011, and continues to grow like crazy in many countries still.

But, some have suggested that it is not really a global brand—at least not yet. Indeed, despite the popularity of the internet in China, Facebook has a low profile in some countries. In China, for example, there are only about 500,000 users in an Internet-hungry nation of roughly 1.3 billion—many millions more of whom use Tencent and other Chinese social media products. Still, as the growth rates for Facebook show, underestimating the website would be a mistake. The company has made some impressive strides in two nations—Russia and Indonesia—that might not strike people as great markets to leap into. Yet, Facebook has done exactly that, armed with an understanding of the culture of both countries and how that culture impacts customers' willingness to use the firm's services.

In Russia, local networking sites are quite popular—an important signal to Facebook. Indeed, Facebook launched its Russian site in 2010 and saw its user base jump nearly 400 percent in the first eight months. One of the factors that attracted Facebook to the country is the fact that Russians average almost ten hours per month on social networking sites—more than twice the global average. Many parts of Russia are isolated and frigid for much of the year, making online interaction an attractive option.

But a bigger reason for the pull of social networking is the Russian cultural tradition of using informal networks as sources of information, often for sheer survival. Given Russia's long history of closed institutions and opaque systems that cannot be trusted or relied on, informal networks can be a powerful substitute. Plus, with historically limited press and civil freedoms, Russians often feel hemmed in personally. Yet, unlike in China, Russian authorities allow pretty much anything to happen online. Moreover, Facebook gives its Russian customers a measure of control, allowing them to create and then vote on Russian names for various website features. Finally, Russia is a very relationship-oriented society, one in which connections are key for everything from securing good jobs to "fixing" problems with officials. This also bolsters the attractiveness of social networking online. Even though there are only about 6 million Russian Facebook users now, this understanding of the market could pay off in much larger numbers of users from this nation of 150 million people.

In Indonesia, many citizens of the world's largest Muslim country love to converse and share stories and, increasingly, they want to do it online. Thanks to skyrocketing growth, Indonesia has already become Facebook's fourth-largest market in the world, despite the fact that less than 20 percent of the over 250 million Indonesians have Internet access. The country trails only the U.S., Brazil, and India as the largest markets for Facebook. Interestingly, Facebook recognized that certain elements of Indonesia's culture make citizens there especially open to using social networking. First, friendships are very important in Indonesian society.

Combined with a tendency to embrace trends, a desire for publicity, and relatively little concern about privacy, Indonesians are ideal customers for Facebook.

That said, however, Indonesia does have some peculiarities as a market for social networking. Few Indonesians have bank accounts or credit cards, so the advertising model that Facebook uses to make money in the U.S. (i.e., where people routinely buy something after clicking on ads) does not apply to nearly the same degree. Instead, Facebook is trying to construct partnerships with other firms in ways that will allow Indonesian customers to barter for goods or use online "currency"—while still making money somehow on these transactions. In any case, another unusual aspect of Indonesians' social networking behavior is their tendency to use avatars—often with completely different physical characteristics—instead of their own photos to represent themselves on Facebook. Indonesians who interact online about their real lives while using idealized avatars as self-images underscore why Facebook cannot take foreign markets at face value. Instead, Facebook and other companies need to better understand how culture impacts social networking complexities in different markets.[46]

The Implications of Culture for International Management

Up to this section, a brief and general commentary about the implications of culture for management has been discussed. We have also noted that culture can potentially impact just about everything—from how international business strategy is formed, to encouraging Facebook use. We will explore these topics and more in greater detail in chapters to follow. For now, however, let's turn our attention to an examination of how culture may affect what people want from their jobs, as well as how individuals view leadership. The chapter concludes with some specific, practical suggestions for moving beyond the kind of "sophisticated stereotyping" that often comes with the limitations of current culture frameworks.

Culture and What People Want from Work

Work Centrality

How central is work in the lives of employees? Do employees work primarily for relationships, money, or for the job itself? The answers have important implications for how managers should approach their jobs in various cultures. Research suggests that what we want from work may, to an extent, depend on our culture. For instance, a survey of 14,000 employees from eight countries (Belgium, Britain, Germany, Israel, Japan, the Netherlands, the U.S., and the former Yugoslavia) found that *work centrality* (how important work is in the lives of employees) varied across countries. Americans fell in the middle of the pack, while the British had the lowest work centrality scores and the Japanese the highest. In fact, the Japanese not only had the highest centrality score, they were also significantly ahead of the other seven countries as a group.[47]

Some have suggested that work centrality in Japan may have eroded in recent years. While this may be true, the tendency to view work as a critical part of life will undoubtedly persist at some level in Japanese culture. Why? One reason is that it is hard to imagine long-standing Japanese traditions being completely undercut in just a decade or two. For centuries, Japan was a society made up of small, isolated farming communities. This isolation required hard work and cooperation to ensure community survival. This agrarian system began changing significantly only within the last 80 years. The legacy of this system in modern industrial Japan is the value placed on hard work and group solidarity.[48]

Other Work Features

But what about other aspects of work? Figure 4.9 summarizes the importance of 11 different work goals across eight countries. You will notice that employees in most countries ranked interesting work first or second in importance. Good pay was also an important goal for most employees, although Dutch and Japanese employees ranked it lower. Substantial differences across countries were found for most of the remaining work goals. For example, job security was very important to Germans, but not very important to Israelis. Japanese felt that achieving a good match between job demands and their talents was the most important work goal, while most countries rated it fifth or lower. Finally, while having autonomy was the most important work goal for Dutch employees, British employees rated it near the bottom.[49]

Work Goal	Country Studied							
	Belgium	Germany	Israel	Japan	Netherlands	U.S.	Former Yugoslavia	U.K.
Interesting work	1	3	1	2	2	1	2	1
Good pay	2	1	3	5	5	2	3	2
Interpersonal relations	5	4	2	6	3	7	1	4
Job security	3	2	10	4	7	3	9	3
Match of job/skills	8	5	6	1	6	4	5	6
Lots of autonomy	4	8	4	3	1	8	8	10
Opportunity to learn	7	9	5	7	9	5	4	8
Work variety	6	6	11	9	4	6	7	7
Good hours	9	6	7	8	8	9	10	5
Safe working conditions	11	11	9	10	10	11	6	9
Opportunity for promotion	10	10	8	11	11	10	11	11

Figure 4.9 Rankings of the Importance of Work Goals by Country.

Note: Ranking of work goals ranges from 1 = most important to 11 = least important.

Source: Adapted from MOW International Research Team. (1987). *The Meaning of Working*, 123. London: Academic Press.

Nevertheless, these results suggest that providing interesting work will have a positive effect on workers in all eight countries. If these findings offer generalization for other nations and cultures, managers could view "interesting work" as something that employees universally want from their jobs. The results also suggest that managers need to adjust their approach to match the values of specific cultures. Of course, this adjustment must be made cautiously. After all, cultures change. Moreover, individual values, needs, and goals may diverge from existing cultural norms in any case.

Other studies have produced similar findings and implications. One survey, for example, found that both American and Asian executives valued hard work. But Americans tended to value personal achievement much more than the Asians, while the reverse was true for respect for learning. Also interesting was the fact that there was considerable divergence in values among Asians managers. Executives from Japan, for instance, were more concerned with harmony than their counterparts from Singapore and Hong Kong.[50]

Value Convergence?

There has been considerable interest in discovering whether cultural perspectives on values and various work features and behavior are converging. One clever investigation compared the relationship between personal characteristics and evaluations of managerial effectiveness in Canada, Hong Kong, and China. The characteristics examined tend to be valued in Anglo countries (e.g., achievement motivation, interest in realizing your highest potential, intellectual ability). The idea was that if cultural values affect the importance of managerial characteristics, then executives in Canada, Hong Kong, and China should differ in terms of how they rate the effectiveness of the managers that work for them. Chinese executives, for instance, might not see a relationship between "Western" criteria and managerial effectiveness. On the other hand, if attitudes toward leadership are converging as industrialization proceeds worldwide and countries like China become more "modern," then the criteria for effective management should be similar in all three countries.[51]

The results painted a mixed picture about the convergence/divergence issue. Canadian executives, for example, felt that interest in realizing your highest potential was most important for managerial effectiveness. Chinese executives, however, felt that a manager's intellectual ability was most important. These results support the idea that culture continues to effect which characteristics are seen as critical for effective management. That said, although the rankings were different, many of the characteristics were viewed as signs of effectiveness by all executives.

This supports the convergence idea since only "Western" characteristics were included. In fact, the Chinese executives in the study all worked for large, modern firms in urban areas and had been exposed to North American management techniques. So the results may reflect the ongoing evolution of Chinese leadership, with "traditional" values being slowly eroded by Western philosophies. An evolution in values has also been observed in many former communist countries such as eastern Germany over the last several decades.[52] Nevertheless, it would be a mistake to assume that local values will be completely supplanted by "Western" values in China (or elsewhere) anytime soon—if ever.

Indeed, research continues to suggest that convergence forces are typically slowed or offset by aspects of the local cultural environment. We will return to this in later chapters on work behaviors such as decision making, leadership, and negotiation.[53]

How Individuals and Corporations Can Make Better Sense of Culture

This discussion underscores the complexities associated with culture, a point that has been touched on throughout the chapter. So far we have presented a series of cultural frameworks and dimensions and also discussed their limitations, including the broad-brush portraits they often paint of cultures around the world. Even if we view these "sophisticated stereotypes" as helpful and useful, they may, at least to some extent, already be outdated. After all, cultures may be stable most of the time, but they are certainly not static.

Yet, sometimes managers carry around cultural stereotypes about different parts of the world that can derail effective decision making. Fortunately, Flextronics CEO Michael Marks avoided this problem when he considered whether to build a manufacturing plant in Mexico. Some of the people around him advised against building the plant, suggesting that the cost savings of manufacturing in Mexico would be eaten up by local employees and their "siesta culture." Mr. Marks ignored this stereotype-driven advice and built the plant anyway, a facility that ended up producing over $1 billion in revenues inside of five years. Indeed, Mr. Marks felt that the experience highlighted the "corrosive effect of stereotypes" on the ability to make good international business decisions. Of course, cultural stereotyping is typically more subtle than the Flextronics example. As Mr. Marks put it, "[m]anagers often pick up the impression that the Chinese are good at this, the Germans are good at that, and so on. But I have learned that in every place that we operate, in every country, the people want to do a good job . . . This isn't to say that we approach every region with a cookie-cutter uniformity. We may need to train workers differently in different parts of the world."[54]

To be able to effectively train workers in various parts of the world, managers must understand employees—including the ways in which their culture and context impact how they learn as well as what they need to learn. So how can managers working in a new country—or international corporations, for that matter—do a better job of accurately figuring out the cultures they have to operate in? Let's start with some suggestions for international managers:

- **Approach other cultures with the idea of testing your "sophisticated stereotypes."** In other words, be aware of any cultural stereotypes that you might possess and treat them not as "truths," but as hypotheses to be tested. The most effective international managers change their stereotypes about people from other cultures and countries during the course of interacting with them.
- **Find cultural informants and mentors to help.** Look for someone who: (1) can really make sense of cultural nuances, paradoxes, and internal logic; and (2) is willing to share his or her insights and information. After all, the more you understand a culture, the more tolerant and effective you will become.

■ **Carefully assess information that seems inconsistent with cultural stereotypes.** Managers can "plateau" in their learning about another culture without realizing it. This may occur when managers have done pretty well, at least initially, in other cultures and, as a result, become less open to deeper learning. In doing so, managers may be more likely to make bad decisions based on faulty assumptions or a superficial understanding of the culture. Managers can avoid this trap by seeking deeper meaning and by looking for and analyzing behavior that seems paradoxical to a culture's basic values (e.g., why are many U.S. executives autocratic if Americans pride themselves on equality and egalitarianism?).[55]

■ **Learn mental maps that will increase effectiveness in different cultures.** This does not mean trying to uncover *all* of the rules of a different culture. What it does mean is that understanding the core values behind the mental maps used in a culture will help you behave more appropriately in that context. And doing so will increase both your effectiveness and self-confidence.

As an example of many of these points (especially the last) consider profiles of Thai culture compared with the profile of their largest trading partner, the U.S. While some of these values (presented in Figure 4.10) can be developed from an understanding of where each country falls on the Hofstede or GLOBE dimensions, sometimes the core values can surprise. Likewise, as we noted earlier, divergence within a culture seems to be occurring in Thailand. Traditional values of respect for elders and reluctance to express emotion are being challenged by the latest generation.[56]

Thai Culture	U.S. Culture
Traditional Buddhist values of giving more than taking, resisting material attachments	Need for achievement and material reward as sign of success
Desire to have trust in business relations built through traditional social networks built over time	Need for rules, regulatory procedures, and laws
Desire for face-to-face business contact, based on the above trust	Need to use the increased productivity of e-commerce via the web and public displays of data/performance
Need to take care of employees, avoid lay-offs and protect investors from taking a "haircut" (and thus losing face)	Need to accelerate restructuring (e.g., cutting ration of non-performing loans through bankruptcy laws)
Taught to be humble and very considerate of others' feelings	Not inconsiderate of others, but taught to stand out, speak up and be yourself
A strong sense of hierarchy in government and business alike (knowing one's place)	Less position-driven respect accorded to those in power

Figure 4.10 A comparison of U.S. and Thai Business Practices/Approaches.

Source: Adapted from Niffenegger, P., Kulviwat, S., and Engchanil, N. (2007). Conflicting cultural imperatives in modern Thailand: global perspectives. In C. Rowley and M. Warner (eds) *Management in South-East Asia*. Routledge: New York.

Finally, what about suggestions at a broader level? Here are some ideas for international corporations to consider if they want to make better sense of culture:

- **Put people who have cognitive complexity in international positions.** The last thing that international companies should want is a black-and-white thinker. Instead, experts suggest they should select people based on their ability to handle alternative viewpoints as well as plenty of ambiguity. Employees with such skills are best equipped to make sense of the complexities and paradoxes inherent in all cultures.

- **Emphasize in-country training for people going overseas.** Too often, cultural training takes place in a classroom environment in the home country and emphasizes concepts and facts rather than hands-on experience. If at all possible, put people on the ground in the culture where they will be going to work and challenge them to figure out answers to actual cultural problems. That is likely to produce more motivation to figure out what is going on.

- **Assess cultural expertise among personnel posted in foreign countries.** The idea here is that not everyone will be on the same page from a cultural learning perspective. There will be different levels of understanding. Part of this variation may reflect individual differences in skills as well as the amount of time spent in the country. In fact, a good reason to assess cultural expertise is to help the firm figure out how long personnel should stay in a country to achieve the cultural understanding needed to function well.

- **Become a learning organization when it comes to cultural understanding.** In short, put mechanisms into place that will help share and disseminate knowledge about different cultures. For example, have expatriates report their insights and understanding about a culture once they return home. This type of sharing can both increase the firm's collective know-how about different cultures and help expatriates make sense of their cross-cultural experiences.[57]

Chapter Summary

We started by claiming that culture has a pervasive impact on the management of international business (decision making, negotiation, leading, and more). The importance of understanding culture, at least for management, has never been higher because of the ongoing growth of international business.

But, *culture* is a complex concept that can have roots in historical events, geography, shared traditions, economic developments, language, and religion, among other things. Plus, cultures are constantly evolving, presenting something of a moving target for managers. Thus, managers need to be careful not to oversimplify culture.

The chapter reviews several efforts to cluster countries by their shared cultural values. Ronen and Shenkar found eight major *country clusters*. Geography, language, and religion are all factors that contribute to shared cultural values across specific groups of countries. Hofstede's effort significantly added to the ability to cluster countries on work-related cultural dimensions. Hofstede argued that all cultures could be described in terms of four basic dimensions: *individualism–collectivism, masculinity–femininity, high–low power distance, and high–low uncertainty avoidance*. By crossing pairs of these dimensions, Hofstede produced some valuable *cultural maps* that allow international managers to identify countries in terms of various combinations of cultural dimensions and how they cluster together.

Other recent efforts have tended to support Hofstede's views and have also added to our knowledge about developing countries. In particular, the GLOBE dimensions provide a more contemporary view. The dimensions were validated using managers from many different countries and companies across several different industries. The findings validated some of Hofstede's research. GLOBE also uncovered its own unique dimensions as well, such as humane orientation and performance orientation, which are predictive of behavior across cultures.

The chapter concludes with practical suggestions for managers to move beyond the kind of "sophisticated stereotyping" that comes with the limitations of current culture frameworks. Some of these include testing one's viewpoints and finding cultural mentors to help understand cultural differences. It is important to rely on people who have "cognitive complexity" in global assignments and to provide in-country training for people going overseas.

Discussion Questions

1. Describe the basic cultural dimensions proposed by Hofstede and the GLOBE research team. What are their similarities, differences, and limitations?

2. How might international managers use information about cultural dimensions? Why is understanding culture such an important part of success in international business?

3. Are there any work-related goals that appear to be universal? Which work-related goals vary significantly across countries? How might cultural values impact these work-related goals?

4. How can companies and international managers go beyond the "sophisticated stereotyping" that a superficial understanding of cultures might produce? What are some of the challenges or difficulties associated with doing so?

Up to the Challenge?

The Steady Rise of the World's Largest Democracy

At the beginning of this chapter we described some of the many challenges that India faces as the country tries to nurture its economy. There are many concerns, to be sure, but these may be more than offset by a variety of factors that may encourage growth. One of those encouraging factors is the set of cultural values that seem to stimulate entrepreneurship as well as the prevailing conditions that support entrepreneurs.

In a nutshell, entrepreneurs really function in a social context. Consequently, societal culture can play a role in inhibiting or enhancing the kind of entrepreneurial problem-solving seen in India today—all of its challenges notwithstanding. Specifically, cultural values that encourage helpfulness, cooperation, relationship building, and bootstrapping—particularly as mechanisms for overcoming obstacles in society—seem to help spur entrepreneurial innovation. India generally scores high on these attributes—including what GLOBE refers to as "humane orientation." Likewise, India scores highly on in-group collectivism, where strong family connections and ties are reflected in some of India's most prominent and entrepreneurial companies. Moreover, when entrepreneurship is held up as being socially desirable in a country—by the media and educational institutions—it can, over time, strengthen and support cultural values that encourage entrepreneurial activity.

But, India is a complex place, one with plenty of built-in contradictions. Because of bureaucratic barriers and increasing domestic competition, some of India's best companies, such as Godrej Consumer Products, are looking abroad to places like Africa to growth their revenues—where their efficient and inexpensive business models are well suited to create products tailored to local demands. Indeed, many companies, including foreign multinationals, feel that India remains a very challenging place to do business. Many Indian roads are abysmal and slowed by checkpoints where officials demand bribes from truck drivers, adding to business costs.

Likewise, companies often must maintain their own backup power and sanitation systems because of unstable utilities in the country. Moreover, while India has plenty of innovative entrepreneurs, it is woefully short of engineers and other trained professionals, has too few outstanding universities, and lacks a strong primary education system. The government is also somewhat unpredictable and laws are routinely challenged in court, making it difficult for businesses to predict what will happen next. One Western businessperson noted that China was much easier to operate in compared to "the freewheeling chaos of India."

The big question, of course, is whether India's cultural support for its unique, problem-solving "frugal innovators" can continue to lift the country up faster than its challenges and weaknesses hold it back. It remains to be seen whether the optimists or the pessimists are right in the end about India.[58]

International Development

Understanding Your Orientation toward Individualism–Collectivism

Purpose

To develop a greater understanding of your own attitudes toward individualism and collectivism.

Instructions

Assume that you are in the U.S. or Canada and want to have a good career in an American or Canadian corporation. Answer the following questions about your behavior in the workplace. Using the accompanying scale, please place the appropriate number in the blank before each question.

5	4	3	2	1
Strongly agree	Agree	Not sure	Disagree	Strongly disagree

1. ___ I would offer my seat on a bus to my supervisor.
2. ___ I prefer to be direct and forthright when dealing with people.
3. ___ I enjoy developing long-term relationships with the people with whom I work.
4. ___ I am very modest when talking about my own accomplishments.
5. ___ When I give gifts to people whose cooperation I need in my work, I feel I am indulging in questionable behavior.
6. ___ If I want my subordinate to perform a task, I tell the person that my superiors want me to get that task done.
7. ___ I prefer to give opinions that will help people save face rather than give a statement of the truth.
8. ___ I say "no" directly when I have to.
9. ___ To increase sales, I would announce that the individual salesperson with the highest sales would be given the "Distinguished Salesperson" award.
10. ___ I enjoy being emotionally close to the people with whom I work.
11. ___ It is important to develop a network of people in my community who can help me when I have tasks to accomplish.
12. ___ I enjoy feeling that I am looked upon as equal in worth to my superiors.
13. ___ I have respect for the authority figures with whom I interact.
14. ___ If I want a person to perform a certain task, I try to show how the task will benefit others in the person's group.

Now, imagine yourself working in one of the following countries. Choose the country about which you have the most knowledge because of actual overseas experience, reading, having friends from that country, classes that you have taken, and so forth.

Japan	Mexico	Brazil
Philippines	Hong Kong	Thailand
Taiwan	Peru	Venezuela
India	Argentina	Greece

If you do not have enough knowledge about any of these countries, imagine yourself working on a class project with three foreign students from any of these countries.

The next part of the exercise is to answer the same 14 questions, but to do so while imagining that you are working in one of the countries listed above or working on a class project with three students from that country. Imagine that you will be living in that country for a long period of time and want to have a good career in a corporation *there*. Use the same scale and numbers as before.

5	4	3	2	1
Strongly agree	Agree	Not sure	Disagree	Strongly disagree

1. ___ I would offer my seat on a bus to my supervisor.
2. ___ I prefer to be direct and forthright when dealing with people.
3. ___ I enjoy developing long-term relationships with the people with whom I work.
4. ___ I am very modest when talking about my own accomplishments.
5. ___ When I give gifts to people whose cooperation I need in my work, I feel I am indulging in questionable behavior.
6. ___ If I want my subordinate to perform a task, I tell the person that my superiors want me to get that task done.
7. ___ I prefer to give opinions that will help people save face rather than give a statement of the truth.
8. ___ I say "no" directly when I have to.
9. ___ To increase sales, I would announce that the individual salesperson with the highest sales would be given the "Distinguished Salesperson" award.
10. ___ I enjoy being emotionally close to the people with whom I work.
11. ___ It is important to develop a network of people in my community who can help me when I have tasks to accomplish.
12. ___ I enjoy feeling that I am looked upon as equal in worth to my superiors.
13. ___ I have respect for the authority figures with whom I interact.
14. ___ If I want a person to perform a certain task, I try to show how the task will benefit others in the person's group.

Scoring

The scoring of this exercise is different from most in that it involves comparison of the two sets of numbers: your set of numbers for imagining a career in the U.S. or Canada and your set for imagining a career in one of the other listed countries.

Let's call the first time you answered the questions the "first pass" and the other time the "second pass." In scoring, give yourself 1 point according to the following guidelines.

1. Give yourself a point if your number in the second pass is higher than in the first pass.
2. Give yourself a point if your number in the first pass is higher than in the second pass.
3. A point if number is higher in the second pass.

4. A point if number is higher in the second pass.
5. A point if number is higher in the first pass.
6. A point if number is higher in the second pass.
7. A point if number is higher in the second pass.
8. A point if number is higher in the first pass.
9. A point if number is higher in the first pass.
10. A point if number is higher in the second pass.
11. A point if number is higher in the first pass.
12. A point if number is higher in the first pass.
13. A point if number is higher in the second pass.
14. A point if number is higher in the second pass.

If you scored 6 or more points, it means that you are sensitive to the cultural differences summarized by the concepts of individualism and collectivism. You are sensitive to the fact that different behaviors are likely to lead to the accomplishment of goals and to success in one's career depending on the emphasis on individualism or collectivism in the culture.

Source: From Brislin, R. W., and Yoshida, T. (eds) *Improving Intercultural Interactions: Modules for Cross-Cultural Training Programs.* Copyright © 1994 by Sage Publications. Reprinted by permission of Sage Publications, Inc.

From Theory to International Practice

The Cultural Minefield of International Gift Giving

Purpose

This activity explores cultural differences in the gift-giving process. You will have the opportunity to learn something about the complex historical, religious, and linguistic factors that have shaped gift giving in particular countries.

Instructions

Read the background material provided. Your instructor will give each group a specific country to research outside class. A variety of websites are available that offer additional detail and resources about international gift-giving issues. For instance, you may want to consult Expat Exchange, an online forum that is full of advice about working and living abroad. And of course, that includes gift giving (see www.expatexchange.com/).

Your group should be prepared to present your findings in a subsequent class (10–15 minutes per group) and/or prepare a group report. Alternatively, your instructor may make this an individual assignment and have you write a report. Be prepared to take part in a general class discussion on the specific countries assigned. In any case, you should focus on answering these gift-giving questions for the country assigned:

1. What gifts might be appropriate for the country in a business context or business relationship?
2. When should gifts be given, generally speaking?
3. What about gift giving if you are visiting the country in question on business?
4. How should gifts be wrapped? What gift wrap colors are appropriate or inappropriate?
5. What presentation issues come into play (e.g., when should a gift be presented during a visit)?
6. What other delivery issues might come into play?
7. What gifts should be avoided altogether?

Some Background on Gift Giving in an International Context

Differences in cultural values around the world can make managing an international business a tricky proposition. Even behavior that has the best of intentions—like gift giving—can be complex and have great potential to give offense. In many countries, it is appropriate to give foreign clients, contacts, customers, and employees a gift as a sign of appreciation. What constitutes an acceptable gift, however, can vary widely. The failure to understand local rules can create hard feelings or even lead to the loss of overseas business.

This begs the question of what you should give as gifts in other countries. Many experts recommend giving something that is unique to your own country or that would otherwise be difficult for the recipient to obtain. For an American, this might mean giving Native American handicrafts if you are from the American southwest, or books about the U.S. in general. But in other cases, it might be best to research the cultural, religious, and holiday traditions of a particular country to figure out what might make an appropriate gift. Better yet, get to know your foreign contacts well enough so that you begin to understand their individual hobbies, tastes, and so on.

Giving gifts overseas, however, means more than just finding an appropriate item. In many countries, there are fairly elaborate rules regarding how gifts should be wrapped and presented. For instance, yellow and red have positive connotations in India. Likewise, white is a bad choice for many Asian countries (it's associated with death) while gold or red would be better selections. Then there is the presentation of the gift itself. In many Asian countries, using both hands to give and receive gifts is a sign of courtesy. If you find yourself in an Islamic country, however, you would want to present a gift with just the right hand since the left hand is viewed as unsanitary.

Timing gift giving is also important. The Christmas season is generally pretty safe because most countries celebrate a major holiday around this time period. Usually, giving gifts in private is the best bet. Japanese, however, typically engage in gift giving after business is concluded, while the Chinese usually present gifts at the beginning of a visit. In any case, do not necessarily expect Asians to praise aspects of the gifts you give; it is considered impolite to open gifts in front of the giver. Finally, it should be obvious that we are just scratching the surface here on gift giving overseas. If you have a foreign trip coming up and you are looking for specific gift-giving advice, do your homework and call the embassy of the country that you will be traveling to.

For a brief snapshot of what we have been talking about, take a look at some recommendations of what to give, when to give, and what to avoid giving for the four countries listed here.[59]

Country	Good Gifts	When to Give Gifts	Gifts to Avoid (with explanation)
China	Ties, pens, modest items	Chinese New Year (January or February)	Clocks (the Mandarin word for clock is similar to "final resting place")
India	Sweets, nuts, fruit	Hindu Diwali Festival (October or November)	Leather goods (cows are sacred to Hindus)
Japan	Americana, liquor	Oseibo (January 1)	Four of anything (associated with death)
Saudi Arabia	Compasses, cashmere	Id al-Fitr (December or January)	Liquor (Islam prohibits alcohol consumption)

Notes

1. *The Economist.* (2011). Chasing the dragon: How the Asian superpowers compare on measures of economic development, October 3, available at: www.economist.com/blogs/dailychart/2011/10/comparing-india-and-china (retrieved May 12, 2013).
2. *The Economist.* (2010). A bumpier but freer road, October 2, 75–77.
3. Hofstede, G. (1993). Cultural constraints in management theories. *Academy of Management Executive*, 7, 81–94; Triandis, H. C. (1996). The psychological measurement of cultural syndromes. *American Psychologist*, 51, 407–415.
4. Adler, N. J. (2002). *International Dimensions of Organizational Behavior* (4th ed.). Cincinnati, OH: South-Western; Thomas, D. C., Au, K., and Ravlin, E. C. (2003). Cultural variation and the psychological contract. *Journal of Organizational Behavior*, 24, 451–472; Shenkar, O. (2001). Cultural distance revisited: Towards a more rigorous conceptualization and measurement of cultural differences. *Journal of International Business Studies*, 32, 519–535.
5. Earley, P. C., and Singh, H. (2000). New approaches to international and cross-cultural management research. In P. C. Earley and H. Singh (eds) *Innovations in International and Cross-Cultural Management*, 1–14. Thousand Oaks, CA: Sage.
6. Gupta, V., and Fernandez, C. (2009). Cross-cultural similarities and differences in characteristics attributed to entrepreneurs: A three-nation study. *Journal of Leadership & Organizational Studies*, 15, 304–318; Begley, T. M., and Tan, W. L. (2001). The socio-cultural environment for entrepreneurship: A comparison between East Asian and Anglo-Saxon countries. *Journal of International Business Studies*, 32, 537–553.
7. Granato, J., Inglehart, R., and Leblang, D. (1996). The effect of cultural values on economic development: Theory, hypotheses, and some empirical tests. *American Journal of Political Science*, 40, 607–631.

8. Newman, K. L., and Nollen, S. D. (1996). Culture and congruence: The fit between management practices and national culture. *Journal of International Business Studies*, Fourth Quarter, 753–779.

9. Gupta, A. K., and Govindarajan, V. (2002). Cultivating a global mindset. *The Academy of Management Executive*, 16(1), 116–126.

10. Osland, J. S., and Bird, A. (2000). Beyond sophisticated stereotyping. Cultural sensemaking in context. *Academy of Management Executive*, 14, 65–79.

11. Ronen, S., and Shenkar, O. (1985). Clustering countries on attitudinal dimensions: A review and synthesis. *Academy of Management Review*, 10, 435–454.

12. Ronen and Shenkar, Clustering countries on attitudinal dimensions.

13. Shenkar, O. (2001). Cultural distance revisited: Towards a more rigorous conceptualization and measurement of cultural differences. *Journal of International Business Studies*, 32, 519–535.

14. Alston, J. P. (1989). Wa, Guanxi, and Inhwa: Managerial principles in Japan, China, and Korea. *Business Horizons*, March–April, 26–31.

15. Alston, Wa, Guanxi, and Inhwa; Bond, M. H. (1991). *Beyond the Chinese Face*. Hong Kong: Oxford University Press; Chen, M. (1995). *Asian Management Systems: Chinese, Japanese and Korean Styles of Business*. London: Routledge.

16. Balfour, F. (2007). You say guanxi, I say schmoozing. *Business Week*, November 19, 84–85.

17. Balfour, You say guanxi, I say schmoozing.

18. Ihlwan, M. (2008). Samsung under siege: Allegations of governance abuses help shed light on how the founding family maintains its grip on the conglomerate. *Business Week*, April 28, 46–50; also see Japanese example: Taylor, A. (2009). Toyota's new man at the wheel: Akio Toyoda, the new president and a grandson of the founder, outlines his vision for the company's future. *Fortune*, July 6, 82–85.

19. Chen, *Asian Management Systems*.

20. Bass, B. M. (1990). *Stogdill's Handbook of Leadership: A Survey of Theory and Research*. New York: Free Press; McFarlin, D. B., Sweeney, P. D., and Cotton, J. C. (1992). Attitudes toward employee participation in decision-making: A comparison of European and American managers in a U.S. multinational. *Human Resource Management*, 31, 363–383.

21. Egri, C. P., Khilji, S. E., Ralston, D. A., Palmer, I., Girson, I., Milton, L., Richards, M., Ramburuth, P., and Mockaitis, A. (2013). Do Anglo countries still form a values cluster? Evidence of the complexity of value change. *Journal of World Business*, 47, 267–276; Lenartowicz, T., and Johnson, J. P. (2003). A cross-national assessment of the values of Latin American managers: Contrasting hues or shades of gray? *Journal of International Business Studies*, 34(3), 266–281.

22. Adler, *International Dimensions of Organizational Behavior*; Cox, T., and Blake, S. (1991). Managing cultural diversity: Implications for organizational competitiveness. *Academy of Management Executive*, 5, 45–56.

23. Kumbula, T. S. (1993). As apartheid falls, black education becomes (at last) a serious issue. *Black Issues in Higher Education*, 10, September 23, 15–18.

24. McFarlin, D. B., Coster, E. A., and Mogale-Pretorius, C. (1999). Management development in South Africa: Moving toward an Africanized framework. *Journal of Management Development*, 18, 63–78; Thomas, A., and Bendixen, M. (2000). Management implications of ethnicity in South Africa. *Journal of International Business Studies*, 31, 507–519.

25. Sivakumar, K., and Nakata, C. (2001). The stampede toward Hofstede's framework: Avoiding the sample design pit in cross-cultural research. *Journal of International Business Studies*, 32, 555–574.

26. Hofstede, G. (1980). Motivation, leadership, and organization: Do American theories apply abroad? *Organizational Dynamics*, Summer, 42–63; Hofstede, G. (2001). *Culture's Consequences* (2nd ed.). Thousand Oaks, CA: Sage; Hofstede, G. (1984). *Culture's Consequences*. Newbury Park, CA: Sage; Hofstede, Cultural constraints in management theories; Hofstede, G. (1991). *Cultures and Organizations: Software of the Mind*. London: McGraw-Hill U.K; Hofstede, G. (1996). An American in Paris: The influence of nationality on organization theories. *Organizational Studies*, 17, 525–537.

27. Imada, T. (2012). Cultural narratives of individualism and collectivism: A content analysis of textbook stories in the U.S. and Japan. *Journal of Cross-Cultural Psychology*, 43, 576–591; see also Morling, B., and Lamoreaux, M. (2008). Measuring culture outside the head: A meta-analysis of individualism–collectivism in cultural products. *Personality & Social Psychology Review*, 12, 199–221. (Note: but also see Lamoreaux, M., and Morling, B. (2012). Outside the head and outside individualism–collectivism: Further meta-analyses of cultural product. *Journal of Cross Cultural Psychology*, 43, 299–327, where the authors find less support for other Hofstede dimensions such as power distance being manifested in actual products such as books, and more.)

28. Gelfand, M. J., Erez, M., and Aycan, Z. (2007). Cross-cultural organizational behavior. *Annual Review of Psychology*, 479–514; Triandis, H. C., and Gelfand, M. J. (1998). Converging measurement of horizontal and vertical individualism and collectivism. *Journal of Personality and Social Psychology*, 74, 118–128.

29. Morris, M., Podolny, J., and Ariel, S. (2000). Missing relations: Incorporating relational constructs into models of culture. In Earley and Singh (eds) *Innovations in International and Cross-Cultural Management*, 52–91.

30. Hui, M., Au, K., and Fock, H. (2004). Empowerment effects across cultures. *Journal of International Business Studies*, 35, 46–60.

31. Fock, H., Hui, M. K., Au, K., and Bond, M. H. (2013). Moderation effects of power distance on the relationship between types of empowerment and employee satisfaction. *Journal of Cross-Cultural Psychology*, 44, 281–298.

32. Hofstede, *Culture's Consequences* (2nd ed.); Hofstede, Cultural constraints in management theories.

33. Bond, *Beyond the Chinese Face*; Hofstede, Cultural constraints in management theories.

34. Dowling, P. J., and Nagel, T. W. (1986). Nationality and work attitudes: A study of Australian and American business majors. *Journal of Management*, 12, 121–128.

35. Taras, V., Steel, P., and Kirkman, B. L. (2012). Improving national culture indices using a longitudinal meta-analysis of Hofstede's dimensions. *Journal of World Business*, 47, 329–341; see also: Leung, K., Bhagat, R., Buchan, N. R., Erez, M., and Gibson, C. B. (2011). Beyond national culture and culture-centricism: A reply to Gould and Grein (2009). *Journal of International Business Studies*, 42, 177–181.

36. Vargas, J. H., and Kemmelmeier, M. (2013). Ethnicity and contemporary American culture: A meta-analytic investigation of horizontal–vertical individualism–collectivism. *Journal of Cross-Cultural Psychology*, 44, 195–222.

37. Kirkman, B., Lowe, K., and Gibson, C. (2006). A quarter century of *Culture's Consequences*. *Journal of International Business Studies*, 37, 285–320; Leung, K., Bhagat, R., Buchan, N., Erez, M., and Gibson, C. (2005). Culture and international business. *Journal of International Business Studies*, 36, 357–378; Smith, P. (2006). When elephants fight, the grass gets trampled. *Journal of International Business Studies*, 37, 915–921.

38. McSweeney, B. (2002). Hofstede's model of national cultural differences and their consequences. *Human Relations*, 55, 89–118; van Oudenhoven, J. P. (2001). Do organizations reflect national cultures? A 10-nation study. *International Journal of Intercultural Relations*, 25, 89–107.

39. Hofstede, G., Van Deusen, C. A., Mueller, C. B., Charles, T. A., and The Business Goals Network. (2002). What goals do business leaders pursue? A study in 15 countries. *Journal of International Business Studies*, 33(4), 785–803.

40. Fountain, H. (2005). The ultimate body language: How you line up for Disney. *The New York Times*, September 18, Section 4, 4; Bradsher, K. (2005). Hong Kong Disneyland faces overcrowding. *The New York Times*, September 8, Section 4, 6; Fan, M. (2006). Disney culture shock. *The Hong Kong Standard*, November 22, 6.

41. Trompenaars, F. (1993). *Riding the Waves of Culture*. London: Brealey; Trompenaars, F., and Hampden-Turner, C. (1998). *Riding the Waves of Culture: Understanding Cultural Diversity in Global Business* (2nd ed.). New York: McGraw-Hill.

42. Ali, A. (1988). A cross-national perspective of managerial work value systems. In R. N. Farmer and E. G. McGoun (eds) *Advances in International Comparative Management*, Vol. 3, 151–170. Greenwich, CT: JAI Press; Trompenaars, *Riding the Waves of Culture*.

43. House, R., Hanges, P. J., Javidan, M., Dorfman, P. W., and Gupta, V. (2004). *Culture, Leadership, and Organizations: The GLOBE Study of 62 Societies*. London: Sage.

44. Brewer, P., and Venaik, S. (2011). Individualism–collectivism in Hofstede and GLOBE *Journal of International Business Studies*, 42, 436–445.

45. Ihlwan, M. (2008). Samsung under siege: Allegations of governance abuses help shed light on how the founding family maintains its grip on the conglomerate. *BusinessWeek*, April 28, 46–50.

46. *The Economist*. (2011). Social media in Indonesia: Eat, pray, tweet, January 8, 64; Ioffe, J. (2011). In Russia, Facebook is more than a social network. *Bloomberg Businessweek*, January 3–9, 32–33.

47. MOW International Research Team (1987). *The Meaning of Working*. London: Academic Press.

48. Meek, C. B. (1999). Ganbatte: Understanding the Japanese employee. *Business Horizons*, January–February, 27–35; Zimmerman, M. (1985). *How to Do Business with the Japanese*. New York: Random House. Segers, R. T. (2008). *A New Japan for the Twenty-First Century*. New York: Routledge.

49. MOW International Research Team, *The Meaning of Working*.

50. Sherer, P. M. (1996). North American and Asian executives have contrasting values, study finds. *The Wall Street Journal*, March 6, B11.

51. Okechuku, C. (1994). The relationship of six managerial characteristics to the assessment of managerial effectiveness in Canada, Hong Kong, and People's Republic of China. *Journal of Occupational and Organizational Psychology*, 67, 79–86.

52. Geppert, M. (1996). Paths of managerial learning in the East German context. *Organization Studies*, 17, 249–268; Kostera, M., Proppe, M., and Szatkowski, M. (1995). Staging the new romantic hero in the old cynical theatre: On managers, roles and change in Poland. *Journal of Organizational Behavior*, 16, 631–646.

53. Hofstede, Van Deusen, Mueller, Charles and The Business Goals Network, What goals do business leaders pursue? A study in fifteen countries.

54. Marks, M. (2003). In search of global leaders. *Harvard Business Review*, August, 43.

55. Van de Vliert, E. (2006). Autocratic leadership around the globe. *Journal of Cross-Cultural Psychology*, 37, 42–59.

56. Klausner, W. (1998). Thai culture in transition. Bangkok: The Siam Society (cited in Niffenegger, P., Kulviwat, S., and Engchanil, N. (2007). Conflicting cultural imperatives in modern Thailand: Global perspectives. In C. Rowley and M. Warner (eds) *Management in South-East Asia*. Routledge: New York.

57. Osland and Bird, Beyond sophisticated stereotyping: Cultural sense-making in context.

58. House, R., Hanges, P. J., Javidan, M., Dorfman, P. W., and Gupta, V. (2004). *Culture, Leadership, and Organizations: The GLOBE Study of 62 Societies*. London: Sage; Srivastava, M. (2010). The untold wealth of unknown cities. *Bloomberg Businessweek*, October 4–10, 9–11; Srivastava, M., and Sharma, S. (2010). Corporate India finds greener pastures—in Africa. *Bloomberg Businessweek*, November 8–14, 61–62; Stephan, U., and Uhlaner, L. M. (2010). Performance-based vs. socially supportive culture: A cross-national study of descriptive norms and entrepreneurship.*Journal of International Business Studies*, 41, 1347–1364.

59. Gutner, T. (1996). Never give a Mandarin a clock and other rules. *BusinessWeek,* December 9, 192; Murphy, K. (1999). Gifts without gaffes for global clients. *BusinessWeek,* December 6, 153.

perception, interpretation, and attitudes across cultures

Learning Objectives

After reading this chapter, you should be able to:

- recognize the impact of culture on your perceptions, interpretations, and resulting attitudes;
- diagnose some of the important ways that perceptual effects can affect our interactions with people from different cultures and then better understand their ways of interacting;
- classify and distinguish cultures along several important perceptual dimensions;
- recognize the importance of, and be able to explain, some of ways that cross-cultural attitudes are formed and the impacts they have.

International Challenge

Desperately Seeking Latin Culture

The TV show *Desperate Housewives* was a Disney Company production that ended a successful eight-year run, with Emmy Awards, Golden Globe Awards, and critical acclaim to its credit. If you have never seen it, you will have plenty of opportunity to catch up, as the complete series has been made available on DVD, and it will likely be shown in syndication. This hit show follows the lives of a group of women, seen through the eyes of a dead neighbor. The characters slog through domestic struggles on Wisteria Lane, a street in the fictional city of Fairview. The idyllic suburban neighborhood setting belies what really goes on: secrets, crimes, and mysteries, much of it happening behind closed doors. If you like dark comedy that focuses on relationships, you would probably like *Desperate Housewives*.

For the 2006–2007 TV season, Disney announced that it would begin production of the show for South American audiences. Mr. Fernando Barbosa, a senior vice-president for Buena Vista (Disney) Productions was in charge of the production and had high hopes, partially because *telenovelas*, the region's counterpart to American soap operas, dominate the prime-time ratings. *Housewives* would thus be likely to resonate with this audience. "Barriers are breaking down . . . *Housewives* shares certain characteristics with the telenovela, but it's based on more real life and isn't as dramatic . . . Latin American audiences want alternatives and we're responding to that," said Mr. Barbosa.

Buena Vista set to making three versions of the series, each tailored to a different area of Latin America, and all three of which were different from the U.S. version. It was felt that in order for *Housewives* to succeed, it must win over demanding Latin viewers, such as 29-year-old receptionist Maria Jose-Garcias. "I'll watch this Spanish version, but I don't know if I'm going to like it," Ms. Jose-Garcias said in Spanish. "They are all great actresses in the cast and that's definitely an attraction. But the U.S. and Argentina are two totally different societies, each with their own customs, and I wonder if it will translate."

Ms. Jose-Garcias laid out the task for Buena Vista/Disney—and for you here. As you read this chapter, try to think of some of the ways that perception, interpretation, and attitudes might differ between U.S. and Latin cultures. What might Buena Vista do differently in the Spanish versions of the show? We do not expect you to identify all the subtleties that Disney used—that is why they make all the money here! At the end of the chapter, we will review some differences between the two versions and we hope that you will be able to flag some of these as you read through this chapter.[1]

Perception, Interpretation, and Attitudes Across Cultures

In the first four chapters, we looked at topics that are wide in scope and effect. Among these were differences in legal structure, political systems, and ethical behaviors. Differences in how countries approach these issues are relatively easy to see and have direct connections to how business is done across borders. Yet, there are many more subtle processes that, while tougher to pinpoint, can help businesspeople interact more effectively in an international environment. One of the most important of these processes is that of perception. The term *perception* refers to the selective mental processes that enable us to interpret and understand our surroundings. These include attending or selecting the events in the first place, processing and evaluating the information that is selected, and then making sense of what we attended to and processed. As it turns out, culture can have an impact on all these processes—in many cases, without us even knowing it or without any second guessing. This is because we almost always take perception for granted and give our perceptions and observations great credibility. We know what we saw and heard and we trust those perceptions. As well, we should do so in order to function in our various cultures. Yet, in the definition above, a key description is the word *selective*.

We know a good deal about perception and one key finding is that we do not perceive all that is going on around us at any one instant. What you are doing right now is a good example. In addition to processing the words on this page, many other things are also occurring around you. You may be listening to music, someone might be walking and talking out in the hallway, noises could be coming from outside, etc. We do not commonly attend to all these various events. Instead, we selectively attend to stimuli that are important to us or that help us make decisions. And, we certainly do not perceive things at random, but instead we impose order on what we are exposed to and what we see. In fact, you may know that a defining symptom of schizophrenia is the inability to organize and selectively process one's perceptions. So, being selective is a good thing and functional for us.

If our job is to impose order on an inherently chaotic environment, how does this happen, and what role does culture play? It is likely that members of a culture teach us what is important to perceive in our interactions with others. Experts say that some of what people in one culture select and perceive may be different from what is needed in other cultures. These "needs" are explicit and out in the open sometimes, such as when an Asian business partner spends a lot of time asking you about your family, your interests and your work experience—things you may find extraneous to your need to complete a negotiation and get back to work. Or, they may be much more subtle or "automatic," occurring without you being completely cognizant of their operation. Have you ever been to a crowded and noisy party, maybe completely engrossed in a conversation with someone, relatively inattentive to all the talking going on? But, then, out of nowhere among all the noise you hear your name spoken. How did you attend to your name among all the noise but not to other noise? Likely, your name is important to you and of the people talking, you heard this above the rest—as they say, "your ears were burning." This so-called "cocktail party" effect may apply to culture as well. Perhaps there are subtle filters operating just below the surface that help us process culturally useful information, such as what it means to be a leader or something as basic as the use of first names among business partners. In other words, culture may subtly sensitize us to the information and behavior that is important for effective interaction. We do not perceive things at random.[2]

Differences in Perceptions of People and Events

Does research support our conjecture about perceptual differences across cultures? And even if there are differences in perception, are there also some similarities in what people look for in forming impressions of others or making sense of events?

Perception of Others

One group of researchers provided a partial answer to our question about culture and perception.[3] They asked groups of Chinese and Australians to read detailed descriptions of a fictitious person, including how conscientious, outgoing, and sensitive they were. Participants were then asked to predict how these people might behave. The goal was find out which specific pieces of information would be *selected* and *emphasized* by the two groups—defining features of our definition of perception.

The two cultural groups were chosen deliberately: the Chinese because their culture is more group oriented and the Australians because their culture is individually oriented (see Chapter 4). It was expected that the Chinese would selectively pick out trait descriptions that involve the consideration of others, whereas the Australians might emphasize more person-centered qualities when forming impressions. The researchers found this exact pattern. When forming an impression, the Chinese were more influenced by a person's conscientiousness toward others, whereas the Australians focused on outgoingness in forming their impressions. Of all the information that was presented, the Chinese and Australians selectively used culturally relevant traits to form impressions. One lesson to learn here is that it would benefit us to understand how other cultures form opinions of people with whom they negotiate, communicate, and otherwise do business, a topic we will turn to in Chapter 7.[4]

There is plenty of other evidence for this culture effect on perception. In other studies, these same researchers argued that some cultures are more naturally conscious and respectful of power differences among people, whereas other cultures give less weight to authority.[5] Participants were again chosen from cultures in which the importance of status varied dramatically. Americans were chosen because they accord relatively little importance to status, whereas Chinese were chosen because they value status highly. The researchers predicted that the Chinese would be more careful in their treatment of higher-status persons than would Americans, so much so that a high-status Chinese might be able to even insult another person with little recrimination.

Of course, it is difficult to observe a personal insult firsthand. Instead, researchers had people read a story about a business meeting during which a manager publicly insulted an employee. There were two different versions of the story: in one version, the "insulter" was a high-status manager, while in the other, he was of low-status. Participants were asked to read one version and then provide their perceptions of the "insulter." Neither group liked the insulter. But, interestingly, Americans made no distinctions between the high- and low-status managers who insulted others. Their perceptions were generally negative. The Chinese, however, were less critical of the insulter when he was a high-status manager.

These results demonstrate that culture allows (or directs) one to moderate perception and interaction depending on a person's status. These results have wide-ranging implications for leadership. A case in point is the *shusa* role (chief engineer) at Toyota. Each of the 38 *shusas* had tremendous power, including complete responsibility for a vehicle from design through sales life, and accountability for the vehicle's success. They were highly respected and granted almost absolute authority. When the Toyota president told the shusas to drive up profitability by cutting costs in 1996, they did so with gusto. Yet, feedback did not emerge when it was clear that these cuts were too deep, nor even when customers began to raise questions about the vaunted Toyota quality. Industry observers and Toyota executives alike believe that the *shusa* system was responsible for the company's lack of attention to feedback and public defensiveness and resulting decline in sales. Fortunately, Toyota learned from these mistakes and recently eclipsed its competition to become the largest company in the world.[6]

Perception of Events

Do these findings extend to how we perceive everyday work events?[7] One study addressed this by again using Chinese and Australian subjects because of their contrasting group and individual orientations. All participants read a list of common, everyday social events (such as arriving late to class, going out with friends, eating lunch) and then rated the events on nearly 30 different scales (e.g., boring–interesting, pleasant–unpleasant, etc.).

A complex statistical technique was then used to reduce all of these responses to just a few common dimensions. The results showed that there were different dimensions found for the two groups. The Chinese, for example, organized their perceptions of these events mainly along an individual versus group dimension. Said differently, the Chinese were attentive to events involving other people. They were more sensitive to these types of events and thought that they were more important than everyday actions that did not include other people. The Australians, however, rated these events involving others as more enjoyable than the Chinese. Apparently, group events imply more "fun" to Australians, whereas to the Chinese they conjure up the perception of social obligation. Studies using different methods in different cultures also show variation in how we interpret events.

Implication of Research on Perceptions of People and Events

Overall, this research suggests that culture shapes perceptions about life events and the people involved in those events. An important point to mention here is that perceptions often seem to operate "automatically." But, automatic does not necessarily mean neutral or unbiased. In fact, these studies suggest that we use filters and organizing tools that reflect key aspects of our culture (i.e., how group-oriented is another person?).

One unintended effect is that we might quickly form impressions of business partners that are based on our own cultural filters, with little appreciation of the filters of others. As an example, Westerners seem to prefer abstract and universal principles, whereas East Asians are more likely to seek rules that are specific to the situation at hand—these views can clash. One study asked managers what they would do about a subordinate whose work had been below average for about a year, after 15 years of above average service. About 75 percent of Canadians and Americans said they would let the employee go, whereas this figure was only 20 percent for those from Korea and Singapore. It appears, therefore, that those in Eastern cultures are more likely to take extenuating factors, such as years of service, into account when making decisions. Westerners emphasized more analytic and absolute views ("performance is down and must be addressed"). These were more detached from the actual person and his or her background.[8] In practice, reactions and opinions such as these may be "automatic"—done with little thought. Yet, this does not mean that they are unchangeable. Research has shown that Asians who live in the West (and Westerners who live in the East) can understand and adopt these different cultural patterns and tendencies. The following International Insights feature discusses the relatively mindless act of exchanging a business card and what that act might mean in different cultures.

International Insights

Getting "Carded" in Japan: Perception and Business Card Ritual

Business cards in the U.S. show little variation. Most are ordered and constructed via a template with little thought devoted to the card style. The same is true about the actual exchange of those cards with others. Maybe this is because the exchange routine is well known to all—an introduction is made, small talk follows, and business cards are exchanged.

This is so familiar that you are probably wondering why we even bother describing it. We do so because other cultures exchange business cards differently. In fact, if you are unaware of cultural rituals and the resulting perceptions, you may be committing a terrible *faux pas*. In Japan, the *meishi* (business card) is accorded much greater significance than in the U.S. It starts with the construction of the card itself, typically printed on the finest paper. The layout subtly accentuates the importance of the company rather than that of the (less important) individual. An American card will list one's name first, with a title underneath in smaller print, and the firm's name and address below or in a corner. The Japanese *meishi* always presents the company name first and most prominently, then the employee's rank, followed by his or her name—reflecting this decreasing order of importance. The *meishi* is usually bilingual, with Japanese on one side and English on the other.

The actual mechanics of exchanging cards is an elaborate and meaningful act in Japan. First, individuals carry plenty of cards with them. Not having a card is equivalent to refusing a handshake in the U.S. The cards should be presented, not passed, with both hands. The employee name should be facing the receiver as the card is presented. A quick, small bow, is given as the card is presented. (Japanese employees must practice the "house style" bow during training they receive after joining the firm.) Finally, a card is taken with both hands and time is spent studying it. The card should not be shoved into a pocket, and it is impolite to write on the card itself. The *meishi* represents an individual's identity and should be treated respectfully. If a meeting is starting, the card (or cards) should be placed in front of you and left there until the meeting is over, when they should be picked up and placed within a specific business card holder (never just casually within a pocket). When the time comes to exchange business cards, take the business card holder out and place the new card within the holder in order to protect it. All of this is done to show that the business card is truly valued.

Some time ago we travelled to Japan, having read in advance about this business card exchange custom. We were relieved that we had practiced, but we also made a mistake in a later trip, not realizing how far it extended. After a long flight with delays (about 25 hours total), we arrived exhausted at our hotel outside Tokyo, ready to check in and to get some sleep. Instinctively, McFarlin took out his credit card to pay and he tossed it out on the counter (as we all may have done in the U.S.). Unfortunately, this act offended the hotel clerk who perceived it as a sign of disrespect. We should have presented the card as we would have a business card. The clerk glared at us thereafter when we strolled through the hotel lobby.[9]

Differences in the Perception of Time

If you are still not convinced that cultural differences in perception are important, you are not alone. Some people feel that perception—like beauty—is in the eye of the beholder. In other words, they believe that the study of perception is too subjective to be of great value. Researchers in international management answered this criticism with a series of studies on the perception of time. They chose to study time because of its objectivity. Everyone has a watch, waits for a bus or plane according to a timed schedule, arranges a meeting for a given time, and is worried about being five minutes late for an interview. Ten minutes is ten minutes, time is time—right?

The answer to this question is an emphatic *no*! Even though we all use a globe-wide time standard (Greenwich Mean Time), there are wide differences in perceptions of this most objective of things. To start, consider how time is perceived in some cultures. In Western cultures, time is perceived as a commodity ("time is money," "you are losing/ saving time," "time is running out," etc.). In many Eastern cultures, however, time is seen as more flexible and fluid. Westerners commonly refer to strict scheduling of events according to the clock, whereas in some Eastern and Muslim cultures, views revolve around events and people. "Event" time in Arab cultures has been characterized by the following: "There are not precise hours for meals; they are eaten whenever the preparation is complete and eating is leisurely. The notion of an exact appointment is unknown; they agree only to meet 'at the next market.'"[10] Researchers have systematically studied this topic in much more detail.

Research on Time Perception Across Cultures

Researcher Robert Levine became interested in culture and time when he took a teaching position in Brazil for a year.[11] On the way to his first class meeting he began to worry about his watch since many of the clocks he glanced at (on public buildings, other people's watches) showed varying times. He did, however, arrive in his classroom a few minutes before the start of his class. But no one was there! Instead, many of his students came late, several after a half-hour, a few around an hour late, and even a few others later than that. Interestingly, no one seemed to be bothered by being late—all wore smiles and gave friendly hellos as they entered class. Because he had been a U.S. professor for years, Levine was very surprised by this behavior. Students are expected to arrive on time in the U.S. He also noticed that his Brazilian students did not get up and leave when class was over. Levine was used to being told when class time was over (the ubiquitous shifting of books, backpacks, etc.). In Brazil, however, few people left on time and many lingered to ask questions and interact—some actually staying a half-hour or more, leaving Levine to do the signaling that it was time to go.

These anecdotes led Levine to conduct a study of American and Brazilian students' perceptions of time. In one study, he asked both groups what might be considered "late" for a lunch appointment with a friend. The average American defined "late" as 19 minutes or more, whereas the Brazilians were more forgiving, defining lateness as about 34 minutes or more. He also found that these perceptions affect impressions of people who were late. Brazilians were less likely to blame others than were Americans—they typically felt that unforeseen circumstances were important causes of lateness. Americans were more likely to blame the individual and to attribute the lateness to a lack of caring. Even more interesting, Brazilians believed that people who were consistently late were more successful than those who were on time, reasoning that they were late because they had more friends to talk to, more partners with whom to do business, etc., and therefore the lack of punctuality "equals" success. Americans generally felt that punctuality was critical and that lateness is something definitely to be avoided.

Levine was not completely satisfied with this study of time. He wanted to show that the effects were not the result of a language barrier or translation problems, and he wanted to study several more countries. The problem clearly facing Levine, however, was

Country	Measures of Time Perception		
	Bank Clock Accuracy	Walking Speed	Post Office Speed
Japan	1	1	1
United States	2	3	2
United Kingdom	4	2	3
Italy	5	4	6
Taiwan	3	5	4
Indonesia	6	6	5

Figure 5.1 Measures of the Pace of Time.*

* Numbers are the ranking of each country on the measures of pace of time (1 = top ranking).

Source: Adapted from Levine, R. V., and Bartlett, K. (1984). Pace of life, punctuality, and coronary heart disease in six countries. *Journal of Cross-Cultural Psychology*, 15, 233–255.

exactly how to study time without relying on language and/or self-reports. He solved this problem in a very clever way by devising several objective indicants of time, ones that did not rely on language or self-report.[12] First, he checked the accuracy of bank clocks by taking a sample of 15 city banks in various countries and comparing their times with the time provided by the telephone company (Greenwich Mean Time). Banks were of special interest because of their relative formality and because they are tied closely with activity in other countries (e.g., monetary exchange) and thus an industry where time is closely monitored. Results showed that bank clocks in Japan were the most accurate—averaging only about 30 seconds off—with U.S. clocks not far behind in accuracy. Clocks in Indonesia were the least accurate, averaging over 3 minutes late (see Figure 5.1).

Figure 5.1 also shows that walking speed was another way that time perceptions were measured. In a sample of large cities in these countries, Levine measured out a 100-foot stretch of a busy downtown street and then clocked how long people took to walk that distance. He was careful to randomly choose people who were walking alone in order to add control to the study. Once again the Japanese were at the top of the list—they took about 21 seconds to walk the distance (a pretty good clip if you try it!), with the British and Americans tied as very close seconds (about 22 seconds each). The Indonesians took about 27 seconds on average to traverse this distance. The difference among countries doesn't seem that long, but if you consider that the whole "trip" only took about 20–25 seconds, then the difference is significant (6 seconds is a 30 percent difference).

Finally, he measured how long it took a postal clerk in these countries to serve a customer. In each country, including the U.S., the researchers presented a clerk with a handwritten note, in his or her native language, requesting a stamp for a normal letter, and gave each clerk an equivalent of a $5 bill. Once again, there was wide variance in the service times, which ranged from a low of 25 seconds in Japan to a high of 45 seconds in Italy.

So what does all this mean? We think it shows that very subtle processes operate within cultures that affect our perceptions of the world, even about very objective features, such as time. And, research shows these differences extend to other "objective" topics such as profit and other business priorities.[13] Chinese appear to pay more attention to history when thinking about events, whereas English speakers seem more attentive to recent events, moving away from the past (e.g., common phrases such as "looking forward" or "putting the past behind us"). These may be tied to the structure of each language.[14] If we can understand these different views, there is less potential for conflict. One way to better understand these differences is to classify cultures on this time dimension.

Classifying Countries by Their Emphasis on Time

The studies shared so far illustrate how far culture extends into perception, but effects are not restricted to just clocks and walking speed. We can classify groups of countries around their conception of time. And, this can help predict how people in those cultures make purchases, view advertisements, and negotiate.[15] It appears that there are at least two different ways that time is generally experienced across cultures: *monochronic* time and *polychronic* time.[16] Roughly, this distinction refers to paying attention to (and doing) one thing at a time versus doing many things at once. Like most concepts we will discuss in this book, there is considerable variation within cultures and countries in how people view time. Nevertheless, let's focus on cross-national mean differences.

In a monochronic culture, time is divided up precisely, with certain slots reserved for certain activities. A schedule is sacred and to violate it is to face considerable irritation because of the monetary value placed on time. Researchers suggest that the choice of economic language ("saving" or "losing" time) to describe it is no accident—it reflects their monochronic view of time. This view is common in most business conducted in the U.S., and probably in many European countries as well. It has been observed that the Swiss and Germans, for example, are monochromic and that they are also known for their expertise in timepieces.

Polychronic cultures, in contrast, take a more flexible view of time and this seems very unfamiliar and difficult for Americans and others from monochromic cultures to understand. Experts point out, for example, that some Latin cultures (typically polychronic) would much rather finish an impromptu conversation on the street rather than abruptly and rudely terminate it in order to get to an appointment. Polychronic cultures do not have a strictly economic view of time and translations of phrases such as "time is money" often do not make complete sense. In Spanish, for example, the closest saying might be the phrase "to pass time."

Time seems to bounce around in a polychronic culture, and "interruptions" are often not seen as such. The word *interruption* implies an unscheduled and unwanted derailing of an activity. In a polychronic culture, however, the unscheduled is not unusual and so naturally fits in with the way life flows. Two or more activities can be engaged in concurrently or intermittently. An American businessperson in Spain, for example, may resent sitting in a lobby beyond her appointment time while her polychronic contact entertains several other people at once. Since time is so valuable in a monochronic culture, to be kept waiting is a sign of rudeness and disrespect. A monochronic American might want an apology. In turn, the polychronic Spaniard may feel that the American

Monochronic Time	Polychronic Time
• Does one thing at a time	• Does many things at once
• Task oriented	• People oriented
• Comfortable with short-term relations	• Prefers longer-term relations
• Sticks to plans	• Plans subject to change often
• More internally focused	• More externally focused

Figure 5.2 Differences between People Who Have Monochronic or Polychronic Time Orientation.

has an overly demanding and self-important attitude. Experts contend that cultural misunderstandings have been very costly for business, as shown in the following:

> *A French salesman working for a French firm recently bought by Americans found himself with a new American manager who expected instant results and higher profits. Because of the emphasis on personal relationships, it can take years to develop customers in polychronic France, and, in family-owned firms, relationships with customers may span generations. The American manager did not understand this, and ordered the salesman to develop new customers within three months. The salesman knew this was impossible and had to resign, asserting his legal right to take with him all the loyal customers he had developed over the years. Neither side fully understood what had happened.*[17]

Figure 5.2 presents some characteristics of people in monochronic and polychronic cultures, some of which have been researched empirically.[18] Americans generally are very monochronic relative to others and are widely viewed as having less patience than they should. In fact, one expert quotes a Japanese businessperson as saying "You Americans have one terrible weakness. If we make you wait long enough, you will agree to anything."[19] To give you a better sense of this dimension and to help identify your time orientation, we include a scale you can complete at the end of this chapter.[20]

Interpretation of Perceptions

Our discussion shows that culture can predispose us to selectively focus on some things (e.g., the use of time), and place less weight on others (e.g., past performance). We do not mean to imply, however, that all we see is fraught with such perceptual bias. Many times what we in others is what is really there. Yet, even though we may "see" the same thing as others, we must still *interpret* what we saw. We have to make sense of what caused certain behavior and what that means. Consider a manager who completes a project successfully and is presenting the results in a meeting. It is possible that nearly everyone at the meeting perceives that the project is a success. Yet, to take action, we likely need to interpret *why* the manager succeeded. If we see this success as resulting from a lucky break or the fact that it was a plum project destined to succeed, it will have different implications for the future than if we believe that the performance came from hard work and lots of skill. The topic of how we answer "why" questions like this is the purview of *attribution theory*.

Attribution Theory

This theory has been tested extensively in the U.S. and more recently in many other countries. It predicts that we have a driving need to figure out what makes other people tick. We can never really know the answer to this question since we cannot get inside someone's head to truly read his or her motives. So, our next best method is to use *behavior* to infer what he or she is really like. Accordingly, we spend a lot of time scanning and evaluating behavior to figure out others. Said differently, because we cannot ever really know what other people are like deep down, our best proxy is to use their behavior to infer or attribute characteristics they may have.

Self-Attribution Effects

One of the most reliable findings in the hundreds of studies done on this topic is known as the *self-serving attribution bias*. This refers to our tendency, when making attributions about our own behavior, to take credit for success (*internal attribution*) and to blame failure on other causes (*external attribution*). This finding underscores our recognition of the importance of perception in management and a study illustrates what we mean.

Researchers interviewed nearly 700 people from five countries—the U.S., India, Japan, South Africa, and the former Yugoslavia.[21] Participants completed a form that measured their attributions about a variety of life events widely viewed as a success or failure (e.g., performing well at a job). Americans showed the typical self-serving bias: they took more credit for success than (blame) for failure. In fact, to an extent, this self-serving bias was observed in all the countries in this study. In comparing across countries, however, the researchers noted several interesting differences. First, the causal attributions of the Japanese were more internal for failure than were the attributions of people from any other country. The Japanese were more likely to take responsibility for a failure. If these results are accurate, then the stereotype of the American as the "step-up, take-charge, buck-stops-here" manager is not supported by these data.

The Japanese were also the least likely to take credit for success. In fact, this latter effect was dramatic: while the scores of Indians and Americans were over 8 on a 10-point scale and the remaining country scores were over 6.0, the Japanese average score was only 3.9. The results of this research were also at least partially supported by another more recent study.[22]

This study showed two important things. First, the self-serving bias has some cross-national applicability. People from countries as diverse as India, South Africa, and the U.S. have a tendency to take credit for success and to externalize failure. Second, the effect is not universal. The Japanese showed a strong tendency toward responsibility for failure and modesty regarding success. Clearly, the Japanese are strongly concerned with themselves as members of a group, more so than as individuals per se. Accordingly, self-effacing behavior as well as a strong sense of duty toward the work group is common. We might conclude, therefore, that in group-oriented cultures modesty is valued, whereas in individually oriented cultures (such as the U.S.) a bolder assertion of competence and credit is common. One recent study took this a step further and looked at the corporate reports of U.S. and Japanese firms. These documents often include explanations for the previous year's performance, something these researchers looked at closely. Overall, the U.S. reports tended to provide a much more positive view of firm performance than did the Japanese reports. American executives who authored these highlighted their successes and provided less information about disappointing results than did their Japanese counterparts. The researchers also meticulously went through a sample of those reports, coding the explanations (attributions) that were made. No difference was found in the explanation of positive events—both groups tended to take credit for their success. And, in contrast to earlier studies, the Japanese were more likely to externalize blame for negative performance. The researchers suggested that because of the anonymous nature of these reports, the norms of humility among Japanese were not as strong as they may be in face-to-face interactions. Besides suggesting that these reports may not be a great source of real information, they also point out that even when performance is in black and (red), it is subject to attributional interpretation.[23]

Attributions about Others

A subsequent set of studies looked at the attributions or causes we assign to *others'* behavior.[24] In one study, Japanese university students read a story about a man who had worked nearly two years for an organization. There were, however, several different versions of the story. Even though most details about the story were the same for everyone, about half were then told that the man was demoted to a lower position after these two years (the "failure" condition). The other half were told that he was promoted to a higher position (the "success" condition). The nationality of the man was also varied in the stories. Equal numbers of subjects were told that the man was either (1) a Japanese citizen working in Japan, (2) a U.S. native working in the U.S., or (3) a citizen of a developing country who also worked in that country.

After reading the materials, the Japanese students made attributions about the cause of the success or failure. It was predicted that the Japanese would make self-serving attributions for people from all three countries. The researchers also predicted an even stronger effect, however, when people were asked to interpret the cause of behavior for someone within (as opposed to outside of) their own group. This in-group bias is similar in form to the self-serving effect. An in-group bias occurs when an individual is more self-serving for members of his or her own cultural group. But, the predictions were not supported—the Japanese students did not show the in-group bias when interpreting the behavior of someone from Japan. In fact, if anything, there appeared to be a pattern that showed a more generous pattern of attributions for people from the other countries (the U.S. or a developing country). These findings are consistent with the earlier study showing that Japanese were less self-serving than those of several other countries. Japanese tended to be modest; they were more likely to assign responsibility to themselves for failure and to deemphasize credit for success.

In this study only the Japanese made attributions about others. In a follow-up study, researchers compared people from other countries.[25] Americans and people from several developing countries also read and reacted to the same descriptions of the man just discussed. Americans were more likely to give credit for success (internal attribution) than were subjects from developing countries. Another study also found a similar effect in Japanese and American views of their political and corporate leaders.[26] Taking both studies into account, we can say that Americans are more likely to attribute success to the individual—especially compared to the modest Japanese.

In fact, researchers have found similar effects in other group-oriented cultures, including Chinese participants.[27] They were asked to rate another person who was either self-effacing (did not take personal credit for success) or was self-serving (took credit for success). The self-effacing person was much better liked by the Chinese. This effect is not always found, but it is robust enough that it seems to explain attributions about very bad events. One study found that English-language newspapers were more personal and that Chinese-language newspapers were more situational in their explanations of the same crime.[28] One story, which attracted press attention in both the U.S. and China, dealt with a Chinese graduate student in the U.S. who murdered his Ph.D. advisor and several others after losing an award competition. Researchers assembled all of the articles that were written on the topic in the U.S. and China and then coded the "attributions" about the student's crime into internal (personal) or external (situational) categories. American newspaper reporters were more likely to emphasize internal attributions about the student (quotes included: "very bad temper," "sinister edge to his character well before the shooting," "darkly disturbed man"). The Chinese reporters, however, were more likely to emphasize situational causes of the murder, including relationships ("did not get along with his advisor," "isolated from the Chinese community") pressures in Chinese society ("a victim of the Chinese educational policy") and aspects of American society ("murder can be traced to the availability of guns").[29]

Implications of Cross-Cultural Attribution

In general, Asian cultures are more likely to explain the behavior of others in terms of situational factors, whereas Westerners have a penchant for attributions about people as the root cause. But, what happens after people offer their explanations? Asians seem to be more attuned to the consequences of events compared to Westerners. Consider how Japanese and Americans react to car accidents. Americans took more responsibility for damage to their car than did the Japanese. But, interestingly, the Japanese thought more about the consequences of the accident: they felt badly about delaying traffic and were worried about causing another accident further back in the line of traffic. Clearly, the Japanese showed more concern for interrelationships than did Americans, which is expected given their cultural backgrounds.[30]

So, even when many people agree about what they saw, culture can affect the interpretation or assignment of causes as to why something happened. Each study we reviewed made it clear that someone succeeded or failed; there was no ambiguity about these events in this set of studies. Yet perception still had an effect on the interpretation of outcomes that occur to the self and others. The International Insights feature discusses this topic by examining a well-known TV interview.

International Insights

Attributions on TV

An interesting story highlights the significance of the attribution process better than the research we reviewed.[31] Barbara Walters is famous for her interviews of notable people from many walks of life. Several years ago, she interviewed Muammar al-Gaddafi, the leader of Libya at the time. Tensions between the U.S. and Libya were quite high during this time (prior to the Libyan revolution) and the interview centered on this friction. After the interview, there was little media about the interview content itself and much more about Mr. Gaddafi's behavior. During much of the interview, Mr. Gaddafi shifted his eyes away from Ms. Walters and appeared reluctant to look her in the eyes at all. Ms. Walters herself remarked, "he wouldn't look me in the eye. I found it disconcerting that he kept looking all over the room but rarely at me." The prevailing view was that Mr. Gaddafi was shifty and evasive and that the behavior was indicative of someone who was, at best, not telling the whole truth.

It is likely that he was not, but that is beside the point here. Our point is instead similar to that made by the attribution researchers. Here we have a case in which people saw the same thing: eyes shifting, an unwillingness to look someone in the face, etc. But the interpretation of the same event—the attribution—could vary dramatically across cultures. Had we asked an Arab, for example, to explain Mr. Gaddafi's behavior, it probably would be at variance with the negative opinion of Americans. To an Arab, Mr. Gaddafi would have been perceived as showing proper respect to another person, especially to a woman. To stare at a woman is considered very rude in Arab culture. Thus, instead of attributing an unwillingness to look at Ms. Walters eye-to-eye as shifty and untrustworthy, the very same behavior is interpreted as the height of politeness by another culture. This story demonstrates that attributions are important—especially across nations and cultures.

Attitudes

If your perceptions occur over and over again, this might be one way you'd form an attitude. An *attitude* is a learned tendency to react emotionally toward some object or person. According to social psychologists, we can have attitudes about nearly everything, including ourselves, others and groups. Many such attitudes have been studied cross-culturally.

Attitudes Toward the Self

We have views about many aspects of our lives, including how much control we feel over our lives and how much we like ourselves, among others. In this section we will focus on attitudes toward the self that are work-related or have direct implications for management.

Interdependent and Independent Selves

The broadest difference in self-attitudes deals with our degree of autonomy or uniqueness. The Western view of the self as independent and individualistic can be seen in cultures that emphasize uniqueness, self-reliance, and individual achievement.[32] American culture is a good example because it highlights independence in so many different ways: parents encourage their children very early on to be independent, school is by and large structured to foster independent activity, and performance on the job is typically evaluated at the individual level. In contrast, many non-Western views of the self are difficult to separate from others and from situations. Great emphasis is put on qualities such as paternalism, interdependence of people, solidarity, and group cohesion. Viewed from this perspective, the self is not a standalone entity but instead is changeable and deeply affected by others. Long-standing proverbs or sayings provide insight into this difference. The Japanese saying that "the nail that sticks out gets hammered down" refers to the need for people to fit in well with others.[33] In contrast, a common Western saying is, "The squeaky wheel gets the grease." Figure 5.3 provides a summary of these differing attitudes about the self.[34]

Self-Descriptions

How do people describe themselves in various cultures? If the preceding distinction is accurate, we should see widely varying self-descriptions between Western and non-Western cultures.[35] To examine this, researchers used a simple approach: they asked U.S. and Japanese students to describe themselves in a very unstructured way. The students were asked to respond, in any way they wished, to the question "Who am I?" and were allowed up to 20 responses to this question.

Then the researchers had some hard work to do. They took all of the responses and placed them into categories. One category was how often the students mentioned *abstract* versus *concrete* self-descriptions. Abstract self-descriptions included general responses

Interdependent Self (non-Western)	Independent Self (Western)
Defines self as part of the group	Defines self apart from group
Focuses on similarity to others	Focuses on uniqueness of self
Encourages efforts to sublimate self	Encourages "finding oneself"
Teaches children dependence on/to others	Stresses independent children
Fears exclusion from others/group	Fears inability to separate from group/stand up
Can "read the mind"/intentions/feelings of others	Believes in importance of "saying what's on your mind"

Figure 5.3 Two Views of the Self.

Sources: Adapted from Markus, H. R., and Kitayama, S. (1998). Culture and the self: implications for cognition, emotion, and maturation. *Psychological Review*, 98, 224–253; Triandis, H. C. (1989). The self and social behavior in differing cultural contexts. *Psychological Review*, 96, 506–520.

such as "I am extroverted" or "I am sensitive," whereas concrete descriptions would include statements such as "I am happy when I work with my friend" or "In social situations, I tend to hold back." If it is true that Westerners have more independent views of the self, then their self-descriptions should be more abstract and devoid of specifics or qualifiers.[36] Likewise, non-Westerners should describe themselves in ways that are specific and embedded in the social situations. This is exactly what was found: Americans were more likely to use general trait descriptions of themselves and less likely to use situational descriptions than were the Japanese.[37]

Studies in different countries show similar results. In one, participants from India and the U.S. were asked to describe several close friends.[38] Nearly 46 percent of the descriptions made by Americans were the abstract, context-free variety (e.g., "he is a tightwad"; "she is selfish"), with only 20 percent of Indians making general statements like these. The Indians were much more likely to make situation-specific descriptions ("he is hesitant to give money away to his family"). Other studies found that Americans were more than twice as likely as Indians to attribute the behavior of others to abstract dispositions ("he is dishonest") than to situational circumstances ("it is not right, but in this situation, she needed the money").[39]

Why Are Self-Views Important at Work?

If some cultures emphasize fitting in rather than standing out, we should also see differences in job-related variables such as performance evaluations. In the U.S., self-ratings of job performance are typically higher than corresponding ratings by supervisors or outside raters. This "leniency bias" had led some experts to express misgivings about the use of self-ratings in annual evaluations.[40] But, we would expect that this leniency bias might be more common in the U.S. than in more interdependent cultures.

This was the premise for a study of nearly 1,000 employees of various organizations in Taiwan.[41] Supervisors and employees were asked to make a variety of ratings of the employees' performance. The ratings for each employee–supervisor pair were then compared. As predicted, the Taiwanese did *not* show a leniency bias—they were more modest in their self-ratings. Given that there is pressure not to stick out from the group in this interdependent culture, this modesty in self-ratings might be expected. It is important to note that ratings were done anonymously, so the modesty effect is not due to some impression management effort, but instead probably does reflect an internalized attitude.

A wider-ranging study looked at workers and supervisors from two Asian (e.g., Korea, Japan) and two Western countries (e.g., the U.S., Mexico).[42] This study also included nearly 1,000 employees and an elaborate set of controls (e.g., gender, age, religion) but still found the modesty effect in self-ratings by Asians. Mind you, we should not lump all Asian cultures together here.[43] Perhaps it is a specific set of attitudes in a culture (such as those stressing order and respect for social hierarchy), not East vs. West per se, that produces the modesty effect.[44] As a result, at least some Western countries might also show modesty effects in self-ratings and other work-related outcomes. The next section discusses some of these attitudes that may directly affect performance on the job.

Attitudes about Work

People spend a lot of time at work and getting ready to go to work. Accordingly, it should be no surprise that attitudes toward work are one of the most studied issues in the field of international management.

Job Satisfaction

The single most studied attitude is job satisfaction. Thousands of studies exist, mostly featuring American employees, most of which show that Americans are relatively happy about their jobs. Yet, a common shared opinion is that Americans rank woefully low in job satisfaction when compared to other countries. And, because of this dissatisfaction, Americans are portrayed as fickle and fidgety, not committed to a company but instead ready and willing to move to a new job at the drop of a hat.

Yet, the research on differences in job attitudes shows a very different effect and some other surprising ones as well. Accordingly, we should put more confidence in research studies that systematically examine attitudes and beliefs—especially those conducted on representative samples from two or more countries. Systematic studies based on large, representative samples in different countries are in short supply. They are just plain hard and expensive to collect. Nevertheless, there are some, including one such project conducted by researchers at Indiana University in conjunction with colleagues in Japan.[45] They selected companies randomly so that the sample represented a wide range of industries; many other studies surveyed workers in only one or two specific industries, such as the auto or electronic industries. Next, a representative sample of employees from organizations reflecting these varied industries was chosen. Again, a lot of previous research included non-representative samples of workers. All in all, this study surveyed over 8,000 employees from over 100 randomly selected factories in central Japan (51 factories) and in Indiana (55 factories).

The results of this study contradict what many believe about Japanese and American workers and underscore the value of such elaborate and complete studies. For one, it was found that U.S. workers were much more satisfied with their jobs than were the Japanese. The researchers went to great lengths to deal with cultural and language differences that might have affected the results. One important potential problem they controlled for was a tendency for Americans to be overly positive and for the Japanese to underplay positive attitudes as neutral, if not bleak. Several patterns in the data, however, eliminate this as a problem. For one, the responses by both groups to different types of job satisfaction questions jumped around. Responses to the question, "All in all, how satisfied would you say you are with your job (1 = not at all, to 5 = very much)?" showed that Americans were much more satisfied than the Japanese. By itself, this result could be explained by the Japanese tendency to be modest. But responses to the question "If your good friend told you that she was interested in working at a job just like yours at this company, what would you say?" The pattern here was the same, as U.S. respondents were more likely to recommend the job to their friends. This question is behavioral and it focused on others. As a result, it would be less subject to the modesty explanation. Finally, an even stronger pattern of effects was found on another question: Nearly 70 percent of Americans said they would take their job again compared to only about 24 percent of the Japanese.

A set of other relevant studies show similar results—studies that use a variety of measures and methods.[46] One important one, for example, showed that again the Japanese were less satisfied than workers in several other countries. Yet, the specific pattern of Japanese responses (to their pay level, working conditions, co-workers, etc.), varied considerably.[47] In some cases, they indicated low satisfaction, but in other cases they were among the most satisfied. Thus, the tendency for Japanese to be either systematically bleak or modest in their self-evaluations is less of an issue than was suspected. After all, if bleakness is the driving force, why does it come into play for some aspects of job satisfaction, but not for others? These findings tell us that many Japanese are willing to state their level of satisfaction, and some might be more willing to do so than others. In fact, older, more senior workers—the very people most likely to hold traditional Japanese values of modesty and self-deprecation—are the ones most likely to say they are happy with their jobs. Newer research has expanded upon these conclusions for both of the countries of study and the approaches used. One study compared the degree of job satisfaction across countries that vary in their cultural values. The responses of nearly 130,000 employees (across 39 countries) of a multinational company were collected. It was found that job level (blue vs. white collar) was positively related to satisfaction in individualistic cultures, but not collective ones. This is especially true for jobs that allow for a real opportunity to use one's skills.[48]

Overall, culture appears to influence job satisfaction and other related measures such as pay satisfaction as well. Existing research shows that, in general, employees from Western (and capitalist/developed) cultures have higher job satisfaction than those in Eastern (and Communist/Socialist/less-developed) cultures. It also shows that the meaning of job satisfaction to employees across cultures is similar, suggesting that the purported "modesty" effect we discussed may not play a large role.[49] Finally, extrinsic job features (e.g., pay) seem to predict job satisfaction across cultures, while intrinsic characteristics (e.g., responsibility, growth potential) were more important in wealthy countries who were high in individualism and low in power distance. Finally, it is important to know that other factors such as one's religious affiliation, education level, age and more are also important predictors of work values and attitudes across culture.[50]

Organizational commitment

Another important work attitude is commitment to one's organization, yet there are far fewer systematic studies of commitment across country and culture. As for job satisfaction, most existing studies have been conducted within the U.S., Canada, and other Western countries.[51] One exception to this trend is a survey of over 1,600 employees from a wide variety of firms within the U.S., Japan, and Korea.[52] Workers in these countries were asked to read and complete a standard measure of organizational commitment (e.g., "I am willing to work harder than I have to in order to help this company," and "I would turn down another job for more pay in order to stay with this company").

U.S. workers showed significantly higher levels of commitment than either Japanese or Korean employees. The commitment levels of the latter two groups were not different from one another. This finding is similar to those for job satisfaction in that it contradicts the popular belief that Japanese or Koreans have higher commitment to their firms than, for example, Americans. Other studies that employ even more controls have found similar effects.[53] For questions such as "I am willing to work harder to help the company succeed" and "I am proud to work for this company" (among others), U.S. employees scored higher than the Japanese. Finally, it is important to note that there is a distinction between organizational and work commitment. The former refers to allegiance to one's company, whereas work commitment refers to the importance of work in one's life (regardless of the firm you work for). There, different results are found. In fact, it looks as though culture is not nearly as strong a predictor of work commitment as it is for organizational commitment. Instead, a far more important predictor was a person's occupational level. Work commitment by occupational level was "remarkably similar" across the 20 countries. In particular, as an employee rises in the ranks within an organization—whether that firm is in Korea, the U.S., South Africa, or Israel—so did his or her work commitment.[54] These results also show that sometimes variables (such as occupational level) can be more important predictors than culture or nationality. In this case, there was more commonality among people in the same occupation across country than among those in different occupations within a country. Indeed, a recent statistical summary of research on commitment shows that macroeconomic variables (e.g., unemployment rates) may be a better predictor of commitment than cultural ones, although culture still exerts an impact.[55]

Conclusions about Job Attitudes

It does appear that there are culturally tied differences in job-related attitudes, even if there are also other predictors as well. A promising and relatively new approach to this is the concept of employee engagement—a concept developed by Gallup and used in the U.S. for years. Engagement is measured by 12 factors that are strongly related to productivity and other work outcomes. While others use this term, Gallup has the most reliable and sophisticated view of it and research to support it. The 12 factors are in some ways a combination of satisfaction and commitment (e.g., quality of co-worker relations, personal alignment with firm's mission, support by company in job, etc.). Gallup recently completed yet another large-scale study, this time across borders. Nearly 47,000 employees in 120 countries participated in the study and we provide a sample of their results in Figure 5.4. Gallup sets a high bar for their definition of an employee to be engaged and emotionally connected to their work and may explain why only 11 percent of employees around the world fit this definition. A whopping 62 percent are not engaged; they may be emotionally detached, perhaps doing little more than the minimum job requirements. And, 27 percent are actively disengaged. These are employees who view the workplace negatively and are likely to spread those views to others. This measure is documented as an important predictor of many organizational outcomes such as turnover, absenteeism, and productivity. We present results, by a sample of countries, of degree of engagement in Figure 5.4. This measure may be the key item used to monitor international differences going forward.[56]

Country	Engagement Levels		
	% Engaged	% Not Engaged	% Actively Disengaged
Australia	18	61	21
Brazil	29	61	10
Canada	20	64	16
China	2	67	31
Costa Rica	31	60	9
Egypt	13	55	32
Germany	11	66	23
India	8	55	37
Israel	14	72	14
Kuwait	25	60	15
Mexico	23	58	19
Russia	7	56	38
Saudi Arabia	13	75	12
Sweden	20	66	14
Turkey	11	58	31
United Arab Emirates	25	67	8
United Kingdom	20	58	22
U.S.	28	54	18
Global Mean	11	62	27

Figure 5.4 Employee Engagement Around the World.

Note: Engagement is based on the use of the extremely well-validated Q12 measure devised by Gallup. This research is based on national samples in 120 countries, n = over 47,000; only sample countries shown above.

Source: Data adapted from Gallup Consulting. (2010). *The State of the Global Workplace: A Worldwide Study of Employee Engagement and Wellbeing*, 1–32; available at: www.gallup.com/strategicconsulting/157196/state-global-workplace.aspx.

Attitudes about Others and Groups

Attitudes about the self and work are one thing, but our attitudes toward other groups and cultures might be even more important. A rising number of managers now interact with colleagues from different cultural groups and countries, with many working and living as expatriates in foreign countries. So it now may be more essential than ever to understand other groups.

What are our attitudes toward other countries and people? Most of us have views about people from other countries. Some of these views are undoubtedly incomplete and inaccurate and more like thumb-nail sketches or stereotypes. Stereotypes are inferences about what other people must be like based on group membership, including racial, religious, and cultural or national groups. A notable percentage of Americans may think the French are romantic, that Germans are technically oriented, and the

Japanese good at details. Of course, we even have stereotypes about people from other regions, provinces, or states in our own country, so *cross-country* stereotypes are hardly a surprise.

Attitudes Toward Other Countries

People around the globe have attitudes about Russians, Chinese, Germans, and Americans, among many others. These attitudes are undoubtedly acted upon at times. For example, let's say that Americans are widely viewed as inventive, perhaps because many features of American pop culture and technology are popular around the world. Indeed this is true—large national surveys of many countries show that significant portions of many countries do have this view. For example, 85 percent of Indians, 76 percent of Germans, and 72 percent of Chinese view Americans as innovative. Some of these same nations may believe that Americans are self-focused and make little or no effort to understand other perspectives.[57] These negative attitudes may be harder for Americans to accept, but either way (and more than ever), it is necessary to understand those views.

Toward that end, several ongoing surveys have been undertaken, the most comprehensive of which is the Pew Global Attitude Project. Figure 5.5 presents some data on favorability ratings for six different countries collected by this group. First, please note that ratings of these six countries are shown for ten other countries, as well as those from the target country itself. For example, in the upper left of the figure you will see that Americans give themselves an 80 percent favorability rating. Traveling

Rating given by . . .	Favorability Ratings of . . .					
	U.S.	Germany	France	Japan	China	Russia
U.S.	80	66	52	66	40	37
Germany	52	65	72	70	29	33
France	69	89	68	83	40	36
Japan	72	78	72	77	15	22
China	43	54	59	21	94	48
Russia	52				62	85
Egypt	19	62	60	63	52	31
India	41	47	46	60	23	30
Pakistan	12	31	25	43	85	20
Spain	58	72	66	65	49	36
Turkey	15	43	18	46	22	16

Figure 5.5 Favorable Opinions of U.S. and Four Other Countries by Other Nationalities.

Note: Table entries reflect the percentage of respondents in each country expressing favorable attitudes toward their own and other countries; missing cells indicate data not collected.

Source: Adapted from Global Public Opinion (2012/2008). *Pew Global Attitudes Project.* Washington, D.C.: Pew Research Center.

down that first column, however, you will see that other countries vary considerably in opinions of the U.S., from a high of about 72 percent by Japanese to a low of only 12 percent for the Pakistanis. Americans do not seem to harbor illusions about their reputation: in 2006, nearly 7 in 10 Americans said that the U.S. is "generally disliked" by other countries. This is the most negative self-view of any country surveyed. This view is overly negative, however, since about 52 percent of people from other countries have favorable views of Americans (with wide regional differences between Muslim countries and Western European countries). This positive view of one's home country is common. Most believe that their country is popular around the world. For example, nearly nine in ten Canadians say that their country is generally liked, and they are joined by Indonesia (86 percent), Jordan (84 percent), India (83 percent), France (80 percent), and China (68 percent) where natives believe that others hold very positive views of their country. These negative views that Americans believe others possess is apparently water off their back. As noted, 80 percent of Americans hold their own country in high regard, second only to the Chinese at 94 percent (see Figure 5.5). Finally, please note that the favorability ratings of the other countries also vary, although the Germans, French, and Japanese are generally viewed positively by people in these ten countries.[58]

Do these general favorability ratings extend to other, more specific characteristics of people in each country? The answer seems to be yes. Since your authors are Americans, we present the U.S. as one example of this in Figure 5.6. There, data collected on large and representative samples of people in 16 different countries a few years ago, also by the Pew Global Attitudes Project, are summarized. Respondents were asked to rate several positive traits (e.g., hardworking, honest) and several negative ones (e.g., greedy, rude). Americans generally rate themselves better than do people from other countries, and very highly on the positive traits of honesty (68 percent) and hard-working (85 percent). Others did not necessarily share this view. In fact, people in all but four other countries saw Americans as less honest and hard-working than Americans rated themselves. To be fair, however, other nationalities do see Americans as hard-working, with all but China providing ratings over 60 percent. On the negative side, fewer countries would use the word "honest" to describe Americans, with some countries, including allies such as the Turks, providing the lowest ratings of all (only 16 percent). Americans are viewed as "greedy," especially by other Americans, but are not often seen as "rude" by others.[59]

Stereotypes and International Management

As you well know, most people who complete these surveys have never interacted with individuals from other countries—these views and stereotypes are formed from news outlets, television, online media, and other methods. But what if you had actual contact with individuals from these other nationalities? Would your interaction with them reduce their stereotypes and generally improve their attitudes? To address this "contact" question, researchers studied managers from different cultural backgrounds who did work together.[60] Four different groups of managers—British, Japanese, Singaporean, and American—were asked to rate themselves and the other groups on two main dimensions:

| Positive Characteristics | | | | Negative Characteristics | | | |
| Hard-working | | Honest | | Greedy | | Rude | |
Country	% Agree	Country	% Agree	Country	% Agree	Country	% Agree
France	89	U.S.	63	U.S.	70	Jordan	64
U.S.	85	India	58	Turkey	68	Indonesia	58
Indonesia	84	Britain	57	Netherlands	67	Turkey	55
Netherlands	84	France	57	Lebanon	66	Canada	53
India	81	Germany	52	Britain	64	Pakistan	51
Jordan	78	Lebanon	46	Jordan	63	Lebanon	50
Canada	77	Netherlands	46	Canada	62	Russia	48
Britain	76	Spain	45	Indonesia	61	China	44
Spain	74	Poland	44	Russia	60	Spain	38
Russia	72	Canada	42	Pakistan	59	France	36
Lebanon	69	Jordan	37	Spain	58	U.S.	35
Germany	67	China	35	China	57	Britain	29
Poland	64	Russia	32	Poland	55	India	27
Pakistan	63	Pakistan	27	Germany	45	Netherlands	26
Turkey	61	Indonesia	23	India	43	Poland	21
China	44	Turkey	16	France	31	Germany	12

Figure 5.6 Positive and Negative Features Associated with Americans by Other Nations.
Source: Table based on data collected by *Pew Global Attitudes Project* (2006), available at: http://pewglobal.org.

(a) expectations about typical performance levels (high or low), and (b) ratings of management style (open vs. closed).

The study found that U.S. and Japanese managers saw themselves as better performers than they were seen by any of the other groups. Another interesting finding was that expatriates highly rated their host nationals, people with whom they had a lot of contact. This was not true, however, if interaction was minimal (e.g. if there was no employment relationship). The results on the management style measure were also provocative. U.S. managers perceived themselves as being much more open (e.g., extroverted, frank, decisive) than the other groups. And, in this case, the opinion was shared by the other nationalities since the U.S. group was rated higher by all other groups. The Japanese managers saw themselves as slightly closed (e.g., introverted, cautious, secretive), but actually are regarded as considerably *more* closed by all the other managerial groups.

So, perhaps contact with another group can help tackle these stereotypic views of others. As we saw in Figure 5.5, some of the most negative opinions of Americans reside in Muslim/Arab countries. A huge number of students from these countries come to study in the U.S. each year and many of the colleges they attend work hard to make sure that this cross-cultural contact improves understanding of each culture.[61] For their part, some in Saudi Arabia are also trying to tackle negative attitudes of Americans with a new reality TV show. The Middle East Broadcasting Center (MBC) show called *On the Road in America* tracks Arab students traveling across the U.S. on a ten-week trip and their encounters that portray Americans in a more appealing light. The show was produced in 2007 and it is too early to gauge its effort but it would be naïve to believe that views formed over centuries could be reversed in such a short period of time, particularly as the U.S. continues to react to security threats post–September 11, 2001. Nevertheless, the effort to bring people in contact with one another is laudable, even if that contact is through the usual medium of television.[62]

Overall, the results of this study of managerial contact suggest that firms need to be aware of these attitudes and the effect they may have on relations among various managerial groups (e.g., nationals and expatriates). Likewise, it might point to the need to do your cultural homework when studying in another country or working with or for a foreign national. Understanding that other culture and conveying that information could "earn you points," especially if that foreign national is your boss. In the accompanying International Insights feature we provide an interesting look at this very situation.

International Insights

Making the Right Impression on your Chinese Boss or Partner[63]

China is now the world's second largest economy, having gotten there faster than any country in history. You hardly need to visit China to see all of the impressive effects of their economic affluence, although if you did travel there you would see gleaming cities, bullet trains, and cranes dotting the horizon of most cities. You do not have to visit because the impact of this prosperity can be seen in the magnitude of Chinese investment that is flowing into many countries, including the U.S. Right now, the U.S. is not only heavily indebted to China, but Chinese investment in U.S. firms could top $2 trillion in a decade. Thus, you could be working for a Chinese boss sooner than you think (if not already).

To help prepare people for this reality, *Businessweek* consulted a set of China experts for advice on how to impress your Chinese boss. They provided suggestions about how to better understand Sino-American attitude differences. Here are a few to know and embrace:

1. Greetings: You are the employee—it is your obligation to greet the boss first. "A high-ranking person should never, never initiate a handshake." Extend your hand to that of your boss. Do not use a Western "killer" grip. It should be a limp grip to express respect and humility. Most Chinese view handshaking as a form of excessive touching anyway. Do a light bow and move on.

2. Business cards: Get a lot of them and use them—the Chinese still do. But, do not use ones that you make on your home printer. Make sure that they are professionally done. When you receive someone else's card, read it over, show that you are impressed, and place it on the table in front of you during the meeting where you can continue to show respect.

3. Gifts: There is a lot of good advice out there that you can fetch easily. A few tips, however, are: do not give clocks, even if you have a stock of them with the firm's logo to share. They conjure up thoughts of death and are not considered in good taste. Do not go overboard with a fancy watch, as "too much 'bling' is garish and embarrassing to the recipient." Get a Western-brand watch such as a Disney character watch, as those would be appropriate and appreciated.

4. Gestures: Big, bold Western (American) type waves, signals, and movements are not something to shoot for; think more subtle and rounded. Pointing with one finger is rude, as it implies a demeaning "hey you . . . come here" attitude. To get someone's attention, one expert suggests gesturing with the entire hand, not like a karate chop, but more of a graceful orchestra conductor with hand pointed down and all fingers moving back and forth.

5. Food: All of what you know or think is familiar is not. Acquaint yourself with the regional delicacies. For example, be ready to eat your weight in "offal" (called "variety" meats or "organ" meats in the West) in some provinces. One expert relayed a business meal in China that included raw pig groin and chewy donkey penis. Another meal also included pig bladder, pig tongue, and jellyfish.

6. Smoking and drinking: To gain your boss's or partner's respect, "channel your inner Don Draper" (the character from the hit AMC TV show *Mad Men*). Smoking remains popular in China and cigarettes are exchanged freely. Even if you declare that you do not or cannot drink (because of personal or health reasons), you will be forced to anyway unless there is physical evidence that demonstrates you cannot. The notion is that it is easier to talk business over baijiu, a Chinese distilled alcoholic beverage. As the saying goes, "if we are good friends, then bottoms up; if not, then just take a sip."

The "In-Group" as a Cause of Stereotypes

In addition to cross-cultural contact and media portrayals, research shows that humans have a tendency to rate our "in-group" higher than an "out-group." Group members tend to emphasize their own positive characteristics and accentuate the negative traits of other groups, findings observed in studies of perceptions between Americans and Russians, Arabs and Israelis, and Catholics and Protestants.[64] In some cases, these stereotypes can manifest themselves in a pattern called *mirror imaging*. This occurs when each group perceives similar positive traits for themselves but opposite negative traits in the out-group. Americans, for example, may recognize and perceive wide differences among themselves while seeing all Russians as relatively similar. Some point out that this contrast is only natural since we have lots of experience with our in-group and are relatively inexperienced with the out-group. This pattern is especially likely to occur between groups under conflict (e.g., Arabs and Israelis; Indonesians and Chinese-Indonesians).[65]

If true, then once again, increased contact and interaction with people from different cultures (out-groups) should result in a more articulated perception. This notion was tested with a sample of Americans and Chinese.[66] Researchers assessed the actual amount of contact that each group had with the other, including both primary contact (*actual* experience in China/U.S.) and secondary contact (number of Chinese/U.S. friends, how often they read about China/U.S., etc.). The perceived similarity of the other cultural group was also measured with questions such as "The more I know Chinese, the more similar they are to each other" and "In the U.S., all people tend to behave alike." Results showed that increased contact with the out-group did result in greater heterogeneity of opinions. For example, the more contact the Chinese had with Americans, the more likely they were to see variety in the Americans' attitudes, behavior, and dress.

Familiarity gained through inter-group contact not only resulted in a more varied set of attitudes, it also increased the *accuracy* of group perceptions.[67] Ratings of Japanese and U.S. managers working together for a Japanese-owned commercial bank were compared.[68] These managers were asked to rate themselves and the other group on various traits. If accuracy is defined as ratings by others that are similar to one's own, then a good deal of accuracy was found. For example, both the Japanese and U.S. managers perceived U.S. employees to be more extroverted, outspoken, and less patient than the Japanese. Similar effects were also found among Chinese and U.S. exchange students who had a good deal of interaction with one another.[69] This was replicated in another study that found Chinese perceived Americans to be as heterogeneous as a group of Chinese, in contrast to the usual in-group/out-group effect noted earlier.[70]

The authors suggested that this result reflects the greater variety in Americans than in the Chinese and that the ratings were rightfully influenced by this "reality." If so, we might expect similar results in Japan, where the non-Japanese-born population is only about 2 percent. This view reflects the "kernel-of-truth" hypothesis: that stereotypes of another group may partially be based on some objective characteristics of that group.[71]

More recent evidence, however, suggests that this may apply only to general or abstract features of groups (e.g., heterogeneity). After all, most of us know that stereotypes are oversimplified judgments that may or may not accurately characterize a specific person, set of people, or a country for that matter. In a National Institutes of Health study, over 80 other researchers from around the globe looked at this issue. They wanted to see if there was a correlation between the supposed features of a national character and the specific features of personality or character of people from that country. They obtained the views of nearly 4,000 people from 49 different countries. As shown previously, they also found that national character stereotypes or attitudes were pretty consistent across countries, but they were *not* closely correlated with average ratings of individuals from those countries. In other words, specific views about people from other countries (their outgoingness, warmth, etc.) seem to be unfounded stereotypes that don't well describe their actual features.[72]

The Effects of Attitudes and Stereotypes

One reason to understand these attitude differences across countries is that they may impact whether, and how, business might be conducted. Take advertising as an example. It is very difficult to customize ads to individuals (web tools aside). Instead, most traditional ads are more likely to gain traction, if not market share, by appeals using abstract values or attitudes. Indeed, some research shows that good ads are tailored to central features about a country's culture. One study collected over 400 web-based ads for a variety of different products in the U.S. and Korea and then coded themes highlighted in the ads. Korean ads were much more likely to feature relationship and family themes as opposed to an American focus on individuals. More generally, ads seem to conform to basic cultural values. Anti-smoking ads in nine countries were examined and it was found that ads in individualistic countries typically portrayed the negative consequences to the person. In collective countries, however, messages were oriented toward the bad effects on other people around them.[73]

Tracking ads and their stereotypic themes can provide insight into general trends of a country. Marketers in China, for instance, claim that macho attitudes among men, which many thought had long since passed, have reemerged in droves. One study in Shanghai and Chengdu, conducted by ad agency Leo Burnett, suggested that Chinese men do not relate to males that they often see in TV ads. One participant put it best by saying, "they lack male qualities and it seems that they are just playing supporting roles to women." Burnett now recommends that its clients emphasize power and "face" to exemplify Chinese machismo, rather than brawn or physique. "Brands should suggest or reinforce a feeling of control." Surveys also show that more and more Chinese men believe their focus should be on their career and that a woman's place is at home. One observer noted this about traditional socialist values of gender equality: "now those values have really become a joke. If you are making the same money as your wife, you are a loser." Chinese men mentioned Harrison Ford as their prototype male, saying that Ford often plays "a steady, decisive leader." Some authors have traced these attitudes to the history of humiliation that the Chinese have perceived—something that also helped explain the importance and tremendous pride taken in the Beijing Olympic Games in 2008.[74]

Another interesting example of such effects concerns India, where color TV transmission was first broadcast in 1982.[75] Because there were no Indian manufacturers, the government allowed domestic firms that produced black-and-white TVs to import "knocked-down" sets (kits with all the parts, but unassembled) to be assembled and sold in India. Identical kits from German, Japanese, and Korean suppliers were imported and put together with Indian brand names. The German and Japanese TV sets commanded much higher prices than did the Korean sets. It was common for Indian consumers to bring along a screwdriver to a store in order to open the back of the set to determine the country of origin. These views go both ways and also change over time. Indian consumers are now very wary of the "made in China" label. And, finicky Japanese consumers are notoriously wary of low prices or discounters, equating this with low quality. Yet, Japan is the world's largest market for luxury brands. As a result, Wal-Mart has had great trouble expanding in Japan.[76]

Those in marketing have long known about country-of-origin stereotypes and still try capitalizing on those. Even well-known brand names carefully monitor their image and even signature products across countries. McDonald's, the beef-centric largest fast-food franchise in the world, has dropped pork and beef from its menus in India, adding the McVeggie burger and McSpicy Paneer. Its competitor, Yum! Brands (e.g., KFC, Pizza Hut), leads in some countries, such as China, where it earned 44 percent of its revenue in part because of early adaptation to Chinese tastes. This included adding fried shrimp and egg tarts to KFC's offerings, and seafood pizza and Thai fried rice in Pizza Huts. Many have learned this lesson and domestic options abound, so Yum! and others are experiencing revenue declines for the first time in China. Kraft has customized its iconic Oreo to have an orange/mango flavor for the Asia Pacific market and a peanut butter one for Indonesia. The green tea version in China was developed recently after its unchanged U.S. recipe languished for years. While Chinese consumers found Oreos too sweet, Indian ones were the opposite, as they thought the cookies were too bitter, so these were successfully adjusted too. To help, Kraft included the Cadbury name on the package (they bought the firm in 2010) taking advantage of the brand recognition in India.[77]

Country of origin effects can be seen clearly on electronic, word-of-mouth product recommendations. Comparisons of Chinese and U.S. online discussion boards found that the Chinese were much more likely to engage in country-of-origin discussions, often requesting this information from others. Discussions included intense anti-Japanese threads, strongly advising that consumers purchase indigenous Chinese equipment and avoid Japanese products. The resulting advice was not correlated with independent measures of product quality.[78] Indeed, the opposite can occur, as shown in the Global Innovations feature.

International Insights

There is No "i" in Havana

A *Businessweek* reporter accidentally dropped her iPhone into the toilet. She pulled it out quickly, but the phone was dead. She was leaving for Cuba the next day so stopped by the Apple store to get it repaired, only to hear Grant, the Apple store associate, say "it's toast . . . we don't deem it really, like, worth it to replace the inner parts." The reporter did not take Grant's advice to buy a new one ($650) right away, as it would not work in Cuba anyway. While in Havana, however, she passed by a small electronics store and on a whim asked for repair advice. She got the name and address of an individual who said he could fix it—he does every day. He took the phone completely apart and within 20 minutes had resuscitated it. But, it now would not hold a charge. The individual who worked on it, however, would not accept payment and could not be convinced to accept anything for his work. The next day in the hotel, the reporter approached the porter for advice, as he was using his i3 processor. The reporter explained her problem and was pointed to a well-dressed young man named Roberto at the bar. Roberto went up to his apartment, returning with a new, sealed iPhone battery that he installed, putting her back in business. Roberto, a student, took an 8gb flash drive as payment. The repair market in California technology, which is better than from Apple, is reminiscent of how the previous generation capitalized on Cuban ingenuity by repairing cars from Detroit.[79]

Summary of Attitudes and Stereotypes

The insidious thing about stereotypes is that it is easy to forget that they are specious ways to make predictions about individuals. We can be "right" by chance if we are "right" at all. One great example of this is a study of characteristics believed to be associated with liars. Across 75 different countries one clear, pan-cultural result that emerged was that people *believed* that liars avert their gaze when lying. Yet, a body of research clearly shows that gaze aversion has little to no association with lying— some avert their gaze, others do not.[80] So, seeing someone avoid looking at you (as in the Muammar al-Gaddafi example provided earlier within this chapter) might not "confirm" that he or she is lying. Worse yet, instead of real and substantial contact with someone from another culture, we may be more likely to have a brief personal encounter and use that as further evidence that all group members are very similar (homogenous). A reasonable perspective on this problem is to recognize that our personal knowledge is very limited, perhaps to a handful or even only one or two persons of another culture. Therefore, to categorize a whole group of people (e.g., Arabs, Americans) as having a single trait is a huge and specious leap of inference. Yet, these perceptions and attitudes can have a real impact, regardless of their veracity. For example, some American expatriates report difficulty obtaining a job in a foreign country, even though they are very qualified and successful in the U.S. This can occur even in a country and culture similar to the U.S., as in Great Britain where some job-seekers are advised to "temper your American eagerness" and to be "more like the Brits, more reserved."[81]

One objection to all of this is that the field of international management itself engages in this stereotyping. After all, in this chapter thus far, we have tried to distinguish Japanese from Americans, Brazilians from Germans, and so on. Although this is generally true, please note that we have usually emphasized relative differences. We certainly are not saying that all Japanese are dissatisfied with their jobs or that all Brazilians do not care about punctuality. We instead refer to observed statistical differences between groups. As you probably know, most statistical tests involve a difference (American vs. Japanese job satisfaction scores, for example) over a pooled variance. The fact that there *is* variance or differences within groups proves our point. In this book, moreover, we have taken an empirical approach—one based on data, not just opinions of a few people.[82]

Chapter Summary

In this chapter, we highlighted the importance of our perceptions and the important role they can play in cross-cultural interaction. Culture affects the way we process information about people and events. Interestingly, these perceptual differences even extend to cultural views about time—one of the most objective factors in our lives. We saw that *monochronic cultures* perceive time as an economic commodity that should be carefully monitored and measured, in contrast to *polychronic cultures*, which view time as fluid and flexible.

Perception is one thing, but we also have to make sense of our perceptions and we discuss the topic of *attribution* next in this chapter. Attribution theorists say that humans are obsessed with asking why something happened. Just because an event catches our attention, doesn't mean that we all interpret it the same way. Indeed, research shows that some cultures make typically more modest attributions about their successes. Other cultures, however, seem to encourage a *self-serving attribution*, in which people take credit for success and externalize blame for failures.

If a perception tends to occur over and over again, we may form an attitude about that topic. Accordingly, we next discussed the topic of *attitudes*—both about the self and about others. Again, there seem to be some cultural determinants of how we view ourselves as well as a tendency to view out-groups (e.g., those from different cultures) in common ways. The chapter concludes with a discussion of national differences in work attitudes and how stereotypic views play a role in interacting with others.

Discussion Questions

1. Compare the effect of cultural background on the tendency to perceive events, people, and groups. Can you think of examples of such an effect?
2. Think of the ways that your *attributions* could affect your perceptions in cross-cultural interactions. What might be the effect in performance evaluations, in meetings, and for a firm's human resource practices as a whole—especially when managing cross-culturally?
3. Reflect on the differences—if any—between the stereotyping process within and across cultures and the process of classifying and distinguishing cultures that we have been engaged in throughout this book. What are your perceptions toward another nation (e.g., France) and why do you have these attitudes? Do you think cross-cultural contact and interaction hold promise for breaking down stereotypes?

Up to the Challenge?

Putting the Culture Back into *Housewives*

At the beginning of this chapter, we introduced Disney's recent venture: a South American version of the popular U.S. TV series *Desperate Housewives*. Recall that Disney officials thought that the existing popularity of the South American telenovelas boded well for the success of *Housewives* in this market. But, remember what a potential Argentine customer said—that "the two societies have their own customs . . . I wonder if [Disney is] going to be able to translate that."

What are some of the things you may have picked up throughout this chapter that could help Disney "translate" the series for a Latin audience? There is no doubt that cultural differences in perception were very much on the minds of producers of *Amas de Casa Desesperadas*, the Spanish translation of the show, despite Disney's demands that they stick to the original American version. Marcos Carnevale, one of the Argentine writers (and directors) acknowledged that "the Mouse" was watching closely, but also declared that certain details in the original script did not make sense when transferred to a Latin setting. For instance, the U.S. show featured a hunky plumber who lives on swanky, upper-middle-class Wisteria Lane—someone unlikely to make enough money in Latin America to afford such a house. For credibility in the Latin audience, this character was changed to a wealthier plumbing supply company owner who had more "airs" about him. Also, scenes involving burials or wakes (an occasional show subject) had to be altered because funerals are different in Latin America than in the U.S. Features about status, wealth, and power are more important in Latin cultures and the producers thus had to be careful in considering this.

A variety of other seemingly small details had to be considered and changed in order to add cultural credibility as well. For example, the death penalty has been largely outlawed in South America. Reference to it in the script was altered. Ditto for things such as Thanksgiving (changed to Easter) and other country differences. There were also some challenges with the characters themselves. Bree Van de Kamp is a hyper-uptight WASP character, played in the American version by Marcia Cross. She was written out of the Latin script and substituted by Vera, the daughter of a military officer and fervent Catholic with extreme leanings. Likewise, the nouveau riche couple in the U.S. show, Carlos and Gabrielle Solis, played by Ricardo Chavira and Eva Longoria, were changed to Ecuadorians so that they could serve as the corresponding ethnic couple on the block (the equivalent of Hispanics in the U.S. show).

The appearance of some characters also had to be modified to better fit the culture. In the U.S. version, Eva Longoria became a star and sex symbol by playing a "bantam Latin spitfire" type—a cultural cliché that would not make sense in Latin America. Instead, her character was changed to one that more closely reflected an icon of beauty there. Mr. Carnevale, the director of the Latin version of the series, encouraged these changes and instructed his cast to "not merely imitate the original characters" and "not to flee from typically Latin American body language." Even when the narrative remained the same, Carnevale still said "but we are Latins, and we have to communicate as Latins. We touch more, kiss more and cry more, and our version had to reflect that." Thus, many topics discussed in this chapter and book played a role in Disney's cultural fine-tuning. To improve effectiveness in doing business in another culture, you probably need to recognize and consider accommodations for differences—in Latin America or elsewhere.

International Development

Measuring Your Perceptual Orientation to Time

Purpose

To get a feel for your views about time in order to better understand different views across cultures.

Instructions

In this chapter we documented the importance of studying perceptions. One area on which we focused our discussion was the perception of time. Some cultures may be relatively monochronic in their perception of time, whereas other cultures may be more polychronic. A scale has been developed to measure monochronic and polychronic perceptions of time. We present the brief four-item scale here so that you can fill it out. Read each item and then choose a number from 1 to 5 that reflects your feeling about the item.

1	2	3	4	5
Strongly agree		Neutral		Strongly disagree

1. ___ I do not like to juggle several activities at the same time.
2. ___ People should not try to do many things at once.
3. ___ When I sit down at my desk, I work on one project at a time.
4. ___ I am comfortable doing several things at the same time.

Now simply add up all your four scores to create a total. The lower your score (below 12), the more monochronic your orientation; the higher your score (above 12), the more poly-chronic you probably are. How does your score compare to the average for U.S. students (3.03) and for students in Brazil (4.15)?

We also encourage you to think about the experience you might have interacting in a business setting with someone who is very mono- or polychronic in orientation. As experts suggest, we might interpret extreme monochronic behavior as pushy and overly demanding and extreme polychronic behavior as unconcerned or reflecting a tightly knit group that is difficult to join or enter. Furthermore, people with a monochronic orientation share some characteristics. For one, they are very task oriented and they tend to stick with their plans—sometimes at all costs. The task orientation also tends to make them more oriented toward the short term in their relations with others. The polychronic person, in contrast, tends to emphasize relations over tasks and thus is more open to changing plans and schedules. When these two types of people meet in a business setting—either within or across cultures—there is great potential for frustration and conflict.

Source: Bluedorn, A. C., Kaufman, C. F., and Lane, P. M., (1992). How many things do you like to do at once? An introduction to monochronic and polychronic time. *Academy of Management Review*, 6, 17–26. Copyright © 1992 by The Academy of Management. Reprinted by permission.

From Theory to International Practice

Conducting a Cultural Audit of China

Purpose

To familiarize yourself with attitudes toward another culture and to get experience preparing to deal with cultural patterns and attitudes in that country

Instructions

For this project, you should consider yourself an employee of a smaller firm in western Ohio who has little or no experience in China. Yet, the firm—that who grows and manufactures silicon—is seeking to move some of its operations to China in order to be closer to some of its customers and to capitalize on the resulting cost savings.

Your assignment is to produce a "cultural audit" that will better prepare your company for this move. Your goal here is to produce a short manual that will provide an overview of what it is like to do business in China—to provide a "how to" approach that will allow your representatives and executives familiarity with some cultural protocol. You are encouraged to touch on the topics that you have covered thus far in the book (Chapters 1–4) as well as this chapter. If your instructor has asked you to read chapters in a different order, then he or she will advise you on what to eliminate or to add in this report. Almost certainly, however, this will include some treatment of Chinese perceptual tendencies as well as their attitudes toward the U.S. and ours toward them.

Resources

• **CIA World FactBook** (https://www.cia.gov/library/publications/the-world-factbook/index.html): This widely referenced document provides a wealth of information about nearly every country in the world. While most of this information deals with basic economic, governmental, and demographic data, it will provide useful information for this exercise.

- **China–Britain Business Council—CBBC** (www.cbbc.org/): This site offers some very useful background information on understanding basic Chinese business practices. You will find detailed information on any number of different issues that may arise in doing business in China.

- **The Embassy of the PRC in the U.S.** (www.china-embassy.org/eng /) and **the Embassy of the PRC in the U.K.** (www.chinese-embassy.org.uk/eng/): These sites, the Chinese embassy in the U.S. and in the U.K., offer a lot of background information on the topics that are the subject of this exercise.

- **U.S. State Department Information on China** (http://travel.state.gov/travel/cis_pa_tw/cis/cis_1089.html): As the title of this page shows, the U.S. State Department offers information on China that you might find helpful.

Global Innovations

Online and at the Head of the Line for Internet Business in China

Web commerce continues its tremendous growth, with the U.S. leading the way ($180 billion, 2010). Business is also growing in China ($70 billion, 2010), in part because of the size of the online population, already the world's largest at about 485 million in 2011—that is with two-thirds of the population not yet online. It is easy to see why predictions show that online revenues in China will eclipse those of the U.S. by a good margin in 2015. Another reason for growth seems to be the distinctly Chinese flavor that the Internet has taken on there.

Online companies in China began, like many others around the globe, by copying Western models of structure and function. But, they seemed to have really blossomed by coming up with clever, country-specific innovations. In fact, Western Internet firms have struggled to replicate their domestic success in China (notwithstanding success as investors). Experts seem to point to a reason why: "the beauty of the Internet is that it easily adapts to local conditions." And, apparently it has done just that, growing more Chinese by the year. Indeed, *The Economist* recently went as far as to say, "the Chinese Internet is the best example of the argument that, far from creating uniformity," networks are shaped by local conditions and forces.

One such force is the young but relatively less well-off Chinese consumer who is hungry for hip products, services, and apps. And, Tencent is a firm catering to them. It started out by replicating AOL's chat service, called ICQ, and then quickly grew (actually to the point of bidding to purchase ICQ in 2010). Growth resulted in part from adding appeal to the very large, young audiences in China who use their phones, homes, and Internet cafés to cheaply communicate with each other and generally have fun. Tencent now has over 500 million free (active) user accounts and other offerings, just invested $300 million in Facebook, and purchased a 10-percent stake in the Russian Digital Sky Internet service. This makes Tencent the third largest Internet company in the world behind Amazon and Google and the biggest social network in China. It makes money not just from advertising but from sales of virtual goods and social games. They developed micropayment memberships (about $1.50/month) that allow users to dress up their avatar for face-offs against others in online shows, to buy a tool in an online game, or more. A whopping 10 percent of Tencent's active users pay for such memberships, over three-quarters of the firm's total revenue. Meanwhile some of the biggest Internet players, Facebook and Zynga, are nowhere in China.

Another good example of Internet business with Chinese features is Taobao Marketplace, an Internet auction site similar to eBay. For years, eBay has spent lots of money in China but has not gotten very far. Meanwhile, Taobao is China's biggest C2C marketplace. Taobao was started in 2003 by Alibaba (another Chinese giant). In response to eBay's purchase ($180 million) of Eachnet, the Chinese leader at the time, Taobao started offering free listings to sellers. Plus, they added other features desired by Chinese consumers, including an IM tool for buyer–seller communication, and a trustworthy, escrow-based payment tool (Alipay) that pays after delivery (most deals are still cash on receipt). Taobao became the undisputed market leader in mainland China within two years: market share jumped from 8 percent to 59 percent between 2003 and 2005, while eBay dropped from 79 percent to 36 percent during this time. Apparently, many dorm rooms in China now double as warehouses, stored full of goods waiting to be sold. These part-time entrepreneur/students work extremely hard.

Similarly Baidu, which has 75 percent of China's search engine market, is different than its U.S. counterpart, Google. Google appears to be engineering dominated (they tape math problems to restroom doors to busy idle minds). Baidu, no technical slouch itself, says it is "focusing more on products and satisfying our users' needs." On its website, Baidu declares that "our deep understanding of Chinese language and culture is central to our success and this kind of knowledge allows us to tailor our search technology for our users' needs." One example mentioned is that there are about 38 ways of saying "I" in the Chinese language. It is important to "recognize these nuances to effectively address our users' requests."

China has its online challenges, to be sure, especially for foreign firms—including regulation, censorship, and other state-related issues. But, the industry is also poised to grow even bigger for a variety of economic and industry-related reasons.

Sources: *The Economist*. (2011). An Internet with Chinese characteristics, July 30, 71–72; www.businessinsider.com/the-10-asian-tech-companies-that-are-putting-american-ones-to-shame-2010-12?op=1#ixzz2JOFgzaTa; also, the websites of Tencent, Taobao, and Baidu provided information used in this section.

Notes

1. Rohter, L. (2006). How do you say "desperate" in Spanish? *The New York Times*, August 13, 1–4.
2. McArthur, L. Z., and Brown, R. M. (1983). Toward an ecological theory of social perception. *Psychological Review*, 90, 215–238.
3. Bond, M. H., and Forgas, J. (1984). Linking person perception to behavioral intention across cultures: The role of cultural collectivism. *Journal of Cross-Cultural Psychology*, 15, 337–353.
4. This comment applies equally to cultures that may share fundamental similarities, such as the U.S. and Australia. Simply sharing characteristics does not imply that one culture understands the other, as is apparently the case with the U.S. Bryson, for example, shows that Australia has

a very low profile among Americans and they generally know little of the country; Bryson, B. [2000]. The land down where? *The Wall Street Journal,* September 15, A18.

5. Bond, M. H., Wan, K. C., Leung, K., and Giacalone, R. A. (1985). How are responses to verbal insult related to cultural collectivism and power distance? *Journal of Cross-Cultural Psychology,* 16, 111–127.

6. Taylor, A. (2010). How Toyota lost its way. *Fortune,* July 26, 110.

7. Forgas, J. P., and Bond, M. H. (1985). Cultural influences on the perceptions of interaction episodes. *Personality and Social Psychology Bulletin,* 11, 75–88.

8. Miyamoto, Y., Nisbett, R. E., and Masuda, T. (2006). Culture and the physical environment: Holistic versus analytic perceptual affordances. *Psychological Science,* 17, 113–119; Nisbett, R. (2003). *The Geography of Thought: How Asians and Westerners Think Differently . . . and Why.* New York: Free Press; Masuda, T., and Nisbett, R. E. (2001). Culture and attention to object vs. field. *Journal of Personality and Social Psychology,* 83, 922–934.

9. Archer, H. (2001). Doing business in Japan: the secrets of *meishi,* available at: www.shinnova. com/part/99-japa.

10. Alon, I., and Brett, J. M. (2007). Perceptions of time and their manifestations in Arabic-speaking Islamic and Western cultures. *Negotiation Journal,* January, 55–73.

11. Levine, R. V., and Wolff, E. (1985). Social time: The heartbeat of culture. *Psychology Today,* March, 28–35; Levine, R. (1997). *A Geography of Time: The Temporal Misadventures of a Social Psychologist, or How Every Culture Keeps Time Just a Little Bit Differently.* New York: Basic Books.

12. Levine, R. V., and Bartlett, K. (1984). Pace of life, punctuality, and coronary heart disease in six countries. *Journal of Cross-Cultural Psychology,* 15, 233–255.

13. Brodowsky, G. H., Anderson, B. B., Schuster, C., Meilich O., and Venkatesan, M. V. (2008) If time is money, is it a common currency? Time in Anglo, Asian, and Latin cultures. *Journal of Global Marketing,* 21, 245–257.

14. Ji, L., Zhang, Z., and Messervey, D. (2009). Looking into the past. *Journal of Personality and Social Psychology,* 96, 761–769; Yong, A. (2008). Cross-cultural comparisons of managerial perceptions of profit. *Journal of Business Ethics,* 82, 775–791.

15. Brodowsky, If time is money is it a common currency?; Macduff, I. (2006). Your pace or mine? *Negotiation Journal,* January, 31–45.

16. Hall, E. T. (1983). *The Dance of Life: The Other Dimension of Time.* New York: Anchor Books.

17. Hall, E. T., and Hall, M. R. (1990). *Understanding Cultural Differences: Germans, French, and Americans.* Boston: Intercultural Press.

18. Usunier, J.-C., G. (1991). Business time perceptions and national cultures: a comparative survey. *Management International Review,* 31, 197–217.

19. Hall, E. T. (1960). The silent language in overseas business. *Harvard Business Review,* May–June, 87–96.

20. Bluedorn, A. C., Kaufman, C. F., and Lane, P. M. (1992). How many things do you like to do at once? An introduction to monochronic and polychronic time. *Academy of Management Review,* 6, 17–26; Kaufman, C., Lane, P., and Lindquist, J. (1991). Exploring more than 24 hours a day: A preliminary investigation of polychronic time use. *Journal of Consumer Research,* 18, 392–401.

21. Chandler, T. A., Sharma, D. D., Wolf, F. M., and Planchard, S. K. (1981). Multi-attributional causality: A five cross-national sample study. *Journal of Cross-Cultural Psychology,* 12, 207–221; Choi, I., Nisbett, R. E., and Norenzayan, A. (1999). Causal attribution across cultures: Variation and universality. *Psychological Bulletin,* 125, 47–63.

22. Kashima, Y., and Triandis, H. C. (1986). The self-serving bias in attributions as a coping strategy: A cross-cultural study. *Journal of Cross-Cultural Psychology,* 17, 83–97.

23. Hooghiemstra, R. (2008). East–West differences in attributions for company performance: A content analysis of Japanese and U.S. corporate annual reports. *Journal of Cross-Cultural Psychology,* 39, 618–629; also see: Zhang, A., Reyna, C., Quian, Z., and Yu, G. (2008).

Interpersonal attributions of responsibility in the Chinese workplace: A test of Western models in a collectivistic context. *Journal of Applied Social Psychology*, 38, 2361–2377.

24. Smith, S. H., Whitehead, G. I., and Sussman, N. M. (1990). The positivity bias in attributions: Two cross-cultural investigations. *Journal of Cross-Cultural Psychology*, 21, 283–301.

25. Smith, S. H., Whitehead, G. I., and Sussman, N. M. (1990). The positivity bias in attributions: Two cross-cultural investigations. *Journal of Cross-Cultural Psychology*, 21, 283–301.

26. Zemba, Y, and Young, M. J. (2012). Assigning credit to organizational leaders: How Japanese and Americans differ. *Journal of Cross-Cultural Psychology*, 43, 899–914.

27. Bond, M. H., Leung, K., and Wan, K. (1982). The social impact of self-effacing attributions: The Chinese case. *Journal of Social Psychology*, 118, 157–166; Zhang, Interpersonal attributions of responsibility in the Chinese workplace.

28. Morris, M. W., and Peng, K. (1994). Culture and cause: American and Chinese attributions for social and physical events. *Journal of Personality and Social Psychology*, 67, 949–971; See also Khan, S. S., and Liu, J. H. (2008). Intergroup attributions and ethnocentrism in the Indian subcontinent: The ultimate attribution error. *Journal of Cross-Cultural Psychology*, 39, 16–36.

29. Matthews, R. (2005). Where East can never meet West: Studies reveal fundamental cultural differences that affect how we do business because of how we perceive reality. *Financial Ties*, October 21, 13; Begley, S. (2003). East vs. West: One sees the big picture, the other is focused. *The Wall Street Journal*, March 28, B1.

30. Maddux, W. W., and Yuki, M. (2006). The "ripple effect": Cultural differences in perceptions of consequences of events. *Personality and Social Psychology Bulletin*, 32, 669–683. See also: Zemba, Y., Young, M. J., and Morris, M. W. (2006). Blaming leaders for organizational accidents: Proxy logic in collective- versus individual-agency cultures. *Organizational Behavior and Human Decision Processes*, 101, 36–51; Choi, I., Dalal, R., Kim-Prieto, C., and Park, H. (2003). Culture and judgment of causal relevance. Journal *of Personality and Social Psychology*, 84, 46–59.

31. Barnum, C., and Wolniansky, N. (1989). Taking cues from body language. *Management Review*, June, 59–60.

32. Miller, J. G. (1988). Bridging the content–structure dichotomy: Culture and self. In M. H. Bond (ed.) *The Cross-Cultural Challenge to Social Psychology*, Vol. 11. Beverly Hills, CA: Sage.

33. Weisz, J. R., Rothbaum, F. M., and Blackburn, T. C. (1984). Standing out and standing in: The psychology of control in America and Japan. *American Psychologist*, 39, 955–969.

34. Markus, H. R., and Kitayama, S. (1998). The cultural psychology of personality. *Journal of Cross-Cultural Psychology*, 29, 63–87; Markus, H. R., and Kitayama, S. (1991). Culture and the self: Implications for cognition, emotion, and motivation. *Psychological Review*, 98, 224–253.

35. Bond, M. H., and Cheung, T. (1983). College students' spontaneous self-concept. *Journal of Cross-Cultural Psychology*, June, 153–171.

36. Triandis, H. C. (1989). The self and social behavior in differing cultural contexts. *Psychological Review*, 96, 506–520.

37. See also Cousins, S. D. (1989). Culture and self-perception in Japan and the U.S. *Journal of Personality and Social Psychology*, 56, 124–131.

38. Schweder, R. A., and Bourne, E. J. (1982). Does the concept of the person vary cross-culturally? In R. A. Schweder and R. A. Levine (eds) *Culture Theory: Essays on Mind, Self, and Emotion*, 158–199. New York: Cambridge University Press.

39. Miller, J. G. (1984). Culture and the development of everyday social explanation. *Journal of Personality and Social Psychology*, 46, 961–978. See also a study by Stipek, D., Weiner, B., and Li, K. (1989). Testing some attribution–emotion relations in the People's Republic of China. *Journal of Personality and Social Psychology*, 56, 109–116. Based on a carefully done study, these researchers concluded that there is little support for characterizations of Chinese as being particularly other-oriented and of Americans as being relatively more self-focused. The difference in results is difficult to explain. The only real difference of note is that this study is the newest of the lot and thus may reflect some of the recent changes occurring in China, particularly among the young and educated. Regardless, the general pattern of findings we present in

this section appears to reflect some differing views of the self, perhaps reflective of a Western independent self and a non-Western interdependent self.

40. Mabe, P. A., III, and West, S. E. (1982). Validity and self-evaluation of ability: A review and meta-analysis. *Journal of Applied Psychology*, 42, 280–297.

41. Farh, J.-L., Dobbins, G. H., and Cheng, B.-S. (1991). Cultural relativity in action: A comparison of self-ratings made by Chinese and U.S. workers. *Personnel Psychology*, 44, 129–147.

42. Kelly, L., Whatley, A., and Worthley, R. (1993). Self-appraisal, life goals and national culture: An Asian–Western comparison. *Asia Pacific Journal of Management*, 7, 41–58.

43. Yu, J., and Murphy, K. R., (1993). Modesty bias in self-ratings of performance: A test of the cultural relativity hypothesis. *Personnel Psychology*, 46, 357–363.

44. For an overview see Heine, S. J., (2003). Making sense of East Asian self-enhancement. *Journal of Cross-Cultural Psychology*, 34, 596–602; Brown, J. D. (2003). The self-enhancement motive in collectivistic cultures: The rumors of my death have been greatly exaggerated. *Journal of Cross-Cultural Psychology*, 34, 603–605.

45. Lincoln, J. R., and Kalleberg, A. L. (1990). *Culture, Control, and Commitment: A Study of Work Organization and Work Attitudes in the U.S. and Japan*. Cambridge: Cambridge University Press; Near, J. P. (1986). Work and nonwork attitudes among Japanese and American workers. *Advances in International Comparative Management*, 2, 57–67; Near, J. P. (1989). Organizational commitment among Japanese and U. S. workers. *Organization Studies*, 10, 281–300.

46. Lincoln, J. R., Hanada, M., and Olson, J. (1981). Cultural orientations and individual reactions to organizations: A study of employees of Japanese-owned firms. *Administrative Science Quarterly*, 26, 93–115; Lincoln, J. R., and McBride, J. (1987). See also: Hattrup, K., Mueller, K., and Aguirre, P. (2007). Value importance in cross-cultural research: Comparing direct and indirect measures. *Journal of Occupational and Organizational Psychology*, 80, 499–513.

47. Warr, P. (2008). Work values: Some demographic and cultural correlates. *Journal of Occupational and Organizational Psychology*, 81, 751–775.

48. Huang, X., and Van de Vliert, E. (2004). Job level and national culture as joint roots of job satisfaction. *Applied Psychology: An International Review*, 53, 329–348.

49. Diener, E., Oishi, S., and Lucas, R. E. (2003). Personality, culture, and subjective well-being: Emotional and cognitive evaluations of life. *Annual Review of Psychology*, 54, 403–425; Judge, T. A., Parker, S. K., Colbert, A. E., Heller, D., and Ilies, R. (2001). Job satisfaction: A cross-cultural review. In N. Anderson, D. S. Ones, H. K. Sinangil, and C. Viswesvaran (eds) *Handbook of Industrial, Work, and Organizational Psychology*, 25–52. Thousand Oaks, CA: Sage; Gelfand, M. J., Erez, M., and Aycan, Z. (2007). Cross-cultural organizational behavior. *Annual Review of Psychology*, 58, 479–514.

50. Gelfand, Erez, and Aycan, Cross-cultural organizational behavior; Huang, X., and Van de Vliert, E. (2003). Where intrinsic job satisfaction fails to work: National moderators of intrinsic motivation. *Journal of Organizational Behavior*, 24, 159–179; Warr, P. (2008). Work values: Some demographic and cultural correlates. *Journal of Occupational and Organizational Psychology*, 81, 751–775.

51. Randall, D. M. (1993). Cross-cultural research on organizational commitment: A review and application of Hofstede's value-survey module. *Journal of Business Research*, 26, 91–110.

52. Luthans, F., McCaul, J. S., and Dodd, N. G. (1985). Organizational commitment: A comparison of American, Japanese, and Korean employees. *Academy of Management Journal*, 28, 213–219.

53. Lincoln and Kalleberg, *Culture, Control, and Commitment*.

54. Gomez-Mejia, L. R. (1984). Effect of occupation on task-related, contextual, and job involvement orientation: A cross-cultural perspective. *Academy of Management Journal*, 27, 706–720; Gelade, G. A., Dobson, P., and Gilbert, P. (2006). National differences in organizational commitment: Effect of economy, product of personality, or consequence of culture? *Journal of Cross-Cultural Psychology*, 37, 542–556; Hattrup, K., Mueller, K., and Aguirre, P. (2008). An evaluation of the cross-national generalizability of organizational commitment. *Journal of Occupation and Organizational Psychology*, 81, 219–240.

55. Fischer, R., and Mansell, A. (2009). Commitment across cultures. *Journal of International Business Studies*, 40, 1339–1358.

56. Gallup Consulting. (2010). The state of the global workplace: A worldwide study of employee engagement and wellbeing, available at: www.gallup.com/ strategic consulting/157196/state-global-workplace.aspx (retrieved December 10, 2012).

57. Hymowitz, C. (2000). U.S. executives reply to criticism leveled by foreign counterparts. *The Wall Street Journal,* September 19, B1; Hymowitz, C. (2000). Companies go global, but many managers just don't travel well. *The Wall Street Journal,* August 15, B1.

58. Pew Research Center (2006). U.S. image up slightly, but still negative: American character gets mixed reviews. Image of the American people. (2006). Pew Global Attitudes Project: Pew Research Center, available at: http://pewglobal.org/reports; *The Economist.* (2003). Living with a superpower, January 4, 17–20.

59. Pew Research Center, U.S. image up slightly, but still negative.

60. Stening, B. W., Everett, J. E., and Longton, P. A. (1981). Mutual perception of managerial performance and style in multinational subsidiaries. *Journal of Occupational Psychology*, 54, 255–263.

61. Institute of International Education (2012). *Open Doors Report, 2012,* available at: www.iie. org/en/Research-and-Publications/Open-Doors (retrieved December 20, 2012).

62. Khalaf, R. (2007). TV aims to bridge reality gap between US and Arab world. *Financial Times*, February 13, A1–2.

63. Spitznagel, E. (2012). Impress your Chinese boss: A guide to Sino-American business relations. *Bloomberg Businessweek*, January 9, 80–81.

64. Bizman, A., and Amir, Y. (1982). Mutual perceptions of Arabs and Jews in Israel. *Journal of Cross-Cultural Psychology*, 13, 461–469,

65. Rodgers-Spencer, J., Williams, M. J., Hamilton, D. L., Peng, K., and Wang, L. (2007). Culture and group perception: Dispositional and stereotypic inferences about novel and national groups. *Journal of Personality and Social Psychology*, 93, 525–543.

66. Hong, Y., Liao, H., Chan, G., Wong, R. Y. M., Chiu, C., Wai-man IP, G., Fu, H., and Hansen, I. G. (2006). Temporal causal links between outgroup attitudes and social categorization: The case of Hong Kong. *Group Processes and Intergroup Relations*, 9, 265–288; Lee, Y.-T., and Ottati, V. (1993). Determinants of in-group and out-group perceptions of heterogeneity: An investigation of Sino-American stereotypes. *Journal of Cross-Cultural Psychology*, 24, 298–818.

67. McAndrew, F. T., Akande, A., Bridgstock, R., Mealey, L., Gordon, S. C., Scheib, J. E., Akande-Adetoun, B. E., Odewale, F., Morakinyo, A., Nyahete, P., and Mubvakure, G. (2000). A multi-cultural study of stereotyping in English-speaking countries. *Journal of Social Psychology*, 140, 487–502; Iwao, S. and Triandis, H. C. (1993). Validity of auto- and heterostereotypes among Japanese and American students. *Journal of Cross-Cultural Psychology*, 24, 428–444; Vassiliov, V., Triandis, H. C., Vassiliov, G., and McGuire, H. (1972). Interpersonal contact and stereotyping. In H. C. Triandis (ed.) *The Analysis of Subjective Culture*, 89–115. New York: Wilby.

68. Omens, A. E., Jenner, S. R., and Beatty, J. R. (1987). Intercultural perceptions in U.S. subsidiaries of Japanese companies. *International Journal of Intercultural Relations*, 11, 249–264.

69. Maitland, A. (2006). A survey of 200 chief executives in France, Germany, and the UK find national differences alive and well. *Financial Times*, January 9, 10; Bond, M. H. (1986). Mutual stereotypes and the facilitation of interaction across cultural lines. *International Journal of Intercultural Relations*, 10, 259–276.

70. Lee and Ottati, Determinants of in-group and out-group perceptions of heterogeneity.

71. Bond, Mutual stereotypes and facilitation of interaction across culture.

72. Terracciano, A. (and 86 others). (2005). National character does not reflect mean personality trait levels in 49 cultures. *Science*, 312, October 7, 96–100; Cookson, C. (2005). Study confounds national stereotypes. *Financial Times*, October 7, 8.

73. An, D., and Kim, S. (2006). Relating Hofstede's masculinity dimension to gender role portrayals in advertising. *International Marketing Review*, 24, 181–207; Miller, C., Foubert, B., Reardon, J., and Vida, I. (2007). Teenagers' response to self- and other-directed anti-smoking

messages. *International Journal of Market Research*, 49, 515–533; Hynes, G. E., and Janson, M. (2007). Global imagery in online advertisements. *Business Communication Quarterly*, December, 487–492; Holt, D. B., Quelch, J. A., and Taylor, E. (2004). How model behavior brings market power: Consumers associate global brands with good quality. *Financial Times*, August 23, 10.

74. Schell, O. (2008). Olympics: It's impossible to understand what the Games mean to the Chinese without understanding their history of humiliation. *Newsweek*, August 4, 39–41; Fowler, G. A. (2003). Marketers take heed: The macho Chinese man is back. *The Wall Street Journal*, December 18, B1.

75. Khanna, S. R. (1986). Asian companies and the country stereotype paradox: An empirical study. *Columbia Journal of World Business*, Summer, 29–38.

76. Banjo, S. (2012). Japan, ready for Wal-Mart? *Wall Street Journal*, September 28, B6; Einhorn, B., and Mehrotra, K. Made in China makes India uneasy. *Bloomberg Businessweek*, February 27–March 4, 14–15.

77. Burkitt, L. (2012). China loses its taste for Yum! *The Wall Street Journal*, December 3, B9; Gasparro, A., and Jargon, J. (2012). In India, McDonald's plans vegetarian outlets. *Wall Street Journal*, September 15, B7; Einhorn, B., and Winter, C. (2012). Want some milk with your green tea Oreos? *Bloomberg Businessweek*, May 7–13, 25–26.

78. Fong, J., and Burton, S. (2007). A cross-cultural comparison of electronic word-of-mouth and country-of-origin effects. *Journal of Business Research*, 61, 233–242; Guth, R. A., and Chang, L. (2002). Sony finds it's a small world. *The Wall Street Journal*, December 18, B1.

79. Becque, E. B. (2012). "The Havana genius bar." *Bloomberg Businessweek*, September 17–23, 98.

80. DePaulo, B. M., Lindsay, J. J., Malone, B. E., Muhlenbruck, L, Charlton, K., and Cooper, H. (2003). Cues to deception. *Psychological Bulletin*, 129, 74–118; The Global Deception Research Team (2006). A world of lies. *Journal of Cross-Cultural Psychology*, 37, 60–74.

81. Skapinker, M. (2004). The myth of national stereotypes. *Financial Times*, March 8, 12; Dunne, N. (2003). Plugging into European jobs no easy task: American executives may find cultural differences a barrier to workplace success abroad. *Financial Times*, August 22, 7; White, E. (2003). Europeans take a satiric jab at the U.S. *The Wall Street Journal*, August 28, B1.

82. Osland, J. S., and Bird, A. (2000). Beyond sophisticated stereotyping: Cultural sense-making in context. *Academy of Management Executive*, 14, 65–77.

chapter 6

---

communicating effectively across cultures

Learning Objectives

After reading this chapter, you should be able to:

- explain the value of communications savvy in international business.
- recognize the options you have for getting across your message, as well as the cultural pluses and minuses associated with each.
- pinpoint communication barriers and understand that even language proficiency is no guarantee that miscommunication will not occur.
- analyze the sources of communication problems across cultures and potentially fix them.

International Challenge

A Small Firm Needs a Communication Boost to Get the Chips Off Their Shoulders . . . and Off Their Shelves

In late 2006, the board of California-based chip designer Teknovus, Inc., began looking for a new chief executive. The firm was only four years old but was in need of a boost in order to expand, let alone hold onto, what were seen as finicky customers from their primary customer base—Asia. Plus, if they wanted to become an attractive target for purchase by some of the big players, they knew they needed to get moving. As a first step, they hired Greg Caltabiano as their new CEO.[1] Mr. Caltabiano is an engineer by training, but also has an MBA from Stanford and post-graduate studies under his belt at University Center, Tokyo, as well as at the world-renowned INSEAD graduate business school in France. Plus, Mr. Caltabiano spent 14 years based in China and Japan, most recently as a general manager for a telecom firm. Mr. Caltabiano seemed to fit the position qualifications well because the firm sold most of its semiconductors to customers in Asia from its northern California offices in Petaluma (a city just north of San Francisco). The firm really needed someone who understood and could manage across different cultures.

Several years ago, it was not uncommon for Teknovus's customers to interact mostly with sales managers assigned to their region and only occasionally problem-solve with their engineers. Yet, because of the nature of the product application (fiber-optic communication networks), it was necessary for the Asian telecom staff and the local carriers that operate the networks to seek help from Teknovus's engineers. When overseas customers requested new features or bells and whistles, Teknovus engineers sometimes balked at these requests. For example, when Japanese customers apparently sought detailed reports for problems they were experiencing, U.S. engineers were both confused and frustrated by the request. Likewise, when Teknovus's engineers at the home office in California complained about repeated requests from the Seoul, Korea, office to change the technical specifications of some chips, explanations were slow in coming.

What should Mr. Caltabiano have done? Ironically, he was leading an advanced telecommunications systems company but messages from key customers abroad were slow in coming and confusing to the Teknovus engineers, who needed clarity. Think about these problems and try to jot down some advice for Teknovus to make necessary adjustments. Then, at the end of the chapter, cross-check those with some of the steps actually taken by Mr. Caltabiano. You may be surprised at some of his solutions to these communication challenges.

Communicating Effectively Across Cultures

We studied cultural differences in perception and attitudes in Chapter 5. There is good reason to believe that there are noticeable effects of culture on what we see and the resulting attitudes we form. This can be very functional for interaction with members of a culture, but these perceptual filters can present bigger challenges across cultures. In Chapter 6, we pick up right where we left off because once you perceive and interpret others, you often need to communicate your feelings or reactions. That is where your prowess and insight into different ways of thinking is critical, especially in an international environment. Communication can help clear up shortcomings in your perceptions or it could also obfuscate them as well. Both sides are discussed in this chapter.

The Value of Communications Savvy in International Business

While it may seem obvious that communication occurs in many different forms, managers sometimes get into trouble by operating as though communication is the same everywhere, language differences aside. To an American, for instance, a gap in conversation can be seen as an opportunity to respond. Long pauses are uncomfortable and create a desire to fill in the silence. But in Finland and Japan, longer periods of silence in conversation are normal, even expected. Pauses may be used to carefully consider what has been said; responding too fast may create offense.[2]

So, in negotiation situations with the Japanese, unprepared Americans may be uncomfortable with silence, perhaps seeing it as dissatisfaction with the offer they put on the table. For their part, Japanese negotiators may feel it is important to consider offers seriously and signal that consideration by pondering matters in silence. They may not understand signs of German impatience. Even worse, some experienced negotiators may be aware of another party's tendency to fill in silence and could use this as an effective negotiating ploy. Miscommunication can cause firms to lose potential partners, to fail to deliver their product or service, and generally distort and damage relationships. These problems underscore the importance of effective communication in international business.[3]

But, even speaking the "same" language has pitfalls, such as what can happen when Americans are posted to places such as Australia or the U.K. Not only is the "English" different, but so is the communication style. There are differences in the use of the same terms, of sarcasm and understatement, irony and emotion. And, differences like these can cause problems if not properly understood. Likewise, nonverbal communication matters too. Leaning back low in your chair might be acceptable in the U.S., especially if you want to convey a relaxed and familiar atmosphere. In other countries, though, it might be viewed as irritating, inattentive, and offensive. The bottom line, as one expert put it, is that "what blows deals is a failure to understand communication styles."[4]

Here then, we will review various forms of personal communication, both verbal and nonverbal. We will also examine some barriers to good communication across cultures and suggest ways to overcome them.

Spoken and Written Communication

The single most important way that we communicate is through language, both spoken and written. As we saw in Chapter 5, language can shape our perceptions, but it can also provide important insights into our cultural values. Let's look at the role that language plays in international communication.

Languages of the World

Experts believe that there are at least 3,000 distinct languages currently spoken in the world, not to mention many more thousands of off-shoots or dialects. Only about 100 of these have more than 1 million speakers. And, only a handful of languages account for most of our communication on the planet (see Figure 6.1). This figure shows that there are over 1.1 billion Mandarin speakers, only a fraction of whom reside outside of China, whereas many of the estimated 500 million English users are second-language speakers. Keep in mind that experts disagree on the numbers presented in this figure.

Language	Approx. Number of Native Speakers (in millions)	Language	Approx. Number of Native and Secondary Speakers (in millions)
Mandarin Chinese	1,100	Mandarin Chinese	1,120
English	330	English	480
Spanish	300	Spanish	320
Hindi/Urdu	250	Russian	285
Arabic	200	French	265
Bengali	185	Hindi/Urdu	250
Portuguese	160	Arabic	221
Russian	160	Portuguese	188
Japanese	125	Bengali	185
German	100	Japanese	133

Figure 6.1 Widely Spoken and Influential Languages Used Around the World.
Source: Weber, G. (1997). Top languages: The world's 10 most influential languages. *Language Today*, 3, 12–18.

For instance, some believe there might be upwards of 0.5 billion English speakers in China and India over the last 20 years.

Mandarin is largely limited to China, and a few other languages are also limited mostly to only one nation (e.g., Polish, Japanese, and Greek). Others are spoken across many borders (e.g., English, Spanish). The reverse is true as well—there are several languages spoken within the borders of one country. English and French are both commonly spoken in Canada, for example, and are more prevalent in some provinces than others. Likewise, India officially recognizes 16 languages.

We would expect greater cultural similarity within a country that has one dominant language (e.g., France) whereas borders may be less important proxies for culture in a multilingual society. Nevertheless, the dominant language in any one country or region can affect (and even define) a particular culture. Consider the Chinese government's efforts to continue to promote Mandarin as the official national language in a country that arguably has the most linguistic diversity on Earth. But, Mandarin is difficult for people from Shanghai and its surrounding provinces to understand. There, various dialects of Wu are common. Some have said that the eight languages of China are as different as Spanish is from French.[5]

While language usage certainly speaks to its impact, in Figure 6.2 we present data that more directly addresses language influence on business. The figure shows several measures of the role of language in world business. These data show that English, Japanese,

Language	Economic Strength	Language	Gross Language Product (GLP)	Language	Traded GLP
English	4,271	English	7,815	English	2,338
Japanese	1,277	Japanese	4,240	German	1,196
German	1,090	German	2,455	French	803
Russian	801	Spanish	1,789	Chinese	803
Spanish	738	French	1,557	Japanese	700
French	669	Chinese	985	Spanish	610
Chinese	448	Portuguese	611	Italian	488
Arabic	359	Arabic	408	Portuguese	138
Italian	302	Russian	363	Malay	118
Portuguese	234	Hindi/Urdu	114	Arabic	85

Figure 6.2 English in Business: Indices of Global Language Impact.

Notes

1. All figures are in billions of U.S. dollars.

2. All measures are estimates: *Economic strength* is the rank of the economies of the countries where native speakers live; *gross language product* takes into account all countries in which a language is spoken and allocates the GDP of each proportionate to the languages spoken there; *traded GLP* is based on the notion that language popularity follows markets, with the "merchant" speaking the customer's language; this is thus more of a measure of native speakers' trade internationally.

Source: Graddol, D. (2000). *The Future of English: A Guide to Forecasting the Population of the English Language in the 21st Century*. London: The British Council and The English Company (U.K.), available at: www.britishcouncil.org/learning-elt-future.pdf. (retrieved January 29, 2013).

French, Spanish, and German are especially influential.[6] These data are a decade old and undoubtedly Chinese would be among the most influential in today's economy.

Language Fluency

The large number of languages throughout the global community presents several challenges to international managers. One self-evident challenge is that in order to be effective, you need to communicate in the common language spoken where business is occurring. Alternatively, you must be willing to place trust in a translator. This seems to be a special challenge for Americans, especially relative to foreign competition, because Americans speak few second or third languages. Roughly 80 percent of U.S. households speak only English at home. This figure is even higher in Britain—about 90 percent speak only English.[7] Some suggest that Americans' relative lack of interest in other languages results from being relatively isolated geographically and, as a result, there is no great need to learn additional languages. This explanation, however, does not hold up well in the face of the large numbers of immigrants and ethnic minorities in the U.S.—numbers that have only increased during the last four decades. Plus, technology has made the rapid transmission of information much easier, rendering geographic isolation more illusory than real. The old adage that you "sell in a customer's language" also argues against this point.

Instead, critics suggest that part of the reason for Americans' lack of foreign language proficiency may be ethnocentrism—the tendency to be more inwardly focused on one's own culture. This may result in a relatively low value placed on learning other languages. Again, the same can be said about the British, who in 2004 dropped the requirement that all 14–16-year-olds should study at least one foreign language.[8] The effects were quick—the number of British students studying foreign languages went into free fall. There are, however, some promising signs within the U.S. Nearly 1.4 million college students are studying a foreign language (over 50 percent study Spanish) and more U.S. students are traveling abroad than ever before.[9]

One factor that has made it easy for Americans to be complacent about being monolingual is that the rest of the world increasingly uses English in business interactions. English is the language for international air traffic, regardless of city of departure or arrival. It is also the most commonly used language in academic research. Peruse French job ads and you will find that most management and professional positions require *anglais courant* (fluent English). English is the official language of oil firm Totalfina, the second largest company in France—this in a country that ferociously protects its language.

But why is English becoming more pervasive in international business circles? First, a good deal of business on the Internet is conducted in English and U.S. firms were early adopters. In the process, the Internet is exposing people everywhere to English more than ever. Even though estimates of web content in English have dropped over the last decade (from 75 percent in 2001 to 27 percent in 2011), English is still the most common web language. Other languages are well represented (24 percent in Chinese, 8 percent in Spanish, and 5 percent in Japanese in 2011), with Chinese content having proliferated—from only 9 percent in 2007 to the current figure of 24 percent. Likewise, the number of Chinese-speaking Internet users has mushroomed by 1,500 percent in the last decade (compared to a 300 percent increase in English-speaking web users during that time). Overall, however, nearly 80 percent of the Japanese and German populations are on the web—the highest percentage on the planet (with others far behind).[10]

A second reason for the widespread use of English in international business is the sheer size of the American economy, and the global reach of U.S. multinationals. These effectively make using English "good business sense," at least in the minds of some. Moreover, English is fairly simple, grammatically speaking, and makes for an easily learned "common tongue" in business. So, for instance, when French pharmaceutical firm Rhone-Poulenc merged with German competitor Hoechst a few years ago, English was made the common language of the merged companies.[11]

There are many different languages spoken throughout the European Union (EU). Yet today, more than half of the people in the European Union claim to be reasonably conversant in English. In fact, a survey of 16,000 people living in EU countries found that almost 70 percent agreed with the statement "everyone should speak English." And the Dutch are closest to already being there, with more than 80 percent indicating that they speak English. English has also been weaving its way into local languages around the world, with Europe no exception. The French term for a self-service restaurant is *le self* and the Russians call denim pants *dzhinsi* (roughly pronounced "jeansy").[12] Germany has become so beset with English phrases that some now refer to it as *Denglisch*. German executives may conduct media interviews in a *pressebriefingraum* (press briefing room) and then go work out their stress at a *Businesssportcenter*. But like the French before them, some German officials worry about the intrusion of English into their culture. One member of the German parliament decried the trend, calling it a "flood of Anglicisms descending on us from the media, advertising, product description and technology."[13] In China, estimates are that over 350 million people are learning English, with perhaps 150 million already speaking.

This global trend seems likely to continue. English is the most common language studied in schools in the EU. And, countries such as South Korea have reemphasized their already strong commitment to English, with plans to recruit 23,000 new English teachers. Some Koreans have even raised the issue of making English the country's official language to strengthen national competitiveness.[14] In Singapore, the percentage of households speaking Mandarin and local dialects at home has steadily declined over the last two decades, whereas those speaking English have dramatically increased.[15] If you add up all of the people who speak English with some competence as a second language to those native English speakers, English speakers have become among the most numerous in the world.[16] Overall, English is the most popular second language in Europe, Africa, Japan, and China, among other places. Consequently, it is probably no exaggeration to consider English the language of international business.[17] Lots of data suggest that this is likely to continue, including in Japan, which has long had a reputation of having a relatively closed culture. Yet, even in Japan there are some firms providing elaborate training in English, with a few even making English the required language for business transactions. Read about what Rakuten, the giant online retailer, is doing about English within its firm in the Global Innovations feature.

Global Innovations

They Have Ways of Making You Talk: A Japanese Firm Requires English

English is the most popular second language to study in the world. Many people already speak it, and millions more are studying it. Japan is considered relatively isolated, and not quick to adopt the conventions of other cultures, including language. Yet, in corporate Japan there is a huge move to the adoption of English in the conduct of commerce.

Consider the Rakuten Corporation, the largest online retailer in Japan. Every Monday morning, about 2,000 employees in the company's Tokyo headquarters meet for an *asakai* (company meeting). Since March of 2010, those meetings as well as corporate officer meetings and board meetings have been held in English. Megumu Tenefusa, Vice President of Public Relations, said that the firm is increasing the number of foreign nationals. And, "in order to globalize the company, everyone from top management to regular employees should be able to speak English." Most current employees are Japanese, although hiring will likely increase the number of non-Japanese now employed by the firm. Despite this, even if the meeting included all Japanese, soon even those meetings will be held in English.

This Japanese rival to Amazon has big plans. It is already a nearly $4 billion company, and recent acquisitions in the U.S. and Europe will be followed by more. Rakuten says that its English-only policy is "crucial to its goal of becoming a global company." The firm's employees seem to be OK with this move, or are at least taking it in stride. Rakuten provides in-house English lessons for employees. They declined to say what Test of English for International Communication Exam (TOEIC) score is required for employees. The TOEIC is an exam required by foreign students studying in the U.S. and other countries. Management did say, however, that English proficiency is necessary for promotion. In the meantime, the company has even changed signs in the cafeteria to English; they need to be able to know and order "tofu hamburg steak curry" in English if they want the company-provided free meals. More significantly, CEO Hiroshi Mikitani (who has an MBA from Harvard and is fluent in English) recently gave the earnings report entirely in English. Japanese reporters asked questions (in Japanese) and Mr. Mikitani answered in English, with an accompanying translation.

A few Japanese firms in addition to the Rakuten Corporation have more or less adopted English. Sony, for example, conducts many meetings in English, as does Nippon Sheet Glass Company, but each has no official language policy. Nissan Motor Co., and some other firms that have been acquired by foreign companies, have made English a common language. But it is rare for a company such as Rakuten, that is dominated by Japanese management, to take such a step. The extreme approach by Rakuten has resulted in some rare public criticism, by observers and by other Japanese firms. At a recent press conference, for example, Takanobu Ito, CEO of Honda, said that forcing Japanese workers to speak to each other in English is "stupid." Others lament that this policy is the first step toward the disappearance of the mother tongue—and ultimately, the fall of Japan.

These arguments do not faze Mr. Mikitani, CEO at Rakuten—nor even do criticisms that his own English leaves something to be desired. Instead, his reply is that lack of English speaking is a huge problem for the country: "Japan is the only country with many well-educated people who can't speak English." Indeed, data supports his statement. According to the International Monetary Fund, Japan had the lowest scores of the TOEFL test (Test of English as a Foreign Language), out of all 34 of the advanced economy countries. The last word, however, might be Mr. Mikitani's if their tremendous growth is any judge![18]

When people adopt a second language it is often because that language is useful in business interactions. English is the medium of business, finance, science, the Internet, broadcasting, and even the government in South Africa and other African countries.[19] In China, for instance, speaking English means better jobs, better pay (often double), and foreign travel opportunities. It is no wonder that teaching English is big business, with up to $3 billion annually spent on English-language training in Asia alone.[20] Some businesses are there to help. A slew of small- to medium-sized firms have been created to handle the international demand for learning English. McKinsey & Co. estimates that more than 300 million Chinese are studying English and that foreign-language business there is worth $2.1 billion annually.[21] One such business with millions of Chinese customers features Li Yang, the "Elvis of English," who teaches a program called "Crazy English." Part teacher, preacher, and drill instructor, he teaches English to groups of 10,000 or more in football stadiums. Through his bullhorn, he screams "How are you?" and the crowds yell that back to Mr. Yang. "I'm in the pink," he answers the crowds, who again repeat that back. The company's tag line of "Conquer English to make China Strong" is appealing to millions.[22] Another strong sign of the importance of communication is the entry of Disney into the foreign-language instruction business. Parents in China spend $1,000 to send their kids to twice-a-week (for a year) English classes held by Disney because they "want their kids to be international" and because Disney is a "familiar and trustworthy brand."[23]

That said, other languages really are not going away, in business or otherwise. For instance, the World Trade Organization's costs related to language have soared over 120 percent since it was founded in 1995. Language service to the more than 140 WTO members eats up 22 percent of its budget. The same is true in European Union meetings in Brussels. Although there are three "procedural" (working) languages, with English being the lingua franca, there are in fact 23 official EU languages. For example, Maltese is one of those, even though it is only spoken by about 400,000 people. About 1.4 million speak Estonian and nearly 6 million speak Catalan in Spain. This creates significant problems. Consider the need to translate 23 official languages into each other: it results in 506 different combinations. Even when there were only ten official languages, the EU could not find interpreters for some pairs of languages. A "relay" system needed to be developed. For example, if a Finnish document needed to be translated to Portuguese, the Finnish might first be translated into French, then a Portuguese translator fluent in French would complete the relay. The need for translators cannot keep up with the demand of some 12,000 EU meetings that take place every year. In 2002, the EU cost for interpreters was $143 million, and translation costs were $465 million—even as English becomes more and more common in the EU.[24]

What does "competence" in English, or any other language that you might speak, really mean—regardless of whether you are in the EU or not? There is no one definition, but there is little doubt that many people overestimate their language skills. And, as noted, perception and decision making may be linked to cultural values regardless of what language is spoken. So communication in international business is likely to have plenty of rough edges to it, even when a "common" language is used. Those rough edges can often create real problems and even great danger, as illustrated in the following International Insights feature.

International Insights

The Best Care in the Air Is Cross-Cultural: Miscommunication Can Be Dangerous to Your Well-being

Seconds before a Korean Air Lines (KAL) flight landed in a storm in South Korea, First Officer Chung tried to abort the landing by grabbing control of the plane from Captain Barry Woods. The aircraft's black box recorded what happened when the plane was only 30 feet above the ground and about to land. Captain Woods shouts: "Get your hand . . . get off. Get off! Tell me what it is . . ." Seconds later loud, terrible sounds are heard over the grunts of Mr. Chung and an alarm bell. The plane crashed and burst into flames. Astonishingly, all 157 people aboard escaped with their lives.

The crash reflects a rising occupational hazard—language obstacles. As fast-growing Asian airlines scour the world for pilots, cockpit crews have become more culturally and linguistically diverse. The problem in Korea, say foreign pilots, is acute. "It's like an air show up there, and it's hard to tell where everything is because the Koreans are all speaking Korean," said an American who flew for Asiana Airlines for years before taking a job with a U.S. firm. "There are a lot of opportunities to get hurt."

Under Korean law, foreign pilots must be matched with a Korean first officer so that communication with the control tower is effective. Unfortunately, Korean first officers receive only a rough familiarity with English as they go through flight school. Worse yet, communication may be further hindered by the hierarchical Korean culture that discourages co-pilots from asking questions or volunteering information. This value placed on high power distance makes it difficult for Korean flight officers to be proactive enough in providing information to pilots. Likewise, asking questions is often regarded as disrespectful. Showing lack of experience or knowledge, even in an airline cockpit, may be considered a loss of "face" or reputation. In fact, one American who trained many Korean pilots said that in the hundreds of preflight briefings he gave, trainees did not ask a single question.

These cultural factors make flying in Korea more risky than should otherwise be the case: Korea's airlines have higher fatal accident rates than other airlines. Investigators acknowledged that miscommunication contributed to this particular KAL accident. During the final approach, Captain Woods asked First Officer Chung to turn on the windshield wipers. Because he did not respond, the captain repeated the request. A few seconds later, Mr. Chung replied: "yeah . . . wind shears." Apparently, Mr. Woods' order to "get off the controls" also caused confusion. Experts say that a clearer command would have been "do not touch the controls." Both pilots were charged with criminal neglect—all were thankful for no loss of life. Another Korean Air Lines flight, however, was not so lucky. The airplane crashed, killing all 228 people on board. The recovered black box revealed that even after altitude alarms sounded, the co-pilot and flight engineer did not bring this up with the pilot; only 6 seconds before impact did the co-pilot make mention of the problem.

This is a wider issue, as shown in a crash of a Saudi 747 and Air Kazakhstan jumbo jet. Over 350 people died in this mid-air collision over New Delhi, India. This collision occurred after Indian air controllers ordered the Saudi jet to climb and hold at 14,000 feet and the Kazakhstan jet to descend to, and hold at, 15,000 feet. These instructions, however, were misinterpreted by the Kazakhstan crew—among other communication problems, they converted the feet to meters. Many airlines now train crew members on culturally based safety features. One is to actively voice concerns and to repeat them if the pilot does not respond. Fortunately, KAL's more recent safety record has been outstanding. With over 70 percent of air travel accidents due to pilot/crew error, safety in this case is in part tied to language competence.[25]

Competence in another language pays dividends in international business, including in air travel. Yet, even as English remains the lingua franca of world business, great reliance on English as the only language spoken by many Americans represents a competitive disadvantage—one that will continue to cause problems as the ferocity of foreign competition escalates. Unfortunately, many American firms continue to underplay the value of having managers who are fluent in other languages. In one survey, American managers felt that while cross-cultural understanding was valuable, foreign language skills were not as important. The general belief was that language problems could be overcome by using translators or by hiring foreign nationals.[26] Not surprisingly, studies show that American businesspeople have the lowest foreign language proficiency of any major trading nation in the world.[27] And as shown in Figure 6.3, the U.S. has received poor grades for knowledge of foreign cultures and languages. In a survey of over 10,000 business people from around the world, the results show that the U.S. had the lowest rating of any country. This latest data, while nearly a decade old, might still provide a similar picture about Americans' standing given the information we have reviewed here and earlier.

Country	Language and Culture Knowledge	Country	Language and Culture Knowledge
Belgium/Luxembourg	7.7	Korea	5.5
Switzerland	7.7	Indonesia	5.3
Netherlands	7.5	India	5.2
Denmark	7.3	Canada	5.1
Hong Kong	7.3	Japan	4.9
Sweden	7.2	Pakistan	4.9
Malaysia	7.2	France	4.8
Turkey	6.8	Brazil	4.8
Chile	6.8	Australia	4.2
Taiwan	6.8	U.K.	4.1
Germany	6.8	South Africa	3.5
Mexico	5.8	U.S.	2.8

Figure 6.3 Knowledge of Foreign Languages and Cultures: Executives' Views of Other Countries.

Note: Ratings provided by a large sample of executives from over 40 countries across the globe of these countries (1 = intercultural understanding is often lacking in the business community to 10 = management has understanding and knowledge of foreign cultures and languages).

Source: Adapted from The World Economic Forum. (2002). *The Global Competitiveness Report, 2002*. Geneva, Switzerland: The World Economic Forum.

Communicating in Foreign Languages: Plenty of Room for Error

The lack of foreign language skills can put you at a clear disadvantage in international business. Just because you speak Mandarin, English, or Russian, however, your problems are far from over. Even with great proficiency, many snags can arise in verbal communication, including dialect variations, accent problems, regional usage differences, and more—even when speaking the same language.

Because of these challenges, international managers must be sensitive to the possibility that what they *intended* to communicate was not what was *heard* or *understood* by other parties involved. This was learned by a large U.S. telecom company that replaced its expatriate managers in Thailand with American-born Thais (ABTs) and American-born Chinese (ABCs). The company's belief was that the replacements would be more culturally attuned to doing business in Asia. Yet, in actuality, those new managers often automatically assumed that they were communicating well. They were less likely to make any special efforts to check with their colleagues and subordinates to see if this was in fact true. This was not arrogance, but just an assumption that their messages were getting through. As experienced managers have said, often these problems cannot be solved by expanding your vocabulary list. Instead, employees on cross-national teams should work to clarify a discussion of items such as deadlines and requests, rather than assume that nuances will be understood. American managers at Reuters Group, a financial information provider, told their Thai employees that they would "like" a project to be done by a certain date. When it was not finished by that date, the managers were upset. The problem here was not vocabulary, but instead a cultural interpretation. The Thais had taken this request as a preference rather than a demand or order (as in "I'd like some water" as opposed to "Please get me some water"). Similarly, after his presentation to employees of a recently acquired Estonian bank, a Swedish banker was advised that he should be more forceful. The banker's presentation (in English) was fine. Estonians, however, expect leaders to show a more authoritative/forceful style, which is not as common in Sweden. One piece of advice was to change use of the phrase "it is good" to "it is vitally important" and to directly address the fears of the Estonians rather than to sidestep their feelings. Similarly, some Japanese firms are training employees to actually be more "rude" (i.e., more direct, less formal). Interestingly, they have found that English helps accelerate this effect. A Japanese manager reported that instead of conducting interviews in Japanese, he does some in English. He says that ordinarily, answers to even mundane questions tend to be veiled in courtesies, whereas in English the Japanese feel more comfortable answering directly. As one expert put it, "a lot of people arrive [in another country] thinking they need grammar practice, when what they need is management skills."[28]

Along the same lines, there are many native speakers who do not interact with foreigners and thus have rarely needed to be crystal clear. Consequently, they may struggle to accommodate to different usage of English by many non-native speakers. In some cases, those non-native speakers may be better at using English with one another than native speakers.[29] This even includes conversations between British and American managers—individuals who share the "same" language. Consider, for instance, the phrase "let's table the proposal." To Americans, it means that the proposal will be put aside indefinitely. To the British, however, it means that the proposal needs action immediately. There are many other examples of differences (e.g., an American flashlight is a British torch, American band-aids are British plasters, the American subway is the British tube, and the American toilet is the British loo), that it is easy to see why Irish playwright and co-founder of the London School of Economics, George Bernard Shaw, said that the U.S. and Britain were "a people separated by a common language."

Misunderstandings between British and Americans are likely to be cleared up fairly quickly given that the core language is the same. Resolving problems is much more difficult in conversations involving distinct languages, especially if managers are not fluent enough to check any translations provided. Consider an Indian who speaks no Spanish, talking with a Spaniard who speaks no Punjabi. They may understand each other well by speaking in a streamlined, simplified English—a watered-down form without grammar or structure, but understandable nonetheless. Talking in this so-called "Easy English," or "Globish," with a vocabulary of about 1,500 words, is becoming more and more common.[30]

Even if managers can avoid some of these communication problems, they can still make major errors that can harm their international business. For instance, Swedish manufacturer Electrolux once used the phrase "nothing sucks like an Electrolux" to promote their vacuum cleaners. Besides being vaguely obscene, this phrasing could be interpreted as something less than a rousing evaluation of the product—a chancy ad even if the double entendre was deliberate! IKEA has found that some of its Swedish names for products do not go over well in Thailand, such as the *Jatterba* vase and pot, which among Thais sounds like a crude term for sex. IKEA turns new product names over to a set of Thai employees who work to modify them to avoid such problems, while keeping the same Swedish charm that you will see in Seattle, Orlando, or Cincinnati.[31] Figure 6.4 presents additional communication blunders committed by companies as they tried to do business internationally. It shows two main types: errors in translation and errors that violate local norms and culture.[32] Even mighty Microsoft tripped up on an earlier, Spanish version of the thesaurus in its popular Word© program. Apparently, the program likened Indians to man-eating savages, "lesbian" was equated with "vicious" and "perverse," and "cannibal" and "barbarian" were suggested substi-

---

Examples of Translation Errors

- The *Redalen* is the name of a bed sold by IKEA in its stores around the world. In Thailand, however, it is very similar in meaning to a sexually suggestive term.
- A foreign airline operating in Brazil advertised plush "rendezvous lounges" which in Portuguese implies a room for making love.
- One German translation of the phrase "Come alive with Pepsi" literally meant "Come alive out of the grave with Pepsi."
- A memo from an African subsidiary of Dutch electronics giant Philips referred to "throat-cutting competition" instead of "cut-throat competition."
- A sign on the elevator in a Romanian hotel read: "The lift is being fixed. For the next two days we regret that you will be unbearable."
- A sign in the window of a Paris dress shop said: "Come inside and have a fit."
- A sign in a Japanese hotel read "You are invited to take advantage of our chambermaid."
- A Bangkok dry cleaner tag line read: "Drop your trousers here for best results."

Examples of Failing to Appreciate Local Norms and Cultural Values when Communicating

- A U.S. firm in Europe handed out fake coins with "$1 billion" emblazoned on them. Instead of spreading goodwill, this was widely seen as American pomposity and superiority. Europeans wondered why the dollar sign was used instead of local currency.
- In Britain, a General Mills breakfast cereal package showed a clean-cut child saying, "See kids, it is great!" Although a prototypical American ad, the product received a poor reception; it failed to reflect that English families are less child-centered when making food purchases.
- A foreign appliance company used an ad in Middle Eastern markets that showed a refrigerator full of food, including a large ham. At the minimum, the ad was insensitive since Muslims are forbidden to eat pork.
- A Listerine ad in Thailand showed a boy and a girl, obviously enthralled with one another. After Listerine learned that the public depiction of romantic relationships was in bad taste, the ad was adjusted to show two girls discussing bad breath, to a better reception.

Figure 6.4 Language Blunders Abroad.

Source: Adapted from Ricks, D. A. (1983). *Big Business Blunders: Mistakes in Multinational Marketing*. Homewood, IL: Dow Jones Irwin.

tutes for the Spanish word for black people. "Occidental" was matched with "white," "civilized," and "cultured." The Mexican press, among others, was merciless in its criticism. For its part, Microsoft was very apologetic and sheepish.[33] Consider also that Microsoft, as well as the companies discussed in Figure 6.4, likely hired professionals to develop and translate their ads but still had problems. Face-to-face and other "real-time" communications are likely to produce even more problems.

Imagine a meeting between American and Japanese managers. In Japan, it is generally considered inappropriate to say "no" in a blunt or direct fashion. The Japanese tend to avoid explicitly saying "no" to the other party so that both sides retain face (reputation). Instead, they rely on a variety of indirect ways to decline an offer, proposal, or invitation. A person not savvy about such cultural norms may not understand that "I will consider your proposal" could actually mean "no." It is so common for the Japanese to avoid direct negatives that the Japan Export Trade Organization provides a pamphlet to foreigners to help them understand the difference between a "yes" and a "no."[34] In Figure 6.5 we present some common phrases that mean "no" but which allow for the bad news to be cushioned. Even the structure of the language itself seems to be designed in part to preserve this harmony. The verb in Japanese comes at the end of a sentence. A communicator can present the subject and object first, then alter the verb after gauging reactions. Further, the speaker can add a sentence ending that changes the overall meaning in order to preserve harmony.[35]

Some researchers have gone even further with this point, suggesting that language might be a good indicator of underlying cultural values, such as individualism or collectivism. As a case in point, consider that languages vary in the freedom that they give

Phrase That Really Means "No"	A Common but Incorrect American Interpretation
"That would be very hard to do."	Some adjustments are needed, but the deal is still possible.
"It is very difficult."	The matter is difficult but not impossible.
"I will consider it."	The issue is under consideration for future use.
"I shall give it careful consideration."	Even more attention will be given to the proposal.
"We shall make efforts."	Energy will be put into exploring options.
Silence/delay in response	The other party is thinking about the topic or they are offended by our message; time is being wasted.
A change of subject	The new topic is more important now.
"I'll think about it."	The issue is still alive and under consideration.
"I'll do my best, but I'm in a delicate position."	It will be extremely tricky, but he or she will give it a shot.
"Yes, but . . ."	Conditional agreement

Figure 6.5 Ten Ways to Avoid Saying No in Japanese.

Sources: Adapted from Imai, M. (1975). *Never Take Yes for an Answer.* Tokyo: Simul Press; Ueda, K. (1978). Sixteen ways to avoid saying "no" in Japan. In J. C. Condon and M. Saito (eds) *Intercultural Encounters with Japan. Communication—Contact and Conflict*, 185–195. Tokyo, Japan: Simul Press.

to drop pronouns in a sentence. In English, for instance, it is not proper to drop the subject in a sentence such as "I went to a movie last night." "Went to the movie last night" is not a complete sentence and does not inform the listener who went to the movies. In Japanese and other languages, however, communicators *are* likely to drop the subject: "Went to the movie last night" is an acceptable sentence. In a study of 39 languages spoken in over 70 cultures, it was found that when the main language permitted pronoun drop, those countries were much more likely to be individualistic. The authors suggest that dropping pronouns deemphasizes the importance of the person or subject of action. Conversely, requiring the pronoun (for example "I," "he," or "she") makes the individual the prominent focus of attention, taking the focus away from the context in which they act.[36] In general, it seems that everyday conventions (such as dropping pronouns) in collectivist societies keep the values of *inter*dependence salient in people's minds. Other common practices in individualistic cultures (such as a focus on specific people) keep those *in*dependent values at the forefront.[37]

In most cultures it can be tough to confront someone directly, but easier if they are approached indirectly and with subtlety. To a degree, therefore, it is probably universal to try to cushion bad news to some degree. But Americans in particular are often irritated when they feel that they are being "strung along" or not given a "straight answer" when the news is bad.[38] Going back to our Japanese example, the problem is that Americans *should* be hearing a "no" but they are not. In other words, the Japanese are probably working very hard to maintain harmony and to show consideration for the feelings of others when they need to communicate a "no." A flat-out refusal would certainly be the worst option to take for many Japanese. Conversely, many Japanese perceive the communications of Americans as "blunt," "too insensitive," "overly critical," or just plain "prying." Of course, it would behoove both sides to gain a better understanding of the other.[39]

Compliments as Communication

Communication is not all about confronting or avoiding. Sometimes it is best to listen, watch, and acknowledge features about others that you admire—probably a good communication tool in any culture. Yet, it is interesting to observe that methods of smoothing interpersonal interaction, such as the use of compliments, differ across cultures. For instance, research shows that Americans praise each other much more frequently than do the Japanese. That is, they directly provide critical and complimentary feedback. In the process, Americans are also much more likely to praise physical appearance and personal traits than are Japanese. Why do researchers find effects like these? It could be that the great value placed on the individual self in U.S. culture may lead Americans to be especially solicitous of compliments that make them feel better or stand out, so much so that there is great difficulty in accepting a mistake and apologizing.[40]

There are wide differences across cultures in terms of how often praise is given, what is praised, and how people respond to praise. For instance, Egyptians tend to have a "complimenting" culture. While they may not compliment as much as Americans, their salutations tend to be longer and have more depth. On one occasion, a host complimented an Egyptian dinner guest on his necktie. The Egyptian promptly took off the tie and gave it to the person who offered the praise. The host politely refused the gift several times but found it neatly folded on the couch after the party was over.[41] Generations of American children have been told that "sticks and stones may break my bones, but names will never hurt me." Interestingly, Egyptians have a nearly opposite saying: "A sharp tongue cuts deeper than the sword." Clearly, there are differences in the types and frequencies of compliments (and insults) given across cultures. Some cultures are very stingy with their praise, while others may be willing to give you the ties off their shirts. This behavior, like other communication, can be linked to underlying cultural norms.[42]

Criticism as Communication

The opposite of compliments are *criticisms*. Once again, differences across cultures exist. One study found that Americans and Japanese tend to use distinctly different styles when criticizing. The Japanese are more likely to use "passive" forms of criticism, such as references to a third party, as well as humorous or ambiguous comments. Americans are much more apt to criticize directly, sometimes with overt anger that might also be accompanied by constructive suggestions. It appears that the need for group harmony in collectivist cultures and an effective self in individualistic cultures may impact how people deliver critical comments. This can be important in the area of performance evaluations where feedback is often shared among those differing in cultural background. It is easy to see how an American could be communicating in a much more negative and blunt way than they may have intended.

Having said this, people in all cultures can, and sometimes do, lose their temper, even in a work setting. Then, criticism can spill over into verbal abuse—something that unfortunately occurs too often in American work settings.[43] Even then, however, the form of "verbal abuse" doled out by others seems to be culture-driven. In one study, researchers reasoned that if communication and attention is focused on specific people in individualistic cultures, then verbal insults should also be focused on the person (e.g., "You are stupid," "I hope your project fails."). This is exactly what they found. Insults in collective cultures showed more concern with the person in relation to other/in context (e.g., "I wish a financial failure on you and your firm.").[44] These are still certainly insults, just ones contextualized in other non-personal ways.

As suggested previously, this could help explain why it is difficult to directly say "no" in some cultures. Many foreigners have been irritated by the apparent "unwillingness" of many Chinese to say "no" directly to a request or question. Instead, they may say that the request is "complicated" or that "the responsible person is busy at the moment." Similarly, some feel that many Spaniards might sooner take a business loss than openly admit that they made a mistake. These are common observations in more group-oriented cultures, and ones that can be seen in individualistic cultures as well, perhaps just not as commonly. Yet, studies show that collective cultures take social rejection to heart more than do those from individualistic cultures.[45] Nonetheless, causing someone to lose face by admitting mistakes and through publicly expressed hostility or rejection are things to be avoided.

Russian culture is a variant on this—a so-called practical interdependence. Russians are very free with their advice to other Russians, as well as others from different cultures. Because advice can help foster practical interchange, Russians generally view this practice as useful and even an obligation. Research comparing native Russians with Russian-Americans and other cultures shows they give advice freely, and found it tough to change this even when the advice was not solicited. Likewise, similar Russian directness and frankness was also observed in parental discussion boards.[46]

Embarrassment as Communication

It might take a lot of advice to embarrass or offend a Russian, but what happens once offense is given or a loss of face or reputation does occur? Again, there seem to be cultural differences in people's responses to these situations. In one study, again among Japanese and Americans, participants were asked to describe recent embarrassing situations that they had experienced. The Japanese tended to mention predicaments involving in-group relations (e.g., interactions with family, a spouse, friends, and co-workers); Americans were more likely to mention relations with out-group members (e.g., acquaintances, friends of friends, strangers, etc.). Also interesting were the *reactions* to these social predicaments. Most of the Americans (65 percent) felt embarrassment, but only a small portion of the Japanese had this reaction (5 percent). On the other hand, the Japanese were much more likely to feel shame (42 percent) in response to the loss of face than were Americans (4 percent). These findings are supportive of the perspective that communication patterns of Japanese and Americans reflect very different points on the individual–collective dimension of culture.[47]

Apology, Regret and Forgiveness as Communication

An interesting follow-up issue is how people resolve their embarrassments, regardless of whether they caused the problem or were the "recipient" of the embarrassing moment. One option is to apologize for creating the problem or at least for playing a part in the social mess. As a general default strategy, it might be the best thing to do. Instead, Japanese and Americans (among others) tend to react differently in situations where one person harms (either physically or psychologically) another person. Earlier in the chapter we presented the communication errors that occur and contribute to commercial airline accidents. When accidents occur, there is always a systematic effort made to determine the cause. Some years ago, a Japan Airlines (JAL) flight crashed into Tokyo Bay at Norita International Airport. Twenty-four people died and many others were hurt. After the accident, the president of JAL publicly apologized, bowing deeply to all those affected during a press conference, showing his respect and sympathy. In addition, he personally visited each family affected by the tragedy and offered up his resignation and a promise of consideration from the company. It is difficult to imagine the management of a Russian or American airline engaging in the same course of action in a similar situation.

Researchers have examined how apologies such as these are communicated across cultures. In one study, Japanese and Americans were asked to describe a recent incident in which they had apologized to another individual. The Japanese preferred to apologize directly and extensively (as in the airline example), without offering explanations and reasons for their actions. Thus, Japanese can be direct in their styles. Interestingly, Americans, while not quite as direct as the Japanese, also generally preferred to apologize directly. American apologies were not as intense, however, and they offered many more justifications and attributions to explain their behavior. The Japanese were highly sensitive to lapses in their social obligations and went to great lengths to try to make amends. The American tendency to provide many explanations may reflect the higher value placed on the self in an individualistic culture, which may make the admission of failure or guilt more difficult. The concern for the collective or group may in turn make it easier to express such feelings for the Japanese. A large-scale review of similar reactions suggests that East Asians score highly on the willingness to accommodate the needs of others.[48]

Experts suggest that international companies should help their employees understand that the type of apologies and explanations provided by people may have a cultural basis different than their own. Managers who fail to adjust their communication strategies risk provoking conflict and creating misunderstandings in cross-cultural situations such as negotiations, cross-cultural teams, and performance appraisals, to name just a few.[49] Several years ago, Japan's largest milk company, Snow Brand, produced and distributed milk that made thousands of people very sick. The firm developed a program of apology. The firm asked 2,000 of its employees to personally visit and apologize to the more than 14,000 customers affected. As an example, two employees visited Yumi Ito, a woman whose young daughter got sick, and they profusely apologized (bowing in respect so deeply that their heads touched the floor). Even Mrs. Ito thought the spectacle was "too painful to watch" and she refused the cash and gift certificates they presented. She did finally accept them when told by the bowed employees that "we won't be able to go back to our company if you don't take these."[50]

While Mrs. Ito accepted the company's detailed apology, how well are such regrets generally accepted? Like many of the other communication concepts discussed here, there are big individual differences. The authors of this book are both parents, with children who would rather visit the dentist or give up an iPhone for a week than apologize to their siblings, let alone forgive and forget a transgression. So it is within any culture, but there are also broad cross-cultural differences that have also been studied. Some collective cultures, such as that of the Congo, think of forgiveness as interpersonal, whereas individualistic cultures (such as in France) emphasize personal responsibility. One study that looked at views of forgiveness in these two countries found that the willingness to forgive was more common in the Congo. Likewise, the views of forgiveness in individual cultures such as France were less encompassing (e.g., "forgiveness is basically approving of what someone did") than in the Congo. The authors explained the findings as resulting from the Congolese view of the harm doer as being cut off from society because of the damage they caused. A big goal of the justice system is to reintegrate the offender back into society.

In France, the personal sanction or punishment is at the core of the judicial system (with neither apology nor forgiveness a requirement or special concern). Similarly, many Americans were surprised by the actions of the Truth and Reconciliation Commission conducted in South Africa after the end of apartheid. There, people who were arrested and found guilty of many terrible things publicly asked for, and were granted, forgiveness by the tribunals. The Commission did receive its share of criticism, including from the three main ethnic groups, and from both apartheid supporters and those in opposition (e.g., the African National Congress).[51]

Finally, the study found that when people from many different cultures (e.g., China, Japan, Russia, the U.S.) reflect on common events in their lives they are more likely to regret things that they *did not* do rather than things that they *did* do. Likewise, these varying cultures did not differ in the type of regret that they expressed—their regret was mostly focused on the self as opposed to the social group, with little difference found among countries. So, even though responses to transgressions and offense are different, there seems to be a more general tendency to ruminate on the things we didn't do or should have done.[52]

Written Communication

One way to avoid all these potential problems is to communicate via letter or e-mail. If you do not speak the language well, you can at least hire someone with writing expertise to carefully craft the message before sending it. But neither option is as simple as it seems on the surface, for several reasons. For one, this can be expensive. Also, costs aside, hiring writing help is impractical much of the time, given the volume of written communication businesspeople have to deal with.

According to one estimate, the average corporate e-mail user can expect 50 to 75 new messages per day, a figure that many think is grossly underestimated! For international managers, the e-mail volume is likely to be much higher. In fact, the growth of international business may account for a good chunk of the rising use of e-mail. Believe it or not, some managers may spend upwards of 50 percent of their office time on e-mail. After all, the convenience of e-mail is seductively attractive—a manager in Dayton, Ohio, can quickly fire off a memo to a counterpart in New Delhi, India, without having to think about what time it is on the other side of the world.

On the other hand, research shows that there may be different rates of use and preferences for communication media, including e-mail, texting, tweeting, and more. In one study, for example, researchers found that students (a group often at the vanguard of new tech applications) varied in their willingness to experiment with technology. Those from high uncertainty avoidance countries were less willing to adopt newer communication methods. The same is true of executives and managers—those from high uncertainty avoidance and power distance countries perceived various information systems as less useful and rated them less favorably than their counterparts from countries low in these dimensions.[53] A similar finding was also reported for internet adoption rates in the U.S., Japan, and a number of other countries. While most of these countries now have high rates of internet usage, their rate of adoption was negatively correlated with degree of country collectivism, uncertainty avoidance, and power distance.[54] These data show some cultural hesitation in adoption of new communication technologies, something we might predict would extend to even newer social media methods that are developed.

Finally, a more recent study compared the preferences of Chinese and Australian managers for texting, e-mail, phone, letters, and more. Because of the Chinese tendency toward higher power distance and avoiding uncertainty, researchers predicted, and found, that they preferred using the phone and texts over the other methods. Australians, however, were more comfortable with more "lean" communication methods, such as e-mail. E-mail offers few, if any, nonverbal cues. Importantly, though, while culture did play a big role in the results here, the researchers found that other variables present in all cultures (e.g., gender, age, and experience) were more important than culture in predicting communication preference. Younger people in both cultures, for instance, were more comfortable with most methods. Likewise, some have suggested that because of increased culture exchange and knowledge, business communicators have been taught to understand and adopt communication strategies from other cultures. Nevertheless, the research still underscores the point that extensive communication, even if only virtual, has cross-cultural complications.[55]

Nearly 70,000 people from 238 global companies were asked the question "What method of communication is the hardest for you to handle in English?" Even though the phone is a rich form of communication and preferred by some, if English was the language of communication, it still presented significant problems. In fact, the phone was cited as the hardest to handle in English by 77 percent of the respondents, with face-to-face meetings (64 percent) and e-mails (63 percent) also being mentioned.[56]

But volume of communication and convenience of sending it does not necessarily make for good communication.[57] How could you construct a letter, or an e-mail to get your point across, make your order clear, or request some key information? If you are an American, you probably would: (1) use English, (2) keep the letter short and to the point, (3) stress the use of the personal tone (personal pronoun), and (4) avoid flowery or exaggerated language.[58] If you were French, however, you would probably be less concise (maybe the letter would spill onto a second page), and your introductions and conclusions would be much more formal and polite. Americans might perceive these parts of the letter to be "old fashioned" or "too formal."[59] Japanese writers often prefer to hint at something, partly because their language itself is ambiguous and partly because, as noted previously, being overly direct could be seen as condescending or an affront to one's face.

Figure 6.6 illustrates this difference in writing style across two versions of a letter that was actually sent to Chinese companies by an American firm looking for business. The first version, written by the company owner (an American) is simple, clear, and direct. Yet, it received no response from the potential customer. The letter was rewritten by a Chinese employee of the firm and is also presented in Figure 6.6. Note that it incorporated relevant cultural conventions. For example, it is typical to begin with set phrases about one's family, the season or weather, and also to close with comments that are similar in form. Likewise, further paragraphs present the purpose of the letter, also appropriately couched in cultural norms (comments about the seasons and demonstrating a humble attitude). Even bad news would be presented very indirectly. This longer letter did receive replies from the customer and inquiries from other customers.[60] This letter shows that there are differences in writing styles among countries and cultures. Clarity, for example, is not a universally valued feature. In fact, in some cultures, this

Dear Sir:

Your name and address were referred to me by the Ohio Department of Agriculture, Asia Office. They stated that you had expressed an interest in our products and requested further information.

I am therefore enclosing a brochure that lists our products and services. Please let me know your specific requirements and I'll be happy to provide you with further details.

Thank you for your participation in the Ohio Department of Development Trade Show. I look forward to your reply.

Sincerely,

Fred Pestello
Director of Sales
Midwest Equipment Company

Enclosure

Dear Mr. Qui:

I hope you have had a safe journey home and that you and your family are in good health. Here in the middle part of the U.S., where you graciously visited, continues to have wet weather. We are thankful for the rain, however, after our two years of drought.

Our company, Midwest Equipment, wishes to thank you very much for your participation in our state Department of Development Trade show and for stopping by our booth.

Our firm is located in Springboro, Ohio, in the heart of a fertile agricultural area of the country. We have over 35 years of experience in selling agricultural equipment. Our company has trade relations with more than 15 countries around the world. And, we are well known for our excellent service and good quality products.

Several years ago, we sold over a dozen machines to a Chinese firm. We wish to establish relations with China on a regular basis. We would like to know whether our agricultural equipment, such as tractors and combines, could benefit you in any way. I will be very happy to provide you with further information.

I am also enclosing two price lists of our equipment, one is the regular prices, the other is the pricing for demonstrators.

May your seasons be fruitful and plentiful.

Sincerely,

Tan Wen-lan

Figure 6.6 Examples of Two Different Versions of a Letter to a Potential Asian Customer.

Note: The letter on the left is the original version, written by the company V.P. The revised version on the right was written by a Chinese employee of the firm.

Source: Adapted from Boiarsky, C. (1995). The relationship between cultural and rhetorical conventions: Engaging in international communication. *Technical Communication Quarterly, 4*, 245–259.

style can be viewed as simplistic, even patronizing. Other cultures use ambiguity and indirectness as a tool to save face and to give instructions politely. People in those cultures view the simple version as a bit unsophisticated.[61]

People learn these styles early on in life and they are imparted for functional reasons—the styles tend to convey basic values. A recent study demonstrated this by looking at the stories presented in children's textbooks in Japanese and U.S. schools. Those stories were carefully coded on several different dimensions. An analysis showed

Writing Element	Foreign Letters Received Using Writing Element (percent)	U.S. Letters Sent Using Writing Element (percent)
Use of personal tone (personal pronouns, informal language, etc.)	25	37
Impersonal tone (formal, passive voice)	25	6
Exaggerated courtesy	44	19
Obvious compliments	16	6
Words omitted from sentences	38	6

Figure 6.7 An Analysis of Letters Written to and Received from Foreign Countries.

Source: Adapted from Kilpatrick, R. H. (1984). International business communication practices. *Journal of Business Communication*, 21, 33–44.

that the stories in American textbooks highlighted themes of individualism (e.g., self-direction and personal achievement). The Japanese textbooks, however, emphasized themes of collectivism, including such topics as conformity and group harmony.[62]

It should be of little surprise, then, that when these students later become business-people, similar effects are observed. One elaborate study of business writing involved asking 100 major U.S. corporations for copies of letters that they sent to foreign companies, as well as letters that they received from those foreign firms. Samples of letters were collected from over 20 countries (e.g., Brazil, Mexico, Italy, Thailand, India, and Caribbean countries). The results are summarized in Figure 6.7. As you can see, American-written letters tend to use an informal, casual tone, especially in contrast to the more formal third-person letters that they often receive from other countries. Likewise, Americans appear to avoid "exaggerated" courtesy and compliments that other cultures are likely to consider important. Perhaps one lesson to be learned is that if you want to impress someone from another culture, do your best to imitate that person's written communication style.[63]

That said, keep in mind our earlier warnings about the pitfalls inherent in what you might be conveying when sending written communications abroad. You may be successful at trying to be more subtle or being more elaborate than you normally would, but you could still create communication problems in other ways. Suppose for a minute that you send an e-mail to a Japanese business partner about projected profits. Even if you have done everything else right, the use of the word "profit" may imply something about long-term collective growth to your Japanese counterpart. To Americans, however, the meaning of the word tends to be multifaceted, with a core theme of personal gain. Managers from Singapore and Malaysia, particularly those of Muslim faith, may be more oriented toward profit as a bottom-line concept in contrast to Australian managers where profit also stirs awareness of corporate social responsibility.[64] If your letter had been sent to a Russian, it is possible that the word "profit" (*prybl*) could even conjure up a less than positive vision.[65]

When people define the same words or objects differently and think that their message is getting through, it is called *bypassing*. Consider the meaning of "Mickey Mouse." In the U.S., it might be reflective of some "all-American" values, as the Walt Disney Company is considered wholesome and family-focused. In Japan, the character conjures up images of something safe and reliable, whereas in France it may not activate many images at all. Likewise, the concept of souvenirs for visitors invokes a fun part of a travel experience for Americans, a legitimizing memento for Japanese, and a tacky waste of money to the French.[66] Because bypassing is so common, you may not even know it is happening until well after the communication process is over.

You may wonder if it is possible to come to grips with these problems on a systematic basis. Difficulties abound, no doubt. Some occur simply because we fall into our more common and comfortable way of talking and acting—then we believe we're getting through to the other party. One example is the use of sports analogies, words that have seeped into our business language—as illustrated in the following International Insights feature. In practice, these words are often amplified by our nonverbal communication, which is the subject of our next section.

International Insights

Many Americans "Strike Out" When Communicating Cross-Culturally

From air traffic control, to TV programs, to business meetings, English seems to be the ticket. Yet, while English may be the preferred tongue of international business, even experienced and fluent foreign managers sometimes find themselves tongue-tied with Americans. Oddly, but increasingly, this seems linked to Americans' strong preference for sports idioms. In fact, U.S. executives use so many of these idioms that they do not know when they are "striking out" with their communication.

Paula Shannon, a seasoned executive at a large Boston-based offshoring services firm with offices in 25 different countries, has experienced this a lot. One of her "favorite" sports expressions used in business is a reference to the "hail Mary pass"—a long-shot effort that needs to be done. Yet, without a working knowledge of American football, few foreign execs would understand the saying. If anything, by using it you might establish your "American centricity and risk a religious offense" at the same time, says Ms. Shannon. Many other sayings from American football are used in the boardroom, including "red-zone selling" (when the stakes get higher as the sale is about to close . . . or when you are close to the end zone in football), as well as "going long" (being bold) and "throwing a screen" (bringing help). The CEO of a Fortune 500 electronics company that does business in over 50 countries remembers wanting to change the meeting agenda at a global retreat in Italy. When he stood up and announced, "I'm calling an audible" (being spontaneous), only the Americans understood.

There are hundreds of baseball euphemisms; if we mentioned more than a handful we would be "running up the score" (being selfish/bragging). While the game is played more widely than football, many still need to translate what it means to "hit a home run" with their presentation. If not, they may have to "manufacture some runs" (smaller victories) by "choking up" (being careful) and "playing small ball in the late innings" (going with the odds). Dieter Zetsche, until recently the CEO of DaimlerChrysler, is a German national, born in Turkey and fluent in English. Once during an interview with an American newspaper, a reported told him that he was about to get a question from "left field." After pausing a second, the savvy Zetsche responded that it was "okay . . . as long as you don't throw me a curve ball" (be unpredictable). Not everyone is like Mr. Zetsche and can "hit one out of the ballpark"; many seem to have "two strikes against them" (are behind) to start with. Ms. Shannon from the Boston offshoring firm noted that these sayings are not just reflective of the American "man-cave" where flat-screen TVs, clickers, and sports are king, but that American women do not "need a raincheck" or someone to "pinch hit" as they are also capable of "stepping up to the plate" (taking a chance) with sports language. Both men or women can "throw this idea around the horn" (brainstorm) or "hit one in the bleachers" (have a great idea/win). So, women are hardly "throwing smoke," "covering all the bases," or going "the whole nine yards" with their communication (all mean to get something done). Neither men nor women appear to be "taking one for the team"—instead it is up to those foreign partners to "steal the signs" (predict competition) of real communication so the conversation can "move from the catbird seat" to the "peanut gallery." All this makes non-native English speakers feel like they are "out in left field" (away from central activity) and "right off the bat" too. Maybe Americans are "playing hardball" (being tough), leaving others "off base" (out of sorts).

Just when a foreigner thinks that he or she has got a lot of these terms mastered, the Americans come up with more—covering even more sports. Maybe basketball season will open just in time for your next meeting. It did for one CEO of a recruiting firm who was meeting with executives of an Indian company in London. One of his colleagues tried to convince the Indian partners to remove a clause in a contract because it would benefit neither side by characterizing it as a "jump ball" situation. They had discussed this for about 10 minutes when one of the Indians said, "I'm not quite clear what you mean by the jumping ball." Obviously, this is not a language problem per se—Indians are, and have been for hundreds of years, widely fluent in English. It just shows that knowing the same language does not make for a "slam dunk"—mistakes are "par for the course."

Some experts say that sports jargon is common in business because both share and feed on competition. And, increasingly, foreign executives understand these euphuisms, although the same might not be true for American's understanding of foreign sports (as in the use of the terms "own goal," "hitting a six," in "the pit," and a "sticky wicket," which are terms from soccer, cricket, and rugby). Either way, if you want to "hit a grand slam" with your international communication efforts, be aware of your use and overuse of these terms.[67]

The advice for written documents used across culture is first to keep things simple. Complex word choice, use of acronyms, and idioms invite confusion. Avoid local expressions and try to use the most common meaning of a word. Finally, but not exhaustively, invite questions or comments—before you send the document as well as from the recipient afterward. One very interesting example is how Caterpillar, the world's largest maker of tractors and excavators, dealt with these problems. They developed their own language program, called Caterpillar Fundamental English (CFE), to be used overseas in operating and repair manuals. The CFE is a greatly condensed, 800-word version of English. The 500 nouns, 70 verbs, 100 prepositions and remaining words are taught in 30 lessons. A similar approach was also taken by EADS, the European Aircraft Consortium (it makes Airbus commercial jets) for its repair manuals.[68]

Nonverbal Communication

As if the challenges linked with verbal and written communication are not enough, we also need to consider the role of nonverbal communication. Nonverbal communication is the transmission of messages without the use of words or writing. Above and beyond what is *being* said, often *how* it is said carries plenty of information value. How you stand (e.g., slouching vs. standing up straight) and what you wear (e.g., a business suit vs. jeans and an untucked shirt), for example, can add (or take away) credibility from your presentation. So can your facial expression, eye contact (or lack of it), physical movements, and any hand gestures that you use (or do not use).[69] These are all examples of nonverbal communication, which can vary across countries and cultures. First, however, it should be noted that much of this research has been overly popularized. It is important to know that nonverbal behavior is complex, easily misinterpreted, and often situation specific. So, we need to be as careful as the researchers discussed in the coming sections were in drawing conclusions about nonverbal behavior.

Interpersonal Space and Gestures

One important nonverbal behavior has to do with the amount of interpersonal space we prefer to have between ourselves and others in social interaction. We regularly make very subtle choices about this distance, but that space varies dramatically depending on the activity and with whom you are interacting. For instance, women tend to have a closer interpersonal space than men do, and friends are physically closer than strangers. Americans and northern Europeans prefer about 2–3 feet of personal space when conducting business. Asians prefer closer to 1½–2 feet, whereas Latinos and Arabs might even choose a much closer personal space. You can imagine the effect of these differences in a cross-national business interaction. If an American likes about 3 feet between himself and another individual, and an Arab businessperson likes about 1 foot between individuals, what is likely to occur? The Arab could perceive the American as stuffy and standoffish, whereas the American businessperson might see the Arab as pushy. Many experts believe that knowledge of cultural space differences can avert a negative perception that could otherwise interfere with a business transaction.

While interpersonal space is a choice, it is more often than not a habit, based on little or no thought. Gestures, however, are usually more direct and deliberate and designed to amplify a message or to act as a stand-alone form of communication. Such gestures might include a shoulder shrug, a thumbs-up sign and many other, sometimes country-specific, gestures. Native speakers have an ability to rapidly size up these valuable signals and their meaning. But, for someone trying to interact well in a different culture, or doing business cross-culturally, it is much tougher. One recent study videotaped a series of real and fake gestures and then asked a group of non-native students in the U.S. to rate their meaning. The results showed that an accuracy in judging the gestures was positively associated with length of stay within the U.S. and with ratings of inter-cultural competence provided by observers and friends. The latter result shows that those who can accurately read gestures are seen as more culturally aware and able to decipher communication nuances in a more sophisticated way.[70]

Emotions and Touch

Closely related to interpersonal space and gestures are the emotions that people express or project across their interpersonal space. Interestingly, behavior (such as emotion shown through facial expressions) can be a common communication method across cultures. Research shows that facial expressions of anger, happiness, and sadness can be recognized reasonably well across cultures.[71] On the other hand, studies also show that our accuracy in figuring out the various emotions gets worse as the cultures become more dissimilar.[72] There may even be the equivalent of nonverbal "accents" among cultural groups. Just as linguistic accents (e.g., pronunciations) can provide clues about someone's ethnic or country origin, various features of nonverbal behavior such as emotions can be clues to those same origins. For instances, one study demonstrated that when Japanese Americans and Japanese nationals expressed emotions in photos, observers were able to detect these subtle cues and more accurately identify the person's culture (American or Japanese). When Australians and Americans were photographed showing happy expressions, and when videoed while walking or waving a greeting, observers were also able to correctly peg their respective nationalities.[73]

These studies suggest that we might observe subtle traces of nonverbal accents that can point others to features about us. Consider some key values that Thais learn early in their childhood. There is *sam ruam*, which reflects a need to be moderate and neutral in one's emotions and to strongly avoid a demonstration of anger. Likewise, Thais are also taught *kreng jai*, the need to refrain from offering opinions that could offend out of respect for others. Outward expressions of emotions are viewed as inappropriate and crude. So, for example, the use of a more Western "in your face" method of negotiation is not well received by a typical Thai, although you'd have to watch closely for the cultural "accent." Likewise, a Thai would likely not tell you to take off your shoes as you enter their house nor express angst, even though it might be important to them. That would be impolite. Instead, you'll get respect, even if it's not deserved.[74]

Likewise, the extent of the use (or misuse) of touch is called haptics and can be a communication tool. In general, Americans tend not to use touch all that much, except with people with whom they are very familiar or intimate. Touching in some cultures, however, is a natural and expected part of social interaction and communication. One interesting study looked at differences in touching by observing people as they sat in outdoor cafés in four different countries. During a one-hour timed period, there were 180 touches in San Juan, Puerto Rico, 110 in Paris, 1 in Gainesville, Florida, and none in London.[75] Another study showed that Americans had two to three times greater physical contact with their parents and about two times the amount of contact with friends than do the Japanese.[76]

Arabs tend to use a lot of touching, eye contact, and other nonverbal behavior. The British, however, are the opposite in their nonverbal style, generally avoiding touch and prolonged eye contact. After interacting with each other, many Arabs might feel that the British are aloof and distant, while many British might wonder why Arabs are so interpersonally aggressive and invasive. But, can this be overcome by preparing before one goes overseas? This was the basis for a study that examined the effect of nonverbal training on impressions of people from other cultures. A group of Britons were trained to perform nonverbal behaviors appropriate to Arab culture (such as extensive touching, closer distance, etc.). Next, this group and a control group that did not receive training interacted with Arabs. Later, the Arabs expressed more liking for the Britons who had received the training than those who had not.[77] This study underscores that nonverbal communications do differ across cultures and can have an impact on relationships but that training can help mitigate unintended effects on partners.

Vocal Qualities as Nonverbal Communication

Vocal qualities such as speed of speech and the loudness of your voice can also project an image and add credibility to a message. This topic has been the subject of a considerable amount of cross-cultural research. One study compared the impression conveyed by a message that was delivered either quickly or slowly, even though the message content was the same. This was done by having Korean and American participants watch a videotaped speech about the perils of smoking. Although the content of the information presented was always identical, the presentation was varied so that the message was delivered at either a slow, normal, or fast speech rate using a technology that retained natural sound.[78]

After listening to the message, the Koreans and Americans rated the speaker and the speech on a number of characteristics. Americans thought that a relatively fast voice conveyed power and competence. For the Korean subjects, however, a slow delivery was more effective in increasing the credibility of the speaker. One explanation for this difference is that Koreans live in a more collective culture and, as a result, are more concerned with measuring their words carefully so as not to offend others.[79] Likewise, Egyptians and many Middle Eastern/Arabic countries use phrases that reflect a more colorful and emotional stance toward others (e.g., "my most esteemed colleague," or "my honored guest"). These emotional and complimentary communication patterns are reflective of a value placed on creating a sense of warm friendship and personal relations among business partners. In the Muslim faith, readings of the Koran aloud in mosques reflects great oratory skill and is considered a profound occasion. Likewise, the public "cry" for prayer in this faith, not seen in some other faiths, is another example of emotionally laden communications.[80]

Context

Our discussion of non-verbal behavior so far reminds us that *how* something is communicated carries importance above and beyond what is being said at times. Yet, while nonverbal behavior can provide "background" for understanding them, an even more subtle form of communication is that due to *context*. Almost all of our interactions occur within some kind of context. For instance, an identical statement could mean dramatically different things, depending, of course, on the context. Many of us know this intuitively but others, such as those quoted "out of context," have learned firsthand the value of proper context. So, you could say that the need for context is relatively universal. Nevertheless, many experts claim that some cultures are more or less reliant on context in their communications and other interactions with others.

Figure 6.8 shows how some cultures and countries differ in the general reliance on context. In low-context cultures, such as in the United States or Australia, our interpretation of people's behavior importantly depends on what is actually said or written. These messages are often precise, with the words themselves carrying most of the real message. If you did business in such cultures, it would be common for communications to be explicitly stated, discussed, and mutually agreed upon and written down before any deal could go forward.

Culture/Country Example	Degree of Context
Chinese Korean Japanese French Arab	**HIGH** • What is unsaid but understood carries more weight than written/verbal. • Relies on trust for agreement. • Personal relations add to business.
Greek	
Spanish	
Italian	
English	
American Scandinavian German Swiss	**LOW** • A focus of specifics of what is written or said. • Handshake is insufficient. • Trust secured with legal agreement; personal relations can detract from business.

Figure 6.8 Comparing High- and Low-Context Cultures.
Source: Adapted from Hall, E. T. (1976). *Beyond Culture*. Garden City, NY: Anchor Press.

High-context cultures often approach a business event very differently. The context itself often provides people with information that can be used to interpret what might otherwise be an ambiguous message. Put plainly, people may not require or expect much detailed, explicit information. Instead, verbal or written information can take a back seat to what is generally understood via the context. Consequently, high-context cultures tend to be concerned with long-term relationships, a person's word or reputation, and establishing trust over time. High-context cultures, such as Japan, prefer face-to-face communication because this mode allows for more subtlety than the written messages preferred by low-context cultures.

The Japanese and similar cultures tend to worry that spelling everything out would be a condescending putdown. Of course, the flip side is that Japanese sometimes say that Americans do not want to take the time to understand their business environment and are overly focused on the short term. If the Japanese understood the low-context culture embraced by many Americans, they would know that Americans' insistence on detailed contracts is a business necessity rather than an indicator of a lack of trust. Those documents allow for a permanent and explicit record of a message. This rational, fact-based style contrasts with the more indirect, intuitive style that is valued in high-context cultures. As an example, consider the well-crafted ad by the Nice Company, a Chinese detergent producer. China is a high-context culture. The company's understanding of the Chinese consumer showed in an ad which depicted a young girl helping her mother, who had just been laid off, do the laundry. It strongly connected with the Chinese concept of *dongshi*, which is the appreciation of family and societal responsibilities, and it sought after the aspect of parenthood in China.[81]

Researchers argue that differences in context may explain common cross-cultural problems that arise in international business. For example, a German manager working for a French company was terminated within a year because his performance fell short of expectations. The German was shocked, especially because "nobody told me what they wanted me to do." A French employee who resigned from a German company had the opposite experience. The French employee became fed up with being constantly told what to do by his German boss. He felt both his pride and his intelligence were threatened. Both examples are failures due to context. The French tend to be high context and typically would expect the German employee to pick up on a message or requirement. The low-context German employee, in contrast, would expect intervention and explicit direction by the French manager. Unfortunately, that intervention came way too late.[82]

This interesting difference in expected verbal input carries across cultures and also exemplifies the notion of context. Research found that people who were extremely verbal were perceived as more attractive by Americans (low context), but those who were less verbal were seen as more attractive by Koreans (high context).[83] At the same time, it is not wise to "beat around the bush" in those low-context cultures. While being more verbal is desirable, low-context communication will be more effective if concrete, specific, and logical statements are made. It is rare to see a message that is simultaneously translated well to both cultures. One writer, however, described a sign that he saw in Switzerland that was presented in three languages—German, English, and French. The words were modified to reflect the varying context of these three countries. In German, the sign read "Walking on the grass is forbidden"—a direct, unambiguous message for this low-context

Communication Feature	Degree of Context	
	Low	High
General approach	direct/explicit	indirect/complex
Degree of precision	literal/exact	approximate/relative
Dependence on words	high	low
Nonverbal dependence	low	high
View of silence	negative; poor/no communication	positive; good communication
Attention to details	high	low
Value placed on intentions	low	high

Figure 6.9 Characteristics of Communication in Low- and High-Context Cultures.
Source: Adapted from Victor, D. A. (1992). *International Business Communication,* 153. New York: Harper Collins.

country. The English version read "Please do not walk on the grass"—a message leavened a bit from the German to reflect the somewhat higher context. Finally, the French version read "Those who respect the environment will avoid walking on the grass"—a much higher-context message reflective of that cultural tendency in France.[84] Figure 6.9 presents more communication characteristics of high- and low-context cultures

Chapter Summary

This chapter discussed the pivotal topic of communication across cultures. Communication comes in many different forms, yet managers sometimes mistakenly assume that is interpreted the same everywhere, actual language differences aside. The single most important way that we communicate is through the spoken word. Some countries, such as the U.S., are largely monolingual and thus foreign-language skills rank among the weakest in the world. Yet, some U.S. firms feel that these "deficits" are not a big problem because English tends to be the de facto language of world business. Native English speakers, however, still run the risk of communication problems across borders and cultures.

Differences are also apparent in written communication styles. Americans tend to keep their letters and memos informal, short, and "to the point," generally avoiding flowery or exaggerated language. Other cultures have written communication norms that require background information and other social customs. Even if you understand the communication style of an international business colleague, you could still experience *bypassing*—a miscommunication that occurs when the same words are defined differently. *Nonverbal communication* is the transmission of messages without the use of words or writing and can help people better interpret what is being said, but is hardly foolproof. Overall, global firms are getting savvier about their communication processes, especially those who use training.

Discussion Questions

1. Explain why both spoken and written communication presents many challenges to cross-cultural communications.
2. How might various dimensions of culture (e.g., collectivism, power distance, and uncertainty avoidance) affect the types of communication discussed in this chapter?
3. How would a country's position on the context dimension affect its communication patterns? Have you seen differences among your international peers at your university?

Up to the Challenge?

Advances in Intercultural Communication—the Low-Tech Way

At the beginning of this chapter we described challenges facing Greg Caltabiano, a newly hired chief executive of a small, privately held, California-based telecommunications firm. It appeared as though, at the minimum, his U.S.-based engineers needed a better understanding of the firm's Asian customers, because Asia was the location of the majority of their sales. For their part, the engineers felt that they were being given confusing, and sometimes conflicting, messages from customers, as well as feedback that came late in the design process. Overall, this important communication left something to be desired, at least from a cross-cultural communication standpoint. Mr. Caltabiano's experience fit the position requirements well and it was hoped that his 14 years in Japan and China working for another telecom firm and his understanding of cross-culture communications would greatly benefit the firm.[85]

Mr. Caltabiano spent the next two years building communication bridges between his Teknovus employees and their customers and staff overseas. One of his first actions was to start sending employees on short visits to Asia so they might better understand, on a first-hand basis, the cross-cultural challenges faced at home. Over a relatively short period of time, 70 of the firm's 95 engineers traveled and met customers and others with whom they only previously communicated with via long-distance. In turn, Teknovus's new hires overseas are required to visit the U.S. Both sets of employees say that this increased contact has resulted in much greater responsiveness to customer needs—something that is overlooked too often in even domestic engineering firms. The effects seemed to have taken root. In just three years, sales more than doubled to $50 million. New market shares in China and the addition of Japanese customers now included in their product-planning are very positive signs.

Experts such as Professor Mary Brannen, a professor at the prestigious INSEAD business school in France, applaud these and related efforts. "International operations are often plagued by mistrust and frustration . . . [In order] to build mutual understanding, employees must learn about different customers and the reasons for those differences," says Professor Brannen. It was not uncommon several years ago for Teknovus's customers to interact mostly with sales managers assigned to their region, and only occasionally to problem-solve with their engineers. Yet, because of the nature of the product application (fiber-optic communication networks), it was necessary for the Asian telecom staff and the local carriers that operate the networks to seek help from Teknovus's engineers. Previously, when overseas customers requested new features or bells and whistles, Teknovus engineers sometimes resisted when, say, a Japanese customer wanted detailed reports for problems that they encountered.

Mr. Caltabiano attacked communication problems by first elevating the status of the foreign offices. He eliminated the U.S.-based sales director and instead had the country directors report to him. Likewise, he had U.S. employees become liaisons that represent overseas offices at meetings and more, and their role was to defend their interests—even to skeptical colleagues. Recently, when the engineers became frustrated because of so many changes to technical specs by Teknovus's Korean office, the liaison was able to soothe concerns by showing this was a big customer and capable of being even bigger. Employees were also urged to phone their counterparts, rather than only e-mail them, in hopes of improving communication. This helped the engineers learn, among other things, that Japanese customers want detailed reports for problems because they in turn are often asked by their partner companies to explain those issues. "It's not torture . . . it's how they do it," said a Teknovus employee. The overseas visits continue to pay dividends and are in part what has led those Japanese firms to include Teknovus early in their (sensitive) development plans. Headquarters engineers now visit the Japanese office monthly to demo new products and to network. As the General Manager in Japan said, "until now, I'd mostly felt that I was explaining the local market" to the California-based engineers. "Now, each person experiences it for themselves." So, apparently, good old-fashioned face-to-face communication and attention to customers still works these high-tech dominated days.

In a recent *Wall Street Journal* article, Mr. Caltabiano offered some communication tips to others trying to bridge the overseas divide:[86]

- Try to go beyond what is actually said—the words—to a larger meaning.

- When you are experiencing a lot of conflict, look for communication problems first as the source.

- Encourage more direct interaction between U.S. employees and foreign-based employees and customers; make sure that voices are heard at headquarters.

- Assign someone to monitor and improve international communications.

International Development

Moshi, Moshi: Overcoming Cultural Barriers to Communication

Purpose

To understand how culture can impact verbal communication in a telephone conversation and to suggest alternative ways to conduct telephone conversations effectively in a given cross-cultural context.

Instructions

Read the following telephone transcript. John Smith, an American marketing manager from Weyerhaeuser, is trying to speak with his Japanese counterpart at Rising Sun Company, a Mr. Yamamoto, about a possible business deal.

The conversation

The phone rings and a woman answers.

Woman: *Moshi, moshi* ["Hello, Hello"].
Smith: Hello, this is John Smith. May I please speak with Mr. Yamamoto?
Woman: Oh, I'm sorry. Who is calling, please?
Smith: This is John Smith calling for Mr. Yamamoto.
Woman: I'm sorry, what is the name of your company?
Smith: I'm calling from Weyerhaeuser.
Woman: I'm sorry, could you spell that, please?
Smith: W-E . . .
Woman: I'm sorry, "W-Z"?
Smith: No, W-E-Y-E-R-H-A-E-U-S-E-R. Is Mr. Yamamoto there?
Woman: Oh, Weyerhaeuser. Thank you very much. Your name please?
Smith: John Smith.
Woman: And who do you wish to speak to?
Smith: As I said, Mr. Yamamoto.
Woman: I'm sorry, which department? We have many Yamamotos.
Smith: Uh . . . of course. Mr. Yamamoto in the international marketing department.
Woman: Thank you very much, wait just a minute please.

(Smith is put on hold. Music plays in the background. Meanwhile, a phone rings in a big room where many employees are working at their desks. Someone passing by picks up the phone.)

Man: Moshi, moshi.
Smith: Hello, Mr. Yamamoto?
Man: Oh no, this is Suzuki. Who is calling, please?
Smith: This is John Smith calling for Mr. Yamamoto.
Man: I'm sorry, what is the name of your company?
Smith: Weyerhaeuser.
Man: Could you spell that, please?
Smith: W-E-Y-E-R-H-A-E-U-S-E-R.
Man: Thank you very much. Just a minute please.
(On hold again. Music plays).
Man: I'm very sorry, but Mr. Yamamoto is in a meeting. Could you call again later?
(Intensely frustrated, Smith hangs up the phone after "wasting" an international call.)

Your instructor will divide the class into small groups of three to six to answer the following questions (15–20 minutes). Your group can present its answers, followed by a general class discussion about international communication and its implications (30 minutes). Alternatively, your instructor may lead a general class discussion about the following questions:

- Why is Smith so frustrated? Would you be in this situation? What cultural factors explain Smith's reaction (and perhaps yours)?

- What mistakes did Smith make, in your opinion? Why? How do Japanese culture and business practices fit in here?

- How would you recommend that Smith approach the call if he had to do it all over again? What specific advice would you offer? Why?

- What if the cultural context was different? For instance, what if Mr. Smith was trying to reach a counterpart in Cairo? How might that shape Mr. Smith's approach to the conversation?

Source: Elashmawi, F., and Harris, P. H. (1993). *Multicultural Management: New Skills for Global Success*, 108–111. Houston: Gulf. Reprinted by permission.

From Theory to International Practice

We Have Ways of Making You Talk: Researching a Foreign Language

Purpose

To examine a few basic elements of a language with which you are not familiar and to appreciate a few of the problems that foreign nationals might have as they take their basic language tools and apply those to English.

Instructions

Step 1

Select a language with which you are not at all familiar. Research some basics about this language and prepare a few statements and greetings from the language to present to class (more detail on this is provided below). Your instructor might want to assign individual students or groups to various languages in order to make sure that several different ones are covered and to make sure that the groups have no familiarity with the language basics. Either way, we recommend looking at the following website that provides briefings on many different languages spoken throughout the world: http://123world.com/languages/index.html. It is unlikely, for example, that many students (or professors!) are very familiar with languages such as Afrikaans, Arabic, Dutch, Farsi, Hindi, Japanese, Russian, Swahili, Turkish, or many others, and this site will provide many such choices.

Step 2

Once you have chosen a language, you should begin to gather information that will give you a bit of insight into some basic features of the language and those speaking it. In particular, we recommend that you discover the following (with possible supplements provided by your instructor):

- Where is the language spoken as the primary one, and how many people speak it? Where else has it been adopted (if at all)?

- What are the origins of the language and how is it related to others and other families of language?

- What is unique or specific to the language (e.g., its grammar, syntax, accent marks, etc.)?

- Present several basic phrases in that language to the class/in your report. If the report is given verbally, you should try to pronounce those phrases or use some of the sources below to present the phrases to the class (several sites offer .wav files that most any class computer could read so that the phase could be heard in a native tongue).

- What types of challenges might native speakers of this language face when communicating to English speakers? That is, what are some transfer issues if they tried to speak in English (e.g., their tones, accents, sounds that are wildly different) and if their communication was translated into English by others?

- Do you have any recommendations for communication training or a possible set of guidelines or advice to give speakers of this language?

Step 3

Once you have chosen a language and considered the questions from Step 2, you can begin your research. There are several good sources to begin your work on this assignment, using the following suggestions as a starting point.

Resources

- **The Linguist List** (http://linguistlist.org/sp/Dict.html): this super site, run by Eastern Michigan and Wayne State Universities, presents an amazing number of bilingual and multilingual dictionaries and translation tools. Some of the nearly 200 such dictionaries offer complete translation of phrases that you enter in English.

- **The Linguist List Subpage** (http://linguistlist.org/sp/LangAnalysis.html#25): this page is also part of The Linguist List, but it could be missed in all the wealth of information provided on the site. Presented here are a large number of links to language families and many language meta-sites. Some of these will be helpful for the background research required in this assignment.

- **Other sources for your research:**
  - http://globaledge.msu.edu/global-resources/language-resources
  - www.ethnologue.com
  - http://www.ilovelanguages.com/index.php?category=Languages
  - http://babel.uoregon.edu/.

Notes

1. Dvorak, P. (2009). Frequent contact helps bridge interaction divide. Chip-designer Teknovus improves Asian ties by raising status of overseas offices, encouraging staff visits. *The Wall Street Journal*, June 1, B4.

2. Adair, C. (2000). Don't get into cultural hot water. *The Toronto Star*, August 9, G6.

3. Damerow, R., and Bailey, K. M. (2011). The language of business. *BizEd*, September/October, 70–71; Jandt, F. E. (2001). *Intercultural Communication: An Introduction*. Thousand Oaks, CA: Sage.

4. Adair, Don't get into cultural hot water.

5. *The Economist*. (1999). Chinese whispers, January 30, 77–79.

6. Graddol, D. (2000). The future of English. A guide to forecasting the population of the English language in the 21st century. The British Council: The English Company (UK), Ltd, available at: www.britishcouncil.org/learning-elt-future.pdf (retrieved January 29, 2013). Note that these data are a decade old and that there are disagreements about these numbers. For example, the National Language Commission of China itself questioned these numbers. They estimated that only 53 percent of China could speak Mandarin, and even many of those people actually prefer to speak a more familiar Chinese language. See *Taipei Times* (2005). Half of all Chinese people cannot speak Mandarin: Report, May 23.

7. U.S. Census Bureau. (2007). *Factfinder*, available at: http://factfinder.census.gov; *The Economist*. (2006). They all speak English: As bilingualism becomes the norm worldwide, the future of English has moved. December 13, 4–6; U.S. Government. (2009). Americans breaking out of their English-only shells: Better resources, opportunities encourage U.S. foreign language students, available at: www.america.gov/st/washfile-english/2006/March/20060302142421aje srom0.4190485.html#ixzz0JBQD0RQn&C.

8. *The Economist*. (2006). God's worst linguists. If the world is learning English, why on earth should the British learn the world's languages? December 13, 1–3; *The Economist*, They all speak English; Dulek, R. E., Fielden, J. S., and Hill, J. S. (1991). International communication: An executive primer. *Business Horizons*, 34, 20–25.

9. Anon. (2004). 1.4 million students studying foreign language. *MLA Newsletter*, Winter–Spring; Commission on the Abraham Lincoln Study Abroad Fellowship Program (2005) *Global Competence and National Needs: One Million Americans Studying Abroad*. Washington, DC: Lincoln Commission.

10. Graddol, D. (2008). *English Next: Why Global English May Mean the End of English as a Foreign Language*. London: British Council, available at: www.britishcouncil.org; *Financial Times*. (2001). Multilingual website widens the way to a new online world, February 7, 1; Miniwatts Marketing Group. (2011). Internet world users by language. Internet world statistics, May 31, available at: www.internetworldstats.com/stats7.htm (retrieved January, 31, 2013).

11. Dyer, G. (2012). The triumph of English. *Pittsburgh Post-Gazette*, May 27, B1, B4; Fox, J. (2000). The triumph of English. *Fortune*, September, 18, 209–212.

12. Daniels, J. D., Radebaugh, L. H., and Sullivan, D. P. (2004). *International Business: Environments and Operations*. Upper Saddle River, NJ: Pearson Prentice Hall.

13. *Miami Herald*. (2001). Experts: English language faces increasing corruption. March 25, 21A.

14. Song, J. A. (2008). South Koreans step up to learn English. *Financial Times*, April 3, 19.

15. Graddol, D. (2008). *English Next*.

16. Boone, J. (2006). Native English speakers face being crowded out of market. *Financial Times*, February 15, 8; *The Economist*. (2001). English is still on the march. February 24, 50–51; Fox, The triumph of English.

17. Tietze, S. (2008). *International Management and Language*. New York: Routledge. See also: Charles, M. (2007). Language matters in global communication. *Journal of Business Communication*, 44, 260–282.

18. Matsutani, M. (2010). Rakuten to hold all formal internal meetings in English. *The Japan Times Online*, May 18, available at: http://search.japantimes.co.jp (retrieved January 2, 2010); Wakabayashi, D. (2010). English gets the last word in Japan. *The Wall Street Journal*, August 6, B1, B2. Matsutani, M. (2010). Rakuten's all-English edict a bold move, but risky too. *The Japan Times Online*, July 16, available at: http://search.japantimes.co.jp (retrieved January 2, 2010).

19. *The Economist.* (2011). Tongues under threat: English is dangerously dominant, January 22, 58.

20. *The Economist.* (2012). Twtr: Which tongues work best for microblogs? March 31, 71; Dvorak, P. (2007). Plain English gets harder in global era. *The Wall Street Journal*, November 5, B1; Boone, Native English speakers face being crowded out of market; Ling, C. (2001). Learning a new language. *The Wall Street Journal,* March 12, R18.

21. Dvorak, Plain English gets harder in global era.

22. McCrum, R. (2010). English + Microsoft = Globish. *Newsweek*, June 12, 31–33.

23. Areddy, J. T., Sanders, P., and Lin, B. (2009). Chinese learn English the Disney way. *The Wall Street Journal*, April 28, B1, B5;

24. Ortega, A. (2006). How Brussels is coping with the growing tower of Euro-babel languages. *Financial Times*, January 27, 5; Dempsey, J. (2002). Brussels faces a real tongue twister: EU enlargement will test the Commission's commitment to linguistic diversity. *Financial Times*, January 26, 6.

25. *The Wall Street Journal.* (1999). Korean airlines faulted on safety by internal study, April 8, A1; Nicholson, M. (1996). Language error seen as cause of Indian air disaster. *Financial Times*, November 14, 18; Glain, S. (1994). Language barrier proves dangerous in Korea's skies. *The Wall Street Journal*, October 4, B1.

26. Fixman, C. S. (1990). The foreign language needs of U.S.-based corporations. *The Annals of the American Political and Social Science Association*, 511, 25–46.

27. Dulek, Fielden, and Hill, International communication: An executive primer.

28. Dvorak, Plain English gets harder in global era; Boone, J. (2006). Native English speakers face being crowded out of market. *Financial Times*, February 15, 8; Flintoff, J. P. (2001). Sayonara to ceremony: The Japanese are having to learn to be more rude and are using English to help them. *Financial Times*, May 5, 1; see also these case study examples of similar problems experienced by many other companies: www.globalenglish.com/m/successful_results/case_studies/.

29. Quotes and examples taken from: Dvorak, Plain English gets harder in global era; also cited: Barnes, W. (2008). Tricky feats of cross-cultural communication. *Financial Times*, August 7, 18.

30. McCrum, English + Microsoft = Globish.

31. Hookway, J. (2012). IKEA's products make shoppers blush in Thailand. Swedish retailer hires local linguists to police racy translations. *The Wall Street Journal*, June 5, B7.

32. *Advertising Age.* (1987). Viewpoint: Letters, June 29, 20; Ricks, D. A. (1983). *Big Business Blunders: Mistakes in Multinational Marketing.* Homewood, IL: Dow Jones Irwin.

33. Chai, B. (2011). In "Chinglish," language barriers are a bad sign of current times. *The Wall Street Journal*, October 10, B6; Clark, D. (1996). Hey, #!@*percent amigo, can you translate the word "gaffe"? *The Wall Street Journal,* July 6, B6.

34. Victor, D. A. (1992). *International Business Communication.* New York: Harper Collins.

35. Koide, F. (1978). Some observations on the Japanese language. In J. C. Condon and M. Saito (eds), *Intercultural Encounters with Japan. Communication, Contact and Conflict*, 173–179. Tokyo, Japan: Simul Press.

36. Kashima, Y., and Kashima, E. S. (2003). Individualism, GNP, climate, and pronoun drop. *Journal of Cross-Cultural Psychology*, 34, 125–134; Kashima, E. S., and Kashima, Y. (1998). Culture and language: The case of cultural and personal pronoun use. *Journal of Cross-Cultural Psychology*, 29, 461–486.

37. Kemmelmeier, M., and Cheng, B. Y. (2004). Language and self-construal priming : A replication and extension in a Hong Kong sample. *Journal of Cross-Cultural Psychology*, 35, 705–712. Gardner, W. L., Gabriel, S., and Lee, A. Y. (1999). "I" value freedom, but "we" value relationships: Self-construal priming mirrors cultural differences in judgment. *Psychological Science*, 10,

321–326; Trafimow, D., Silverman, E. S., Fan, R. M.-T., and Law, J. S. F. (1997). The effects of language and priming on the relative accessibility of the private self and the collective self. *Journal of Cross-Cultural Psychology*, 28, 107–123.

38. Barnlund, D. C. (1989). Public and private self in communicating with Japan. *Business Horizons*, 32, 32–40; Tung, R. L. (1984). How to negotiate with the Japanese. *California Management Review*, 26, 62–77.

39. Barnlund, Public and private self in communicating with Japan; Haneda, S., and Shima, H. (1982). Japanese communication behavior as reflected in letter writing. *Journal of Business Communication*, 19, 19–32.

40. Barnlund, D. C., and Araki, S. (1985). Intercultural encounters: The management of compliments by Japanese and Americans. *Journal of Cross-Cultural Psychology*, 16, 9–26.

41. Almaney, A., and Alwan, A. (1982). *Communicating with Arabs*. Prospect Heights, IL: Waveland Press, cited in G. L. Nelson, W. El Bakary and M. Al Batal. (1993). Egyptian and American compliments: A cross-cultural study. *International Journal of Intercultural Relations*, 17, 293–313.

42. Copeland, L., and Griggs, L. (1985). *Going International*. New York: Random House.

43. McFarlin, D. B., and Sweeney, P. D. (2000). *Where Egos Dare: The Untold Truth about Narcissistic Leaders and How to Survive Them*. London: Kogan-Page.

44. Semin, G. R., and Rubini, M. (1990). Unfolding the concept of person by verbal abuse. *European Journal of Social Psychology*, 20, 463–474; Gudykunst, W. B., and Nishida, T. (1993). Interpersonal and intergroup communication in Japan and the United States. In W. B. Gudykunst (ed.), *Communication in Japan and the United States*, 149–214. Albany: SUNY Press.

45. Garris, C. P., Ohbuchi, K., Oikawa, H., and Harris, M. (2011). Consequences of interpersonal rejection. *Journal of Cross-Cultural Psychology*, 42, 1066–1083; Copeland and Griggs, *Going International*; Victor, *International Business Communication*.

46. Chentsova-Dutton, Y., and Vaughn, A. (2012). Let me tell you what to do: Cultural differences in advice-giving. *Journal of Cross-Cultural Psychology*, 43, 687–703.

47. Imahori, T. T., and Cupach, W. R. (1994). A cross-cultural comparison of the interpretation and management of face: American and Japanese responses to embarrassing predicaments. *International Journal of Intercultural Relations*, 18, 193–219; Sueda, K. and Wiseman, R. L. (1992). Embarrassment remediation in Japan and the U. S. *International Journal of Intercultural Relations*, 16, 159–173.

48. Barnlund, D. C., and Yoshioka, M. (1990). Apologies: Japanese and American styles. *International Journal of Intercultural Relations*, 14, 193–206; Smith, P. D. (2011). Communication styles as dimensions of national culture. *Journal of Cross Cultural Psychology*, 42, 216–233.

49. Tata, J. (2000). Toward a theoretical framework of intercultural account-giving and account evaluation. *The International Journal of Organizational Analysis*, 8, 155–178.

50. Dvorak, P. (2000). Japanese dairy pours on the apologies: Snow Brand puts humility first after big recalls. *The Wall Street Journal*, July 12, A21.

51. Kadiangandu, J. K., Gauche, M., Vinsonneau, G., and Mullet, E. (2007). Conceptualizations of forgiveness: collectivist-Congolese vs. individualist-French viewpoints. *Journal of Cross-Cultural Psychology*, 38, 432–437; Sandage, S. J., and Williamson, I. (2005). Forgiveness in cultural context. In E. L. Worthington (ed.), *Handbook of Forgiveness*, 41–56. New York: Routledge.

52. Gilovich, T., Wang, R. F., Regan, D., and Nishina, S. (2003). Regrets of action and inaction. *Journal of Cross-Cultural Psychology*, 34, 61–71.

53. Thatcher, J. B., Srite, M., Stepina, L. P., and Liu, Y. (2003). Culture, overload and personal innovativeness with information technology: Extending the homological net. *Journal of Computer Information Systems*, 44, 74–81; Leidner, D. E., Carlsson, S., Elam, J., and Corrales, M. (2000). Mexican and Swedish managers' perceptions of the impact of EIS on organizational intelligence, decision making, and structure. *Decision Sciences*, 30, 633–661.

54. LaFerle, C., Edwards, S. M., and Mizuno, Y. (2002). Internet diffusion in Japan: Cultural considerations. *Journal of Advertising Research*, 42, 65–79.

55. Guo, Z., Tan, F. B., Turner, T., and Xu, H. (2008). An exploratory investigation into instant messaging preferences in two distinct cultures. *IEEE Transactions on Professional Communication*, 51, 396–415; However, see: Wang, J. (2010). Convergence in the rhetorical pattern of directness and indirectness in Chinese and U.S. business letters. *Journal of Business & Technical Communication*, 24, 91–120; and Ding, D. D. (2006). An indirect style in business communication. *Journal of Business & Technical Communication*, 20, 87–100.

56. Survey data cited in Dvorak, Plain English gets harder in global era.

57. Hymowitz, C. (2000). Flooded with e-mail? Try screening, sorting, or maybe just phoning. *The Wall Street Journal,* September 26, B1.

58. Kilpatrick, R. H. (1984). International business communication practices. *Journal of Business Communication*, 21, 33–44.

59. Varner, I. I. (1988). A comparison of American and French business correspondence. *Journal of Business Communication*, 25, 55–65.

60. Boiarsky, C. (1995). The relationship between cultural and rhetorical conventions: Engaging in international communication. *Technical Communication Quarterly*, 4, 245–259; see also Haneda, S., and Shima, H. (1982). Japanese communication behavior as reflected in letter writing. *Journal of Business Communication*, 19, 19–32; Johnson, J. (1980). Business communication in Japan. *Journal of Business Communication*, 17, 65–70.

61. Tim Weiss (1997). Reading culture: Professional communication as translation. *Journal of Business & Technical Communication*, 11: 321–338.

62. Imada, T. (2012). Cultural narratives of individualism and collectivism: A content analysis of textbook stories in the United States and Japan. *Journal of Cross-Cultural Psychology*, 43, 576–591.

63. Kilpatrick, R. H. (1984). International business communication practices. *Journal of Business Communication*, 21, 33–44.

64. Yong, A. (2008). Cross-cultural comparisons of profit. *Journal of Business Ethics*, 82, 775–791; Sullivan, J. J., and Kameda, N. (1983). The concept of profit and Japanese–American business communication problems. *Journal of Business Communication*, 19, 33–39.

65. Rajan, M., and Graham, J. L. (1991). Nobody's grandfather was a merchant: Understanding the Soviet commercial negotiation process and style. *California Management Review*, Spring, 223–239.

66. Brannen, M. Y. (2004). When Mickey loses face: recontextualization, semantic fit and the semiotics of foreignness. *Academy of Management Review*, 29, 593–616.

67. Adapted from and quotes taken from: Jones, D. (2007). Do foreign executives "balk" at sports jargon? *USA Today*, March 30. 1, 4.

68. *Financial Times*. (2008). A word in your ear: keep it slow and simple, August 25. Cited by R. W. Griffin and M. W. Pustay. (2013). *International Business*. Upper Saddle River, NJ: Pearson.

69. Hall, E. T. (1983). *The Dance of Life*. Garden City, NY: Anchor Press; Hall, E. T., and Hall, M. R. (l990). *Understanding Cultural Differences*. Yarmouth, ME: Intercultural Press.

70. Binkley, C. (2008). Americans' learn the global art of the cheek kiss. *The Wall Street Journal*, March 26, B1, B6; Molinsky, A. L., Krabbenhoft, M. A., Ambady, N., and Choi, Y. S. (2005). Cracking the nonverbal code: Intercultural competence and gesture recognition across cultures. *Journal of Cross-Cultural Psychology*, 36, 380–395; see also: McCarthy, A., Lee, K, Itakura, S., and Muir, D. W. (2008). *Journal of Cross-Cultural Psychology*, 39, 716–729.

71. Tracy, J. L., and Robins, R. W. (2008). The nonverbal expression of pride: Evidence for cross-cultural recognition. *Journal of Personality and Social Psychology*, 94, 516–530; Matsumoto, D., and Willingham, B. (2006). The thrill of victory and the agony of defeat: Spontaneous expressions of medal winners of the 2004 Athens Olympic Games. *Journal of Personality and Social Psychology*, 91, 568–581; Ekman, P., and Friesen, W. B. (1987). Universals and cultural differences in the judgments of facial expressions of emotion. *Journal of Personality and Social Psychology*, 53, 712–717.

72. Elfenbein, H. A., and Ambady, N. (2002). On the universality and cultural specificity of emotion recognition: A meta-analysis. *Psychological Bulletin*, 128, 203–235; Mesquita, B., Frijda, N. H., and Scherer, K. R. (1997). Culture and emotion. In J. W. Berry, P. R. Dasen, T. S.

Saraswathi, Y. H. Poortinga, and J. Pandey (eds), *Handbook of Cross-Cultural Psychology: Vol. 2. Basic Processes and Human Development* (2nd ed.), 255–297. Boston: Allyn & Bacon.

73. Marsh, A. A., Elfenbein, H. A., and Ambady, N. (2007). Separated by a common language: Nonverbal accents and cultural stereotypes about Americans and Australians. *Journal of Cross-Cultural Psychology*, 38, 284–301; Marsh, A. A., Elfenbein, H. A., and Ambady, N. (2003). Nonverbal "accents": Cultural differences in facial expressions of emotion. *Psychological Science*, 14, 373–376.

74. McCann, R. M., and Giles, H. (2006). Communication with people of different ages in the workplace: Thai and American data. *Human Communication Research*, 32, 74–108.

75. Knapp, M. (1980). *Essentials of Nonverbal Communication*. New York: Holt, Rinehart and Winston.

76. Barnlund, D. C. (1975). *Public and Private Self in Japan and the United States: Communication Styles of Two Cultures*. Tokyo: Simul Press; Barnlund, Public and private self in communicating with Japan.

77. Collett, P. (1971). Training Englishmen in the nonverbal behavior of Arabs: An experiment on intercultural communication. *International Journal of Psychology*, 6, 209–215.

78. Lee, H. O., and Boster, F. J. (1992). Collectivism–individualism in perceptions of speech rate: A cross-cultural comparison. *Journal of Cross-Cultural Psychology*, 23, 377–388.

79. Peng, Y., Zebrowitz, L. A., and Lee, H. K. (1993). The impact of cultural background and cross-cultural experience on impressions of American and Korean male speakers. *Journal of Cross-Cultural Psychology*, 24, 203–220.

80. We thank an anonymous reviewer for these comments and insights.

81. Williamson, P., and Zeng, M. (2004). Strategies for competing in a changed China. *Sloan Management Review*, 45, 85–91.

82. Hall, E. T. (1976). *Beyond Culture*. Garden City, NY: Anchor Press; Hall, E. T., and Hall, M. R. (1990). *Understanding Cultural Differences*. Yarmouth, ME: Intercultural Press.

83. Elliot, S., Scott, M. D., Jensen, A. D., and McDonough, M. (1982). Perceptions of reticence: A cross-cultural investigation. In M. Burgoon (ed.), *Communication Yearbook 5*. New Brunswick, NJ: Transaction Books.

84. Victor, D. A. (1992). *International Business Communication*. New York: Harper Collins.

85. Dvorak, P. (2009). Frequent contact helps bridge interaction divide. Chip-designer Teknovus improves Asian ties by raising status of overseas offices, encouraging staff visits. *The Wall Street Journal*, June 1, B4.

86. Dvorak, Plain English gets harder in global era; Skapinker, M. (2008). A word in your ear: keep it slow and simple. *Financial Times*, August 26, 9.

Case 2: Chiba International, Inc.

Ken Morikawa, the general manager for administration of a Japanese manufacturing plant under construction in rural Georgia, was troubled. This morning his American personnel manager, John Sinclair, had walked eagerly across the temporary open-plan office and announced: "I've found a professor of Japanese at Georgia State University who is willing to help translate our corporate philosophy. I would like to hire him for the job."

Ken felt pressured. He thought that John Sinclair, like many Americans, was expecting too much of Japanese companies. The company philosophy that he, Ken, had learned to live by in Tokyo would continue to guide him, but he did not feel that Americans would welcome or even understand a Japanese company philosophy.

Ken had a very large task to do in supervising the building of a plant that might ultimately provide jobs for up to 2,000 employees in an area where very few workers had had any industrial experience. He wished to show that his was a company that cared about the welfare of its workers and their job security, and could be trusted to treat them fairly and not lay them off. He believed that such a philosophy, if it could be properly explained to workers and carefully implemented, would help to build high morale among the employees and consequently improve productivity.

Ken also wanted to ensure that high morale be maintained as the workforce expanded to full capacity. Indeed, aside from issues of ease of transportation and distribution, the characteristics of the local workforce, their "Japanese" work ethic, had been one of the primary reasons for establishing the plant here. He believed that the training costs involved in transforming very "green" workers were well worth it, to avoid people who had picked up "bad habits" or had had their morale lowered in previous industrial jobs. In Japan, teaching company philosophy is an important part of the company's introductory training program. But will it work here?

Ken wondered if his new administrative duties were lowering his concern for personnel matters. Ever since he had had to read Alfred Sloan's *My Years with General Motors* during the company training program and had written a review that focused on human resource issues, he had held positions related to his field. Even though he had majored in mathematical economics in college, his first assignment had been in the personnel "design center," which controlled training and salary administration for white-collar employees. After two years he was sent to a district office as a salesman. He returned after 13 months to the employee welfare section of the personnel department at the head office, administering such programs as house loans and recreational activities. Eight years with the company had passed by the time he was sent to an American college to study personnel-related subjects and improve his English.

After receiving his MBA he returned to the head office. His most recent assignment before coming to Georgia was in personnel development research, planning new wage systems. It was expected that in his new job in Georgia he would eventually hand the reins over to an American general manager and remain only in an advisory capacity. However, he felt that it was at this vital stage that the corporation depended on his human relations expertise to set the scene for future success. Was he neglecting an area in which he had been trained to be sensitive?

He brought the subject up at lunch with John Sinclair. "Let me tell you something, John. I have a hunch why the Japanese are more successful in achieving high quality and productivity than Americans have been recently. It has to do with application, rather than ideas. Many great ideas have come from the United States, but the Japanese concentrate on applying them very carefully. Americans emphasize creating something new and then moving on. The Japanese meticulously analyze a problem from all angles and see how a solution might be implemented.

"As they say, Rome wasn't built in a day. I'm not sure our American workers will understand what it really means to have a company philosophy. Let's take is slowly and see what kind of people we hire and then see what best meets their needs."

John, who had worked at a rather traditional U.S. company for 11 years and had become increasingly interested in how Japanese companies managed their U.S. employees, had been eager to join a Japanese company. He wanted to see in action such "Japanese" strategies as long-term employment, the expression of a company philosophy, and careful atten-

tion to integrating the employees into the company. He answered comfortingly, "Ken, I know you hate conflict. But I also know that you think it important to gather information. One of our purchasing agents, Billy, told me about a Japanese company that he recently visited, Chiba International. Apparently, they already have a fully developed company philosophy and I understand that they are doing very well with it. Why don't we go out to California and talk with their management and try and understand how and why they concentrated on communicating their philosophy?"

"And soak up some sun, too," beamed Ken. "You're on!"

The Company

Chiba International Inc. in San Jose, California, makes high-precision, sophisticated electronics parts used in the final assembly of customized and semi-customized integrated circuits— particularly the expensive memory chips used in computers and military hardware. In such products, reliability is everything, price a lesser consideration. The similar but cheaper parts that manufacturers use once a product reaches a high volume are left for others to make.

Chiba International is a subsidiary of Chiba Electronics Company. *Nihon Keizai Shimbun*, Japan's preeminent business paper, recently ranked Chiba Electronics as one of the foremost companies in Japan on the basis of its management earnings stability and performance, ahead of such better-known giants as Sony, Matsushita Electric, and Toyota Motor. Chiba Electronics Co. has 70 percent of the world market for its products. Chiba International likewise has a 70 percent share of the U.S. market.

Chiba International started in the United States 12 years ago, with a small sales office. A manufacturing plant that had been losing $100,000–200,000 a month was acquired from an American competitor. The American management was terminated, and a team of Japanese headed by a Canadian-born Japanese-reared executive succeeded in turning it around within two years.

Today 14 out of the 24 top executives and 65 out of 70 salesmen at Chiba are Americans. All of the employees in other categories are also American.

Chiba's Philosophy

As the sun rises brilliantly in the sky,
Revealing the size of the mountain, the market,
Oh this is our goal.
With the highest degree of mission in our heart
we serve our industry,
Meeting the strictest degree of customer requirement.
We are the leader in this industry and our future path
Is ever so bright and satisfying.

"That's a translation of our company song," said a high-ranking Japanese executive, one of the group of Japanese and American managers who had agreed to meet with Ken and John. "But we haven't introduced it to our employees yet. That's typical of the way we brought the company philosophy to our employees—slowly and carefully. Every line worker gets a leaflet explaining our company philosophy when he or she starts work. We don't have a specific training session on it and we don't force them to swallow it. It's up to them to digest and understand it."

"What about when you acquire a company as you have done over the past few years?" asked John.

"The same thing. It's very gradual. If we force it, it causes nothing but indigestion. Here it has been easy, the work is very labor intensive, repetitive, tedious assembly. In other places the soil is different. At one, for example, almost all the employees are exempts. They understand the philosophy but won't necessarily go by it. Engineers and technical people also seem to be less receptive than people in sales, personnel, and administration. In other sites, though, where the technology is more similar to this, we have had no problem at all."

One of the other managers present in the group, this one American, interrupted to show Ken and John a copy of the leaflet. It was quite rhetorical in tone, but a few paragraphs struck them as particularly interesting.

Management Philosophy
Our goal is to strive toward both the material and spiritual fulfillment of all employees in the Company, and through this successful fulfillment, serve mankind in its progress and prosperity.

Management Policy
Our purpose is to fully satisfy the needs of our customers and in return gain a just profit for ourselves. We are a family united in common bonds and singular goals. One of these bonds is the respect and support we feel for our fellow family co-workers.

Also, the following exhortation:

When there is a need, we all rally to meet it and consider no task too menial or demeaning; all that matters is that it should be done! We are all ready to sweep floors, sort parts, take inventory, clean machines, inspect parts, load trucks, carry boxes, wash windows, file papers, run furnaces, and do just about anything that has to be done.

Meetings

"Daily meetings at the beginning of each shift are held in the courtyard," explained the group. "All the workers stand in lines (indicated by metal dots in the asphalt). Each day, a different member of management speaks for about five minutes. On Mondays, executives speak, on Tuesday, personnel and administration are represented, Wednesdays are about safety concerns, and on Thursdays and Fridays, members of production and sales speak. They all are free to say whatever they like. The shift workers tend to develop favorites, especially among the more extroverted sales managers.

"Then a personnel coordinator delivers news about sports events and so on, and perhaps a motivational message, and goes on to lead the group in exercises for one minute. These calisthenics are voluntary, but most of the employees join in. After that, the large group breaks up for brief departmental meetings."

"Again, in the departmental meetings, a speaker is chosen for the day and speaks for about five minutes. Even people at the lowest exempt level find themselves speaking. Then the department manager discusses yesterday's performance, today's schedule, and any other messages, such as that housekeeping is inadequate or that certain raw materials are in short supply."

"Once a month, there is an announcement of total company performance versus plans. This is important, as all company employees share at the same rate in the annual company bonus, which is based on profitability and usually equals about one month's salary or wages."

Another Japanese manager continued, "Years ago, there were complaints about having so many meetings, but I haven't heard any for a long time now. The employees like to hear important announcements and even less important ones, such as who is selling theater tickets, bowling league reports, and tennis match dates."

The American personnel manager chimed in: "I was the one who came up with the idea of exercises. I saw it on my visit to Japan. They are just a part of the rituals and symbols that you need in order to get better mutual understanding. The atmosphere was right and the timing was good. Even so, because they weren't mandatory, it took about one-and-a-half years until everyone joined in. Now most people understand the meaning behind it. If we were to stop it now, we'd get complaints."

"Besides the morning meeting, we have several other meetings. On Mondays, we have a very large liaison meeting for information sharing. All the executives attend: sales managers and staff managers, the plant manager and the assistant plant manager. On Tuesdays, we have a production meeting attended by the production managers and any staff involved with their problems. On Monday at four o'clock every second week we have a supervisors' meeting, mainly for one-way communication to them. On the alternating weeks we have a training meeting. The whole personnel department also meets every week."

"Less formally, we have many sales meetings about, for example, new products. We have combination sales and production meetings, which are called on an as needed basis. Team meetings on the production line are also called whenever needed."

"All these formal meetings are supplemented by many company-sponsored activities. We have a company bowling league, tennis matches, softball, fishing, and skiing. We often organize discount tickets. We're planning the Christmas party. Each employee can bring a guest, so it costs us about $40,000. Our company picnic costs $29,000."

"It sounds very well worked out for the nonexempts," commented John. "How about for the exempts?"

Sales Force

They started with the largely American sales force.

"They're a very different species. They have tremendous professional pride. Most of the American sales engineers have a very arrogant take-it-or-leave-it attitude. Our attitude is almost the complete opposite. We try to serve our customer's needs, almost like a geisha girl, who makes her customer feel that he is the only one served by her.

"We try to communicate the following motto to them:

S incerity
A bility
L ove
E nergy
S ervice

"Sincerity is the basic attitude you need to have, as well as the ability to convince the customer. You must love the products that you sell or you can't convince the customer. You must have energy because at the end of the day it's always the case that you could have done one more thing or made one more sales call. Finally, the mentality of serving the customer is the most important."

"We communicate that to our sales force and they like it, especially when they don't have to tell white lies to customers or put up with harassment from customers. We also want them to be honest with us, even about their mistakes. Quite often we depend on the salesmen's input for our understanding of customers, so an objective daily report by telex or phone is very important to us.

"No one in our company works on a commission basis, not even salesmen. We would lose market share for products that are difficult to promote. Also, the nature of different sales territories would make commissions unfair.

"We don't really have a marketing department. We feel that it is an expensive luxury, and, while we have a vice-president in charge of marketing, his is almost a corporate sales staff function."

U.S. Management

John was curious about how American line managers reacted to working in a Japanese company.

A Japanese manager explained: "When Americans join us, they expect the usual great deal of internal politicking. They scan people in meetings, looking for those with real power, looking, to use our expression, for whose apple he should polish. It takes time for them to realize that it's unnecessary."

"When we interview American executives for a job, we do it collectively, so five to ten interviewers are present. This usually puzzles the interviewee. He wonders whom he will report to. We reply that he will be hired by the company, although he may report to one individual. As in Japan, the company will take care of him, so it does not depend on his loyalty to one individual."

"What about your company criteria for hiring managers?" asked John.

"His way of thinking, not necessarily his ability. Although a Harvard MBA is welcomed, it is not essential. In fact, no one here has one. We don't provide an elegant fit to his social elite. There are no private offices. Salary and benefits are up to par for the location (and industry) but not especially high. We work long hours."

"We're looking for devotion and dedication as well as an aggressive attitude. We conduct two or three long interviews for an important position. We ask questions like, 'What is your shortcoming?' We're interested in not the answer itself but in the kind of thinking behind it. We do make mistakes sometimes, but our batting average is good."

"Sometimes there's a very deep communication gap between Japanese management and U.S. management because we believe in dedication and devotion to the company. They do, too, but only to a certain point. We often tell them that the joy of working for the company can be identical to personal happiness with the family. I ask my wife for her understanding of that, and I work six days a week from seven o'clock to ten o'clock. Their wives place demands on them to come home at six o'clock. U.S. executives put personal and family happiness first. I'm not telling you which is right. But it is second nature for me to

think about the future of the company. So long as I have challenging assignments and job opportunities, I will put the company before my personal happiness."

"What do American interviewees feel about all of this?" asked John.

"One problem is that they ask, 'What's my real future? Can I be considered for President?' There's no real answer because it probably will be a Japanese. However, we don't like to close the doors to a really capable American."

"The issue of communication between Japanese and Americans is still a problem. After the Americans go home, the Japanese get together at seven or eight o'clock and talk in Japanese about problems and make decisions without the Americans present. Naturally this makes the Americans feel very apprehensive. We're trying to rectify it by asking the Japanese managers not to make decisions alone and asking the Americans to stay as late as possible."

"More important, if we could really have our philosophy permeate the American managers, we Japanese could all go back to Japan and not worry about it. Our mission is to expedite that day by education and training."

"So far, however, there is a gap. Americans are more interested in individual accomplishment, remuneration, and power. When they are given more responsibility, they don't feel its heavy weight, rather they feel it extends their sovereign area so that they have more of a whip. That creates power conflicts among U.S. managers."

"Let me tell you, though," summarized the American personnel manager, "I like it. I was recruited by a headhunter. Now, I've been with the company five years and the difference from my former employer is astounding. I don't have to get out there and be two-faced, fudging to keep the union out, hedging for the buck. In general, it's hard to find an American employer that really sincerely cares for the welfare of the low-level employee. This company went almost too far in the opposite direction at first. They wanted to do too much for the employees too quickly, without their earning it. That way, you don't get their respect."

Financial People

"Our financial people throughout the company are proud because of our impressive company performance. Only 20 percent of our financing is through debt, in contrast to many Japanese companies. We also have a rather unique way of treating some of our raw materials internally. We try to expense everything out. It's derived from our founder's very conservative management. We ask the question: 'If we closed down tomorrow what would our liquid assets be?' In line with that, for example, internally we put our inventory at zero."

"We follow the 'noodle peddler theory.' The noodle peddler is an entrepreneur. He has to borrow his cart, his serving dishes, and his pan to make ramen. He has to be a good marketer to know where to sell. He has to be a good purchasing director and not over-buy noodles, in case it rains. He could buy a fridge but he would need a lot of capital, the taste of noodles would deteriorate, and he would need additional manpower to keep an inventory of the contents of the fridge. The successful noodle peddler puts dollars aside at the end of the day for depreciation and raw materials for tomorrow. Only then does he count profits. That's also why we don't have a marketing department. The successful peddler doesn't have time to examine opportunities in the next town."

"This is the way a division manager has to operate. In order to maximize output with minimum expenditure, every effort is made to keep track on a daily basis of sales, returns, net shipment costs, and expenses."

Open Communication

"I understand all that you've said so far," mused John, "but how exactly do you take all these abstract philosophical ideas and make them real?"

"Oh, open communication is the key. We have a fairly homogeneous workforce. Most are intelligent, some are even college graduates. Most are also very stable types with dependents or elderly parents they send money to."

"We're lucky, but of course it's not as homogeneous as in Japan where everyone has experienced one culture. So here, the philosophy has to be backed up by a great deal of communication."

"We mentioned the meetings. We also have a suggestion box and we answer all the suggestions in print in the company newspaper. Also, one person from personnel tours the plant all day, for all three shifts, once a week, just chatting and getting in touch with any potential problems as they arise. It's kind of a secondary grievance system. We're not unionized and I guess we'd rather stay that way as it helps us so much with flexibility and job changes among our workforce."

"In the fall, when work is slow, we have many kompas. You may not know about this, John. A kompa is a small gathering off-premises after work. Eight to eighteen people participate and the company pays for their time and refreshments. They're rarely social, they have an objective. For example, if two departments don't get along and they need to work together, they might hold a kompa. A kompa can take place at all levels of the company. Those groups that do it more frequently tend to move on from talking about production problems to more philosophical issues."

Appraisal and Reward Systems

"It all sounds great," sighed Ken, "just as good as Japan. But tell me, how does it tie in with wages and salaries, because people here are used to such different systems?"

"Well, we don't have lifetime employment, but we do have an explicit no-layoff commitment. We are responsible for our employees. This means that employees also have to take responsibility and have broad job categories so we don't have to redo paperwork all the time. We have tried to reduce the number of job classifications to the raw minimum, so we have two pay grades covering 700 workers. At the higher levels, we have three pay grades for craftsman and two for technicians."

John ventured, "I guess an example of your job flexibility in action is the mechanic you mentioned when we toured the plant."

"Yes, the person you spoke with was a dry press mechanic. He's doing menial labor this week, but his pay hasn't been cut and he knows he wouldn't be taken off his job if it weren't important."

"We don't hire outside, if we can avoid it," added the personnel manager. "Only if the skill is not available in-house. The bulk of our training is on-the-job. We don't utilize job postings. We promote when a person's skills are ripe or when there is a need."

"The job of a 'lead' or team leader is the steppingstone to supervisor. It's not a separate job status within our system, but the lead is given a few cents an hour extra and wears a pink, not a yellow, smock. The lead is carefully groomed for his or her position, and although a lead might be demoted because a specific need for them no longer existed, a lead would rarely be demoted for lack of skills or leadership ability."

"Rewards are for service and performance. Plant workers, unskilled and semi-skilled, are reviewed every six months. The lead completes the evaluation form (see Exhibit C.1). This is checked or confirmed by the supervisor and the overall point score translates into cents per hour. There are two copies, one for the supervisor and one for the employee. Depending on the supervisor, some employees get a copy, some don't."

"The office clerical staff are all reviewed on April 1 and October 1. A similar review form for managers is used to determine overall letter scores. All the scores are posted on a spreadsheet and compared across departments, through numerous meetings of managers and personnel people, until the scores are consistent with one another. Then the scores are tied to dollars. Some managers provide feedback, some don't."

EXHIBIT C.1 Evaluation Form.

Employee's Name	Clock No.		Dept.	Shift	Over Last 6-Month Period			
					Days Absent	Number Tardies	Number Early Exit	Work Days Leave of Absences
Employee's Job Title	Anniversary							
Rate on Factors Below:					Numerical Score			
					L	S	M	F
1. LOYALTY/ DEDICATION	Faithful to the company cause, ideals, philosophy, & customers; a devoting or setting aside for company purposes.							
2. SPIRIT/ ZEAL	Amount of interest & enthusiasm shown in work; full of energy, animation, & courage; eagerness & ardent interest in the pursuit of company goals.							
3. COOPERATION	A willingness & ability to work with leaders & fellow employees toward company goals.							
4. QUANTITY OF WORK	Volume of work regularly produced; speed & consistency of output.							
5. QUALITY OF WORK	Extent to which work produced meets quality requirements of accuracy, thoroughness, & effectiveness.							
6. JOB KNOWLEDGE	The fact or condition of knowing the job with familiarity gained through experience, association, & training.							
7. SAFETY ATTITUDE	The willingness & ability to perform work safely.							
8. CREATIVENESS	The ability to produce through imaginative skill.							
9. ATTENDANCE	Includes all types of absence (excused or unexcused), tardies, early exits, leave of absences from scheduled work.							

10. LEADERSHIP	The ability to provide direction, guidance, & training to others.				
OVERALL EVALUATION OF EMPLOYEE PERFORMANCE:					
Supervisor's Approval			Personnel Dept. Approval		
Do Not Write Below This Line — For Human Resource Department Use Only					
Present Base Rate	New Base Rate	Effective Date of Increase	Refer to instructions on the back side of this paper.		

"Exempt staff are reviewed on April 1, and, as a separate process, the spreadsheet procedure just outlined is carried out. At least two managers review any exempt employee, but feedback is usually minimal. The reason is that we encourage feedback all year. If there are no surprises for your subordinate at review time, then you've managed well."

"Agreements on reviews for exempt personnel take place in many meetings at various levels. The process is very thorough and exceptionally fair, and contributes to the levels of performance we get."

Quality and Service

A question from John as to how Chiba International was doing as a result of all this elicited much pride.

"Turnover is two and a half percent a month, which is very satisfactory for our kind of labor given a transient society. We rarely have to advertise for new employees now. The community knows about us. But we do select carefully. The personnel department does the initial screening, and then the production man-agers and supervisors get together and interview people."

"The lack of available technically trained people used to be a big problem, but over the years we've developed the expertise internally. Our productivity is now almost as high as in Japan."

Ken and John asked what other aspects of the company they had not yet discussed. They were told that quality and, hence, customer service was another central part of the philosophy.

"Our founder, Mr. Amano, firmly believes in zero defect theory. Doctor Deming taught us the concept of quality control. Unfortunately, many American companies did not emphasize this. During World War II, the concept of acceptable quality level was developed in the United States. The idea was that with mass production there will be some defects. Rather than paying for more inspectors on the production line, real problems, for example with cars, could be identified by the consumer in the field and repaired in the field."

"We don't allow that. We have 100 percent visual inspection of all our tiny parts. They only cost $50 per 1,000 units.

We inspect every finished package under a microscope so we have 130 inspectors, which is about one-sixth of our production staff."

"The company's founder, Amano, has said to us, 'We try to develop every item our customers want. Being latecomers, we never say no, we never say we can't.' Older ceramic manufacturers would evaluate a proposal on a cost basis and say no. Yet we have been profitable from the start."

As the interview drew to a close, one Japanese manager reflected that Mr. Suzuki has a saying: *ability × philosophy × zeal = performance.*

If the philosophy is negative, performance is negative because it's a multiplicative relationship.

"But in our company, which now numbers 2,000, we must also start to have different kinds of thinking. The Japanese sword is strong because it is made of all different kinds of steel wrapped around one another. The Chinese sword is also very strong, but, because it's all one material, it's vulnerable to a certain kind of shock. We must bear that in mind so that we have differences within a shared philosophy."

"We're thinking of writing a book on our philosophy, addressing such issues as what loyalty is, by piecing together events and stories from our company history. This would be a book that would assist us in training."

Ken and John walked out into the parking lot. "Whew!" sighed John. "It's more complicated than I had thought."

"Oh, yes! You need a great deal of patience," responded Ken paternally.

"So we'd better get started quickly," enthused John. "Where shall we begin? Perhaps I should call the translator."

Assignment Questions

1. Can Japanese management practices work in the United States without adaptation? Why or why not? What cultural values are relevant?

2. How should Ken and John adapt Chiba's California practices to their situation? What problems will they run into (cultural and otherwise)?

3. What aspects of the Japanese approach used by Chiba are the most interesting or unusual to you? Why?

part III

capitalizing on international opportunities

chapter 7

managing conflict and conducting effective negotiations

Learning Objectives

After reading this chapter, you should be able to:

- identify several important causes of cross-cultural conflict;
- understand how other cultures commonly interpret and react to conflict;
- pinpoint some of the more effective methods of managing cross-cultural conflict, including the critical role played by effective negotiations;
- identify the four stages of international negotiation and appreciate how cultural values impact the progress through each stage.

International Challenge

Two Sides of a Common Border: Negotiations between Mexicans and Americans

Two companies, a Swedish firm and an American firm, were vying for a lucrative contract from the Mexican government. Both had already passed several hurdles, leading to an invitation to Mexico City in order to present their proposals to ministry officials. The American team, made up of senior technical experts and lawyers from the New York office, put a lot of effort into producing an impressive, high-tech, and hard-hitting presentation. Their tag line was simple: "We can give you the most technically advanced equipment at a price others can't match." This team met several times with senior management before they made the trip to Mexico City. Agenda topics included several key points of emphasis and possible concessions to make to the Mexicans in order to win the contract. The team also received the green light from management to make needed decisions on the spot.

The American team flew down for a week, staying at one of the top hotels in Mexico City. They had an elaborate conference room reserved so that they could deliver their best possible presentation to ministry officials. In an effort to do their due diligence and to impress, they brought all necessary equipment with them, instead of asking for material upon arrival. They also express-mailed outlines of the presentation to Mexican officials two weeks before the meeting and included a detailed presentation schedule and other activities in an enclosed memo to the officials. For their part, the Mexican officials dutifully thanked the Americans and said that they looked forward to meeting with the team and to finding out more about their proposal and their firm. The ministry officials, in turn, provided the Americans with information about the history of their agency, as well as the top members of the current ministry. The Americans flew in a full day before the presentation to avoid any travel problems and met that afternoon at the conference room to set it up and make sure all was a "go." Finally, at the agreed-upon time the next day, the Americans were all ready to present and to impress.

Unfortunately, the Mexican ministry officials were not—in fact, no one from the ministry was there yet when the agreed-upon meeting time arrived. Instead, various ministry officials arrived to the room gradually over the next hour. They offered no apologies to the perplexed Americans, but instead began to chat amiably about a variety of non-contract-related matters. The American team leader was feeling some pressure from both the situation and his team members—should he act "leaderly" and get the meeting going, or should he let the Mexican officials provide the right signal? Finally, after nearly an hour of glancing at his watch and scanning nervously, the team leader assertively suggested that the meeting should start. For their part, the Mexicans seemed surprised, but politely agreed and took their seats.

The presentation began with informal introductions of the American team members by the team leader. The presentation itself was flawlessly delivered, thanks to the endless practice put in. But, about 20 minutes into the presentation, the minister himself with an entourage of other officials, walked in. When he figured out what was going on, his demeanor turned unpleasant. Angrily, he asked the Americans to start the presentation from the beginning again. They complied and started over. Again, the presentation was going well until about 10 minutes later when an aide arrived with a message for the minister that he delivered to him in hushed tones. Not wanting to anger him again, the American presenter stopped to wait until the message was delivered, but the minister signaled for him to continue. He did, but a few minutes later, a number of audience members were talking among themselves. By this time, the Americans were very frustrated, but they slogged on and finished. At the end, when invited to ask questions, the minister's only comment was to wonder why the Americans had focused so much on the technical details—why had they told the Mexicans so little about their firm's history?

Later, during lunch, the Americans felt that they had to be very forceful about keeping the conversation focused on the topic at hand: the contract and any outstanding issues or problems. Most of the conversation was (again) seemingly casual, having little or nothing to do with their possible business—similar to what they had experienced before the presentation started. The Americans were surprised by the many questions about their individual backgrounds and personal experience, including their qualifications. The minister breezed in during the lunch, had a brief but casual conversation with the American team leader and then left. He did not return.

Over the next several days during their time in Mexico City, the Americans repeatedly contacted the Mexican officials for a follow-up conversation or meeting. Were there additional questions about the specs? Could they provide more detail about the technical features of their implementation? Were there any initial reactions or was more information needed? They reminded ministry officials of the schedule that they shared ahead of time and the fact that they needed to return to New York soon. In short, they wished to start the negotiation process. The Mexican response was the same to each of these forays across the rest of the week: "We need time to examine your proposal among ourselves here first." The Americans reached the end of the week extremely frustrated. After all, the ministry officials had had the proposal for several weeks before the meeting even took place and had also had multiple opportunities for elaboration of the specs and other elements. The Americans left Mexico empty-handed, only to later find out that the contract was awarded to the Swedish firm with whom they were competing.

As you work on this chapter, you will learn how cultural values can impact conflict and negotiation. The tactics and methods used may have a cultural component that's useful to know. You will also read about how managers can overcome the challenges represented in this and related negotiation situations. In the meantime, keep an eye out as you read for cultural sources of conflict between the groups. Think about the characteristic negotiation tactics and strategies that might be used by the Mexican and American negotiators. Then, take a look at the Up to the Challenge? feature at the end of this chapter for some insights into this exchange.[1]

A World of Conflict

In the previous chapter, we provided lot of examples of why and when communication in a global business setting can be a formidable challenge. There are many ways in which a message can be distorted, confused, or missed altogether across cultures, leaving the door wide open for potential differences and disagreements. Miscommunication can lead to conflict. In this chapter, we will review some of the causes of conflict and follow up with how to manage it effectively in an international context. One important conflict management tool is the skill needed to work and negotiate with your partner or adversary. As you will see, the general view of negotiation (as well as the tactics that are used) is the result of many factors. One of the most prominent factors is culture.

Not all conflict is bad, even though it may seem so when you are in the middle of it. Actually, conflict can have positive results. For one, it can help focus attention on critical tasks. It also allows for different perspectives to be put on the table and can clarify issues. Positive or not, conflict is incredibly common: American managers spend about 20 percent of their time at work dealing with conflict situations.[2] Combined with cross-cultural communication problems we reviewed in the previous chapter, we would have to believe that conflict occupies an even greater portion of time for those with international responsibilities.

Cultural Causes of Conflict

Conflict occurs when disagreements and friction arise in the course of social interaction because of opposing interests. Cultural differences in communication styles and the resulting confusion can contribute to these causes. Compounding the challenge for today's managers is the need to act more like diplomats than ever before, with an increasingly burdensome set of "missions" to carry out that can stir up serious disagreements. For example, international managers may have to handle foreign labor strife, negotiate with overseas vendors, tend to unsatisfied clients, deal with partners, manage suppliers, lobby governments, soothe relations with outside groups over environmental or other issues, and somehow convince employees with conflicting interests to work together.[3] That is a plateful of duties.

Given the stakes, though, international managers need a good understanding of the basic causes of conflict. We have already addressed some of these, at least indirectly. For instance, *language* difficulties are one major cause—a mix-up due to a poor translation can cause confusion and anger on both sides of the negotiating table. We also know that differing *cultural norms* may give rise to conflict, especially when each side lacks an appreciation or understanding of the other's frame of reference. Many an American has been greatly offended to be kept waiting well beyond a scheduled appointment time in a foreign country, with individuals even storming out at this "offense."[4] The resulting conflict in this example could have been avoided had the American been aware that she was bringing her monochronic perspective of time into business done in a polychronic culture.[5] Additionally, had the meeting actually taken place, different norms about the directness of communication (e.g., low vs. high context) might have been a source of further conflict.

Different *decision-making methods* can be yet another potential source of conflict. Some international firms are highly centralized, with power concentrated among a few people at the top. Others operate in a more dispersed fashion, with decision-making control decentralized and pushed down into lower ranks. In Chapter 4 we showed that employees in high power distance cultures may have a preference for centralized and hierarchical decision making. In such cultures, attempts to spread out decision making, such as involving employees in goal-setting, can backfire. An example of this is in Figure 7.1. It is possible that this conflict between an American manager and a Greek employee could have been avoided if the American manager had understood the Greek preference for centralization.

Words Spoken	Interpretation by Each Party
American: How long will it take you to finish the report?	*American*: I asked him to participate. *Greek*: His behavior makes no sense. He is the boss. Why doesn't he tell me?
Greek: I don't know. How long should it take?	*American*: He has refused to take responsibility. *Greek*: I asked him for an order.
American: You are in the best position to analyze the time requirements	*American*: I press him to take responsibility for his actions. *Greek*: What nonsense—I'd better give him an answer.
Greek: Ten days.	*American*: He lacks the ability to estimate his time; this estimate is totally inadequate.
American: Take 15. Is it agreed? You will do it in 15 days?	*American*: I offer a contract. *Greek*: These are my orders: 15 days.

Figure 7.1 The Road to Conflict Is Paved with Interpretation: A Conversation between a Greek and an American.

Source: Triandis, H. C. (1977). *Interpersonal Behavior.* Pacific Grove, CA: Brooks/Cole Publishing Company, a division of International Thomson Publishing, Inc. Reprinted by permission.

Finally, the propensity for people in a given culture to be involved with conflict in the first place can drive disagreement. Some cultures go to great lengths to avoid friction between individuals and groups. In collective cultures, various social mechanisms are in place to prevent direct conflict from occurring in the first place. For example, in the previous chapter, we discussed the Japanese practice of using alternate ways to say "no" to avoid confrontation and smooth interpersonal relations. Ironically, this tendency can be extremely frustrating and conflict-provoking when it is used *across* cultures.

The risk of damaging conflict may be highest when a cultural mismatch occurs. When an American, who has a tendency to value open and lively discussion, interacts with a less outspoken Japanese, styles can clash. Although a tendency to be blunt may be seen as laudable and effective within American culture, few traits may be more off-putting to the Japanese. The same can be said about the Thai culture, where kids are taught at a young age to be *sam* ruam—to keep their feelings inside. Conflict in the form of outward expression of anger is seen as ignorant, crude, and immature. In fact, one study found that the Thais are so sensitive to others' negative comments that they downgrade their ratings of interaction with others (feel they're less supportive, helpful) more than do Americans viewing the same behavior.[6] A wider view of this is provided in Figure 7.2, where you will see features about conflict across five different countries.

Views of Conflict	Country				
	China	**Germany**	**Japan**	**Saudi Arabia**	**U.S.**
Avoid conflict?	Yes	No	Yes	Yes/no	No
Degree of directness?	Indirect	Direct	Indirect/subtle	Indirect; face-related concerns are high	Direct
Use of third party/ mediation	Preferred (but a familiar mediator)	Not first choice, but as a way to break deadlock	Can be used, but not common	Yes; go-between can often smooth relations and air difficulties	Not first choice/ but when used, mediator unfamiliar with parties to conflict
Face-saving tendency?	High	Low	High	High	Low
Common reaction to conflict	Discomfort, embarrassment, redirection	Can disagree openly and be blunt. Initial discomfort, but not reluctant to mix it up/ represent themselves	Discomfort, embarrassment, silence	Discomfort; undaunted by lack of progress due to social issues; will stay the course	Initial discomfort, but not reluctant to mix it up/ represent themselves

Figure 7.2 Examples of Differences in Approaches to Conflict in Five Different Countries.

Keep in mind that these are general tendencies; you could easily meet a Thai who is comfortable with out-and-out conflict and an American who shies away from a tussle like it is the plague.

Managing Conflict Effectively

Conflict Styles

If a manager spends a decent amount of time each day dealing with conflict, then how does she typically react to this strife once it raises its head? The quick answer to this question is that there seem to be common and characteristic ways that all of us use to resolve conflict once it occurs. The more effective international managers use those styles to minimize any damage or lingering effects, if not capitalize on the conflict to make positive change. Figure 7.3 shows a layout of these styles.[7] Basically, this approach balances concern for your own outcomes against concern for the outcomes of others with whom you interact. Various combinations of concern for self and the needs of others result in the five distinct styles that are portrayed in the figure. There has been plenty of research done on these styles, although most studies focus on American organizations. The research shows that, even within a culture, there are individual differences in style preferences. You can probably think of someone whose common approach to conflict is to confront it head-on (*competition*), and another who prefers to try to ignore conflict altogether (*avoidance*). The same can be said about *accommodation* (giving in to the other during conflict) and *compromise* (each gives a bit to reach a mutual resolution).

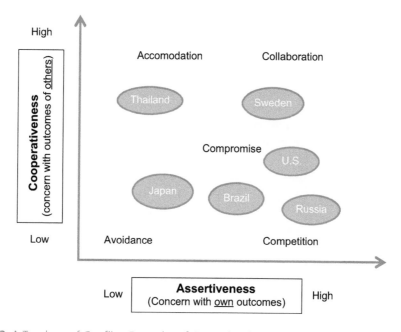

Figure 7.3 A Typology of Conflict: Examples of General Styles by Country.

The collaboration style is the most difficult style to enact and the least common style to possess. This integrative approach is often called a "win–win" where both parties gain (without great compromise) because someone thought of a new, inventive solution. Once people learn or choose a style, they tend to stick with that approach—it becomes part of their personality. For our purposes, however, research does show that some general, culture-based tendencies exist that can distinguish how sets of people tend to handle conflict.

Culture and Characteristic Style

Overall, it appears that, relative to some other nationalities, Americans like a good argument. One study compared Japanese and Americans on a scale that measured the tendency to either embrace or avoid arguments. The results showed that the Japanese were less inclined to argue in the first place, but even once they were involved, their degree of argumentativeness was less than that of the Americans'.[8] Based on this and other studies, some experts have gone so far as to say that Americans feel stimulated by an argument and enjoy the intellectual challenge that it provides.[9] Whether or not that is true, the same cannot be said for the Japanese or some other nationalities. The Japanese are not fond of open conflict, may even feel mortified that it has occurred, and worry that it could disturb group harmony. Based on these findings, it is reasonable to conclude that Americans tend toward the competitive conflict management style while Japanese tend to fall in the avoidance area shown in Figure 7.3. That said, we remind you that these generalizations may not apply to *individual* Americans or Japanese who may use different forms of conflict resolution, but rather to these nationalities as a whole.[10]

Other studies have compared the conflict styles of people from many other countries and cultures. In general, this research finds that people from collectivist cultures tend to *prefer* an avoidance style while people from individualistic cultures tend to prefer a direct, competitive style of dealing with conflict. Examples of countries with a collectivist orientation include China, Japan, Korea, and Mexico, while the U.S. has been the primary individualistic culture studied.[11]

From a Western, and specifically an American, viewpoint, a basic assumption is that conflict is something that should be approached. A manager who "ducks" conflict situations, or fails to approach conflict head-on, can be labeled as *passive aggressive* by colleagues. Yet, in many cultures, avoiding conflict is the better part of valor—at least among one's own in-group. One researcher examined this issue in a study of young adults in Hong Kong and the U.S. They were asked to read about a conflict situation and then to make judgments about what actions they might take if they were involved. Members of both nationalities indicated that they would be more likely to pursue the conflict if the stakes were large and/or if the other party was an "out-group" member. Importantly, though, the Chinese participants were less likely to engage in conflict with an "in-group" member and more likely to engage with an out-group member than were the American respondents.[12] So, as suggested earlier, Americans prefer more active, confrontational approaches, while Koreans, Chinese, and Mexicans tend to use more avoidance-type approaches when handling conflict.[13]

The Meaning of Conflict

We need to understand, however, that avoidance does not necessarily mean the same thing across borders and cultures.[14] For instance, in a collective culture the basis for the value of avoidance is a high concern for others, whereas in individualist (typically Western) cultures it is believed to reflect low concern (compare with Figure 7.3). One study, for example, found that Australians (individualists) rated the competitive style higher and the avoidance style lower than did Chinese students. But, at the same time, when their reputation (or "face") was threatened, respondents from both countries preferred to use direct, assertive approaches to defend themselves.[15] So, it may be that it is the type of conflict that distinguishes cultures.

Plus, more recent research suggests that the reason for the conflict is also a differentiator of cultures. Consider, as an example, if someone asked you to do something but did not offer a good reason for the request. What if you were making photocopies and someone came in and, nearly out of breath, asked, "Can I use this machine because I have to make copies?" Of course they have to make copies—that is why you are there too! Why should you stop and let the other person step in? What would you do in this situation? Would you say no? Would you sidestep the request? Or would you let the individual cut in before you finish?

Researchers set up an experiment that looked at this very situation. Across a series of four studies, Americans and Chinese rejected requests from others when they were not provided with a good reason. Both groups agreed to the request when it was presented with a very good reason (e.g., when a co-worker explained that their boss urgently needed a memo copied to meet an unexpected deadline). It was only when the request occurred in the context of a moderately good reason for needing to jump ahead that differences between groups were found. Then, Americans were more assertive in rejecting the requests than were the Chinese. It appears that under these conditions, Americans' sense of self and the Chinese sense of others are more likely to be activated. This seems to account for the pattern of responses that were observed.[16]

Parties Involved in the Conflict

Experts in conflict resolution also say that preferences may vary depending on *who* is party to the conflict. Managers from Turkey and Jordan, for example, tend to use an overall conflict-handling style that is not much different from their American counterparts. But when peers are involved, Turkish and Jordanian managers tend to avoid conflict; with subordinates, they take a much more forceful approach when conflict erupts.[17]

A similar finding was observed in another study, this time with Chinese, Japanese, and U.S. managers. Researchers studied how these managers might react to a disagreement from the role of a third party—a role that is common in dispute resolution. A simulation was used whereby an argument between two managers occurred and in which a third manager (the study participant) became involved. Respondents were then asked to predict features of the conflict resolution (e.g., What was the final outcome? Who decided it?, etc.). While the results are complex, they do point to the contribution of cultural values in third-party conflict resolution. Briefly, the researchers found that U.S.

and Japanese managers acted in ways we might predict from their typical cultural values (Japan being more hierarchical and traditional than the U.S.). The Chinese managers, however, were much more sensitive to situational cues (e.g., the status of those involved) as evidenced by their deference to those of higher status in their resolution decision. So, while the studies do highlight the impact of culture, they also suggest that culture may be only part of the answer in working through cross-group conflict. A detailed understanding of norms and context can also help predict effective conflict resolution behavior.[18]

Yet, this effect goes both ways: norms can actually emerge from cultural preferences in the first place. Conflict preferences are deeply rooted in culture and extend to many different settings. Consider a ubiquitous business process such as dividing up resources (e.g., raises, promotions) that can be conflict laden. Employees in individualistic cultures often prefer an *equity norm*.[19] In determining pay raises, for example, individual contributions should drive the size of a raise for these individualistic cultures such as American and Australian—"people should get what they have earned or deserve". In these cultures equity is the natural way of doing business. This is the norm for figuring out who deserves what. In collective cultures, however, people have a tendency to prefer an equality norm (every group member gets a more or less equal share of rewards).[20]

These preferences may in part result from inherent cultural differences in dealing with conflict. The Japanese say "the nail that sticks up gets hammered down"—a direct, out-in-the-open conflict style is a "nail" that sticks out in Japan and some other collectivist cultures. In the U.S., however, there are many myths and stories that celebrate rugged individualists (the "nails") who oppose and conflict with the majority ("the squeaky wheels who get the grease"). Finally, the tendency to engage in conflict in the first place is also related to the cultural dimension of uncertainty avoidance. Those cultures high on this value tend to avoid conflict. Clearly, then, there are cultural prescriptions about how to deal with conflict. While individualism may be a virtue for Americans, it can have negative connotations (e.g., selfishness) in other cultures.[21]

The Role of "Face" in Intercultural Conflict

What Is "Face"?

While we have said that conflict may be inevitable across cultures, this does not mean that it occurs with equal frequency across borders. In fact, we have already documented that some cultures generally avoid conflict if possible. More importantly, however, is that cultures typically have mechanisms in place to stifle conflict from happening in the first place. One of these is the notion of "face" or reputation.

This concept is a prime example of the contrasting issues of interpersonal conflict on the one hand and decorum among people on the other. "Face" has a lot to do with the need to obtain and maintain both self-respect and the respect of others. One expert sets this squarely in the area of conflict and negotiation by defining it as "the interaction between the degree of threats or consideration one party offers to another, and the degree . . . of respect put forth by the other party."[22] If there is any behavioral concept that might cut across most cultures, it could be that of face. After all, pride and the respect of others are of great important to most people.

Face can be lost in many ways, including via personal insult (whether intended or not), being forced to make unnecessary concessions, highlighting a failure, mocking cultural values, or damaging a relationship that has been cultivated over time (among many other causes). But, the processes and dynamics of *how* face plays out in and across cultures are different. Some cultures place more value on the importance of respect for others. One of the sharper contrasts that can be drawn is that between some Asian cultures and the general American set of behaviors associated with face. The accompanying International Insights feature demonstrates this and provides some advice to all about being careful and respectful to those in other cultures.

International Insights

Get Out of My "Face": The Importance of Respect Across Cultures

There is little doubt that concern for the respect of others is important in all cultures. But, this notion of "face" is especially important in many Asian cultures. One expert has gone as far to say that "to speak or act in a way that causes an Asian to lose face is tantamount to physical assault in the West." While this statement might be hyperbole, it underscores what many see as an important factor in business communication in Asia. Face is not one-sided here though—it's important to maintain face for others. All 100 Chinese managers in a recent study, for example, said that face was mutual—that it should be returned when it is given.[23] For example, if you were to ask an Asian for directions to the post office, they might actually take you there, even if it is out of the way. If they do not know where it is, they may still point and say, "That way." To not know is to potentially lose face. Conversely, you may not receive valuable and much needed feedback if that information has the potential to be critical of you because doing so may cause *you* to lose face.

The concept of face can explain why some Westerners may perceive Asians as indirect. Americans pride themselves on how direct, frank, and honest they are, and they expect similar behavior when dealing with others. Asians are also very honest people, yet directness, frankness and related features can be prime sources of face loss. Conflict can occur based on how each culture expresses these values, with social norms in Asia often favoring concern for reactions and feelings of others. Schooled in these social demands of face, however, many Asians understand the tacit rules about if and when to covey overt feedback or bad news. These "rules" might sometimes lead to more directness for Asians as well. For example, how do Americans and Chinese react to an angry business partner? As a business partner became more angry (in a negotiation) Chinese reacted by stating higher demands; Americans compromised to the angry partner. The same is true for Americans who know how to decode their rules: feedback should be delivered quickly and directly to those affected. [24]

How does one resolve this culture clash? The solution for Americans is somewhat complex and difficult to enact. One technique is to try to use a more indirect approach to conveying information or resolving conflict. For example, a Western product engineer might ask for any suggestions regarding product design that an Asian may be asked to build. That way, the Asian does not feel compelled to avoid discussion of problems or issues with the design— something that he or she might otherwise do to preserve the reputation of the American. Then, the face of all parties is preserved. Another option might be to work through a third party to convey or solicit news that affects the face of others. The third party could be carefully chosen to be of appropriate status and can have time and background to craft the feedback.

Regardless of the tactics used, the general rule to follow is: do not mistake a smile as a solid connection with your business contact. Quite the contrary—it is actually easy for an American to create resentment and even not pick up on it. If you did offend, it is not likely that you will be told, since no one wants you to lose face. Alternatively, you might be told in such a subtle fashion that you would miss the message anyway. For example, you will find that things will slowly become more difficult, no one will seem very cooperative, and not much will be accomplished. We present a good set of advice within the text itself, but here we will share one suggestion for Westerners that will go a long way toward helping all maintain face and smooth interactions. This expert says, "go slow, be calm, never loud. Listen more than you talk." This is probably good advice for doing business anywhere, especially in Asia.

Social Complexities of Face

To be sure, we have simplified here. For one, face may be different from concepts such as dignity. It appears that face effects result from information provided (or inferred) from others, whereas dignity effects emanate from internal judgments are more impervious to outside impacts. Likewise, the effects of culture on face can be more complex than first assumed, including the involvement of certain social triggers that can make face more important. A recent study looked at one of those triggers—the impact of status in an accounting firm, a setting in which information sharing is vital. Researchers compared Chilean and Chinese managers, countries chosen because of their similar ranking on the Hofstede dimensions (e.g., collectivism, power distance). The study compared the amount of information shared about errors committed by staff accountants when a supervisor was or was not present at a meeting. The results showed little difference between countries when supervisors were *not* present at the meeting, but much less information was shared by the Chinese when their managers *were* at the meeting.[25] Accordingly, we might say that the presence of a superior activates a stronger need to maintain face for Chinese.

Practice Advice about Face

Overall, research provides a complex picture about what face is, and how to give it and keep it. This is understandable since so much is wrapped up in this concept (status, personal worth, family, work success, etc.). For a Westerner not used to doing business in Asia, for example, navigating in and around face-related issues can be daunting and full of mistakes. Fortunately, experts have provided some general suggestions to keep in mind when navigating around problems with face in conflict and negotiation situations.[26]

- In parts of Asia, there is a very fine line between being frank and being rude; subtle, high-context communication is the norm.
- As a rule, you should compliment but never criticize—even if asked for criticism. Your host may test you on small things, saying, "People here are poor workers, aren't they?" If you say "yes," you will fail the test and should start packing. Some go so far as to say that if you cannot think of the correct answer—one that saves face for everybody—then you should not even try to do business in Asia.
- Asians may laugh if you say something that causes loss of face or indirectly demeans their culture or country. Do not mistake the laugh for anything other than defensive— as a way to save face.
- If you ask a question in Asia and do not get an answer, don't push it. Save it for a later time and different (private) setting. Or, put in more blunt Western terms, if you want to maintain face for all, then keep the lower half of it shut!
- Avoid public displays of strong emotions. Never show anger, even if you feel it. It will do you no good and you will be labeled a "peasant."
- Do not be in a rush, as it is an attack on the face of others. To Asians, your sense of urgency says that they are not important enough to spend time with and that you have better places to be.

Taking your time and showing respect to others is good advice in any culture, because it displays consideration of others. But, some claim that obeying these social rules is akin to capitulating to the demands of an Asian partner. Parts of both positions are likely true. But, acknowledging differences does not mean you have to be a pushover. In fact, Westerners could use face to their advantage. Sometimes simply saying, "I would lose face at home if I were to agree to this deal" will carry more weight than a rational, numbers-based argument. Nevertheless, one expert advises those doing business in Asia to "be firm, but avoid obstinacy and rudeness. A calm and relaxed stubbornness is advised. Be persuasive in a gentle way."

Other Responses to Conflict

Taking time to understand the values and needs of a business partner from a different culture is certainly of value. And, this can help one avoid or minimize conflict that gets in the way of doing business. Some experts, however, think that some conflict is ubiquitous, and it's hard to argue when we look around the world today. So, if conflict is inevitable, how do we deal with it once it raises its head? If the conflict is egregious enough, it will be tough to completely look the other way. Instead, people might hold a grudge and/or look for ways to get back at the offending party. To examine this, researchers compared Chinese and American managers of real firms. They read a brief story that asked them to imagine themselves in conflict with a colleague who had taken their idea and presented it to their shared boss as his or her own. Both the American and Chinese managers expressed a desire to get back at the perpetrator. There were differences, however, in their approach to this revenge. Americans were more likely to choose a direct approach, such as confronting the colleague or reporting them to the boss. The Chinese more commonly chose an indirect approach, such as criticizing the colleague to others. The Chinese were also more bent on teaching a moral lesson and shaming.[27]

Instead of getting even or 'filing away' a slight, we may go through a formal process our organization has set up to resolve conflicts. For example, a disinterested third party might be able to approach conflict with a more level head. Earlier in this chapter, we mentioned a study that looked at how third parties might react to disputes brought to their attention, based on their traditional cultural values (and prevailing norms). This reliance on typical values in a culture brings up related questions here. For instance, is it more likely for someone to seek out third parties or mediators in individualistic as opposed to collective-type cultures? Given our discussion, this is a reasonable prediction. After all, consider the degree of attention paid by third parties (labor mediators and arbitrators) in many Western countries. In combination with the tendency to underplay conflict, why would we expect a Chinese employee to draw more attention to conflict by involving other people?

Yet, despite this logic, research shows that Chinese *do* rely on third parties to help resolve conflict. In fact, there is a long social tradition of using mediation. But, not all mediators are the same. It appears that the Anglo-American tradition is to seek third parties who are dispassionate and disconnected from disputes, what one American observer stated should be "a eunuch from Mars." At the heart of this preference is that people with no interest or connection to the conflict would render the best judgment. This approach is exactly opposite to the Chinese tradition—they prefer mediators who are/were involved and knowledgeable about the specific conflict and situation.[28]

Work–Family Conflict

One area in which traditional values seem to produce conflict is in the area of work–family interchange. In many cultures, people work hard and put many hours into their work. Sometimes, this comes at the expense of time with family and creates a well-documented set of problems that you are probably all too familiar with, given the emphasis on technology and constant communication capabilities. So while it is reasonable to expect that while employees will experience work–family conflict, its nature may be quite different across borders—a topic that researchers are starting to explore.

One study suggested that individualistic cultures such as the U.S. may place a higher value on personal family time than do more collectivistic societies. This prediction seems to run counter to our image of Americans as career-obsessed and our perception of Chinese as intensely family-oriented. But the basic idea is that when push comes to shove, individualistic Americans will put self-interest (for example, time with family) above collective interest (work). The more collectivistic Chinese may do just the opposite, putting work before family. Another perspective on this issue is that in the U.S., careers are viewed as vehicles for personal achievement. A "good family person" will not let personal ambitions harm the family. In contrast, Chinese employees often view work as a vehicle for bringing prosperity and honor to their families. So, working 70 hours a week and thus not seeing much of your family, even if that extended family lives with you, would be considered a personal sacrifice that you are making for the family rather than a selfish statement about your career objectives.

In short, family demands may cause greater conflict in the U.S. than in China, while the reverse may be true for work demands. And that is exactly what the study found. Of course, more research needs to be done to tease out the exact role of culture and other factors such as economic development. Plus, we also have evidence that the latest generation of wealthy, young, urban professionals in China (an explosively growing segment) is increasingly challenged by the balance between work and family. We illustrate this with a story about the Fan family in the accompanying International Insights feature. Like so many other issues in international management, one size may not fit all when it comes to work–family conflict. Managers should first try to identify the source of work–family conflict before pouring effort and money into trying to design "balanced" workplaces that reduce employee strain and stress.[29]

International Insights

Conflict in the Middle Kingdom: The Fan Family Feud

In Confucianism (an ethical and philosophical system developed from the teachings of the Chinese philosopher Confucius), a deep respect for parents and ancestors known as filial piety is a virtue to be held above all others. Taking care of one's parents and bringing a good name to them and to other ancestors are key values taught to all. For thousands of years, extended families have lived together, with the younger family members deferring to the older ones. China's dramatically expanding economy, however, is testing those long-held beliefs. Cracks in the social structure are beginning to show, including in the Fan family from Nanchang.

Life followed the traditional guidelines for the Fans when the children were young. The father, Hamlin Fan, now pines for those old days. Qun, his oldest son, looked after his two younger siblings while his parents were at work. The Fans worked hard and had big dreams for their children: they would do well in school, land good jobs, marry well, have children, and support them as parents into old age. Unfortunately, times got the best of all this filial duty. The children came of age when economic reforms in China began to bloom—new opportunities, lifestyles, and jobs. Qun jumped in head first, opting for a job with a Western pharmaceutical firm where he learned marketing techniques. He used this experience to start his own consulting business, providing advice to drug companies in China. Now his firm has 12 employees, and generates more than $1.3 million of sales.

As the business grew, relations with his parents became strained, in no small part because he relocated to Beijing. Now when he talks with his parents on the phone, he does not share many life details because they do not approve of his choices. He and his wife drive their own cars, eat out often, employ housekeepers (including one for their dog), and grab Starbucks on the run to and from their new two-story house in a wealthy Beijing neighborhood. They spend more money on luxuries such as imported foods, Coach bags, and dog treats than Qun's parents' monthly income. "If my parents saw me spending this kind of money, I'd be embarrassed," said Qun. Qun bought his parents a new apartment and takes them sightseeing when in town a few times a year, but his first priority now is to his *xiao jiating*—his marriage-based family. He and his spouse have ignored "suggestions" by his parents to have a baby.

Qun's younger brother, Jun, in another reversal of tradition, is living with his parents after a divorce. Jun and his ex-wife had a son, and Jun's mother spent a long time living with them and caring for the child when it was born. His ex-wife regarded Mrs. Fan's presence as an intrusion: "it would be better if the older generation didn't live with us, but I couldn't refuse," she said. She eventually left Jun and their son and is now living with her boyfriend, running a business that teaches English. Jun spars with his parents over how he raises the now 9-year-old boy. The elder Mr. Fan says, "I talk and no one listens." Jun says that it is important to show love to your children and that his father did not do that for him when he was a child. Jun did move to Beijing at one time and spent a year working for his older brother. But, his performance was weak and he missed his son (left in his parents' care). He left the job and returned to his parent's' home. His brother said that Jun was not cut out for the job, and instead approached it as though he was still at a state-run company. "He drank a cup of tea, and then did only what I told him to do."

The Fans' youngest child, Min, similar to her two older brothers, went against tradition. Instead of settling at home in Nanchang after college, she left for the big city. Now Min lives in Guangzhou, is married, and has a child and a successful career with an insurance company. She too does not return to Nanchang often because of work demands.

The elder Fans are at a loss. Their oldest son has a social standing that they never dreamed of and which far exceeds their own; their younger son is struggling financially and personally yet does not listen to advice; and their daughter is 1,000 miles away with a blossoming career of her own. Mr. Fan often spends time alone in his bedroom and Mrs. Fan escapes by playing mahjong every afternoon. Their experience is not isolated. Increasingly, younger Chinese are seeking privacy from their extended family. Some, like Qun Fan, can buy their parents apartments. Others violate Chinese filial obligations by putting their parents in nursing homes (occupancy is up 40 percent the last decade).

Time might be the biggest casualty in today's China. Some do not understand the latest generation and have turned to TV for an answer. A popular series in China is a show called *Chinese-Style Divorce*, and it gets plenty of attention. The producer said that the impetus for the show was his view that families suffer as people fight to get ahead financially and professionally. "Everyone is focused on making money; it destabilizes society." For centuries, outsiders have tried changing China and all have failed. Perhaps this latest change, coming from *inside* and centering on work–family conflict, may finally do that. For the Fan family, it has already happened.[30]

Understanding International Negotiation

Culture can play a role in creating and dealing with conflict, thus dealing with conflict can be especially valuable in a cultural negotiation setting. There has been quite a bit of research about how the negotiation process unfolds and the factors (including culture) that impact it.

Knowing how to manage conflict, in order either to stop it from occurring in the first place or to suppress any negative effects after it does arise, is a valuable asset. One very important tool to accomplish this is the ability to negotiate well. Negotiation is the process of communicating back and forth with another person or group to work toward a joint decision or agreement. All negotiations have four key elements:

- multiple parties (two or more) are involved;
- mixed motives typically exist (i.e., areas of disagreement or conflict, but also some interests in common);
- movement of positions held by the parties often occurs over time;
- there is a goal of reaching an agreement.

Negotiation is such a common feature of life, let alone business, that it has been studied a great deal and via a number of different perspectives. This section focuses on an approach to international negotiations called the *comparative* perspective. The primary emphasis of this approach is on what happens between negotiators during face-to-face interactions and how those interactions shape the outcomes that result (as opposed to country-to-country negotiation or other forms). Accordingly, attention is paid to how cultural factors may affect the way the negotiation process unfolds between individuals or small groups of negotiators.[31] Consider the Global Innovations feature on how culture plays a role in negotiations that literally have life or death consequences.

Global Innovations

Getting to "Yes": Negotiating Safely in a Hostage Crisis

Terrorism is a worldwide menace that has only recently been studied in depth. Officially, most governments and companies say that they do not negotiate with terrorists. Yet, in practice most do.[32] Data suggest that more *should*. While a few successful assaults on terrorists come to mind—for example, the 1976 Entebbe raid in Uganda, which freed Israeli and Jewish hostages from Popular Front for the Liberation of Palestine (PFLP) captors—they are unfortunately not common. These are more than offset by tragedies resulting from such actions, such as the 2002 raid in a Moscow theater, where Chechen rebels held roughly 900 individuals hostage—over 200 hostages were killed. Data show that more people die from raids by authorities than at the hands of terrorists. So, it can be of great value to negotiate. Consequently, rules have been developed to improve success in freeing hostages, including some culturally based suggestions that could help in those negotiations.

Consider the 2002 kidnapping of a Dutch medical aid volunteer in Dagestan, a Russian Federation Republic. Dutch negotiators talked with the Russian kidnappers for nearly two years before the hostage was released. Although it was ultimately successful, the negotiation process used by both parties was complicated by varying culture styles. Dutch authorities said that the Russian criminals were oblique and ambiguous, and the Russians reacted negatively to the characteristically direct style of the Dutch.

An important recent study looked at this issue further by meticulously coding transcripts of 25 different crisis negotiations in which police interacted with perpetrators from a different culture. The sample was unique in that many audiotapes about the incidents were available, including statements made by the criminals who had held the hostages. All in all, nearly 7,000 separate conversations across the 25 crises were coded, with an equal number seen from the police and the perpetrators. The hostage-takers were classified as being from low- or high-context societies. Remember that low-context (LC) cultures prefer direct communication methods—ones that rely on what people say or write. High-context (HC) cultures are more likely to rely on indirect messages—ones best interpreted within a cultural framework. Most cultures use both HC and LC communication, with one type perhaps being more common (e.g., in individualistic cultures, LC is more common; in collective cultures HC messages are more common).

These researchers found that across the hostage situations (some involving kidnapping, extortion, etc.), LC perpetrators of the crime were more likely to use more direct, persuasive arguments during negotiations (e.g., "You just said you have the money available . . . go bring it to us right away."). These LC criminals were more likely themselves to respond to persuasive arguments of negotiators with compromises. LC perpetrators were also more likely to communicate direct threats than were HC criminals, especially early in the negotiation time period (e.g., "I will kill the hostage if I don't get the money soon."). Overall, though, the effect of culture in this negotiation situation was more likely to occur in the later phases of negotiation, when the initial crisis mode had passed, providing opportunity for more common cultural styles of those involved to surface. Finally, there was some evidence that HC perpetrators were more flexible in their styles and may have adapted more to their police counterparts. The same was true for police, who tended to compromise more when they negotiated with a HC criminal versus one from an LC culture.

What sort of touch points might come into play between Western (LC cultures typically) and Asian (much more HC) negotiators? We know that Westerners are more likely to value direct messages and will reciprocate with definitive replies. They will likely spend less time on background information and instead they will get right to a persuasion phase and likely take a "win–lose" orientation. Asians, however, are more likely to be reticent and cautious during negotiations. We know from research that the Japanese (at least) are more likely to be seeking a win–win or a long-term approach in their negotiations, something accelerated by collection of background information on the other party. We also know from Hofstede's research in Chapter 4 that Asians might be less receptive to risk than would Westerners. All these differences could impact the course of negotiations, a prediction confirmed by this hostage negotiation research.

Above all, we know that crimes are committed by criminals! That means these situations are volatile and complex and infused with violence—with luck regularly playing a role in success. Nevertheless, this research suggests that negotiators who are sensitive to the cultural backgrounds of those involved in the crisis might end up with better outcomes for all.

Preparation for International Negotiations

This section presents a four-stage model of how international negotiations unfold. First, however, it is best to consider all of the planning and preparation that should go into a negotiation prior to beginning those four important steps—and often before any face-to-face interaction even begins. In many cases, work done in preparation of negotiation could smooth your movement across those four important stages.

Experts have long advised that negotiators put more thought and work into preparing for negotiations, rather than focus solely on the back and forth banter that is really only the end portion of negotiation. Yet, for many, some of this advice still goes unheeded. Over 30 years ago, one expert cautioned American executives to pay close attention to the Japanese negotiating style. He reasoned that if Americans did a good job of studying Japanese customs and negotiation tactics, the U.S. would be much better off. He thought that this kind of "homework" would help prevent the U.S. trade deficit with Japan from rising to the then "impossible level of $4 billion" (the U.S. trade deficit with Japan was $63 billion in 2011; the trade deficit with China was $295 billion).[33]

Cross-Cultural Advice

Much of this preparation advice is still sound, yet not heeded as much as one might expect.[34] Why don't people typically take the advice? The answers apply to any negotiation. First, few employees receive training in the art of negotiation, wherein preparation can be emphasized. Second, employees are busy and thus put off preparation while working on more pressing issues (such as an actual proposal, other work, attending meetings, etc.). Therefore, when there is little opportunity available, preparation is given a back seat. Third, many consider the essence of negotiation to be the ability to repel efforts by the other side to improve their outcomes while assertively putting forward one's own across the table. Yet, those who practice negotiation often consider information acquisition to be the key feature of good negotiators. Students applying for their first jobs typically do not receive training in negotiation and also believe that negotiation is simply the final process of a give and take over salary desires via a test of wills. But, if they had done their preparation months before reaching a phone call or face-to-face negotiation, research shows, they would have higher starting salaries.[35]

Consider the following general suggestions that experts say should be reflected on before undertaking an international negotiation:[36]

- Do not underestimate the complexity of international negotiation. It is replete with opportunities to fail.
- Take whatever steps are necessary to gain an in-depth understanding of the other side—not just on contractual issues, but how negotiating styles, view of the process, and values may come into play. It is a big mistake to think that everyone thinks the same as you or your team.[37]
- Seek outside help from consultants and trainers if the necessary expertise or knowledge is missing inside the company.

- Use interpreters that are hired by your company if there is a language barrier between sides. Do not rely on the other side to provide this resource.
- Consider the use of an international negotiating team.
- Be prepared to spend significant time and effort on the preparation process. You and your team will undoubtedly pay later if you are impatient or cut corners.

Allowing Time

Americans in particular seem to face continuous challenges in allowing enough time for proper preparation. An American manager leaving the U.S. for a negotiation in Asia should be prepared for a stay that is longer than expected. It is possible to spend only a few days on the ground in a location such as Japan or China and quickly wrap up a negotiation, particularly if you have experience there or have worked with the other party before. But, often this is not the case. For example, when the authors of this book were in Shanghai a few years ago, we spoke with an executive from an American automotive company. He groused that he had already "wasted" a week in the country without getting anything done other than eating and drinking with officials. He was angry about having to pick between spending an indefinite period of time in the country or simply calling the effort a failure and going home. Businesspeople in some Asian countries expect a good bit of time to be spent on establishing a rapport, whereas Americans want to "get down to business." Worse yet, some foreign negotiators are savvy to Americans' time sensitivities and may end up using this against them.

Bringing Friends

One piece of advice provided is to use a negotiation team. Once again, however, some employees and businesses ignore this advice because they believe that teams are cumbersome and feel that they're better off going it alone. American negotiating teams, for instance, are small, in part because of the costs associated with larger groups. In other cases, the team is small because of the negotiators' confidence in their own abilities, although that confidence can be misplaced. Either way, Americans may find themselves "outnumbered." The sheer number of details, let alone the language and cultural issues, often reduces the odds of a successful outcome for an understaffed negotiation team.[38]

Even with a solid team in place, members may not be properly prepared or understand how best to work with the team's translator. Experts will often recommend plenty of advance meetings with your interpreter and, ideally, including them from the start. Companies that follow this advice have more success in negotiations. A survey of over 100 multinationals revealed that nearly 90 percent felt that the presence of a bilingual team member improved the quality of their negotiation process. About the same percentage of firms thought that this helped speed up the process. Among those firms without a bilingual team member, most indicated that they would include one in future negotiations. Other experts suggest that negotiating teams should be multicultural, and ideally consist of employees from both the home country and the country represented by the other side. A multicultural team such as this could make bargaining perspectives, traditions, and tactics clearer for all sides and help resolve any culturally driven impasses.[39]

Basic Familiarity with Customs and Norms

Regardless of the size and composition of the negotiating team, familiarity with the prominent features of the host country's culture and customs pays big dividends. When asked about this, Japanese managers said that the most important factor for ensuring success in negotiations with U.S. firms was the willingness of Americans to devote time, effort, and patience to building relationships. Not far behind was "cultural awareness," which referred to familiarity with (Japanese) business norms, customs, and practices. It is likely that an understanding of norms and practices is important in most all international negotiations. Fortunately, these complex cultural factors can be studied and understood well before the actual negotiation process begins.[40]

We do not, however, want to create the impression that preparation will automatically lead to successful negotiations. As with any business venture, competition plays a role, as do political considerations and various other factors. Yet, while these complexities make for no guarantees, preparation that is done correctly will only improve your odds of success.

Even if you are well prepared and display behaviors and tactics that are customized to your counterparts, those efforts to "adapt" will be viewed more positively in some cultures than in others. Training may not always have the intended or desired effects. Even after they went through identical training in negotiation tactics (separately), when Danish and Spanish negotiators in one study met to discuss business, each team still stuck with their own nationality's bargaining styles, as opposed to working with the opposing team's style. The Spaniards tended to connect relationships to the issues at hand and were willing to attack the other side, while the Danes preferred to focus on the issues and avoid direct conflicts. Consequently, Spaniards were likely to view the Danes as being too focused on the business issues while being emotionally distant, while the Danes were likely to view the Spaniards as uncooperative and confrontational. This suggests that training alone, while helpful, is unlikely to completely suppress deep-seated styles.[41]

Training in Advance

Finally, consider that whatever its drawbacks and limitations, more training is usually going to be more desirable than less training. That is where large firms have an advantage over small ones. Research has found that larger firms tend to do better and to find more success in international negotiations than their smaller counterparts because of the resources that often accompany size. Big firms are more likely to have the money for consultants, trainers, interpreters, and an overall hands-on role-playing of negotiations.[42] Larger firms often also have the luxury of taking more time to prepare, as there are more employees to cover the work and projects going on elsewhere within the company.[43]

Training in a high-context approach—or at least the flexibility to use this style—would serve most Western negotiators well. While there is no direct research to support our claim, some work does speak to this issue. For example, one elaborate study had participants from high-context countries (Russia, Japan, China, and Thailand) and low-context countries (Germany, Israel, Sweden, and the U.S.) participate in a simulated negotiation. The researchers taped the interactions between group members and later transcribed and coded all that was said during the 90-minute bargaining session. The

285

findings show that the high-context negotiators used more flexible and complementary tactics than did the low-context negotiators. This suggests that the high-context approach allowed negotiators to pull more information from the low-context group without signaling that they were completely cooperating or giving in. Additionally, the high-context participants were better able to mimic the opposite approach; low-context negotiators found it difficult to switch styles to the high-context approach.[44]

A Four-Stage Model of the Negotiation Process

Overview of the Stages

Regardless of the amount of preparation, or lack of preparation, eventually you must begin interaction and negotiation. Experts suggest that the complete negotiation process can be divided up into four main stages.[45] The first stage is called nontask sounding. This is often a relatively long stage, especially outside of the U.S. The basic purpose of this stage is to establish a rapport with a potential business partner and to get to know the other party. It is very much related to the preparation issues outlined previously. Seemingly, interaction at this stage is not directly related to the task of negotiating but instead involves "sounding out" the other party. Negotiating must be considered as a wider process, however, encompassing preparation all the way to signing a contract and following through on agreements made during the process.

The next stage involves the task-related exchange of information. This stage involves an exchange of the two parties' needs and preferences as well as an explanation of background issues. Following this is the persuasion stage of negotiations, in which, as the label suggests, there are overt attempts to modify each other's positions. All three of these stages lead to the final agreement stage, in which bargains are agreed upon and contracts signed. There is a good deal of research comparing cultures across these four stages.[46]

Stage 1: Nontask Sounding

First, consider nontask sounding—the effort to establish rapport and to get to know the other party. This is common in a lot of social interaction across cultures, especially when meeting someone for the first time. Importantly though, this does not mean that nontask sounding unfolds the same way everywhere. In fact, there are often great differences among negotiating parties as to how they approach this stage.

One important feature in the nontask sounding stage is the amount of time spent on entertaining one's guests in an effort to feel them out and establish a personal relationship. You may, for example, encounter people who want to know about you and the company you represent in great detail. They may wish to know your company history, your personal qualifications, features about your family and much more. Knowing where you fit within the company and your history with it can be of value too. In fact, the other party may even center themselves within the company when first introduced. For instance, in many Asian cultures we might introduce ourselves by saying, "We are the University of Dayton's Paul Sweeney and Dean McFarlin." Obviously, in the U.S. we would almost certainly introduce ourselves by saying, "Hi, I'm Paul Sweeney and this is Dean McFarlin; we're with the University of Dayton." This is a subtle difference, but substantial in its underlying meaning. It reflects what we have already discussed—that people in individualistic cultures such as the U.S. tend to give primary emphasis to the person, while people in collectivistic cultures give primacy to the group (the organization, in this case). In this example, the first introduction places emphasis on our university of employment. The second introduction places emphasis on us, individually.

But nontask sounding goes well beyond this. What to an American might seem to be discussions about irrelevant personal details or tangential issues can instead mean a great deal to a Chilean or Philippine negotiator. In fact, it might be vital from their perspective to have these discussions early on. Those from low-context cultures like the U.S. often do not want a lot of personal "background" before undertaking negotiations. Generally, their goal in negotiations is a "context-less" agreement (one that is explicit and in writing). Spending enormous amounts of time to get to know the other party, therefore, is relatively unimportant and possibly an impediment to reaching that goal. The perspective of people from high-context cultures such as Chile and the Philippines is often very different. These negotiators commonly find it very important to spend a significant amount of time on nontask sounding. The personal and organizational information that they seek provides the perspective that is critical for understanding messages in their culture. Figure 7.4 summarizes this and other differences that might be observed between high- and low-context cultures in the nontask sounding stage.

Stage of Negotiation	Low-Context Culture	High-Context Culture
Stage 1: Nontask sounding	• Briefly exchange social niceties • Will get to the point (i.e., Stage 3) quickly • Not especially concerned with status of other group	• Will want to know all about you and your company • Long presentations, meetings in order to get to know you • Give careful attention to age, rank, status of other negotiators
Stage 2: Task-related exchange of information	• Relatively brief stage • Young, ambitious, likely to do well	• Among the longer stages • Advantage given to older, higher-status team member
Stage 3: Persuasion	• Argumentative • The most important stage • "To the point" negotiating style • Cost–benefit approach; face saving not very important	• Declarative • The least important stage • More guarded style • Face saving very important
Stage 4: Concession/ agreement	• Favor or require detailed written contract • Decision/agreement is impersonal • Profit motive determines agreement	• Less emphasis on long contracts • Deal is sealed on the basis of the contextual variables • Good setting necessary for final agreements

Figure 7.4 Behavior in the Stages of Negotiation: Differences in Low- and High-Context Cultures.

The amount of time spent on what Americans and other low-context negotiators might consider "meaningless" interaction can vary across cultures. In high-context cultures, it really *does* matter in ways that impact final outcomes. For example, one study showed that for Brazilian and Japanese negotiators, interpersonal comfort was much more likely to lead to outcomes that satisfied their negotiating partner than it was for Americans. This finding highlights the role of nontask sounding in building the personal relationships that are essential for successful negotiations in high context cultures.[47]

Another sign of a culture's emphasis on this "getting to know you" stage is the emphasis that negotiators place on status. The status of the participants involved in the negotiation, while often not directly relevant to the issues being discussed, is important to some. Once again, the distinction between high- and low-context cultures is useful for explaining this point. Negotiation among equals is much more common in low-context cultures such as the U.S. American negotiators often downplay status in any number of ways (e.g., by using first names, dressing casually, and soliciting input from all team members). In many other cultures and countries (especially high-context ones), title and status are very important and interactions are more formal.[48] It would be rare, for example, for a high-context negotiator to address the other party by his or her first name. The Chinese, for instance, are very aware of status differences among people on negotiation teams and prefer to negotiate with the head of the foreign company.[49] This is also an apparent preference among Japanese, French and Mexican negotiators, among others.[50]

One's rank or position provides background for upcoming negotiations with high-context negotiators, but it is less important in low-context cultures. One study had groups of English, French, Germans, and Americans participate in a simulated negotiation. The French (i.e., the highest context of the four groups) were most interested in, and affected by, the status of other negotiation team members. Another study gathered observations from more than 700 business people from 11 different cultures. The cultures ranged from very low context (e.g., the U.S., Germany) to very high context (e.g., Korea, China, Taiwan) and discovered that high status and personal relations mattered more to people from high-context cultures. In Japan, status distinctions can be based on age, gender, and relative position in the firm. So if you are an older male who is higher up in the firm, the odds are that your status will impress a Japanese bargainer.[51] In the low-context U.S., however, Americans often want to establish equality between people, even where it clearly does not exist.[52]

Stage 2: Task-Related Exchange of Information

This second stage involves the exchange of both parties' needs and preferences. Negotiators can also place different weight on this phase. In high-context cultures, long and in-depth explanations of initial bargaining positions are expected. This exchange and the meetings that go along with it will probably be drawn out and involve many questions about the issues on the table. The long-term approach taken by high-context cultures also means that you are likely to see an initial offer that is not very favorable. The belief is that a poor initial offer will leave plenty of room to maneuver in later stages. This was verified in research on groups of businessmen from the U.S., Japan, and Brazil who were asked to participate in simulated negotiations. The Japanese asked for higher profit outcomes than their American and Brazilian counterparts in their initial offer. The American negotiators, however, were more likely to offer a price that was closer to the eventual terms agreed upon by both parties. And, both the Americans and Brazilians were irritated at the Japanese for their "greedy" initial offers. A second study with the same three cultural groups found that American bargainers could reduce their irritation and improve their outcomes by stretching out this second stage. In particular, the more Americans encouraged information exchange from their bargaining partners, the better their financial outcomes were in the negotiation.[53]

This finding was accentuated by a more recent study of actual negotiation transcripts of Japanese and American businesspeople. Early first offers generated higher gains for the Japanese and lower ones for American negotiators. But, exchange of information prior to the first offer resulted in a turnaround of this effect—U.S. negotiators received higher gains.[54] Overall, experts suggest that the probability of success in international negotiation increases as the negotiators are motivated to search for new information and are flexible in their approach during the process.[55]

Stage 3: Persuasion

While the earlier findings are clear and consistent, Americans are still often skimpy in the attention that they pay to task-related information exchange. Sure, Americans may spend some time talking about sports or their families and are willing to exchange product and other information, but relatively little time compared to other cultures. Instead, a slight glance at the wristwatch is enough to move an American onto the next stage of negotiations. Persuasion involves explicit attempts to modify each other's positions. To Americans, this is the most important step in the negotiating process. And it is the stage during which they expect to spend most of their time. But how the persuasion stage unfolds in other cultures may end up surprising many Americans and others who share their general traits.

First let's examine the amount of time spent at this stage. As stated, Americans usually spend relatively little time and effort in the earlier two stages in order to spend greater amounts of time in this third phase. Other cultures, such as the Thais, take the time to sound each other out earlier and therefore they spend relatively less time engaging in the kind of overt persuasion many Americans are used to.

Next, what about the actual tactics used to persuade? As you might expect, most Americans believe that this stage is where the "real" negotiating takes place and therefore pay very close attention to the interactions that occur here. Throughout the persuasion phase, Americans will often compromise and make modifications to their initial bargaining position. In fact, they commonly make concessions throughout all stages of negotiations. Unlike American bargainers, however, Japanese negotiators tend to wait toward the end of negotiations before making any concessions.[56] Consequently, Americans may go too far and give too much away in an effort to compromise in this persuasion stage.[57] Interestingly, while Americans may be among the best in the world at compromising, the meaning of the word *compromise* and related terms can differ dramatically across cultures, as shown in the following International Insights feature.

International Insights

The Devil Is in the Details: The Meaning of Compromise Across Cultures

If you are wondering about how important language is in international business, consider the language of negotiation. Take the word *compromise*, which generally has very positive connotations for Americans. The U.S. was founded on compromise and many famous compromises have made up its history. Americans may be among the world's best compromisers. It follows, of course, that compromise has been an essential part of American business dealings as well. To be sure, for many Americans, a compromise or concession is a very strong sign of good faith and fair play between parties.

Interestingly, however, the word *compromise* has some very different meanings in other cultures. And many of those meanings are far more negative than those conjured up by Americans. In the Middle East, for example, compromise carries with it many negative associations, such as in the phrase "his virtue was compromised." Similarly, the Persian word for *mediator* translates to "meddler." In many Latin American cultures, compromise presents an issue of personal honor. There, compromise could connote giving in, and that raises many issues of face and personal integrity for Mexicans which can be problematic in negotiations. Russians typically see compromise as a sign of weakness. To concede even a minor point can sometimes suggest a loss of control or the excessive influence of another's will. As a result, negotiations with Russians can be confrontational.

Likewise, many other terms that relate to the negotiation process are open to different interpretation. The word *aggressive* may be an insult to the British or Japanese, while to Americans such a characterization may indicate a tough, respected bargainer. We do not mean to imply that words carry most of the weight in determining success of negotiations—they do not. But, it may pay to become aware of national sensitivities.[58]

Another reflection of the American belief that persuasion is where the real negotiation takes place is that they now are ready to "lay their cards on the table." Basically, this means that Americans often give, and expect to receive, frank information during this stage of negotiations. It has been found that Americans often believe that the ideal position for both parties should be put on the table, so to speak, at which time progress can be made—often on an issue-by-issue basis—toward some kind of compromise. One study reported that Americans were more likely to share information directly with negotiation partners than were those from five other countries (Brazil, France, China, Japan, and Russia). Negotiators from Russia, Japan, and China were more likely to use indirect strategies to communicate in negotiations.[59]

In another study, which looked at the appropriateness of various bargaining methods, Americans were less likely to endorse tactics such as bluffing, feigning threats, or misrepresenting information than were Brazilians.[60] Setting aside the preference for being "up front," the American style often does not mesh well with the bargaining approaches used in other countries and cultures. This American approach to negotiation stems from an idealistic moral philosophy, rather than a focus on the relative consequences of specific actions. Other cultures, such as the Saudis, embrace a more relativist philosophy which affords more flexibility in their approach.[61] An example is when a Chinese negotiator makes sudden demands that are presented as non-negotiable. Such demands often throw Westerners off if they are not well prepared and can provide an advantage to the Chinese—a tactic not generally viewed as viable for some Westerners.[62] Similarly, another study using a simulated bargaining session found that Chinese negotiators used more competitive approaches (persuasive communication, threats) and fewer cooperative methods (such as multiple offers or attempts, and a focus on long-term outcomes).[63] With sufficient patience and some more flexibility, research shows that Americans might find that concessions will appear from the Chinese (and from others) occasionally at the last minute.[64]

Figure 7.5 presents some elements of what might be considered the stereotypic American negotiating style. Most of these elements play a role here in the persuasion stage of negotiations, but also apply to other stages. Put simply, the quintessential American style resembles that of the frontiersman or cowboy in the old West. This "John Wayne" style of interaction may work well within the U.S., but these characteristics that are key features of American individualism can be received very poorly on a foreign stage. Even in the U.S., it pays to be flexible and it is rare for any one successful negotiator to consistently use more than a couple of these behaviors presented in Figure 7.5. After all, negotiation is by definition *inter*dependent—some of the most successful negotiation approaches used in Western countries are more long-term oriented and focus on benefits for both parties. Consequently, a review of the behaviors shown in Figure 7.5 can benefit potential negotiators.[65]

Let's take this a step further and consider what might happen when the prototypic "John Wayne" negotiator meets a Japanese (or other high-context) negotiator. The American might quickly present a complex set of arguments, concluding their presentation with an offer that is not too far from what they eventually expect. The Japanese may be surprised by the abruptness of the offer but will probably consider it given that she likely knows that Americans prefer to "get to the point." What she may not know, however, is that the American offer is pretty close to the final offer available to the American to make. In fact, in many cultures and countries, bargainers leave themselves considerable room to maneuver. Accordingly, the Japanese may counter by asking for a lot. But Americans may show irritation, something that can harden positions and result in less exchange of information.[66] This is exactly what happened in a study based, once again, on a simulated negotiation session. American negotiators initially asked for a "fair" price—one closer to their final offer—whereas Japanese negotiators initially asked for much higher profit options, a position that upset the Americans.[67]

Despite feelings such as these, Americans would press on by trying to deal with one issue at a time, despite most likely experiencing more frustration and anger. The Japanese typically do not like dealing piecemeal with issues; instead their concessions are commonly bunched toward the end of the process. Even if Americans are very persuasive, they may receive a silent response—which the Americans may interpret as stonewalling or stalling. A cultural analysis can pinpoint their source of frustration here.

American Style	Prescriptions for Use in Other Countries
1. **Just call me John:** Americans downplay status and titles, as well as other formalities like lengthy introductions.	1. **Follow local customs:** Our informality simply out of place in most other cultures; foreign clients are more comfortable when we follow their customs.
2. **Get to the point:** Americans, like no others, want to dispense with the small talk and get down to business.	2. **Getting down to business:** This is defined differently across cultures; getting to know the other party is important in many countries.
3. **Lay your cards on the table:** We expect honest information at the bargaining table ("You tell me what you want and I'll tell you what I want").	3. **Hold something back:** Foreign executives seldom lay everything on the table; the negotiating process is expected to take time with concessions made along the way.
4. **Don't just sit there, speak up:** Americans don't deal well with silence: we get into trouble by feeling pressured to fill in silence with possible concessions.	4. **Silence can be a powerful negotiating tool:** Consider its use, but also be aware of its use against you.
5. **Don't take no for an answer:** We are taught to be persistent and not to give up; negotiation is mostly persuasion.	5. **Minds are often changed behind the scenes:** If an impasse is reached, ask more questions; take a recess; try a more subtle approach.
6. **One thing at a time:** Americans approach a negotiating task sequentially ("Let's settle the quantity issue first, and then discuss price").	6. **Postpone concessions:** Until you've had a chance to get all issues on the table; don't measure progress by the number of issues that have been settled.
7. **A deal is a deal:** When we make an agreement, we give our word. We expect to honor the agreement no matter the circumstances.	7. **What we take as a commitment:** Means different things in Tokyo, Rio, or Riyadh; deals—particularly new ones—are more uncertain than we're used to.

Figure 7.5 Some Elements of the Stereotypic American Negotiating Style.

Source: Adapted from Graham, J. L., and Herberger, R. A. (1982). Negotiators abroad—don't shoot from the hip. *Harvard Business Review*, July–August, 160–168.

The Americans may have used their on-the-spot latitude to grant a concession. But the Japanese may not have the same amount of discretion; their decision-making style is to take time after hearing an offer to discuss it as a group and, ideally, reach a consensus. This approach is more common in high power distance countries (e.g., Mexico and India, and Japan to a somewhat lesser degree). Consequently, the Japanese negotiators are not likely to react immediately to an offer.[68]

If they are frustrated enough at this point, Americans counter with a very aggressive tactic. They might tell the Japanese, "If you can't lower your price, we will have to go with another supplier." This may be the worst thing to do. The mere directness of this approach will be off-putting to the Japanese. It would be much more appropriate if this option were presented through a third party or, if it must be done directly, then in a completely different way. For example, the American might say, "Lower prices on your part would go a long way toward us not having to develop other options." Additionally, other tactics such as repeating the explanation of your position in more detail, asking questions, playing dumb, or even silence, can go a long way.[69]

Indirect approaches, however, are not the first choice for Americans as they are in many parts of the globe. Consider the following scenario presented by experts in international negotiation: You are a member of an American firm who has contracted with a Chinese bicycle manufacturer. You have received convincing data that this manufacturer has had some quality problems in the past and that the bikes in your order have an annoying rattle. They are supposed to ship to Hong Kong next week. What would you do? Would you (a) Go to the plant to see to the quality problem yourself, instructing the plant manager that the rattling has to be fixed before shipping? Or (b) Go to the plant and test some bikes yourself, taking the plant manager for a ride near the factory and afterwards ask her if other bikes rattle, if the rattling will be a problem for buyers, before leaving the plant?[70] If you are like most Americans, your first instinct is to choose the first option—many do. But, it may not be the best choice.

This brief story is true and had a happy ending when the actual American took the indirect approach (option b). Gently asking for the plant manager's view helped—the bikes arrived on time with no rattle. The American ordered more, so both parties came out of this well. This indirect confrontation is more common in collective cultures; it does not imply blame or make the problem personal. The issue does not morph from a problem with rattling bikes to the *people* who made the rattling bikes; the indirect approach gets across the message without communicating disrespect. For this reason, an intermediary or third party is often a useful way to fix a problem in Asia as well.[71]

Stage 4: Agreement

Many negotiations do come to a conclusion where an agreement is reached. Agreements are the culmination of all the concessions and persuasion used in the earlier stages. That said, an agreement is only as good as the follow through. In other words, all of the considerable time and effort invested into the previous three stages could be wasted if both parties involved in the negotiation do not behave in a way that is consistent with the final agreement. Recognizing this fact, many American companies will insist that elaborate formal contracts be signed that bind each party to specifics. In some parts of the world, this preference is sometimes viewed as a negative or even something to resist outright; those negotiators are loath to seal the deal with a final, written contract that spells out responsibilities in great detail. Instead, they hope that the ties that they spent so much time building and strengthening in the earlier stages of the process will now pay off. They hope that the general trust established via an extended nontask sounding phase will allow a much more general agreement to be drafted and acknowledged by each party.[72] Despite this inclination, most foreign firms nowadays expect a lengthy formal contract to be requested if they are negotiating with U.S. companies.

The Chinese have similar views about the form of a good agreement. Instead of a specific contract, they prefer broad agreement about general principles. Some say that the Chinese want broad agreements because they believe that if all parties agree to the principles, the details can be worked out later by people of good intention and trust.[73] Of course, Americans and other Westerners often take the position that if trust exists, then the Chinese should be willing to make clear commitments. Who is "right" depends on the specific case. One thing, however, is certain: Americans tend to slight the process of establishing broad principles. To the degree that this impacts trust with partners, this can be problematic. Regardless, it can pay to make an assessment of the degree of trust and then adjust one's actions accordingly. In fact, Figure 7.6 presents advice for negotiators based on their judgment of the level of trust that exists between them and their partner.

These principles, however, are the standards that some use to evaluate future agreements. In some cases, Americans and others consent to agreements with little input, perhaps because they believe that since general principles can be interpreted to support most positions, then there is no sense sweating over those. Nevertheless, experts recommend that Western firms provide serious input into this process, including laying out their ideas on business concepts such as quality products, profit, and shareholder return, instead of just going through the motions.

Whether it is broad or narrow, however, even the very notion of a contract can have different implications across countries. For example, in Russia a party to a contract can only do what is expressly allowed. Generally, in the U.S. you can do anything that is not *prohibited* by contract (provided it is legal).[74] Again, an agreement is only good if it is kept. Whether other parties live up to their end of the agreement depends on, at least in part, the potential long-term impact. This impact, in turn, is determined by the trust we have in the other parties and our satisfaction with the agreement. Making sure the other party feels they also got a good deal, therefore, pays off in the long run.[75] Global competition is so fierce today that general principles are probably worth abiding by in order to communicate effectively and negotiate a lasting agreement.

Level of Trust in Relationship		
Trust Exists	**Trust is Possible**	**Trust Not Possible**
• Operate as though trust exists.	• Put superordinate goals forward.	• Extend offers on multiple issues at the same time.
• Work to understand counterpart.	• Point to a shared future.	• Have your team look for signs and signals in negotiating partner behavior/discussion.
• Emphasize interests and features in common with other party.	• Separate people from issues and focus on the latter.	• Provide concessions in a reciprocal manner.
• Cross-check what was said (restate what you heard).	• Try to break an impasse by taking breaks, suggesting other approaches.	• When deadlocked, use emotion to communicate (apologize, sympathize, and otherwise relate to partner).
• Keep the elements of the agreement open/tentative until the end.	• Consider the use of a third party/mediator.	• Show expertise or authority to improve effectiveness.
	• Form an argument for a common enemy.	

Figure 7.6 The Trust Factor in International Negotiations: Advice for Those in Short Supply.
Source: Adapted from Gunia, B., Brett, J., and Nandkeolyar, A. (2012). In global negotiations, it's all about trust. *Harvard Business Review*, December, 26–27.

Chapter Summary

Conflict occurs all too often in international business, and important causes include differing cultural norms, decision-making styles, and the characteristic cultural tendency to engage in or avoid conflict in the first place. We discussed different styles that cultures use to deal with conflict issues once they arise. These approaches balance concern for your own personal outcomes against concern for the outcomes of others. For instance, Americans tend to use a competitive style (high in own concern/relatively low in other concern) whereas Thais use a more avoidant style, shying away from overt conflict with others.

An important way to minimize, and possibly eliminate conflict is through negotiation. We focused on four common stages of the negotiation process itself, and also highlighted the importance of preparation. Preparation should include learning about the other side (about their culture and how that impacts negotiation), seeking outside experts when necessary, using translators and a multicultural negotiating team, and generally being willing to prepare fully.

Once preparation is complete, the actual negotiations typically proceed through four main stages and we showed how different cultures put more or less weight on each stage. For example, Americans tend to undervalue the first stage of negotiating—*nontask sounding*—relative to other cultures. This "getting to know one another" phase is viewed by Americans as best kept brief and perfunctory, whereas it is a relatively long and important stage for some other cultures. The final three stages, *task-related exchange*, *persuasion*, and *agreement*, all have cultural ties as well. Finally, we examined some mistakes that can be made in an international negotiation process as well as some techniques that may result in more beneficial outcomes for each of these stages.

Discussion Questions

1. In our discussion of conflict we highlighted negative implications and effects. Explain some *positive* effects that might result from intercultural conflict.
2. How might Asians, Latinos, and Americans (U.S.) characteristically deal with conflict? More importantly, think through why each group's typical style might create a sense of frustration when interacting with the others.
3. Reflect on how an American, a Mexican, and a Saudi might move through the four stages of negotiation (you may wish to refer back to Chapter 4 to see each country's standing on Hofstede's dimensions). How might each stage be approached and what areas might each nationality emphasize?

Up to the Challenge?

The Mexican and American Negotiation Gap: Returning El Norte, Empty-Handed

At the beginning of the chapter, we presented a negotiation scenario between Mexican government officials and American managers. The American team flew to Mexico City to present their proposal with the hope of hammering out and negotiating the terms of the large contract. The cross-cultural differences that they faced, along with plenty of anger, frustration, and misunderstanding, are more common than we all might expect. What is your take on this situation? What were the reasons for the breakdown? Compare your guesses with ours that are presented just below here.

In a nutshell, the Mexicans displayed more concern for relationships and background information than their American counterparts before and during negotiations. The Mexicans tended to use stories and allegories to support their points before the presentation and during the lunch afterward and they acknowledged the work done by the Americans. They also tended to be more effusive in their early communication and during their informal meetings during lunch. On the other hand, they also held some topics near and dear—such as the importance accorded to their boss, the minister—something that was shared in response to the receipt early on of the American proposal and schedule.

The Americans, in contrast, "played by their own rules," or at least the rules that they should use if they were dealing with other Americans. On the positive side, they approached the presentation with due diligence—they prepared to the hilt and did their homework. But, good technical preparation was not the problem here. In fact, the inclusion of a lawyer on the American team was probably done to ensure that any contract might be free of threats to the firm. This could suggest to the other party that if there are problems later, the first stop might be Mexican courts. Yet, for many cultures, including Mexican, business is more personal. Some go as far to say that you would just as soon bring a lawyer to the opening of a business relation as you would during the opening of a romantic relationship. Business "prenuptials" in many collective cultures are informal.

The Americans also tended to focus more on moving things along, with repeated references to time and requests for more information. Indeed, even at the lunch afterward, the Americans pressed for reactions whereas the Mexicans kept the conversation light. This business during lunch emanated from different views about punctuality (late start of presentation and late arrival of players). In Mexico, this is a lot less important than the cultivation of a good atmosphere and relations. That said, the Americans were willing (to a point) to accommodate the Mexican officials, agreeing, if only because they did not know what else to do, to wait around an hour beyond the appointed start time. The Mexicans were more concerned with establishing a positive working relationship first, preferring to explore options jointly rather than to consider specific details. This was signaled in their early communications that confirmed the joint meeting with the Americans. These differences are common across individualistic (U.S.) and collective (Mexican) cultures. Americans tend to worry less about relationships and are focused more about persuading and securing agreement in a negotiation.

And, while the Mexican officials accommodated the American team leader's request to eventually start the meeting, they were also a bit taken aback since their leader, the minister, had not yet arrived.

The offense taken by the minister and his staff raises another cultural red flag. Power distance between these two countries is great. Mexicans are relatively high on this dimension—leaders carry significant power and are looked to for important decisions. The U.S. is lower in power distance—differences between managers and subordinates are less significant and lower-level managers enjoy more decision control. The U.S. managers were empowered by their management back in New York to make decisions on the ground in Mexico City. The questions raised by the Mexicans during the early meetings might have been efforts to determine the seniority levels of the American team. The Americans might have considered including the CEO, the president, or a board member of the firm so that the Mexican minister may have felt that the negotiation was conducted on equal terms.

In summary, the reactions of each side may have been influenced by cultural differences. Do you have any suggestions about how each side might better respond and adapt to the other, or have been better prepared to do just that? Could the Americans have done anything to salvage the situation—even after the offense taken by the minister? As we noted in this chapter, perhaps the biggest mistake a manager can make is to be unfamiliar with the norms and typical behaviors of another culture. If the Americans had been better prepared for potential cultural disconnects during the negotiations, things might have indeed gone more smoothly.[76]

International Development

Assessing and Comparing Your Conflict Management Style

Purpose

To diagnose and assess your characteristic approach to conflict once it arises.

Instructions

You will complete a scale of conflict management and then compare your scores with those from several different cultures. It is easy to complete this scale. For each of the 15 items, indicate how often you rely on that specific tactic by circling the appropriate number. Your instructor will then provide an easy scoring sheet that you can use to calculate your scores on several subscales that measure approaches to conflict. After this, you instructor may have you pair up with another person in class to discuss your scores and also to speculate how your scores compare with those from different cultures. Alternatively, your instructor may choose to make this a class exercise with open discussion. Data will be presented on scores of college students from other cultures to provide comparison points. The instructor will draw out implications of differing styles and what this could mean for cross-cultural interactions.

The Scale

Complete the scale by choosing a number that reflects your view about each item:

1	2	3	4	5
	Rarely	Sometimes		Always

1. ___ I argue my case with my co-workers to show the merits of my position.

2. ___ I negotiate with my co-workers so that a compromise can be reached.

3. ___ I try to satisfy the expectations of my co-workers.

4. ___ I try to investigate an issue with my co-workers to find a solution acceptable to us.

5. ___ I am firm in pursuing my side of the issue.

6. ___ I attempt to avoid being "put on the spot" and try to keep my conflict with my co-workers to myself.

7. ___ I hold on to my solution to a problem.

8. ___ I use "give and take" so that a compromise can be made.

9. ___ I exchange accurate information with my co-workers to solve a problem together.

10. ___ I avoid open discussion of my differences with my co-workers.

11. ___ I accommodate the wishes of my co-workers.

12. ___ I try to bring all our concerns out in the open so that the issues can be resolved in the best possible way.

13. ___ I propose a middle ground for breaking deadlocks.

14. ___ I go along with the suggestions of my co-workers.

15. ___ I try to keep my disagreements with my co-workers to myself in order to avoid hard feelings.

Source: Rahim, A (1989). *Managing Conflict: An Interdisciplinary Approach*. New York: Praeger.

From Theory to International Practice

Characteristic Features of Negotiation Behavior in Countries around the World

Purpose

To explore the difficulties that can occur when negotiating with people from other cultures.

Instructions

Divide into groups. Your instructor will assign each group one culture to study in order to provide a wider sample of different countries and cultures. Outside of class, do research to find three dominant cultural values and their corresponding behaviors for your assigned culture. Several websites might be useful in your research. Your instructor might also suggest other sites at which to find information. Consider the following:

- **Global Negotiation Resources**—This site provides a wealth of information on over 50 countries, including cultural perspectives and preferences—especially as they might apply to negotiation: www.globalnegotiationresources.com/resources/countries/

- **Negotiation.biz**—This site is a resource for those interested in studying cross-cultural negotiation. It provides a variety of specific information regarding characteristics and values of various countries that might impact negotiation: www.negotiation.biz

- **U.S. Department of State Country Background Notes**—This site presents a wealth of information about every country on the globe. This information is used by Foreign Service Officers and others who spend considerable time overseas: www.state.gov

- ***The Economist* Country Profiles**—*The Economist* magazine is well known, but its Intelligence Unit, while less well known, is an invaluable resource for anyone interested in international business. Information can be obtained by country: www.economist.com/countries/

- **The CIA World Factbook**—This is a complete and detailed source of information about all countries on the globe, useful for this exercise and others as well: https://www.cia.gov/library/publications/the-world-factbook/

Based on your research, each group should:

1. meet with your group to discuss each cultural value and some of the behavior it produces;

2. next, make some predictions about how negotiators from that culture act as a result;

3. finally, come up with a strategic negotiating response for each of the predicted negotiating behaviors.

In class, your group will have 10–15 minutes to present its research findings and suggested negotiating strategy. The instructor will wrap things up with a discussion of cultural differences and their relationship to international business negotiations.

Source: Adapted from Whatley, A. (1979). *Training for the Cross-Cultural Mind*. Washington, D.C.: SIETAR.

Notes

1. Fox, C. (2006). International negotiator. *British Journal of Administrative Management*, June/ July, 20–22; Posthuma, R. A., White, G. O., Dworkin, J. B., Yanez, O., and Swift, M. S. (2006). Conflict resolution styles between co-workers in US and Mexican cultures. *International Journal of Conflict Management*, 17, 242–260; Heydenfeldt, J. A. G. (2000). The influence of individualism/collectivism on Mexican and U.S. business negotiation. *International Journal of Intercultural Relations*, 24, 383–407; see also: www.globalnegotiationresources.com/cou/Mexico.pdf .
2. Thomas, K. W., and Schmidt, W. H. (1976). A survey of managerial interests with respect to conflict. *Academy of Management Journal*, 10, 315–318.
3. Saner, R., Yiu, L., and Sondergaard, M. (2000). Business diplomacy management: A core competency for global managers. *Academy of Management Executive*, 14, 80–92.
4. Ricks, D. A. (1983). *Big Business Blunders: Mistakes in Multinational Marketing*. Homewood, IL: Dow Jones Irwin.
5. Alon, I., and Brett, J. M., (2007). Perceptions of time and their impact on negotiations in Arabic-speaking Islamic world. *Negotiation Journal*, January, 55–73.
6. McCann, R. M., and Giles, H. (2006). Communication with people of different ages in the workplace: Thai and American data. *Human Communication Research*, 32, 74–108.
7. Thomas, K. W. (1976). Conflict and conflict management. In M. D. Dunnette (ed.) *Handbook of Industrial and Organizational Behavior*, 889–935. Chicago: Rand McNally.
8. Prunty, A. M., Klopf, D. W., and Ishii, S. (1990). Argumentativeness: Japanese and American tendencies to approach and avoid conflict. *Communication Research Reports*, 7, 75–79.
9. Klopf, D. W. (1991). Japanese communication practices: Recent comparative research. *Communication Quarterly*, 39, 130–143.
10. Niikura, R. (1999). Assertiveness among Japanese, Malaysians, Filipino, and US white collar workers. *Journal of Social Psychology*, 139, 690–699; Fao, A., Hashimoto, K., and Rao, A. (1997). Universal and culturally specific aspects of managerial influence: A study of Japanese managers. *Leadership Quarterly*, 8, 295–312.
11. Holt, J. L., and DeVore, C. J. (2005). Culture, gender, organizational role, and styles of conflict resolution: a meta-analysis. *International Journal of Intercultural Relations*, 29, 165–196; Ting-Toomey, S., Gao, G., Trubinsky, P., Yang, Z., Kim, H. S., Lin, S. L., and Nishida, T. (1991). Culture, face maintenance, and styles of handling interpersonal conflict: A study in five cultures. *International Journal of Conflict Management*, 2, 275–296.
12. Leung, K. (1988). Some determinants of conflict avoidance. *Journal of Cross-Cultural Psychology*, 19, 125–136.
13. Posthuma, White, Dworkin, Yanez, and Swift, Conflict resolution styles between co-workers in US and Mexican cultures; Tinsley, C. H., and Brett, J. M. (2001). Managing workplace conflict in the United States and Hong Kong. *Organizational Behavior & Human Decision Processes*, 85, 360–381; Morris, M. W., Williams, K. Y., Leung, K., Larrick, R., Mendoza, M. T., Bhatnagar, D., Li, J., Kondo, M., Liu, J.-L., and Hu, J.-C. (1998). Conflict management style: Accounting for cross-national differences. *Journal of International Business Studies*, 29, 729–748.
14. Tinsley and Brett, Managing workplace conflict in the United States and Hong Kong.
15. Brew, F. P., and Cairns, D. R., (2005). Styles of managing interpersonal workplace conflict in relation to status and face concern: A study with Anglos and Chinese. *The International Journal of Conflict Management*, 15, 27–56.
16. Cheng, C., and Chun, W. (2008). Cultural differences and similarities in request rejection: A situational approach. *Journal of Cross-Cultural Psychology*, 39, 745–764; Gelfand, M. J., Major, V. , Raver, J. , Nishii, L., and O'Brien, K. (2006). Negotiating relationally: The dynamics of the relational self in negotiations. *Academy of Management Review*, 31, 427–451.
17. Kozan, M. K. (1989). Cultural influences on styles of handling interpersonal conflicts: Comparisons among Jordanian, Turkish, and U.S. managers. *Human Relations*, 42, 787–799.

18. Brett, J, M., Tinsley, C. H., Shapiro, D. L., and Okumura, T. (2007). Intervening in employee disputes: How and when will managers from China, Japan, and U.S. act differently? *Management & Organization Review*, 3, 183–204.
19. Leung, K., and Iwawaki, S. (1988). Cultural collectivism and distributive behavior. *Journal of Cross-Cultural Psychology*, 19, 35–49.
20. McFarlin, D. B., and Sweeney, P. D. (2001). Cross-cultural applications of organizational justice. In R. Cropanzano (ed.) *Justice in the Workplace: From Theory to Practice*, Vol. 2, 67–95. Mahwah, NJ: Erlbaum.
21. Victor, D. A. (1992). *International Business Communication*. New York: HarperCollins.
22. Cardon, P. W. (2006). Reacting to face loss in Chinese business culture: An interview report. *Business Communication Quarterly*, December, 439–443; Ting-Toomey, S. (1990). *A Face Negotiation Perspective Communicating for Peace*. Thousand Oaks, CA: Sage; Cardon, P. W. (2009). A model of face practices in Chinese business culture: Implications for Western businesspersons. *Thunderbird International Business Review*, January/February, 51, 19–36.
23. Dong, Q., and Lee, Y. (2007). The Chinese concept of face: A perspective for business communicators. *Journal of Business and Society*, 45, 204–216; Redding, S. G., and Ng, M. (1983). The role of 'face' in the organizational perceptions of Chinese managers. *International Studies of Management and Organization*, 11, 92–123; Ho, D. Y. (1994). Face dynamics: From conceptualization to measurement. In S. Ting-Toomey (ed.) *The Challenge of Facework: Cross-Cultural and Interpersonal Issues*, 269–286. Albany, NY: State University of New York Press; Cardon, P. W. (2006). Reacting to face loss in Chinese business culture. *Business Communication Quarterly*, December, 439–443.
24. Adam, H., Shirako, A., and Maddus, W. W. (2010). Cultural variance in the interpersonal effects of anger in negotiations. *Psychological Science*, 21(6), 882–889; Liu, M. (2009). The intrapersonal and interpersonal effects of anger on negotiation strategies: A cross-cultural investigation. *Human Communication Research*, 35, 148–169; Reeder, J. A. (1987). When West meets East: Cultural aspects of doing business in Asia. *Business Horizons*, January–February, 69–74.
25. Schulz, A. K. D., Salter, S. B., Lopez, J. C., and Lewis, P. A. (2009). Revaluating face: A note on differences in private information sharing among two communitarian societies. *Journal of International Accounting Research*, 8, 57–65; see also: Bond, M. H., and Hwang, K. (1986). The social psychology of the Chinese people. In Y. Kim, D. Cohen, and W. Au (eds) *The Psychology of the Chinese People*, 213–266. Hong Kong: Oxford University Press; Kim, Y., Cohen, D., and Au, W. (2010). The jury and abjury of my peers: The self in face and dignity cultures. *Journal of Personality and Social Psychology*, 98, 904–916.
26. Reeder, When West meets East.
27. Adam, Shirako, and Maddus, Cultural variance in the interpersonal effects of anger in negotiations; Liu, The intrapersonal and interpersonal effects of anger on negotiation strategies; Tinsley, C. H., and Weldon, E. (2003). Responses to normative conflict among American and Chinese Managers. *International Journal of Cross-Cultural Management*, 3, 183–194.
28. Fu. H. Y., Morris, M. W., Lee, S., and Chiu, C. Y. (2002). Why do individuals follow cultural scripts? A dynamic constructivist account of American–Chinese differences in choice of mediators to resolve conflict. *Academy of Management Proceedings*, CM, D1–D6.
29. Makela, L., and Suutari, V. (2011). Coping with work–family conflicts in the global career context. *Thunderbird International Business Review*, 53, 365–375; Coffey, B. S., Anderson, S. E., Zhao, S., Liu, Y., and Zhang, J. (2009). Perspectives on work–family issues in China: The voice of young urban professionals. *Community, Work and Family*, 12, 197–212; De Cieri, H., and Bardoel, E. A. (2009). What does "work–life management" mean in China and Southeast Asia for MNCs? *Community, Work and Family*, 12, 179–196.
30. Chen, K. (2005). China's growth places strains on a family's ties: Brothers with different goals split over business venture, as father feels ignored. *The Wall Street Journal*, April 13, A1, A15.
31. Tinsley, C. H., Turna, N., Weingart, L. R., and Dillon-Merrill, R. L. (2012). How cultural stereotyping influences intercultural negotiation. In B. M. Goldman and D. L. Shapiro (eds) *The Psychology of Negotiations in the 21st Century Workplace*, 269–291. New York: Routledge;

Sebenius, J. K. (2002). The hidden challenge of cross-border negotiations. *Harvard Business Review*, March, 76–85; Graham, J. L. (1983). Brazilian, Japanese, and American business negotiations. *Journal of International Business Studies*, 14, 47–62.

32. See: Special issue of the journal *International Negotiation* (2004, Vol. 8), Zartman, W. (ed.), that was focused on terrorism and features about such crimes, including an article by Faure, G. O. (2004). Negotiating with terrorists: The hostage case. *International Negotiation*, 8, 469–494; Giebels, E., and Taylor, P. J. (2009). Interaction patterns in crisis negotiations: Persuasive arguments and cultural differences. *Journal of Applied Psychology*, 94, 5–19; Salacuse, J. (2009). Negotiating: The top ten ways that culture can affect your negotiations. *Ivey Business Journal*, September/October, 1–6; Taylor, P. J., and Donald, I. J. (2004). The structure of communication behavior in simulated and actual crisis negotiations. *Human Communication Research*, 30, 443–478.

33. See: U.S. Bureau of the Census. (2011). *Exports, Imports and Trade Balance by Country and Area*, available at: www.census.gov/foreign-trade/Press-Release/2011pr/final_revisions/exh13tl.txt (retrieved February 10, 2013); Van Zandt, H. F. (1970). How to negotiate in Japan. *Harvard Business Review*, November–December, 45–56.

34. Gulbro, R., and Herbig, P. (1996). Negotiating successfully in cross-cultural situations. *Industrial Marketing Management*, 25, 235–241.

35. Fisher, R., and Ury, W. (1990). Getting to Yes: Negotiating Agreement Without Giving In. New York: Penguin Books.

36. Weiss, S. E. (1994). Negotiating with "Romans"—Part 1. *Sloan Management Review*, 53, 51–61.

37. *Financial Times*. (2003). Avoid the trap of thinking everyone is just like you, August 29, 7.

38. Volkema, R. J. (2012). Why people don't ask: Understanding initiation behavior in international negotiations. *Thunderbird International Business Review*, 54, 625–637; Graham, J. L., and Herberger, R. A. (1983). Negotiators abroad—don't shoot from the hip. *Harvard Business Review*, July–August, 160–168; see also Sebenius, J. K. (2002). Caveats for cross-border negotiators. *Negotiation Journal*, 18, 121–133.

39. Gulbro and Herbig, Negotiating successfully in cross-cultural situations; Tung, R. L. (1984). How to negotiate with the Japanese. *California Management Review*, 26, 62–77; Volkema, R. J. (1999). Ethicality in negotiations: An analysis of perceptual similarities and differences between Brazil and the United States. *Journal of Business Research*, 45, 59–67.

40. Tung, How to negotiate with the Japanese; Van Zandt, How to negotiate in Japan.

41. Grindsted, A. (1994). The impact of cultural styles on negotiation: A case study of Spaniards and Danes. *IEEE Transactions on Professional Communication*, 37, 34–38. Pornpitakpan, C., and Giba, S. (1999). The effects of cultural adaptation on business relationships: Americans selling to Japanese and Thais. *Journal of International Business Studies*, 30, 317–338.

42. Ghauri, P., and Fang, T. (2001). Negotiating with the Chinese: A socio-cultural analysis. *Journal of World Business*, 36, 303–309; Graham, J. L., and Lam, N. M. (2003). The Chinese negotiation. *Harvard Business Review*, October, 82–91.

43. Gulbro and Herbig, Negotiating successfully in cross-cultural situations; Tse, D. K., Francis, J., and Walls, I. (1994). Cultural differences in conducting intra- and inter-cultural negotiations. *Journal of International Business Studies*, 25, 537–555; Volkema, R., and Fleury, M. (2002). Alternative negotiating conditions and the choice of negotiation tactics: A cross-cultural comparison. *Journal of Business Ethics*, 36, 381–397.

44. Adair, W. L., and Brett, J. M. (2005). The negotiation dance: Time, culture, and behavioral sequences in negotiation. *Organizational Science*, 16, 33–51.

45. Graham, J. L., and Sano, Y. (1986). Across the negotiation table from the Japanese. *International Marketing Review*, 3, 58–71.

46. Graham, J. L. (1985). The influence of culture on the process of business negotiations: An exploratory study. *Journal of International Business Studies*, 16, 81–96.

47. Graham, J. L., and Mintu-Wimsat, A. (1997). Culture's influence on business negotiations in four countries. *Group Decision and Negotiation*, 6, 483–502; Li, J., and Labig, C. E. (2001). Negotiating with Chinese: Exploratory study of relationship building. *Journal of Managerial Issues*, 13, 342–348.

48. Herbig, P. A., and Kramer, H. E. (1992). Do's and don't of cross-cultural negotiations. *Marketing Intelligence and Planning*, 10(2), 10–13.

49. Banthin, J., and Steizer, L. (1988/89). "Opening" China: Negotiation strategies when East meets West. *Mid-Atlantic Journal of Business*, 25, 1–14; Tung, R. L. (1982). U.S.–China trade negotiations: Practices, procedures, and outcomes. *Journal of International Business Studies*, Fall, 25–37.

50. Campbell, N. C. G., Graham, J. L., Jolibert, A., and Meissner, H. G. (1988). Marketing negotiations in France, Germany, United Kingdom, and the US. *Journal of Marketing*, 52, 49–62; Tung, How to negotiate with the Japanese.

51. Trompenaars, F., and Hampden-Turner, C. (1998). *Riding the Waves of Culture: Understanding Diversity in Global Business*. New York: McGraw-Hill.

52. Campbell, Graham, Jolibert, and Meissner, Marketing negotiations in France, Germany, the United Kingdom, and the United States; Graham, J. L., Mintu, A. T., and Rodgers, W. (1994). Explorations of negotiation behaviors in ten foreign cultures using a model developed in the United States. *Management Science*, 40, 72–95.

53. Graham, J. L. (1983). Brazilian, Japanese, and American business negotiations. *Journal of International Business Studies*, 14, 47–62; Tung, How to negotiate with the Japanese.

54. Adair, W., Weingart, L., and Brett, J. (2007). The timing and function of offers in U.S. and Japanese negotiations. *Journal of Applied Psychology*, 92, 1056–1068; Adair, W., Brett, J., Lempereur, A., Okumura, T., Shikhirev, P., Tinsley, C., and Lytle, A. (2004). Culture and negotiation strategy. *Negotiation Journal*, January, 87–111.

55. Brett, J. M. (2000). Culture and negotiation. *International Journal of Psychology*, 35, 97–104.

56. Graham, J. L. (1988). Negotiating with the Japanese: A guide to persuasive tactics (Parts I and II). *East Asian Executive Reports*, 10, November, 6, 19–21 and December, 8, 16–17.

57. Barnum, C., and Wolniansky, N. (1989). Why Americans fail at overseas negotiations. *Management Review*, October, 56–57.

58. Herbig and Kramer, Do's and don'ts of cross-cultural negotiations.

59. Adair, Brett, Lempereur, Okumura, Shikhirev, Tinsley, and Lytle, Culture and negotiation strategy.

60. Volkema, Ethicality in negotiations: An analysis of perceptual similarities and differences between Brazil and the United States.

61. Al-Khatib, J. A., Malshe, A., and AbdulKader, M. (2008). Perception of unethical negotiation tactics: A comparative study of US and Saudi managers. *International Business Review*, 17, 78–102.

62. Stewart, S., and Keown, C. F. (1989). Talking with the dragon: Negotiating in the People's Republic of China. *Columbia Journal World Business*, 24, 68–72.

63. Liu, M. (2009). The intrapersonal and interpersonal effects of anger on negotiation strategies: A cross-cultural investigation. *Human Communication Research*, 35, 148–169.

64. Sheer, V. C., and Chen, L. (2003). Successful Sino-Western business negotiation: Participants accounts of national and professional cultures. *Journal of Business Communication*, 40, 50–85; Weiss, J. (1988). The negotiating style of the People's Republic of China: The future of Hong Kong and Macao. *Journal of Social, Political and Economic Studies*, 13, 175–194.

65. Graham and Herberger, Negotiators abroad—Don't shoot from the hip.

66. Liu, M. (2009). The intrapersonal and interpersonal effects of anger on negotiation strategies: A cross-cultural investigation. *Human Communication Research*, 35, 148–169.

67. Graham, J. L. (1985). The influence of culture on the process of business negotiations: An exploratory study. *Journal of International Business Studies*, 16, 81–96; Graham and Herberger, Negotiators abroad—Don't shoot from the hip.

68. Graham, Negotiating with the Japanese: A guide to persuasive tactics (Parts I and II); Graham and Herberger, Negotiators abroad—Don't shoot from the hip.

69. Graham, Negotiating with the Japanese: A guide to persuasive tactics (Parts I and II).

70. Negotiation scenario taken from: Brett, J. M.., and Gelfand, M. J. (2005). Lessons from abroad: When culture affects negotiating style. *Negotiation*, January, 3–5.

71. Brett and Gelfand, Lessons from abroad: When culture affects negotiating style.

72. Oh, T. K. (1984). Selling to the Japanese. *Nation's Business*, October, 37–38.

73. Banthin, J., and Steizer, L. (1988/89). "Opening" China: Negotiation strategies when East meets West. *Mid-Atlantic Journal of Business*, 25, 1–14.

74. Pettibone, P. J. (1990). Negotiating a joint venture in the Soviet Union: How to protect your interests. *Journal of European Business*, 2, 5–12; Choi, C. J. (1994). Contract enforcement across cultures. *Organization Studies*, 15, 673–682.

75. Adler, N. J., Graham, J. L., and Gehrke, T. S. (1987). Business negotiations in Canada, Mexico, and the U.S. *Journal of Business Research*, 15, 411–429.

76. Fox, C. (2006). International negotiator; Posthuma, White, Dworkin, Yanez, and Swift, Conflict resolution styles between co-workers in US and Mexican cultures; Heydenfeldt, The influence of individualism/collectivism on Mexican and U.S. business negotiation.

chapter 8

taking stock
developing international strategy

Learning Objectives

After reading this chapter, you should be able to:

- describe basic international strategic concepts and the theory of national competitive advantage;
- identify types of international strategies and the firm and industry factors that affect them;
- describe the steps involved in the process of creating international strategy;
- identify the organizational features that help companies develop and implement their international strategies successfully.

International Challenge

Localization and Integration: One Company's Solution to the "Either–Or" Dilemma

Global behemoths such as GE have a tendency to segregate their corporate headquarters from operations that they establish in other countries—particularly ones designed to capitalize on low-cost labor and production in emerging markets. Of course, they are happy to sell products to customers in those countries, and they like saving money by manufacturing there. Ultimately, however, many such firms remain fundamentally unchanged despite this global outreach. Corporate offices sometimes even have a palatable air of "we know best" which is a mindset that features ideas and strategic directives that flow one way. All too often it seemed as though Siemens remained distinctly German, Panasonic retained its Japanese footprint, and GE remained singularly American, despite each company's widespread global presence.

At least, that used to be the case for these firms—GE in particular. For decades, GE (like many multinationals from developed countries) favored a *glocalization* strategy for product development. The essence of this approach is to create products at home and then push them out to be made and sold to the rest of the world, with perhaps some adaptations made for local markets. This was a terrific way to minimize research and development costs while still allowing products to be tailored to local conditions after the fact. It also had the positive effect of minimizing risks because key development and proprietary concerns were under corporate control. Likewise, the multinational may have great confidence in its brand's ability to appeal to other markets, including emerging ones. Such was the case for GE.

Yet, change has a way of altering strategies. GE reasoned that with rich countries growing slowly, in addition to the rapid rise of countries such as China, India, and Brazil, it needed to start to back away from glocalization. The growth opportunities—and threats from rising competitors—were often both coming from emerging markets. GE felt it needed to create cheaper products designed for those developing markets overseas. Failure to do this would mean that local companies in developing markets would fill in the gap and then take their cheap, innovative products into wealthier markets, interfering with GE's existing business there. In fact, this is precisely what happened to Panasonic's healthy business based on its glocalization strategy in China. The results for Panasonic were awful, including layoffs of over 10,000 employees before the company changed strategies. The bottom line is that products created in rich nations are often too expensive and too feature-laden to penetrate deeply into emerging markets. With much lower per capita incomes, a large set of customers in emerging markets are often perfectly happy with technology that offers good, but not great, performance at an extremely cheap price, with room to spare for those in the market with more expensive tastes as well.

As some experts have observed, all too often "multinationals may be *in* global markets, but they're regularly not *of* them."[1] Instead, local initiatives are expected to stay local. But, what is remarkable about GE, and is frankly surprising about any global giant, is when they go to an emerging market in search of low-cost manufacturing and the like, yet come back a different company. This seemed to be the case for GE. Consider the fact that some of its newest and most exciting products were a portable ultrasound machine and a hand-held electrocardiogram (ECG) device. Both devices are relatively inexpensive and very innovative. Yet, the most unexpected aspect of both products is that they were developed *in* emerging markets *for* emerging markets. The ultrasound was developed in China and the ECG in India—both sold in their respective countries *before* being sold in the U.S. Think about this reversal of business and how GE made the transformation. What strategic issues and tactical options could it develop to move from a traditional glocalization approach to one where innovation is fostered in those markets? As you read through the chapter, you will run across some such options. At the end of the chapter, take a look at the Up to the Challenge? feature to see what steps GE took to address this strategic challenge.[2]

International Strategy: Deciding How to Compete Abroad

Business is about competition. Management's job is to figure out how to outperform competitors in ways that allows the firm to grow and to become more profitable. That "how to"—the steps and actions that a company's leadership pursues to accomplish its objectives—is the essence of strategy. Developing and implementing company strategy is tough going and gets tougher when borders are crossed. As seen already, multinationals often face a diverse quilt of cultures, values, and practices. In addition, they typically encounter an array of opportunities (e.g., promising markets) and threats (e.g., risk, moves by competitors) in foreign locales. Determining the best way to operate in markets around the world can be a very complicated task. Consequently, developing an overall plan for competing abroad and choosing market entry options that make sense can mean all the difference when operating internationally.[3]

This chapter focuses on basic strategies that firms can pursue abroad as well as how to develop them. (Chapter 9 will cover specific foreign market entry options.) Generally speaking, the process of formulating international strategy involves setting international goals and then following through with whatever approach the company adopts. The stakes are high. Today, more than ever, companies must be able to anticipate and react quickly to competitors' moves, while being nimble in the face of rapid changes in markets and technology. Otherwise, they risk losing their ability to compete effectively.

For instance, while multinationals often see China as a great place to manufacture, conduct product research, and sell (especially given China's dramatically rising middle and upper income groups), some experts consider it among the toughest markets in the world because of the cultural, legal, and social differences with many other countries. Increasingly, droves of aggressive local companies are emerging to challenge established international firms. Ford Motor Company's recent push into China offers a look at these very issues. As is well known, China is large and rapidly evolving and Ford wants to grow there in a big way—it has three plants in China (one with local partner Chonqing Changan) that can collectively produce over 600,000 cars per year. Yet, Ford's production capacity lags that of key rivals Toyota and General Motors. Moreover, Ford is nowhere close to being the top automotive brand in China's tough marketplace. Indeed, in 2009, Ford was behind three Chinese car companies (Chery, BYD, and Geely) as it tried to climb up from eleventh place in sales. While it has had great success with its Ford Focus (the largest-selling car in China), it has also dealt with supplier and management problems. Nevertheless, it recently set a two-year goal to double market share to 6 percent by 2015.[4] Figure 8.1 shows that Ford has made little progress relative to other brands in China through 2012 and looks to jump production significantly.

Rank	Auto Company	Home Country	Market Share (2011)
1st	Volkswagen (includes Audi)	Germany	15.9%
2nd	GM (includes Buick, Chevrolet)	USA	9.6%
3rd	Hyundai (includes Kia)	South Korea	9.4%
4th	Toyota	Japan	6.5%
5th	Nissan	Japan	6.4%
6th	Honda	Japan	4.5%
7th	Chery	China	4.3%
8th	BYD	China	3.4%
9th	Great Wall	China	2.8%
10th	Ford	USA	2.5%
11th	Suzuki	Japan	2.3%
12th	Mazda	Japan	1.7%

Figure 8.1 Race for the Top: Car Brand Sales Leaders in China.

Sources: Adapted from Focus2Move. (2012). *Chinese Car Market*, available at: www.focus2move.com/item (retrieved November 25, 2013); Dolan, M., Shirouzu, N., and Bellman, E. (2009). Ford makes push to boost Asian presence. *The Wall Street Journal*, September 23, B2.

China's development underscores the point that companies need to respond to growth opportunities wherever they exist. Moreover, advances in communication and transportation have made it easier for all companies to source the best parts, materials, products, and labor from anywhere in the world in ways that best meet their needs. Consequently, you might think that the importance of location as a competitive weapon isn't what it used to be. After all, if everyone can source globally (e.g., manufacture garments in Bangladesh because labor is cheap), then there is no unique advantage to doing so. But this overlooks how important it is to figure out where the best places are to manufacture, to innovate, to buy supplies, and to sell products in the first place. It also overlooks the challenges associated with managing globally distributed work once those choices are made. Regardless, there is little doubt that when it comes to innovation and long-term success, location still matters a great deal.[5]

For instance, the world's best consumer electronics firms are based in Asia, the best entertainment firms are in the United States and India, and the best in leather fashions comes from Italy. Understanding how and why these clusters of excellence exist around the world underscores why strategic planning may be the most important task facing international managers.[6] Despite the potential value of having a coherent international strategy, a surprising number of companies enter overseas markets with goals but no coherent strategy. This failure to plan can lead to a variety of problems, including underestimating what is needed in a foreign setting (resources, key supplies); the inability to predict foreign environment and adapt accordingly; and competing poorly.[7] Regardless of the level of competition or company overseas sophistication, all international strategies should provide answers to the same basic questions, including:

- What products or services will be sold abroad?
- Where and how will services be delivered or products made?
- What resources are necessary and how will they be acquired?
- How can competitors be outperformed?[8]

In the past, developing international strategy was often the exclusive purview of top executives. Some contemporary firms involve people who are closer to the marketplace in the creation of international strategy. The idea is to react more quickly to specific changes in an evolving international environment. For instance, line managers can sometimes be in a great position to spot trends, understand competitors, and test new ideas than senior management. If the goal of strategy development is to stay agile and to quickly take advantage of international opportunities, then involving people who understand the marketplace best should help this process.[9]

In fact, some companies such as Hewlett-Packard even involve suppliers and customers in strategic planning to help identify new business opportunities. Overall, research suggests that the best strategic planning process is one that builds in flexibility and openness to change. For those firms who are in rapidly changing environments (such as the dwindling, low-margin laptop business), companies may have to modify, amend, and tweak their international strategies as they go, or even dump them altogether if conditions warrant.[10]

Accordingly, the next section discusses some company-level international strategies and outlines the strategy development process, including the special strategic challenges facing small firms. The chapter's conclusion examines some organizational features that companies should have (or should cultivate) to successfully develop and implement their strategies.

Basic Strategic Concepts for International Competition

Chapter 1 provided a snapshot of the economic powers that are emerging and challenging the dominance of established players such as Germany, Japan, and the U.S. The past several years have seen dramatic increases in the growth of international business, much of it fueled by rapidly developing countries such as Brazil, India, and especially China. Moreover, developing markets are spawning multinationals of their own—companies that are hungry to compete not just in their home markets, but everywhere. Often, these emerging local giants (e.g., Chinese appliance maker Haier) have lower costs and innovative ideas—a combination that should worry more established multinationals from developed countries.[11]

Another important trend to mention is that small and medium-sized companies have contributed greatly to the recent growth in international business. In fact, they actually account for a bigger slice of international trade than do large firms. For instance, the 50 largest American exporters (e.g., Boeing) account for only about a third of exported merchandise, with small and medium-sized firms producing most of the rest. And while multinationals can be a threat to smaller firms, especially if they are poorly run, many small companies are more nimble, more inventive, and more connected to local markets than the globe-trotting giants.[12]

Nevertheless, large multinationals continue to be the focus of research on international strategy because of their enormous influence and impressive global reach. The Japanese giant Mitsubishi Corporation actually represents a family of companies with interrelated ownership. This ownership structure, called *keiretsu,* is common in Japan but is slowly fading away. One family member is usually a trading company (called a *sogo shosa*) that helps market products from the rest of the corporate family to the outside world. In this role, Mitsubishi at one point sold as many as 100,000 products to some 45,000 customers around the world.[13]

General Business-Level Strategies

So, how do international companies actually compete? Fundamentally, all companies make money through value creation. They offer products or services that customers want. Everything else being equal, the more value companies create, the more profitable they will be—because customers are more willing to buy their products or services, even at a higher price. Naturally, things typically are not so simple. Competing products or services from other firms often dilute the value that a company offers customers, putting downward pressure on the price that can be charged. Consequently, profitability often depends on whether companies can create value for customers in the face of competition while also reducing costs.[14]

Generally speaking, there are three basic business-level strategies that companies can pursue to create value, and ultimately, profitability—either alone or in combination. One way companies can meet international customer demands is by differentiating their products or services from those of competitors. In doing so, they provide unique or superior products that customers are willing to pay for. That is what Mercedes-Benz does in offering what it believes are the world's most sophisticated production cars. But a Mercedes is not cheap. Thus, another way to provide value is through cost leadership—offering cheaper products or more efficient services than competitors. For example, Asian computer manufacturers have done well by combining efficient manufacturing operations and inexpensive labor, allowing them to undercut competitors on price (e.g., Taiwan's Acer). Finally, firms embracing a niche strategy focus on a specific line of products or services relative to competitors who operate more broadly. By serving a specific market segment, firms hope to do a better job of responding to customers and meeting their needs (e.g., on price, differentiation, or both) than do competitors. Italy's Ferrari S.p.A. is an example of a firm that has pursued a niche strategy. The company focuses exclusively on upscale sports cars, which offer superior performance relative to competitors.[15]

Building the Value Chain

Regardless of the basic approach used to attract customers, companies can add value by changing any of their primary activities (e.g., manufacturing or marketing of products) or supporting activities (e.g., information technology), either alone or in combination. As Figure 8.2 suggests, a firm can be thought of as a linked set of these primary and

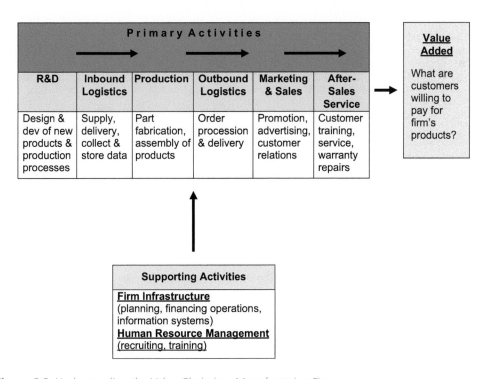

Figure 8.2 Understanding the Value Chain in a Manufacturing Firm.

supporting activities, referred to as a value chain. Consequently, a company's international strategy also involves the choices it makes in terms of how value chain activities are configured (e.g., where do value chain activities happen?) and coordinated (e.g., is there tight control from headquarters or local control?).

Often, companies change value chain activities to improve their core competencies. Core competencies are skills that are hard for competitors to imitate and can be located anywhere in a value chain. For instance, one firm's competitiveness might rest on its logistical execution (e.g., Wal-Mart's sophisticated distribution system), while another firm's competence is its ability to innovate (e.g., 3M's history of creating unique products), and yet another's is based on its manufacturing prowess (e.g., Toyota's production quality). If firms have a core competency that helps them outperform competitors, then they possess a distinctive competence. Said differently, they attract more customers because they have the best logistics, are the most innovative, or have the highest production quality.

Because international business should continue to grow over the long term, one view is that firms compete best by moving different value chain activities to wherever location economies exist. For instance, if the cheapest and most productive labor for assembling a certain product is in Vietnam, then that is where a company should locate its production operations. If the best product designers are found in the U.S., then that is where R&D activities should be located. Naturally, this is a bit of an oversimplification. For instance, transportation costs may offset any savings from the use of cheap, but distant, skilled labor. Balancing these tradeoffs and making the right decision in the end regarding potential location economies is a big challenge for management.[16]

Indeed, locating certain value chain activities in places that offer positive benefits gives companies a source of competitive advantage compared to firms that fail to do so. For instance, software development and maintenance firms may gain an edge over rivals by locating those activities in India, a source of inexpensive and well-trained programmers. Others use a complex patchwork of locations for various value chain activities. Consider what Hewlett-Packard does in bringing a new server to market. The concept for a server is hatched by the firm's designers in Singapore, with managers in Houston providing final approval. Next, parts and components are engineered in Taiwan. Final product assembly then happens in many locations, including China, India, and Australia, with most of the servers staying in those markets.[17]

The pros associated with dispersing value chain activities to various locations can be offset by various cons, such as coordination difficulties due to cultural differences. Thus, the goal is to capitalize on location while effectively integrating operations across those locations. This is easier said than done. Location economies, such as low labor costs or plentiful raw materials, only offer a sustainable competitive advantage if it is hard for other firms to follow suit. In other words, there is nothing terribly unique about moving plants to low-wage locations or sourcing materials from certain overseas locations. You may be at a disadvantage if your competitors operate in a low-wage environment and you do not, everything else being equal. But, jumping on the low-wage bandwagon alone will not set you apart. Instead, locations that somehow help companies continually improve their processes, marketing savvy, or capacity for innovation can do more to provide a long-term competitive advantage. Put simply, it is the ability to constantly change and adapt that allows many international firms to outperform competitors.[18]

Locations and Competitiveness

Our discussion to this point suggests that competitiveness is a complex concept involving industry features and the locations at which they do business. Of course, companies compete. But in a sense, nations also compete to create innovations and provide goods and services that international markets demand. What is at stake is nothing less than whether countries can continue to offer a rising standard of living for their citizens.[19]

How do nations become competitive and why is it that certain nations seem to produce firms that are very successful in specific industries? For instance, why have American companies tended to lead in computer software, but Asian companies have tended to lead in consumer electronics? The theory of national competitive advantage tries to answer such questions. It argues that four factors shape the competitive context among nations and the firms based there. These factors, presented in Figure 8.3, represent a combination of national and firm-specific characteristics. Understanding how they interact can help explain why industries and companies tend to do better or worse in particular locations. Each of these factors is considered next.

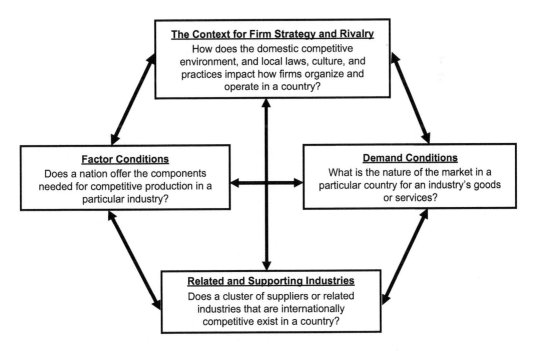

Figure 8.3 Location Factors That Help Explain International Competitive Advantage.

Source: Adapted from Porter, M. E. (1990). The competitive advantage of nations. *Harvard Business Review*, 90, 77.

313

Factor Conditions

Does a nation offer the components needed for competitive production in a particular industry, such as abundant raw materials, capital, business infrastructure, and skilled labor? With the right combination of conditions, home-grown competitors can spring up, do well domestically, and eventually become formidable international competitors. For instance, the prime grape-growing land in California and a large pool of expert winemakers are key reasons why the United States is a worldwide leader in this industry.

Demand Conditions

What is the nature of the market in a particular country for an industry's goods or services? Large, sophisticated home markets often force firms to become more responsive to demanding customers, which may foreshadow where international markets are ultimately headed. This early awareness can help firms stay ahead of competitors from other countries. For instance, the American desire for convenience and speed has spawned efficient fast food companies (e.g., McDonald's), many of which have done well overseas where similar desires have subsequently emerged.

Related and Supporting Industries

Does a cluster of suppliers or related industries that are internationally competitive exist in a country? If so, they can provide superior and mutually beneficial access to components, technology, and innovation thanks to shorter lines of communication and established working relationships. For instance, Italian shoe companies owe much of their overseas success to the close relationships they have developed with local leather suppliers, shoe component manufacturers, and specialized equipment firms.

Firm Strategy, Structure, and Rivalry

How does the domestic competitive environment, as well as local laws, culture, and business practices, impact the ways in which firms organize and operate in a particular country? Tough domestic competition forces firms to be more innovative, productive, and cost efficient—characteristics that may serve them well in international markets. For instance, Honda's excellent performance in the U.S. auto market is partially a consequence of its intensive competitive struggles with formidable homegrown rivals in Japan (e.g., Toyota and Nissan). Likewise, management practices can also make it easier or harder for firms in certain countries to compete in specific industries.[20]

Implications of the Four Factors

As Figure 8.3 illustrates, the four factors driving national competitive advantage can interact to affect how successful firms are in international markets. For example, just having demanding domestic customers may not be enough to give a firm in a particular country a competitive advantage. But if that firm also faces tough domestic competition and existing factor conditions support its efforts to develop more innovative products (e.g., technology infrastructure is excellent), then a competitive advantage may result when the company tries to sell internationally. A combination of factors may help explain why successful American software firms such as Microsoft have also done well abroad. Conversely, a combination of factors may explain why Italian leather and wool goods firms, some with histories dating back several hundred years, have seen their long-running success recently put at risk by upstart Chinese competitors. Being in a cluster of related industries with well-developed relationships and a tradition of craftsmanship helped the Italian firms prosper for many years. The local business environment, however, made it difficult for them to respond quickly to Chinese competition. Specifically, as low-cost, but high-quality Chinese companies started winning customers away, the Italian firms were hamstrung by local labor laws that made human resource moves difficult.[21]

Overall, the theory of national competitive advantage is useful for thinking about how country-specific factors can affect a firm's international competitiveness. That said, questions about the theory remain. For instance, having a positive domestic environment does not necessarily mean that a particular industry or company will thrive in a particular location. Conversely, companies have emerged from locations without some of the positive factors specified by the theory and still become formidable international competitors.[22]

The role of government is another controversial aspect of the theory of national competitive advantage. According to the theory, governments can act to facilitate the development of industries in a nation (e.g., by passing laws that influence firms' ability to compete). The exact nature and impact of government action on the creation of competitive firms, however, is not completely understood. But like it or not, many national governments are now engaged in helping their companies develop, innovate, and compete. Dozens of countries are making strategic bets on innovation in various ways. Consider these examples:

- Singapore is focused on encouraging innovation in digital media, green technology, and life sciences. Life sciences start-ups can receive tax credits, facilities, staff training, and grants from the government.
- China wants to become a world-class innovation country by 2020 and has provided incentives to ten top universities to turn out more research and technical experts in a variety of fields.
- Finland has spent almost $1 billion to launch an "innovation university" designed to foster new, commercially viable innovations that cut across multiple areas of technology.[23]

These four factors spelled out by the theory of national competitive advantage generally drive the international strategies used by certain firms. Companies need to make strategic decisions and often reflect on and take advantage of the conditions that they face in specific countries. When firms are operating in many countries across a variety of different industries, they need to consider developing larger, corporate-level strategies. In essence, they need to find ways to effectively manage operations that stretch across a diverse array of both products and countries.[24]

Corporate Strategy Options in International Business

Corporate strategies are used by multinationals as a guide for adding value (e.g., based on differentiation or low cost) to their business-level strategies across countries. It is common for firms to slowly evolve through several levels of internationalization if they are successful competitors in each. In fact, small companies often first enter international markets by exporting and only later do they establish overseas facilities. Some of these firms eventually build subsidiaries in dozens of countries and form alliances with other companies. Nevertheless, this evolutionary pattern of international development, one that is often followed by multinationals in rich, developed countries, has been giving way recently. Instead, newer multinationals from developing and emerging markets (e.g., China, India, and Mexico) have tended to grow and expand much more rapidly. These multinationals have grown out of difficult home markets—ones often plagued with weak business infrastructures, legal systems, and financial institutions. As a result, they have developed the ability to handle tough environments, something that allows them to move into foreign markets quickly and adapt well to local circumstances.[25]

In general, foreign market entry decisions are driven by a variety of features, including the nature of the industry the firm is in, the particular market being entered, the firm's strengths and weaknesses, and the firm's stage of international development. Chapter 9 considers the many options for entering foreign markets.[26]

When it comes to strategy, multinationals use various options that reflect the needs of their different business units or product lines. GE offers an astonishing array of products that cut across several industries. These include appliances, electrical equipment, jet engines, lighting, medical diagnostic systems, and plastics (and this is not a complete list!). The degree to which GE can compete by tailoring its products to local customers' needs (versus selling the same product everywhere in the same way) varies considerably across business units. That has implications for the international strategies that those units need to pursue. It may help to think of diverse multinationals such as GE as networks of relationships that exist among many dispersed organizations, each with somewhat different goals, perspectives, and strategies. Nevertheless, the presentation here simplifies things by treating multinationals as if they used a single strategy to guide all of their international operations.[27]

Industry Pressures for Global Integration and Local Responsiveness

Consider that a multinational's international strategy often reflects the nature of the industry in which it competes. For instance, in some industries, products or services have to be tailored to customer preferences, traditional practices, local distribution methods, legal requirements, and government regulations within individual markets. After all, the multinational may face different local competitors in each. Such is the case for many food, home, and personal care products, where local tastes for things such as flavors and scents vary considerably (e.g., pizzas are ubiquitous but toppings vary noticeably—such as octopus in Japan). In other industries, customer preferences may matter less than the web of laws and regulations that govern the development, manufacture, and distribution of products. The pharmaceutical industry is a good example of the impact of laws on strategy.

Tradition may also matter in addition to customer preferences, meaning that products have to be customized to match. For instance, in North America, people drive on the right side of the road and want steering wheels on the left side of their cars. In the U.K. however, cars are driven on the left side of the road, with preferences for steering wheels on the right. Many other regional differences in cars exist for a variety of reasons, including the price of fuel. In Europe, high gas prices mean people prefer smaller and more fuel-efficient cars than their North American counterparts, where gas is comparatively cheap.

On the other hand, in some industries products can basically be sold anywhere in the world on a nearly identical basis, with little or no modification across countries (e.g., computer chips, chemicals, passenger aircraft). Overall, the degree to which companies have to tailor their products or services to satisfy local market demands is a function of the pressure for local responsiveness in their respective industries.

Likewise, industries vary in terms of how much pressure for global integration exists. This force pushes companies in an industry to be very efficient and to capture economies of scale. All eyes are on improving profitability by simplifying operations and cost cutting. This depends on the number and prowess of competitors in an industry. When competitors are few or weak, a company with unique or superior products is likely to face low pressure for integration. When more formidable competitors emerge, however, companies may look to integrate and coordinate all their value chain activities. This is often done on a worldwide basis with an eye toward improving their global efficiency and responsiveness to such competitive threats. For instance, in low-cost locations, multinationals may try to concentrate their manufacturing. This can help firms reducing control and coordination challenges. Integration pressures may lead firms to source globally—searching far and wide for talent, supplies, and components, thus creating an integrated web of value chain activities around the world. Integration is especially appealing in industries where customer needs are becoming similar or where delivering high-quality service to customers worldwide is key. Nonetheless, the bottom line is that global integration pressures are higher in some industries than others.[28]

There are five common corporate strategies used by multinationals, all of which typically reflect responses to varying levels of this pressure for global integration and local responsiveness discussed so far. Figure 8.4 summarizes these strategies on those two dimensions.

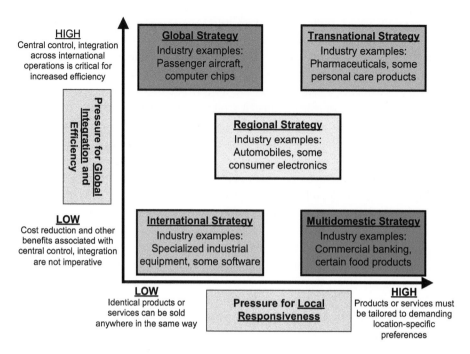

Figure 8.4 Five International Strategies: Responses to Pressures for Local Responsiveness and Global Integration.

Sources: Adapted from Beamish, P. W., Morrison, A. J., Rosenzweig, P. M., and Inken, A. C. (2000). *International Management: Text and Cases* (4th ed.), 143. Burr Ridge, IL: Irwin McGraw-Hill; Daniels, J. D., and Radebaugh, L. H. (2001). *International Business: Environments and Operations* (9th ed.), 529. Upper Saddle River, NJ: Prentice-Hall; Hill, C. W. L. (2008). *Global Business Today.* (5th ed.). New York: McGraw-Hill/Irwin.

The International Strategy

When companies face low pressure to tailor their products or services across foreign markets as well as low pressure to become more efficient and cut costs, they often choose to pursue an international strategy (also referred to as an export strategy or home replication strategy). Companies using this approach sell the same or similar products everywhere—often first created for their home markets. They typically perform all their product development in the home market but may sometimes establish manufacturing, marketing, or distribution facilities in important foreign markets. Headquarters, however, still maintains control over operations and decision making (see Figure 8.4).

This international strategy is a good fit for companies in industries where serious competitors are few and they can offer unique, specialized products that serve similar (if not identical) needs across a variety of markets. Many domestic firms find themselves using an international strategy when they first start doing business abroad, typically by selling products created for their home markets. U.S. motorcycle maker Harley-Davidson, for instance, is known for its iconic products. It holds a strong position in the U.S. market for heavy bikes, where it earns some 70 percent of its total revenue. But in recent years, Harley has distributed its U.S.-built bikes around the world—most recently India, where it started selling 12 of its most expensive models in 2009 and has no competition in the "luxury" end of the Indian market. In its earlier days, Procter & Gamble (P&G) followed a similar path. All products were created in Cincinnati, Ohio, and then distributed overseas. Now, P&G faces much tougher, more entrenched competitors than it did 20–30 years ago and thus no longer pursues an international strategy.

Nevertheless, many companies continue to follow an international strategy today, often in very specialized niche markets where they have a dominant position. For instance, Germany is known for producing firms with unique combinations of skills when it comes to the development and production of specialized industrial equipment. These firms have successfully integrated mechanical engineering prowess with sophisticated information technology systems using some of the finest manufacturing specialists in the world. This combination has proven hard for competitors to beat. This in turn buffers German firms from having to focus too much on costs—which is a good thing, given Germany's high wage rates and taxes. Firms in countries such as Brazil, China, and India are increasingly turning to these German corporations for their specialized equipment needs. Examples include Kuka, a German robotics company that makes industrial robots for specialized auto industry applications and, more recently, theme park rides. Another example is Centrotherm Photovoltaics, another German firm that makes the world's best solar-cell producing machines. These are in demand by solar energy cell companies such as China's Asia Silicon.[29]

The Multidomestic Strategy

In other industries, the pressure to tailor products and services to meet local preferences is high, even if integration and cost effectiveness pressures remain relatively low. In such circumstances, companies may opt for a multidomestic strategy, which focuses on closely aligning products and services to the specific demands found in foreign markets. This can work well if the value-added associated with these customized products allows the firm to charge higher prices or creates more demand for company products. Because of the intense focus on localizing products, firms often cede enormous control to managers in specific countries. This independence allows them to best respond to local conditions. As a result, product variations—along with management approaches—may vary considerably across countries. Subsidiary managers in specific countries are allowed to run their operations more or less as intact companies, with little interference from headquarters. The notion is that this is how to best provide tailored products and services for the local market.

While this allows for maximum tailoring to local conditions, the multidomestic strategy can be duplicative, inefficient, and lead to product proliferation. It can also inhibit information sharing as country managers simply act in their own best interest or even compete with each other for resources. Beauty product giant Avon experienced some of these problems a few years ago. The company earns 70 percent of its revenues overseas, much of it in developing markets such as Russia and China. It gave tremendous autonomy to country managers: they had discretion to develop, manufacture, and market their own products. Over time, bloat resulted, with overhead costs soaring to

$2.5 billion because of inefficiencies company-wide. Product proliferation had also increased dramatically (for example, 13,000 products were offered in the Mexican market alone). As business in key markets began to slow, these costs and inefficiencies became intolerable for Avon. The company decided to restructure and to step away from its multidomestic approach, cutting management layers and centralizing marketing and manufacturing on a global basis. This underscores that firms may need to move away from the multidomestic strategy if they encounter problems or if stronger competitors emerge that ratchet up pressures for greater efficiency, cost savings, and innovation.[30]

Companies can put up with these drawbacks in the right circumstances. For instance, in the commercial banking and beverage industries, multinationals must respond effectively and quickly to a diverse set of local preferences and needs. Put simply, in these industries, what will satisfy customers can vary from country to country. In response, multinationals may need to modify their products, marketing, service delivery methods, and/or pricing. In some industries requiring local responsiveness, differences in local needs may obliterate any advantages that might otherwise be obtained with centralized or integrated operations. Centralizing production of certain food products makes little sense for companies such as Nestlé and Unilever (both of which operate hundreds of manufacturing facilities worldwide). Transportation costs would offset any savings from economies of scale, and centralization would make it more difficult to offer an array of products tailored for specific locations in the first place.[31]

The Global Strategy

At the other end of the spectrum are industries in which country-specific preferences for products or services are minimal and global integration can lead to cost reductions and efficiencies necessary for profitability. In these industries, the same standardized products or services can be sold everywhere with relatively few, if any, adjustments. For example, as a key competitor in the production of commercial aircraft, Boeing operates in an industry that has become increasingly global over the years. It sells commercial aircraft worldwide with few major differences across countries. This is not to say, however, that no differences exist. Boeing typically offers customers around the world a limited set of variations on a particular plane, usually to accommodate the individual needs of specific airlines (e.g., for passenger capacity, aircraft range, size of first-class cabin, etc.).[32]

In any case, multinationals operating in industries where requirements for local tailoring are low and pressures for global integration are high often pursue a global strategy—an approach where products or services are standardized as much as possible for sale everywhere while goals and directions are set on a worldwide basis. Indeed, with a global strategy, company headquarters serves a key integrating and controlling role, maintaining central control over operations worldwide—to promote efficiencies, economies of scale, and learning. Company operations are simplified and this makes it easier for management to respond to changes in the marketplace. All of this also tends to improve and promote product or service quality. This is essentially the situation at prominent computer chip makers such as Intel. The company has chip-making plants in only a handful of countries (including the U.S., China, Costa Rica, Ireland, and Israel), despite the fact that its products are used globally. The key for Intel is to be able to supply key customers such as Hewlett-Packard and Dell on a just-in-time basis while keeping costs low and margins high. Indeed, companies pursuing global strategies may avoid scattering value chain activities around the world. Instead, they often prefer to concentrate important value chain activities such as manufacturing and product development in key places to cut costs and increase efficiencies.[33]

Boeing has historically followed this approach in competing against Airbus, its European rival. For example, Boeing operates a design center in Moscow, where several hundred employees develop parts for various planes. Boeing also coordinates oversees suppliers (e.g., Xian Aircraft in China and Mexmil in Mexico) that produce parts, and partner firms that both design and build key aircraft components (e.g., Mitsubishi). In essence, Boeing is an exporter of commercial aircraft. All of its planes are assembled in the United States (albeit with an increasing percentage of parts coming from foreign suppliers) and then sold to airlines around the world.[34]

That said, a global strategy also has serious drawbacks. For instance, it can prove difficult for management to effectively coordinate highly dispersed international operations and activities. Undeniably, Boeing is a poster child for this particular problem. The company ran into trouble with one of its latest planes, the 787 Dreamliner. Years behind schedule, this high-tech plane is Boeing's most complex to date (at the time of this book's publication). Because of the high development costs, Boeing not only decided to outsource a great number of components to other companies, but it also asked them to do much of the design work and assume the financial risks—instead of simply manufacturing parts using Boeing blueprints. Unfortunately, this significantly increased the complexity of Boeing's supply chain, creating management headaches that Boeing was ill equipped to deal with and burdening subcontractors with new challenges. The result was poor quality and missed deadlines.

In response, Boeing moved production of some components back in-house and took steps to reassert its control and improve its ability to coordinate subcontractors. Boeing literally set up a worldwide control room for the Dreamliner labeled the "Product Integration Center." From the Center, managers can see the Dreamliner assembly line as well as monitor dozens of TV screens displaying parts shipments and technical queries from around the globe—information that helps Boeing keep the assembly process on track. The Center, which is open 24 hours a day, provides real-time communication and translators so that Boeing can effectively interact with subcontractors from countries as diverse as Sweden, Russia, Japan, Italy, Korea, France, Britain, and Australia.[35] While this has helped, Boeing continues to have trouble with the 787 as it has been deployed.

The Transnational Strategy

In some ways Boeing has it "easy"—at least relative to industries in which it is important to both tailor products or services to local market preferences *and* operate on an integrated basis worldwide to improve efficiency. Firms facing these challenges may want to move value chain activities to wherever they can be done "best" (e.g., cheapest, most efficiently, with the highest value-added, etc.), while still adapting to important local preferences.

This approach is the essence of a transnational strategy. To some extent, this approach represents a "best of both worlds" blend of global and multidomestic approaches. It involves firms seeking economies of scale and location advantages world-wide while still acting locally with their products or services out of competitive necessity. Increasingly, it is also a strategy that companies embrace because of the potential to transfer knowledge and innovations around the company from wherever they surface, which may prove especially important when competing in other markets. Yet, it also offers high potential for conflict and management headaches given the competing demands of local responsiveness and global efficiency. Indeed, standardizing products to the extent possible promotes the goal of global efficiency—standardization makes for simpler operations.[36]

Accordingly, companies that pursue a transnational strategy sometimes want to tilt the balance toward the global side regarding product standardization. For instance, P&G moved to simplify its personal care product lines and formulas worldwide. Today, the firm's Vidal Sassoon hair care products use a single fragrance worldwide. To satisfy local tastes, however, less fragrance is used in markets where customers prefer subtlety (such as in Japan) and more is used where customers like intense scents (such as some European countries). This often proves to be a delicate balancing act for companies. On the one hand, moving toward similar products or services worldwide simplifies things for companies by improving efficiency and reducing costs. But going too far risks alienating customers if significant preference differences exist across markets that are not adequately captured with a move toward greater standardization.[37]

As a result, firms pursuing a transnational strategy must tweak and juggle the often competing demands for local responsiveness and global integration. One approach is to create products that have many identical underlying components (which can be manufactured in a few central locations where location economies are best). Products can then be assembled in plants in important markets, where specific features or parts can be added to the final product that are particularly important given local preferences. This is essentially what the Illinois-based company Caterpillar does to keep its costs low while also localizing its products to a degree. And it is working. Caterpillar sells products in 180 countries and is arguably the world's top provider of earthmoving equipment for agricultural, construction, mining, and logging applications. While most of its components plants are in the U.S., manufacturing and assembly also takes place in 60 different facilities within 23 countries. Needless to say, balancing product localization and integration requires vigilant management. In fact, multinationals using a transnational strategy must quickly transfer their core competencies throughout their worldwide organization and be prepared to take advantage of new or improved core competencies wherever they are developed.[38]

Another Alternative: The Regional Strategy

Despite the positive hype sometimes associated with global and transnational strategies, they may not always be best. Indeed, multinationals sometimes have great difficulty figuring out just how responsive they should be to local preferences. Some products fall into an area where lifestyles and tastes are converging worldwide (favoring a global strategy), while others are in an area where customers still hold on to their own unique preferences in specific countries (favoring a multidomestic strategy). And in some cases, the reality is somewhere in between, with regional tastes and preferences instead of significant country-by-country differences. Consider Pringles, P&G's 40-year-old snack brand. Today, Pringles are sold in dozens of flavors, typically created for regionwide palates. While Americans are familiar with a variety of Pringles flavors (such as "original," "ranch," "salt & vinegar," and "pizza"), some flavors developed for other markets may lead to some head-scratching. For instance, in Asian markets, unique Pringles flavors include "seafood" and "aromatic crispy chicken." In the Middle East, flavors include "ketchup," and in Western Europe, popular flavors include "grilled shrimp and pepper," and "Jamon Serrano."[39]

Figure 8.5 lists factors that tend to favor global versus multidomestic strategies. As you can see, the formation of regional trading blocks (e.g., NAFTA) appears under the multidomestic column. Yet, some multinationals that compete in supposedly "global" industries might be better off pursuing a regional strategy. This approach allows managers in a regional area such as South America to make decisions, set goals, and respond to customers' needs. Part of this strategy also involves achieving efficiencies and economies by leveraging any location advantages that may exist within or even across regions (e.g., minimize production costs by locating plants in cheap labor nations within a region).

For instance, at one point France's Thomson Consumer Electronics used a regional strategy for its television lines. Plants in Britain, Spain, Germany, and France each made

Factors Favoring a Global Approach	Factors Favoring a Multidomestic Approach
• Converging income across industrialized nations, rising middle-class incomes in developing countries	• Industry standards and regulations governing business activities remain diverse across nations
• Increasing similarity of consumer lifestyles and tastes worldwide	• Customers continue to demand products and services tailored to their local needs
• Rapid advances in technology, communications and transport; globalized financial markets	• Being seen as a "local" company is often a competitive asset
• Increasing worldwide trade, formation of global alliances among companies	• Global organizations are hard to manage and control
• Reduced trade barriers, more open markets, and privatization of state-dominated economies	• Globalization can undercut unique competencies of foreign subsidiaries
• Emergence of nations with productive, low-cost labor (e.g., Ecuador and Indonesia)	• Formation of regional trading blocks and agreements (e.g., the North American Free Trade Agreement or NAFTA)

Figure 8.5 Two Sides of the Coin: Factors Favoring Global and Multidomestic Strategies.

Sources: Adapted from Morrison, A. J., Ricks, D. A., and Roth, K. (1991). Globalization versus regionalization: Which way for the multinational? *Organizational Dynamics*, 19, 17–29; Yip, G. S. (1995). *Total Global Strategy*. Englewood Cliffs, NJ: Prentice-Hall.

specific types of televisions for the European market. Thomson's North American operations were run independently and focused on producing televisions with the RCA and GE labels just for that market, largely using regional suppliers of components. While this regional approach lacked the worldwide integration found in a transnational strategy, it offered more local product customization than a global strategy would. That said, a regional strategy does allow more geographic coordination than a multidomestic strategy (where multinationals set up quasi-independent subsidiaries to serve specific national markets).[40]

Overall, a regional strategy often represents a good alternative for companies in certain industries—where it is not possible to be truly global but where some customization pressures exist across regional or national markets. Moreover, the increasing impact of regional trade agreements and the fact that a large chunk of international commerce is intraregional makes regional approaches a good bet for many multinationals. For example, consider the automobile industry. While there are differences in national preferences and regulations, there are also broad regional differences (e.g., cars across Europe are generally smaller and more fuel-efficient than cars in North America). Toyota has been using regional strategies to compete for some time. For instance, the company relies on a limited number of vehicle platforms which are designed for adaptability and on top of which Toyota can apply regional customization. This gives Toyota economies of scale while still delivering customization at a reasonable cost. Indeed, key Toyota factories around the world produce a small number of unique models designed to be sold throughout their respective regions. Toyota also takes truck and minivan engines and transmissions made in its Asian plants and distributes them to assembly facilities serving markets in Asia, Latin America, and Africa. These components are not used in the U.S. or Canada because of differences in North American conditions (e.g., bigger engines are needed).[41]

When Strategy Provides a Competitive Advantage

At this point, you may be wondering when a firm's international strategy choices actually provide a competitive edge. Of course, executing a strategy well is important. Moreover, competitors change and evolve—today's strategic success for a firm may be tomorrow's disaster if management fails to adjust to more effective competition. But it is important to note that strategy itself can provide an important competitive advantage, at least in the short run. This depends, in part, on the degree of alignment between the industry and the strategies typically used by competitors.

For example, a multinational's global strategy may offer a competitive advantage when key competitors are relying on a multidomestic approach and the underlying character of the industry actually favors globalization (e.g., where customer preferences are becoming the same everywhere and global economies of scale are possible). In short, if a multinational uses a global strategy in an under-globalized industry, such as when competitors rely on strategies that do not fit the industry's underlying character, it should enjoy a competitive advantage. In fact, research supports the idea that the match or mismatch between the actual strategies used by international competitors in an industry and its underlying potential for globalization affects the relationship between multinational strategy and performance. Figure 8.6 summarizes these points.[42]

Underlying Industry Character	Strategy Used by Key Competitors	Resulting Level of Globalization in Industry (and example)	Implications for Firm Strategy and Performance vs. Competition
Favors global strategy	Multidomestic	Under-globalized (credit card industry)	Global strategies may offer real competitive advantages and higher performance relative to multidomestic strategies
Favors global strategy	Global	Optimum (ship-building industry)	Global strategies may result in good performance but may not offer a competitive advantage relative to other firms
Favors multidomestic strategy	Multidomestic	Optimum (funeral industry)	Multidomestic strategies may result in good performance but may not offer a competitive advantage relative to other firms
Favors multidomestic strategy	Global	Over-globalized (tire industry)	Multidomestic strategies may offer real competitive advantages and higher performance relative to global strategies

Figure 8.6 When Strategies Matter Most: Taking Advantage of Mismatches between Industry Character and Competitors' Strategic Choices.

Source: Adapted from Birkinshaw, J., Morrison, A., and Hulland, J. (1995). Structural and competitive determinants of a global integration strategy. *Strategic Management Journal*, 16, 637–655.

How Culture Can Impact Strategic Choices

International strategy should be developed carefully and via a process that is shaped by a firm's context. For instance, European multinationals have smaller home markets relative to their American counterparts. This may explain why they tend to give foreign subsidiaries more autonomy, as well as why foreign sales tend to account for a larger percentage of total sales in European multinationals. Conversely, the large U.S. market may be one reason that American multinationals have been slower to internationalize than their European and Japanese counterparts. But these patterns also reflect the influence of culture on how managers interpret the "rules of the game" in international business.[43]

In essence, managers from different countries may bring different views about time, risks, and goals into the strategic planning process. For example, many Japanese multinationals have a tradition of centralized control, with all roads leading back to Japan. This tradition has been linked to several cultural factors, including Confucian values, the importance of in-group networks, and a desire to avoid uncertainty. Cultural values can also impact the methods used to develop international strategy. For example, when developing their strategies, companies based in countries with high individualism (such as the United States) tend to rely more on subjective information than on quantitative data or forecasting methods.[44]

Perceptions about culture matter too. For example, the wider the perceived cultural gap between headquarters and foreign subsidiaries, the tighter the management control from headquarters tends to be. Perceived similarity can also shape strategy. Firms often make their first forays abroad in countries thought to have familiar cultures and business practices. The rationale, of course, is that starting with foreign markets that are similar to the home market is "safer." But when judgments about similarity are inaccurate, problems result. The high failure rate of Canadian retail firms entering the American market, many of which assumed that the U.S. was merely a larger version of Canada, is a case in point. Perceptions notwithstanding, real differences in tastes, values, and business practices exist between Canada and the U.S.[45]

Finally, culture can impact the ownership positions firms take in their foreign operations. Companies based in high power distance, high uncertainty avoidance countries (such as France) are more likely to maintain majority ownership over foreign subsidiaries than multinationals based in low power distance, low uncertainty avoidance countries (such as the U.S.). Managers with a low power distance perspective tend to be more comfortable sharing control of overseas operations with a partner, such as in a joint venture. Overall, international managers should consider how their values and perspectives shape their strategy development and implementation efforts.[46]

The Process of Developing International Strategy

Culture fit or not, firms should develop international strategies that fit their competitive contexts. But how is international strategy developed in the first place? While this process can vary, in many cases management follows a series of steps in developing international strategy. These steps are outlined in Figure 8.7.

Step 1: The Mission Statement

To clarify direction, many firms start the process of developing an international strategy by creating a mission statement. This statement summarizes firm values and overall purpose. Ideally, the mission will express common goals in a way that succinctly captures management's vision for the firm. For example, in its mission statement, motorcycle maker Harley-Davidson describes itself as "an action-oriented, international company—a leader in its commitment to continuously improve the quality of mutually beneficial relationships with stakeholders." Other firms eschew mission statements or produce them after much of the strategic planning process is complete.[47]

Step 2: Conducting a SWOT Analysis

Assuming a mission statement is developed first, performing a SWOT analysis is typically the second step in strategy development. SWOT stands for strengths, weaknesses, opportunities, and threats. It involves an assessment of the company's internal circumstances and external environment. A SWOT analysis usually involves environmental

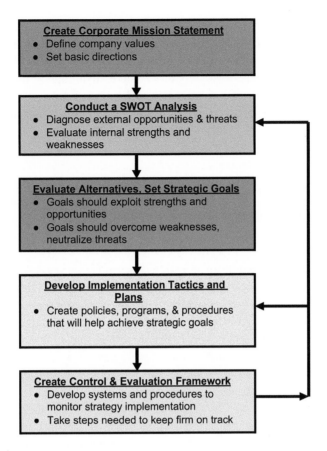

Figure 8.7 The Process of Developing International Strategy.

Source: Adapted from Griffin, R. W., and Pustay, M. W. (2005). *International Business: A Managerial Perspective* (4th ed.), 322. Upper Saddle River, NJ: Prentice-Hall.

scanning, a process in which information about the internal and external situation facing the firm is systematically collected and evaluated. The external side of this assessment is known as an environmental analysis. Here, the company assesses both promising international opportunities for its products or services (e.g., unmet demand or weak competition in certain markets), as well as any threats in foreign markets that might preclude those opportunities from being fully realized (e.g., inadequate business infrastructure, political instability, onerous government regulations, increasing competition, etc.).[48]

Ideally, firms will examine opportunities and threats at a multinational, regional, or country-specific level. At the multinational level, companies assess how worldwide trends might impact their businesses. For instance, many consumer product companies are optimistic about their long-term prospects for international growth because of rising disposable incomes in developing countries such as China. But assessing external opportunities and threats is easier said than done, particularly for companies that have been largely domestic in their orientation. Such firms may lack the staff or expertise to conduct an environmental analysis of international markets. Consequently, these firms may fail to perceive international opportunities or significant foreign threats.[49]

In any case, it may be hard for companies to take advantage of international opportunities because of both internal weaknesses and pressure from competitors. See the following International Insights feature regarding Kraft Foods' international challenges for an example.

International Insights

Krafting Strategy for International Markets

Kraft is an American food icon. Its more than five dozen brands (including Velveeta, Oscar Mayer, Triscuit, Planters, Toblerone, and Maxwell House) are household names. As the largest food corporation in the U.S., Kraft is a giant, with sales of $42 billion in 2008. But Kraft is somewhat of an also-ran overseas. Less than 42 percent of Kraft's sales come from outside North America and only 20 percent come from rapidly developing markets such as China and India. By comparison, McDonald's earns over 50 percent of its revenues abroad and Coca-Cola exceeds 80 percent. Walk through supermarkets in Australia, for instance, and Kraft products are relatively scarce. Referring to Kraft, one Australian supermarket owner noted, "They would be classified as a slow-moving line." In Great Britain, one of Kraft's strongest foreign markets, the company only ranks eighth in size among food companies.

Strategically, Kraft says that it wants to "rewire the organization for growth" and "drive down costs without compromising quality." But Kraft's dominant market, the U.S., is saturated. Indeed, the food business in the U.S. is cut-throat. Brand loyalty is undercut by supermarket brands and intense price competition. Take salad dressing, for example. Many shoppers just buy what is on sale—be it Kraft, Wish-Bone, or Hellmann's.

So, Kraft is looking to overseas markets, particularly in developing countries, for more rapid growth. The global competition is formidable and includes the likes of Anglo-Dutch Unilever, Switzerland's Nestlé, and France's Groupe Danone. All three moved rapidly into fast-growth emerging markets in Latin America, Eastern Europe, and Asia. Nestlé and Unilever both realize over 30 percent of their sales from developing countries alone. In contrast, one expert said Kraft still tilted too much toward the U.S. and Canada, noting that "A truly global organization would have a quarter to one-third of its business in North America."

Indeed, Kraft's forte (pricey convenience foods and snacks) often have a tough time in foreign markets where basic products are what many people can afford. For instance, while Kraft's visibility in India is low, competitor Unilever has done well by pushing staples such as rice and salt. But the good news is that Kraft has a plan for boosting revenues in developing markets. First, it wants to expand the range of products and brands it sells in countries where it already operates. Second, the company also wants to acquire local competitors, particularly in beverages and snacks, as a way to quickly enter new emerging markets and tap into rising middle-class populations. Recently, Kraft has targeted other multinationals to quickly raise its profile in key developing markets. For instance, in late 2009 Kraft offered to buy U.K.-based confectioner Cadbury PLC for nearly $17 billion. With strong gum and candy brands, Cadbury is the leading confectioner in high-growth emerging markets, including Egypt, India, Mexico, and Thailand. In India alone, Kraft's acquisition of Cadbury would vault it into a leadership position in a confectionery market, projected to grow 15 percent annually as the Indian middle class expands and spends more on candies.

Internally, Kraft has also made changes to put itself more on a growth footing. The company recently reorganized around five global product units, with country managers holding responsibility for local merchandising efforts. As one senior manager put it, the "challenges we face . . . demand that we become a more unified, global company" while at the same time strengthening the "local expertise that has built our success." How well these moves help broaden and deepen Kraft's international reach in the years ahead, especially relative to its competitors, remains to be seen, but it hopes to swat the competition with this new strategy.[50]

Analyzing the environment from a regional perspective involves looking at emerging trends in a geographic area. For example, South American governments have generally loosened regulations and improved their business infrastructures in recent years, creating opportunities for multinationals specializing in construction, energy, and communications.[51]

While many Western multinationals have shied away from Africa because of perceptions about poverty, instability, and infrastructure problems, Chinese companies have displayed no such reluctance. Indeed, Chinese mining, energy, automobile, and construction companies see such negatives as opportunities. For example, Chinese car companies Geely Group and Chery Automobile view Africa as an ideal proving ground—a region full of price-sensitive customers who might find their cheaper products appealing. Geely and Chery hope that their African experience will eventually result in the kind of recognition and success now enjoyed by South Korea's Hyundai Motor Co.[52]

Other Chinese firms feel that they can address needs in Africa that were once concerns in China. As the director of a Chinese well-digging firm put it, "China doesn't need many new water wells. But Africans struggle to find drinking water every day." Chinese consumer-products firms view Africa as a region where they can avoid tough competition from Japanese, European, and American multinationals. That led office-supply company Shanghai Hero Co. to build a new facility in South Africa, giving it easy access to the wider African market. This is not to say everything has gone smoothly for Chinese companies—in some countries (such as Zambia), resentment against the wave of Chinese investment is palpable. Complaints have included abusive labor practices, unsafe working conditions, and attitudes toward locals that smack of "colonialism." Exaggerated or not, these charges underscore the greater role Chinese firms now play in markets around the world.[53]

Finally, environmental analysis can also be country-specific, assessing whether the cultural, legal, economic, and political circumstances in a particular country are opportunities or threats. For example, at one point multinationals wanting to do business in Saudi Arabia had to consider the fact that the Saudi economy was growing twice as fast as its electricity-generating capacity. Multinationals unwilling to risk power interruptions canceled or delayed plans to build new facilities as a result. Others installed generators to keep things running during blackouts.[54]

It is important to note that cultural values and prior experiences shape managers' scanning tendencies. Depending on their backgrounds, managers may pay attention to different things in the environmental scanning process. One study found that Nigerian managers paid more attention to governmental issues than did Americans, while the opposite was true for technology issues. In Nigeria and other developing countries, political instability can drastically affect business. The U.S., in contrast, is politically stable, but has a volatile technological environment. Overall, managers coming from these contexts need to adjust their environmental scanning efforts when considering opportunities elsewhere.[55]

The internal side of a SWOT analysis is known as an internal resource audit. This audit involves identifying key business success factors for the firm. For example, in the pharmaceutical industry, business success factors might include product efficacy and patents held, while in the automotive industry styling, quality, and fuel efficiency might be key factors. In short, business success factors can vary across industries. Business success factors can also vary over time as well as from country to country. In essence, firms want to see how internal resources stack up against the demands that they will face in foreign markets.[56]

For instance, a key success factor for Wal-Mart, particularly in the U.S., are huge stores offering a wide range of products, combined with a sophisticated distribution system. In fact, Wal-Mart's computerized warehouses and its ability to negotiate and influence suppliers with large orders help it keep prices low in the U.S. When it first opened stores in Mexico, however, Wal-Mart's Mexican suppliers wanted to ship smaller orders directly to stores, not warehouses. Wal-Mart initially underestimated the difficulties of creating a Mexican version of its American distribution system and experienced lower initial sales in Mexico as a result. But the company has learned it was inexperienced and inflexible when it came to foreign markets. Wal-Mart now understands that what worked in America may not work elsewhere—and not just in Mexico. For instance, in Sao Paulo, Brazil, huge stores were impossible to build in traffic-clogged streets, so Wal-Mart stores have a smaller footprint. Wal-Mart is also paying more attention to local and regional preferences in Brazil, both for products and for how they are presented to customers. For instance, fruits and vegetables are piled high with large colorful displays—typical of what customers would see in a traditional Brazilian market. Today, Wal-Mart continues to expand abroad. According to its website, Wal-Mart has over 11,000 stores in 27 countries and saw $466 billion of revenue in fiscal 2013.[57]

So, the internal resource audit should include an evaluation of both internal strengths (such as a skilled workforce and superior technology) and weaknesses (such as high debt, poor name recognition, and lack of international experience) relative to competitors. Firms typically want to build on distinctive strengths that would be tough for competitors to copy in the short term (i.e., strengths that might provide a sustainable competitive advantage). To identify strengths that are truly distinctive, management should be able to answer "yes" to the following questions:

- Can the strength help the firm exploit opportunities or avoid threats?
- Is it rare/unique, or do competitors have similar "value-added" capabilities?
- Is the strength difficult or expensive for competitors to duplicate?
- Can the firm take advantage of the competitive potential of strengths?[58]

For instance, in the 1990s Japanese electronics giant Matsushita built a network of 150 plants across dozens of countries, providing a buffer against currency and economic fluctuations in particular locations. Dispersed manufacturing, combined with cutting-edge technology and world-class brands, gave Matsushita a global reach that few competitors could match. In 2005, the company renamed itself Panasonic Corporation to forge a stronger link between customers and its most famous brand. Today, Panasonic has over $90 billion in revenues and some 300,000 employees.[59]

Step 3: Deciding on an International Strategy and Setting Goals

After the SWOT analysis, the typical next step is for the firm to adopt an international strategy. Ultimately, goals should flow from the SWOT analysis. The firm needs to exploit strengths and opportunities while neutralizing competitive threats and internal weaknesses. Goals should reflect decisions about how broad or narrow the breadth and depth of the firm's international operations will be. For instance, the company will need to decide if it will operate in a limited number of countries or many, and whether it will offer all products and services abroad or just a subset.

Once general goals such as these are set, more specific objectives can be developed. Goals should be achievable and have a specific time frame for accomplishment. Areas where international goals might be set include: profitability (such as to grow an international profit by 25 percent), production (such as to increase the ratio of foreign to domestic production from 50 to 75 percent), marketing (such as to improve marketing effectiveness in Europe), and R&D (such as to disperse R&D capability worldwide), just to name a few.[60]

Consider how Mercedes-Benz defined some of its strategic goals. Mercedes is a luxury brand that embodies German craftsmanship and quality. But German labor costs, among other things, made it very difficult for Mercedes to export cars to North America at a profit. So, Mercedes decided to move a substantial amount of manufacturing capacity to the U.S. Mercedes built an assembly plant in Alabama, allowing the firm to manufacture at a lower cost in a key market. Mercedes also bought more components from non-German suppliers. On one hand, achieving these and related strategic goals may dilute Mercedes' image as the embodiment of German craftsmanship, ultimately hurting sales. On the other hand, Mercedes' sales suggest that the risk of being seen as "less German" was worth taking, at least so far.[61]

Step 4: Developing Implementation Tactics and Plans

After strategic goals have been set, companies should develop specific plans and tactics that involve deployment of corporate resources (material, money, people, etc.) to achieve them. New procedures, processes, or facilities may also have to be developed to achieve company goals, including specific steps designed to neutralize competitors. Basically, a support system must be in place to actually move the firm from where it is to where it wants to be internationally. For example, in the late 1990s, Hyundai began manufacturing its small Santro model in the Indian city of Chennai. This was the result of Hyundai's assessment that, to beat the rising tide of competition in the Indian market, it had to be fully committed and design its products with local as well as other markets in mind. Consequently, Hyundai sank $1.2 billion into building a world-class manufacturing plant in Chennai, investing far more than rival multinationals. With two plants and a capacity of 600,000 cars annually, Hyundai is the second largest auto exporter in India. It owns almost 20 percent of the market in India, good for second place and better than local Indian rival, Tata Motors.[62]

That said, firms often underestimate what is needed to compete effectively abroad. Pepsi's decision in the 1990s to increase international revenues some 300 percent may be a case in point. To achieve this goal, the firm quickly expanded its global presence. Unfortunately, this expansion backfired. By the late 1990s, Pepsi was actually losing money overseas and pulled out of some important international markets. Today, small local competitors are giving both Pepsi and Coca-Cola a run for their money in developing markets such as in Peru, Mexico, and even Iran. With lower overhead costs, cheaper prices, and local knowledge (that spawned effective guerrilla marketing tactics), small firms such as Peru's Kola Real can cut into the once fat margins of Pepsi and Coke.[63]

This underscores the idea that to secure a competitive advantage abroad, multinationals must carefully design and execute actions that support their strategies and improve key value chain activities. For example, multinationals can neutralize a common advantage of home-grown competitors—greater understanding of the local market—by developing products tailored to local tastes. In Japan, local soft-drink maker Suntory Ltd introduced "Asian tea" drinks in response to local tastes. But Coca-Cola countered by developing and offering an Asian tea for the Japanese market. Of course, such tactics carry risks. Adapting products for specific markets can increase costs or prove wrongheaded, as restaurant chain TGI Fridays discovered in South Korea. Customers turned up their noses at its adapted menu, which included a variety of local items, because they expected an "American" dining experience. This example highlights the difficulty of teasing out when and how adapting products to local preferences makes competitive sense.[64]

Companies in other industries also face daunting challenges. An example is Texas Instruments' (TI) semiconductor group who wanted to establish a manufacturing and technology presence quickly to better absorb market growth wherever it occurred. That meant getting capital-intensive facilities and plants up and running fast to preempt competitors. To achieve this, TI developed new tactics and practices, including the formation of a ten-person team to facilitate new plant construction worldwide. The team developed procedures (e.g., to cut through red tape quickly, find high-quality local vendors) that enabled TI to bring world-class chip manufacturing plants online eight months faster than competing firms.[65]

Step 5: Putting Control and Evaluation Procedures in Place

This final step involves the control and evaluation procedures designed to ensure that strategy implementation efforts stay on track so that all of the work done to this point is not wasted. It is also about ensuring that companies can quickly adjust, if not reinvent, their strategies as business circumstances change. Clearly, the development and implementation of international strategy is a dynamic, ongoing process.[66]

For example, starting in the 1980s and 1990s, Japanese car companies such as Nissan, Honda, and Toyota all built car plants in the U.S. in order to meet the needs of the American market. When growing export demands needed to be met around the world, Japanese plants in the U.S. shifted gears and ramped up production in response. As a result, Japanese firms at one point were actually shipping more cars abroad from their U.S. plants than GM, Ford, and Chrysler combined. This shift in strategy allowed Japanese automakers to take advantage of lower U.S. production costs relative to Japan. Moreover, the type of cars that emerging markets were clamoring for happened to be the ones that the Japanese firms were already making in the U.S. Toyota's American plants helped it sidestep import restrictions in Taiwan and South Korea on cars built in Japan. This strategic flexibility is one reason why Japanese car companies have proven to be such formidable international competitors.[67] This section concludes with a Global Innovations feature about McDonald's and Jollibee, a competitor in the fast food business in the Philippines and the competitive flexibility that each has shown.

Global Innovations

A Strategic Fast Food Fight: McDonald's Faces Tough Local Competition from Jollibee in the Philippines

McDonald's is an international giant. With over 34,000 outlets in 119 countries, its footprint is indeed global. But the fast food is a tough business. McDonald's is up against other American firms such as Burger King, Subway, and Yum! in foreign markets. But, it also faces a dizzying array of local competitors eager to take a bite out of the Big Mac. One of those is Jollibee Foods, known as "the McDonald's of the Philippines." Jollibee has over 750 outlets in the Philippines and another 95 in ten other countries including the U.S. (26 stores), Canada and eight other Asian and Middle Eastern Countries (and it operates over 2,000 outlets counting all its brands).

Needless to say, McDonald's is one of the best-known companies in the world, with a reputation for high quality, cleanliness, and fast service. It is excellent at picking high-traffic store locations and successfully enticing families and children with jungle gyms, signature characters, and licensed toys. Yet, Jollibee has thrived in the face of the McDonald's challenge in its home market. Today, Jollibee sits on top of the fast food market in the Philippines. While McDonald's has grown in the nation over the past several years, Jollibee has grown faster. The bottom line is that Jollibee has been successful despite having to deal with McDonald's.

What strategic recipe did Jollibee create to more than hold its own against McDonald's in the Philippines? And, how might McDonald's respond, not just in the Philippines but elsewhere? Jollibee decided that it had to copy aspects of McDonald's approach, including the same type of clean and speedy service, and adhering to its "FSC" excellent standards (food, service, and cleanliness). Employee training is taken very seriously and pay leads the industry in the Philippines. Jollibee also makes much of its own food products in centrally located commissaries. It also markets itself to kids with in-store novelties and signature characters—just like McDonald's does worldwide.

That said, Jollibee decided that a key to succeeding against McDonald's was to "act locally," more so than the Big Mac. So, anytime a customer approaches a Jollibee counter, employees say, "*Magandang umaga po*"—welcome to Jollibee. The first part of this phrase is a traditional Filipino greeting that underscores the company's local heritage and creates an atmosphere of humble Filipino hospitality. On top of that, Jollibee prices its food lower than comparable items at McDonald's. Jollibee's menu is geared more toward Filipinos' sweet-and-spicy tastes than McDonald's. For example, Palabok Fiesta is a noodle dish topped with smoked fish, deep fried pork skin, bean curd, and onions. Along with spicy flavors, Jollibee customers can opt for rice with their meals instead of fries, another local preference. In addition to palates, Jollibee is also mindful of lifestyle, as with its development of indigenous characters that epitomize the Filipino spirit of "everyday happiness."

Of course, how well Jollibee will compete against McDonald's in the years ahead remains to be seen. McDonald's is well known for its flexibility and it responded to Jollibee's success by spicing up its own menu in the Philippines. Ironically, Jollibee's own foreign expansion exposed it to some of the same difficulties that McDonald's initially encountered in the Philippines and other locations. For instance, in the U.S., Jollibee found that it had to make adjustments, including offering larger portions than it does in the Philippines. It also tended to locate outlets in areas with large populations of Filipino expatriates.

In any case, competitors of McDonald's—regardless of their origins—should not underestimate the power of the Big Mac. Over the years, McDonald's has evolved its strategic business model. For example, in response to concerns about healthy eating, McDonald's added salads and fruits in many locations. While outlets worldwide conform to company requirements, McDonald's allows for a surprising amount of tailoring to local conditions. These variations in offerings and services are designed to help the company stand out in local markets.

For instance, take something that seems pretty simple—an apple. In the U.S., customers receive apple slices in packets (with the skin removed). But in Europe, the apple skins are left on. In Australia, customers are simply handed a whole apple. Next, consider the Big Mac. While it is the most popular item worldwide, local variations in the product abound. For example, a Big Mac's meat patty is made of beef in the U.S., but chicken in India. McDonald's also offers service variations in some markets. For example, in China many outlets are open 24 hours a day and the company offers "dessert kiosks" which just sell drinks and sweets.

In crowded, traffic-choked cities around the world, McDonald's delivers. In Cairo, Egypt, a call center handles orders and motorbikes then deliver all over town from nearby outlets. McDonald's has expanded this model to cities where drive-thrus are impractical, including Beirut, Sao Paulo, Shanghai, and Manila (Jollibee's home). McDonald's also capitalizes on cross-fertilization of ideas, such as when outlets in Australia came up with the idea of selling gourmet coffees. They are now sold all over the U.S., and "Starbucks-like" cafés located inside existing restaurants are growing in Europe. This underscores the firm's willingness to look for innovations anywhere that can be applied elsewhere.

Yet, more variety can mean higher costs, more operational complexity, and perhaps a blurring of what it means to be McDonald's. As one critic put it, "People go to McDonald's to eat burgers." Some of McDonald's American competitors have attacked this problem by offering a separate line of restaurants aimed at local tastes. Yum! Brands made in China, for example, have kept its Pizza Hut and KFC outlets, but have also opened a new fast-service chain offering just Chinese food. The dilemma about how much to cater to local tastes versus sticking to the "core" food and service concept is not going away soon. And, as Jollibee has demonstrated, there is no shortage of local competitors who think they can take a bite out of the Big Mac. All this is food for strategic thought. It raises issues about the kinds of challenges McDonald's and other firms face with foreign expansion and how far to go to "localize" menus and dining experiences. So, while Jollibee is on top in its home market, it too will need to constantly assess a changing environment and innovate to keep McDonald's at bay.[68]

Organizational Requirements for Successful International Strategy

This final section briefly discusses four organizational features that have important implications for multinationals' ability to successfully develop and implement their international strategies. These include:

1. Corporate structure: the way that reporting relationships and units are organized.
2. Management processes: the planning, budgeting, coordination, and performance appraisal activities and systems used to run the firm.
3. Human resources: the people who staff the firm worldwide.
4. Corporate culture: the expectations, values, beliefs, and unwritten rules that guide employee behavior in the company.

Multinationals must build characteristics into these organizational features that will support strategy development and implementation. When firm characteristics and strategic demands are aligned, better performance results.[69]

For example, a global strategy requires a corporate structure with some centralized authority to assist global product development and to make global decisions. This does not necessarily mean that "headquarters" calls all the shots. But some structure must exist to coordinate worldwide operations and to make decisions, often with input from local operations. For instance, South Korea's LG Electronics credits much of its recent marketplace success to a new structure where every product has an executive who takes total responsibility for it—from the research and development stage until it is no longer sold anywhere in the world. Known inside LG as Product Business Leaders (PBLs), these executives help the company spot problems quickly, allowing mistakes to be corrected (which in some cases may mean pulling losing products off the market). PBLs at LG spend much of their time visiting markets around the world to assess reaction to company products—while also interacting with product developers, factory managers, and marketing personnel. As one senior executive at LG put it, before the PBL system was developed, "we didn't have people who owned the performance of a product." Leadership training and development is also built into this program and it is considered a launching point for career success at LG.[70]

Management processes that facilitate coordination and strategic decision making are also critical if companies are to respond quickly to the competitive environments they face. For example, some firms can have more success developing and implementing global strategies by using teams of key employees from different countries to make decisions with worldwide implications. Such teams can bridge cultural and geographic barriers to develop and execute complex global strategies effectively.[71]

Likewise, management processes may include specific capabilities that help the firm outperform competitors in areas that are important to customers. In the semiconductor industry this might involve developing cutting-edge chips more quickly than competitors. Identifying and developing capabilities that are complex and diffused through the company (i.e., that cut across functions) and that rely on well-developed interfaces (e.g., sophisticated networks of informal communications) are best because they are tough for competitors to imitate.[72]

The structures and processes designed to support an international strategy are themselves supported by a firm's culture and human resources. For example, cultural values that emphasize global flexibility and responsiveness help give the firm an identity that fosters its ability to execute a global strategy. Figure 8.8 illustrates how corporate

General Area	Specific Corporate Feature Necessary
Corporate Structure	• Centralized global authority • No international division • Strong business dimension
Management Processes	• Global strategy information system • Global strategic planning • Cross-country coordination • Global budgeting
Human Resources	• Global performance review and compensation • Use of foreign nationals • Frequent travel • Statements and actions of leaders
Corporate Culture	• Global identity • Commitment to worldwide employment • Interdependence of businesses

Figure 8.8 Corporate Features That Support a Global Strategy.

Source: Adapted from: Yip, G. S. (1995). *Total Global Strategy.* Englewood Cliffs, NJ: Prentice-Hall.

structure, culture, human resources, and management processes should be aligned to support a global strategy. Of course, for other strategies, these organizational features will be different. For instance, a corporate structure in which decision authority for products, marketing, and so on is largely delegated to subsidiaries in specific countries makes sense for firms using a multidomestic strategy.

Designing a Fair Strategy Development Process

Finally, companies should pay attention to how strategy is created. It turns out that if the processes used to create strategies are perceived to be fair, then local managers are more likely to implement them. This is especially the case when any new strategy is a significant departure from the status quo. Among other things, instituting a fair process for strategy development means that:

■ headquarters executives make a serious effort to familiarize themselves with local operations;
■ two-way communication occurs when strategy is being developed;
■ headquarters executives are consistent across subsidiaries in making decisions;
■ local employees are encouraged to challenge headquarters' strategic perspectives and decisions;
■ the strategic decisions ultimately made are fully explained to local employees.

While this process is complex, it involves engaging the involvement of local employees, fully explaining strategic options, and clarifying performance expectations. If this is done reasonably well, multinationals can improve local employee trust and commitment in headquarters management. Committed employees who trust the company will be more likely to cooperate and act in ways that ensure company strategies are executed successfully abroad. After all, it is one thing to strategize, but people need to jump in and enact the good ideas. This "jumping in" process is the subject of Chapter 9.[73]

Chapter Summary

Figuring out how a company should compete abroad is part of international strategic management. Unfortunately, a surprising number of companies enter overseas markets without a clear, well-designed approach. This can lead to problems, including the poor use of resources abroad and failing to anticipate operational problems in foreign environments (among others). All international strategies should help firms decide (1) what products/ services will be sold abroad, (2) where and how services will be delivered or products made, (3) what resources are necessary and how they will be acquired, and (4) how competitors will be outperformed.

At a business level, firms make money through value creation, offering products or services that customers want. One way to do that is by differentiating products from those of competitors. Another tack is the cost-leadership approach. Finally, a niche strategy involves focusing on a specific line of products or services relative to competitors who operate more broadly. A company can also add value by changing any primary or supporting activities in its value chain. International strategy is ultimately about how value chain activities are configured and coordinated.

Five corporate-level strategies used by multinationals were discussed as a function of industry pressures for local responsiveness and global integration: international strategy, multidomestic strategy, global strategy, transnational strategy, and regional strategy.

The chapter also outlines the process of creating international strategy, which consists of five key steps, including developing a mission statement, conducting a SWOT analysis, the actual selection of a strategy and goals, followed by the development of implementation tactics and plans. Finally, steps have to be taken to monitor strategy implementation on an ongoing basis. The chapter concludes by noting that features such as corporate structure, management processes and corporate culture all need to be aligned with a firm's international strategy to maximize performance.

Discussion Questions

1. What is the value of having a coherent international business strategy?

2. What factors determine national competitive advantage?

3. Explain the differences between international, global, transnational, and multidomestic strategies. What roles do industry and firm characteristics play in the choice of strategy?

4. What is a SWOT analysis? What do you do with the results?

5. What organizational features are needed to successfully develop and implement a global strategy?

Up to the Challenge?

General Electric Upends "Glocalization" in Favor of "Reverse Innovation"

As we mentioned in the opening feature, two of GE's newest and most exciting products in 2009 were a portable ultrasound machine and a hand-held electrocardiogram (ECG) device.

Both devices are inexpensive and innovative and both were developed *in* emerging markets *for* emerging markets (the ultrasound in China and the ECG in India) before being sold in the U.S. This represented the start of GE's move away from a "glocalization" approach—creating products at home but moving them out to the world with adaptations for local markets to a new unique strategy. Glocalization offered many advantages, including reduced R&D costs while still allowing for tailoring to local conditions. GE recognized that it needed to create cheaper products specifically designed for developing markets overseas to combat indigenous competition in India, China, and Brazil. Local firms there were filling in the gaps with less expensive yet innovative products. GE's versions were expensive and too feature-laden to penetrate deeply into emerging markets. Customers there were perfectly happy with technology that offered good, but not great, performance at an extremely cheap price.

Indeed, many developing countries have weak infrastructures and huge populations, making the development of inexpensive, inventive technologies very attractive. This is certainly the case in China when it comes to health care, because many facilities outside of urban areas are relatively basic with rudimentary technology. Because of this, developing nations have started to become leaders in everything from low-cost medical devices to cheap solar panels to rechargeable batteries. In turn, this produces local competitors who can grow into formidable multinationals in their own right. This is something GE learned firsthand—running into aggressive Chinese companies as it competed for power system business in Africa.

GE also felt that any innovations it produced in emerging markets could be brought back into wealthier markets—a process it ultimately dubbed *reverse innovation*. Products created for the needs of developing nations can in fact sell very well in rich countries if they offer new innovations. In the case of GE's Chinese-developed ultrasound device, this meant a lower-cost machine that was portable, space-saving, and energy efficient. Moreover, cheaper products from developing markets can be upgraded to satisfy more demanding developed markets while still offering innovations at a reasonable price. For example, GE added imaging applications to its portable ultrasound for sale in the U.S. Likewise, GE invested money to further develop technology in an aircraft engine created in the Czech Republic—an engine that will be used in the turboprop market in developed nations.

But GE also has had to make some major internal changes for reverse innovation to work. The company was structured for decades around the glocalization concept, with research and development looking out from the U.S. to developing markets instead of the reverse. Initially, GE managers in India and China had their ideas for new product developments shot down by higher-ups within the U.S. To combat this, GE created local growth teams (LGTs) to independently develop products and technologies in emerging markets. LGTs are free to develop their own approaches, strategies, and products. They can manage their own intact value chains and emphasize local recruiting. LGTs are also free to innovate from scratch, the rationale being that simply tinkering with existing global products will not lead to breakthrough innovations. Having LGTs report to a senior manager at GE was also important. A manager with the clout to handle conflicts between LGTs and global business leadership, provide resources, and smooth the way for products developed in emerging markets to find their way into developed countries was invaluable.

Today, GE has over a dozen LGTs in India and China. For the most part, these teams have been quite successful. GE's portable ultrasound created a niche now worth almost $280 million in annual sales worldwide. But some managers raised on glocalization are having trouble adapting and not all LGTs have developed breakthroughs. Nevertheless, GE vows to push ahead—and we will all be watching to see what happens.[74]

International Development

Conducting a Company Situation Analysis

Purpose

To practice your skills in analyzing and assessing company strategies and to find out more about a company's international business situation relative to competitors.

Instructions

Your instructor will divide the class into groups of three to six people. Each group should interview a senior manager (preferably one with responsibility for a major line of business) at a local company that has some international activity. Ideally, the interview should focus on a specific line of business. For instance, if you interview managers at diversified companies, you should focus on a specific product line sold abroad since strategies are often different across business lines. The interview itself should cover the issues listed here. Ideally, the manager should answer questions for the business line he or she is responsible for in the company and also should answer the same questions for two or three major competitors.

1. The nature of management
- Are any foreigners in senior management positions?
- How extensive is the cross-cultural training for managers?

2. Company strategy
- Is the company's vision global, transnational, regional, or domestic?
- How willing is the firm to embrace alliances with foreign firms?
- Do units in different foreign locations operate independently or as a single global company?
- How important is environmental scanning in the company?
- To what extent does the home country control key decisions?

3. Operational issues
- Where are the firm's major facilities located (home country or abroad)?
- Are product development decisions centralized or decentralized?
- Are manufacturing decisions centralized or decentralized?

After the interview is completed, each group should make an assessment about the basic strategy employed by the company (and its major competitors). Each group should then develop recommendations about what the company can do to either close the gap with competitors in terms of international practices or maintain the advantages the company already enjoys.

Depending on the class time available, your instructor may ask you to conduct additional research about the company interviewed and its industry before you come up with group recommendations. These recommendations could be part of your group presentations or even written up and given to the companies interviewed.

Assuming a more basic assignment, each group should make a 15-minute class presentation about their findings (allow 20 minutes if presentations are to include the group's own recommendations). Your instructor will then lead a class discussion (another 15–20 minutes), focusing on these issues:

- How "globalized" were the companies interviewed? Did they generally tend to be ahead or behind their competition in this regard? Why or why not?
- What industry, firm, or competitive factors might account for the differences or similarities observed across firm practices?

An Alternative Approach to the Exercise

If the class size is too large or other constraints such as time or the availability of executives make an interview approach impractical, your instructor may convert this activity into a library research assignment. You may be asked to do an in-depth analysis of the strategic approach taken by an international company or even an industry group. If so, you may also be asked to use the interview questions listed to predict the responses that senior managers in the company or industry might make.

From Theory to International Practice

Making Moves on a Global Stage

Purpose

To experience making strategic moves in an international context and to anticipate the possible reactions of competitors

Instructions

Your instructor will divide the class into six groups. Each group will be assigned to analyze one of the following pairs of competitors. The pairs consist of an American multinational and a foreign rival that compete against each other in specific markets. Your instructor may assign other pairs of companies as well.

- **Power generation:** General Electric (www.ge.com) vs. Siemens AG (http://w1.siemens.com/entry/cc/en/)

- **Laptops/PCs:** Dell (www.dell.com) vs. Acer (www.acer-group.com/public)

- **Cell phones:** Samsung (www.samsung.com/us/mobile/cell-phones) vs. Motorola Corp. (www.motorola.com)

- **Automobiles:** Ford Motor Company (www.ford.com) vs. Toyota Motor Corp. (www.toyota-global.com/)

- **Printers:** Hewlett-Packard Co. (www.hp.com) vs. Canon Inc. (www.canon.com)

- **Food:** Kraft Foods Inc. (www.kraftfoodscompany.com/home/index.aspx) vs. Nestlé S.A. (http://nestle.com).

Each group will be asked to select one product category or product type in which each of its paired companies compete. Next, each group will be asked to assess where the American firm in its pair stands relative to its foreign rival in that product category or type. Specifically, groups will be asked to assess the foreign rival's potential ability to react to increased pressure in that product area (i.e., the level of motivation to defend a position in a product area) as well as the degree of importance of that product area to the American firm. Each group will also assess the relative clout of both firms (i.e., which firm is better able to take strong competitive moves or better defend against the same?). Finally, each group will develop recommendations for how the American firm in its pair can do a better job competing against its foreign rival (e.g., what specific competitive moves might be made and why?). More details of how each group should go about this competitive assessment, as well as possible competitive moves that might be tried, can be found in this article: MacMillian, I. C., van Putten., A. B., and McGrath, R. G. (2003). Global gamesmanship. *Harvard Business Review*, May, 62–73.

All groups should read this article before starting in earnest. Depending on the class and time available, your instructor may ask each group to write a report summarizing its assessment and recommendations. The scope and length of that report will be defined by your instructor. In addition, your instructor may ask each group to give a 10–15 minute presentation about its findings.

Notes

1. Wakayama, T., Shintaku, J., and Amano, T. (2012). What Panasonic learned in China. *Harvard Business Review*, December, 109–113.
2. Immelt, J. R., Govindarajan, V., and Trimble, C. (2009). How GE is disrupting itself. *Harvard Business Review*, October, available at: http://hbr.harvardbusiness.org/2009/10/how-ge-is-disrupting-itself/ar/pr.

3. Hill, C. W. L. (2008). *Global Business Today* (5th ed.). New York: McGraw-Hill/Irwin; Hitt, M. A., Ireland, R. D., and Hoskisson, R. E. (2005). *Strategic Management: Competitiveness and Globalization* (6th ed.). Cincinnati, OH: South-Western.

4. Dolan, M., Shirouzu, N., and Bellman, E. (2009). Ford makes push to boost Asian presence. *The Wall Street Journal*, September 23, B1, B2; Chang, L. (2003). Making money in China. *The Wall Street Journal*, June 17, A15.

5. Kumar, K., van Fenema, P. C., and von Glinow, M. A. (2009). Offshoring and the global distribution of work: Implications for task interdependence theory and practice. *Journal of International Business Studies*, 40, 642–667; Ghemawat, P. (2001). Distance still matters: The hard reality of global expansion. *Harvard Business Review*, September, 137–147.

6. Porter, M. E. (1998). Clusters and the new economics of competition. *Harvard Business Review*, November–December, 77–90.

7. Phatak, A. V. (1995). *International Dimensions of Management* (4th ed.). Cincinnati, OH: South-Western.

8. Gary, L. (2001). Strategy as process. *Harvard Management Update*, July, 8; Porter, M. E. (1990). The competitive advantage of nations. *Harvard Business Review*, 90, 73–93.

9. Hamel, G. (2001). Innovation's new math. *Fortune*. July 9, 130–131.

10. Brews, P. J., and Hunt, M. R. (1999). Learning to plan and planning to learn: Resolving the planning school/learning school debate. *Strategic Management Journal*, 20, 889–913.

11. Immelt, Govindarajan, and Trimble, How GE is disrupting itself; *The Economist*. (2001). Economic size, May 12, 110.

12. Prashantham, S., and Birkinshaw, J. (2008). Dancing with gorillas: How small companies can partner effectively with MNCs. *California Management Review*, 51(1), 6–22; Rose, R. L., and Quintanilla, C. (1996). More small U.S. firms take up exporting, with much success. *The Wall Street Journal*, December 20, A1, A11.

13. Smith, L. (1995). Does the world's biggest company have a future? *Fortune*, August 7, 124–126.

14. Hill, C. W. L. (2008). *Global Business Today* (5th ed.). New York: McGraw-Hill/Irwin.

15. Hitt, Ireland, and Hoskisson, *Strategic Management: Competitiveness and Globalization*; Porter, The competitive advantage of nations.

16. Hill, *Global Business Today*; Hill, C. W. L. (1998). *International Business: Competing in the Global Marketplace* (2nd ed.). Burr Ridge, IL: Irwin/McGraw-Hill.

17. Buckman, R. (2004). H-P outsourcing: Beyond China. *The Wall Street Journal*, February 23, A14.

18. Porter, M. E. (1998). *Competing Across Locations: Enhancing Competitive Advantage Through a Global Strategy*. Boston, MA : Harvard Business School Press.

19. Lodge, G. C., and Bell, M. (1995). *Is the United States Competitive in the World Economy?* Boston, MA: Harvard Business School Press (Publication 9-795-129).

20. Porter, The competitive advantage of nations.

21. Rhoads, C. (2003). Threat from China starts to unravel Italy's cloth trade. *The Wall Street Journal*, December 17, A1, A10.

22. Grant, R. M. (1991). Porter's "competitive advantage of nations": An assessment. *Strategic Management Journal*, 12, 535–548; Luo, Y., and Park, S. H. (2001). Strategic alignment and performance of market-seeking MNCs in China. *Strategic Management Journal*, 22, 1411–155; Murtha, T. P., and Lenway, S. A. (1994). Country capabilities and the strategic state: How national political institutions affect multinational corporations' strategies. *Strategic Management Journal*, 15, 113–129.

23. Kao, J. (2009). Tapping the world's innovation hot spots. *Harvard Business Review*, March, 109–114; Spencer, J. W. (2003). Global gatekeeping, representation, and network structure: A longitudinal analysis of regional and global knowledge-diffusion networks. *Journal of International Business Studies*, 34, 428–442.

24. Hitt, Ireland, and Hoskisson, *Strategic Management: Competitiveness and Globalization*; Li, P. P. (1993). How national context influences corporate strategy: A comparison of South Korea and Taiwan. In S. B. Prasad and R. B. Peterson (eds) *Advances in International Comparative Management*, Vol. 8, 55–78. Greenwich, CT: JAI Press.

25. Guillen, M. F., and Garcia-Canal, E. (2009). The American model of the multinational firm and the "new" multinationals from emerging economies. *The Academy of Management Perspectives*, 23(2), 23–35.

26. Craig, C. S., and Douglas, S. P. (1996). Developing strategies for global markets: An evolutionary perspective. *Columbia Journal of World Business*, Spring, 70–81.

27. Ghoshal, S., and Bartlett, C. A. (1990). The multinational organization as an interorganizational network. *Academy of Management Review*, 15, 603–625; Malnight, T. W. (1996). The transition from decentralized to network-based MNC structures: An evolutionary perspective. *Journal of International Business Studies*, 27, 43–65.

28. Cavusgil, S. T., Knight, G., and Riesenberger, J. R. (2008). *International Business: Strategy, Management, and the New Realities*. Upper Saddle River, NJ: Prentice-Hall.

29. Bellman, E. (2009). Harley to ride India growth. *The Wall Street Journal*, August 28, B1, B2; Ewing, J. (2009). Amazing machines may lead Europe out of recession. *Business Week*, August 24 and 31, 60–61; Hill, *Global Business Today*; see also www.harley-davidson.com/wcm/Content/Pages/Company/company.jsp?locale=en_US.

30. Byrnes, N. (2007). Avon: More than cosmetic changes. *Business Week*, March 12, 62–63; Ewing, Amazing machines may lead Europe out of recession; Hill, *Global Business Today*.

31. Bartlett, C. A., and Ghoshal, S. (1989). *Managing Across Borders: The Transnational Solution*. Boston, MA: Harvard Business School Press; Hout, T., Porter, M. E., and Rudden, E. (1982). How global companies win out. *Harvard Business Review*, September–October, 9–108; Lovelock, C. H., and Yip, G. S. (1996). Developing global strategies for service businesses. *California Management Review*, 38, 64–85; Luo, Y. (2001). Determinants of local responsiveness: Perspectives from foreign subsidiaries in an emerging market. *Journal of Management*, 27, 451–477.

32. Lunsford, J. L. (2003). Boeing may risk building new jet despite a lack of U.S. customers. *The Wall Street Journal*, October 15, A1, A13.

33. Hitt, Ireland, and Hoskisson, *Strategic Management: Competitiveness and Globalization*; MacMillian, I. C., van Putten., A. B., and McGrath, R. G. (2003). Global gamesmanship. *Harvard Business Review*, May, 62–73; Ramstad, E., and Juying, Q. (2006). Intel pushes chip production deep into China's hinterlands. *The Wall Street Journal*, May 23, B1, B3.

34. Holmes, S. (2003). A plane, a plan, a problem. *Business Week*, December 1, 40–42; *Business Week*. (2002). Boeing's high-speed flight, August 12, 74–75.

35. Michaels, D., and Sanders, P. (2009). Dreamliner production gets closer monitoring. *The Wall Street Journal*, October 7, B1, B2.

36. Cavusgil, Knight, and Riesenberger, *International Business: Strategy, Management, and the New Realities*; Morrison, A. J., Ricks, D. A., and Roth, K. (1991). Globalization versus regionalization: Which way for the multinational? *Organizational Dynamics*, 19, 17–29; Prahalad, C. K., and Doz, Y. L. (1987). *The Multinational Mission: Balancing Local Demands and Global Vision*. New York: The Free Press.

37. Schiller, Z., Burns, G., and Miller, K. L. (1996). Make it simple: That's P&G's new marketing mantra—and it's spreading. *Business Week*, September 9, 96–104.

38. Luo, Y. (2003). Market-seeking MNEs in an emerging market: How parent–subsidiary links shape overseas success. *Journal of International Business Studies*, 34, 290–309; Bartlett and Ghoshal, *Managing Across borders: The Transnational Solution*. See also: www.cat.com/corporate-overview/offices-and-facilities.

39. *Dayton Daily News*. (2009). Crunch time: P&G may be ready to sell-off Pringles, July 11, A8; Birkinshaw, J., Morrison, A., and Hulland, J. (1995). Structural and competitive determinants of a global integration strategy. *Strategic Management Journal*, 16, 637–655.

40. Hitt, Ireland, and Hoskisson, *Strategic Management: Competitiveness and Globalization*; Morrison, A. J., Ricks, D. A., and Roth, K. (1991). Globalization versus regionalization: Which way for the multinational? *Organizational Dynamics*, 19, 17–29.

41. Ghemawat, P. (2005). Regional strategies for global leadership. *Harvard Business Review*, December, available at: www.hbrreprints.org.

42. Birkinshaw, Morrison, and Hulland, Structural and competitive determinants of a global integration strategy.

43. Johansson, J. K., and Yip, G. S. (1994). Exploiting globalization potential: U.S. and Japanese strategies. *Strategic Management Journal*, 15, 579–601; Mosakowski, E. (2000). Strategic colonialism in unfamiliar cultures. In P. C. Earley and H. Singh (eds) *Innovations in International and Cross-Cultural Management*, 311–337. Thousand Oaks, CA: Sage; Rosenstein, J., and Rasheed, A. (1993). National comparisons in strategy: A framework and review. In S. B. Prasad and R. B. Peterson (eds) *Advances in International Comparative Management*, Vol. 8, 79–99. Greenwich, CT: JAI Press; Yip, G. S. (1995). *Total Global Strategy*. Englewood Cliffs, NJ: Prentice-Hall.

44. Wacker, J. G., and Sprague, L. G. (1998). Forecasting accuracy: Comparing the relative effectiveness of practices between seven developed countries. *Journal of Operations Management*, 16, 271–290.

45. Horning, C. (1993). Cultural differences, trust and their relationships to business strategy and control. In Prasad and Peterson, *Advances in International Comparative Management*, Vol. 8, 155–174; O'Grady, S., and Lane, H. W. (1996). The psychic distance paradox. *Journal of International Business Studies*, 27, 309–333.

46. Erramilli, M. K. (1996). Nationality and subsidiary ownership patterns in multinational companies. *Journal of International Business Studies*, 27, 225–248; Tse, D. K., Pan, Y., and Au, K. Y. (1997). How multinationals choose entry modes and form alliances: The China experience. *Journal of International Business Studies*, 28, 779–803.

47. Atwater, L. E., and Atwater, D. C. (1994). Strategies for change and improvement. In B. M. Bass and B. J. Avolio (eds) *Improving Organizational Effectiveness Through Transformational Leadership*, 146–172. Newbury Park, CA: Sage; Yukl, G. (2008). *Leadership in Organizations* (7th ed.). Englewood Cliffs, NJ: Prentice Hall.

48. Griffin, R. W., and Pustay, M. W. (2005). *International Business: A Managerial Perspective* (4th ed.). Upper Saddle River, NJ: Prentice-Hall.

49. Phatak, A. V. (1995). *International Dimensions of Management* (4th ed.). Cincinnati, OH: South-Western.

50. Misquitta, S., and Rohwedder, C. (2009). Kraft covets Cadbury's know-how in India. *The Wall Street Journal*, September 10, B1; Ball, D. (2003). Nestlé craves fatter profits. *The Wall Street Journal*, August 19, B5; Ellison, S. (2004). Kraft CEO to revamp company; Holden gets a new global post. *The Wall Street Journal*, January 9, A9; Ellison, S. (2003). Kraft's stale strategy. *The Wall Street Journal*, December 18, B1, B6; See also www.kraftfoodscompany.com.

51. Friedland, J. (1996). In this "great game," no holds are barred: U.S. power companies seek to dominate Latin gas markets. *The Wall Street Journal*, August 14, A10;

52. Miller, J. W. (2007). Africa's new car dealer: China. *The Wall Street Journal*, August 28, B1, B2.

53. Kahn, J. (1996). China finds a promising market in Africa. *The Wall Street Journal*, July 19, A9; Trofimov, Y. (2007). In Africa, China's expansion begins to stir resentment. *The Wall Street Journal*, February 2, A1, A16.

54. Pearl, D. (1996). Saudis, of all people, find industry hobbled by a lag in electricity. *The Wall Street Journal*, August 20, A1, A8.

55. Sawyer, O. O. (1993). Environmental uncertainty and environmental scanning activities of Nigerian manufacturing executives: A comparative analysis. *Strategic Management Journal*, 14, 287–299.

56. Phatak, *International Dimensions of Management*.

57. See http://corporate.walmart.com/our-story/ (retrieved December 10, 2013); Bustillo, M. (2009). After early errors, Wal-Mart thinks locally to act globally. *The Wall Street Journal*, August 14, A1, A10.

58. Barney, J. B. (1995). Looking inside for competitive advantage. *Academy of Management Executive*, 9, 49–61; Phatak, *International Dimensions of Management*.

59. Schlender, B. R. (1994). Matsushita shows how to go global. *Fortune*, July 11, 159–166, see also www.panasonic.net.

60. Griffin and Pustay, *International Business: A Managerial Perspective*; Phatak, *International Dimensions of Management*.

61. Choi, A. (1995). For Mercedes, going global means being less German. *The Wall Street Journal*, April 27, B4; Taylor, A. (2000). Bumpy roads for global automakers. *Fortune*, December 18, 278–292.

62. *The Economist*. (2008). A global love affair: A special report on cars in emerging markets, November 15, 8.

63. Ellis, E. (2007). Iran's cola war. *Fortune*, March 5, 35–38; Luhnow, D., and Terhune, C. (2003). A low-budget cola shakes up markets south of the border. *The Wall Street Journal*, October 27, A1, A18.

64. Gupta, A. K., and Govindarajan, V. (2001). Converting global presence into global competitive advantage. *Academy of Management Executive*, 15, 45–56.

65. Burrows, P., Bernier, L., and Engardio, P. (1995). Texas Instruments' global chip payoff. *BusinessWeek*, August 7, 64–66.

66. Phatak, *International Dimensions of Management*.

67. Bremner, B., and Dawson, C. (2003). Can anything stop Toyota? *BusinessWeek*, November 17, 114–122; Brown, S. F. (2004). Toyota's global body shop. *Fortune*, February 9, 120B–120F;

68. Lichauco de Leon, S. (2013). Billionaire Tony Tan Caktiong takes Jollibee foods global. *Forbes Asia*, January 30, available at: www.forbes.com/sites forbesasia/2013/01/30/billionaire-tony-tan-caktiong-takes-jollibee-foods-global/ (retrieved December 10, 2013); Gross, M. (2009). Jollibee brings a Filipino addiction to Queens. *The New York Times*, March 11, available at: http://events.nytimes.com; *The Economist*. (2008). Here comes a whopper, October 25, 78; Arndt, M. (2007). Knock knock: It's your Big Mac. *BusinessWeek*, July 23, 36; Bellman, E. (2009). McDonald's plans expansion in India. *The Wall Street Journal*, June 30, B4; Liu, L. (2009). Europe's new McCafé culture. *BusinessWeek*, October 5, 70; also see www.jollibee.com.ph; www.mcdonalds.com.

69. Johansson, J. K., and Yip, G. S. (1994). Exploiting globalization potential: U.S. and Japanese strategies. *Strategic Management Journal*, 15, 579–601; Yip, *Total Global Strategy*.

70. Ramstad, E. (2009). Korea's LG dials up cellphone growth, gaining market share on rivals. *The Wall Street Journal*, July 21, B1, B5; Yip, *Total Global Strategy*.

71. Snow, C. C., Snell, S. A., Davison, S. C., and Hambrick, D. C. (1996). Use transnational teams to globalize your company. *Organizational Dynamics*, 24, 50–67.

72. Bartmess, A., and Cerny, K. (1993). Building competitive advantage through a global network of capabilities. *California Management Review*, 35, 2–27.

73. Kim, W. C., and Mauborgne, R. A. (2005). *Blue Ocean Strategy: How to Create Uncontested Market Space and Make the Competition Irrelevant*. Boston, MA: Harvard Business School Press. Kim, W. C., and Mauborgne, R. A. (1991). Implementing global strategies: The role of procedural justice. *Strategic Management Journal*, 12, 125–143; *Sloan Management Review*. (1993). Making global strategies work, Spring, 11–25.

74. Immelt, J. R., Govindarajan, V., and Trimble, C. (2009). How GE is disrupting itself. *Harvard Business Review*, October, available at: http://hbr.harvardbusiness.org/2009/10/how-ge-is-disrupting-itself/ar/pr.

chapter 9

jumping in

foreign market entry and ownership options

Learning Objectives

After reading this chapter, you should be able to:

- describe the stages of international development that firms may pass through and how these stages relate to foreign market entry;
- understand the strengths and weaknesses of various foreign market entry options that do not require ownership as well as those that do require some ownership responsibilities;
- identify the different types of strategic alliances between international companies and why they are used.

International Challenge

General Electric Powers up in China . . . But at a Technological Price

For over two decades, GE has had success in China selling its many products—everything from hair dryers and washing machines to jet engines and power-generating turbines. GE's focus is understandable given the economic growth in China. For example, the demand for power generation was projected to grow by leaps and bounds. While China is the world's largest consumer of coal, it has also recognized the need for development of renewable energy and has invested heavily in that. In 2009, GE turbines were installed when China launched its biggest biogas energy plant, turning chicken waste into electric power with reduced greenhouse gas emissions. GE also opened the firm's first wind turbine assembly facility in China, a wholly owned plant designed to supply the huge wind power needs there. The gearbox is a key part of the technology for GE's wind turbine and was to be jointly developed with partner Nanjing High Speed and Accurate Gear Company (NGC). GE provided technical prowess and brought NGC management to the U.S. for training and leadership development.

Yet, GE's efforts to sell power turbines in China underscore the conundrum faced by many who eye booming Chinese demand with relish. On the surface, the competitive context facing GE's power turbines seems clear. Specifically, GE's potential Chinese customers are mostly regional utilities and independent energy-producing firms. Today's most advanced power turbines are sophisticated pieces of technology that pump out huge amounts of electricity from their high-tech blades. Consequently, GE's main competitors at the moment are mainly other multinationals, such as Vestas (Denmark), Siemens (Germany), and Alstom (France). In contrast, multinationals in comparatively low-tech industries such as personal care (for example, shampoo makers such as P&G and Unilever) see China as many different and difficult local markets driven by specific preferences. These firms often face many local competitors that operate cheaply and possess in-depth knowledge about local customers.

But a few years ago, GE faced big challenges of its own when it tried to win a contract that could be worth billions to provide power turbines to several regional utilities in China. On the one hand, China represented a big growth market for GE's power turbines because soaring economic development caused electricity demands in China to skyrocket in recent years. At the time, China determined it must spend over $10 billion annually on new power plants well past 2011 just to catch up.

On the other hand, in competing against Siemens and Mitsubishi for the turbine business, GE faced Chinese negotiators who wanted access to *all* of the technology that allowed GE to develop its cutting-edge turbines. Government officials asked GE to pass along its proprietary technology to a couple of Chinese firms that wanted to be able to construct the turbines on their own. Clearly, China wants its companies to be global players in high-tech manufacturing industries. There is the rub—China's strategy the past decade or so has been to dangle access to its growing internal markets in exchange for the transfer of the most critical technologies.

As you might suspect, GE was torn. While access to China's growing market for power turbines was important, the Chinese demand for 100 percent of their technology was hard to swallow, especially because the process of developing advanced power turbines cost some $500 million. As one GE executive put it, "we're interested in protecting the technology that we made significant financial investment in." In essence, companies such as GE face a tradeoff—pursue short-term profits at the risk of creating formidable local competitors in the long run, thanks to transfers of technology, or keep its technology and get shut out of a key market. Indeed, multinationals such as Motorola, Samsung, and Ericsson all either formed joint ventures with local partners or established research and development centers in China as vehicles for responding to Chinese demands for the transfer of technology. GE is now doing the same in certain areas, like the earlier example of GE's partnership to develop wind turbine gearbox technology.

So, here is the challenge. What should GE do in response to these technology transfer demands? Is there a way that GE can protect itself, at least to some degree, and still gain access to the Chinese market for power turbines? What might the role of the U.S. government be, if any, in all of this? Think about these questions as you read through our sections on modes of entry in foreign markets and their associated pros and cons. If you can, do some research on the power turbine industry and the technologies involved. Because several years have passed since GE faced this decision, you can then take a look at the Up to the Challenge? feature at the end of the chapter for a glimpse at how GE actually responded.[1]

Taking the Plunge

This chapter examines the options companies have for entering foreign markets. Of course, the options that companies select are often a direct reflection of their corporate-level international strategies. As you will see, foreign market entry options vary considerably in terms of the managerial and financial resources that need to be committed for companies to be successful. But which specific entry method companies select usually depends on how management sizes up the following sets of factors:

■ company objectives for foreign markets (e.g., desired market share, profitability);

■ the environment in specific foreign countries targeted for entry (e.g., cultural, economic, and legal context, quality of the business infrastructure);

■ company capabilities and resources (e.g., technical, managerial, financial);

■ the competitive context in targeted foreign markets (e.g., existing as well as potential future competitors);

■ attributes of the products or services to be sold within targeted foreign markets (e.g., certain products may be impractical to ship because they are perishable, too heavy, fragile, or so complex that they require on-site support);

■ the risk–reward equation (e.g., do the risks associated with entering a particular foreign market stack up well against the potential rewards and help the company achieve its objectives).

Other factors shaping company choices include the pros and cons of the various entry options as well as the firm's level of international development (and how successful it is). Many of these factors are considered within this chapter. Yet, it is also important to emphasize that entering foreign markets may not always be the best move for companies. Unfortunately, some companies seem to feel that they must "go global" because of a perception that "everyone" is involved in international markets one way or another. The bottom line is that entering foreign markets has to make sense for each individual company. Consequently, management should step back and ask some tough, basic questions before proceeding—questions that address the potential costs, benefits, and capabilities of the firm as they relate to foreign market entry options. These questions are summarized in Figure 9.1. Of course, addressing such questions can be part of the process

What Are the Potential Benefits of Going Global?	Will the Costs of Going Global Outweigh the Benefits?	Does the Firm Have the Management Skills Needed to Globalize?
When and where would the benefits of global moves show up in financial statements?	What costs are associated with the benefits of moves to globalize?	What specific management skills are needed to realize benefits of going global?
Is the understanding of each benefit clear, and what is the value of each benefit?	What do company skeptics say about the costs of globalizing and the impact on performance in foreign markets?	Has the company demonstrated that it has the talent and skills needed to execute the globalization moves under consideration?
Is there any hard evidence that other firms have realized these benefits under similar conditions?	What's the best alternative use of the resources the company plans to spend on executing its strategy to globalize?	Can the firm effectively develop the management skills needed to execute any planned globalization moves?

Figure 9.1 Thinking About Globalizing Your Company Somehow? Ask Questions in Three Areas before Taking the Plunge.

Source: Adapted from Alexander, M., and Korine, H. (2008). When you shouldn't go global. *Harvard Business Review*, December, 70–77.

of developing a company's international strategy in the first place, something covered in Chapter 8. Nevertheless, companies need to avoid "bandwagon" thinking and carefully consider the alternatives before taking the plunge. As you read through this chapter, keep the questions in Figure 9.1 in mind as we review the pros and cons of specific foreign market entry options.[2]

Stages of International Development

It is useful to first understand how a firm's embrace of international markets evolves over time. Historically, companies have gradually expanded their international activities in a series of relatively distinct stages. In essence, as companies accumulated experience, knowledge, and capabilities overseas, their involvement in international markets grew accordingly. This allowed companies to effectively manage the complexities associated with more sophisticated international operations.[3]

For instance, a small company might first dip into foreign markets by exporting. Perhaps the company saw potential foreign markets as attractive. Or perhaps it was concerned about negative trends in its domestic market. Either way, the company reached a tipping point and was willing to experiment and to dip a proverbial toe into foreign markets. In such cases, exporting is a common option for small firms because large capital outlays are not required (e.g., to build expensive plants overseas). But as companies grow and evolve, however, they may move from relying on exports to building manufacturing facilities overseas. Yet, the international developmental process is anything but exact. Many firms do not evolve in a clear sequence of steps or move in a linear fashion through developmental stages. For instance, companies can jump from exporting to establishing an international division without establishing an overseas sales subsidiary first. Likewise, overseas acquisitions may allow firms to leapfrog some steps. Later in this section, we will take a closer look at the different evolutionary path that some multinationals from emerging economies have taken to grow and develop.[4]

But first, consider the dichotomy between service and manufacturing firms. A manufacturer is more likely to go through a gradual series of stages as it expands internationally. Global car giant Toyota is a good example. It began by exporting cars from its home base in Japan, slowly expanding its presence overseas by building local manufacturing capabilities in key markets such as the U.S. In recent years, Toyota has been aggressively expanding its manufacturing base in China.[5]

In contrast, service companies essentially have to jump in with both feet when they decide to enter foreign markets, often through acquisitions. Unlike manufacturing firms, service companies do not have the luxury of starting out slowly and gaining experience (e.g., by exporting a product overseas) before setting up operations abroad. For instance, GE Capital, the financial services arm of parent GE, lends money and offers insurance worldwide. It has arguably become a master at setting up foreign operations quickly, either building them from scratch or rapidly integrating foreign acquisitions. Some years ago, GE Capital bought troubled Toho Mutual, a Japanese insurance firm. GE Capital quickly installed its own procedures while scrapping Toho Mutual's seniority-based personnel system.[6] Naturally, the success of this approach depends on how well the company executes its procedures and the extent to which local difficulties hamper operations. For instance, Western banks and other financial services firms that barreled into Eastern European markets a few years ago ran into cultural, recruiting, and legal obstacles that ate into potential profits, especially after paying millions to snap up local banks.[7]

Nevertheless, many firms evolve through relatively distinct stages as they become more sophisticated in their international operations. Not surprisingly, there are different perspectives as to how to define such stages.[8] Nevertheless, many experts assume that companies can be successful in any stage and that the time companies take to progress through internationalization stages varies. Figure 9.2 presents a basic framework for understanding the process of internationalization that involves six stages.

Stage 1: Exporting

A domestic company often begins internationalizing by exporting its products or services to foreign customers. This stage may include marketing of products or services abroad, perhaps through an export department run by a manager and small support staff. Such departments are typically considered ancillary to the firm's domestic sales and marketing activities, at least initially. Alternatively, domestic firms that are new to international business may turn to banks or consulting firms to handle many export-related activities and provide the necessary expertise (such as dealing with documents, currency issues, shipping, and letters of credit). For many years, L.L. Bean was a good example of a Stage 1 firm. This Maine-based outdoor clothing company got its start in 1912 and, while it has bricks and mortar retail outlets, L.L. Bean has been mainly known for its direct-to-the-consumer sales approach, first by mail-order catalog and later by e-commerce. The company began by serving only the U.S. market but eventually began exporting to customers in other countries. Today, L.L. Bean ships its products to over 160 countries. It does, however, obviously face a variety of challenges as an exporter, including import restrictions on textiles in some European nations as well as U.S. government restrictions on exporting to certain countries (such as North Korea, Syria).[9]

Stage 2: Sales Subsidiaries

As overseas sales continue to grow, firms may feel that it is best to contract with distributors or representatives to represent their products abroad, such as to promote products, to answer questions, and to provide follow-up service, etc. For example, in Japan, L.L. Bean established local customer service operations, including service representatives, to help Japanese customers who have questions. Indeed, once a firm such as L.L. Bean decides to open overseas sales offices or retail operations, it is essentially moving to Stage 2. The company arguably reached that milestone in 1992, when it opened its first overseas retail operation in Japan. As of 2008, the company had over a dozen retail outposts in Japan and had launched its first store in China. Likewise, Milwaukee-based motorcycle maker Harley-Davidson was the quintessential example of a Stage 2 firm for many years. Strong growth in foreign markets prompted Harley-Davidson, which exports just over 30 percent of its motorcycles, to establish overseas offices and retail outlets for better marketing and sales support.[10]

Stage 3: International Division

Indeed, Harley-Davidson has continued to expand its sales and retail presence overseas (its first dealership in China opened in 2006). That said, the company has also moved to Stage 3, which involves assembly or manufacture of products overseas. Specifically, Harley-Davidson established its first foreign assembly operation in South America, shipping motorcycle kits to Brazil for final assembly and subsequent sale. While the vast majority of Harley-Davidson motorcycles are still assembled in the U.S., the company's move to assemble products in Brazil is a common and natural progression from the creation of overseas sales subsidiaries. Yet, sometimes companies move from exporting to an international division in one fell swoop. Regardless, having an international division means that a more sophisticated organizational structure is in place to oversee all foreign business activity and to support future international expansion. Usually, an international division also means that the company has placed a greater emphasis on hiring personnel who are knowledgeable about international business and can monitor foreign markets.[11]

Stage 4: Multinational

Stages 4–6 describe the more complex multinational operations that may evolve over time. In Stage 4, multinational companies recognize that while headquarters plays a key role in important strategic decisions, foreign operations often do best when staffed by local employees who understand the local environment. In fact, the role of the foreign subsidiary in Stage 4 is to serve the needs of the national or regional market where it is located. But expanding and localizing foreign operations or activities is expensive and can distract from a firm's core brand, especially in challenging times. For example, Harley-Davidson acquired Italian performance motorcycle maker MV Agusta Group in 2008 in order to give it a more significant footprint in Europe with popular brands that could complement its own. But in late 2009, Harley-Davidson reversed itself and put MV Agusta up for sale, concluding that the money spent on acquiring and running the company was "diverting investment dollars away from the Harley brand."[12]

Stage	Area of Concentration
Stage 1	Exporting
Stage 2	Sales subsidiaries
Stage 3	International Division
Stage 4	Multinational
Stage 5	Global or transnational
Stage 6	Alliances, partners, and consortia

Figure 9.2 Common Stages in the Process of Corporate Internationalization.

Source: Adapted from Briscoe, D. R. (1995). *International Human Resource Management*. Englewood Cliffs, NJ: Prentice-Hall.

On the other hand, achieving the right balance between headquarters' control and local fine-tuning may sometimes mean playing up a foreign subsidiary's local roots. For instance, to enter the Brazilian market, American retailer J. C. Penney bought Lojas Renner, a family-run regional department store chain. But rather than turning Lojas Renner into just another J. C. Penney outpost, the company kept things local. After running into trouble in other countries, J. C. Penney realized that successful retailing is often a localized phenomenon. So, J. C. Penney wanted to keep the local expertise that was the backbone of Lojas Renner's outstanding reputation for service and value. Consequently, J. C. Penney kept the Lojas Renner name on storefronts in Brazil and kept the local management team in place. Those steps, along with J. C. Penney's financial help, allowed Lojas Renner to grow more than 100 percent within two years.[13]

There are many other retailers that also try to localize their operations to succeed. For example, France's Carrefour, the world's second-largest retailer after Wal-Mart, operates in dozens of countries and states that over 90 percent of the products in its stores are local in origin. As one Carrefour executive explained, "In China, we are Chinese; in Spain, we are Spanish." Dutch competitor Ahold goes even further, operating under different store names and emphasizing local brands in the more than two dozen countries where it operates. As Ahold's CEO put it, "Everything the customer sees, we localize. Everything they don't see, we globalize." Yet, successful multinationals can stumble if they are complacent. For instance, in 2009 Carrefour pulled out of Russia a mere month after it had opened a second store there. Analysts suggested that the company was not fully prepared to compete in the Russian market and decided to cut its losses and regroup.[14]

Wal-Mart is another company that has had its share of tumbles in foreign markets. In Germany, for instance, Wal-Mart did not fully understand local shoppers, government regulations, and the pervasive role of German unions, much less the competitive landscape. Indeed, Wal-Mart has been criticized abroad for everything from "abusing" local suppliers to committing cultural snafus in foreign markets. For example, Japanese employees initially resisted Wal-Mart's "10 foot rule," which pushes employees to offer help to customers who come within 10 feet (in most Japanese stores the custom is to wait for customers to ask for assistance). But Wal-Mart has learned—it now relies much more on local management expertise and adapts its retailing approach where needed when operating outside of the U.S. In 2003, Wal-Mart had over 1,300 stores in foreign locations. By 2013, of its over 11,000 stores nearly 60 percent (6,350) were outside of the U.S., and accounted for a significant portion of the firm's revenue. In short, Wal-Mart has lost some of its "headquarters knows best" mentality.[15]

Stage 5: Global or Transnational

A more global or transnational orientation marks companies in Stage 5. Of course, some companies never reach this stage, perhaps because their industries do not require operational integration worldwide. As discussed in Chapter 8, companies that operate on a global or transnational basis try to ignore geographical boundaries in terms of their ongoing operations. In short, they will build product, source materials, or perform services anywhere in the world if doing so somehow minimizes costs and maximizes returns. For instance, computer-peripherals maker Logitech International has dual headquarters (in Silicon Valley and Switzerland) and bases its top manufacturing executive in Taiwan (a hub of low-cost Asian computer component suppliers and manufacturers) so that he or she can make faster decisions about where it can source product. Of course, managing this effectively is no easy chore, requiring flexibility, the ability to bridge cultures and time zones, interdependence across all units, and a global perspective, among other things. A transnational orientation, however, also will allow for location-specific tailoring of products or services where necessary, often to a surprising degree. For large, diverse companies such as GE, assessing whether the firm operates "globally" or "transnationally" really makes little sense. Instead, each business unit (such as plastics, medical imaging, etc.) must decide how local it needs to be to succeed against the competition.[16]

Stage 6: Alliances, Partners, and Consortia

Stage 6 highlights the fact that firms are increasingly linking up to leverage their combined resources such as people, equipment, technology, expertise, and research. For many multinationals, partnerships, joint ventures, and alliances help tap resources that they believe are either too expensive or otherwise impossible to secure alone. For instance, Daimler, Mitsubishi, and Hyundai partnered to jointly develop a new engine. By sharing key technologies and minimizing development costs, the three companies hope to use the engine, in a variety of configurations, in cars sold in Europe, Asia, and the U.S. As one auto executive put it, "You collaborate or die. You must achieve economies of scale."[17]

   The process of transferring technology via alliances can put a firm's technology advantage at risk. Many countries have developed laws that help their firms protect their technological edge (see Chapter 2). A related issue for small and large firms alike is the ability to prevent misuse of legal but questionable use of patents. For example, large companies sometimes engage in patent flooding. This involves applying for many different patents dealing with small variations on technology originally developed by one's competition or a small, start-up firm. The following International Insights feature provides a specific example of how this shattered a partnership between a small U.S. firm and large Japanese one.

International Insights

U.S. Firm Battled a Japanese Giant to Protect Its Technology

Dr. Steven Case, founder and former chair of Cyberoptics, invited Yamaha Motor Co. to visit the firm. The meeting was a great success and led to a beneficial agreement between companies. But, the five-year alliance ended in U.S. District Court when Cyberoptics sued Yamaha for contract and patent violations. It charged Yamaha (the well-known maker of motorcycles) with using a deluge of patent filings to poach the technology that Cyberoptics had developed—a practice called "patent flooding."

At the time, patent flooding was more common in Japan, while it was generally viewed as a questionable practice in the U.S. Flooding occurs when a firm files for many separate, but isolated, patents that closely resemble a rival's patent of larger scope. This handcuffs the innovating firm and ties it to the firm that "flooded" the patents surrounding its product. Otherwise, it finds itself slapped with lawsuits by the "flooder," claiming infringement. To avoid the problems and costs, many firms (particularly smaller ones) are cornered into exchanging patent rights or paying fees to be able to launch their product.

The Cyberoptics case is similar, and because of its relatively small size there was a lot on the line. The firm supplies optical laser sensors and image analysis systems to makers of electronic equipment. Cyberoptics' problems began when Dr. Case met with Yamaha engineers at an Anaheim, California, hotel. There, Cyberoptics demonstrated its new product to an impressed Yamaha who bought 500 systems over the next five years. Dr. Case stated in court documents that during a visit to Yamaha he came up with a way to improve the effectiveness of Yamaha's robots. While there, he jotted down an outline of his invention on a napkin, which became one of many documents entered into evidence (something that Case claims he signed and dated). Other documents allegedly also support Cyberoptics' claim that Yamaha made only slight changes to its inventions when it subsequently filed 26 patents in several countries that represent only slight variants of the Cyberoptics product. Another company alerted Cyberoptics of the Yamaha patents and, once informed, it filed suit alleging Yamaha violated the agreement that neither company could file patents on their collaboration without mutual consent. Dr. Case claimed that the patents were very similar to those he had sketched out on the napkin.

For Yamaha's part, it denied the allegations and claimed that Cyberoptics was informed of the applications and that the napkin was nothing more than a duplication of existing Yamaha diagrams that its engineers showed Dr. Case. Yamaha countersued for defamation, saying that the charges were false and slanderous. While the facts were being sorted out in U.S. Federal Court, Cyberoptics continued to spend time and money to protect its technology. Eventually the lawsuits were settled out of court.

Lawsuits such as this show why worries among smaller firms may be warranted. The sheer number of similar cases led the U.S. to raise patent flooding by Japanese firms, and the Cyberoptics case in particular, as an issue between countries a few years ago. As early as 1996, Japan was added to the U.S. watch list of countries with weak patent protection. Yet, despite a global treaty designed to stop flooding, the issue persists. Some think it has gotten worse.

U.S. firms are getting into the act themselves with an onslaught of litigation brought about by domestic patent "trolls." Trolls are not inventors with creative ideas they want to protect. Instead, they are people with some capital who typically buy up a slew of patents that might slightly overlap with existing patents or products. They then engage lawyers to sue anyone and everyone who might be using or selling the claimed "inventions" as small parts of their products or processes. Lawyers euphemistically call the trolls "non-practicing entities"—leave it to Americans to develop a market in patent "derivatives." Trolls, in fact, filed the majority of the roughly 4,700 patent suits in 2012, many of which were against small companies and start-ups that often cannot afford to fight back.[18]

Despite the increasing popularity of such between-company linkages, building trust between partners can be quite difficult. This might be especially true when the firms involved are separated by cultural differences, such as in the Cyberoptics–Yamaha case. Even these gaps, however, can be bridged. For instance, one study found that American automotive suppliers developed greater trust with Japanese automakers operating in the U.S. than with American automakers. One factor that seemed to make a difference was the greater tendency for the Japanese firms to be helpful—they sent consultants to help American partners for months on end without charge. In short, to build trust in partnerships, you may have to give it first.[19]

Emerging Market Multinationals: A Different Evolutionary Path

The stages of internationalization just described may not hold for every firm. Indeed, there is increasing evidence that the traditional path to internationalization—slow expansion into foreign markets as firms gain the knowledge and experience needed to manage greater risks abroad—simply does not hold for new multinationals that come from emerging market economies. In short, many emerging market multinationals have internationalized very quickly. Moreover, they have done so after growing in home markets that often come with many disadvantages such as weak business infrastructures, poor intellectual property protections, political instability, and opaque legal systems, as well as the fact that they must often compete against wealthy, experienced multinationals from developed markets. Figure 9.3 summarizes key developmental differences between traditional multinationals and emerging market multinationals.[20]

Ironically, these home market challenges often make emerging market multinationals better equipped than "traditional" multinationals when it comes to coping with difficulties in developing countries. They are often more nimble as well—lacking stifling corporate bureaucracies and entrenched cultures that have built up over decades in more established multinationals. Consequently, they often expand internationally by entering other emerging markets as well as more developed countries as they build their capabilities to compete with established multinationals, such as in the U.S. or Europe. One of the ways that they "upgrade" their competitive capabilities is by buying or forming alliances with sophisticated multinationals in developed countries. Between 2008 and 2009, for instance, Chinese energy companies such as China National Petroleum Corp, Chinalco, Cnooc, and Sinopec put over $40 billion on the table to buy, sometimes unsuccessfully, energy firms from Argentina (YPF), the U.K. (Rio Tinto), Switzerland (Addax Petroleum), and Norway (Awilco Offshore). Sometimes, developing country multinationals bargain with more established multinationals for reciprocal market access. Many Chinese multinationals behave just this way, using their strong position at home to entice established Western multinationals into partnerships—trading home market access and know-how for access to technology or even developed country market access. A good example would be Chinese appliance maker Haier, whose products, up until fairly recently, were not found in American stores.[21]

Development Dimension	Traditional Multinationals from Developed Countries	Multinationals from Emerging Markets
Firm adaptability	Generally *low* due to ingrained cultures and structures that may lead to inertia	Generally *high* because of scant international history, allowing for nimble, innovative responses
Capabilities in unstable/ difficult business and political environments	Generally *weak*; these firms evolved in stable political contexts/good infrastructures	Generally *strong* since these firms evolved in markets with business and political instability
Competitive advantages	Generally *strong* thanks to deep, well-developed resources available in the firm	Generally *weak*; with limited resources that need to be upgraded relative to traditional multinationals
Path of expansion	*Simple*, evolving from closer to more distant nations	*Complex*, often simultaneous entry into developed and emerging markets
Typical foreign market entry mode	*Internal*, with wholly owned foreign subsidiaries	*External*, relying on acquisitions and alliances
Speed of internationalization	*Gradual*, often evolving through distinct stages	*Accelerated*, often rapidly moving into several markets in multiple ways

Figure 9.3 Comparing the Old with the New: Developmental Differences between Traditional and Emerging Market Multinationals.

Source: Adapted from Guillen, M. F., and Garcia-Canal, E. (2009). The American model of the multinational firm and the "new" multinationals from emerging economies. *Academy of Management Perspectives*, 23(2), 23–35.

Foreign Market Entry Options

Our discussion so far suggests several options when it comes to entering foreign markets and this section presents those choices in more detail, along with their respective pros and cons. As noted earlier, the choice of entry mode reflects several factors, including the challenges that exist in certain foreign markets and the capabilities that firms have to overcome them. Other important factors shaping entry choices include firm goals and opportunities in foreign markets.[22]

Entry Options without Ownership

First, we consider entry options that do not involve ownership of overseas facilities or plants and then move to entry routes that involve at least partial ownership of overseas assets.

Exporting: A Popular and Flexible Alternative

Compared to some options, exporting is a relatively easy, cheap, and flexible way to enter foreign markets. These features explain both the ongoing popularity of exporting and why it is often a company's first exposure to international business. Exporting involves sending goods or services to other countries where they can be sold. Exporting might be initiated for two reasons. First, it is an inexpensive way for companies to increase their revenues: opportunities in foreign markets may entice firms to begin exporting. Second, and conversely, weakening domestic demand may prompt firms to diversify their markets by exporting, soaking up excess domestic capacity in the process.[23]

A major plus of exporting is that it involves no foreign ownership requirements. Because there is no need to outlay a firm's capital, it is a low-cost market entry option. Exporting also allows companies to shield themselves from risks in certain markets, to sidestep foreign investment restrictions, and to shift gears relatively painlessly (export agreements can generally be terminated fairly quickly and inexpensively). Moreover, once companies start exporting, they can use customer feedback to tailor their products and increase their overseas business. Yet, quick profits may not be the primary motivation for small firms to begin exporting. Instead, learning about new markets, new technologies, and new ways of doing things may also be valuable motivations.[24]

Cost containment is not an issue limited to small firms. Manufacturing products in one place and then exporting them abroad can help bigger companies, such as Boeing, take advantage of economies of scale. When the dollar is weak relative to foreign currencies, those big American exporters can reap major financial rewards. In late 2009, the dollar slid against major foreign currencies. This made the price tag for big-ticket products exported by Caterpillar, General Electric, and IBM cheaper for foreign customers. As a result, all three companies were able to undercut foreign rivals on price while continuing to make money. For instance, Caterpillar's ability to stay ahead of Japanese rival Komatsu, particularly in growing countries such as India and China, was helped tremendously when the weaker dollar made its exported construction and mining equipment less expensive. Currency fluctuations can cut both ways, like in 2005 when the value of the dollar increased significantly—effectively hiking prices for U.S. firms.[25]

The Costs and Challenges of Exporting

This underscores the point that exporting also has costs and challenges to consider. For instance, to be successful exporters, firms must:

- select products that sell well overseas (requiring possible product modifications);
- understand export rules and prepare to deal with voluminous paperwork;
- find overseas customers (and adapt marketing and advertising to reach them);
- deal with currency fluctuations, language issues, tariffs, and transport delays;
- obtain letters of credit/financing from foreign customers; and
- hire freight forwarders to ship products and distribute them overseas.

A single export transaction may involve many steps, several banks, and dozens of documents. Learning about, much less executing, these aspects of exporting all require time and effort—as well as hefty price tags in some cases. Fortunately, there is plenty of help available. American companies, for instance, can turn to a variety of local, state, and federal agencies for help (e.g., the U.S. government's www.export.gov website). Firms can also hire export management companies to handle some, most, or all of their export-related chores, including ones that specialize in specific markets or industries. Export management companies can be retained on a long-term basis or temporarily while the firm learns enough to handle things itself.[26]

Nevertheless, let's consider some specific exporting challenges in more detail. While exporting is typically less expensive than perhaps building a new plant overseas, some large firms end up making substantial foreign direct investments to support their export-ing activities. To help sell the cars it exported to Japan, Chrysler at one point spent $100 million to buy Japanese car dealerships, sank another $10 million on a parts distribution center outside Tokyo, and dropped $180 million more to modify its cars for the Japanese market. So much for "cheap" exporting![27]

Another challenge for exporting firms is dealing with tariffs and trade barriers. For instance, at one point Boeing faced a steep 40 percent import tariff on planes that it was trying to sell in Russia to cash-strapped local carriers. Of course, foreign exporters can also face hurdles in the U.S. In 2002, for example, steel companies in Europe and Asia howled about lost export sales to the U.S. resulting when the American government briefly imposed tariffs as high as 30 percent. More recently, the U.S. government did the same to imported Chinese tires, slapping on tariffs as much as 35 percent in 2009. China's response was to levy tariffs on American imports of auto parts and poultry products.[28]

In addition to tariffs and other regulatory barriers that boost costs, exporters also face logistical challenges. Communications can be difficult because of the distance from customers (e-mail and other communication technology notwithstanding). Moreover, certain modes of transportation are too slow, too unreliable, or too expensive for par-ticular types of exported goods. In many situations, the key to overcoming these draw-backs is to find a foreign distributor who has both the knowledge and the resources to market imported products successfully.[29] For another look at how export rules can impact U.S. firms, see the following International Insights feature.

International Insights

Trouble Can Find American Exporters at Home

Optical Associates is a small company that makes components for semiconductor firms. It had been doing well in the exporting game, at least until it shipped equipment to an Indian nuclear facility without obtaining an export license. U.S. authorities told the firm that it had violated federal export restrictions by selling to "forbidden entities." Optical Associates was fined $100,000 and prohibited from exporting to India for three years. Other examples of fines include IBM, which paid a whopping $8.5 million fine for shipping computers to a Russian nuclear lab and Northrop Grumman, which paid $15 million in fines for exporting without the needed licenses. Raytheon paid a similar fine in 2013 for export violations that *it* reported. And, United Technologies agreed to pay a $75 million fine for the sale of software (later used by China to develop its first attack helicopter) that violated export laws.

Some might say that companies should know better. Regardless, the stakes for staying out of trouble have never been higher. In 2008, the Department of Justice announced a new program (Counter Proliferation Initiative) to more aggressively seek out, prosecute, and fine those found in violation of exporting critical technology. A general rise in international trade, combined with ongoing threats from terrorism and weapons development, has led the U.S. to do more about, as well as to expand upon, export restrictions to dozens of countries. Even allies such as Israel are subject to restrictions on products such as high-speed computers and encryption software.

Yet, critics charge that export laws have become complex and difficult to fathom, costing firms a bundle in lost business, late shipments and government penalties. Plus, the complexity of global business has made it more difficult for firms to follow the law in the first place. As one manufacturing executive put it, "When you're sourcing from 10 to 15 countries for a product, or you're part of a supply chain, knowing who your customers are can be more difficult than you think."

Naturally, big companies, particularly those in sensitive industries, tend to have the best resources for coping with the daunting array of export restrictions—including export managers and software to help track and comply with export regulations. But for smaller firms, the intricate and cumbersome regulations are intimidating. Most U.S. firms have taken the position that while export restrictions are needed, the regulations governing them should be simplified (e.g., less paperwork, shorter license approval times, etc.). In the meantime, American firms interested in exporting may want to keep the following principles in mind.

- Firms can run into trouble not because of their products. Any prohibited technology, information, or data that is disclosed to restricted foreign entities or countries may trigger action by the U.S. government.
- Export laws and regulations are complicated. For instance, defense-related products fall under the control of the Directorate of Defense Controls (State Department) while products that may have "dual use" are under the Bureau of Industry and Security (Commerce Department).
- U.S. exporters need to ensure that they have appropriate export control procedures in place and that their personnel or agents fully grasp applicable export laws. Compliance training is a necessity.
- Come clean and disclose any illegal exports. Penalties are less severe when violations are unintentional or companies voluntarily share their mistakes (such as the Raytheon example mentioned previously). Firms that "put their heads in the sand" when it comes to U.S. export laws do so at their own peril.[30]

Types of Exporters and Types of Exporting

Data show that small firms (those with fewer than 500 employees) are more likely to be exporters. Interestingly, small firms run by managers who embrace risk taking and innovation are the most successful exporters—they export a higher percentage of total sales and have higher export growth rates than competitors run by more conservative bosses. A good example might be Frontier Foods, a small Australian food company. Some years ago, Frontier began exporting a variety of cheese products to China. This was a daring step because most Chinese at the time had no experience with cheese, were concerned about digestion problems, or disliked the taste. But Frontier's risky move worked, thanks in part to a burgeoning middle class in China (and more openness to new tastes) as well as the soaring growth of fast food operators and Western-type supermarkets in China. Within seven years, China accounted for 70 percent of the firm's revenues.[31]

Corporate giant Boeing and other large firms also export. Indeed, Boeing engages in the three different types of exporting. When it sells a plane to a foreign airline, Boeing is engaged in *direct exporting*—where sales of a firm's products or services directly involve foreign customers. The many U.S. companies that supply Boeing with parts or components, however, are involved in *indirect exporting*. This occurs when a domestic firm sells a product to another domestic firm, which in turn exports the product often after changing it in some fashion. The final major type of exporting is an *intracorporate transfer*. In this case, a firm located in one country sells a product to an affiliated company in another country. For instance, Ford plants in Mexico produce fuel tanks that are then exported to Ford car assembly plants in the U.S. Intracorporate transfers such as these account for about one-third of international trade worldwide and about 40 percent of all imports to, and exports from, the U.S. Figure 9.4 shows a breakdown of intracorporate transfers in U.S. imports and exports.[32]

Overall, exporting and importing are deeply woven into the fabric of international business. Honda is another good example of a company that uses exporting and importing extensively, often in very inventive ways. The company operates a variety of facilities in the U.S., including a major assembly plant in Marysville, Ohio. Honda makes creative use of its $1 billion trading arm, Honda Trading America Corporation (HTAC). To help supply its American operations, Honda ships parts and components from Japan to the U.S. At one point, however, the transport ships involved went back to Japan empty after

U.S. Trade Flow	Intracorporate Transfer Source	
	American Multinationals	**Foreign Multinationals**
Imported goods	Products imported from overseas subsidiaries to U.S. parent firm	Products imported from foreign parent company to a subsidiary in the U.S.
Exported goods	U.S. parent firm exports products to its overseas subsidiaries	Foreign-owned subsidiaries in the U.S. export products to parent firm abroad

Figure 9.4 Sources of Intra-Corporate Transfers in U.S. Imports and Exports.

Source: Adapted from Koretz, G. (1997). A new twist in trade numbers, *BusinessWeek*, May 12, 24.

unloading their cargos in the U.S. But, thanks to HTAC, those ships now return to Japan fully loaded with everything from scrap metal to frozen salmon to soybeans. Next to Honda's Marysville auto plant sits a huge HTAC warehouse that sorts and packages soybeans grown under contract by over 100 American farmers. Soybeans are loaded onto rail cars and sent to California, then put on ships bound for Japan. HTAC exports around 800,000 bushels of American soybeans to Japan—about 14 percent of the high-end foreign soybeans sold there. Profits from this soybean venture help buffer Honda from downturns in the auto market and have introduced many American farmers to exporting. Sounds like a win–win to us.[33]

Licensing

Another inexpensive and flexible foreign market entry option is licensing. This option is often used when foreign investment or ownership restrictions are in place or firms want to reduce their financial exposure in risky foreign markets. It also makes sense when high tariffs render importing goods too expensive or when product customization needs to be done locally. Likewise, when a company in a competitive industry wants to sell a product abroad that is older or has dated technology, margins may be slim. Heavy investments in overseas markets, therefore, make little sense given the low potential returns. Licensing then represents a low-cost entry option that permits the firm to still make good money on the product.[34]

In general, licensing is a contractual agreement in which one company (the licensor) sells a foreign firm (the licensee) the right to use its brand names, trademarks, copyrights, patents, manufacturing technology, or any other intellectual property. This shows that licensing can cover a wide variety of circumstances. For instance, companies such as Coca-Cola, Disney, and Harley-Davidson have licensed their logos and brand names to clothing makers around the world. High-tech firms such as AT&T and Intel license their expertise, know-how, and technologies to foreign companies as well. Agreements last for several years and often include an option to renew. Typically, once the licensee understands the licensor's technology or intellectual property, the licensor has little or no involvement with the licensee's activities. In many cases, the license granted comes with specific restrictions (e.g., licensed products can only be sold in a particular location for a fixed amount of time).[35]

The advantages are clear. For one, the licensor obtains quick access to foreign markets and an immediate benefit in the form of royalties, fees, or even payment in kind (i.e., products, know-how, or intellectual property) from the foreign licensee. Royalties can be paid up front in the form of a flat fee or as a percentage of sales value. Regardless, these benefits accrue to the licensor without having to set up costly overseas plants or expend significant capital. Consequently, licensing is often very attractive to small or medium-sized companies since they lack the capital to pay for ownership entry options. With licensing, firms have no reason to have any presence in foreign markets, much less spend money there. It is also a great way to test out new foreign markets and learn about them before making a more significant financial commitment. Large firms can also use licensing to preempt (or block) rivals in foreign markets. For instance, Microsoft used controversial long-term licensing agreements with government agencies and schools in over a dozen African countries to both build its presence on a continent with only 10 million computers, for a population of 750 million, while also locking out competitor Linux from key customers.[36]

But licensing also has risks and drawbacks. For example, firms wishing to license their intellectual property to foreign companies should carefully craft the terms, conditions, and boundaries of the licensing contract. The contract should clearly spell out the obligations of both the licensor and the licensee. Typically, the licensor wants the licensee to make narrow or limited use of its intellectual property and to avoid passing trade secrets to competitors. Negotiating such terms is rarely easy because the two sides involved usually have conflicting motives. For instance, the licensor often wants a fairly short-term agreement, especially if it is using licensing as a way to test a market before jumping in with major investments of its own. On the other hand, the foreign licensee often wants a longer agreement, one that will allow it to recoup costs associated with producing and distributing the licensed product.[37]

Even when an equitable licensing deal is struck, there are still major risks. For instance, the licensor gives up considerable control by definition and can be hurt if the licensee produces shoddy goods or otherwise behaves in ways that damage the licensor's reputation. The lack of control also makes it more difficult for licensors to take advantage of location economies. Finally, firms that end up licensing their important technologies and production processes to foreign companies may be "educating" a potential competitor. Indeed, firms often overestimate their ability to control technologies once licensed.[38]

Franchising

In key respects, franchising is a more elaborate version of licensing. Imagine having a contract that allows a foreign entrepreneur or firm to operate a business using the methods, procedures, products, trademarks, and marketing strategies created by another company. Moreover, that contract involves longer commitments between the parties and requires tighter controls (e.g., strict adherence to specific operating rules) than what is found in a licensing agreement. This is the essence of *franchising*.

The company offering the business system (including methods, trademarks, products, and so on) is the franchisor, while the firm that agrees to run the business using those methods and products is the franchisee. Service firms, particularly in the food and lodging industries, are most likely to enter foreign markets as franchisors. Sometimes franchisors seek out a master franchisee in doing so. In other words, they find a company or group of investors willing to coordinate all franchising operations in a specific foreign market. This *master franchisee* then runs the franchisor's businesses in the foreign market and may even bankroll the entire operation, or conversely, sub-franchise to other independent businesses there. McDonald's is perhaps the quintessential example of a well-known franchisor operating all over the world. The company looks for foreign firms or entrepreneurs to run its restaurants in a particular country and sometimes seeks out master franchisees. In exchange for use of company trademarks, operating procedures, products, and various support services (such as training and logistics help), the foreign franchisee pays McDonald's a fee. The franchisee commonly has to fork over a portion of revenues to the franchisor. Perhaps the most important aspect about franchising, however, is that franchisees must adhere to strict guidelines about how the business has to be run. That is one reason why McDonald's restaurants operate similarly worldwide despite the fact that many are run by franchisees.[39]

Besides being able to enter many foreign markets quickly and cheaply, franchisors typically have attractive brand names to offer foreign franchisees, who in turn offer the franchisors in-depth knowledge of local markets. The greater control franchising offers is another key advantage compared to licensing. Similar to licensing, franchising also allows the franchisor to shift costs (and risks) to the franchisee. So, when a foreign firm signs a deal to run a 7-Eleven convenience store, that firm often has to come up with the money to start up the business. This requirement allows franchisors, especially established ones such as 7-Eleven and Subway, to expand quickly worldwide at a relatively low cost.[40]

The success of franchising giants such as KFC has led smaller fast food companies to dip into international markets (A&W, Au Bon Pain, Big Boy, and Schlotzky's Delicatessen, are just a few). Smaller franchisors, however, sometimes cannot support franchisees to the same extent that bigger firms such as Subway can (e.g., with global supply networks, extensive employee training programs, etc.). Consequently, franchisees may have to scramble to find suppliers or to make necessary menu changes on their own. One Big Boy franchisee in Thailand ended up with a menu oriented toward Thai locals and European tourists instead of the chain's trademark "American" hamburgers. As the franchisee put it, "We thought we were bringing American food to the masses. But now we're bringing Thai and European food to the tourists."[41]

Nevertheless, franchising has challenges that even the biggest firms have to grapple with. For instance, control issues remain a concern. Firms often have high standards that franchisees may not be motivated to duplicate. In fact, a brand name and the expectations that go with it are precious commodities that the franchisor must protect. Customers come to McDonald's, for example, with high expectations of speed, cleanliness, and food quality. Foreign franchisees that do not live up to these expectations can hurt the overall McDonald's reputation. Sometimes the franchisor will replace weak franchisees by setting up company-owned outlets in foreign countries if local firms can't meet the franchisor's standards. In other cases, disagreements between franchisors and franchisees can spark distracting conflicts. For instance, McDonald's got into a tiff at one point with some Brazilian franchisees who complained that McDonald's was opening too many new restaurants near existing outlets, cutting into sales. Some Brazilian franchisees also claimed that McDonald's was ripping them off, demanding a 17-percent cut of sales as a rental fee (almost twice what U.S. franchisees supposedly pay). McDonald's rejected these complaints, arguing that Brazilian franchisees were "spoiled" by their early profits and that the rental fee helped it recoup the cost of building restaurants in Brazil and providing technical help to local franchisees.[42]

Indeed, these control and franchisee management issues are one reason why a few companies in this industry have decided to limit their exposure to franchising. Starbucks is a case in point. With over $13 billion in annual revenue and some 21,000 stores worldwide in 2013 (with over 7,000 locations outside of the U.S., within 62 countries), Starbucks is a big company but not as large as McDonald's. More than 60 percent of its U.S. stores are company owned. Likewise, about 40 percent of its stores in foreign markets are owned by the company, with many of the remainder being joint-venture operations instead of franchisee outlets. Because it tends to rely more on company-owned stores, Starbucks has lower profit margins and higher expenses than McDonalds and other fast food chains. But, Starbucks feels that having greater control over more of its stores is a tradeoff it is willing to make.[43]

Overall, the overseas growth opportunities for franchisors continue to be very bright. For a closer look at why American franchisors are finding foreign markets so attractive, see the accompanying Global Innovations feature.

Global Innovations

McDonald's and Other U.S. Franchisors Find Foreign Growth Is Golden

How is this for a plan? To escape the sluggish and slow-growing American market, you decide to search for better fortunes abroad. In the process, you entice foreign investors, entrepreneurs, and companies to bankroll your international expansion. Sound far-fetched? Not if you are an American franchisor.

In fact, in recent years, U.S. franchisors such as McDonald's, Subway, and the women's fitness center chain Curves International have been plowing into hot developing markets where the middle class is growing rapidly, including Brazil, China, India, and Central and Eastern Europe. Through mid-2013, almost half of McDonald's nearly 34,000 units were outside of the U.S.—in over 119 countries. For years now, Europe has been the stronghold for McDonald's, representing well over half of its international revenue. Yet, the Asia/Pacific region has been the hotbed for recent growth, with the number of restaurants nearly doubling between 2006 and 2011, compared with just a 15-percent jump in U.S. revenue during that period. To realize this growth, McDonald's and other U.S. franchisors have been looking for—and finding—master franchisees, groups of entrepreneurs or businesses willing to bankroll operations themselves. In doing so, they often pay hefty fees to the franchisors for the right to control a big territory or even a country. There they can act like a miniature franchisor and sell outlets to smaller franchisees.

The biggest American franchisors are often the most sought after abroad because of their instant name recognition and low risk. Especially attractive are the kind of relatively simple, turnkey operations offered by franchisors such as Subway. Simple operations mean lower prices and fewer barriers to entry for foreigners looking to invest as a Subway franchisee. Subway restaurants, now the world's largest franchisor with over 41,000 outlets, has one of the lowest total franchisee fee structures. This resulted in the opening of more foreign operations, including nearly 2,000 the last three years—now with about 10,000 locations outside the U.S., in over 100 countries.

If you are a female in a foreign country who wants to get into better shape, you can probably find a local Curves International fitness franchisee ready and eager to help. While Subway opened 1,400 new overseas outlets between 2008 and 2009, Curves International was opening over 600 fitness centers outside the U.S. during the same period. Right now, Japan is Curves International's largest foreign market, where it has over 700 centers. But the company also opened its first centers in China and India between 2009 and 2010. Now, foreign locations represent over half of its 7,000 total units. This flip is due to increasing international demand and a precipitous decline in the number of U.S. stores that occurred between 2007 and 2010. Nevertheless, one intriguing possibility for more international growth is in the Middle East, where Curves International's core concept—fitness centers for women—may play well because religious customs dictate that men and women use separate facilities in public.

The future, at least for now, looks bright for American franchisors wanting to expand abroad—where foreign customers apparently want to eat hamburgers and submarine sandwiches and then pump iron and sweat it off.[44]

Management Contracts

In an international management contract, one company provides a foreign firm with specific services, technical help, or managerial expertise for either a flat fee or a percentage of sales. Usually the contract is for a specific period of time. Like other entry modes considered, this is a relatively low-risk way to increase international revenues because no ownership costs are involved. For example, Marriott has run hotels overseas for years under management contracts without actually owning them. Likewise, Disney actually owns minority stakes in its theme parks in Paris, Tokyo, and Hong Kong—the company derives much of its income in these locations by providing various management services.[45]

The operation of complex infrastructure facilities is another area where management projects often come into play. For instance, some years ago Argentinean oil producer Yacimientos Petroliferos Fiscales SA (YPF) used management contracts at its main refinery in La Plata. The technical help that was provided under contract by U.S.-based Hughes Tool Co. helped YPF modernize the plant and cut the cost of oil production in half. Later, Chevron Corp. supplied executives under a management contract with YPF to help run the ongoing operation. Likewise, U.S. Steel's consulting group provided managers and engineers to help Slovakia's Vychodoslovenske zelziarne AS (or VSZ) modernize and refine its automated steelmaking equipment. U.S. Steel later bought VSZ.[46]

Turnkey Contracts

Sometimes management contracts are a consequence of international *turnkey contracts*. Typically, turnkey contracts include all of the steps needed to design, build, and operate large-scale facilities in foreign locations. When a project is complete, the facility may be run for a short time by the contractor to ensure smooth operations. In many cases, however, a facility will eventually be turned over to the company or government who issued the contract. Most turnkey contracts involve building expensive, complex facilities (e.g., power plants, dams, airports, oil refineries). Typically, the contracts themselves are hundreds, if not thousands, of pages long and are the result of protracted meetings and negotiations with foreign customers. It may take a year or more to land a turnkey contract because of all that is involved.[47]

Some countries lack the internal expertise needed to construct such complex facilities and turn to foreign firms for help. This often provides a forum for local companies to learn about the technology and processes associated with building these facilities. This is exactly why Colorado-based engineering firm CH2M Hill has had such success. The firm's reputation is impeccable and includes helping local engineers and technical experts develop their own skills. These very factors helped the firm land a $5.3 billion expansion of the Panama Canal, a project targeted for completion in 2014. One CH2M Hill executive noted that because the U.S. owned and ran the Panama Canal until 1999, sensitivities were high. In awarding the contract Panama looked for "a partner they can trust, who won't take over their project" and who would "leave the Panamanian engineering and construction community stronger."[48]

Turnkey projects are especially attractive when more direct forms of foreign investment are impossible or when political or economic instability makes such investments risky. On the other hand, turnkey projects are often limited, one-shot deals that can transfer know-how to potential competitors. Moreover, sometimes foreign governments scuttle, delay, or raise costs for already approved projects.[49]

Certain countries, such as India, seem to put more obstacles in the way of foreign companies than others. Although free market reforms continue to make India a good place to do business, bureaucracy, convoluted regulations, and shifting political pressures remain sources of frustration. Indeed, multinationals may have to deal with the central government as well as one or more of 35 state governments. For instance, several agreements to build power plants were signed between Indian governments and foreign firms in the early 1990s. A decade later, financing troubles were still being worked out for certain projects, while on others some of the American, French, and South Korean firms involved had given up and pulled out. As of 2010, some 200 new plant and infrastructure projects worth almost $100 billion were on hold, thanks to a three-way tug of war between government agencies, farmers seeking higher land prices, and companies wanting to build. Many of these projects had been delayed for years and involved foreign firms such as Luxembourg steelmaker ArcelorMittal, South Korean steelmaker Posco, and Japanese car giant Nissan. Nevertheless, multinationals are still attracted to opportunities in India, thanks to the country's growing middle class and its desire for better business infrastructure.[50]

Contract Manufacturing

An increasingly popular option in recent years, *contract manufacturing* allows companies to outsource their manufacturing operations to other firms, either in whole or in part. The advantages associated with this option are many. Companies can avoid spending capital to build and maintain expensive plants as well as paying the workforces needed to run them. For instance, shoe companies such as Nike are able to focus on critical value-added areas, such as marketing and shoe design, because all of their manufacturing is done under contract, mostly in low-wage Asian countries. Likewise, California-based Vizio, Inc., a popular provider of inexpensive flat-panel TVs, relies completely on contract manufacturers in Asia to make its product line—which now also includes Blu-ray video players. As the LCD TV market leader in the U.S., Vizio believes that contract manufacturing kept it profitable as prices for electronics fell steeply in 2008–2009 while also allowing them to focus on marketing and product design. Other household names in consumer electronics have also been moving to contract manufacturing as a way to lower costs. Sony, for instance, announced in 2009 that it would sell its LCD television plant in Mexico to Taiwan-based Hon Hai Precision Industry Company, which would continue making TVs on Sony's behalf.[51]

Contract manufacturing also means that firms have ceded control for product quality and timely delivery to someone else. Moreover, contract manufacturing may bring unwelcome attention to companies. For instance, Nike has taken public relations hits in recent years because of the alleged mistreatment of workers for contract manufacturers operating in Indonesia and Vietnam. In addition, contract manufacturing is part of the debate about the outsourcing of jobs from developed countries such as the U.S. Manufacturing workers in a variety of American industries continue to be under pressure due, in part, to the rising tide of contract manufacturing across industries. For example, many American furniture makers have increasingly looked to companies in China to produce furniture on their behalf. In the process, dozens of plants in the U.S. were closed and thousands of employees' contracts terminated, sparking political debates and hurting the images of some firms.[52]

Entry Options Involving Ownership

As firms become larger and more multifaceted, some progress from strategies like exporting to those involving actual ownership of overseas facilities. Moving to ownership position can also reflect a desire to make more money abroad, something made easier with ownership control. Ownership also allows firms to more closely coordinate worldwide operations. Overall, companies typically pursue ownership options for foreign market entry with one or more motives in mind. Three general sets of motives exist: market-based, where entering foreign markets provides opportunities to sell to new customers; efficiency-based, such as opening overseas plants to lowering production costs; and resource-based, such as the ability to obtain technologies or raw materials available in a foreign market. Figure 9.5 provides more detail about these ownership motives. Overall, however, these motives must be balanced against the greater expense and risk that ownership typically entails.[53]

Wholly Owned Foreign Subsidiaries: The Greenfield Approach

One straightforward ownership option for firms is the Greenfield approach. Here, a firm would enter a foreign market by establishing (from scratch) a wholly owned foreign subsidiary there. Doing this means scouting for, and then buying, a piece of property on foreign soil that can accommodate subsidiary operations. Once this site is acquired, construction can begin on the facility. Later, workers can be hired to staff the new operation. That is exactly what Swedish appliance maker Electrolux AB did between

Source of Motivation for Ownership Options		
Market-Based	**Efficiency-Based**	**Resource-Based**
Being able to access new customers and opportunities in new markets	***To tap government incentives while avoiding trade barriers***	***To gain managerial or technical expertise that exists in a foreign market***
For instance, car companies have built plants in the U.S. and China to tap into the world's largest automotive markets	By building plants or partnering with firms in local markets, firms avoid import tariffs and realize government tax reductions or subsidiaries for setting up shop	Firms wishing to learn and innovate may want to establish facilities where world-class know-how exists, (e.g., the U.S. for software or Japan for industrial robotics)
To be able to directly compete against important rivals in their own markets	***To lower production/ sourcing costs***	***To obtain critical raw materials***
Forcing rivals to defend their own turf can make it more difficult for them to expand elsewhere	Can explain growth of new factories built in places like China, India, and Mexico— countries with inexpensive production costs and cheap labor	In many cases, companies simply have to go where the resources exist given their industries (e.g., mining, oil production)
To follow important customers	***To have production located closer to customers***	***To obtain the assets or knowledge of a foreign partner***
Suppliers may follow customers overseas to grow sales and keep competitors at bay (e.g., Japanese parts firms followed Toyota when they built plants overseas)	Having factories located close to key markets overseas can yield pluses, especially if customer needs are changing rapidly or they require close attention	Opening foreign facilities with local partners allows firms to tap their expertise in product development, marketing and manufacturing

Figure 9.5 Why Firms Pursue Ownership Options in Foreign Market Entry: Three Key Motivations.
Source: Adapted from Cavusgil, S. T., Knight, G., and Riesenberger, J. R. (2008). *International Business: Strategy, Management, and the New Realities*, 421–423. Upper Saddle River, NJ: Prentice-Hall.

2004 and 2012. It opened new plants in lower-cost locations such as Mexico primarily to reduce production expenses.[54]

The main advantage of a Greenfield approach is maximum control. For instance, proprietary technology can be protected more easily than with other foreign market entry options. This is particularly the case when the firm is ahead of competition. Intel Corporation's newly built $2.5 billion computer chip factory in Dalian, China, is wholly owned for just that reason—the firm worried that a joint-venture or partial government ownership would have meant transferring sensitive technology and manufacturing expertise to various entities in China. While it took years to complete, once it was finished in late 2010 Intel was able to tap another key advantage of a Greenfield approach—being able to hire an entire workforce fresh, with no negative prior history to worry about. This

Dalian plant is only part of Intel's nearly $5 billion recent investment in China. It also built an assembly/test site in Chengdu and research sites in Beijing and Shanghai.[55]

Moreover, the Greenfield approach allows firms to pick a site that maximizes location economies (e.g., being close to target markets or low-cost local labor) and then put a modern facility on it. As the Electrolux example illustrates, location economies explain why companies have spent billions in recent years to build new plants in low-cost locations. Mexico provides an excellent low-cost manufacturing platform, especially for firms that want to be close to the large American market. There are about 3,000 plants employing over 1 million Mexican workers set up by multinationals, many literally just across the border from the U.S. Such *maquiladora* facilities allow the parent company to pay duty only on the value that local Mexican labor adds to exported products. This arrangement, combined with low Mexican wage rates, proximity to the American market, and access to the U.S. transportation system, lowers overall production costs.[56]

Likewise, China continues to be a magnet for Greenfield plants, including the high-tech variety, thanks to government land incentives, low costs, and a growing internal market for more expensive products. Those positives prompted South Korea's LG Display Company to announce in 2009 that it would be building a $4 billion plant in Guangzhou, China, to manufacture large, sophisticated LCD display panels. Due to some bureaucratic problems, construction was delayed until 2012, with the plant expected to open in 2014. Samsung has beaten them to the punch and has already begun production in 2013 on its flat-panel plant in Suzhou.[57]

There are also, however, significant downsides to a Greenfield option. Building a Greenfield facility takes time and is very expensive (both of which are shown in the LG case above). While facilities are under construction, companies may be particularly vulnerable to the whims of the host government, such as raised taxes or onerous environmental requirements. Nor does recruiting and training a new workforce happen overnight, especially in a new culture and unfamiliar legal environment. Unfortunately, firms sometimes ignore these realities and push too fast to set up new foreign subsidiaries. For instance, U.S.-based Lincoln Electric lost money for the first time after the firm built 16 new plants in 11 countries within a four-year period. The company ended up closing plants in four countries and switched to exporting and alliances as its main international entry modes.[58]

Wholly Owned Foreign Subsidiaries: The Acquisition Approach

Multinationals can also establish wholly owned foreign subsidiaries by purchasing existing foreign companies. This *acquisition approach* usually involves complicated negotiations and financial transactions. There may also be legal, competitive, or political hurdles to surmount, especially if the multinational is acquiring a foreign company with a strong local reputation or one that is state owned. Over the past 20 years, countries transitioning to market-based economies have engaged in large-scale privatization efforts—with governments selling off state-owned enterprises or assets to private companies or individuals. For instance, many of China's state-owned businesses have been privatized because they were poorly equipped to survive, particularly when matched against foreign firms. China viewed privatization as one way to convert state-owned businesses into more effective competitors. Often that means having foreign companies purchase or otherwise invest in state-owned enterprises. But turning around moribund state-owned enterprises is rarely simple or cheap.[59]

In any case, China still has plenty of government-owned firms operating, some of which are owned at the local level and are looking to make foreign acquisitions of their own to better compete. Consider Beijing Auto, owned by the city of Beijing's municipal government. A small player in the Chinese market, Beijing Auto sought to acquire foreign car companies as a way of accessing new technologies and achieving better market penetration at home and abroad. For instance, in 2009, Beijing Auto bid for a controlling interest in GM's Europe-based Adam Opel GmbH operation. In rebuffing the bid, GM was concerned that it would have to later face a Beijing Auto armed with Opel (i.e., GM) technology in China, a market the company considers critical. This underscores how competitive concerns can sometimes derail foreign acquisitions.[60]

When firms do successfully complete a foreign acquisition, they may encounter some of the major risks associated with an acquisition approach. Specifically, acquiring another firm, whether private or state-owned, also means buying all the problems that acquired company had, such as poor labor–management relations, debt, and inferior product quality. On top of that, cultural and managerial differences between the multinational and the foreign firm being acquired can be difficult to overcome, at least in the short run. Interestingly, recent research suggests that long-term performance of a foreign acquisition may be better when the cultural distance between the acquiring and the acquired firm is larger rather than smaller. Companies, especially from highly developed countries, may be more cautious before stepping into culturally distant markets (e.g., exercise more diligence in investigating acquisitions, etc.). If so, then they may be more prepared and less prone to make mistakes. Moreover, acquiring another company in a vastly different cultural environment may help the acquiring firm build strengths that improve its competitiveness. In short, while "culture clashes" are perhaps inevitable with foreign acquisitions, they are not necessarily debilitating over a longer time period.[61]

Regardless, there is no doubt that foreign acquisitions can present significant challenges, cultural or otherwise, in the short term. For instance, U.S. Steel acquired steelmaker Vychodoslovenske zelziarne AS (VSZ) for $1.2 billion in 2000. U.S. Steel's goal in buying VSZ, a former state-owned enterprise in Slovakia, was to position itself to supply steel to the developing countries of Eastern Europe. Along with the acquisition, however, came antiquated equipment, management corruption, lousy customer service, a bloated workforce of 17,000, and resistance to the "American business culture."[62]

These challenges are hardly unique. For example, Ispat International, a London-based steelmaker, spent $1 billion to buy Kazakhstan's huge Karmet steelmaking complex in 1996. Among the problems Ispat inherited (besides outdated equipment) were 12 former KGB agents who initially refused to leave their gadget-filled spy suite and hundreds of workers who showed up drunk every day. Ispat felt that some 40 percent of Karmet's 38,000 employees were unneeded while the local union saw the company as a rich target and wanted a 75-percent wage hike. The company spent hundreds of millions of dollars to upgrade the complex.[63]

Nevertheless, one important advantage that acquisitions have over a Greenfield approach is that they are quicker to complete. The multinational is, in many cases, buying a working foreign facility, complete with workforce, equipment, product, distribution system, brand names, and reputation. The ability to enter foreign markets quickly, especially in response to competitors' moves, is an attractive option as international competition intensifies and demands for worldwide efficiency rise. This may explain why 48 percent of manufacturers in one survey said that the best international entry strategy was to acquire existing foreign plants. Only 31 percent said the best bet was to build Greenfield facilities. In fact, speed explains Nestlé's acquisition of Polish chocolate maker Goplana. The Swiss giant felt that building a new plant would delay its entry into Poland by two years. Waiting that long would prevent Nestlé from seizing a large share of one of Eastern Europe's largest markets.[64]

Besides speed, multinationals also target foreign companies for acquisition precisely because they have assets, such as successful brands or unique technologies that represent valuable competitive advantages. When added to the multinational's "portfolio," these advantages have the potential to add revenue quickly. For instance, from 2007 to 2009, Dutch multinational Philips Electronics NV snapped up medical equipment firms in China, India, and Brazil—all key markets where the firm wanted to grow quickly. With each acquisition, Philips picked up product lines designed for the local market (e.g., cheaper, simpler x-ray machines, other medical equipment), then upgraded the acquired plants and products to sell elsewhere. Similarly, in 1996 Coca-Cola acquired Parle Exports, India's top soft-drink supplier. This gave Coke all of India's local soft-drink brands, plus 50-odd bottling plants. As a result, Coke owned brands accounting for some 60 percent of the Indian soft-drink market. Conversely, Indian IT firm Wipro bought U.S.-based American Management Systems Inc. and NerveWire Inc. in 2003. Wipro hoped that this acquired expertise would help it better compete in the IT consulting business.[65]

A common question for acquisitions is whether to buy or to build. Cross-border acquisitions ("buying") may not always be best, especially relative to a Greenfield approach ("building"). Recent research suggests that what determines the better option for long-term growth is complex and depends on how the acquiring firm is structured and managed. For instance, if a firm operates foreign units as a tightly interconnected network, then a Greenfield approach may be the better path to growth than an acquisition. If, on the other hand, foreign units operate more independently, then an acquisition approach may be the better choice. In any case, an often-stated reason for large foreign acquisitions is that consolidation and size in "global" industries results in greater efficiencies. But savings from acquisitions are often overestimated, undercut by the complexities inherent in cross-border deals.

Managers also need to ask themselves whether their industry is really becoming more globally concentrated or if they are simply following a trend, perhaps because of ambition. Consider Korean construction equipment maker Doosan's nearly $5 billion acquisition of U.S.-based Bobcat in 2007. By the middle of 2009, Bobcat sales were down nearly 60 percent. While a recession certainly did not help, ex-Doosan employees argued the firm overpaid for Bobcat because of "national pride" in the face of rival bidders (independent analysis suggested Doosan overpaid by 20 percent or $1 billion).

Is your industry really becoming more concentrated globally?

		Yes	No
Is your company pursuing foreign acquisitions as part of an effort to consolidate globally?	**Yes**	Foreign acquisitions are most likely to pay off	Overexpansion is the likely outcome of foreign acquisition
	No	Failing to pursue foreign acquisition risks putting the firm at a disadvantage	Not pursuing a foreign acquisition is appropriate

Figure 9.6 Will Foreign Acquisitions Pay Off? A Decision Matrix.

Source: Adapted from Ghemawat, P., and Ghadar, F. (2000). The dubious logic of global megamergers. *Harvard Business Review*, 78, 71.

Figure 9.6 presents a simple decision matrix for determining whether a foreign acquisition is the right move. While it looks simple, making the actual decision is very difficult and is getting even more complex. Nevertheless, managers should avoid the various types of traps in thinking about these issues, such as getting caught up in the hype, wanting to match the "big deals" made by competitors, or rushing into a deal without vetting the impact.[66]

A positive case in point is DuPont's recent acquisition of Danish biotechnology firm Danisco. In November 2010, DuPont CEO Ellen Kullman's phone rang. On the other line was the CEO of Danisco, who explained that his firm was "in play" and a European chemical company had offered to buy it. His question to Kullman was "Are you interested?" Bids were being accepted only until January. While this had the potential to similarly entice DuPont, Kullman kept her head. She was interested, and the company was prepared. DuPont regularly scans the environment and Danisco was already on its acquisition radar and already a JV (joint venture) partner. It knew that Danisco recently changed shareholder voting rules, making it a little easier for a buyer. Kullman assembled the key due diligence team and they worked from Thanksgiving until January, with people eating and sleeping at the office. They worked until the last 30 minutes before the bid was due, questioning all data and assumptions and relying on their previous analysis of the firm. As Kullman said, "You can't fall in love with a deal; you have to fall in love with what it does for our company. And even then it has to be at the right price." Subsequently, they spent considerable time thinking through the integration of Danisco into DuPont.[67]

Alliances and Partnerships

A cheaper alternative to acquisitions is to pursue various types of alliances and partnerships with other firms. There are several options available here.

Joint Ventures

Some alliances, such as joint ventures (JVs), involve shared ownership, but ownership of a foreign operation need not be complete. A JV is a strategic alliance between two companies that is set up as a separate legal entity. Joint venture ownership can be split 50/50 between the parent companies or one firm can have a more dominant stake. Partners that hold more than a 50-percent share usually do so to have tighter control over the JV.[68] Firms with sophisticated technology seek a controlling stake in JVs, especially if the local partner's role is largely to supply local market expertise. That is the approach that U.S.-based appliance maker Whirlpool took to quickly position itself in key Asian markets. In the mid-1990s, Whirlpool started JVs with four Chinese and two Indian firms. Whirlpool bought controlling stakes in each to balance costs with maximum control. This expensive rapid expansion and effective local competitors, however, eventually caused Whirlpool to pursue cheaper alternatives.[69]

Not all international JVs involve manufacturing a final product. Sometimes they are designed to procure raw materials, produce components, or deliver services. Creating one may also involve construction of Greenfield facilities, the acquisition of existing firms, or both. Finally, JVs may have more than two partners and their form and purpose can vary considerably.[70]

That said, a common goal for many international JVs is to market, produce, and distribute a product in a particular foreign country or region. Often the partners are a large multinational and a smaller local company, as is the case with Whirlpool and its Asian counterparts. It is easy to see why both parties would be attracted to a JV. For example, the multinational might provide product design and technological expertise desired by a local company, while the local partner might provide marketing know-how and knowledge of local culture, laws, and business practices sought by the multinational. In short, both sides benefit.[71]

Cost, knowledge, and risk sharing are also major reasons for creating these alliances. This can be especially important for firms that want to be the first to position themselves in risky emerging markets. For instance, Pratt & Whitney (a unit of United Technologies) signed a JV agreement with Russia's Aviadvigatel in 1995 to put engines on Russian-built jets, even though big profits were unlikely in the near future. Likewise, UT's Otis Elevator unit was among the first U.S. firms to enter China in the early 1980s.[72]

JVs, however, are not limited to partnerships between large multinationals and much smaller local firms. Increasingly, the costs and risks of entering global markets or developing a salable product encourage even large multinationals into JVs with each other. In 2004, for instance, Honda and GE Aviation formed GE Honda Aero Engines, a 50/50 JV headquartered in Cincinnati, Ohio, to develop, certify, manufacture, and market a new small engine for light business jets. In 2007, the firm began building a new plant in North Carolina with the goal of starting mass production of engines in late 2010. Jet engine development is technically complex, expensive, time consuming, and subject to certification requirements and government oversight. The joint venture setup was attractive because of the shared development risks and costs as well as the size of the potential market (roughly 200 engines worldwide per year). In other words, with this alliance both firms had a better chance of recovering the costs of designing and producing the engine.[73]

Joint ventures can also provide access to markets that otherwise would be difficult to penetrate, such as China, where JVs can be either equity based or contractual in nature. Having a local firm as a partner in such markets can also be a buffer against pressures from foreign governments and changes in local regulations. A local partner can also allay some of the mistrust that certain countries may feel toward foreign multinationals due to fears of exploitation or a history of colonialism. Many developing countries, for instance, are concerned that foreign multinationals will overwhelm local firms, but JVs can help allay these fears and help local firms to be more competitive.[74]

As noted with earlier entry strategies, this could also hurt multinationals if key technologies or know-how is transferred to a local partner. Like licensing, the joint venture may turn local firms into formidable competitors later. JV contracts can be written so as to disallow transfer of critical technologies. But obtaining agreement on this may be tough as some countries strongly desire technology transfer. In addition, experience has shown that cultural and managerial conflicts can plague JVs. Decisions about selecting partners, setting goals, managing the venture, and performance appraisal strategies can be thorny. Indeed, research suggests that as many as ten decision factors impact joint venture performance—many of which are multi-faceted and complex.

Nevertheless, making good decisions here is critical if the JV is to perform well. One way to minimize conflict is to use a *delegated arrangement* in which the partners agree to step back from the management of ongoing operations and instead either hire new executives or reassign executives already working for the partners. But this might simply shift conflict to who will be hired or transferred. Given these challenges, management should think carefully about the partnering process and all the decision questions that need to be addressed if a JV is to function well (see some of these process and questions in Figure 9.7).[75]

A common theme of many of the questions listed in Figure 9.7 is, once again, concern about control. Indeed, one of the largest disadvantages of JVs has to do with these very issues. Crucial decision making may be hampered because of the need to consult with the JV partner, especially if the partners do not see eye to eye on matters. Joint ventures also may fail to provide the level of control multinationals need to take full advantage of location economies or coordinate worldwide operations. A common way to minimize these disadvantages is for the multinational to have majority control over the JV. Of course, foreign companies do not want to play second fiddle in many cases. So, finding a partner willing to accept a minority position can be difficult. While taking a majority position means greater control, it also means greater financial risk.[76]

Nevertheless, the additional financial commitment may be worth it. For example, having a dominant position in a Chinese JV can pay big dividends, giving management from the senior foreign partner more leverage over key business decisions. Not surprisingly, one study found that American managers felt U.S.–Chinese joint ventures were more efficient and profitable when dominant control is maintained.[77]

This sounds as though a multinational's ideal joint venture is one in which it can run things as usual despite having a local partner. Indeed, multinationals often seem most satisfied with alliances where they can ignore the local partner, at least on certain issues, and run operations their own way. But acting in that manner could lose the

Developing the Partnership	Decision Questions to Address
Evaluating the Strategic Rationale for a Joint Venture	• What are our *goals*? Are we in this for the long haul or just the short term? • What *resources* are needed to achieve our goals and how do we obtain them? • Is a joint venture really our best option?
Choosing the Best Partner	• Are our goals aligned with our partner's goals? • Does the partner have the resources we need and will they provide them? • Does the partner have any international joint venture experience? • What are the partner's motives and are we compatible as companies?
Negotiating Terms of the Partnership	• What are the business practices in the country where the joint venture will be? • Who will manage the joint venture? How will performance be assessed? • What equity split is appropriate? • Are all assumptions on the table? Any unresolved issues remaining?
Implementing and Managing the Joint Venture	• How should we handle disputes and any potential need to renegotiate terms? • If outcomes are poor, how do we improve? When should we terminate the joint venture? • Are we learning and can the parent firms leverage any new capabilities?

Figure 9.7 The Joint Venture Partnership Process: Decision Questions That Must be Answered.
Source: Adapted from Beamish, P. W., and Lupton, N. C. (2009). Managing joint ventures. *Academy of Management Perspectives*, 23(2), 88.

learning and opportunities provided by the partner's perspective. When this happens, it undercuts one of the major benefits of establishing a JV in the first place. Moreover, when multinationals ignore their foreign partners or otherwise are not paying close attention, the results can be disastrous, even when the multinational has a dominant position in the JV. The accompanying International Insights box discusses this issue.[78]

International Insights

Danone's Chinese Joint Venture Turns Sour

It seemed like a good match. Groupe Danone SA of France formed a 51 percent joint venture with Shanghai-based Hangzhou Wahaha Group in 1996 to produce soft drinks, juices, and milk products for the Chinese market. Aimed at a valuable and growing consumer products segment in China, Danone's stake in the JV was worth over $500 million and included some 40 different operations—a stake that gave it access to one of China's leading brand names, Wahaha.

In 2007, however, Danone publicly released its complaints against Hangzhou Wahaha, a highly unusual step in China where disputes are typically handled in face-saving fashion behind closed doors. Danone accused Wahaha of illegally selling Wahaha-branded products by using distributors outside of the ones selected by the JV. After two bitter years of charges and counter-charges, including back-and-forth lawsuits, Danone announced in 2009 that a settlement was reached and it would be exiting the partnership and selling its 51 percent stake. This left Danone to basically start over from scratch in China with a much smaller presence—after losing perhaps $100 million or more. Danone's first foray without Hangzhou Wahaha involved a yogurt product launched through a new, wholly owned subsidiary, one lacking the impressive distribution network of its former Chinese partner.

So, what went wrong? Granted, running joint ventures in China can be a challenge, especially because partners' motives are often different. The foreign multinational is after efficiency, profits, and market access while the Chinese partner is more focused on securing better technology and increasing employment. Indeed, foreign joint venture partners have complained about theft of technology and the lack of adequate redress from Chinese courts.

Danone alleged that Zong Qinghou, Hangzhou Wahaha's billionaire founder, had set up and run a parallel set of operations outside of the joint venture, surreptitiously run by his spouse and daughter, to produce a Wahaha line of drinks. Danone claimed that its joint venture agreement entitled it to 51 percent of the profits from anything with the Wahaha name on it, which it did not receive from these parallel plants. Mr. Zong replied by saying that he had Danone's permission to set up the plants, that the joint venture agreement was "outdated" anyway, and that the French company was only interested in making quick profits.

Part of the problem may have been that Danone was arguably piggybacking on Mr. Zong's earlier success in creating the Wahaha brand and developing a distribution network. Moreover, Danone apparently had been content to let Hangzhou Wahaha run the show, playing little or no role in managing its joint venture operations in China. As one analyst put it, to operate joint ventures successfully in China, companies need to build a business together "from the ground up." That did not appear to be the case with Danone. Despite owning 51 percent of the joint venture, Danone allowed Mr. Zong to operate them with almost no supervision or review. In any case, the former partners have both moved on, choosing not to cry over spilled milk.[79]

Figure 9.8 summarizes the key pluses and minuses of the market entry options that we have presented in this chapter.

Other Types of Strategic Alliances

JVs are actually just one of many possible strategic alliances. That said, making alliances work well requires trust between the parties, a clear set of shared objectives, and a

Non-Ownership Modes	Pluses	Minuses
Exporting	• Fairly inexpensive, no ownership risks • Relatively easy foreign access • Can move in/out of markets quickly • Can leverage skills and capabilities of foreign partners, distributors	• Missed location economies • Logistical and communication challenges • Learning compromised due to distance • Exposed to trade barriers, tariffs, currency fluctuations
Licensing	• Inexpensive, flexible, generates quick revenues via current intellectual property • Good when trade barriers preclude exporting or ownership restrictions exist • No ownership costs, good for testing risky markets or preempting rival firms	• Risky where intellectual property protection is weak, especially with complex products • Control ceded to licensee may inhibit coordination • May create new competitors
Franchising	• Low-cost, low-risk, quick market entry • Offers more control than licensing • Established brand names attract franchises with local market knowledge	• Maintaining control can be a challenge • Conflict due to franchise not adhering franchisors' standards • Requires monitoring of franchisees
Management contracts	• Very inexpensive • Low-risk revenue	• No long-term presence • May create competitors
Turnkey contracts	• An option if direct investment isn't feasible • Lowers risk if long-term instability exists	• No long-term presence • May create competitors • Vulnerable to political changes
Contract manufacturing	• Low financial risk, reduced manufacturing costs • Allows firm to focus on value-added areas	• Less control (lower product quality) • Learning is compromised • Public image may suffer

Ownership Modes	Pluses	Minuses
Greenfield subsidiaries	• Allows extremely high control • Offers location economies • Can pick own site, workers, technology	• Setup expensive and time consuming • Requires considerable global expertise • Risky due to ownership
Acquired subsidiaries	• Allows high control • Rapid entry compared to Greenfield • Offers location economies • Taps acquired firm's technology/knowhow	• Risky due to ownership • Cultural differences may be formidable • May be 'buying' problems (e.g., shoddy products, bad equipment)
Joint ventures	• Less financial and business risk than wholly owned subsidiaries • Leverages partner's resources, know-how, market knowledge	• Risks transferring some control or technology to partner • Still some ownership risk • can be a headache to manage

Figure 9.8 Pluses and Minuses of Foreign Market Entry Options.

Sources: Adapted from Cavusgil, S. T., Knight, G., and Riesenberger, J. R. (2008). *International Business: Strategy, Management, and the New Realities.* Upper Saddle River, NJ: Prentice-Hall; Griffin, R. W., and Pustav, M. W. (2004). *International Business* (4th ed.). Upper Saddle Ridge, NJ: Prentice-Hall.

forward-thinking management style. One success story, at least so far, is the Renault–Nissan partnership. In 1999, France's Renault took a 37-percent equity stake in struggling Nissan. Making this partnership work and moving from losses to profits in the process is arguably thanks in no small measure to Renault's charismatic leader, Carlos Ghosn. As Mr. Ghosn confidently put it, "there is only one global alliance that has added value, and that is Nissan and Renault."

Even as the car market skidded in 2008, Mr. Ghosn was nevertheless pursuing new projects and joint ventures to keep the alliance moving forward—including electric vehicles in Denmark, building a new factory in Morocco, rehabbing a shoddy Soviet-built plant in Russia, and designing a $3,000 car for the Indian market. Interestingly, part of the Renault–Nissan alliance's success has been Ghosn's effective management of, as he puts it, "the contradiction between synergy and identity." According to Ghosn, each corporate partner must maintain its unique identity ("because it is the basis of motivation") while still embracing common goals.[80]

Features of Alliances

Other types of alliances are typically narrower in scope, are less stable, and are shorter in duration than most JVs. These partnerships may also lack the formal structure and independent legal status found in JVs. As such, they are formed when multinationals believe that a cooperative arrangement is the best way to advance their own self-interest in specific areas. For a variety of reasons, including ease of market entry, the sharing of risk, and the ability to realize competitive advantages quickly, the use of strategic alliances has grown in recent years. The advantages associated with alliances are especially critical in less developed countries—where deregulation has created more demanding and competitive markets. Other entry options provide similar advantages. Strategic alliances, however, are often a better way for a multinational to learn "invisible skills" from a foreign partner. These skills are informal, tacit forms of expertise or know-how that can only be learned through the close contact possible in cooperative relations. Often, they are quite complex and evolve from a specific cultural context, such as Honda's expertise in developing and producing engines. This proficiency has been applied to diverse products (Honda cars, motorcycles, lawn mowers, and now, even jet turbines) and reflects a complex blend of know-how in flexible manufacturing, customer service, quality control, product development, and just-in-time materials management.[81]

Production Alliances

Acquiring such expertise is often part of the motivation behind production alliances. These involve firms that agree to manufacture products or deliver services in a shared facility that is either built from scratch or owned by one of the partners. Prior to its acquisition by Boeing, McDonnell-Douglas and Shanghai Aviation Industrial Corp. had a production alliance to assemble jetliners in China using kits shipped over from the U.S. The alliance was seen by the Chinese as a way to learn how to develop and build commercial aircraft. Costs can also be part of the equation. H. J. Heinz, for instance, asked food business competitors Unilever and Nestlé to consider sharing production facilities as a way to reduce manufacturing overheads.[82]

R&D and Financial Alliances

Another way for multinationals to stay ahead of rapidly changing technology is to enter into a research and development alliance. These involve joint research aimed at the development of new services, products, or technologies. Often partners agree to cross-license any new developments that result from joint research so that all participating firms can equally share in any applications. HP's cooperative arrangement with Japan's Canon Corp. to develop new printer technology is an example. Also, financial alliances are formed by partners whose primary goal is to reduce the monetary risks of doing a particular project. Such was the case when IBM and Toshiba entered into an alliance to share the cost of developing new computer chip manufacturing facilities.[83]

Marketing Alliances

Finally, marketing alliances are designed to share marketing-related expertise or services. These are often formed by companies wanting access to the other partner's markets and who are willing to pool resources to get it. This is probably the type of alliance that the general public is most aware of and it has become standard practice in the airline business worldwide for nearly a decade. Specifically, most of the world's major airlines are members of one of three competing global alliances: Oneworld, Sky Team, and Star Alliance. Each of these alliances has at least one major American carrier. American Airlines is part of Oneworld, Delta is part of Sky Team, with US Airways and United a part of Star Alliance. Alliance members fluctuate to an extent given the fortunes of the airline business and the circumstances of individual airlines. Continental, for example, switched from Sky Team to rival Star Alliance in late 2009 where it stayed until it merged with United in 2013. Likewise, in 2010 both Sky Team and Star Alliance were unsuccessful in their efforts to persuade Japan Airlines to leave Oneworld and join their group instead. Their reasoning was simply—both Star Alliance and Sky Team covet Japan Airline's Pacific and Asian routes, lucrative assets for alliances aimed at sharing passengers in a global flight network.[84]

Knitting together these networks requires code-sharing agreements among alliance members. For instance, this would allow member airlines to sell customers "seamless" tickets for flights from American cities to various European destinations and then on to Middle Eastern and Asian capitals. In essence, such alliances allow airlines to tap into the strength of each other's route structures while offering customers integrated trip planning, airport services, and frequent flyer miles. For example, to fly from Cincinnati to Moscow, with a quick mini-vacation in Rome, Delta could fly customers to New York, where they would take an Alitalia flight to Rome before boarding an Aeroflot plane for the final leg to Moscow. This allows Delta to tap into Alitalia's and Aeroflot's overseas routes while the other airlines can do the reverse, tapping into Delta's extensive route structure inside the U.S. And for Delta customers, it means earning frequent flyer points on all legs of the roundtrip.[85]

Cost efficiencies are an important benefit of these alliances. Members can share check-in locations, personnel, airport lounges, and planes. Yet, their major benefit is on the marketing side. As Sky Team explains, the alliance offers improved brand recognition, market positioning, customer service, and increased reach to additional destinations. Even though the airline business rebounded in 2012 from previous lean years, marketing alliances are looking better than ever.[86]

Chapter Summary

Chapter 9 began by considering the six stages that many companies go through in their international development. We then considered options for entering foreign markets, starting with modes that do not require ownership of facilities. This includes exporting and licensing. Licensing can be a very risky proposition, especially when proprietary technology is involved. Franchising involves the contractual right to operate a business using the methods, procedures, products, trademarks, and marketing strategies created by another company. Management contracts, turnkey projects, and contract manufacturing are also examples of entry modes not requiring any ownership.

We then considered modes of entry involving ownership, including wholly owned foreign subsidiaries. A form of entry that only requires partial ownership is a joint venture, an alliance between two companies set up as a separate legal entity that offers benefits for both partners. It comes with challenges and management hassles that also accompany other types of strategic alliances.

Discussion Questions

1. What are the different stages that companies may pass through as they develop internationally? Can you think of examples of firms that have progressed through all the stages? What about examples of firms that have remained very successful in a particular stage?

2. Compare and contrast the various foreign market entry options that do not involve ownership. Under what circumstances would each option be ideal?

3. Likewise, compare and contrast the various foreign market entry options that involve ownership. Under what circumstances would each option be ideal?

4. Describe the different international alliances that may exist between firms. What are some of the management headaches associated with such alliances?

Up to the Challenge?

GE Antes Up (Some) Technology to Power China's Growing Market

Facing a choice between taking a pass on a lucrative contract to supply power turbines to Chinese utilities vs. having to transfer key technologies to potential competitors, GE eventually chose a middle-ground approach. In doing so, GE eventually won the biggest single slice of the turbine market at the time (a contract to supply 13 turbines, worth about $900 million). It may largely account for why GE took the lead in terms of world market share in 2012 (at 15.5 percent).

The company concluded that technology transfers were necessary to compete for a piece of the Chinese market. GE passed along some, but not all, of the critical technologies (e.g., designs, manufacturing processes, etc.) necessary to produce its most sophisticated power turbines. It did so via an agreement to set up two joint ventures where it had a majority stake. The first was with a state-owned firm, Harbin Power Equipment Ltd., which was allowed to assemble GE turbines in one of its plants. The second joint venture with Shenyang Liming Aero-Engine Group allowed it to produce certain turbine blades. This required the transfer of technologies involving blade metallurgy and turbine combustion systems. That said, GE was able to keep some critical technologies secret—it held on to the cooling system design for the first row of turbine blades as well as its proprietary thermal coating. These first-row blades were produced at one of GE's U.S. plants, then sent to the Harbin plant for installation in the final product.

But, GE's actions raise questions about whether it is creating new, potential competitors and whether the U.S. government played a role in GE's ability to protect its technology. First, GE reasoned that the threat of creating new competitors by transferring technologies was not imminent. The experience of other multinationals suggested that having critical technologies simply was not enough to quickly turn Chinese companies into serious global competitors in advanced manufacturing. It felt that the Chinese firms did not have the technical expertise to take full advantage of the technology. It knew that after joint ventures with firms such as Ericsson and Nokia dissolved, Chinese firms were not able to manufacture advanced telecom equipment.

GE's own experience was similar. Earlier, GE had licensed its turbine technology to Chinese companies, and in the 1980s it also formed joint ventures with state-owned firms to produce small, less sophisticated power turbines. Competitors in the turbine business formed joint ventures with Chinese firms at the same time, all involving the transfer of technology. The net result of all this was that Chinese firms mastered the ability to produce steam-driven turbines, but not before GE subsequently developed newer, more advanced turbines. Put simply, Chinese firms had been unable to keep up with advancing technologies pursued by the likes of GE and Siemens.

As far as the government's role, U.S. firms can sometimes use trade law as a reason to protect their technologies. Indeed, U.S. export regulations are such that GE is prohibited from transferring cooling system technologies for turbine blades since they are also applicable to aircraft engine design. At one point, Intel used U.S. export restrictions on sensitive technologies to blunt Chinese demands to build a cutting-edge silicon wafer plant in China.

Overall, GE felt it could maintain control over its most critical technology and still land a big chunk of the Chinese business. It plans to continue to develop more advanced turbines while its Chinese counterparts scramble to digest and develop enough expertise to reproduce GE's current turbines. Chinese officials admit that, at least in the short run, they remain dependent on GE for key components and technology. As one official put it, "The foreigners are now agreeing to tell us how and where to dig a hole, but we still do not know *why* to dig a hole there."

But is this all a risky pipe dream on GE's part? Isn't there a real risk that Chinese firms will scale the learning curve faster in the future and develop enough internal expertise to catch up, if not surpass, their partners? Clearly, Chinese companies want to continue to acquire sophisticated technologies, either by forming joint ventures with foreign companies, licensing technology, or inventing it themselves. Indeed, while some of their products may still lag GE's in complexity, Chinese competitors to GE have been stepping into foreign markets around the globe. Shanghai Electric and Dongfang Turbine both won contracts to supply equipment to power plants in India and Belarus. Other Chinese firms are building power plants in Kenya, Nigeria, Pakistan, Senegal, and Yemen—posing yet another challenge for GE to deal with in the years ahead.[87]

International Development

Using the Global Practices Instrument

Purpose

To hone your ability to assess the internal environment of an international company from a strategic perspective.

Instructions

The Global Practices Instrument measures the extent to which corporate practices embrace an international perspective and reflect a clear international strategy. Select an internationally oriented company that you might be interested in learning more about (alternatively, your instructor may assign a company to you) and then do some Internet research to answer the questions by circling the appropriate number. In doing so, be sure to keep industry factors in mind, such as that industries vary in terms of the extent to which products or services have to be tailored for local markets. A good place to start for basic information is Hoover's online information service for business, which will allow you to search for companies by industry or location (www.hoovers.com). Alternatively, you can pick a company on the *Fortune* Global 500 list (http://money.cnn.com/magazines/fortune/global500/2009/index.html), or, if you are more interested in the international strategies used in fast-growing companies, start with the *Inc.* magazine list of the 500 fastest-growing firms (http://inc.com/inc5000/2009/the-full-list.html).

Of course, whether a particular international strategy orientation is appropriate for a specific company is another matter entirely. Likewise, a company may have a reasonable international strategy but may not execute it very well. These are issues that you should consider once all the answers are in. Put another way, how well do you think the company's existing strategy matches what it should be doing? If the match is poor, what recommendations would you have? If the match is good, what suggestions, if any, do you have for improving the firm's execution (e.g., in terms of market entry options or other management-related issues)?

Global Practices Instrument

A. Management Team

1. The firm's vision and culture is:

Domestic	1	2	3	4	5	Global

2. The senior management team . . .

Does not include foreigners	1	2	3	4	5	Includes many many foreigners

3. Key jobs in all countries are held by . . .

HQ employees	1	2	3	4	5	Local employees

4. Top managers travel the world . . .

Rarely	1	2	3	4	5	Often

5. Top management's familiarity with local culture in key markets:

High	1	2	3	4	5	Low

6. Number of foreign nationals on company's board of directors:

None	1	2	3	4	5	Three or more

B. Strategy

1. The strategy for each country, region, or profit center in the firm is:

| Independent | 1 | 2 | 3 | 4 | 5 | Under one global plan |

2. Firm's philosophy about forming alliances or coalitions in foreign markets versus using wholly owned subsidiaries or acquisitions:

| "Go it alone" | 1 | 2 | 3 | 4 | 5 | "Share to gain" |

3. Units in specific foreign locations operate as . . .

| Separate companies | 1 | 2 | 3 | 4 | 5 | One global company |

4. In the company, environmental scanning of foreign markets is . . .

| Somewhat important | 1 | 2 | 3 | 4 | 5 | Extremely important |

5. The extent to which decisions made in the firm reflect home-country concerns and control:

| A great deal | 1 | 2 | 3 | 4 | 5 | Very little |

C. Operations and Products

1. The primary focus of the company is . . .

| Exporting | 1 | 2 | 3 | 4 | 5 | Fully global operations |

2. The company's major operating facilities are mainly located in:

| The home country | 1 | 2 | 3 | 4 | 5 | Around the world |

3. Production processes and product design decisions are . . .

| Mostly decentralized | 1 | 2 | 3 | 4 | 5 | Mostly centralized |

D. Scoring

Add up the points for each area:

A. Management team (score range is 6–30): _____ divide by 6 = _____ average.
B. Strategy (score range is 5–25): _____ divide by 5 = _____ average.
C. Operations/products (score range is 3–15): _____ divide by 3 = _____ average.

To see where the firm is on the continuum between purely domestic and fully global, compare averages with the following scores:

Domestic	Moving Toward Global	Approaching Global	Global

1.0	1.5	2.0	2.5	3.0	3.5	4.0	4.5	5.0

Source: Adapted from Lussier, R. N., Baeder, R. W., and Corman, J. (1994). Measuring global practices: Global strategic planning through company situational analysis. *Business Horizons*, September–October, 58–60.

From Theory to International Practice

Exporting Your Technology Products

Purpose

To better understand the process of exporting and the benefits and challenges that come with it.

Instructions

For this exercise, we want you to imagine that you work for a firm that makes equipment, and software to drive it, that is useful in the chemical and biological industries. Most of your sales are to drug firms, academic institutions, and other research and development labs, and you are looking to expand your business overseas. That means that you will need to research issues related to the export of your products to other countries. Choose three countries from separate continents that might be in a position to purchase your products/services. Your instructor may put the class in groups to complete the project, in which case each person (or pair of students) can be responsible for a continent. Once you target your countries, you should prepare a report that addresses the following items:

1. Do you need an *export license* from the U.S. Bureau of Industry and Security (USBIS; formerly the Export Administration) for any of your products? Use the following website for more information: www.bis.doc.gov/licensing/exportingbasics.htm. You may also wish to view a consolidated federal government export site (www.export.gov/about/index.asp) for more information.

2. To answer Question 1, you may have to determine a commodity classification for your product. All commodities, technology, or software is subject to the licensing authority of the government via the Commerce Control List (CCL). Go to www.bis.doc.gov/policiesandregulations/index.htm#rp and begin the classification process for at least two of your products.

3. U.S. law places the burden on exporters to classify their products and services and to then request an export review by USBIS prior to receiving their classification. Look closely at the guidelines for an export license after you classify your product (www.bis.doc.gov/licensing/index.htm#factsheets and www.access.gpo.gov/bis/ear/ear_data.html). If your instructor requires it, obtain and complete the application form (www.access.gpo.gov/bis/ear/pdf/forms.pdf; scroll through this list of many different applications). This part of the assignment asks you to simulate the required application process (but not to submit it). Nevertheless, you can give an oral report of your findings to the class.

4. What are some examples of countries that are barred from possible exports from the U.S.? If none of the countries you have chosen is barred, be sure to note at least one such country. Conversely, if each of the countries you chose cannot receive your exported product, choose at least two countries that can. (One source for this is: www.access.gpo.gov/bis/ear/ear_data.html; see country chart.)

5. Finally, show that you have performed due diligence in familiarizing yourself with warning signs/red flags of possible problems with your export partner (www.bis.doc.gov/complianceandenforcement/redflagindicators.htm).

Notes

1. Pruitt, A. (2009). *Making Power out of Chicken Waste in China*, September 29, available at: www.energyboom.com; Stein, M. A. (2009). Going clean. *The Wall Street Journal*, October 19, R7; *The Economist*. (2009). Selling foreign goods in China: Impenetrable, October 17, 73–74; Kranhold, K. (2004). China's price for market entry: Give us your technology, too. *The Wall Street Journal*, February 26, A1, A6; See also: www.ge-energy.com/wind and www.freedoniagroup.com/Turbines-In-China.html.
2. Alexander, M., and Korine, H. (2008). When you shouldn't go global. *Harvard Business Review*, December, 70–77; Cavusgil, S. T., Knight, G., and Riesenberger, J. R. (2008). *International Business: Strategy, Management, and the New Realities*. Upper Saddle River, NJ: Prentice-Hall.
3. Guillen, M. F., and Garcia-Canal, E. (2009). The American model of the multinational firm and the "new" multinationals from emerging economies. *Academy of Management Perspectives*, 23(2), 23–35.
4. Cavusgil, Knight, and Riesenberger, *International Business: Strategy, Management, and the New Realities*; Negandhi, A. (1987). *International Management*. Boston, MA: Allyn & Bacon.

5. Shirouzu, N. (2003). As Toyota pushes hard in China, a lot is riding on the outcome. *The Wall Street Journal*, December 8, A1, A12.

6. Rohwer, J. (2000). GE digs into Asia. *Fortune*, October 2, 165–178; see also www.gecapital. com.

7. Walker, M. (2003). Banking on Europe's frontier. *The Wall Street Journal*, November 25, A14.

8. Milliman, J., Von Glinow, M. A., and Nathan, M. (1991). Organizational life cycles and strategic international human resource management in multinational companies: Implications for congruence theory. *Academy of Management Journal*, 16, 318–339.

9. Black, J. S., Gregersen, H. B., and Mendenhall, M. E. (1992). *Global Assignments: Successfully Expatriating and Repatriating International Managers*. San Francisco: Jossey-Bass; See also www.llbean.com.

10. Aeppel, T. (2009). Harley-Davidson profit plunges. *The Wall Street Journal*, October 16, B5; see www.llbean.com; www.harley-davidson.com.

11. See www.harley-davidson.com.

12. Aeppel, Harley-Davidson profit plunges.

13. Landers, P. (2001). Penney blends two business cultures. *The Wall Street Journal*, April 5, A15, A17.

14. Spencer, M. (2009). Carrefour, in shift, to exit Russia as it reports 2.9% drop in sales. *The Wall Street Journal*, October 16, B5; Ellison, S. (2001). Carrefour and Ahold find shoppers like to think local. *The Wall Street Journal*, August 31, A5; Zellner, W., Schmidt, K. A., Ihlwan, M., and Dawley, H. (2001). How well does Wal-Mart travel? *Business Week*, September 3, 82–84.

15. See http://corporate.walmart.com/our-story/our-business/locations/; Bellman, E. (2009). Wal-Mart exports big box concept to India. *The Wall Street Journal*, May 28, B1; Bianco, A., and Zellner, W. (2003). Is Wal-Mart too powerful? *Business Week*, October 6, 100–110; Zimmerman, A., and Fackler, M. (2003). Wal-Mart's foray into Japan spurs a retail upheaval. *The Wall Street Journal*, September 19, A1, A6.

16. Hamm, S. (2003). Borders are so 20th century. *Business Week*, September 22, 68–72; Rohwer, GE digs into Asia.

17. Ball, J., Zaun, T., and Shirouzu, N. (2002). Daimler explores idea of "world engine." *The Wall Street Journal*, January 8, A3; Tse, D. K., Pan, Y., and Au, K. Y. (1997). How MNCs choose entry modes and form alliances: The China experience. *Journal of International Business Studies*, 28, 779–803.

18. Rader, R. R., Chien, C. V., and Hricik, D. (2013). Make patent trolls pay in court, *New York Times*, June 4, available at: www.nytimes.com (retrieved December, 20, 2013); Glain, S. (1996). Little U.S. firm takes on Japanese giant: Yamaha accused of "patent flooding" to gain advantage. *The Wall Street Journal*, June 5, A10.

19. Dyer, J. H. (2000). Examining interfirm trust and relationships in a cross-national setting. In P. C. Earley and H. Singh (eds) *Innovations in International and Cross-Cultural Management*, 215–244. Thousand Oaks, CA: Sage.

20. Guillen and Garcia-Canal, The American model of the multinational firm and the "new" multinationals from emerging economies.

21. Poon, A. (2009). Chinese oil firms bid $17 billion to expand. *The Wall Street Journal*, August 11, B1, B2; Guillen and Garcia-Canal, The American model of the multinational firm and the "new" multinationals from emerging economies.

22. Bogner, W. C., Thomas, H., and McGee, J. (1996). A longitudinal study of the competitive positions and entry paths of European firms in the U.S. pharmaceutical market. *Strategic Management Journal*, 17, 85–107; Daniels, J. D., Radebaugh, L. H., and Sullivan, D. P. (2004). *International Business: Environment and Operations* (10th ed.) Upper Saddle River, NJ: Prentice Hall.

23. Griffin, R. W., and Pustay, M. W. (2005). *International Business* (4th ed.). Upper Saddle River, NJ: Pearson Prentice Hall.

24. Burpitt, W. J., and Rondinelli, D. A. (2000). Small firms' motivations for exporting: To earn and learn? *Journal of Small Business Management*, 38, 1–18.

25. Cavusgil, Knight, and Riesenberger, *International Business: Strategy, Management, and the New Realities*; Carter, C. (2009). Stocks rise as dollar drops. *Dayton Daily News*, October 25, C2.
26. Hill, C. W. L. (2008). *Global Business Today* (5th ed.). New York: McGraw-Hill/Irwin.
27. Updike, E. H., and Vlasic, B. (1996). Will Neon be the little car that could? *Business Week*, June 10, 56.
28. Bradsher, K. (2009). China moves to retaliate against U.S. tire tariff. *The New York Times*, September 14, available at: www.nytimes.com; *The Economist*. (2002). Steel: Rust never sleeps, March 9, 61–62; Holmes, S., and Belton, C. (2001). Boeing: In search of a big bear hug. *Business Week*, November 12, 71.
29. Griffin and Pustay, *International Business*.
30. Shalal-Esa, A. (2013). Raytheon to pay fine for U.S. export control violations, Reuters, available at: www.reuters.com/article (retrieved December 23, 2013); Baker Donelson. (2008). *The U.S. Government is Increasing its Prosecution of U.S. and Foreign Companies that Violate Export Laws*, available at: www.bakerdonelson.com (retrieved June 20, 2010); U.S. Department of Commerce (2001). California company penalized for illegal export to India, April 26, available at: www.bis.doc.gov/news/archive2001/opticalassociates.htm; Gatti, M. M., and Laigaie, D. M. (2008). Businesses beware: penalties climb for export law violations. *The Legal Intelligencer*, February, available at: www.dilworthlaw.com/CM/Publications/whitecol-larlegalupdate-200802.pdf.
31. Wilson, K., and Doz, Y. (2012). 10 rules for managing global innovation. *Harvard Business Review*, October, 85–90; Barringer, B. R., Macy, G., and Wortman, M. S. (1996). Export performance: The role of corporate entrepreneurship and export planning. *Journal of International Management*, 2, 177–199; Buckman, R. (2003). China's determined "cheeseman" no longer stands alone. *The Wall Street Journal*, December 11, B1, B7; Dosoglu-Guner, B. (2001). Can organizational behavior explain the export intention of firms? *International Business Review*, 10, 71–89.
32. Griffin and Pustay, *International Business*; Koretz, G. (1997). A new twist in trade numbers, *Business Week*, May 12, 24.
33. Montgomery, C. (2001). This car company knows (and grows) beans. *Dayton Daily News*, December 9, 1F, 8F.
34. Hill, *Global Business Today*.
35. Cavusgil, Knight, and Riesenberger, *International Business: Strategy, Management, and the New Realities*.
36. Daniels, J. D., Radebaugh, L. H., and Sullivan, D. P. (2004). *International Business: Environment and Operations*; Hill, *Global Business Today*; Stecklow, S. (2008). Microsoft battles low-cost rival for Africa. *The Wall Street Journal*, October 28, A1, A13.
37. Cavusgil, Knight, and Riesenberger, *International Business: Strategy, Management, and the New Realities*.
38. Price, R. M. (1996). Technology and strategic advantage. *California Management Review*, 38, 38–55.
39. Hill, *Global Business Today*.
40. Cavusgil, Knight, and Riesenberger, *International Business: Strategy, Management, and the New Realities*; Griffin and Pustay, *International Business*.
41. Frank, R. (2000). Big Boy's adventures in Thailand. *The Wall Street Journal*, April 12, B1, B4.
42. Jordan, M. (2000). McDonald's strikes sparks with fast growth in Brazil. *The Wall Street Journal*, October 4, A23.
43. Serwer, A. (2004). Hot Starbucks to go. *Fortune*, January 26, 60–74; see also www.starbucks.com/aboutus/Company_Factsheet.pdf.
44. Gibson, R. (2009). U.S. franchises find opportunity to grow abroad. *The Wall Street Journal*, August 11, B5.
45. Cavusgil, Knight, and Riesenberger, *International Business: Strategy, Management, and the New Realities*; Fowler, G. A., and Marr, M. (2005). Disney's China Play. *The Wall Street Journal*, June 16, B1, B7; Griffin and Pustay, *International Business*. See also http://corporate.disney.go.com, www.marriott.com/corporateinfo/default.mi.

46. Matthews, R. G. (2000). U.S. Steel's plunge into Slovakia reflects need to grow. *The Wall Street Journal*, October 12, A1, A10; Solis, D., and Friedland, J. (1995). A tale of two countries. *The Wall Street Journal*, October, R19–23.

47. Gunther, M. (2009). A big new world to engineer. *Fortune*, June 8, 82–86; Cavusgil, Knight, and Riesenberger, *International Business: Strategy, Management, and the New Realities*.

48. Gunther, M. (2009). A big new world to engineer. *Fortune*, June 8, 82–86.

49. Hill, *Global Business Today*.

50. Srivastava, M., and Gopal, P. (2009). What's holding India back. *BusinessWeek*, October 19, 38–44; *The Economist*. (2001). Red tape and blue sparks, June 2, 9–10; *The Economist*. (2001). India's economy: Unlocking the potential, June 2, 13.

51. Cavusgil, Knight, and Riesenberger, *International Business: Strategy, Management, and the New Realities*.

52. Cole, A. (2009). Vizio expects flat panel growth. *The Wall Street Journal*, October 27, B2; Griffin and Pustay, *International Business*; Morse, D. (2004). In North Carolina, furniture makers try to stay alive. *The Wall Street Journal*, February 20, A1, A6.

53. Cavusgil, Knight, and Riesenberger, *International Business: Strategy, Management, and the New Realities*; Yip, G. S. (1995). *Total Global Strategy*. Englewood Cliffs, NJ: Prentice-Hall.

54. Sandstrom, G. (2009). Electrolux profit surges, amid cuts. *The Wall Street Journal*, October 27, B4.

55. Griffin and Pustay, *International Business*.

56. Hadjimarcou, J., Brouthers, L. E., McNicol, J. P., and Michie, D. E. (2013). Maquiladoras in the 21st century: Six strategies for success. *Business Horizons*, 56, 207–217.

57. Reuters. (2013). Samsung display begins LCD production in its first China Plant, October 25, available at: www.reuters.com; Jing, J., Kim, Y. H., and Clark, D. (2009). Another LCD plant set for China. *The Wall Street Journal*, August 28, B4.

58. Griffin and Pustay, *International Business*; Lublin, J. S. (1995). Too much, too fast. *The Wall Street Journal*, September 26, R8, R10.

59. *The Economist*, Red tape and blue sparks; Wonacott, P. (2001). China's privatization efforts breed new set of problems. *The Wall Street Journal*, November 1, A15.

60. Shirouzu, N. (2009). Beijing Auto maps out a global expansion. *The Wall Street Journal*, October 9, B4.

61. Calori, R., Lubatkin, M., and Very, P. (1994). Control mechanisms in cross-border acquisitions: An international comparison. *Organizational Studies*, 15, 361–379; Chakrabarti, R., Gupta-Mukherjee, S., and Jayaraman, N. (2009). Mars–Venus marriages: Culture and cross-border M&A. *Journal of International Business Studies*, 40, 216–236; Olie, R. (1994). Shades of culture and institutions in international mergers. *Organizational Studies*, 15, 381–405; Schweiger, D. M., Csiszar, E. N., and Napier, N. K. (1993). Implementing international mergers and acquisitions. *Human Resource Planning*, 16, 53–70.

62. Matthews, U.S. Steel's plunge into Slovakia reflects urgent need to grow.

63. Barkema, H. G., Bell, J. H. J., and Pennings, J. M. (1996). Foreign entry, cultural barriers, and learning. *Strategic Management Journal*, 17, 151–166; Filatotchev, I., Hoskisson, R. E., Buck, T., and Wright, M. (1996). Corporate restructuring in Russian privatizations: Implications for U.S. investors. *California Management Review*, 38, 87–105; Ramamurti, R. (2000). A multilevel model of privatization in emerging economies. *Academy of Management Journal*, 25, 525–550; Pope, K. (1996). A steelmaker built up by buying cheap mills finally meets its match. *The Wall Street Journal*, May 2, A1, A6; see also www.ispat.com.

64. Kripalani, M., and Einhorn, B. (2003). Global designs for India's tech king. *BusinessWeek*, October 13, 56–58; Steinmetz, G., and Parker-Pope, T. (1996). All over the map: At a time when companies are scrambling to go global, Nestlé has long been there. *The Wall Street Journal*, September 26, R4, R6.

65. Abboud, L. (2009). Philips widens marketing push in India. *The Wall Street Journal*, March 20, B3; Clifford, M. L., Harris, N., Roberts, D., and Kripalani, M. (1997). Coke pours into Asia. *BusinessWeek*, October 28, 72–80.

66. Ihlwan, M., and McGregor, J. (2009). Korea's biggest foreign deal ever bites back. *Business Week*, October 26, 61; Tan, D. (2009). Foreign market entry strategies and post-entry growth: Acquisitions vs. Greenfield investments. *Journal of International Business Studies*, 40, 1046–1063.

67. Kullman, E. (2012). DuPont's CEO on executing a complex cross-border acquisition. *Harvard Business Review*, July–August, 43–46.

68. Griffin and Pustay, *International Business*.

69. Blodgett, L. L. (1991). Partner contributions as predictors of equity share in joint ventures. *Journal of International Business Studies*, 22, 63–73; Ghemawat, P., and Ghadar, F. (2000). The dubious logic of global megamergers. *Harvard Business Review*, 78, 64–72; Rose, R. L. (1996). For Whirlpool, Asia is the new frontier. *The Wall Street Journal*, April 25, B1, B4.

70. Phatak, A. V. (1997). *International Management: Concepts and Cases*. Cincinnati, OH: South-Western.

71. Dimitratos, P, Petrou, A., Plakoyiannaki, E., and Johnson, J. E. (2011). Strategic decision-making processes in internationalization: Does national culture of the focal firm matter? *Journal of World Business*, 46, 194–204; Hill, *Global Business Today*.

72. Ingrassia, L., Naj, A. K., and Rosett, C. (1995). Overseas, Otis and its parent get in on the ground floor. *The Wall Street Journal*, April 21, A6.

73. See: http://gehonda.com/index.html, downloaded on December 30, 2013; *Aviation Today*. (2007). Honda Aero breaks ground for HQ, jet engine plant. December 3, available at: www.aviationtoday.com.

74. Afriyie, K. (1988). Factor choice characteristics and industrial impact of joint ventures: Lessons from a developing economy. *Columbia Journal of World Business*, 23, 51–62; Phatak, *International Management: Concepts and Cases*.

75. Ren, H., Gray, B., and Kim, K. (2009). Performance of international joint ventures: What factors really make a difference and how? *Journal of Management*, 35, 805–832; Hill, *Global Business Today*; Weiss, S. E. (1987). Creating the GM–Toyota joint venture: A case in complex negotiations. *Columbia Journal of World Business*, 22, 23–38.

76. Phatak, *International Management: Concepts and Cases*. Cincinnati, OH: South-Western.

77. Newman, W. H. (1992). Launching a viable joint venture. *California Management Review*, 35, 68–80; Osland, G. E., and Cavusgil, S. T. (1996). Performance issues in U.S.–China joint ventures. *California Management Review*, 38, 106–130.

78. Blumenthal, J. (1995). Relationships between organizational control mechanisms and joint-venture success. In L. R. Gomez-Mejia and M. W. Lawless (eds) *Advances in Global High-Technology Management*, Vol. 5, part B, 115–134. Greenwich, CT: JAI Press.

79. Areddy, J. T. (2009). Danone pulls out of disputed China venture. *The Wall Street Journal*, October 1, B1; Knok, V. W. (2009). Danone gives up China fight, available at: www.forbes.com (retrieved December 12, 2013).

80. Kiley, D. (2008). Ghosn hits the accelerator. *Business Week*, May 12, 48–49; Matlack, C. (2008). Carlos Ghosn's Russian gambit. *Business Week*, March 17, 57–58; *The Economist* . (2001). Halfway down a long road, August 18, 51–53; *The Economist*. (2001). Just good friends, August 18, 53.

81. *Aviation Today* (2007). Honda Aero breaks ground for HQ, jet engine plant. December 3, available at: www.aviationtoday.com; Blumenthal, Relationships between organizational control mechanisms and joint-venture success; Gillespie, K., and Teegen, H. J. (1995). Market liberalization and international alliance formation: The Mexican paradigm. *Columbia Journal of World Business*, 30, 59–69; Serapio, M. G., and Cascio, W. F. (1996). End-games in international alliances. *Academy of Management Executive*, 10, 62–73.

82. Baker, S. (1996). The odd couple at Heinz. *Business Week*, November 4, 176–178; Hamel, G. (1991). Competition for competence and inter-partner learning within international strategic alliances. *Strategic Management Journal*, 12, 83–103; Kahn, J. (1996). McDonnell Douglas' high hopes for China never really soared. *The Wall Street Journal*, May 22, A1, A10.

83. Bremner, B., Schiller, Z., Smart, T., and Holstein, W. J. (1996). Keiretsu connections: The bonds between the U.S. and Japan's industry groups. *Business Week*, July 22, 52–54.
84. Esterl, M. (2009). Star draws 2 airlines closer. *The Wall Street Journal*, October 27, B1, B5; Takahashi, Y. (2009). Japan airlines to cut jobs, pursue alliance. *The Wall Street Journal*, September 16, B3; Done, K. (2003). New bonding could mean altered shape for alliances. *Financial Times*, October 1, 18; See also www.oneworld.com; www.skyteam.com; www.staralliance.com.
85. Esterl, Star draws 2 airlines closer; See also www.oneworld.com; www.skyteam.com; www.staralliance.com.
86. Esterl, Star draws 2 airlines closer.
87. Rajgor, G. (2013). Renewable power generation—2012 figures, available at: www.renewable-power-generation-2012-figures (retrieved December 20, 2013); Lemper, T. A. (2012). The critical role of timing in managing intellectual property. *Business Horizons*, 55, 339–347; Stein, M. A. (2009). Going clean. *The Wall Street Journal*, October 19, R7.

Case 3: Go Global—Or No?

For two years, DataClear has had the data analysis market to itself. But now a British upstart is nipping at its heels. Should DataClear continue to focus on its strong domestic products or expand overseas to head off the nascent international threat?

"Why aren't they biting?" wondered Greg McNally as he laid down another perfectly executed cast. He was fly-fishing in the most beautiful spot he had ever seen, on the Alta River in Norway—reputedly the home of Scandinavia's worthiest salmon. And he had plenty of opportunity to admire the view. No fish were getting in the way.

What a difference from the luck he'd had a couple of weeks earlier trout fishing at Nelson's Spring Creek in Montana. It seemed like so much more time had passed since the two-day offsite he had called there, designed to be part celebration of the past, part planning for the future.

Some celebration had definitely been in order. The company, DataClear, was really taking off, fueled by the success of its first software product, ClearCloud. In 1999, its first full year of operation, DataClear's sales had reached $2.2 million. Now, the following September, it was looking like 2000 sales could easily reach $5.3 million. At the all-staff meeting on the Friday before the offsite, Greg had announced the company's success in recruiting two more great executives, bringing the staff to 38. "I'm more confident than ever that we'll hit our goals:

$20 million in 2001 and then $60 million in 2002!"

Clouds on the Horizon

A New Jersey native, Greg held an MSc from Rutgers and then went West to get his PhD in computer science from UC Berkeley. He spent the next 15 years at Borland and Oracle, first as a software developer and then as a senior product manager. He started DataClear in Palo Alto, California, in the spring of 1998.

At the time, Greg realized that companies were collecting information faster than they could analyze it and that data analysis was an underexploited segment of the software business. It was at a seminar at Northwestern University that he saw his opportunity. Two researchers had developed a set of algorithms that enabled analysts to sift through large amounts of raw data in powerful ways without programmers' help. Greg cashed in his Oracle options and, in partnership with the two researchers, created DataClear to develop applications based on the algorithms.

His partners took responsibility for product development and an initial stake of 20 percent each; Greg provided $500,000 in financing in return for 60 percent of the shares and the job of CEO. A year later, Greg offered David Lester, founder of DL Ventures and a former Oracle executive, 30 percent of the company in return for $5 million in additional funding.

In his previous positions, Greg had shown a knack for leading "fizzy" technical teams, and under his leadership the two researchers came up with a state of the art data analysis package they dubbed ClearCloud (from the clarity the software brought to large data clouds). Two versions, one for the telecommunications industry and the other for financial services providers, were officially launched in September 1998. Clear-Cloud had a number of immediate and profitable applications. For instance, it could be used to help credit card companies detect fraud patterns more quickly in the millions of transactions that occurred every day. Greg conservatively estimated the annual demand from the U.S. telecommunications and financial services sectors to be around $600 million. The challenge was to make potential users aware of the product.

ClearCloud was an instant hit, and, within just a month of its launch, Greg had needed to recruit a dozen sales staffers. One of the first was Susan Moskowski, a former sales rep at Banking Data Systems, who had worked successfully with Greg on several major joint pitches to financial institutions. She had spent two years at BDS's Singapore subsidiary, where she had laid the groundwork for a number of important contracts. She had left BDS to do an MBA at Stanford and joined DataClear immediately on graduating as the new company's head of sales. She was an immediate success, landing DataClear's first major contract with a large West Coast banking group.

Greg realized that ClearCloud had huge potential outside the telecommunications and financial services industries.

In fact, with relatively little product development, Greg and his partners believed, ClearCloud could be adapted for the chemical, petrochemical, and pharmaceutical industries. Annual demand for customers in those sectors could reach as high as $900 million.

But accessing and serving clients in those fields would involve building specialized sales and service infrastructures. Just two months ago, to spearhead that initiative, Greg recruited a new business development manager who had 20 years' experience in the chemical industry. A former senior R&D manager at DuPont, Tom Birmingham was excited by Clear-Cloud's blockbuster potential in the U.S. market. "The databases can only get bigger," he told Greg and Susan. Greg had asked Tom to put together a presentation for the offsite in Montana on the prospects for expanding into these new sectors.

Just two weeks before the outing, however, Susan burst into Greg's office and handed him an article from one of the leading trade journals. It highlighted a British start-up, VisiDat, which was beta testing a data analysis package that was only weeks away from launch. "We're not going to have the market to ourselves much longer," she told Greg. "We need to agree on a strategy for dealing with this kind of competition. If they start out as a global player, and we stay hunkered down in the U.S., they'll kill us. I've seen this before."

The news did not take Greg altogether by surprise. "I agree we've got to put together a strategy," he said. "Why don't we table the domestic expansion discussion and talk about this at our offsite meeting, where we can get everyone's ideas? Unlike the rest of us, you've had some experience overseas, so perhaps you should lead the discussion. I'll square things up with Tom."

Go Fish

In Montana, Susan kicked off the first session with a story of GulfSoft, a thinly disguised case study of her former employer. The company had developed a software package for the oil and gas exploration business, which it introduced only in the United States. But, at almost the same time, a French company had launched a comparable product, which it marketed aggressively on a global basis. A year later, the competitor had a much larger installed base worldwide than GulfSoft and was making inroads into GulfSoft's U.S. sales. When she reached the end of the story, Susan paused, adding ominously, "Today, we have twenty installations of ClearCloud outside the United States—fifteen in the U.K. and five in Japan—and those are only U.S. customers purchasing for their overseas subsidiaries."

At Susan's signal, the room went dark. Much of what followed, in a blizzard of overhead projections, was market research showing a lot of latent demand for ClearCloud outside the United States. The foreign markets in telecommunications and financial services were shown to be about as large as those in the United States—that is, another $600 million. The potential in pharmaceuticals, petrochemicals, and chemicals looked to be about $660 million. Taken altogether that meant a potential market of $1.5 billion domestically and $1.26 billion abroad.

In ending, Susan drew the obvious moral. "It seems pretty clear to me that the only defense for this kind of threat is to attack. We don't have any international sales strategy. We're here because we need one—and fast."

She glanced at Greg for any hint of objection, didn't see it, and plunged ahead. "We know we can sell a lot of software in the United States, but if we want DataClear to succeed in the long run, we need to preempt the competition and go worldwide. We need a large installed base ASAP."

"I propose that for the afternoon we split into two groups and focus on our two options for going forward. Group A can consider building our own organization to serve Europe. Group B can think about forming alliances with players already established there. Based on what you can come back with tomorrow, we'll make the call."

As the lights came back on, Greg blinked. He was dazzled. But he sensed that he needed to do some thinking, and he did his best thinking knee-deep in the river. After lunch, as the two groups got to work, Greg waded into Nelson's Spring Creek. The fish seemed to leap to his hook, but his thoughts were more elusive and ambivalent.

Money, Money, Money

Greg decided he needed a reality check, and that night he called David Lester to review the day's discussion. Not too surprisingly, Lester didn't have a lot of advice to give on the spot. In fact, he had questions of his own. "Instead of focusing on foreign markets in our core industries, what if we focus on developing ClearCloud for the domestic pharmaceutical, petrochemical, and chemical industries and capitalize on the $900 million U.S. market?" he asked. "How much would that cost?" Greg offered a best guess of $2 million for the additional software development costs but hadn't yet come up with a number for marketing and sales; the industries were so different from the ones that DataClear currently focused on. "Whatever the cost turns out to be, we're going to need another round of financing," Greg allowed. "Right now we're on track to generate a positive cash flow without raising any additional capital, but it won't be enough to fund a move beyond our core industries."

"That's not where I was headed," Lester replied. "What if we went out and raised a lot more money and expanded the product offering and our geographic reach at the same time?"

Greg swallowed hard; he was usually game for a challenge, but a double expansion was daunting. He couldn't help thinking of the sticky note he'd posted on the frame of his computer screen a few days after he started Data-Clear. It clung there still and it had just one word on it: "Focus."

Lester sensed Greg's hesitation: "Look. We're not going to decide this tonight. And really, at the end of the day it's up to you, Greg. You've done the right things so far. Keep doing them." Hanging up, Greg was reminded how pleased he was with Lester's hands-off approach. For the first time, he wondered what things would be like if he had a more hands-on venture capitalist as an investor—maybe one with some experience in international expansion.

Greg was also reminded of his own lack of international management experience. Eight years earlier, he had politely turned down an opportunity to lead a team of fifty Oracle development engineers in Japan, primarily because he had been unwilling to relocate to Tokyo for two years. His boss at the time had told him: "Greg, software is a global business, and what you don't learn early about cross-border management will come back to haunt you later."

Options on the Table

At ten o'clock the next morning, Group A took the floor and made their recommendation right off the bat: DataClear should immediately establish an office in the U.K. and staff it with four to six sales people. Britain would be a beachhead into all of Europe, but eventually there would also be a sales office somewhere on the continent, maybe in Brussels. They had even drafted a job description for a head of European sales.

Greg was impressed, if a little overwhelmed. "Any idea how much this would cost in terms of salaries and expenses over the first year?" he asked.

"Conservatively about $500,000 a year, probably more," the group leader replied. "But cost is not so much the point here. If we don't make this move, we'll be killed by VisiDat—or some other competitor we don't even know about yet. Imagine if SAP introduced a similar product. With their marketing machine, they would just crush us."

Tom Birmingham started to object. "Where are we going to find local staff to install and support the product?" he wanted to know. "I mean, this is not just about setting up an office to sell: ClearCloud is a complex product, and it needs a service infrastructure. We'd have to translate the interface software, or at least the manuals, into local languages. We'd need additional resources in business development and product support to manage all this. Selling Clear-Cloud in Europe is going to cost a lot more than $500,000 a year . . ."

Susan was quick to jump in. "Good point, Tom, and that isn't all we'll need. We also have to have somebody in Asia. Either Singapore or Tokyo would be an ideal base. Probably Tokyo works better because more potential clients are headquartered there than in the rest of Asia. We need at least four people in Asia, for the time being." Tom frowned, but feeling that Susan had the momentum, decided to hold his fire.

After lunch it was Group B's turn. They suggested using autonomous software distributors in each country. That would help DataClear keep a tight grip on expenses. Greg spoke up then. "What about teaming up with some local firm in Europe that offers a complementary product? Couldn't we get what we need though a joint venture?"

"Funny you should mention that, Greg," said the presenter from Group B. "We came up with the idea of Benro but didn't have time to pursue it. They might be willing to talk about reciprocal distribution." Benro was a small software shop in Norway. Greg knew it had about $5 million in sales last year from its data mining package for financial services companies. Benro was very familiar with European customers in the financial services sector but had no experience with other industries. "Working with Benro

might be cheaper than doing this all on our own, at least for now," the presenter said.

Susan chose that moment to speak up again. "I have to admit I'm skeptical about joint ventures. I think it will probably take too long to negotiate and sign the contracts, which won't even cover all the eventualities. At some point we will have to learn how to succeed in each region on our own."

That's when Greg noticed Tom studying Susan, his eyes narrowing. So he wasn't surprised—in fact he was a little relieved—when Tom put the brakes on: "I guess I don't see how we can make that decision until we gather a little more input, Susan," Tom said. "At the very least, we need to have a conversation with Benro and any other potential partners. And I know I'd want to meet some candidates to lead a foreign sales office before I'd be comfortable going that route. But my real concern is more fundamental. Are we up to doing all this at the same time we're building our market presence in the United States? Remember, we don't yet have the capability to serve the chemical and pharmaceutical industries here. There are still only thirty-eight of us, and I estimate that building the support infrastructure we need for domestic expansion could cost as much as $2 million—on top of product development."

Before Susan could object Greg struck the compromise. "Tell you what. Let's commit to making the decision in no more than three weeks. I'll clear my calendar and connect with Benro myself. At the same time, Susan, you can flush out some good candidates for a foreign sales office and schedule them to meet with Tom and me."

Casting About

And that's how Greg McNally found himself up a creek in Norway that Sunday morning. Benro's CEO had been interested; Greg was confident that meeting with him on Monday would yield some attractive options. And once the trip was booked, it didn't take Greg long to realize he'd be near some fabled fishing spots.

He also realized it would be a great chance to pick the brain of his old Berkley classmate, Sarah Pappas. A hardware engineer, Sarah had started her own company, Desix, in Mountain View, California, in 1993. The company designed specialty chips for the mobile communications industry. Within seven years, Desix had grown into one of the most successful specialized design shops around the world, with about 400 employees. Like Greg, Sarah had received funding from a venture capitalist. As a lot of demand for Desix's services was in Scandinavia and to a lesser degree in Japan as well, Sarah had opened subsidiaries in both places and even decided to split her time between Mountain View and Oslo.

Greg arrived in Oslo on Thursday morning and met Sarah that evening at a waterfront restaurant. They spent the first half-hour swapping news about mutual friends. Sarah hadn't changed much, thought Greg. But when the conversation turned to potential geographic expansion and he asked her about her experience, Greg saw her smile grow a little tense. "Ah, well," she began. "How much time do you have?"

"That bad?"

"Actually, to be honest, some things were easier than we thought," she allowed. "Recruiting, for example. We never expected to get any great engineers to leave Nokia or Hitachi to join us, but we ended up hiring our Oslo and Tokyo core teams without much trouble. Still, some things turned out to be hard—like coordinating the three sites across the borders. There were so many misunderstandings between Oslo and Mountain View that at first our productivity went down by 40 percent."

The story got worse. Sarah explained how, in 1998, her venture capitalist sought to exit his investment. As an Initial Public Offering seemed inadvisable for various reasons, the parties agreed to sell the company to Pelmer, a large equipment manufacturer. Sarah agreed to stay on for three years but couldn't do much to keep the engineers in her Oslo and Tokyo subsidiaries from leaving. No one had fully anticipated the clash between Pelmer's strong U.S. culture and Desix's local cultures in Oslo and Tokyo. By this point, Sarah felt, the merger had destroyed much that had gone into making Desix a small multinational company.

"I can tell I've been a real buzz killer," she laughed apologetically, as Greg picked up the check. "But if I were you, given what I've been through, I'd stay focused on the U.S. for as long as possible. You might not build the next Oracle or Siebel that way, but you'll live a happier life."

"So you think you made the wrong choice in expanding internationally?"

"Well, no," said Sarah, "because I don't think we had a choice. You, on the other hand, can sell much more product in the U.S. than we could have."

Up to His Waist

The next day brought its own worries, as Greg met with Pierre Lambert, a candidate for head of European sales, whom Susan had identified through a headhunter. Lambert had graduated from the Ecole des Mines in Paris and then worked for four years at Alcatel and five years at Lucent. As they talked, it occurred to Greg that he had no experience in reading résumés from outside the States. Was Ecole des Mines a good school? He noted that Lambert had worked only in France and the United States. How successful would he be in the United Kingdom or Germany? As he wrapped up the interview, Greg figured he would need to see at least five candidates to form an opinion about the European labor market. And Asia would be even harder.

That evening, he compared notes with Tom, who had interviewed Lambert by phone the previous day. Tom expressed some doubts: he suspected Lambert wasn't mature enough to deal with the level of executives—chief information officers and chief scientists—that Data-Clear would be targeting. That call only just ended when the cell phone rang again with Susan on the line. "Greg—I thought you'd want to know. VisiDat just made its first significant sale—to Shell. The deal is worth at least $500,000. This is huge for them."

And now, two days later, here he stood in the glorious, frustrating Alta. He could see the salmon hanging out under the surface. He cast his line again, an elegant, silvery arc across the river, and maneuvered the fly deftly through the water. Nothing.

Greg slogged back to shore and peered into the box housing his extensive collection of hand-tied salmon flies. Was it just that he was so preoccupied? Or were the conditions really so different here that none of his flies would work? One thing was for sure: it was a lot chillier than he'd expected. Despite the liner socks, his feet were getting cold.

Assignment Questions

1. What dilemma or strategic threat is DataClear facing?
2. Would you recommend that DataClear expand into international markets at this point in time? Either way, fully explain the basis for your recommendation.
3. If your answer to question 2 was yes, lay out specific recommendations for exactly how DataClear should proceed to "go global" in the new term. If the answer to question 2 was no, what specific steps should DataClear take to position itself for possible expansion overseas?

part IV

managing people in the international arena

chapter 10

motivating and leading across cultures

Learning Objectives

After reading this chapter, you should be able to

- recognize and adapt motivation practices across cultures;
- explain how effective cross-cultural motivation strategies can be developed;
- determine how a leader's behavior, power sources, and influence tactics can be modified to be more effective across international environments;
- identify the challenges facing managers in multinationals and describe how effective international leaders can be developed.

International Challenge

Can Stodgy South Korean Companies Loosen Up Their Leadership?

It is common to hear stories of organizations that encourage innovative leadership, development of ideas, and speedy decision-making. This prototype is seen as a formula for success in many firms—the old view of a leader acting as referee, naysayer, and keeper of the order is now a distant memory. Yet, in some countries and cultures the concept of leadership conjures up images of paternalism (taking care of employees like parents to offspring), order, and formality. Those descriptions fit the leadership approach of many large Korean companies over the past 50 years, where the power to make key decisions has been concentrated at the top of a rigidly bureaucratic corporate structure.

The paternalistic perspective came to the surface recently at the Bank of Korea (BOK), and especially so when Lee Ju-yeol came to the podium to present his farewell speech to employees in the spring of 2012. Mr. Lee had spent his 35-year career there, rising to the rank of senior deputy governor. Everyone expected a traditional warm "thank you" as he rode off into the sunset, but instead, Lee took the decidedly non-Korean approach of a verbal barrage at his boss, Governor Kim Choongsoo, who sat in the front row of the packed room: "Many feel in chaos now because the values and rules that have been developed over the last 60 years were denied in a single day." The target of his comment was his boss, Mr. Kim, who apparently showed no reaction to these public criticisms. The executive of the Bank of Korea consists of the governor, the senior deputy governor, and five or fewer deputy governors.

What were those long-standing values and rules Mr. Lee referred to in his speech? They involve a traditional leadership approach which flows from Confucian values that emphasize family, loyalty, and seniority. Seniority based on age (even a single year difference) is deeply embedded in Korean society, especially at a traditional organization such as BOK. When meeting strangers or co-workers, Koreans work subtly to figure out one another's age and then use that as a guide for behavior. One effect of these values is that at each level of management, subordinates are often prohibited from questioning their (older) superiors, much less allowed to communicate with other executives further up the line. Some experts feel that this stifles creativity and chokes off growth, putting many Korean companies in danger of falling behind competition.

As bank governor, Mr. Kim felt that there were too many senior officials in high-ranking roles, including many such as Mr. Lee who had been at the bank for decades, and too few working-level employees. A U.S.-educated "outsider," Mr. Kim took the unconventional approach of replacing these high officers after serving only two years as governor. His view was that age-based hierarchies and other traditional leadership practices limit promotion opportunities for younger talent in the organization.

These changes were not without consequences. Mr. Lee's critical speech, itself a break from tradition in its directness, also released some deeply held frustration among many at BOK. One deputy governor who left the bank before Mr. Lee (possibly experiencing the same fate) stated that, "It's a humiliating experience for those who spent the better part of their lives at the bank only to see one day their juniors take control."

So, what are Korean firms to do in today's environment? On the one hand, huge Korean companies such as Samsung, Hyundai, and LG (and the interrelations they share via the chaebol system, which is a South Korean form of business conglomerate) have produced great economic success. And, the hierarchical and closed leadership approach employed by Koreans seems well suited for the culture. The power to make key decisions is concentrated at the top of rigidly bureaucratic corporate structures, often run by wealthy families who act like royalty. This authoritarian nature allows South Korean firms to move quickly (e.g., the Lee family's control over Samsung), but it can also stifle creativity and cause problems, such as the fall of the Daewoo chaebol and the clan-style management it exemplified (Daewoo was the second largest conglomerate in Korea after Hyundai Group, followed by LG Group and Samsung Group—there were about 20 divisions under the Daewoo Group, some of which survive today as independent companies).

In 2011, a special *Wall Street Journal* report raised key questions for the country. While it gave ample credit to the country-level strategy that brought South Korea into the upper echelon of world economies, it was also very critical of current leadership. The report, entitled "The miracle is over: Now what?" advocated a tough, yet important self-examination along the lines taken by BOK above. As you read this chapter, think about this traditional hierarchical system and closed leader style. Do you think a new approach to leadership is necessary or should companies stick with what got them where they are? What features could Korean firms import from other countries to help change the style? Importing new methods of leadership from other cultures is not a panacea, so think through some of the challenges that would be involved in importing. Finally, take a look at the Up to the Challenge? feature at the end of this chapter for some further thoughts on this issue and to learn from some other South Korean firms who seek to change traditional leadership.[1]

Motivating and Leading Abroad: One Size Does Not Fit All

Most Americans agree that firms need motivated and engaged employees in order for the company to succeed. Yet *how* to motivate employees is a frustrating exercise for many. Compounding matters is the challenge of motivating across borders or cultural contexts. Western approaches to motivation typically reflect the individually oriented and goal-driven cultures that produced them in the first place. This may significantly limit their applicability in places where employees embrace different values. Many experts believe that what motivates employees and how they respond to feedback may vary depending on cultural factors.[2]

In fact, cultural values (such as the emphasis placed on hard work) may affect employee motivation in ways that can help explain different economic growth rates across nations.[3] Overall, cultural values may shape the "psychological contract" that employees have with their firms. For example, consider the implications of employees who view work as a "money for effort" transaction, an inherent good in itself, or an opportunity to be part of something important. Each perspective has important but different implications for motivation. While many unanswered questions remain about how motivation processes work across cultures, it is clear that, when it comes to motivation, what works in one culture (or even company) is unlikely to work well everywhere, at least not without some adaption.[4]

Consequently, this chapter starts by explaining how culture may limit the applicability of popular Western approaches to motivation. To be effective, managers need to know which motivation strategies require culture-specific adaptations.[5] The bottom line is that few cross-cultural universals exist when it comes to motivation. Even for similar concepts, such as merit pay, managers often have to tweak their implementation to match local cultural norms, at least initially. For instance, managers in most places would prefer to rely less on formal authority to motivate their employees. Employees everywhere want to be trusted by their superiors and to be fairly compensated. But *how* managers should delegate authority, build trust, and define "fair pay" may vary considerably from place to place.[6] Not surprisingly, cultural values also may have an impact on leadership styles, a related topic tackled later in this chapter.

International managers must understand how cultures can shape employee motivation in particular countries as well as their response to leadership. Moreover, motivation and leadership approaches that run counter to the prevailing culture may still work, especially if given enough time to succeed or if focused on receptive segments of the population (e.g., younger workers who may be more open to new ideas).[7] International managers may also face important regional differences in values *within* countries that impact both motivation and business performance. For instance, regional subcultures in Brazil have distinct motivational tendencies when it comes to work.[8]

Western Motivation Concepts and Their Applicability to Other Cultures

This section addresses the cross-cultural applicability and limitations of some specific motivation theories that have been popular in America and other Western countries.[9]

Maslow's *hierarchy of needs* and Herzberg's *two-factor theory* both focus on explaining what needs actually energize employee behavior. In contrast, equity theory, reinforcement theory, and expectancy theory all examine the process by which employees are motivated to pursue their needs.

Maslow's Hierarchy of Needs

Psychologist Abraham Maslow believed that everyone is motivated by five basic needs that are pursued hierarchically.[10] At the most pure are physiological needs such as food and shelter. Once these needs are met (via decent wages, for example), then employees are motivated by safety needs, which are met via benefits such as life insurance. Next are social needs. These are satisfied when employees feel that they "belong." Esteem needs are met when employees have found self-respect and confidence. Finally, self-actualization needs are motivators after all other needs have been met. They reflect an employee's desire to reach his or her maximum potential. Overall, research shows that needs are not always triggered in the order specified by Maslow, but that all of these needs occur at some point.[11]

Cross-Cultural Applicability

We might expect the motivation to pursue higher-order needs (such as self-actualization) to be the strongest in developed countries, with lower-order survival needs more prominent elsewhere. Put simply, many workers in poor countries may be less interested in self-actualization if their daily survival or safety is in question. That said, this same pattern may also exist within countries. For instance, in one survey, wealthier elites in rapidly developing nations such as India, China, Russia, and Brazil were much more positive about how things were going in their countries (and presumably better positioned to "self-actualize") than the general (and poorer) population at large. All of this underscores a primary finding about Maslow's theory—that cultural values and societal context may impact which needs tend to be pursued most strongly. Moreover, how employees interpret needs-related self-actualization—such as competition and achievement—is shaped by a complex constellation of factors, including culture and the position people occupy in a society.[12]

As an example, having cooperative co-workers and meeting other social needs may rank above self-actualization for some Chinese employees.[13] Other studies find that employees in individualistic societies (such as Australia and Germany) are more likely to be interested in pursuing personal accomplishment than employees in more collective societies (such as Japan and Mexico) and, in turn, less interested in esteem needs than employees in societies embracing "feminine" values (such as Sweden).[14] These ingrained preferences may be slow to change, even in the face of large-scale social upheavals. Indeed, a recent Gallup survey showed that a clear majority of employees in most Western European countries view their supervisor as a "partner" (i.e., someone who involved them in decisions and provided some "self-actualizing" autonomy) rather than an autocratic boss who is uninterested in their opinions. The opposite was true in many Eastern

European nations, perhaps reflecting their previous heritage as communist members of the old Soviet bloc—and the heavy-handed, top-down management that went with it. Figure 10.1 summarizes these results by country. What is particularly fascinating is that those Eastern European employees fortunate enough to work for a "supervisor-as-partner" reported being more satisfied with their jobs than their counterparts toiling under a more autocratic boss.[15]

Eastern European Nations	Majority of Employees View Supervisors as a . . .
Belarus	Autocratic Boss
Czech Republic	No clear majority
Estonia	Autocratic Boss
Hungary	No clear majority
Latvia	Autocratic Boss
Lithuania	No clear majority
Moldova	Autocratic Boss
Poland	Autocratic Boss
Romania	Partner
Russia	Autocratic Boss
Slovakia	Autocratic Boss
Slovenia	Autocratic Boss
Ukraine	Autocratic Boss

Western/Northern European Nations	Majority of Employees View Supervisors as a . . .
Austria	Partner
Belgium	Partner
Denmark	Partner
Finland	Partner
France	Partner
Germany	Partner
Greece	Partner
Ireland	Partner
Netherlands	Partner
Norway	Partner
Portugal	Partner
Spain	Partner
Sweden	Partner
Switzerland	Partner
United Kingdom	No clear majority

Figure 10.1 Partner or Boss? How Employees in European Countries View Their Supervisors.

Source: Adapted from Brown, I. T. (January, 2009). *In Western Europe, More Partners Than Bosses*, available at: www.gallup.com/poll/114076/western-europe-partners-bosses.aspx.

Research on Maslow's ideas is clear—needs simply do not operate in a fixed hierarchy across borders. In essence, Maslow's hierarchy is a philosophy that reflects *American* values. Its emphasis on higher-order growth needs is popular in the United States because American culture values individualism, personal achievement, and risk taking. Nevertheless, to the extent that individuals or nations evolve toward those values, we would expect more receptiveness to higher-order growth needs.[16]

Herzberg's Two-Factor Theory

Herzberg suggested that without decent "hygiene" factors, such as good pay and working conditions, employees will be unhappy and unmotivated. But, just because these needs are attended to does not mean that employees will be highly motivated. If firms want highly motivated employees, Herzberg believed that management must also provide *motivators* such as challenge, responsibility, and autonomy.[17] Hygiene factors are often extrinsic to the job itself (such as pay or poor supervision) and should be dealt with in order to improve the workplace. Motivators deal more directly with doing the job itself—they are intrinsic to doing the job itself (such as challenges, opportunities, etc.). Paying attention to these two main factors (hygiene and motivators) and ensuring that a job has plenty of motivators built in, is often referred to as job enrichment. Hygiene factors are needed to ensure an employee is not dissatisfied, while motivators are needed to encourage higher performance.

Cross-Cultural Applicability

Research has produced a variety of results regarding Herzberg's ideas. For instance, one study found that workers in Zambia generally matched Herzberg's two-factor approach, with growth needs (a motivator) associated with high motivation and bad working conditions (a hygiene factor) associated with dissatisfaction. But other studies suggest that Herzberg's ideas do not fit other cultures as precisely and may work best in a Western context, similar to Maslow's hierarchy model, where efforts to increase individual opportunity and performance are often very attractive to employees.[18]

Consistent with this argument, another study found that British managers, when compared to their French counterparts, were more interested in responsibility and autonomy, but less interested in security, fringe benefits, or good working conditions. This finding suggests that job enrichment efforts might be easier to implement in Britain than in France.[19] It seems that the more that employees value individualism, risk taking (low uncertainty avoidance), and performance (masculine culture traits such as ego-oriented and work-centric), the more likely that Herzberg's motivators will help spur personal achievement. Many employees in the U.S. and Britain fit this description. In Sweden, however, many employees embrace individualism while also being very relationship-oriented (feminine culture traits such as relationship-oriented and family-focused). In these circumstances, efforts to improve interpersonal harmony in the workplace may be more motivating than job enrichment efforts aimed at encouraging individual achievement.[20]

International managers might also find it difficult to implement Herzberg's motivators in developing countries such as Indonesia, India, and Pakistan. These countries are collectivist, high in uncertainty avoidance and power distance, and low in masculinity. Employees who are high in uncertainty avoidance and power distance may be reluctant to make decisions involving risk, or ambiguity. Likewise, many employees who embrace collectivistic values may also react poorly to efforts aimed at enriching jobs on an individual basis. Finally, when feminine values hold sway, job enrichment efforts that focus narrowly on the job itself, without concern for interpersonal issues, may backfire since employees' obligations to family or community are often a priority.[21]

The worldwide trend toward increasingly complex (or enriched) jobs, and the responsibility that goes with them, marches on. Yet the willingness of employees to embrace such jobs still depends, at least in part, on cultural values and context.[22] Fortunately, experts believe that cultural obstacles to implementing job enrichment efforts can be overcome. They suggest that international managers should learn about the local cultural environment in depth before attempting any job enrichment effort. Once managers understand how local values may impact job enrichment, managers can sidestep cultural barriers while leveraging local values in other ways to improve employee motivation.[23]

A case in point is what Thomson, the French electronics giant, did to improve motivation and performance at a plant in Morocco. Its challenge was to convince employees to take on more responsibilities and to make decisions independently. While this sounds like a typical Western job enrichment effort, these motivation changes were accomplished in a culture-specific way. In the process of doing so, openness and trust also increased dramatically. Morocco is a high power distance context, one in which senior executives often expect to wield sweeping authority over many workplace decisions. Consequently, Thomson management decided to lead by example using culturally appropriate methods. Specifically, their efforts to improve motivation were described as a "new moral code, one that everyone would live by." This new code was linked to Islamic values pervasive in Moroccan life. For example, management encouraged employees to embrace greater responsibility as a way of living Islam's emphasis on openness, honesty, and respect for the contributions of others.[24]

It is important to underscore that hygiene factors alone can, under certain conditions, prove highly motivating to employees. For instance, job security and pay often behave as motivators in developing countries, but may also be very motivating in industrialized nations. For instance, according to one survey, Danish employees are the most satisfied workers in the world—perhaps because of outstanding relations between labor and management. This theme of "getting along" is part of Lego's culture, perhaps Denmark's best known company. The very name of the firm is derived from two Danish words that mean "play well."[25] For another look at how a hygiene factor, money, is a big motivator for some Russian women, read the following International Insights feature.

International Insights

Money Drives Russian Women Working for Mary Kay and Avon

Mary Kay Cosmetics and Avon, both American firms, have been successful in Russia for years. Thanks to a burgeoning demand for cosmetics, Russia ranks high among Mary Kay's operations in 35 countries. Likewise, some 70 percent of Avon's revenues come from developing nations—and Russia is one of its three biggest foreign markets. A big key to the success of both firms is the sales force of Russian women. And, for most of them, money is a key motivator. Mary Kay provides sales training and sells its products at a discount to retail prices to its Russian sales representatives who then sell them at full price, preferably to small groups of customers. Women in Mary Kay's Russian sales force typically make several hundred dollars a month while top performers, many of whom have their own offices and administrative staff, can rake in thousands. Either way, Mary Kay's sales force exceeds the average monthly wage in Russia by a considerable margin—which may explain why turnover among Mary Kay's Russian sales force is so low. Avon's experience is similar and the company prides itself on helping its representatives get started, including low-cost loans.

Mary Kay and Avon are attractive to Russian women because they offer financial independence, something that remains relatively rare in Russia. Some women feel that Russia's economic development has left them behind. The majority of Russia's unemployed are women and some Russian organizations still reserve certain jobs for men. When they are employed, women in Russia are often trapped in low-paying jobs and are the first to be laid off. Ironically, these same attitudes toward gender in Russia help make being a Mary Kay or Avon sales representative a socially acceptable job for Russian women—one that can pay very well indeed.[26]

Overall, rather than focus on hygiene factors versus motivators, it might be simpler just to assume that what motivates employees probably varies from place to place more often than not. At the risk of generalizing, implementing enriched jobs that provide autonomy and opportunities for achievement is likely to foster deeper motivation and commitment more quickly in places where individualistic and masculine values are strong (e.g., U.K., U.S.). In contrast, it may be better to improve working conditions and relations among workers if managers want to create a motivated and committed workforce in places where collectivism (e.g., Japan) or feminine values tend to exist (e.g., Sweden).[27]

Equity Theory: You Should Get What You Deserve

Equity theory proposes that an employee's sense of fairness is an important driver of his or her level of motivation at work. If an employee perceives that she has been treated unfairly by an organization or boss, she is motivated to take action to restore a sense of fairness. These judgments of fairness or equity are reached by comparing oneself with similar people at the workplace (peers with the same job title and description, etc.). The theory claims that we consider various outcomes and weigh the possible consequences of actions and rewards that we receive at work (such as pay, recognition, etc.) relative to the amount that we put *into* the job (such as effort, education, skills, etc.). When the comparison of outcomes to inputs is roughly balanced, employees should feel that they have been fairly treated by their organization. If they do not have this sense, employees will spend time and effort trying to restore the balance somehow.[28]

Applying Equity Concepts Across Cultures

Research seems to show that the way that different cultures define, interpret, and assess "fairness" can vary considerably. Moreover, national culture is not the only factor impacting employee views about equity. The corporate context (e.g., firm norms, the nature of the industry) can also shape employee acceptance of equity concepts. For instance, over time a strong merit pay system—one in which higher pay is linked to individual performance—may influence employee attitudes. And, as multinational corporations continue their push abroad, they are helping to shape workforce values in those places. For instance, one study found that Chinese employees working for international joint ventures involving Western firms were increasingly accepting of company norms that distributed rewards based on their performance. This flies in the face of the fact that distributing rewards equally among workers would be more consistent with traditional Chinese values. Yet, how fast and how far such changes will permeate across the broader Chinese workforce remains to be seen.[29]

International managers would be wise to consider the impact of cultural values when it comes to equity concepts. For example, workers in cultures that highly value individualism may still be more motivated by equity and deservingness than employees elsewhere. In such cultures, individual performance is important (inputs) and should be rewarded accordingly based on deservingness (outcomes). On the other hand, in collectivist cultures there may be more openness to seeing rewards distributed equally, regardless of performance, to preserve group harmony and cohesiveness.[30]

As previously stated, however, the link between culture and equity-based rewards is both complex and evolving. Some studies suggest that employees in collectivistic cultures are less likely to apply equity concepts when distributing rewards than employees in individualistic cultures. Other experts, however, suggest a more nuanced view, pointing out that studies have found that employees in collectivistic cultures may be more likely to use equity norms when rewarding efforts to promote group cohesiveness. Still other studies suggest that in-group versus out-group differences may also complicate matters in collective cultures such as China. For example, equality norms (relatively equal distributions, regardless of inputs) may be preferred when distributing rewards to *in*-group members, whereas equity (performance-based) norms are more preferable when rewards were being divvied up to *out*-group members. Finally, some studies have suggested power distance can impact these differences in equity–equality, with low power distance employees preferring equality and high power distance employees preferring equity as the fairest way to distribute rewards.[31]

An alternative perspective emerging on equity theory is that we should focus less on broad fairness rules and more on understanding what goes into the mental equation that employees consider when judging fairness around the globe. Put another way, there may be fewer differences across cultures than we think when it comes to preferences for equity or equality norms. Instead, culture may have a bigger impact on what employees consider to be relevant work inputs and outcomes, as well as how important they are. While everyone may understand and have similar views about broad norms like equity, how these are implemented may be shaped to a large extent by culture. A related example of this is illustrated in Figure 10.2, which shows the results of a survey of nearly 90,000 people across 18 countries (five examples are shown in Figure 10.2). Employees were asked to rank features that attract them to a firm and also to rate various features that engage them once employed there. As the figure shows, there are common features in ranked items, as well as some unique features that are motivating within any one country.

Country	Top Three Attraction Drivers	Top Three Engagement Drivers
Brazil	Competitive base pay Career advancement opportunity Challenging work	Organization rewards outstanding customer service Improvement of my skills over last year Senior management sincerely interested in employee well-being
China	Learning and development opportunity Career advancement opportunity Competitive base pay	Excellent career advancement opportunities Organization encouraged innovative thinking Organization's reputation for financial stability
India	Career advancement opportunity Challenging work Learning and development opportunity	Input into decision making Senior management actions consistent with values Organization's reputation for social responsibility
South Korea	Competitive benefits Competitive base pay Reputation of organization as good employer	Senior management ensures organization's long-term success Unit has skills needed to succeed Organization supports work–life balance
U.S.	Competitive base pay Competitive health care benefits Vacation/paid time off	Senior management sincerely interested in employee well-being Organization's reputation for social responsibility Improvement of my skills over last year

Figure 10.2 What Attracts Employees to a Firm and Engages Them Once They Are There?

Source: Adapted from Tower Perrin. (2008). Closing the engagement gap: A road map for driving superior business performance. *Tower Perrin Global Workforce Study*, available at: www.towersperrin.com/tp/showhtml.jsp?url=global/publications/gws/index.htm&country=global.

Hopefully, researchers will be able to sort this out in the years ahead and offer more concrete advice to international managers in the process. This important information is needed by practicing managers who regularly make compensation and other reward decisions. That said, cultures are not static and this complicates efforts to solve this puzzle. Moreover, the pace of change regarding how employees judge equity and fairness distribution may vary considerably as a consequence of local circumstances. For instance, although we mentioned shifting equity perspectives among Chinese employees at the beginning of this section, there is also evidence to suggest that Chinese managers have been slower to adopt "Western" equity rules to distribute material rewards than, say, their Russian counterparts.[32]

What do these complex findings mean for international managers? Findings suggest that managers should do the following:

1. Think through how their *own* cultural values might affect their use of equity or equality rules in doling out rewards.
2. Take some time to understand how the cultural values of their *subordinates* might affect the use of various inputs and outcomes.

Overall, it is important to be mindful of how traditional values and practices may change in ways that affect how rewards should be allocated. Again, conditions in China not long ago allowed firms located on the coast to keep workers from the interior reasonably satisfied with low pay and no raises (sometimes for years). Job prospects elsewhere were just very slim. But this has changed as the country has developed and opportunities spread. Indeed, many low-paid employees in China already feel pangs of inequity, particularly if they compare themselves to others who seem better off.[33] As discussed later in Chapter 13, this resulted in widespread worker protests and was partially responsible for ethnic strife in some Chinese provinces in the late 2000s.

Reinforcement Theory: Connecting Behavior and Consequences

The central idea behind reinforcement theory is that the best way to motivate is to clearly link valued consequences to the performance of specific employee behaviors. For example, managers can improve employee performance by applying positive reinforcers (e.g., big bonuses). Conversely, poor performance can be eliminated by carefully applying sanctions or punishment (e.g., a pay cut).

Culture, Context, and Reinforcement Ideas

To use positive reinforcement most effectively managers need to know what employees value. Culture and societal context, however, makes this more challenging than it seems. For example, in South Africa many black employees are more motivated when their firm continues to remove the social inequalities left over from apartheid (e.g., the inferior housing still plaguing much of the black majority). This connection between work and life outside of work also reflects African cultural values that emphasize the importance of community and family. Such values are less common in Western management approaches.[34]

Culture may also affect how employees interpret performance-related feedback. For instance, while employees everywhere react more favorably to positive than to negative feedback, this pattern is more pronounced in collectivistic cultures. Moreover, employees in individualistic cultures tend to respond more to individualized performance feedback rather than group performance feedback, with employees in collectivistic cultures doing the opposite. Narrowing our lens even further for a moment, while U.S. employees tend to prefer positive feedback, they will often take steps to explain away or dismiss negative feedback. In contrast, while Japanese employees tend to react even more strongly to negative feedback than Americans, they are also more open to feedback and more likely to respond with behavioral changes. It is very likely that these tendencies are rooted in cultural and societal traditions. Many Americans like to revel in their triumphs, especially individual ones, while finding failure threatening to their self-worth as individuals. In collectivistic Japan, however, critical evaluations may help people maintain a humble posture toward the wider group as well as offer suggestions for improving overall group performance.[35]

Similarly, U.S. and Mexican workers may react differently to positive performance feedback.[36] Americans may see praise as suggesting that even better performance is possible, while Mexicans may see it as recognition that their current performance is good. Mexican workers are also less likely to exceed the informal performance norms of their work groups regardless of the feedback they receive from a supervisor. Compared with Americans, Mexican employees may be more collectivist and tend to pay close attention to group norms.[37]

Cultural values can also present other hurdles for reinforcement strategies. For instance, performance-based pay may not motivate workers in high uncertainty avoidance cultures because pay is put at risk. Using large bonuses or big pay increases alone may also prove difficult in feminine cultures since loyalty to the boss, company, or co-workers is valued above performance. India is an example of a country where cultural values may limit reinforcement strategies. In fact, pay systems in some Indian companies violate reinforcement principles. For example, compensation may strongly reflect employee seniority as opposed to being contingent on behavior. Performance appraisal may also be rudimentary, making "merit pay" seem arbitrary. This may reinforce the resigned fatalism and indifference to good performance (a state referred to *chalega*) that some Indians already embrace because of their socialization experiences. Instead, Indian employees' efforts may be directed to activities aimed at strengthening relationships with supervisors who offer valued rewards.[38]

Overall, managers need to consider how culture affects the elements that employees find motivating as well as how they react to company efforts to link those motivators to desired behaviors. Once again, managers must be willing and able to scale what is often a formidable learning curve to understand what works best in a particular cultural context. This does not necessarily mean that U.S. managers have to avoid Western approaches to reinforcement. What it does mean, however, is that to be accepted by employees, reinforcement approaches may have to be modified to fit local sensibilities.[39]

Expectancy Theory: Setting Goals and Tying in Rewards

Expectancy theory pulls together many of the ideas about motivation that we have presented so far. The expectancy approach assumes that three factors determine employee effort in a given situation, with effort being a strong indicant of motivation.[40] First, employees must believe that working hard will result in good performance. So, if an employee feels it is impossible to hit production goals that have been set, he or she will not exert much effort. Second, employees must believe that rewards are tied to good performance. If this is not the case, then motivation will also suffer. Finally, the available rewards must be valued—motivation and effort will languish if the rewards employees receive are unimportant to them.

Cultural Assumptions of Expectancy Theory

You may have noticed that expectancy theory makes some now-familiar cultural assumptions in that it emphasizes individualistic and masculine values (such as a focus on tasks rather than on relationships). It also assumes that individual workers are rational and control their lives by manipulating effort. All of this fits U.S. culture quite well. But many Asian and Middle Eastern cultures believe that fate helps determine events. Similarly, many Mexicans feel that being from the appropriate family is a real key to success. Likewise, many Saudi Arabians believe that what happens at work is a reflection of God's will. In each case, external forces are important.[41]

Because rewards must be valued to produce motivation, expectancy theory suggests that the rewards used should reflect cultural values. For instance, in one study U.S. managers felt that bonuses should be tightly connected to performance. This fits the expectancy assumption that people are achievement-oriented and can tolerate risk. But the French and Dutch managers in the study were less interested in money and were more skeptical about linking bonuses to performance. And in reality, the bonuses earned by French and Dutch managers were smaller and varied less than did the bonuses earned by Americans. The Dutch tend to have a more feminine cultural orientation and are less individualistic than Americans. As a consequence, Dutch managers are less likely to use pay as a way to "keep score" of personal achievement. Similarly, managers in high uncertainty avoidance cultures, such as France, may be leery of reward systems with large, highly variable performance bonuses.[42]

These cultural differences help explain why the "outrage threshold" for executive compensation is generally lower in Europe than in the U.S. In particular, these differences might affect the second key element of expectancy theory explained earlier—the belief that rewards are tied to good performance. Indeed, European executives in major firms earn only about 40 percent of what their American counterparts take home. In 2009, this averaged roughly $13 million for American CEOs vs. an average of only roughly $3 million (Dutch) to $6 million (British) for European CEOs. Moreover, legal restrictions on executive pay, bonuses, golden parachutes (huge payouts if an executive leaves), and stock options tend to be more severe in Europe than in the U.S. As a result, it is not surprising that (in 2007) the $14 million pay package earned by the CEO of giant Swiss pharmaceutical company Novartis sparked many negative comments about "excessive compensation" in Europe—a sum that is unlikely to provoke a similar reaction in the U.S. That said, pay packages for U.S. executives will produce outrage if they are seen as "exorbitant" by American standards and are not perceived to be strongly linked to performance.[43]

Of course, sensibilities about pay change and evolve. Indeed, some of the outrage that has been seen in Europe regarding "huge" executive pay packages reflects a shift toward U.S.-style compensation. Between 1998 and 2008, for instance, CEO pay jumped up dramatically as European firms tried to keep up in the worldwide search for talent. In fact, foreigners now run several major German and French companies, with U.S.-type incentive and bonuses plans being much more common across the board. After losing talent to U.S. and British rivals in recent years, Deutsche Bank and Bayerische Vereins-bank in Germany began offering American-style performance bonuses that increased total compensation by 50 percent or more. Many other German banks remain uneasy and have relied on smaller bonuses—some even making part of the bonus pay contingent on the ability to work well with colleagues. This also underscores the fact that pay differences persist across European nations. Northern European countries (e.g., Netherlands, Norway, Sweden), along with Germany, tend to have more egalitarian values than their British and French counterparts—and hence tend to pay CEOs less.[44] For a closer look at how performance–reward linkages are evolving in Japan, see the International Insights feature.

International Insights

Global Dining's Message to Its Japanese Employees: Perform or You Are Chopped Liver

The "cut-throat capitalism" of the U.S. is a tough sell for many Japanese. Contentious disputes about pay and performance are rare in Japan, at least in traditional companies. But Japanese firms such as Global Dining may provide a peek into the future. This restaurant chain embraced three innovations that are shocking for many Japanese—plenty of conflict, do-or-die competition between employees, and brutally honest individual performance feedback.

How brutal? One cook sat in front of a group of bosses and peers to demand a big pay increase. They immediately shouted criticisms, including that his cooking was uneven and that sales on his shift were lousy. A quick vote was taken with the humiliated cook being rebuffed. In fact, all employees, from senior leaders to dishwashers, are evaluated against performance criteria in such face-to-face meetings. Those who miss performance targets get no bonuses. Managers who foul up are quickly demoted or fired. But excellent performers are rewarded incredibly well. One young restaurant manager made over $150,000, considerably more than a typical mid-career executive working for a large Japanese firm. Global Dining's CEO summed up the system's philosophy this way: "Just as sharks

417

need to keep swimming to stay alive, we only want people who are constantly craving challenges."

The willingness to embrace this demanding approach is part of a broader debate in Japan regarding traditionally cushy relationships between employees and big firms that often have little to do with performance (e.g., lifetime employment, seniority-based raises, etc.). Japan's prolonged economic difficulties have been driving that debate, so Global Dining is not alone. Companies such as Sony, clothing chain Fast Retailing, and machine parts firm Misumi Corporation are among the bigger Japanese companies that have aggressively recruited young managers willing to live with the ups and downs of a tough pay-for-performance system. Thanks to bonuses, one young Misumi manager earned almost $530,000—a sum that eclipsed the pay of the company president.

But some workers at Global Dining worry about the pressures under such a hardnosed performance management system. Even waiters watch each other closely because everyone votes on raises and bonuses for everyone else (one performance marker is how long it takes a waiter to notice that a customer needs another drink). That said, Global Dining employees may have the last word because the system actually *encourages* criticism of superiors, right up to the CEO level. In fact, at one point, employees complained to the CEO about the bonus formula. Eventually, employees demanded a vote on the issue; the CEO lost, and the formula was modified. One manager who left Global Dining to start his own restaurant said that while performance management was a good thing, his system would be less ruthless. As he put it, "There's a saying, 'too much is as bad as too little.'"

Indeed, the flip side of the challenges that firms such as Global Dining take on is the growing percentage of younger Japanese who are "slackers," perfectly content with humdrum jobs. These workers, labeled *hodo-hodo zoku* ("so-so folks") in Japan, deliberately avoid working hard and refuse to accept more responsibilities, promotions, and even pay raises. As unusual as it may seem in workaholic Japan, only 3 percent of Japanese employees said that they were giving their jobs full effort in a recent 18-nation survey—the lowest of any country. Critics suggest that Japan's crumbling traditions of lifetime employment and generous benefits are causing younger workers to do the minimum amount of work and are thus threatening Japanese productivity in the process. But these employees watched their parents commit themselves totally to their jobs and companies, putting in extraordinarily long hours, only to see them "rewarded" with layoffs and pay cuts during recessions in the 1990s and 2000s. As one "so-so" employee put it, "That's definitely not the life I want." Consequently, companies as diverse as Sanyo Electric and Dai-ichi Mutual Life Insurance are having a hard time just finding employees willing to be promoted into management.

Perhaps the answer for these companies is to take the Global Dining approach and offer more radical alternatives to employees—where there are plenty of risks, but also plenty of bigger rewards. This might entice younger Japanese into signing up if they believe big rewards will really follow from working hard—unlike their parents' experience in the slow, seniority-based approach found in traditional Japanese firms. Yet it remains to be seen whether younger Japanese will gravitate more toward *hodo-hodo zoku* thinking, the "cut-throat capitalism" embraced by Global Dining, or something else entirely.[45]

As interesting as these Japanese examples are, major shifts in attitudes and motivation do not typically happen overnight. For instance, in recent years Japanese have been seeking out foreign companies for employment in ever-increasing numbers. In most cases, this attraction is based on the belief that, relative to their domestic counterparts, foreign firms demand fewer hours while at the same time are more willing to pay for individual performance and to promote based on personal achievement. That said, the percentage of Japanese in the workforce who are employed by foreign companies is still small (less than 3 percent) and trails the percentage in other industrialized nations by a considerable margin (e.g., over 5 percent in both the U.S. and Germany).

So while change is occurring, the starting point is low and the rate of change unclear.[46] In general, the perceived link between effort and performance remains stronger for Americans than for Japanese. The longer history of performance-contingent reward systems in the U.S. likely explains this difference. Finally, Americans still tend to see pay increases, promotions, and personal recognition as more desirable than do their Japanese counterparts. Cultural values that emphasize individual performance and achievement in the U.S. and group cohesion in Japan may be the source of those findings. Consequently, how fast and to what extent Japanese society will become more individualistic is unclear. But the government apparently wants to move in that direction. A few years ago, Japan launched a new education policy designed to help children become more independent and individually oriented.[47]

Conclusions about Motivation Across Cultures

International managers would be well served to take culture and related factors into account when designing and implementing motivation strategies for use abroad.[48] But this is no small challenge, especially because cultural values are a moving target and managers may not appreciate how their own values affect the motivation strategies they use.[49] Consequently, international managers should rely on motivation approaches and tactics that complement rather than conflict with the specific cultures involved. In short, they should strive for cultural synergy in their motivation efforts. This can be done in five basic steps:

1. **Describe the motivation situation.** The first step is to discover if different motivational perspectives exist and if they create conflict. How does the manager view the motivation issue? What perspectives do employees have?
2. **Identify cultural assumptions about motivation.** The next step is to pinpoint the cultural values that explain different perspectives on motivation. The goal is to be able to see things from another culture's perspective.
3. **Determine where cultural overlaps exist.** Next is to determine where similarities and differences exist between cultures in the work environment.
4. **Generate culturally synergistic alternatives.** Once cultural assumptions have been identified, the next challenge is to develop motivation strategies that blend elements of the cultures involved or even go beyond them.
5. **Select, implement, and then refine a synergistic strategy.** The final step involves picking and implementing the best motivation strategy. A key is to have all parties observe the strategy from their own cultural lens and then fine-tune it based on any feedback that is received.

Accomplishing these steps may require conversations with foreign employees, as well as their involvement in the development and implementation of specific motivation programs. To ensure success in these efforts, managers and employees must both possess cultural self-awareness (i.e., awareness of their own values) and cross-cultural awareness (i.e., awareness of others' values). Having both types of awareness increases the odds that the chosen strategy can be implemented in a way that reflects the best of the specific cultures involved. But first, underlying values and cultural frames of reference must be identified. This will help foster an appreciation for alternative perspectives, something that can then be used in generating motivational approaches which accomplish management goals in ways that are sensitive to local cultures.[50]

Effective Leadership in a Global Context

In this section we turn our attention to management, shifting our focus from motivating employees to those who often are responsible for implementing a motivation program: the leaders. At the core, leaders help set things in motion in their organizations—they guide the development of the firm's vision and enable employees to contribute effectively to its achievement. But thanks to globalization, today's leaders face daunting challenges—whether coordinating virtual teams from 10,000 miles away, leading a foreign subsidiary as an expatriate, or running a multicultural department in their home countries. Consequently, effective leadership in international companies requires openness, an appreciation of cultural differences, and the ability to bridge differences quickly—to develop culturally synergistic solutions to international management challenges.[51] Recent thinking is that these global skill sets can be differentiated from a more domestic leader style along three dimensions. Global leadership is more *complex* because it comprises the above skills in addition to some of the same domestic leader skills. The flow of knowledge and information is also both wider and deeper. And, the degree to which leaders must span geography and culture (presence) is in much greater demand from a global manager.[52]

Yet, the specific ways in which "leadership" is practiced can also become blurry once borders are crossed.[53] For instance, perspectives vary about what characteristics leaders must possess to be effective. Nevertheless, leaders exist in every culture. Moreover, some leadership attributes seem to be viewed as positively (or negatively) contributing to a leader's effectiveness in most countries. That said, other leader attributes are viewed differently across cultures. Figure 10.3 presents a few examples of leadership attributes that are considered positive in most cultures, negative in most cultures, and interpreted very differently across cultures. Researchers continue to investigate how leadership attributes travel across cultures. One recent study suggested that self-awareness, an attribute often seen as critical to leadership effectiveness in the U.S., may not be as important elsewhere. Americans embrace the open sharing of inner thoughts and feelings—which promotes managers' self-awareness as they receive feedback from others. On the other hand, in cultures where saving "face" is valued and direct communication is less acceptable, self-awareness may be much less important for leadership success. But even when attributes are generally seen as good or bad in most cultures, how those attributes are manifested varies considerably depending on the cultural context. Finally, even when

Leadership attributes likely to be viewed as "good" in most cultures	Decisive
	Good communicator
	Honest
	Intelligent
	Has integrity
	Positive
	Trustworthy
Leadership attributes likely to be viewed as "bad" in most cultures	Dictatorial
	Egocentric
	Irritable
	Ruthless
Leadership attributes likely to be viewed differently across cultural boundaries	Ambitious
	Enthusiastic
	Individualistic
	Logical
	Sensitive
	Willing to take risks

Figure 10.3 Leadership Attributes Across Cultures: Examples of the Good, the Bad, and the Different.
Sources: Adapted from Frost, J., and Walker, M. (2007). Cross-cultural leadership. *Engineering Management*, June/July, 27–29; and House, R. J., Hanges, P. J., Javidan, M., Dorfman, P. W., and Gupta, V. (eds) *Culture, Leadership, and Organizations: The GLOBE Study of 62 Societies*. Thousand Oaks, CA: Sage.

cultures tend to manifest certain types of leadership behaviors, it doesn't mean international managers should automatically emulate them. Instead, other approaches to leadership will be more effective in the long run.[54]

Consequently, some tough questions are tackled in this section. Do managers behave differently across cultures in leadership roles? Do certain situations require similar leadership behaviors, regardless of culture? Can corporate culture override or weaken other cross-cultural effects with respect to leadership? This section offers some answers to these and other important questions.

Leader Behavior Across Cultures

Leadership concepts, values, and styles continue to evolve around the world, which complicates matters. This evolutionary process can be seen in Russia, Poland, and other countries in Eastern Europe that have undergone social and economic upheaval in over the last decades.[55] Yet, tension between old and new ways of leading is not limited to former members of the Soviet bloc. South Korea has produced some remarkable success stories in recent years, with many Korean brands such as Hyundai, LG, and Samsung now household names in Western markets, including the U.S. There is little doubt that some of this success reflects the impact of shifting leadership cultures in certain top South Korean firms, a point considered more closely in the closing case of this chapter.

Task- vs. Relationship-Oriented Leader Behavior: Cultural Limitations

A common distinction drawn by American researchers is that two basic types of leader behavior exist. *Task-oriented behavior* includes clarifying performance expectations and specific procedures to be followed. Other examples include planning, scheduling, providing technical help, and goal setting. In contrast, *relationship-oriented behavior* includes showing concern for subordinates' feelings, needs, and well-being. Other examples include expressing empathy, warmth, encouragement, consideration, and trust to subordinates. But which type of leadership behavior produces the best performance and in which countries? There is no simple answer. On the one hand, leaders in collectivistic cultures such as Japan may tend to use relationship-oriented behaviors more than leaders in individualistic cultures such as the U.S. On the other hand, when relationship-oriented behaviors are used, employee reaction tends to be relatively positive across a wide variety of cultures. Reactions to task-oriented behavior, however, tend to be more variable across cultures. The bottom line is that depending on the circumstance (which may include cultural factors, organizational context, and employee characteristics) leaders may need to use different combinations of task-oriented and relationship-oriented behaviors to be effective.[56]

Use India as an example. It presents a challenging leadership environment to say the least, as a rapidly developing Asian country where personal relations are critical and complexities abound due to culture, religion, caste, and family ties. Many Indian experts have suggested that a nurturing style of leadership that mixes empathy and concern for subordinates with an emphasis on getting the job done often works best in many Indian work contexts.[57] See the following International Insights feature for more detail on the nurturing style of leadership.

International Insights

Vineet Nayar: Changing the Leadership Culture, 1.2 Billion at a Time

India is a large and rapidly developing Asian country with a number of features shared by the U.S. For example, India is the world's largest democracy with (now) deep-seated political roots. The rule of law is firmly established and detailed. Likewise, India nurtures a free press, a strong judiciary, and well-educated business leaders operating in open capital and labor markets. Yet, there are significant differences, which can create problems if the businessperson is not well schooled on each culture. Likewise, even within such a large country, clashes can occur between old and new ways. This might be especially the case in areas of India in which personal relations are critical and complexities abound due to culture, religion, caste, and family ties.

This may have led to an indigenous and unique leadership style. Many Indian experts have suggested that a nurturant style of leadership that mixes empathy and concern for subordinates with an emphasis on getting the job done often works best in many Indian work contexts. Interestingly, researchers asked sets of Indian executives about this and related leadership issues. Leaders of the 100 largest publicly listed companies (by market capitalization) were asked to order their priorities in running their businesses. These responses were compared to those of similar American executives. A distinctive feature of the Indian approach was the high priority that leaders placed on investing in and power given to their employees. This ranked well above maximizing shareholder value—the highest priority voiced by American executives.[58]

Given this priority, it is no surprise that interesting and unique leadership ideas are coming from India. There is no doubt that large swaths of India remain impoverished, but in the growing tech and business sectors, Indian companies are fighting hard to attract and to retain highly talented and skilled employees who are among the world's best. At HCL Technologies (an information technology outsourcing firm that is the fifth-largest firm in India), even throwing money, perks, and fancy benefits at employees was not enough to stem an atrocious attrition rate. Instead, HCL's CEO, Vineet Nayar, decided to focus on his people. First, he deployed a 360-degree feedback system that collected assessments of over 1,500 managers worldwide (including Mr. Nayar himself) from peers, bosses, subordinates, customers, and more. As Mr. Nayar said, "Our competitive differentiation is that we are more transparent than anybody else in our industry . . . [Employees and customers] like us because there are no hidden secrets." No secrets indeed! HCL routinely puts the results of those 360-degree reviews on the firm's intranet for all to see—including Mr. Nayar's own evaluation. Plus, instead of determining who gets bonuses or promotions, the goal of the system is to encourage democracy. In a reversal of the usual truism (as Mr. Nayar puts it) HCL's goal is "to get the *manager* to suck up to the *employee*."[59]

Other new approaches include an online complaint system that employees can use for any issue and which also tracks complaint resolution. Mr. Nayar also spends his weekends personally responding to the 50 or so electronic questions that he receives from employees every week. His responses are posted for all to see. Mr. Nayar claims that a traditional "command and control" orientation at HCL is giving way to "collaborative management." But, he is not content to let this take its own course—Mr. Nayar has pushed for more rapid evolution. To accelerate this change, in any one year he spends upwards of half his time in town hall meetings with employees, sharing his views and vision and taking questions. He has a personal goal of shaking every employee's hand every year, with the goal (self-stated) of "destroying the office of the CEO" in five years. On his public blog (also titled "Destroying the Office of the CEO") he explains that he wants decision making pushed out of the C-suite and into the hands of where the company meets the client.

Overall, these unique employee-focused approaches may be consistent with the nurturant style of leadership described above. They may be well beyond it! Either way, it has people's attention. While a variety of Western firms have visited India in order to learn about HCL's leadership ideas, none have adopted its 360-degree system so far. CEO Nayar's explanation is simple: "It's too radical for most of them." It is easy to see why Vineet Nayar's well-understood motto is "Employee first, customers second."[60]

Japan has also produced some interesting ideas about leadership in that country. For example, the "PM leader" is a leadership style that combines complementary concern about problem solving and motivation of group performance (performance leadership) with behavior designed to promote interdependence, avoid conflict, and maintain harmony within the group (maintenance leadership). On the surface, these behaviors resemble the distinction between task- and relationship-oriented behaviors drawn by American researchers.

But their implementation in Japan makes it clear that both sets of behaviors are grounded in a very different cultural context. For instance, if a Japanese leader discussed a subordinate's family problems with other employees, this would likely be seen as showing high maintenance leadership. The same behavior in the U.S., however, would most likely be viewed as inappropriate. Similarly, performance leadership behaviors that would be seen as positive in Japan (e.g., the leader being strict about following company policies or urging employees to work to their utmost as a group) would be off-putting to many U.S. employees. U.S. employees typically view leadership as an individual process, and want their leaders to "make tough calls" and to "take charge." In contrast, traditional Japanese leadership tends to have a more communal quality, focusing instead on group performance. Decision making is typically much slower, and involves plenty of consultation with peers and concern for relationships.[61]

These examples from India and Japan underscore that lumping everything into two behavioral dimensions can often mask important cross-cultural differences. In fact, the relationship-oriented behavior described by Western scholars is colder and more egalitarian than the paternalistic Indian version. That "paternalistic version" of relationship-oriented behavior may produce positive reactions from employees in places such as India, the Middle East, and parts of Latin America. Consequently, international managers may get themselves into trouble if they limit leadership to Western views of "task-oriented" and "relationship-oriented" behaviors.[62]

A survey of Iranian employees further illustrates this point. Respondents were asked whether their immediate supervisor showed task-oriented and relationship-oriented behavior styles. The results showed that Iranian supervisors who acted in a benevolent and paternalistic way had the best performance ratings from subordinates. Yet, forcing the Iranian data into task- and relationship-oriented factors produced no significant relationships with leader performance or subordinate satisfaction. This suggests that Western definitions of leader behavior may not fit Persian or Middle Eastern cultures. In Iran, the boundary between work and family relationships is often ambiguous. The warm but firm father figure who plays such a prominent role in Iranian society translates into the work supervisor who is directive but still shows respect for subordinates.[63]

In essence, leadership style must be understood in terms of both its general underlying structure as well as its particular expression in certain cultures. For example, American and Japanese leaders might agree that being supportive (relationship-oriented behavior) is important for success. In the individualistic U.S., a manager might express support by showing respect for subordinates' ideas. In collectivistic Japan, however, a manager might express support by spending more time with subordinates as a group.[64]

A study comparing managers from Britain, Hong Kong, Japan, and the U.S. found that while there was agreement on basic aspects of leadership style, the specific expression of these behaviors varied across the four countries.[65] These differences may explain why American and Japanese managers often encounter enormous difficulties when in leadership roles in each other's "home" environment. Overcoming this may require a blending of leadership strategies that parallel our synergistic recommendations on motivation.[66]

Culture and the Impact of Leader Behavior

The behavior shown by leaders can affect an employee's attitude and performance. But, as with motivation, this effect may change because of cultural background. In collectivist, high power distance cultures such as Japan and Taiwan, task-oriented behaviors may have a stronger positive impact on employees than in individualistic, low power distance cultures such as the U.S. For instance, the criticism that Japanese managers use (often aimed directly at subordinates) would likely seem punitive to many Americans, even though it works well in a Japanese context. In Japan, managers will often balance criticism with plenty of supportive behaviors and go to great lengths to minimize status symbols. On the other hand, Americans are more likely to use status symbols (e.g., a big, fancy office) to project authority.[67]

What happens, however, when American subordinates work under Japanese leadership at a facility within the U.S.? In one study, Japanese managers had less impact on American subordinates than Japanese ones, and had less influence over both groups than American supervisors. American subordinates, however, performed better when a Japanese supervisor was friendly and supportive but worse when an American supervisor did basically the same thing. So, the nationalities of supervisors may affect how their behavior is *interpreted* by their subordinates in specific contexts. Friendliness by an American supervisor may imply weakness, while the same behavior from a Japanese supervisor may be seen as a desire to get things done.[68] But, can different leader behaviors have the same positive effects across cultural contexts? The answer is yes, according to experts testing this question.

In many U.S. companies, for example, participative approaches that involve employees in decision making by supportive supervisors are effective. This participative method is a good match for low power distance cultures, such as the U.S. This style may not work well in high power distance cultures, such as Mexico. There, a paternalistic, autocratic leadership approach would fit better—where managers make most decisions in a way they feel is best for employees (as a parent would for offspring). One study examined this very issue by comparing managers in plants in Mexico and the U.S. Both plants were owned by the same American firm and produced the same product. American managers got their employees involved in decisions by seeking their reactions and feedback to quality improvement options. Mexican managers, however, did not consult with employees, but instead reserved most of those decisions for themselves.[69]

The broader implication here is that foreign outposts can match the level of performance found within U.S. facilities, for example, without having to use a strictly "American" approach to leadership. Consider the U.S.–Mexico comparison in more detail. Many of the initial production problems facing American-owned plants in Mexico may be due to the use of management techniques inconsistent with Mexican cultural values.

Leadership Issue	Management Expectations and Attitudes	
	American Managers	**Mexican Managers**
Valued subordinate behaviors	Initiative, achievement	Obedience, harmony
Key to subordinate evaluation	Performance	Personal loyalty
Leadership style	Loose/informal, communicative, power sharing possible	Close/formal, empathetic, use of directives, little power sharing
Basis of discipline/justice	Uniform application of rules and procedures	Personal relationships
Work environment model	Competitive team	Cooperative family

Figure 10.4 Leadership at the Border: The Expectation Gap between American and Mexican Managers. *Source*: Adapted from de Forest, M. E. (1994). Thinking of a plant in Mexico? *Academy of Management Executive*, 8, 33–40.

These differences surface when U.S. multinationals send poorly prepared Americans to manage Mexican workers. Figure 10.4 describes some of the divergent expectations that may separate American and Mexican managers. Mexican workers sometimes appear passive to Americans. Compared to the U.S., Mexico is less individualistic but higher in power distance and uncertainty avoidance. What seems like Mexican passivity is really due to beliefs that conformity, respect, and personal loyalty to supervisors are important. Indeed, for many Mexican employees, viewing the organization as an extended family makes sense. Just like in a family, people should work cooperatively but within a pre-scribed role. The value Americans place on individual achievement and power sharing may strike many Mexican employees as inconsistent with this view.[70]

American managers also need to be sensitive when interacting with Mexican employees. For instance, honoring status is part of Mexican business. At one plant in Mexico, the ranking union leader was insulted when the American plant manager failed to introduce him to visiting executives. Formality is another way that many Mexicans recognize status differences. American informality can produce problems. For example, one American manager in Mexico tried to reduce status differences by wearing jeans and dropping professional titles. But, the result was that Mexican workers thought he was "unsophisticated." Distance between management and labor is expected. Mexican workers often view autonomy as less important and may respond best to formal but empathetic managers who supervise them closely. Likewise, traditional Mexican supervisors are used to being obeyed without question. They view having to explain an order as a weakness. Consequently, American management efforts to share power and encourage problem solving can be confusing to Mexican employees, although this can be overcome by training that taps into familiar family concepts (e.g., "we are all brothers and sisters in this together").[71]

For their part, U.S. managers in Mexico sometimes feel that local workers are undisciplined and that Mexican workplaces run "loosely." U.S. managers feel that discipline results when policies are applied equally to all workers. Mexicans, however, may view discipline embodied in the form of loyalty to a manager, not a policy manual. One

American plant manager learned this lesson the hard way after he created an elaborate grievance system to prevent labor unrest. He was later shocked when the entire workforce walked out without using the new system to air their complaints. Resolving grievances in Mexico may require a relationship-oriented approach that includes personal expressions of understanding of workers' needs.[72]

Aligning Leadership Behavior with the Cultural Context

This information suggests that international managers may need to adapt their leadership style to match expectations in specific countries to be effective, at least initially. Consider a common cultural mistake that American managers make in Japan—assigning parts of a project to different individuals instead of handing it off (in totality) to a group. In the U.S., giving clear, specialized assignments to each employee is often seen as the best way to organize work. In Japan, however, it would be better to give the entire project to a group of subordinates, letting them tackle it as they see fit. The Japanese view is that interaction among employees provides the structure for organizing work.[73]

Nevertheless, many Americans continue to believe that if they are good managers in Indianapolis or Denver, that they can export that style successfully overseas. One study debunked this idea by comparing Americans managing in Hong Kong and the U.S. on 12 different leader behaviors. As expected, the American managers behaved relatively similarly in both places. But the relationship between behavior and performance was quite different. While eight of the leader behaviors were correlated with overall performance in the U.S., only one behavior was correlated with performance for the Americans in Hong Kong. In short, the same behaviors that "worked" in the U.S. had no impact in Hong Kong.[74]

Of course, U.S. managers are not the only ones who can have trouble adapting their leadership approaches to foreign contexts. Some experts believe that many of the factors that helped the Japanese succeed at home and in the export market became stumbling blocks as they set up operations overseas and/or globally integrated.[75] Also, consider some of the challenges that German giant Siemens has encountered in trying to run its U.S. subsidiaries and its tens of thousands of American employees. One of the complaints from the American side of things is that German leadership is too autocratic, inflexible, slow, and bureaucratic, with many decisions requiring approval from Germany. At Siemens, a management board meets in Germany to make decisions about a variety of strategic and operational issues. When major decisions are involved, another group, the supervisory board (consisting of both employees and shareholders), has to step in and approve the decision made by the management board before the firm can proceed. As you might suspect, some Americans view this leadership approach as cumbersome, one that tends to shut out local input and initiative.[76]

Transformational Leadership: What Is It and Does It Work Across Cultures?

This section considers transformational leadership, a recent—and increasingly popular—perspective in the U.S. A transformational leader is able to galvanize employees, turning poorly performing companies into winners. This happens when the transformational leader creates an emotional bond with employees—something which inspires intense loyalty and outstanding performance. This bond is the result of the leader's:

- **charisma,** which arouses intense emotions among followers based on faith in and identification with the leader;
- **use of inspirational appeals,** that convey a clear and compelling future vision, with very high performance expectations for employees;
- **intellectual stimulation,** that challenges subordinates to think about new ways to do things, overcome problems, and design products as they pursue the leader's vision;
- **individualized consideration** which offers subordinates personal attention, empathy, and communication.[77]

In American firms, transformational leaders can have positive effects on subordinate effort, performance, and satisfaction. This often requires a willingness to cede control to the leader, something that is more likely when subordinates feel vulnerable (such as during a business downturn). Research does show that transformational leaders seem to have the greatest impact in a crisis.[78]

But does this mean that international business, with its rapid changes and competitive threats, is tailor-made for transformational leadership? Some experts believe that "yes," the most successful international managers are transformational leaders. Supporting this are studies showing the positive impact of transformational leadership in places as diverse as Israel, New Zealand, Germany, and Singapore. Still, broad statements about the "global" value of transformational leadership should be treated cautiously for a number of reasons.[79]

First, the nature of the "positive impact" of transformational leadership can vary from place to place. For example, most studies done in Western cultures find improved job satisfaction to be one of the benefits of transformational leadership—something that does not seem to be the case in the Middle East or India. Second, research seems to suggest that regardless of the nature of any positive impacts, they are driven by different aspects of transformational leadership in different cultures or even unique, culture-specific aspects. For instance, research has found that doing one's duty (*dharma*) is a key component of transformational leadership in India while in China showing good moral character and sensitivity to others were important parts of transformational behavior.[80]

Some research suggests that transformational leadership behavior can actually have *negative* effects on innovation in an international context—as it did in one study that examined research alliances between American and Japanese firms. This underscores the impact of the international context (in this case, a complex research-oriented alliance) on leadership effectiveness as well as the need for more research about how transformational leadership works and under what circumstances.[81]

For now, we can say that the appeal of transformational leadership may be somewhat limited in collective cultures where group harmony is highly prized. In countries such as Japan, for instance, a charismatic leader who tries to galvanize individual performance could degrade group cohesiveness. Tweaking a transformational approach to focus on group performance may be a better bet. That said, implementing a transformational approach to leadership will likely be more difficult in Japan than in the U.S. Yet, most research on transformational leadership did not include foreigners or expatriates trying to be transformational leaders with local employees. As discussed previously, U.S. employees react differently to Japanese managers than American managers, even when their behavior is similar. One wonders, for example, whether a Japanese executive would have been seen as successful in taking over Nissan as French executive Carlos Ghosn was a few years ago. Seen as heroic by many Japanese, Ghosn came from Renault and turned struggling Nissan around. Of Lebanese decent, Ghosn was born in Brazil but raised in France. He closed unproductive plants and fired employees (decisions that raised eyebrows in Japan) while pushing for bold new products. Indeed, Ghosn's words on product design speak to his inspirational vision and intellectual stimulation of employees, both hallmarks of transformational leaders: "We are unleashing the imagination of our designers as part of our strategy for the market. You are going to see revolutionary designs from Nissan."[82]

Cross-Cultural Leadership Effectiveness: Pulling Everything Together

Clearly, there is no shortage of approaches to leadership. Unfortunately, when it comes to a comprehensive framework that can account for a variety of individual, organizational, and situational factors, including culture, we still have a long way to go. Nevertheless, our discussion concludes by presenting two content-based leadership frameworks that summarize the impact of culture on international leadership. These are not meant to be exhaustive guides nor should they preclude international managers from thinking critically about their specific leadership situations. Nevertheless, these two frameworks provide some important initial guidance for international managers to consider.

The first framework comes from the Global Leadership and Organizational Behavior Effectiveness (GLOBE) Project. An impressive research effort involving scholars from more than 60 countries, GLOBE described six basic leadership dimensions, identified whether they facilitated leadership effectiveness, and indicated where these dimensions would be most likely and least likely to be displayed by leaders (see Chapter 4). Figure 10.5 summarizes these findings from the GLOBE Project. What is interesting is that two leadership dimensions (charismatic/value-based, team-oriented) were found to contribute positively to effectiveness while one dimension (self-protective) was generally negative—regardless of country or culture. Naturally, there may still be country-specific implementation differences with respect to specific aspects of these dimensions. Overall though, these are the leadership dimensions that seem to have the most consistent impact on effectiveness across countries and cultures. For the remaining dimensions (autonomous, humane-oriented, participative), the results were mixed, with effectiveness much more a function of the cultural context. In short, in the right cultural environment, these dimensions could also prove to be moderately to highly effective.[83]

Leader Behavior Dimension	Description of Leader Dimension	Dimension Effective Across Countries/ Cultures?	Where Is Dimension Most/Least Prevalent?
Autonomous	Encourages individualistic and independent behavior	*Depends*—ranges from facilitating to impeding leader effectiveness	Most in Eastern Europe, least in Latin America
Charismatic/ value-based	Motivates/inspires, has high expectations; all driven by core beliefs	Generally *facilitates* leader effectiveness	Most prevalent in Anglo nations; least in Middle East
Humane orientation	Supportive, generous, considerate, compassionate	*Modestly facilitates* leader effectiveness, but has little impact in some places	Most prevalent in South Asia; least in Nordic countries
Participative	Involves others in making decisions	General *positive* impact on leader effectiveness, but considerable variation	Most prevalent in Germanic countries; least in Middle East
Self-protective	Concerned with safety, security, face-saving	Generally *negative* impact on leader effectiveness	Most prevalent in South Asia; least in Nordic countries
Team-oriented	Focuses on team building, and common goals among members	Generally *facilitates* leader effectiveness	Most prevalent in Latin America; least in Middle East

Figure 10.5 Leader Behavior Dimensions: Effectiveness and Prevalence Across Cultural Boundaries.
Source: Adapted from House, R. J., Hanges, P. J.,. Javidan, M., Dorfman, P. W., and Gupta, V. (eds) (2004). *Culture, Leadership, and Organizations: The GLOBE Study of 62 Societies*. Thousand Oaks, CA: Sage.

The *path–goal leadership* approach is arguably the most proscriptive model of all and predicts that leadership effectiveness is contingent on matching leadership style to the situation. This approach includes four basic leadership styles:

1. **Directive:** The leader provides clear procedures, guidelines, and rules for subordinates to follow when doing their jobs.
2. **Supportive:** The leader focuses on subordinates' needs and overall well-being to maintain positive relationships.
3. **Participative:** The leader consults with subordinates, solicits their opinions, and otherwise involves them in decision making.
4. **Achievement-oriented:** The leader focuses on maximizing subordinate performance by setting lofty goals and challenges, and emphasizes excellence.

To be most effective, leaders should use the style that best fits the demands of a particular situation. In fact, several factors may shape which style produces the highest motivation and performance among employees. For example, tasks that are poorly defined or unpredictable may require more directive leadership, everything else being equal. On the other hand, tasks that are well defined, with clear guidelines for performance, may be a better fit for participative leadership. Similarly, employees who lack experience may benefit from directive leadership, while employees who have well-developed skills may benefit from achievement-oriented leadership.[84]

If we consider Hofstede's cultural dimensions as modifiers of this path–goal approach, some useful applications can be generated for practicing managers. In general, participative leadership should work best in low power distance cultures (such as Sweden), while directive leadership should work best in high power distance societies (such as France). Countries with moderate levels of power distance (such as the U.S.) may find leadership that combines participation with some supportive behavior most attractive. A paternalistic style combining both supportive and directive behaviors should work best in collective societies (remember that collectivism is often associated with high power distance, e.g., Taiwan). Individualistic societies (such as Denmark), which are often associated with low power distance, should embrace participative leadership. Finally, strong uncertainty avoidance cultures may prefer directive leadership (such as Greece), while in cultures more tolerant of ambiguity, participative and achievement-oriented styles might be better received (such as England). It is important to remember that these are merely generalizations, albeit complex ones. International managers will still need to factor in even more complexity of the situation that they are in to determine which approach to leadership will work best in a specific context.[85]

Leadership Development in Multinationals

The leadership challenges discussed thus far can be daunting and add to an already difficult job. After all, leaders are not exactly welcomed with open arms and showered with positive feedback in their own countries where they largely manage their own nationals—let alone while working in a foreign culture. Figure 10.6 demonstrates the results of a study of nearly 30,000 employees who rated their senior management on five different attributes. Ratings included features such as the leader's ability to deal with company challenges and their people-management skills. The highest-rated leaders were from China and India—over 70 percent of employees rated leaders as effective in those countries. Overall, however, the average score given to leaders across the 21 countries was only 55 percent, with Japan bringing up the rear. Japanese leaders received awful ratings: only 35 percent of employees in Japan rated leaders as effective, a dramatic fall from the late 1980s when Japanese leaders drew wide praise for their various management techniques. (These data were collected before a sequence of tragedies in 2011 in Japan when an earthquake resulted in a massive tsunami, and which in turn produced a major nuclear disaster.) True to predictions of the path–goal theory, the study also showed that ratings of effectiveness varied across a number of situational circumstances, such as government vs. private settings and across high-tech vs. low-tech firms.

Many multinationals undoubtedly hope that the increasing similarity (in terms of structure, technology, and strategy) of companies around the world will weaken or overcome cross-cultural differences. But, these convergent forces may be offset by factors that continue to maintain, or even accentuate, cultural differences, as discussed next. Consequently, a safe

Skill/Development Area	A Transnational Manager . . .	A Traditional International Manager . . .
World view	Understands the business environment from a global perspective	Focuses on managing relationships between headquarters and a single foreign country
Culture knowledge	Learns about a variety of cultures	Becomes an expert on a single culture
Approach to learning	Learns from many cultures, creates a culturally synergistic workplace	Works with people in each foreign culture separately or sequentially, integrates foreigners into parent firm culture
Ability to adapt	Able to transition effectively to living in a variety of foreign cultures	Able to adapt to living in a single foreign culture
Cross-cultural interaction	Uses cross-cultural interaction skills daily	Uses cross-cultural interaction skills mainly on foreign assignments
Collaboration	Interacts with foreign managers as equals	Interacts within defined hierarchies of cultural and structural dominance
Foreign experience	Views foreign experience as critical for career development	Views foreign assignments as a mechanism for getting a job done

Figure 10.6 Comparing Transnational and Traditional Skills for International Managers.
Source: Adapted from Adler, N. J., and Bartholomew, S. (1992). Managing globally competent people. *Academy of Management Executive*, 6, 54.

assumption is that managers' effectiveness will continue to depend, at least in part, on how well they adapt their approaches to the cultural circumstances in which they lead. In fact, some U.S. (such as General Electric), European (such as Nokia), and Japanese (such as Sony) multinationals have created comprehensive programs to help develop better international managers. Some experts have gone so far as to say that multinationals also need training programs to help local employees interact more effectively with the international managers they have to work with—again, because of cultural differences.[86]

Other multinationals work to embed their corporate values into the work environment of various countries. They believe that by emphasizing corporate values, a more homogeneous international workforce can be created. This allows managers to use similar (and already tested and successful) leadership strategies everywhere that the firm does business. This assumes, of course, that employees are willing to accept corporate values at the expense of their own. Some successful examples include McDonald's and FedEx.

Building a global workforce with a common set of values is very difficult. Simply working for a multinational may actually accentuate local cultural values. In one study, cultural differences were more pronounced among employees working for a multinational than for employees working for domestic firms. It may be that the contrast accentuates differences that might otherwise blend in better. So, for example, Italians acted more "Italian" when they worked for a foreign firm than when they worked for an Italian company. The same was true for the other nationalities in the study.[87] Resistance is also likely when multinationals push foreign employees to embrace corporate values that explicitly conflict with local values. For example, an American multinational's effort to encourage participative decision making among European managers backfired—merely reinforcing the differences between corporate and local values. The conclusion reached by management was "horses for courses," or that some situations and cultures are more amenable to participative leadership than others.[88]

The Skills Needed for International Leadership

The best option for multinationals may be training and development programs aimed at building international leadership skills and experiences throughout the corporation. But that is just part of the job: firms also need to identify their aspiring international managers early, using valid and reliable methods. For instance, experts suggest that companies screen for personality attributes (e.g., extroversion) associated with greater receptiveness to developmental activities when selecting managers for international assignments.[89]

Once on an international leadership track, it will take managers time to acquire the skills needed to be effective. As the CEO of one international search firm put it, "cultural sensitivity does not always come naturally, so developing global executives often requires helping people to see their own biases." And doing that means more than simply plugging managers into a foreign outpost. Rotating people through international work assignments is just one part of a systematic and proactive effort to design a career plan that takes managers' experience and skills, as well as the company's needs, into account.[90]

Some firms have developed unique training programs for international leaders. At IBM, the most promising international managers are sent in small groups for one-month stints abroad to help solve social and economic problems in developing countries. This Peace Corps-type approach is aimed at teaching managers "how the world works" and exposes them to everything from installing water wells in Filipino villages to battling malaria in Ghana. Many managers return recognizing the need to change their leadership styles.[91] The Global Innovations feature details the public accounting firm PricewaterhouseCoopers' unique approach to leadership development.

Global Innovations

It Takes a Village: Developing an International Leadership Cadre at PwC

Alain Michaud was reflecting on the time he spent in Paraguay and what he learned in his time there. Tahir Ayub talked about his experiences in the Namibian outback. And, Jennifer Chang was wowed by the time she spent in Belize—great experiences all. But, Chang was not reflecting on one of those exotic eco-tourism vacations that are all the rage now. Nor were the others sharing great get-away experiences they found out about in *Travel* magazine. Instead, they were commenting on the impact of an innovative leadership training program called Ulysses© that each had participated in with their firm, PricewaterhouseCoopers (PwC).

In 2000, PwC started Ulysses with the purpose of building a network of global leaders for the firm. The goal was to send promising senior managers and leaders overseas to gain experience in cultural diversity and to better equip them to work and lead in a "global stakeholder society." So, Mr. Ayub, a PwC partner, worked in a Namibian village to help local leaders deal with their community's terrible AIDS crisis. The cultural disconnect was huge—which was something that PwC was looking for in this and other assignments, such as Ms. Chang's in Belize, where she lived among residents in dirt-floored houses and some dreadful poverty. Mr. Ayub and two colleagues had to leave behind their iPhones and the PowerPoint presentations and work from the break of dawn to nightfall to provide help for the community. Others completed similar projects in their eight-week stints.

Does this "walk a mile in someone else's shoes" approach make for an effective leader development tool? PwC thinks so. While the results are hard to quantify, they point to the tangible benefits noticed among participants and their impact on others. Among other things, increased understanding of others, deeper listening skills, and the value of trust in interactions have all been cited by participants.

Likewise, Genesis Park is a related program deployed by the firm. This is a ten-week assignment also designed to develop leadership and innovation. Nascent leaders are nominated by their managers to work on real-life problems in multicultural teams, with input from diverse leaders in their field. The problems are strategic rather than technical and ones that PwC's clients are likely to encounter (e.g., how does PwC enter a new market?). The teams collaborate together, obtain necessary information, throw around innovative and creative solutions, evaluate results, and then prepare recommendations for PwC leadership. The teams live in close quarters during their ten weeks together and are pushed hard. At the start, they are told that they will be challenged "physically, emotionally, professionally, and intellectually." The expected results are surprisingly non-tangible, especially for an accounting firm: leaders become more creative; innovative; better able to understand client and firm problems; and are better able to understand wider personal, political, and global realities. PwC is careful to monitor and to build on the benefits accrued from these and other global leadership development programs.

If you reflect on your view of public accounting firms, it may conjure up images of staid, conservative approaches to problems, managers reactive more than proactive in their stance. Yet, in our opinion, accounting firms are often at the vanguard of modern human resource practices and these innovative leadership programs mentioned are but a couple more examples of global innovation that we have seen.[92]

Regardless of how they acquire it, international managers should have a perspective on cultural issues that is not limited to a particular country or region. The continuing internationalization of business is increasing the need for more and different cross-cultural relationships—something, for example, that Lenovo recognized after they purchased and merged with IBM's PC division. Management worked to train leaders to develop a style that combined Eastern and Western cultural features.[93] This merging of cultures will probably be a more common experience in the coming decade. As a result, a country-based or regional set of experiences and skills is insufficient over the long haul. Ultimately, managers need transnational leadership skills to be effective—some of these are listed in Figure 10.6.

Relatively few multinationals have made a comprehensive and sustained effort to develop managers with transnational leadership skills such as those by IBM or PwC. But, this is changing and more substantial leadership development programs are replacing the limited, modest efforts undertaken by most firms.[94] Chapter 11 will consider international human resources in more detail and illustrate how firms can link leadership development to their business objectives. Some general suggestions for a transnational leadership development strategy are summarized in Figure 10.7 and include ideas for both individuals as well as corporate training programs. Companies serious about preparing their managers for international leadership challenges will take these ideas to heart.[95]

Suggestions for Individuals	Description/Explanation
Be open to new global experiences both emotionally and intellectually	Key skill to develop is tolerance for ambiguity; treat international experiences as learning opportunities
Avoid making assumptions or forcing your values onto others	Focusing on what others in an international context will help you recognize and bridge cultural differences
Do your cross-cultural homework	It's essential to put time into researching the cultures where you'll work—read as much as you can/find mentors to help
Grab opportunities to meet foreign colleagues face to face	Video conferences save money, but there's no substitute for face-to-face interaction to learn/build relationships
Reflect on your limitations	Understanding your strengths/weaknesses will help you make the most out of any international experience

Suggestions for Corporations	Description/Explanation
Emphasize overseas experience for managers	Work experience is a key for developing international managers
Make sure leadership development and key human resource practices are aligned	Building international skills into appraisal and promotion processes reinforces the value of international development
Create support mechanisms for development	This helps track careers and development activity effectiveness
Make senior executives responsible for leadership development	Top management is in the best position to build visible and influential support for international development efforts

Figure 10.7 Individual and Corporate Suggestions for Developing Transnational Leadership Skills.

Sources: Adapted from Conner, J. (2000). Developing the global leaders of tomorrow. *Human Resource Management*, 39, 147–157; and Frost, J., and Walker, M. (2007). Cross-cultural leadership. *Engineering Management*, June/July, 27–29.

Chapter Summary

This chapter discussed the challenge of motivating and leading across cultural boundaries. A key point is that most research on these topics was done by Americans on Americans, with all their accompanying cultural baggage. If managers need to know which motivational approaches and techniques work well overseas, then what might be common wisdom in the U.S. may be inappropriate in other countries. There are relatively few universal approaches when it comes to motivation. But even if the underlying principles (e.g., equity) being used are the same, how they are framed and presented needs to reflect local values to be effective, at least to an extent.

Overall, managers should take cultural variables into account in designing reward systems and motivational strategies. Action steps that international managers can take in order to develop synergistic solutions to motivation issues start with efforts made by managers to understand their own value systems, as well as employees', before tackling motivation issues. This can be valuable in generating motivational approaches that meet goals in ways that are sensitive to local cultural values and dynamics. At the same time, while it is important to be sensitive to host-country norms, we should not take those as fixed or uniform.

Similar conclusions were reached about what makes for effective leadership in an international context. Leader behavior can vary across cultures and that a manager's international effectiveness can be increased by awareness of this fact. Indeed, what constitutes *effective* leadership behavior and style also differs across cultures to some degree. A take-charge, aggressive style may work well in many situations in the U.S., whereas in the Netherlands it may be less successful. It is suggested that multinationals need leaders with transnational skills throughout their ranks.

Discussion Questions

1. What difficulties might international managers encounter when implementing each of the motivation approaches discussed in this chapter? What specific concerns might come up if managers were trying to motivate Japanese employees? Mexican employees?

2. What steps would you take to develop a culturally synergistic approach to motivation challenges? What difficulties might you encounter in trying to implement those steps?

3. Describe how some popular leadership approaches, such as *transformational leadership* and the *path–goal model* might operate in different countries. How can those explain why different leader behaviors can have the same positive effects across cultures?

4. How can corporations identify and develop managers with transnational leadership skills?

Up to the Challenge?

Leadership with Seoul: Korean Firms Are Mindful of Their Roots While Trying New Approaches

This chapter opens with a discussion of the traditional South Korean leadership style—one that may be out of step with the premium placed on creativity and nimbleness that seems to characterize today's global economy. This authoritarian and closed leadership style seems to flow from traditional Confucian values that emphasize family, seniority or age, and loyalty. How can a South Korean firm overcome these ingrained, base values? It will not be easy, as illustrated in the opening feature, due to the emotions raised by changes introduced at the Bank of Korea in terms of promotions and other management practices.

Yet, this has not prevented other Korean firms from trying. Take, for example, SK Telecom—a big Korean provider of cell phones that recently saw business level off in its home market. In the process of considering moves into new markets, particularly China and the U.S., SK Telecom concluded that success would require a revamp of its leadership culture. The changes made were radical, particularly by South Korean standards, and included a flatter leadership structure and incentive systems tied directly to performance. The company started promoting people based on performance and ability instead of age or seniority, giving employees in their 20s leadership of important product teams. The management hierarchy was also pared down, the dress code relaxed, and employees encouraged to voice opinions to their bosses.

The result was more idea flow and free-wheeling discussions that led to new product initiatives. Some old-guard managers struggled to adapt even as they recognized the merits of the new approach. As one of them put it after being challenged by a younger employee with admittedly better ideas, "For a moment I wished it was back in the old days when I could have shut that guy down."

A more well-known Korean firm, LG Electronics (part of the giant *chaebol* LG Group), took a different approach to shaking up its leadership. It put Westerners in top executive roles, luring them from companies like P&G, IBM, HP, and Unilever to run marketing, purchasing, HR, and supply-chain management efforts for the company.

An engineering powerhouse that grew into a good-but-not-great producer of TVs, cell phones, and appliances, LG Electronics had become complacent. The firm decided it wanted to be a premium player in the global marketplace and concluded that it needed to shake up company leadership to meet the challenge. Of course, bringing in the Westerners brought challenges of its own. Executive meetings became feisty as the newcomers pushed and probed the Koreans' thinking. Some Korean managers felt that Western leadership styles clashed too much with Confucian values. Nevertheless, both sides hung in, putting significant efforts into building a bridge between the two cultures. And, having interpreters constantly present also helped.

Korean Airlines conducted a similar staff shuffle in 2012, making a point of promoting a 44-year-old woman as part of its senior leadership team. They explained that "KAL is a very conservative company but, we're moving toward a merit-based system to induce competition." Perhaps the best example of the priority on merit over age occurred when a Dutch soccer coach, Guus Hiddink, took over the national Korean soccer team prior to the last World Cup. He was stunned to see that the internal hierarchy was so strong that younger players felt obliged to pass the ball to older ones. Coach Hiddink promoted better younger players and eliminated the older player preference as part of a revamp. South Korea became the first Asian team to reach the World Cup semifinals and Hiddink became a national hero. Leadership courses even sprung up touting the "Hiddink Way." Today, Korea continues to build toward a new future and a new leadership sensibility. They are doing it by integrating non-traditional aspects of leadership without abandoning their Korean roots.[96]

International Development

How Are Your Cross-Cultural Motivation Skills?

Purpose

To learn more about the challenge of motivating people from different cultures.

Instructions

Several short descriptions of situations involving Chinese, Egyptian, Japanese, Saudi, and American subordinates are presented, along with alternatives for motivating them. Think about, and select, an answer for each situation. Your instructor may ask you to break into small groups to come up with a consensus answer for each example in class. Your group can then make a brief presentation about your answers and rationales. Your instructor can then lead a discussion about the most appropriate answers for each situation.

Motivation Situations

1. You would like to have a Saudi Arabian colleague's help so that you can finish a major assignment. You are most likely to get that help if you say:
   a. "In the name of God, please help me."
   b. "If you help me, I'll buy you dinner."
   c. "My friend, I need your help."
   d. "Let's be the first to finish this assignment."
2. You are a department manager in China. Which of the following would probably work best to motivate your production supervisor to improve performance?
   a. "If our department increases output by 20 percent, you'll get a 5 percent bonus."
   b. "I'm planning to reorganize the department and I'm thinking of promoting you if production increases."
   c. "If your team doesn't meet the quotas, you're fired."
   d. "Why don't you put in some overtime to help make the production quotas?"

3. You are a manager about to conduct a series of performance appraisals on your American subordinates. To motivate them, you will probably want to focus on recognizing the Americans' . . .
  a. promptness
  b. creativity
  c. directness and openness
  d. accomplishments.
4. Last month your Japanese team hit all production targets. Which of the following would be the best way to acknowledge their achievement?
  a. Treat them to a dinner where you give special recognition to the team leader.
  b. Do not mention it, because meeting targets is their job.
  c. Call the oldest team member aside and thank him or her.
  d. Thank the group at your next meeting and ask them to increase production even more.
5. You are managing a factory in Egypt. One supervisor's group is not meeting your production expectations. Which of the following might be the best way for you to draw the supervisor's attention to this problem?
  a. "Increase your group's productivity or you're fired."
  b. "Do you need any help with your group?"
  c. "You'd better take care of your group, or I may have to move to another job."
  d. "Why don't you hold a meeting with your group to find out what's wrong?"
6. You are a manager in a large international company and are about to begin an important project. Mr. Hiro has been assigned to work for you on this project. Because Mr. Hiro is Japanese, which of the following is likely to motivate him?
  a. Being part of a strong, leading international firm
  b. A good raise in his annual salary
  c. A promotion to group leader and a better title
  d. A trip to Hawaii after the project is completed.

Source: Based on materials from Elashmawi, F., and Harris, P. R. (1993). *Multicultural Management: New Skills for Global Business*, 148–151. © 1993 by Gulf Publishing Company. Used with permission. All rights reserved.

From Theory to International Practice

Leadership Transitions in BRIC Countries: Understanding the New Economic Powerhouses

Purpose

To conduct a detailed analysis of how leadership approaches have evolved in what are commonly referred to as the "BRIC countries" (i.e., Brazil, Russia, India, and China). These countries have all experienced rapid economic growth in recent years. Russia and China also have had long experience with authoritarian regimes.

Instructions

All four BRIC countries are expected to continue to play increasingly large roles in the global economy in the years ahead. Consequently, assessing how their business leadership has evolved over the years will help us better understand these countries as well as their associated strengths or weaknesses. Your instructor will assign you one of the BRIC countries to research and will place you into small groups (ideally four to six) to do research on the basic approach to leadership used in a specific BRIC country you are assigned to. This research effort should be done outside of class and focus on:

a. the dominant business leadership approaches used in your assigned country 30 years ago (i.e., before the fall of the Soviet Union);

b. an assessment of how business leadership has evolved in your assigned country since then and why;

c. an analysis of any additional changes in leadership and management practices that need to be made if your assigned country is to become a more formidable global competitor;

d. suggestions for how remaining barriers to change can be overcome (including how changes in leadership values and management practices can be encouraged).

Your instructor may ask each group make a presentation (20 minutes) about its findings to class. This could be followed by a discussion about common as well as unique leadership themes in the BRIC countries as well as the role of cultural values. If your instructor decides to make this an individual assignment, be prepared to take part in a general class discussion on the issues raised.

Research Tips

To get started with your research, you may want to consult the websites below for background information and profiles about BRIC countries. These websites should help you refine your research efforts and act as a gateway to articles, reports, and other websites about leadership issues and management practices in your assigned country:

- **https://www.cia.gov/library/publications/the-world-factbook/index.html:** the CIA World Factbook. It provides in-depth information about individual nations.

- **www.imf.org/external/country/index.htm**: the International Monetary Fund Country Information page.

- **www.worldbank.org:** the World Bank website (see the Data and Statistics subpage for country-specific information).

Notes

1. Nam, In-Soo (2012). New attitudes on age rattle Korean hierarchies. *The Wall Street Journal*, October 18, A12; Yang, J. (2012). Samsung's latest battle is all in the family. *Bloomberg Businessweek*, June 11–17, 25–26; Ihlwan, M. (2008). The foreigners at the top of LG. *BusinessWeek*, December 22, 55–57; Ramstad, E. (2007). Pulling rank gets harder at one Korean company. *The Wall Street Journal*, August 20, B1, B3.

2. Adler, N. J., and Gundersen, A. (2008). *International Dimensions of Organizational Behavior* (5th ed.); Communal, C., and Senior, B. (1999). National culture and management: Messages conveyed by British, French, and German advertisements of managerial appointments. *Leadership and Organizational Development Journal*, 20, 26–35.

3. Granato, J., Inglehart, R., and Leblang, D. (1996). The effect of cultural values on economic development: Theory, hypotheses, and some empirical tests. *American Journal of Political Science*, 40, 607–631.

4. Gelfand, M. J., Erez, M., and Aycan, Z. (2007). Cross-cultural organizational behavior. *Annual Review of Psychology*, 58, 479–514; Huang, X. (2008). Motivation and job satisfaction across nations. In P. B. Smith, M. F. Peterson, and D. C. Thomas (eds) *The Handbook of Cross-Cultural Management Research*, 77–93. Thousand Oaks, CA: Sage; Thomas, D. C., Au, K., and Ravlin, E. C. (2003). Cultural variation and the psychological contract. *Journal of Organizational Behavior*, 24, 451–471.

5. Rodrigues, C. (1990). The situation and national culture as contingencies for leadership behavior: Two conceptual models. In B. Prasad (ed.) *Advances in International Comparative Management*, Vol. 5, 51–68. Greenwich, CT: JAI Press.

6. d'Iribarne, P. (2002). Motivating workers in emerging countries: Universal tools and local applications. *Journal of Organizational Behavior*, 23, 243–256.

7. Yukl, G. (2010). *Leadership in Organizations* (7th ed.). Upper Saddle River, NJ: Prentice Hall.

8. Lenartowicz, T., and Roth, K. (2001). Does subculture within a country matter? A cross-cultural study of motivational domains and business performance in Brazil. *Journal of International Business Studies*, 32, 305–325.

9. Hofstede, G. (1996). An American in Paris: The influence of nationality on organization theories. *Organizational Studies*, 17, 525–537.

10. Maslow, A. H. (1970). *Motivation and Personality* (2nd ed.). New York: Harper & Row.

11. Greenberg, J., and Baron, R. A. (2001). *Behavior in Organizations* (7th ed.). Englewood Cliffs, NJ: Prentice-Hall.

12. *The Economist*. (2007). Where money seems to talk, July 14, 63–64; Gelfand, Erez, and Aycan, Cross-cultural organizational behavior; Hayward, R. D., and Kemmelmeier, M. (2007). How competition is viewed across cultures. *Cross-Cultural Research*, 41(4), 364–395.

13. Shenkar, O., and Von Glinow, M. A. (1994). Paradoxes of organizational theory and research: Using the case of China to illustrate national contingency. *Management Science*, 40, 56–71.

14. Sagie, A., Elizur, D., and Yamauchi, H. (1996). The strength and structure of achievement motivation: A cross-cultural comparison. *Journal of Organizational Behavior*, 17, 431–444.

15. Brown, I. T. (2009). In Western Europe, more partners than bosses, available at: www.gallup.com/poll/114076/western-europe-partners-bosses.aspx; Borg, I., and Braun, M. (1996). Work values in East and West Germany: Different weights, but identical structures. *Journal of Organizational Behavior*, 17, 541–555; Frese, M., Kring, W., Soose, A., and Zempel, J. (1996). Personal initiative at work: Differences between East and West Germany. *Academy of Management Journal*, 39, 37–63.

16. Adler and Gundersen, *International Dimensions of Organizational Behavior*; Ronen, S. and Shenkar, O. (1985). Clustering countries on attitudinal dimensions: A review and synthesis. *Academy of Management Review*, 10, 435–454.

17. Herzberg, F. (1966). *Work and the Nature of Man*. Cleveland, OH: World.

18. Adler and Gundersen, *International Dimensions of Organizational Behavior*.

19. Kanungo, R. N., and Wright, R. W. (1983). A cross-cultural comparative study of managerial job attitudes. *Journal of International Business Studies*, 14, 115–129.
20. Hofstede, G. (2001). *Culture's Consequences* (2nd ed.). Thousand Oaks, CA: Sage.
21. Mendonca, M., and Kanungo, R. N. (1994). Motivation through participative management. In R. N. Kanungo and M. Mendonca (eds) *Work Motivation: Models for Developing Countries*, 184–212. Thousand Oaks, CA: Sage; Robert, C., Probst, T. M., Martocchio, J. J., Drasgow, F., and Lawler, J. J. (2000). Empowerment and continuous improvement in the United States, Mexico, Poland, and India. *Journal of Applied Psychology*, 85, 643–658.
22. Vauclair, C., Hanke, K., Fischer, R., and Fontaine, J. (2011). The structure of human values at the cultural level: A meta-analytical replication of Schwartz's value orientations using the Rokeach Value Survey. *Journal of Cross Cultural Psychology*, 42, 186–205; Schaubroeck, J., Lam, S. S. K., and Xie, J. L. (2000). Collective efficacy versus self-efficacy in coping responses to stressors and control: A cross-cultural study. *Journal of Applied Psychology*, 85, 512–525.
23. Randolph, W. A., and Sashkin, M. (2002). Can organizational empowerment work in multinational settings? *Academy of Management Executive*, 16, 102–115.
24. d'Iribarne, P. (2002). Motivating workers in emerging countries: Universal tools and local applications. *Journal of Organizational Behavior*, 23, 243–256.
25. *The Economist.* (2002). A survey of management: The return of von Clausewitz, March 9, 18–20; Boyle, M. (2001). Nothing is rotten in Denmark. *Fortune*, February 19, 242.
26. *The Economist.* (2009). Ding dong! Empowerment calling, May 30, 70; Banerjee, N. (1995). For Mary Kay sales reps in Russia, hottest shade is the color of money. *The Wall Street Journal*, August 30, A8; also see www.marykay.com/en-US/About-Mary-Kay/Pages/CountrySelector.aspx.
27. Gelade, G. A., Dobson, P., and Auer, K. (2008). Individualism, masculinity, and the sources of organizational commitment. *Journal of Cross-Cultural Psychology*, 39(5), 599–617.
28. Adams, J. S. (1965). Inequity in social exchange. In L. Berkowitz (ed.) *Advances in Experimental Social Psychology*, Vol. 2, 267–299. New York: Academic Press.
29. Choi, J., and Chen, C. C. (2007). The relationships of distributive justice and compensation system fairness to employee attitudes in international joint ventures. *Journal of Organizational Behavior*, 28, 687–703; Fischer, R., Smith, P. B., Richey, B., Ferreira, M. C., Assmar, E. M. L., Maes, J., and Stumpf, S. (2007). How do organizations allocate rewards? The predictive validity of national values, economic and organizational factors across six nations. *Journal of Cross-Cultural Psychology*, 38(1), 3–18; Morris, M. W., and Leung, K. (2000). Justice for all? Progress in research on cultural variation in the psychology of distributive and procedural justice. *Applied Psychology: An International Review*, 49, 100–132.
30. Gelfand, Erez, and Aycan, Cross-cultural organizational behavior; Hofstede, *Culture's Consequences*.
31. Kim, K. L., Park, H. J., and Suzuki, N. (1990). Reward allocations in the U.S., Japan, and Korea: A comparison of individualistic and collectivistic cultures. *Academy of Management Journal*, 33, 188–198; Bond, M. H., Leung, K., and Wan, K. C. (1982). How does cultural collectivism operate? The impact of task and maintenance contribution on reward distribution. *Journal of Cross-Cultural Psychology*, 13, 186–200.
32. Fischer, R. (2008). Organizational justice and reward allocation. In Smith, Peterson, and Thomas, *The Handbook of Cross-Cultural Management Research*, 135–150; Giacobbe-Miller, J. K., Miller, D. J., Zhang, W., and Victorov, V. I. (2003). Country and organizational-level adaptation to foreign workplace ideologies: A comparative study of distributive justice values in China, Russia, and the United States. *Journal of International Business*, 34, 389–406.
33. Wonacott, P. (2002). China's secret weapon: Smart, cheap labor for high-tech goods. *The Wall Street Journal*, March 14, A1, A6; Chen, C. C. (1995). New trends in rewards allocation preferences: A Sino–U.S. comparison. *Academy of Management Journal*, 38, 408–428.
34. Mangaliso, M. P. (2001). Building competitive advantage from Ubuntu: Management lessons from South Africa. *The Academy of Management Executive*, 15, 23–33; McFarlin, D. B., Coster, E. A., and Mogale-Pretorius, C. (1999). Management development in South Africa: Moving toward an Africanized framework. *Journal of Management Development*, 18, 63–78.

35. Bailey, J. R., and Chen, C. C. (1997). Conceptions of self and performance-related feedback in the U.S., Japan, and China. *Journal of International Business Studies*, 28, 605–625; Gelfand, Erez, and Aycan, Cross-cultural organizational behavior.

36. Podsakoff, P. M., Dorfman, P. W., Howell, J. P., and Tudor, W. D. (1986). Leader reward and punishment behaviors: A preliminary test of a culture-free style of leadership effectiveness. In Farmer, *Advances in International Comparative Management*, Vol. 2, 95–138.

37. Hofstede, *Culture's Consequences*.

38. Mendonca and Kanungo, Motivation through effective reward management in developing countries.

39. d'Iribarne, P. (2002). Motivating workers in emerging countries: Universal tools and local applications. *Journal of Organizational Behavior*, 23, 243–256.

40. Porter, L. P., and Lawler, E. E. (1968). *Managerial Attitudes and Performance*. Homewood, IL: Irwin; Vroom, V. H. (1964). *Work and Motivation*. New York: Wiley.

41. Shenkar and Von Glinow, Paradoxes of organizational theory and research: Using the case of China to illustrate national contingency.

42. Pennings, J. M. (1993). Executive reward systems: A cross-national comparison. *Journal of Management Studies*, 30, 261–279.

43. *The Economist*. (2008). Executive pay in Europe: Pay attention, June 14, 77–78; Reilly, D., Ball, D., and Ascarelli, S. (2003). Europe's low pay-rage threshold. *The Wall Street Journal*, September 10, A8, A9.

44. *The Economist*, Executive pay in Europe: Pay attention; Stewart, M. (1996). German management: A challenge to Anglo-American managerial assumptions. *Business Horizons*, 39, 52–54; Walker, M. (2002). Deutsche Bank finds that it has to cut German roots to grow. *The Wall Street Journal*, February 14, A1, A10.

45. Ono, Y. (2001). A restaurant chain in Japan chops up the social contract. *The Wall Street Journal*, January 17, A1, A19; Tabuchi, H. (2008). Slacker nation? Young Japanese shun promotions. *The Wall Street Journal*, November 1–2, A1, A6.

46. *The Economist*. (2008). Sayonara salaryman, January 5, 68–70; *The Economist*. (2002). Foreign firms in Japan: Finding hidden talent, October 26, 58.

47. Ono, Y. (2002). Rethinking how Japanese should think, *The Wall Street Journal*, March 25, A12, A14.

48. Gomez-Mejia, L., and Welbourne, T. (1991). Compensation strategies in a global context. *Human Resource Planning*, 14, 29–41.

49. Schneider, S. C., and Barsoux, J. L. (2003). *Managing Across Cultures*. Harlow, England: Pearson Education; Thomas, D. C. (2008). *Cross-Cultural Management: Essential Concepts* (2nd ed.). Thousand Oaks, CA: Sage.

50. Adler and Gundersen, *International Dimensions of Organizational Behavior*.

51. Aycan, Z. (2008). Cross-cultural approaches to leadership. In Smith, Peterson, and Thomas, *The Handbook of Cross-Cultural Management Research*, 219–238; Gupta, A. K., and Govindarajan, V. (2002). Cultivating a global mindset. *Academy of Management Executive*, 16, 116–126.

52. Mendenhall, M. E., Reiche, B. S., Bird, A., and Osland, J. S. (2012). Defining the "global" in global leadership. *Journal of World Business*, 47, 493–503; Pankaj, G. (2012). Developing global leaders. *McKinsey Quarterly*, 3, 100–109.

53. Dickson, M. W., Castano, N., Magomaeva, A., and Hartog, D. N. (2012). Conceptualizing leadership across cultures. *Journal of World Business*, 47, 483–492.

54. Atwater, L., Wang, M., Smither, J. W., and Fleenor, J. W. (2009). Are cultural characteristics associated with the relationship between self and others' ratings of leadership? *Journal of Applied Psychology*, 94(4), 876–886; House, R. J., Hanges, P. J., Javidan, M., Dorfman, P. W., and Gupta, V. (eds) *Culture, Leadership, and Organizations: The GLOBE Study of 62 Societies*. Thousand Oaks, CA: Sage.

55. Kostera, M., Proppe, M., and Szatkowski, M. (1995). Staging the new romantic hero in the old cynical theatre: On managers, roles and change in Poland. *Journal of Organizational Behavior*,

16, 631–646; Kets De Vries, M. F. R. (2000). A journey into the "Wild East:" Leadership style and organizational practices in Russia. *Organizational Dynamics*, 28, 67–81.

56. Thomas, D. C. (2008). *Cross-Cultural Management: Essential Concepts*; Wendt, H., Euwema, M. C., and van Emmerik, I. J. H. (2009). Leadership and team cohesiveness across cultures. *The Leadership Quarterly*, 20, 358–370; Yukl, *Leadership in Organizations*.

57. Sinha, J. B. P. (1980). *The Nurturant Task Leader: A Model of Effective Executive*. New Delhi: Concept; Sinha, J. B. P. (1984). A model of effective leadership styles in India. *International Studies of Management & Organization*, 14, 86–98; Singh, N., and Krishnan, V. R. (2007). Transformational leadership in India. *International Journal of Cross-Cultural Management*, 7(2), 219–236.

58. *The Economist*. (2011). Out of India: A briefing on the Tata group, March 5, 75–78.

59. Cappelli, P., Singh, H., Singh, J., and Useem, M. (2010). The India way: Lessons for the U.S. *Academy of Management Perspectives*, May, 6–24; McGregor, J. (2007). The employee is always right. *BusinessWeek*, November 19, 80–82.

60. McGregor, The employee is always right.

61. Dvorak, P. (2006). Making U.S. management ideas work elsewhere. *The Wall Street Journal*, May 22, B3; Peterson, M. P., Brannen, M. Y., and Smith, P. B. (1994). Japanese and United States leadership: Issues in current research. In S. B. Prasad (ed.) *Advances in International Comparative Management*, Vol. 9, 57–82. Greenwich, CT: JAI Press; Thomas, D. C. (2008). *Cross-Cultural Management: Essential Concepts*. Thousand Oaks, CA: Sage.

62. Davila, A., and Elvira, M. M. (2012). Humanistic leadership lessons from Latin America. *Journal of World Business*, 47, 548–554; Pellegrini, E. K., and Scandura, T. A. (2008). Paternalistic leadership: A review and agenda for future research. *Journal of Management*, 34(3), 566–593.

63. Ayman, R., and Chemers, M. M. (1983). Relationship of supervisory behavior ratings to work group effectiveness and subordinate satisfaction among Iranian managers. *Journal of Applied Psychology*, 68, 338–341.

64. Doktor, R. H. (1990). Asian and American CEOs: A comparative study. *Organizational Dynamics*, 18, 46–57.

65. Smith, P. B., Misumi, J., Tayeb, M., Peterson, M., and Bond, M. (1989). On the generality of leadership style measures across cultures. *Journal of Occupational Psychology*, 62, 97–109.

66. Tolich, M., Kenney, M., and Biggart, N. (1999). Managing the managers: Japanese strategies in the U.S.A. *Journal of Management Studies*, 36, 587–607.

67. Dorfman, P. W., and Howell, J. P. (1988). Dimensions of national culture and effective leadership: Hofstede revisited. In R. N. Farmer and E. McGoun (eds) *Advances in International Comparative Management*, Vol. 3, 127–150.

68. Peterson, Brannen, and Smith, Japanese and United States leadership: Issues in current research; Thomas, *Cross-Cultural Management: Essential Concepts*.

69. Morris, T., and Pavett, C. M. (1992). Management style and productivity in two cultures. *Journal of International Business Studies,* First Quarter, 169–179.

70. Morris and Pavett, Management style and productivity in two cultures; Pellegrini, E. K., and Scandura, T. A. (2008). Paternalistic leadership: A review and agenda for future research. *Journal of Management*, 34(3), 566–593.

71. d'Iribarne, Motivating workers in emerging countries: Universal tools and local applications.

72. de Forest, M. E. (1994). Thinking of a plant in Mexico? *Academy of Management Executive*, 8, 33–40; Gowan, M., Ibarreche, S., and Lackey, C. (1996). Doing the right things in Mexico. *Academy of Management Executive*, 10, 74–81; Stephens, G., and Geer, C. R. (1995). Doing business in Mexico: Understanding cultural differences. *Organizational Dynamics*, 24, 39–55.

73. Keys, J. B., Denton, L. T., and Miller, T. R. (1994). The Japanese management theory jungle revisited. *Journal of Management*, 20, 373–402.

74. Black, J. S., and Porter, L. W. (1990). Managerial behaviors and job performance: A successful manager in Los Angeles may not succeed in Hong Kong. *Journal of International Business Studies*, First Quarter, 99–112.

75. Black, S., and Morrison, A. J. (2012). The Japanese global leadership challenge: What it means for the rest of the world. *Asia Pacific Business Review*, 18, 551–566.

76. Karnitschnig, M. (2005). Too many chiefs at Siemens? *The Wall Street Journal,* January 20, A12; Karnitschnig, M. (2003). For Siemens, move into U.S. causes waves back home. *The Wall Street Journal*, September 8, A1, A8.

77. See Yukl, *Leadership in Organizations*.

78. Bass, B. M. (1990). *Stogdill's Handbook of Leadership: A Survey of Theory and Research*. New York: Free Press.

79. Bass, B. M., and Avolio, B. J. (1992). Developing transformational leadership: 1992 and beyond. *Journal of European Industrial Training*, 14, 21–27; Brodbeck, F., Frese, F., and Javidan, M. (2002). Leadership made in Germany: Low on compassion, high on performance. *Academy of Management Executive*, 16, 16–30.

80. Aycan, Cross-cultural approaches to leadership.

81. Osborn, R. N., and Marion, R. (2009). Contextual leadership, transformational leadership and the performance of international innovation seeking alliances. *The Leadership Quarterly*, 20, 191–206; Rossant, J. (2002). The fast fall of France's celebrity CEOs, *BusinessWeek*, April 1, 48; Yukl, *Leadership in Organizations*.

82. Takahashi, K., Ishikawa, J., and Kanai, T. (2012). Qualitative and quantitative studies of leadership in multinational settings. *Journal of World Business*, 47, 530–538; Aycan, Cross-cultural approaches to leadership; Taylor, A. (2003). Nissan shifts into higher gear. *Fortune*, July 21, 98–104.

83. Dorfman, P., Javidan, M., Hanges, P., Dastmalchian, A., and House, R. J. (2012). GLOBE: A 20-year journey into the intriguing world of culture and leadership. *Journal of World Business*, 47, 504–518; House, Hanges, Javidan, Dorfman, and Gupta, *Culture, Leadership, and Organizations: The GLOBE Study of 62 Societies*.

84. House, R. J. (1971). A path–goal theory of leader effectiveness. *Administrative Science Quarterly*, 16, 321–339.

85. Mittal, R., and Dorfman, P. (2012). Servant leadership across cultures. *Journal of World Business*, 47, 555–570; Rodrigues, The situation and national culture as contingencies for leadership behavior: Two conceptual models.

86. Chhokar, J. S., Brodbeck, F. C., and House, R. J. (eds) (2007). *Culture and Leadership Across the World: The GLOBE Book of In-Depth Studies of 25 Societies*. Mahwah, NJ: Erlbaum; Gupta, A. K., and Govindarajan, V. (2002). Cultivating a global mindset. *Academy of Management Executive*, 16, 116–126; Herrmann, P., and Werbel, J. (2007). Promotability of host-country nationals: A cross-cultural study. *British Journal of Management*, 18, 281–293.

87. Adler and Gundersen, *International Dimensions of Organizational Behavior*; Laurent, A. (1983). The cultural diversity of Western conceptions of management. *International Studies of Management and Organization*, 13, 75–96.

88. McFarlin, D. B., Sweeney, P. D., and Cotton, J. C. (1992). Attitudes toward employee participation in decision-making: A comparison of European and American managers in a United States multinational company. *Human Resource Management*, 31, 363–383.

89. Caligiuri, P., and Tarique, I. (2012). Dynamic cross-cultural competencies and global leadership effectiveness. *Journal of World Business*, 47, 612–622; Caligiuri, P., and Tarique, I. (2009). Predicting effectiveness in global leadership activities. *Journal of World Business*, 44, 336–346; Adler, N. J., and Bartholomew, S. (1992). Managing globally competent people. *Academy of Management Executive*, 6, 52–65; Spreitzer, G. M., McCall, M. W., and Mahoney, J. D. (1997). Early identification of international executive potential. *Journal of Applied Psychology*, 82, 6–29.

90. Pankaj, Developing global leaders; Meiland, D. (2003). In search of global leaders. *Harvard Business Review*, August, 44–45; Youssef, C. M., and Luthans, F. (2012). Positive global leadership. *Journal of World Business*, 47, 539–547.

91. Hamm, S. (2009). The globe is IBM's classroom. *BusinessWeek*, March 23 and 30, 56–57; also see: Lateef, S. M. (2012). Setting the gold standard. *Training & Development*, July, 50–54 for

another example of a successful global leadership training program at Genpact, a global supplier of business process management and tech services.

92. Please see the PwC page on the Genesis Park program for more details on its operation: www.pwc.com/gx/en/genesis-park/index.jhtml; Hempel, J., and Porges, S. (2004). PricewaterhouseCoopers tests partners by sending them to work in poor nations: It takes a village—and a consultant. *Bloomberg Businessweek*, September 6, 76.

93. Connor, J., Min, Y., and Iyengar, R. (2013). When East meets West. *Training & Development*, April, 54–59.

94. Li, M., Mobley, W. H., and Kelly, A. When do global leaders learn best to develop cultural intelligence? *Academy of Management Learning & Education*, 12, 32–50; Tichy, N. M., Brimm, M. I., Charan, R., and Takeuchi, H. (1993). Leadership development as a lever for global transformation. In V. Pucik, N. M. Tichy, and C. K. Barnett (eds) *Globalizing Management: Creating and Leading the Competitive Organization*, 47–60. New York: Wiley.

95. *Training.* (2013). A summary of the annual global leadership study, May/June, 50, 32–36; Adler and Gundersen, *International Dimensions of Organizational Behavior*; Frost and Walker, Cross-cultural leadership.

96. Nam, New attitudes on age rattle Korean hierarchies; Yang, Samsung's latest battle is all in the family; Ihlwan, The foreigners at the top of LG; Ramstad, Pulling rank gets harder at one Korean company.

chapter 11

---

building an effective international workforce

Learning Objectives

After reading this chapter, you should be able to:

- explain why an international human resource management strategy is critical for achieving international business goals;
- identify global staffing options and their advantages and disadvantages;
- discuss how cultural factors impact the selection and development of international employees;
- describe how firms can manage equal opportunity and diversity issues in their international operations;
- pinpoint the major factors associated with the effective use of expatriates.

International Challenge

Seoul-Searching a Work World Away: One U.S. Expatriate's Cautionary Tale

Linda Meyers's experience in South Korea is a cautionary tale for any expatriate. Meyers welcomed the opportunity to become an expatriate by accepting a management position in human resources at Seoul-based SK Telecom. The prospect of working in Asia's fourth-largest economy while helping SK Telecom become a more global company was exciting. Meyers brought impressive credentials to her new employer, including years of experience as an expatriate consultant helping executives from top U.S. multinationals such as ExxonMobil and HP make successful transitions to their overseas assignments.

Yet, soon after arriving in Seoul Meyers began wondering if she had made a huge mistake. Despite previous job experience that required considerable overseas travel (e.g., several months in the Czech Republic and Ecuador) and her expertise as an expatriate consultant, Meyers was unable to fully grasp the situation, much less operate effectively, at SK Telecom. During the next two years, Meyers came to realize that her direct Western style of addressing situations clashed with the formal and polite style of her Korean colleagues. She also learned that SK Telecom had few Western employees in general and only a handful of women in senior positions. Meyers discovered that she was, in effect, a trailblazer—one of the few U.S. women to serve in an executive capacity at any Korean company. Eventually, Meyers concluded that she and SK Telecom had divergent views about her role in the company. She had become frustrated, demoralized, and exhausted—an outsider who was marginalized and precluded from having the impact she desired.

The signs of things to come started early, when Meyers was initially e-mailed by an SK Telecom recruiter—who assumed she was male. These and other incidents gave her pause, but she eventually took the job feeling it was simply too good to pass up. Once in Seoul, Meyers was surprised that she received no official orientation or even much specific help on how to adapt to her new surroundings. She also noticed how homogeneous things were at SK Telecom and South Korea more generally, where less than 3 percent of the population has foreign roots (vs. roughly 20 percent or more in cities such as London, New York, and Singapore).

But Meyers was completely shocked by the struggles she had communicating with her colleagues inside the company's hierarchical management structure. Her inability to speak Korean was a major impediment, and Meyers felt that she had no choice but to ask for an interpreter to attend certain meetings. Getting information from Korean colleagues who did speak English was also difficult. Forced to ask questions to learn anything, Meyers felt that even her polite questions were interpreted as criticisms.

Nevertheless, after just four months on the job, SK Telecom promoted Meyers, asking her to lead SK Holding's Global Talent group. Meyers became frustrated, however, at her inability to push through any significant changes in HR policies and practices. This was especially vexing because Meyers saw herself as an agent of change for the company—a view that senior leadership at SK Holdings apparently did not share. Meyers felt increasingly ostracized in her new job, hamstrung by the language barrier and what seemed to be a deliberate effort to exclude her from important conversations and meetings with top executives.

Things eventually got so bad that many of her colleagues simply would not speak with her. The other shoe finally dropped in 2009, when Meyers was told that her contract would not be renewed. While disappointed that she did not have the impact on the company that she would have liked, Meyers also felt a sense of relief that she would be leaving. As you read this chapter, think about some of the experiences and insights that Meyers went through and develop your own assessment of the situation. Her experience raises many questions: Who is responsible for expatriate difficulties and adjustment? Why did Meyers encounter so much trouble in Korea, especially considering her prior overseas experience? Think about these and related questions concerning expatriate adjustment as you read this chapter. Then, read the Up to the Challenge? feature at the end of the chapter to read about possible answers to these important considerations.[1]

A Strategic Look at International Human Resource Management

In the previous chapter, we looked at the motivation and leadership challenges facing international managers. Here, we build upon that understanding and begin to consider the broader role that human resource management plays in a global context. International human resource management (IHRM) activities focus on selecting, training, developing, appraising, and rewarding employees for firms operating in a global environment. Granted, human resource professionals, even those working for domestically focused companies, are "international" to the extent that they hire immigrants, assemble multi-cultural teams, and compete against multinationals in their local markets. But, compared to their domestic counterparts, a broader and deeper set of challenges face those responsible for IHRM, especially in larger multinationals.

Some of these many challenges are outlined in Figure 11.1. These include HR complications due to different legal systems and laws, currencies, cultures, compensation packages and tax codes—among many others. Mistakes made in some of these areas involve much bigger stakes than in a domestic setting. Moreover, IHRM professionals must also contribute to the overall international strategic planning process for the firm as well as think strategically within their own functional area.[2] Ideally, human resource executives should be involved in all phases of the development and implementation of a company's international goals.[3]

A strategic perspective on IHRM is essential because companies with a highly trained, flexible, and motivated global workforce may have an advantage over competitors, especially if that workforce directly supports corporate goals.[4] As theorist Michael Porter put it, "[h]uman resource management affects competitive advantage in any firm, through its role in determining the skills and motivation of employees."[5]

Porter is right in that developing an effective international workforce is more difficult for a competitor to emulate than buying some technology (or even securing capital) and can mean the difference between success and failure.[6] There are many positive outcomes that result from the effective management of international human resources. These can include outperforming competitors in terms of identifying new business opportunities, adapting to changing conditions, sharing knowledge throughout the firm, coordinating acquisitions and subsidiaries well, and maintaining a high-performing, committed overseas workforce.[7]

Possible Additional/Unique Responsibilities	Description/Explanation
A wider variety of external variables that must be taken into account when making decisions	Different cultures, laws, languages, currencies, and governments influence IHRM and require broad expertise
Need to manage a wider and more diverse mix of employees	May include parent-country, host-country, and third-country nationals
A larger portfolio of human resource activities and functions	IHRM professionals may be involved with international relocations, work visas, complex and different pay and tax issues for employees
More direct exposure to international risk issues	HR decisions involve greater liability potential (e.g., mistakes made in supporting foreign acquisitions, posting or repatriating managers overseas who fail involve bigger stakes).

Figure 11.1 Additional Responsibilities Facing International Human Resource Management (IHRM) Professionals.

Source: Adapted from Briscoe, D. R., Schuler, R. S., and Claus, L. (2009). *International Human Resource Management* (3rd ed.). New York: Routledge.

In many multinationals, a key and common challenge is how to balance the need to coordinate units scattered around the world against the need for those units to have the control necessary to deal quickly and effectively with local issues.[8] Getting the right mix of control is tough. For example, consider a situation in which the parent firm's national culture differs dramatically from the cultures in its overseas subsidiaries. This may make it harder for the parent firm to share information, technology, and innovations between the home office and foreign outposts. It may also be more difficult to promote needed organizational changes and manage any conflicts that come up between employees in different countries.

Fortunately, IHRM strategies can help deal with such problems.[9] Companies could benefit from the development of an international human resource philosophy. These both describe and guide corporate values about human resources. These strategies in turn shape the broad outline of what constitutes acceptable IHRM practices for employees all over the world. Under this "big tent," individual units can then fine-tune and select specific practices that best fit their local conditions. But this is easier said than done, especially for firms operating in dozens of countries. For instance, multinationals usually find it extremely difficult to design a compensation system that is sensitive to cultural differences yet still meets general guidelines of being seen as fair by employees everywhere. Culture can also impact other "local" human resource management practices, from how benefit packages are constructed to the hiring, firing, and promotion practices that are used.[10]

So, for all of these reasons, the selection of the right IHRM strategy can pay off, even if it is customized to a particular foreign market. Consider multinationals wanting to quickly enter countries with transition economies as they continue to move from being state-dominated to being market-based (e.g., former Russian republics, others). Choosing to enter those markets by buying local firms, building new plants or establishing joint ventures may create significant human resource challenges that undercut performance if not handled well. Consequently, multinationals need to adopt an appropriate human resource management strategy in order to meet transition economy challenges.

Figure 11.2 presents three possible strategies that might be used in transitional markets. The social welfare approach is a "womb to tomb" perspective on employees that was once characteristic of many state-dominated economies. In contrast, a cost-containment approach is characteristic of some Western multinationals that believe in minimizing employee costs in the face of changing business conditions. Neither of these, however, may be the best options in transitional markets. Instead, an invest-in-employees approach may be best for increasing employee motivation and subsequent firm performance. This may be especially true for transition economies in which high uncertainty avoidance and a strong desire for stability both prevail (e.g., Ukraine). Like the social welfare approach, the invest-in-employees approach offers at least some stability to employees—provided they perform. More importantly, it relies on human resource practices that reflect the idea of "investing" in the workforce (e.g., training that can help employees' careers). That being said, the degree to which multinationals should pursue this approach depends on local conditions. Put simply, one size does not fit all—some combination of the strategies in Figure 11.2 may be the best bet, depending on the country circumstances.[11]

	Types of IHR Strategies		
Human Resource Issue	Social Welfare Approach (e.g., used by some state-owned firms in China and Russia)	Cost-Containment Approach (e.g., used by U.S. firms with a cost-cutting mentality)	Invest-in-Employees Approach (e.g., used by Western firms with a high commitment philosophy)
Employee training/ development	Narrow, training tends to be technology-specific	Minimize training expenditures to the extent possible	Wide range of developmental training offered for new and existing employees
Monetary incentives	Pay determined on a group basis and not performance-driven	Individual performance is the primary driver of raises, bonuses	Both individual bonuses/incentives and unit/firm-based profit-sharing are used
Employee health and welfare provisions	Extensive subsidies for housing, health, child care, other needs	Cut back or eliminate subsidies for employee welfare needs	Slowly phase out direct subsidies not directly linked to employee performance
Employee job security	Offers high job security	No job security offered	Moderate level of job security offered
Expected link to firm performance	Negative—may result in poorer performance	Negative—may result in poorer performance	Positive—may result in better performance

Figure 11.2 Effectively Managing Human Resources in Transition Economies: Three Possible Strategies. *Source*: Adapted from Buck, T., Filatotchev, I., Demina, N., and Wright, M. (2003). Inside ownership, human resource strategies and performance in a transition economy. *Journal of International Business Studies*, 34, 530–549.

This caution underscores the idea that developing an effective IHRM system that reflects broad principles while also allowing for some local flexibility is tough to do. Moreover, it begs the question of how such systems are created in the first place. In reality, a variety of developmental processes exist across firms—depending on their level of internationalization, the nature of their industries, and other factors. Many firms develop such systems over time as their international operations grow in size and complexity—sometimes with professional help from experts at consulting firms.[12]

IHRM systems themselves also vary. In some firms, virtually all IHRM functions are run out of corporate headquarters. Others set general policies while asking foreign subsidiaries to customize those policies locally. Then there are firms that look for best practices in IHRM worldwide in order to implement them everywhere that is practical, regardless of origin. In other cases, specific IHRM responsibilities are divided up among corporate headquarters, regional areas, and individual subsidiaries.[13] Finally, some firms organize IHRM functions around the type of employee. It is important to understand how firms choose from among employee types to staff international operations.

Staffing Foreign Operations: A World of Choices

This section explores the options for staffing international operations. For instance, some multinationals reserve human resource responsibilities for parent-country nationals (PCNs) and third-country nationals (TCNs), but delegate decisions about host-country nationals (HCNs) to local units.[14] As already suggested, the strategic choices among these three options (and more) that firms make should be supported by their IHRM philosophy and practices. For instance, a company that earns a significant chunk of its revenue in foreign countries should be led by senior executives who have substantial international experience, including a firsthand understanding of foreign markets, cultures, and business practices.

U.S. multinationals have focused more in recent years upon hiring and promoting top managers with international experience as well as offering international development opportunities to managers lower in the ranks. And, one foreign posting these days is not enough—especially for those who want to rise high within the organization. At Novelis, a Georgia-based aluminum firm, the chief HR officer states that those with high-level ambitions are required to have multiple overseas assignments before they enter the C-suite. At Xerox, rising stars must pass the test of several years' overseas assignments (and eight of ten managers are promoted from within).[15]

Yet, many U.S. multinationals seem "multinational" in name only—at least when it comes to the percentage of board members who are either foreign executives or Americans experienced in running foreign outposts. Indeed, less than half of the firms in the S&P 500 have even one foreign national on their boards. And some firms have boards where only 4–5 percent of the members have significant foreign experience or are foreign nationals, including companies earning over 50 percent of their revenues abroad (e.g., Adobe Systems, Halliburton, and Unisys). At the other end of the spectrum are companies that seem to think that foreign experience matters a great deal when it comes to the board. Consider Colgate-Palmolive and Schlumberger—both firms earn over 75 percent of their revenues overseas and both have boards where at least half of the membership has foreign experience or are foreign nationals.[16]

Staffing international operations can be complex, though, with IHRM professionals facing a dizzying array of choices. Take a look at Figure 11.3—it summarizes many of the different types of employees available to help firms run their international operations.

A traditional staffing option is to recruit parent-country nationals (PCNs) for top management and important technical positions in foreign subsidiaries. PCNs have citizenship in the country in which the hiring multinational is headquartered. Once posted abroad for at least one year, PCNs are referred to as expatriates. Among the most common reasons for sending a PCN on an expatriate assignment are:

- the perceived lack of appropriate expertise in a foreign subsidiary
- the belief that a PCN is the best way to monitor and control foreign operations
- a desire to transfer know-how about local markets back home to the parent firm
- a desire to provide opportunities for high-potential employees to develop their cross-cultural expertise.[17]

Types of Employees	Description
Parent-country nationals (PCNs)	Employees who are citizens in the nation where the multinational is based
Traditional expatriates	PCNs who are sent abroad on assignment for one year or more
Second-generation expatriates	Immigrants who are naturalized citizens of the multinational's home country and who are then posted overseas for one year or longer to a country other than where they were born
Just-in-time expatriates	Expatriates hired outside the multinational on a one-time basis to fill a specific role or particular assignment—hired on an as-needed basis
Short-term international assignees	Employees sent on assignments lasting between a few weeks and a year; increasingly popular option that doesn't require relocation
Frequent business travelers	Employees who must make frequent international trips for their jobs, usually lasting from a few days or weeks to a few months at most
Localized employees	Employees posted to a foreign location and treated as a local employee; the firm/individual may want to be permanently based there
Permanent expatriates	Employees who spend many years, if not their entire careers, in international assignments, going from one foreign posting to another
Host-country nationals (HCNs)	Locals hired to staff foreign subsidiaries or operations
Inpatriates	Typically HCNs who are brought to the multinational's parent country to fill a temporary assignment lasting from months to two years
Third-country nationals (TCNs)	Employees hired to work in a foreign subsidiary or the headquarters of a multinational, but who are actually citizens of another country
Domestic internationals	Stay in their home country, but perform "remote" international work (e.g., interacting with foreign customers by phone, e-mail, video, etc.)
International commuters	Live in one country, but commute to work in another country
Boomerangs	Employees who are hired or chosen to return to their home countries to work for the multinational
Outsourced employees	"Employees" who actually work for global employment firms hired by the multinational to provide workers/staffs for a foreign outpost

Figure 11.3 Types of International Employee Available to Multinational Firms.

Source: Adapted from Briscoe, D. R., Schuler, R. S., and Claus, L. (2009). International Human Resource Management (3rd ed.). New York: Routledge.

A case in point here is CEMEX, a Mexican multinational that had about 100 managers in expatriate roles in 2012. They were assigned overseas because the company decided that local employees did not have the necessary skill level, or motivation level needed to instill the CEMEX corporate culture in the company, of the home managers.[18]

On the other hand, however, sending a PCN abroad is typically the most expensive staffing option. Adding to the expense is that failure rates for expatriate assignments are high. Although estimates for failure rates vary considerably (from under 5 percent to some 70 percent), a rough rule of thumb is that around 25 percent of expatriate postings end in some kind of failure (e.g., premature return or ineffective performance).[19] Perhaps the biggest risk in sending PCNs overseas is their often limited grasp of local cultures and business practices, especially early in the assignment.[20] To offset this, some firms recruit immigrants for positions in foreign subsidiaries back in their ancestral homes. But such employees, sometimes referred to as "boomerangs," can run into trouble, causing issues for themselves and multinationals in the process. Read the following Global Innovations feature to learn why this staffing option holds some great promise yet is not as simple as it seems.

Global Innovations

Want an Alternative to Traditional Expatriates? Try "Boomerangs"

Instead of posting expatriates to foreign countries, some multinationals are experimenting with so-called "boomerangs." These firms are recruiting employees who emigrated abroad and asking them to return to their home country to run the company's business operations there. Firms at the vanguard in the use of boomerangs seem to be more common in countries with dissimilar cultures and languages. For instance, U.S. multinationals have frequently turned to Chinese boomerangs in recent years—often recruiting them while they are living in the U.S. and then sending them back to China to run business units.

It sounds like a terrific idea—in part because the appeal of boomerangs is simple. Companies can fill key positions in important foreign markets with skilled professionals who are on an equal footing with country nationals because of their grasp of the local culture, business practices, and even language. Examples of U.S. firms using boomerangs include Marriott, McDonald's, and Payless Shoes—all of which have returned highly educated and well-trained immigrants to their home nations to offer service support or to lead operations. Payless Shoes sent a native El Salvadoran to run a store in that Central American country and to lay the groundwork for further expansion in the region. This particular manager had left El Salvador at the age of 15 and eventually became a U.S. citizen. By posting her back to her birth country at the age of 35, Payless Shoes had a boomerang manager in place that understood the local culture well and spoke Spanish fluently.

Yet, simple as this seems, there can be significant challenges. Experience shows that boomerangs can struggle to adapt when they find themselves back in their "home" cultures. The reasons for these struggles vary but can include an overestimation of their understanding of the local culture after years spent elsewhere, as well as their inability to change aspects of the local culture they might now find unappealing.

One Chinese executive who returned home after working in the West for a number of different multinationals found the traditional behavior of his subordinates frustrating. When he arrived to visit one branch office in China, the executive found employees waiting for him in a receiving line—a traditional courtesy designed to boost management egos. A little annoyed and embarrassed, he asked the branch manager not to do that again. Likewise, he experienced difficulty persuading his managers not to run to the airport to personally greet him after a trip. His view of the airport scenario was blunt: "To me it's wasting time—they should be working in the office."

Boomerangs can also be surprised at the treatment that they receive from local employees who may not perceive them as locals after so much time away. Some of those employees view the boomerangs' attempts to "act local" as flimsy impersonations that betray their status as overpaid interloper. For example, one executive went back to Japan after more than two decades in the U.S. in order to run Apple Computer's Japanese operations. His Japanese colleagues felt that he was "too American," and he left in frustration after just one year. Likewise, a management consultant returned to her Russian homeland after living for years in the U.S. Despite her fluent Russian, she returned to the U.S. after less than two years, tired of Russian women who found her ambition and accomplishments off-putting.

Companies can help boomerangs overcome such obstacles and eventually succeed. One tactic that works well is to assign locals to serve as "cultural translators" for boomerangs in order to ease their adjustment back into their native cultures. Another option is cross-cultural training designed to help reintegrate back into their local cultures. Apparel giant Levi Strauss does this very thing. One Peruvian Levi Strauss employee was educated in the U.S. but ran into trouble when she was sent to Mexico for a management position. During company training, she realized that her failure to use formal titles when addressing her Mexican colleagues was a key reason why they were being standoffish—they thought that she was being rude.

Unfortunately, some companies seem only to be following or imitating the vanguard firms in their use of boomerangs. They see the success of firms and jump on the band-wagon with little planning, assuming that boomerangs will somehow automatically understand and conquer the ropes in their native countries, even if they have spent years away. Because of this, some estimates show that less than 20 percent of boomerangs receive any cross-cultural training. Yet, the training received at the best companies shows that it would be wise not to assume that boomerangs will automatically snap back into their native cultural environments without any difficulty, especially if they have had a new home for years now.[21]

Consequently, many companies turn to host-country nationals (HCNs), especially to fill lower- and middle-level management jobs. HCNs are individuals from the foreign country where a multinational has set up operations. Some firms are reluctant to put HCNs in top management positions, fearing that it may dilute their control over operations or corporate culture. Still, HCNs offer some potential advantages over PCNs. Typically, HCNs have a superior grasp of the local culture, business practices, and language. HCNs are also less expensive, because expatriates usually entail expensive relocation costs and enticing pay packages. "Going local" to staff foreign operations can also bring public relations benefits and relieve government pressures to create jobs.

The giant Korean firm Samsung uses just this approach. With almost 100,000 employees outside of South Korea (up 300 percent over the last decade), the number of HCNs continues to rise, approaching 70 percent in 2011. One of Samsung's senior HR executives said that "[t]his is a change from the past, when Samsung's overseas operations were mainly run by Koreans." While some firms will wonder if the HCN has the appropriate knowledge to build corporate culture, the advantages of HCNs over PCNs are clear: the former usually have a better understanding of local practices and culture.[22] This seems to be especially true for Western companies doing business in Asia. In fact, a leading HR consulting firm reports that three out of four senior executives hired in Asia by multinationals were Asians already living in the region. It appears that firms want someone who can directly make deals with local businesses and governments—who are now more likely to be equals.[23]

Another popular staffing option is third-country nationals (TCNs), to work either in foreign subsidiaries or at multinational headquarters. TCNs hold citizenship in a country other than the one in which they are working: for example, if a multinational wants someone with expertise in local culture and business practices to fill a management position in a foreign subsidiary. PCNs may have plenty of management experience but lack local knowledge. Likewise, HCNs understand local conditions, but may lack relevant technical skills. A TCN may be the best option, especially if the goal is to groom someone for top management positions in foreign subsidiaries or to effectively run operations in countries that lack home-grown management talent. For instance, an American firm setting up manufacturing operations in Costa Rica may find appropriate candidates in Mexico, a country with a large pool of Spanish-speaking management talent.

Although PCNs, HCNs, and TCNs represent three major staffing categories, they do not describe *all* staffing possibilities or situations. For instance, multinationals often want a talented international *cadre*—a group of managers who can be plugged into any country and successfully represent the company's values. Doing this means selecting managers based on potential and ability, regardless of nationality, and then exposing them to a variety of international experiences. Indeed, some international cadre members essentially spend their careers jumping from one foreign assignment to the next. These people might best be described as permanent expatriates—employees who stay on at one or more foreign assignments for an extended period of years. For example, during a visit to China, an American executive working for a U.S. multinational in Shanghai has been continuously working in various overseas subsidiaries for over 25 years. Developing an international cadre seems to pay off. Multinationals that use regional transfers and TCNs extensively to build their international cadres tend to outperform multinationals that rely on traditional expatriates.

Finally, consider a promising Chinese employee working in Beijing for an American firm. The Chinese employee is sent to the U.S. to fill a temporary position at corporate headquarters for as long as a few years. Such employees are sometimes referred to as inpatriates. Sending foreign employees to the home country is often done to develop skills and strengthen commitment to the parent firm. Likewise, companies can take advantage of what inpatriates can teach them about doing business in particular countries.[24]

Interestingly, some experts urge international firms to strive to have PCNs, HCNs, TCNs, and other types of employees working side by side wherever possible. Their rationale is that a diverse work environment improves innovation and learning, outcomes that ultimately raise subsidiary performance. The role for IHRM professionals in this context is to select the right people and ensure that the advantages of staff diversity are not overwhelmed by its accompanying disadvantages (e.g., more conflict and coordination problems). This can be accomplished by appropriate selection, socialization, and training efforts that make employees aware of staffing goals while improving their international skills.[25]

Selecting and Developing International Employees

Identifying types of employees is one thing, but how do multinationals decide which option is best for a specific overseas position? Experts suggest that such decisions should be made with a firm's international business strategy in mind, taking into account its competitive environment, overseas sophistication, level of internationalization, and the foreign market where the position will be based. One study of a U.S. financial services firm found that overseas branches with higher proportions of American expatriates offered more complex services. In these locations, expatriates could offer greater insights about complex services than their local counterparts. On the other hand, however, branches in foreign countries with fierce local competition—places in which local knowledge was critical—had more HCNs and fewer expatriates.

But the degree to which IHRM is melded with a firm's strategic decision-making, and the specific selection tactics and training approaches used, varies across countries. This suggests that national culture impacts human resource activities. One example is the Chinese emphasis on business contacts that rely on reciprocal obligation (known as *guanxi*), which seeps into the hiring practices, training approaches, and career development activities of many firms in ways not seen elsewhere. There is pressure to reciprocate a favor, and this could extend to one with human resource implications. This type of local, cultural knowledge often needs to be developed in PNCs and even TCNs and should be part of a firm's development programs. The ability to put this knowledge into play can, as we will see in the second part of this chapter, be included in a performance evaluation.

Figure 11.4 summarizes some of the skills that international managers need to succeed. As you can see, this is a formidable list of talents. Fortunately, research shows that even mastering several of these skills goes a long way toward improving managerial effectiveness across cultures.[26] This skill set can help promote a wide understanding, to be sure. Yet, at the same time, it is also important to recognize that stamina and a steady hand play a role in managerial success. With this in mind, read the following International Insights feature on some of the more mundane, yet common, challenges facing most of today's international managers.

Skill Area	Thumbnail Sketch of Desired Competencies
Multidimensional perspective	Has extensive multi-functional, multi-country, and multi-environment experience
Line management proficiency	A successful track record in overseas projects and assignments
Decision making	Successful in making strategic decisions across a variety of situations
Resourcefulness	Has skills to be accepted by host country's government and business elite
Cultural adaptability	Can quickly adapt to foreign cultures, with diverse cross-cultural experience
Cultural sensitivity	Deals effectively with people from many cultures, races, nationalities, religions
Team-building	Can create culturally diverse working groups that achieve organizational goals
Mental maturity	Has the endurance needed for the rigors of foreign posts
Negotiation	Has track record of successful business negotiations in multicultural contexts
Delegation	Has track record of ability to delegate in cross-cultural contexts
Business practices	Can conduct business across borders successfully in a global environment
Change agent	Has track record of successfully initiating/implementing organizational changes
Vision	Can quickly spot and respond to threats and opportunities in the host country

Figure 11.4 Think You Have the Right Stuff? A Skill Profile for International Managers.

Sources: Adapted from Briscoe, D. R., Schuler, R. S., and Claus, L. (2009). *International Human Resource Management* (3rd ed.). New York: Routledge; and Howard, C. G. (1992). Profile of the 21st-century expatriate manager. *HR Magazine*, June, 93–100.

International Insights

Glamour, Grunge, or Both? In the Trenches with International Managers

International management is a term that conjures up a romantic image of travel to exotic locales, generous perks, and a pampered life abroad. But, as is too often the case, this image can contrast with actual experience. At the minimum, the perks are not what they used to be. Companies are putting the brakes on the rising costs of sending expatriates overseas. One way has been through the use of shorter overseas assignments, often to tackle opportunities in growing markets such as in Latin America and Asia, whose firms in turn are sending their employees out to extend their global reach.

Shorter assignments can mean frenetic and exhausting trips. One manager's 11-day trip included stops in six countries. Hardly sleeping, the manager got sick and canceled his final Moscow stop. Another manager earned 17,000 frequent flyer miles on just a four-day trip spanning three continents. Yet, do not assume that jet lag is a small price to pay for going to flashy cities such as Paris or Hong Kong. Managers are increasingly finding themselves in underdeveloped and risky locations where they may travel on dirt roads, stay in lousy hotels, and deal with challenges such as disease, polluted air, bad water, and security threats ranging from street crime to terrorism. One American manager ended up using buckets of sea water for washing (and flushing) in Papua New Guinea after the hotel's water main was blown up by local guerrillas. Another manager found himself in the middle of 500,000 chanting Egyptians in a march protesting U.S. involvement in Iraq on the way to a Cairo business meeting.

Today, companies often restrict travel after a terrorist incident. But, temporary restrictions typically fade, even in the face of terrorism. The reason is simple—fast-growing markets demand attention. On November 26, 2008, 12 coordinated terrorist attacks occurred in the city of Mumbai, India. Several of these targeted locations were favored by foreign business travelers, including the Taj Mahal luxury hotel. Over 100 people were killed by members of a Pakistani extremist group, although hotel employees showed tremendous heroism in saving many customers. Despite the destruction and tragic loss of life (something that has repeatedly occurred in Mumbai since 1993), many companies continued to send employees there, even as they took additional precautions. After the Mumbai attacks, one marketing executive from a Western firm said that his company was undeterred and "would not even think of changing" travel plans to India.

More mundane travel concerns that affect international managers include an often grueling lifestyle and family hardships. One executive at a Boston-based firm spent three out of every four weeks on the road, mainly abroad. When asked what he wanted for Christmas, the executive's son said he "wanted his Dad to be home." Likewise, the children of a manager making ten trips a year to China for a Pittsburgh-based company endured schoolyard taunts about having an absent parent. A Ford expatriate in China with his family saw them struggle with isolation and culture shock in the massive city of Chongqing. The urbanization of many cities has been remarkable, as has the growth of amenities and sights to see. Yet, it can be a difficult adjustment for some.

There are many positives, however, associated with all of this globetrotting, whether it be short term or long term. The Ford manager referenced previously felt that his posting to China helped strengthen family ties, improved his children's education (they attended an excellent school for expatriate children), and provided opportunities for travel within China and Asia. The Pittsburgh-based manager felt that making ten trips to China a year put him "on the frontier" in perhaps the key world market where he was able to make decisions on the spot.

Balancing the pluses and challenges of frequent international travel requires flexibility and adaptability. One BellSouth manager spent much of his time shuttling between Atlanta and various South American countries. He learned to adapt early when his Cuban parents sent him to live in the U.S. at the age of 9. His secret to survival was being able to adapt his style to whatever culture he was in. Over time, he learned to handle big differences in business styles across continents. Also important are foreign language skills, having a mentor, and resilience to travel stress. More mundane survival tactics for assignments include doing whatever is necessary to get enough sleep and exercise—which includes turning off laptops, cell phones, and all other "24–7" technology products in order to protect sleep time. It may also mean not over-scheduling meetings and letting go of the home office. As one PricewaterhouseCoopers veteran put it, when on business overseas, "forget about home" and "focus on why you're there."[27]

Cultural Values and Staffing Needs

Researchers are focusing more than ever on the connections between cultural values and staffing—information that would be valuable for HR practitioners who need to make staffing decisions. For instance, Japanese multinationals tend to use PCNs to run foreign subsidiaries to a greater extent than American and European firms. But, this tendency can change depending on the business conditions in play. For instance, Japanese firms in industries where global integration and control are important tend to be especially heavy users of expatriates. As their experience grows overseas, Japanese multinationals tend to shift toward using more HCNs in subsidiaries. Generally, when higher power distance and assertiveness are valued in their home countries, multinationals tend to use expatriates more often. These decisions reflect the belief that higher levels of control are needed in foreign outposts, tipping the balance in favor of the high-cost expatriate option.[28]

General Staffing Models

There are likely many situations that call for different employee types. It might be helpful, however, to consider some broad perspectives that can guide multinationals' international staffing efforts—even if they are modified later by prevailing conditions. For instance, a geocentric philosophy means that the firm stresses ability and performance when selecting international staff, without regard to nationality. The goal is to develop and train managers who can be good corporate citizens anywhere in the world. Standards for performance are determined collaboratively between headquarters and foreign operations. At the other extreme is an ethnocentric philosophy. In this case, headquarters makes all key decisions and foreign subsidiaries have little autonomy or input. Most or even all important jobs at headquarters and in all foreign operations are held by PCNs.

In between these two extremes are two other philosophies. A polycentric philosophy gives HRM control to the foreign subsidiary, although headquarters still makes broad strategic decisions. Each subsidiary is a semi-independent entity that controls its own staffing needs. As a result, HCNs usually hold top jobs in foreign subsidiaries. These same HCNs, however, rarely move beyond their local subsidiary to headquarters or other foreign locations. Similarly, with a regiocentric philosophy, most foreign employees will not move into headquarters positions. Nevertheless, employees can move from country to country in a particular region.[29]

Developing Managers with International Skills

Many firms embrace the geocentric philosophy as they become more experienced in international business. It can take years to build an international workforce where employees are flexible, open-minded, and expert in several cultures and languages. And because large multinationals operate in dozens of countries, virtually all aspects of the business involve international contact. For these firms, relying on just a small handful of managers with international experience is a recipe for trouble. Ideally, all employees must recognize how differences in cultures, laws, and business practices across borders impact international communications and relationships (see Figure 11.4).

Options for Developing International Managers

But how should firms go about developing employees with appropriate international skills? While there is no clear recipe, many companies rotate promising managers through different foreign assignments over several years. This strategy produces managers with experience across a variety of countries and organizational circumstances, such as managing a start-up operation, an ongoing joint venture, a restructuring, and so on. Indeed, some companies go about this from the ground up. Procter & Gamble, for instance, emphasizes identifying and cultivating talent at local levels worldwide. Promising employees are then plugged into regional talent pools as they develop—eventually, they gain the experiences and abilities needed to fill critical assignments anywhere in the world. This also promotes diversity throughout the P&G global workforce as employees from countries around the globe are fed into the system. To keep track of it all, P&G uses a computerized system that tracks promising employees worldwide by experiences, skills, and success in prior assignments, making it quicker and easier to select someone for an international position when an opening occurs.[30]

Another option is to recruit foreign students who want to work in their home country after graduation—where their language and cultural skills can be put to good use. Likewise, some firms will focus on potential employees who are fluent in multiple languages, open to other cultures, and willing to tackle overseas assignments. Finally, some U.S. companies have had success with training programs that bring high-potential managers from all over the world to work together on a variety of projects in a simulated environment. Such programs build cross-national relationships and improve cross-cultural problem-solving skills. For example, Motorola annually puts up-and-coming international managers through a business simulation that can last weeks. As one manager who went through the simulation said, "[i]t's surprising how realistic and demanding it is." Using such tools can also save firms money. French food giant Danone SA cut its failure rate among expatriate managers from 35 percent to 3 percent in three years by using simulations to evaluate international talent.[31]

In fact, some firms with extensive overseas operations have developed global training programs for employees. Sometimes this includes training for expatriates going to specific countries. Global training programs, however, usually have broader goals, such as developing cultural awareness, working effectively in cross-cultural teams, and building cross-cultural communication skills. Procter & Gamble and Intel Corporation are examples of U.S. firms that have successfully implemented global training programs.[32]

Cultural Differences in Selection and Development Procedures

So far, the chapter has explained that cultural values shape how firms select, develop, and place international staff. For instance, American and British multinationals have used different procedures to select and manage expatriates than their German and

Japanese counterparts.[33] When these cultures and their unique methods interact, conflict can emerge. Consider what an American experienced when he was hired by Samsung to help set up a plant in New Jersey:

> *The hiring process was unique. Many people attended the interviews. Side conversations in Korean were the norm. Decision making inched forward as consensus was painstakingly achieved. The senior people did not commit themselves to a position until their respective staffs had fully and freely expressed their support or concerns for my candidacy. Personal issues were critical. Those items went beyond my wife and me. They penetrated into realms of what my father had done for a living, whether or not my mother worked outside of the home, and what my brothers and sister were doing. They all seemed to have a significance I could not fathom.[34]*

This American was surprised by a hiring process that differed from that normally used within the U.S. To his credit, his professed ignorance of Korean culture and hiring practices prevented him from really understanding what was happening at the time. Likewise, Samsung's Korean managers were clearly unaware that Americans would find the personal questions that they asked shocking and off-limits. In the U.S., such questions are perceived as irrelevant, discriminatory, or both. Plus, some of these questions would be illegal in the U.S., where anti-discrimination laws are extensive and strictly enforced. Many other countries either do not have the same type of legal protections in place when it comes to forms of discrimination (e.g., Thailand) or do not enforce them consistently if they do (e.g., Mexico). In any case, it is no surprise that foreign managers may be unaware of U.S. legal and cultural restrictions on interview questions nor grasp that what is seen as fair with respect to selection procedures can vary greatly. From their perspective, the Korean managers in this example likely felt that they could not make a good hire without understanding the candidate's home life, religious orientation, and family.[35] They may be puzzled if such questions were *not* asked of them if they were interviewing with a U.S. firm.

Selection procedures can be modified to fit the situation, though. For example, traditional American selection and job analysis procedures can be adapted to better fit cultural values that Japanese firms often want to emphasize in their U.S. plants. In one auto parts plant, Japanese management wanted to stress team skills, consensus building, harmonious relationships, and other "Japanese values" when hiring American workers. Yet, these values make the common U.S. practice of openly comparing individual applicants uncomfortable for some Japanese. American managers generally feel that their role is to pick the best candidate for a job, making comparisons between people necessary. Clearly, American and Japanese approaches to selection are different.

Fortunately, the selection system developed at the American plant cleverly blended both approaches. At the plant, groups of job applicants assembled windshield wiper motors. Individual performance within groups was assessed by trained evaluators who arrived at a final score for each person using a consensus decision process. All applicants who reached a predetermined cutoff score were considered qualified and hired to staff the plant. This system cleverly combined individual assessment (American) with consensus decision making for overall evaluation (Japanese). It also allowed Japanese managers to assess issues critical to them, including an applicant's ability to work well in a team.[36]

Finally, the success of any selection or training program depends on how well it matches the values and culture of those employees being trained. For most U.S. managers, self-focused training improves performance more than group-focused training. The opposite is true for many Chinese managers. To Americans, information about their ability to succeed at a task (self-focused training) seems more useful than information about the ability of a group they belong to (group-focused training). Self-focused information is valued in individualistic cultures where performance is usually viewed at the level of an individual employee. In contrast, Chinese managers may pay more attention to information that describes how a group that they belong to should approach a task. As you know, in collectivistic cultures people tend to view themselves as members of a group first and as individuals second. As a result, "performance" is a function of shared responsibilities, which in turn makes information about group behavior more valuable. In a nutshell, firms should take the cultural values of employees into account when designing training programs.

Expatriates: Work a World Away

In this section, we focus on selection and development issues for expatriates in more detail. For a decade or more now, American multinationals have been hiring more locals in foreign subsidiaries, sending headquarters staff out on more short-term overseas trips, and using technology (e.g., e-mail, teleconferencing) to keep people connected worldwide. In part, this might reflect a change to more of a geo- or polycentric philosophy by the multinationals. But, it is also likely that the high cost of sending expatriates abroad is a concern in tough economic times. Increased safety concerns and political turmoil abroad are other considerations that weigh on the minds of managers.

The Need and Presence of Expatriates

Nevertheless, despite these trends, expatriates are not going to disappear anytime soon. Indeed, they have played valuable roles (and will continue to do so) for multinationals as technical experts, international managers, relationship builders—or all three. In many cases, there is simply no better option than to send someone overseas for multiyear assignments. If anything, the expatriate population has actually been increasing in very recent years. This may be due to more companies engaging in international business than ever before, including multinationals rising up from developing markets such as Brazil, China, and India. Moreover, many established multinationals have expanded the number of countries in which they do business and have pushed heavily into emerging markets. This expanded need for expatriates can also explain their rising numbers—which are staggering. In China, over 90 percent of companies on the Global Fortune 500 list operate there. Moreover, the number of foreign employees posted to China (more than 300,000) has doubled over the past several years.[37]

As you might guess, a good portion of those 300,000 foreigners working in China are U.S. expatriates. Indeed, the overall number of Americans who work in foreign countries or travel abroad for business is astounding. Roughly 6 million Americans work abroad in some capacity, and 7.5 million more go on business trips to foreign countries each year. Roughly 1.3 million expatriates work for U.S. multinationals, 80 percent of whom have a partner or spouse that will accompany them. So, if we also count children who accompany an expatriate parent, nearly 3 million people are somehow "involved" in expatriate assignments for U.S. multinationals alone. Some of the big multinationals support huge expatriate populations. For instance, energy giant Royal Dutch/Shell has over 5,000 expatriates posted to 120 countries, while German conglomerate Siemens has roughly 2,000 expatriates posted to over 100 countries.[38]

While it is important to remember that expatriates represent only a small slice of the overseas workforce in most multinationals, there is little doubt that expatriate assignments will continue to be important.[39] Indeed, in one recent survey, Japanese firms were the most likely to report that they were moving toward *longer* expatriate stints overseas. The bottom line is that expatriates often fulfill a variety of critical roles for multinationals, ranging from technical experts to subsidiary managers to relationship builders, either alone or in combination. At times, there is no substitute for a long-term international assignment.[40]

Expatriates: Balancing Risks with Rewards

The role of an expatriate can be a risky proposition. When firms make mistakes in selecting and managing expatriates, the consequences of failure can be expensive for the company as well as for the expatriate. Figure 11.5 summarizes some of these consequences. By failure, we mean expatriates have either returned early, finished the assignment but were ineffective, or left the company soon after coming home—all costly outcomes. As explained earlier, failure estimates vary considerably, with 20 percent being a reasonably accurate value. Failure rates, however, may be creeping upward. A recent survey found that 34 percent of expatriates in 180 multinationals failed—perhaps because larger numbers were posted to challenging places such as Russia, India, and Indonesia. Moreover, U.S. firms tend to experienced higher expatriate failure (common estimates around 20–30 percent) more than either their European or Japanese counterparts (common estimates are around 10 percent). Europeans may do better because they are exposed to a variety of languages and cultures while the Japanese tend to have longer overseas assignments, which may help their adjustment.[41] Likewise, failure rates depend on the location as well. For example, U.S. failure rates are lower in Europe than in more culturally challenging areas.[42]

Expatriates are very expensive, however, even when things go well. Add up all the costs (e.g., higher pay, airfare for family members, moving expenses, housing allowances, education benefits for any children, company cars, taxes, home leave, extensive

Failure Consequence	Description/Implication
Premature return	Estimates of the percentages of expatriates who are asked to come home (or request it) vary on the assignment and situation. Yet, premature return can jeopardize a firm's ability to compete effectively.
Wasted relocation costs	Sending expatriates abroad (plus partner, spouse, children), is very expensive. Wasted costs on relocation can easily top $100,000.
Wasted preparation and support costs	Failure means the firm loses the direct (e.g., training, overseas pay) and indirect costs (e.g., not getting the job done) spent on preparing/supporting an expatriate.
Other indirect costs	Failure hurts the career/confidence of the expatriate and damages relations with local employees, officials, customers, and suppliers (which take time to repair).
Ineffective performance	Even if expatriates stick out their assignments, they may not be performing well (e.g., making poor decisions, hurting local relations, not meeting firm goals).
Turnover after repatriation	When expatriates return from a foreign assignment, it leaves the firm with no return on its $1 million-plus investment for a typical three-year posting.
Negative momentum	As word spreads of the problems expatriates have (e.g., failure, "out of sight, out of mind" issues, lousy repatriation prospects), recruiting becomes harder, making it more difficult to capitalize on overseas opportunities.

Figure 11.5 Expatriates and the Consequences of Failure.

Sources: Adapted from Birdseye, M. G., and Hill, J. S. (1995). Individual, organizational/work and environmental influences on expatriate turnover tendencies: An empirical study. *Journal of International Business Studies*, 41, 787–806; Black, J. S., Gregersen, H. B., and Mendenhall, M. E. (1992). *Global Assignments: Successfully Expatriating and Repatriating International Managers.* San Francisco, CA: Jossey-Bass; Carpenter, S. (2001). Battling the overseas blues. *Monitor on Psychology*, July/August, 48–49; Hauser, J. (1999). Managing expatriates' careers. *HR Focus*, February, 11–12; Poe, A. C. (2000). Destination everywhere. *HR Magazine*, October, 67–75.

training, etc.) and the first year abroad can cost 300 percent of the expatriate's base salary. The tab to post a professional overseas for three years can easily top $1 million (see Chapter 13).[43]

Of course, one might not find a three-year foreign assignment appealing anyway—perhaps because of worries about terrorism, political upheavals, or personal safety. Indeed, the perception is that the world has become a more dangerous place in recent years. Of some 240 foreign locations examined, nearly 30 percent are ranked as high risk, compared to just over 20 percent in 1998. Or, perhaps one is just not the sort of person who would thrive in a challenging foreign environment regardless. If you think *you* are the kind of person who could succeed as an expatriate, multinationals may be interested. Increasingly, multinationals want their top executives to have extensive foreign experience, making an expatriate assignment essential for reaching the corner office. Figure 11.6 outlines some tips if landing a job overseas is part of your career plan.[44]

Tips for Snaring a Job Abroad	Explanation/Description
Learn additional languages	Multilingual professionals are always in demand
For lower-level jobs, leverage any specialized skills	Specialized skills can provide an edge in lower-level jobs if marketed correctly
For higher-level jobs, network like crazy with key players	Focus on people who have clout where you want to go and develop long-term relationships with executive recruiters
Get involved in international professional groups to raise your visibility	Attend international meetings, participate in global bulletin boards, and speak at international conventions—these provide opportunities to meet and pitch people who might hire you for an overseas job
Get noticed in the press about international issues to raise your profile as an expert	Volunteer to write articles, give reporters quotes for their stories about international business topics in newspapers or business publications—a reader with authority may notice and hire you
Seek introductions from foreign suppliers, customers, and officials	These people may be in a position to hire you or to steer you to someone who can in your desired location
Keep track of former colleagues	They may now be working for a new employer in a foreign country and may be in a position to help
Offer to pay for recruiting costs	Offering to cover interview or even relocation costs is expensive, but it may impress a hiring manager overseas and help you compete against local talent that is cheaper to recruit

Figure 11.6 Want an Overseas Job? Better Get Busy.

Source: Adapted from Lublin, J. S. (2005). Job hopping overseas can enhance a career, but it takes fortitude. *The Wall Street Journal*, June 7, B1.

Choosing People for Expatriate Assignments

In choosing expatriates, many factors should be considered in the selection and training process, including the assignment itself (e.g., which competencies are needed and how much interaction is required with local employees or customers), and features about the assignment location (e.g., cultural and socio-economic differences present). Of course, important features of the potential expatriate—including motivation, skills, experience, and family situation—should also matter a great deal.

National Differences in Expatriate Criteria

Across countries and regions, multinationals weigh such features differently and sometimes diverge altogether regarding the factors that they use in selecting expatriates. For instance, U.S. firms tend to emphasize previous performance, technical skills, and a desire to be assigned overseas when choosing expatriates, often because the assignment itself is aimed at fixing problems in overseas subsidiaries. Recently, U.S. multinationals have been paying more attention to personal fit and family circumstances in their selection process. Screening personal factors such as resilience and openness, as well as consideration of family motivation to travel, has become an important tool in the process. On the other hand, in Chinese firms, while managers take skills and performance into account when choosing expatriates, they may place greater emphasis on their relationships with candidates. Chinese firms seem to be less interested in employee development when dealing with expatriate assignments. As a result, expatriate selection is driven by managerial authority, if not favoritism, in many Chinese firms.[45]

European and Scandinavian firms tend to stress flexibility and cultural competencies more than do multinationals from other parts of the world. They also tend to rely on a wider variety of evaluation methods than U.S.-based firms. This suggests that European and Scandinavian firms place more weight on the alignment of candidate skills and attributes with the needs of a specific assignment. Many U.S. firms fail to systematically assess the extent to which location and assignment demands fit with a candidate's family situation, personal attributes, and "soft" skills. The most important factors for expatriate success include certain personal attributes (e.g., tolerance and emotional stability), soft competencies (e.g., motivation and the ability to bridge cultural differences in building relationships), and family context (e.g., the accompanying spouse's or partner's ability or motivation to adapt).[46]

Get to "Yes" and Success

But how do multinationals actually evaluate candidates for expatriate assignments? As you might suspect, evaluation practices can vary, independent of the selection criteria used. Sophisticated Western multinationals may use talent information systems to track large groups of employees and build a pool of potential expatriates. P&G uses just such a database to keep track of 13,000 managers all over the world, with variables that capture experiences in foreign or cross-cultural contexts. From there, a variety of additional techniques can be employed to identify the best individual candidate for the expatriate position, including interviews (ideally including spouses and partners), psychometric tests (measuring such traits as adaptability and emotional maturity), performance in assessment-center training (where candidates are put through various real-world scenarios), and intensive reviews of past accomplishments relevant to the assignment. U.S. companies often use in-depth interviewing when picking expatriates. In addition to any job-relevant qualifications, the interviews are most productive if they examine individual attributes related to expatriate success. The key goal is to pick the person who best fits the requirements of the expatriate assignment.[47]

Getting a handle on the precise factors that lead to success in expatriate assignments will also require some analysis. Much will depend on how well expatriates adjust to their new cultural environment, the nature of the work they are doing overseas, and the interaction needs of their foreign colleagues. Individuals, however, bring different talents, skills, and experiences to the workplace and firms will also differ in how much support is provided to expatriates before and after they leave for an assignment. Consequently, we should expect variance in how expatriates adjust to foreign assignments, perhaps a good amount of it. These variations in adjustment approaches may reflect differences in home cultures as well as the HR practices companies use to support expatriates.[48]

Regardless of how rigorous the selection process has been, an expatriate candidate may, at the end of the day, simply decline the assignment offer. To secure a "yes" from potential expatriates, the financial package will need to be attractive and the job itself interesting and rewarding, offering the potential for advancement rather than a high risk of failure. Expatriate candidates may also decline assignments if their concerns (or those of their family) about the location are not assuaged. Few individuals would want to be assigned to a location that is viewed as politically unstable or physically unsafe.

If there are few job opportunities available for partners or spouses planning to accompany an expatriate, or a lack of strong schools and education programs for any accompanying children, little incentive exists. Issues such as these can be particularly vexing. Not surprisingly, it is often difficult to convince employees to consider an expatriate posting if the culture overseas does not provide for his or her family. Another deterrent is that expatriates themselves are more likely to be demoted rather than promoted after they finish an overseas assignment. Multinationals typically refuse (or are unable) to promise expatriates their old jobs back and instead often place them into open positions that are available after they return (often a de facto demotion). Firms should be clear about how expatriate assignments will develop an employee's career and specify how expatriates will be assigned a new position once they return home.[49]

Some forward-thinking companies have been taking additional steps to tackle these common concerns of potential expatriates. About 25 percent of multinationals factor in the potential loss of a trailing spouse's or partner's job by including job search help, career counseling, or a cash bonus in the expatriate's assignment package. Approximately 90 percent of multinationals offer location visits before employees accept an assignment, and roughly 50 percent offer language or other training for family members who are accompanying the expatriate. For some of the most dangerous locations, extreme offers are made to lure expatriates. Several years ago, a U.S. company offered expatriates an annual $75,000 hardship bonus for working in Iraq. Firms may also give expatriates safety training before leaving, and otherwise address emergency procedures, personal safety, and local politics. If needed, others may provide high-security housing within walled complexes guarded 24/7 by security personnel.[50]

A Selection and Evaluation Process

Regardless of what package is needed by the employee to accept an expatriate position, multinationals should have a systematic process for choosing and evaluating expatriates relative to the requirements of a particular foreign assignment. Firms would do well to follow the recommended process laid out in Figure 11.7—which begins by putting together a selection team and ends with the chosen expatriates preparing for their overseas assignments.

Selection teams should consist of home-country, host-country, and international HR professionals. The role of HR experts is to identify expatriate candidates and help the team use appropriate selection methods. Home- and host-country managers on the team are there to represent the needs of the parent company and foreign subsidiary, respectively. Once formed, the team should determine the job factors (e.g., nature of the work

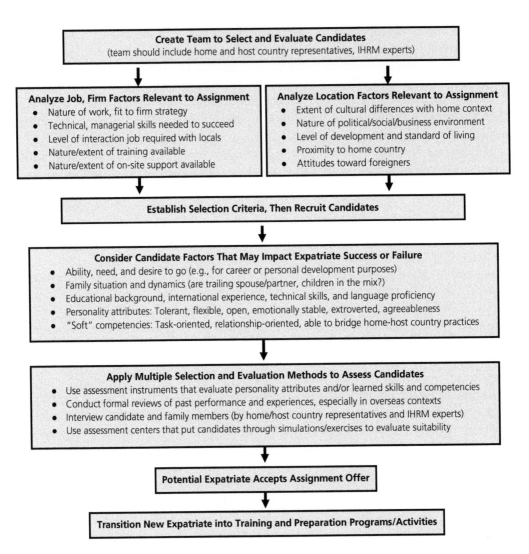

Figure 11.7 A Recommended Process for Effective Selection and Evaluation of Potential Expatriates.

Sources: Adapted from Black, J. S. Gregersen, H. B., and Mendenhall, M. E. (1992). *Global Assignments: Successfully Expatriating and Repatriating International Managers.* San Francisco, CA: Jossey-Bass; Briscoe, D. R., Schuler, R. S., and Claus, L. (2009). *International Human Resource Management* (3rd ed.). New York: Routledge; Downes, M., and Thomas, A. S. (2000). Managing overseas assignments to build organizational knowledge. *Human Resource Planning*, 20, 33–48; and Shaffer, M. A., Harrison, D. A., Gregersen, H., Black, J. S., and Ferzandi, L. A. (2006). You can take it with you: Individual differences and expatriate effectiveness. *Journal of Applied Psychology*, 91, 109–125.

and skills required) and location factors (for example, cultural differences) most relevant to the assignment. Next, the team should establish criteria for judging assignment success and then begin to build a pool of candidates (such as through job postings). Candidates should be carefully assessed on factors known to predict expatriate success and failure, including motivation to go, family dynamics, cross-cultural experience, personal attributes (such as tolerance), and appropriate competencies (such as technical and linguistic requirements). The team should use multiple methods and tools to conduct candidate screening (for example, tests, interviews, exercises).[51]

After the candidate pool has been reduced to a handful of finalists, another set of interviews can be conducted that focus on assignment issues in greater depth. It would be wise at this point to include detailed information about what work and home life will be like in the host country as well as the specific implications of successful assignment completion for expatriates' careers. It is absolutely vital at this point to interview any trailing spouses, partners, or family members. Sending candidates and any trailing family members on pre-assignment trips to the host country may also help them grasp what life abroad will be like. This is also a good mechanism for fleshing out any potential lingering concerns held by the candidate or family members—these should be discussed at length and taken seriously. Once the selection team has had its assignment offer accepted (hopefully by the best-fitting candidate), the next step is to begin efforts to prepare the expatriate to succeed abroad.[52]

Training, Preparation, and Adjustment of Expatriates

Preparing Expatriates

But what constitutes effective preparation for an overseas assignment? First, training and preparation should be an ongoing process, with rigorous efforts made before, during, and even after repatriation. After all, expatriates often experience a culture shock of sorts when they return home, not just at the beginning of their assignment. While a variety of approaches exist, all preparation and training programs should have two basic goals: (1) help expatriates be effective in their assignments as quickly as possible; and (2) minimize adjustment difficulties expatriates and their families face, in both their new environment and after they return. In addition to cultural training and language instruction programs, preparation efforts may also include briefings and counseling on:

- completing the physical relocation (e.g., travel, shipping possessions);
- daily life overseas (e.g., housing, shopping, living conditions);
- family issues (trailing spouse/partner opportunities, educational for kids);
- acclimating to business overseas (e.g., business practices, maintaining relationships, legal issues, political/economic conditions);
- health, safety, and security issues; and
- company history, policies, and personnel in the foreign location.

Unfortunately, many firms provide no significant preparation or training prior to departure (estimates are that between 40 and 70 percent of firms with expatriates fall into this category). And when it comes to small to mid-sized companies, the figure may be on the high end of this range, if not exceed it. Given that evidence shows that training improves the ability to adjust to new cultural environments as well as boost job performance, this training gap is unfortunate.[53]

Cross-Cultural Training

Cross-cultural preparation is a very important component of most expatriate training efforts. So, what should cross-cultural training look like and include? Learning from cross-cultural training involves a three-step process. The first step involves paying attention to cultural differences that explain why foreigners think and behave the way that they do. Next, expatriates must retain knowledge about behavior that is culturally appropriate. In other words, expatriates must think about the new cultural knowledge that they receive and use it to develop a mental framework for their own behavior. This tactic helps expatriates remember how to behave in foreign settings and the consequences of mistakes. The last step involves practicing culturally appropriate behavior that is consistent with expatriates' mental frameworks. This trying-it-out process helps expatriates fine-tune culturally appropriate behaviors and increases their confidence when interacting with foreign colleagues, clients, and suppliers.[54]

Cross-cultural training itself can range from superficial activities that can be covered in a few days to rigorous efforts spanning across months. Figure 11.8 displays the range of training rigor possible and some associated activities. Determining the right mix of rigor and activities is critical. In making this determination, firms should consider how important the assignment is, how long it will last, and the extent to which an expatriate must interact with locals. For instance, if an expatriate's job requires extensive interaction with locals and communication norms in the foreign country are different, then more rigorous training is advisable. This example also underscores the importance of assessing *cultural toughness*. Said differently, this raises the question of how different the culture is in one assignment location from the home culture of the expatriate.

Everything else being equal, the greater the difference from the home culture, the more difficult the expatriate's adjustment process in a foreign country will be. Consequently, more rigorous training is needed for expatriates headed to countries that, to them, are high in cultural toughness. For instance, Americans typically have less trouble adjusting in Europe than they would in Africa, the Middle East, or Asia—all places

Level of Rigor	Time Duration	Activities Included
Low	4–20 hours	Lectures, films, books, area briefings
Moderate	20–60 hours	Everything above, plus role-plays, cases, survival-level language training
High	60–180 hours	Everything above, plus assessment centers, simulations, field trips, in-depth language training

Figure 11.8 Levels of Cross-Cultural Training Rigor.

Source: Black, J. S., Gregersen, H. B., and Mendenhall, M. E. (1992). *Global Assignments: Successfully Expatriating and Repatriating International Managers*. San Francisco, CA: Jossey-Bass), 97. Copyright © Jossey-Bass Inc. By permission of the publisher.

where the cultural values encountered may seem more "foreign." Overall, cultural toughness can negatively affect expatriates' adjustment and even their willingness to accept a foreign assignment in the first place.[55] See the accompanying International Insights feature, which takes a close look at the issue of cultural toughness.

International Insights

Hardship Post or Comfortable Sojourn? Chinese Expats in the West

Things are looking up for Western expatriates in China. Well-worn hotels, poor food, and weak education and hospitality services have given way to glitzy housing developments, fancy restaurants, and high-priced private schools and a university system on its way to the top for children. Rapid growth has made China the place to be for foreign expatriates, who are increasingly accepted within society and are less likely to attract stares, even in far-flung inland Chinese provinces such as Sichuan. Like nearly everywhere, however, not everything is perfect. Air quality and traffic can be big problems in some cities. Likewise, censorship, opaque government rules, and cultural differences present hassles for Western expatriates.

The movement of Western expatriates into China, however, is no longer a one-way street. Thanks to enormous economic clout, Chinese companies are setting up shop and making deals all over the world. As a result, a flood of Chinese expatriates has been sent into Africa, Europe, and the U.S. Yet, the contrast between the shifts made by Western expatriates and their Chinese counterparts could not be starker. Westerners landing in China have left modern democracies with individualist values and slow-growing economies for a more collectivist place with rapid growth, governed by a controlling and bureaucratic regime. And, Chinese expatriates have done exactly the reverse. So, are there differences in what each group of expatriates generally experiences? And, which group might have the greater challenge making the adjustment?

While the answers to these questions are less than precise, anecdotally Chinese expatriates seem to have the more difficult challenge. This is partly because for most Chinese expatriates, the perks and pay fall short of that rewarded to Westerners. As a result, the higher prices that they often encounter in Western cities create hardships. Instead of having maids to cook and clean as they do at home, Chinese expatriates in the West find themselves having "to clean their own toilets," as one expatriate so aptly put it. And, without a generous package to lean on, most Chinese leave their families behind to cut costs. Many Chinese find their time in Western countries lonely—unless they are extroverted, single, are able to communicate easily.

Beyond these challenges, Chinese expatriates may encounter other difficulties. Back home, they tend to be waited on and shown tremendous deference and respect, both in and out of the office. In Western countries, however, they are more likely to be greeted with just a smile, especially outside of work. The entire atmosphere abroad as an expatriate may also be different by group. In Western multinationals, being picked for a stint in China is often highly motivating—an opportunity to learn a fascinating culture, make more money, and receive an indirect acknowledgement of being on the fast track to the top. But in China, winning promotions is often a function of cultivating close relations with key superiors and that is hard to do when you are an expat on the other side of the world. Indeed, when some Chinese managers are tagged for an expatriate assignment, it may signal that they are not well regarded, or that they have some weaknesses that could harm the company. Yet, unlike in most Western firms, Chinese who are employed by state-owned companies cannot refuse an expatriate assignment.

Then there are differences in attitudes and practices that Chinese expatriates must deal with, including the fact that strikes can strand people at train stations and airports, particularly in Europe. While China has labor unrest, it does not extend to public services because of government control. Also, Chinese expatriates often start from behind because Chinese companies are not well-known brands in most Western countries, making it tough to penetrate Western markets. Western directness also tends to throw some Chinese expatriates for a loop. Being peppered with questions by potential customers in China could mortify a Chinese manager making a sales presentation. Yet, such behavior in Western countries is common and may reflect a desire for more information, not negative perceptions of the presenter.

Postings to Western countries also have big pluses for Chinese expats. First, society is relatively transparent and business regulations are clearer. For example, instead of having to tap into your network of contacts to get a business license, one Chinese expatriate marveled that "you just download a form from the Internet and apply." People in Western countries also tend to be friendly toward Chinese expatriates, with little evidence of hostility. So, overall, both types of expatriates have the opportunity to develop their skills and to even enjoy themselves. The latter two outcomes, however, are importantly determined by preparation and mindset—two things good in any business venture and discussed next.[56]

Trends in Expatriate Preparation

Wider and Deeper Training

Some multinationals are going to great lengths to create sophisticated training programs for expatriates. Royal Dutch/Shell, for instance, sent surveys to 17,000 former, current, and potential expatriates, as well as family members, to systematically assess the issues confronting employees in foreign assignments. The company used the results to develop better training and career-management programs. Indeed, such extensive efforts are most likely to appear in companies such as Royal Dutch/Shell, IBM, Unilever, and others that have made expatriate preparation and global management development a board-level priority.[57]

Recently, cross-cultural training programs have focused more on improving open-mindedness by challenging expatriates' prejudices, assumptions, and attitudes about different cultures. This goes beyond the short, superficial courses on overseas business etiquette and dress often used in the past. Instead, the training emphasis today is likely to be on understanding and respecting all cultures. That is the goal that Motorola had in mind when it built a cultural training center to help company managers be more effective in whatever cultural context they found themselves.[58]

Involvement of Families

It was noted earlier that many firms are doing more to address safety, family, and dual-career issues. In part, this is because many of these issues are causing recurring problems. For instance, nearly 90 percent of Fortune 500 firms in one survey stated that dual-career complications will continue to create expatriate selection and performance headaches in the future. Often, the expatriate's family situation is the most important predictor of success or failure—even more important than cultural skills, adaptability, or job knowledge.[59] The good news is that involving spouses, partners, and children in pre-departure cultural training can improve the adjustment of expatriates and their families, especially when combined with other forms of assistance (e.g., help with spouse/partner job searches or lost income replacement).[60]

Training Will Continue to Improve

In the years ahead, companies may step into new areas when it comes to expatriate training and preparation, especially if research shows that they improve success rates. For instance, providing mentors is a promising area. Specifically, companies should consider creating programs that partner expatriates with both a home-country and host-country mentor throughout their assignments. Having a home-country mentor who consistently provides long-distance support, communication, and updates about the home office appears to improve expatriates' knowledge of the organization as well as their promotion chances and job performance.

Likewise, a host-country mentor provides similar benefits. Host-country mentors also appear to facilitate organizational knowledge sharing and teamwork. In other words, expatriates learn to appreciate the host-country assignment more, feel more integrated into host-country staff, and are more likely to share what they know. All of these positive effects are potentially career enhancing—particularly important because expatriates often report that their careers stall or take a step backward after returning home. For companies, it increases the odds that expatriates will be motivated knowledge transmitters who improve the flow of critical knowledge across national boundaries in the markets they serve.[61]

Self-Preparation and Training

Nevertheless, when it comes to training and preparation, expatriates would be wise to look out for themselves. As one expert observed, "[i]t would still be rare to find a company that is using everything that research has shown us about selecting, training, developing, and supporting expatriates." This suggests that expatriates should also help themselves prepare for overseas assignments. For instance, they can sign up for college courses to help build skills and abilities not included in company training. Expatriates can also seek independent advice from firms that specialize in cross-cultural training and relocation (such as from the U.S.-based Cartus Corporation). Soliciting insights from other expatriates is another good option. Finally, if not already provided by the employer, a pre-departure visit to the host country (with the family) can help ease the settling-in process. Once abroad, expatriates can also seek out groups that offer support (such as trip planning, blog and message boards, advice, and, in some cases, expat camaraderie).[62]

Returning Home: The Challenge of Repatriation

Unfortunately, the need for preparation, planning, and training does not end when expatriates leave to return home. A bevy of potential problems also awaits expatriates when once home. These repatriation problems explain the high turnover rate among expatriates. Consider these common repatriation challenges:

- Changes in the home country and in the expatriate's values after several years abroad make "home" seem more "foreign".
- Changes at the home office require major adjustments and new learning.
- New jobs after return can be disappointing (this may be due to a demotion, a disconnect from the overseas job, or an unclear career track).
- There may be problems of reorientation to living conditions in the home country.
- The expatriate may experience feelings of under-appreciation by the firm after performing well overseas.
- Returning home may mean adjustment to a lower standard of living (with no more pay premiums or fancy benefits).[63]

Many companies now realize how expensive it is to neglect these repatriation issues. To the contrary, there is growing recognition that expatriates represent a unique and valued resource once they return—they are individuals who can help the firm because of the important information they have collected, the new competencies that they developed, and the new knowledge that they created during their overseas assignment. Without successful repatriation, all of this will be lost, which could end up being a competitive disadvantage for the firm (and consequently a plus to a competitor!). [64]

Thus, some firms address repatriation issues in depth even before the expatriate leaves for an assignment. For instance, Monsanto, the pharmaceutical, chemical, and agricultural giant, started a repatriation program to combat high turnover among its expatriates. In a nutshell, they found that expatriates' dashed expectations for advancement upon return home were a big part of the turnover problem. Monsanto instituted pre-departure planning for the role that expatriates would have once they returned. The firm also now gives returning expatriates opportunities to showcase their overseas accomplishments publicly and provides counselors to help with readjustment problems. Programs such as these can improve the performance and adjustment of expatriates after they return.[65]

Attacking the "out of sight, out of mind" problem is another key issue. Some companies deliberately bring expatriates back home several times a year to give them visibility and express appreciation for their work. Expatriates can meet with important managers and, ideally, a designated mentor. Return trips also serve to jump-start the adjustment process. The longer that expatriates are away, the more difficult they will find it to return. To combat this, firms can increase the frequency of home visits as the final return date approaches, especially for employees who are gone for more than two years. Consider what happens at Coherent, Inc., a California-based manufacturer of lasers and other high-tech equipment with offices in several countries, including China. The company brings expatriates home for short stints of a few months before their final return. During this time, expatriates complete modest projects. They then return to their foreign postings to conclude their affairs before coming home for good. This months-long period in the U.S. helps reacquaint expatriates with the office, their (new) colleagues, and ongoing projects. It also gives expatriates an extended taste of life back home. Overall, the program has helped cut down the repatriation adjustment period. Figure 11.9 lists some additional steps that firms can take to ease the repatriation process.[66]

Time Frame	Suggestions/Description
Before departure	• Clearly communicate reentry job options, establish career development plan • Appoint home- and host-country mentors to support expatriate • Arrange home visits for visibility
6–9 months before return	• Narrow list of reentry job options, send expatriate job openings/listings • Conduct home office visits to facilitate adjustment, schedule job interviews
3–6 months before return	• Conduct briefings with employee/family about what they've learned • Explain home-country changes that may impact their return • Ask expatriate to list return expectations to minimize misunderstandings • Explain firm's moving policies and repatriation programs
Immediately on return	• Assign employee/family to a welcome home group of former expatriates • Provide a home sponsor to review changes in firm (e.g., policies, products) • Provide returning spouse with career-related assistance • Offer counseling for more serious problems
3–6 months after return	• Provide training for reentry shock, or any negative feelings about return • Ask employee how new skills and experience can be better used by the firm • Reassess adjustment process to identify outstanding problems and offer assistance

Figure 11.9 Before, During, and After: Suggestions for Improving the Repatriation Process.

Sources: Adapted from Shilling, M. (1993). How to win at repatriation, *Personnel Journal* (September), 40–46; Solomon, C. M. (1995). Repatriation: Up, down, or out? *Personnel Journal*, January, 28–37.

Chapter Summary

This chapter discussed the challenges of managing human resources globally as well as the strategic value of international human resource management (IHRM). Aligning IHRM with firm goals is important. Consequently, companies may want to develop approaches to IHRM that both reflect broad principles while also including tactics tailored for use in specific markets.

We also considered the basic options for staffing foreign operations. These include PCNs, HCNs, and TCNs. Some firms are trying to develop an international cadre of managers who can be sent anywhere in the world. Companies are increasingly using boomerangs to improve their effectiveness in foreign markets. Likewise, firms continue to designate valued foreign employees as inpatriates, bringing them to the parent country for various developmental assignments to increase their commitment.

Sometimes firms embrace a particular selection philosophy in making staffing decisions. At one extreme is a geocentric approach, where ability is all that matters. An ethnocentric approach, in contrast, means that only PCNs will be posted in key overseas positions. Polycentric and regiocentric approaches fall between these two extremes. In a polycentric approach, human resource management control is in the hands of the foreign subsidiary, although headquarters still makes key decisions. Likewise, under a regiocentric approach, most foreign employees will not move into headquarters positions. Employees, however, can move from country to country in a particular region.

The chapter concluded with a focus on expatriates, where the consequences of failed assignments are often severe. Firms need to develop a rigorous selection process and use criteria that accurately predict success. Expatriates also need to be prepared to deal with all of the cultural and lifestyle changes that will be encountered abroad. The exact nature and level of training needed should be driven, in part, by the cultural toughness of the foreign location. Preparation is also needed if employees are to be successfully repatriated back to their home countries. Fortunately, companies are moving toward more sophisticated repatriation programs that kick in before the expatriate has even begun the foreign assignment.

Discussion Questions

1. What are some of the unique challenges facing international human resource management professionals?

2. What are some of the pros and cons associated with using PCNs, TCNs, and HCNs? How does culture impact selection and development of international employees?

3. What are the elements of a successful program to select, prepare, and repatriate employees destined for foreign assignments? How can cultural toughness and family issues be managed effectively?

Up to the Challenge?

Trying Fitting in Across an Ocean of Differences

At the beginning of this chapter, we told you about the real-life experiences of a seasoned international business professional, Ms. Linda Meyers. In particular, we relayed her observations about the various interactions and styles of management in South Korea and her (self-acknowledged) lack of preparation for the many cultural differences between managing in the U.S. and Korea. Plus, Meyers was hardly a novice as she had other extensive assignments that ended successfully and was a consultant to other firms about expatriate deployment. So, what happened in Seoul?

On reflection, Meyers felt that she had made some important mistakes. One lesson was summarized by the phrase "easier said than done." The extensive experience that she had in prepping others for expatriate roles did not make it any easier to implement that advice herself. Moreover, much of the training she provided to other soon-to-be expatriates did not have much specific applicability to the SK Telecom environment in Seoul. Despite her own personal preparation efforts to read about and to understand Korean business culture, Meyers judged that her efforts were superficial and that she missed about 80 percent of what she actually needed to know. Another realization was that Meyers's view of progress and change did not align with her more conservative Korean bosses, something that she should have done more work on to clarify in advance.

In terms of her own management style, Meyers also concluded that she should have been more patient when introducing changes to her Korean subordinates. For example, soon after arriving in Seoul, she tried to create a more informal environment by telling her Korean subordinates to stop using her title and instead to address her by her first name. Unfortunately, this backfired and caused her subordinates to lose respect for her and to perceive her as weak. Likewise, Meyers admitted that she tended to jump to the conclusion that every misunderstanding that she had with her Korean colleagues was due to cultural differences or poor treatment because she was a foreigner. After one disagreement with a Korean manager, which she chalked up to a cultural misinterpretation, Meyers spoke to another colleague about how to handle the situation. The Korean manager was very embarrassed and upset when he found out that Meyers had consulted with another colleague about their misunderstanding.

After leaving SK, Meyers returned to her roots, again serving as a consultant to help other people prepare for their expatriate assignments. Her experience in Korea, Meyers believes, ended up making her a better consultant. As she put it, "those years in Seoul taught me to question my own actions and assumptions. I realized that my leadership style had been shaped by a particular environment and that my way was not always best."

As you reflect on this situation, does it surprise you that she encountered so much trouble in Korea, especially given her prior experiences and positions? What are some additional steps that she could have taken to better prepare for her role at SK Telecom (both before she accepted the job as well as after)?

International Development

What Is Your International Orientation?

Purpose

To develop self-insight and knowledge about your level of experience with, and interest in, other countries and cultures. This may help provide guidance about whether you would be attracted to and likely succeed in a foreign work environment.

Instructions

The following items are from the International Orientation Scale. Answer each question and give yourself a score fo each dimension. The highest possible score for any dimension is 20 points.

Dimension 1: International Attitudes

Use the following scale to answer questions Q1 through Q4, placing the appropriate number next to each question.

1	2	3	4	5
Strongly disagree	Somewhat disagree	Unsure	Somewhat agree	Strongly agree

Q1. ___ Foreign language skills should be taught (as early as) elementary school.
Q2. ___ Traveling the world is a priority in my life.
Q3. ___ A year-long overseas assignment (from my company) would be a fantastic opportunity for my family and me.
Q4. ___ Other countries fascinate me.

Add up total score for Dimension 1 (scores will range from 4 to 20).

Dimension 2: Foreign Experiences

Q1. ___ I have studied a foreign language.
   1. Never
   2. For less than a year
   3. For a year
   4. For a few years
   5. For several years.
Q2. ___ I am fluent in another language.
   1. I don't know another language.
   2. I am limited to very short and simple phrases.

3. I know basic grammatical structure and speak with a limited vocabulary.

4. I understand conversation on most topics.

5. I am very fluent in another language.

Q3. ___ I have spent time overseas (traveling, studying abroad, etc.).

1. Never

2. About a week

3. A few weeks

4. A few months

5. Several months or years.

Q4. ___ I was overseas before the age of 18.

1. Never

2. About a week

3. A few weeks

4. A few months

5. Several months or years.

___ Add up total score for Dimension 2 (scores will range from 4 to 20).

Dimension 3: Comfort with Differences

Use the following scale for questions Q1 through Q4, placing the appropriate number next to each question.

1	2	3	4	5
Quite similar	Mostly similar	Somewhat different	Quite different	Extremely different

Q1. ___ My friends' career goals, interests, and educations are _____ to mine.

Q2. ___ My friends' ethnic backgrounds are _____ to mine.

Q3. ___ My friends' religious affiliations are _____ to mine.

Q4. ___ My friends' first languages are _____ to mine.

___ Add up total score for Dimension 3 (scores will range from 4 to 20).

Dimension 4: Participation in Cultural Events

Use the following scale to answer questions Q1 through Q4, placing the appropriate number next to each question.

1	2	3	4	5
Never	Rarely	Sometimes	Often	Always

Q1. ___ I eat at a variety of ethnic restaurants (e.g. Greek, Indian, Thai, German).
Q2. ___ I watch the major networks' world news programs.
Q3. ___ I attend ethnic festivals.
Q4. ___ I visit art galleries and museums.

___ Add up total score for Dimension 4 (scores will range from 4 to 20)

Self-Assessment Discussion Questions

1. First, lay out your total scores on each of the four dimensions. Also, add together your scores on each dimension for a total score (should range from 16 to 80). The higher your score on each dimension (and the higher your total score), the greater your experience with and interest in other countries and cultures.
2. On what dimension is your highest score? Your lowest score? Your instructor may provide comparative data from other students. If so, how do your dimension totals and your overall total score compare to other students?
3. Would you like to improve your international orientation? If so, what could you do to change various aspects of your life? What dimension would you tackle first? Which one would be the hardest to improve?
4. Is an overseas assignment something that is attractive to you? Why or why not? Are there specific places in the world that you would be interested in going to as an expatriate? Places that you would not? Why?

Source: This exercise was prepared by Paula Caligiuri, School of Management and Labor Relations, Rutgers University. Used with permission. As appeared in *Management International: Cases, Exercises, and Readings* by Dorothy Marcic and Sheila Puffer. Copyright © 1994 by West Publishing Company, Minneapolis/St. Paul, Minn., a division of International Thomson Publishing Inc. Reprinted by permission.

From Theory to International Practice

International Human Resource Management in Specific Firms

Purpose

To learn more about the international human resource management challenges facing companies and how they try to cope with them.

Instructions

Your instructor will divide the class into groups of three to six students. Each group should interview at least two managers with human resource management responsibility who work for companies engaged in significant international business activity that requires staff abroad. Examples of activities requiring overseas staff (i.e., expatriates, local employees, or third-country nationals, either alone or in combination) include:

- having offices in foreign countries to help market and sell products or services;

- running foreign subsidiaries that deliver services or manufacture products; and

- joining ventures overseas or forming international alliances to develop technology, build a product, share information, or make international deals.

The goal of the interviews is to assess the international human resource challenges facing the company and to determine what the company is doing to cope with them. Some good general questions to ask might include the following:

- How do you support the company's international business operations?

- What are the key human resources challenges facing your company in its international operations (e.g., staffing foreign operations, not having enough control to deal with local issues)? Why do these challenges exist? To what extent do they reflect cultural, legal, or political differences across countries?

- What human resource strategies, policies, and practices have been developed to overcome these challenges? Have they been successful? Why or why not?

Naturally, other, more specific questions can be developed that are tailored to the specific managers being interviewed. Your instructor may also ask you to research specific international human resource management issues and develop questions aimed at examining how local companies have responded. If interviewing managers is impractical for any reason, your instructor may treat this activity as an Internet research assignment.

Deliverable

To conclude the exercise, each student group should make a 15-minute class presentation about their findings. Alternatively, your instructor may set up this activity as an individual assignment. There are a variety of Internet information sources available for doing research on international human resource management issues. For instance, the following websites may be useful for generating questions, better understanding the employee side of international human resource management, or learning more about specific company practices:

- **www.expatriates.com** (offers an extensive directory of expatriate-oriented links)

- **www.shrm.org** (site of the Society for Human Resource Management, a professional organization that provides a wealth of information and links).

After all groups have presented, the instructor will lead a class discussion (15–20 minutes) that focuses on three issues:

- To what extent do the human resource challenges reported reflect the type of international operations companies are engaged in?

- To what extent do the human resource challenges reported reflect country-specific factors, such as culture?

- What about the quality and appropriateness of the international human resource strategies being pursued by various companies?

Notes

1. Green, S. (2011). The would-be-pioneer. *Harvard Business Review*, April, 124–126.
2. Briscoe, D. R., Schuler, R. S., and Claus, L. (2009). *International Human Resource Management* (3rd ed.). New York: Routledge; Truss, C., and Gratton, L. (1994). Strategic human resource management: A conceptual approach. *International Journal of Human Resource Management*, 5, 662–686.
3. Briscoe, Schuler, and Claus, *International Human Resource Management*; Roberts, K., Kossek, E. E., and Ozeki, C. (1998). Managing the global workforce: Challenges and strategies. *The Academy of Management Executive*, 12, 93–106.
4. Briscoe, Schuler, and Claus, *International Human Resource Management*; Carpenter, M. A., Sanders, W. G., and Gregersen, H. B. (2000). International assignment experience at the top can make a bottom-line difference. *Human Resource Management*, 39, 277–285.
5. Porter, M. E. (1985). *Competitive Advantage: Creating and Sustaining Competitive Advantage*. New York: Free Press, 43.
6. Briscoe, Schuler, and Claus, *International Human Resource Management*.
7. Brannen, M. Y., and Peterson, M. F. (2009). Merging without alienating: Interventions promoting cross-cultural organizational integration and their limitations. *Journal of International Business Studies*, 40, 468–489; Gong, Y. (2003). Toward a dynamic process model of staffing composition and subsidiary outcomes in multinational enterprises. *Journal of Management*, 29, 259–280; Minbaeva, D., Pedersen, T., Bjorkman, I., Fey, C. F., and Park, H. J. (2003). MNC knowledge transfer, subsidiary absorptive capacity, and HRM. *Journal of International Business Studies*, 34, 586–599; Oddou, G., Osland, J. S., and Blakeney, R. N. (2009). Repatriating knowledge: Variables influencing the "transfer" process. *Journal of International Business Studies*, 40, 181–199.
8. Schuler, R. S., and Florkowski, G. W. (1996). International human resources management. In B. J. Punnett and O. Shenkar (eds) *Handbook for International Management Research*, 351–401. Cambridge, MA: Blackwell.
9. Briscoe, Schuler, and Claus, *International Human Resource Management*; Fey, C. F., and Bjorkman, I. (2001). The effect of human resource management practices on MNC subsidiary performance in Russia. *Journal of International Business Studies*, 32, 59–75.
10. Briscoe, Schuler, and Claus, *International Human Resource Management*.
11. Buck, T., Filatotchev, I., Demina, N., and Wright, M. (2003). Inside ownership, human resource strategies and performance in a transition economy. *Journal of International Business Studies*, 34, 530–549; Fey, C. F., Margulis-Yakushev, S., Park, H. J., and Bjorkman, I. (2009). Opening the black box of the relationship between HRM practices and firm performance: A comparison

of MNE subsidiaries in the USA, Finland, and Russia. *Journal of International Business Studies*, 40, 690–712.

12. Brewster, C., and Mayrhofer, W. (2008). Comparative human resource management policies and practices. In Smith, P. B., Peterson, M. S., and Thomas, D. C. (eds) *Handbook of Cross-Cultural Management Research*, 353–366. Thousand Oaks, CA: Sage; Briscoe Schuler, and Claus, *International Human Resource Management*.

13. Beechler, S., and Yang, J. Z. (1994). The transfer of Japanese-style management to American subsidiaries: Contingencies, constraints, and competencies. *Journal of International Business Studies*, 25, 467–491.

14. Bartlett, C., and Ghoshal, S. (1989). *Managing Across Borders: The Transnational Solution*. Boston: Harvard Business School Press; Schuler, R. S., and Florkowski, G. W. (1996). International human resources management. In B. J. Punnett and O. Shenkar (eds) *Handbook for International Management Research*, 351–401; Taylor, S., Beechler, S., and Napier, N. (1996). Toward an integrative model of strategic international human resource management. *Academy of Management Review*, 21, 959–985.

15. Kwoh, L. (2012). Don't unpack that suitcase. *The Wall Street Journal*, B10; Cascio, W., and Bailey, E. E. (1995). International human resource management: The state of research and practice. In O. Shenkar (ed.) *Global Perspectives of Human Resource Management*, 15–36. Englewood Cliffs, NJ: Prentice-Hall.

16. *Business Week* (2008). How global are you? December 8, 12.

17. Downes, M., and Thomas, A. S. (2000). Managing overseas assignments to build organizational knowledge. *Human Resource Planning*, 20, 33–48.

18. Geissler, C., Kuhn, L., and McGinn, D. (2011). Developing your global know-how. *Harvard Business Review*, March, 71–75.

19. Carraher, S. M., Sullivan, S. E., and Crocitto, M. M. (2008). Mentoring across global boundaries: An empirical examination of home- and host-country mentors on expatriate career outcomes. *Journal of International Business Studies*, 39, 1310–1326; Hsieh, T. Y., Lavoie, J., and Sarnek, R. A. P. (1999). Are you taking your expatriate talent seriously? *McKinsey Quarterly*, 3, 71–83.

20. Briscoe, Schuler, and Claus, *International Human Resource Management*; Ready, D. A., and Conger, J. A. (2007). How to fill the talent gap. *The Wall Street Journal*, September 15–16, R4.

21. Browne, A. (2004). Chinese recruit top executives from abroad. *The Wall Street Journal*, November 30, B1, B8; Lublin, J. S. (2006). Is transfer to native land a passport to trouble? *The Wall Street Journal*, June 3, B1, B5; Millman, J., and Zimmerman, A. (2003). 'Repats' help Payless Shoes branch out in Latin America. *The Wall Street Journal*, December 24, B1, B2.

22. Briscoe, Schuler, and Claus, *International Human Resource Management*.

23. Kwoh, L. (2012). Asia's endangered species: The expat. *The Wall Street Journal*, March 28, B6.

24. Latta, G. W. (1998). Global staffing: Are expatriates the only answer? *HR Focus*, July, S1, S2; Woodruff, D. (2000). Distractions make global manager a difficult role. *The Wall Street Journal*, November 21, B1, B18.

25. Gong, Y. (2003). Toward a dynamic process model of staffing composition and subsidiary outcomes in multinational enterprises. *Journal of Management*, 29, 259–280.

26. Brewster, C., and Mayrhofer, W. (2008). Comparative human resource management policies and practices. In Smith, Peterson, and Thomas, *Handbook of Cross-Cultural Management Research*, 353–366; Peterson, R. B., Sargent, J., Napier, N. K., and Shim, W. S. (1996). Corporate expatriate HRM policies, internationalization, and performance in the world's largest MNCs. *Management International Review*, 36, 215–230.

27. Going Global. (2009). Global relocation trends show future expat growth, available at: www.goinglobal.com/newsletter/march09corp_general_global.asp; *The Economist*. (2006). Traveling more lightly, June 24, 77–79; *The Economist*. (2000). International assignments: Nasty, brutish and short, December 16, 70–71; Areddy, J. T. (2005). Deep inside China, American family struggles to cope. *The Wall Street Journal*, August 2, A1, A6; Kahn, G., Ono, Y., Fowler, G., and Choudhury, S. (2008). Frequent travelers wonder if any place is safe. *The Wall Street Journal*,

November 28, A6; Kaufman, J. (1996). Tethered to Pittsburgh for years, an engineer thrives on trips to Asia. *The Wall Street Journal*, November 19, A1, A8; Lublin, J. S. (2005). Globetrotters' tips to boost performance on long business trips. *The Wall Street Journal*, May 31, B1; Lublin, J. S. (2003). No place like home. *The Wall Street Journal*, September 29, R7; Rosman, K. (2007). Expat life gets less cushy. *The Wall Street Journal*, October 26, W1, W10; Silverman, R. E. (2001). Global crossings. *The Wall Street Journal*, January 16, B12.

28. Ando, N., Rhee, D. K., and Park, N. K. (2008). Parent country nationals or local nationals for executive positions in foreign affiliates: An empirical study of Japanese affiliates in Korean. *Asia Pacific Journal of Management*, 25, 113–134; Brock, D. M., Shenkar, O., Shoham, A., and Siscovick, I. C. (2008). National culture and expatriate deployment. *Journal of International Business Studies*, 39, 1293–1309.

29. Briscoe, Schuler, and Claus, *International Human Resource Management*.

30. Ready, D. A., and Conger, J. A. (2007). How to fill the talent gap. *The Wall Street Journal*, September 15–16, R4; Roberts, K., Kossek, E. E., and Ozeki, C. (1998). Managing the global workforce: Challenges and strategies. *Academy of Management Executive*, 12, 93–106.

31. Solomon, C. M. (1995). Navigating your search for global talent. *Personnel Journal*, May, 94–101; Woodruff, D. (2000). Distractions make global manager a difficult role. *The Wall Street Journal*, November 21, B1, B18.

32. Odenwald, S. (1993). A guide for global training. *Training and Development*, July, 23–31.

33. Peterson, R. B., Napier, N. K., and Shul-Shim, W. (2000). Expatriate management: Comparison of MNCs across four parent countries. *Thunderbird International Business Review*, 42, 145–166.

34. Dimmick, T. G. (1995). Human resource management in a Korean subsidiary in New Jersey. In Shenkar, *Global Perspectives of Human Resource Management*, 63–70.

35. Cascio, W., and Bailey, E. E. (1995). International human resource management: The state of research and practice. In Shenkar, *Global Perspectives of Human Resource Management*, 15–36; Daspro, E. (2008). An analysis of U.S. multinationals' recruitment practices in Mexico. *Journal of Business Ethics*, 87, 221–232; Scroggins, W. A., Benson, P. G., Cross, C., and Gilbreath (2008). Reactions to selection methods: An international comparison. *International Journal of Management*, 25, 203–216.

36. Love, K. G., Bishop, R. C., Heinisch, D. A., and Montei, M. S. (1994). Selection across two cultures: Adapting the selection of American assemblers to meet Japanese job performance demands. *Personnel Psychology*, 47, 837–846.

37. HR Spectrum. (2004). Expatriates and your global workforce. January 4, available at: www.hrspectrum.com/insightofweek.htm; ORC Inc. (2004). The 2002 worldwide survey of international assignment policies and practices. January 4, available at: www.orcinc.com/surveys/wws2002.html; Briscoe, Schuler, and Claus, *International Human Resource Management*; Feng, S. (2009). Expatriate localization: A Chinese solution, available at: www.mercer.com; Lublin, No place like home; Martins, A., and Lengre, J. (2007). Expat networking: Helping you improve the success of expat assignments, available at: www.expatwomen.com/tips/expat_networking_helping_improve_success.php.

38. Geissler, C., Kuhn, L., and McGinn, D. (2011). Developing your global know-how. *Harvard Business Review*, March, 71–75; Harzing, A. (2001). Of bears, bumble-bees, and spiders: The role of expatriates in controlling foreign subsidiaries. *Journal of World Business*, 36, 366–379; Hsieh, T. Y., Lavoie, J., and Sarnek, R. A. P. (1999). Are you taking your expatriate talent seriously? *McKinsey Quarterly*, 3, 71–83; Shaffer, M. A., and Harrison, D. A. (2001). Forgotten partners of international assignments: Development and test of a model of spouse adjustment. *Journal of Applied Psychology*, 86, 238–254.

39. HR Spectrum, Expatriates and your global workforce.

40. ORC Inc., The 2002 worldwide survey of international assignment policies and practices; Briscoe, Schuler, and Claus, *International Human Resource Management*.

41. Briscoe, Schuler, and Claus, *International Human Resource Management*; Martins and Lengre, Expat networking: Helping you improve the success of expat assignments; Poe, A. C. (2000). Destination everywhere. *HR Magazine*, October, 67–75.

42. Note that failure rate percentages are a matter of controversy, with a least one research paper showing that what used to be characterized as high failure of expatriates might be more of a perpetuated myth than empirical fact; Harzing, A. (1995). The persistent myth of high expatriate failure rates. *Human Resource Management*, 6, 457–475. As this issue continues to be settled, we suggest that average failure rates of even 10 percent are costly for the firm and the individual expatriate; Christensen, C., and Harzing, A. (2004). Expatriate failure: Is it time to abandon the concept? *Career Development International*, 22, 35–43.

43. Engen, J. R. (1995). Coming home. *Training*. March, 37–40; Hauser, J. (1999). Managing expatriates' careers. *HR Focus*, February, 11–12; Latta, G. W. (1999). Expatriate policy and practice: A ten-year comparison of trends. *Compensation and Benefits Review*, 31, 35–39.

44. Carpenter, Sanders, and Gregersen, International assignment experience at the top can make a bottom-line difference; Harris, N. (2002). Tools to protect traveling employees. *The Wall Street Journal*, March 11, R8; Lublin, J. S. (2005). Job hopping overseas can enhance a career, but it takes fortitude. *The Wall Street Journal*, June 7, B1.

45. Briscoe, Schuler, and Claus, *International Human Resource Management*; Tung, R. L., and Varma, A. (2008). Expatriate selection and evaluation. In Smith, Peterson, and Thomas, *Handbook of Cross-Cultural Management Research*, 367–378.

46. Shaffer, M. A., Harrison, D. A., Gregersen, H., Black, J. S., and Ferzandi, L.A. (2006). You can take it with you: Individual differences and expatriate effectiveness. *Journal of Applied Psychology*, 91, 109–125; Carpenter, S. (2001). Battling the overseas blues. *Monitor on Psychology*, July/August, 48–49; Klaus, K. J. (1995). How to establish an effective expatriate program: Best practices in international assignment administration. *Employment Relations Today*, Spring, 59–70; Tung and Varma, Expatriate selection and evaluation.

47. Garonzik, R., Brockner, J., and Siegel, P. A. (2000). Identifying international assignees at risk for premature departure: The interactive effect of outcome favorability and procedural fairness. *Journal of Applied Psychology*, 85, 13–20; Nichols, C. E., Rothstein, M. G., and Bourne, A. (2002) Predicting expatriate work attitudes: The impact of cognitive closure and adjustment competencies. *International Journal of Cross-Cultural Management*, 2, 297–320.

48. Bolino, M. C., and Feldman, D. C. (2000). The antecedents and consequences of underemployment among expatriates. *Journal of Organizational Behavior*, 21, 889–911; Grant-Vallone, E. J., and Ensher, E. A. (2001). An examination of work and personal life conflict, organizational support, and employee health among international expatriates. *International Journal of Intercultural Relations*, 25, 261–278.

49. Tung and Varma, Expatriate selection and evaluation; Ward, C., and Rana-Deuba, A. (2000). Home and host culture influences on sojourner adjustment. *International Journal of Intercultural Relations*, 24, 291–306.

50. Adler, N. J., and Gundersen, A. (2007). *International Dimensions of Organizational Behavior*. Stamford, CT: Cengage Learning; Black, J. S. Gregersen, H. B., and Mendenhall, M. E. (1992). *Global Assignments: Successfully Expatriating and Repatriating International Managers*. San Francisco: Jossey-Bass; Jordan, M. (2001). Have husband, will travel. *The Wall Street Journal*, February 13, B1, B12; Latta, Expatriate policy and practice; Selmer, J. (1999). Corporate expatriate career development. *Journal of International Management*, 5, 55–71; Swaak, R. A. (1995). Today's expatriate family: Dual careers and other obstacles. *Compensation and Benefits Review*, 26, 21–26.

51. Adler and Gundersen, *International Dimensions of Organizational Behavior*; Black, Gregersen, and Mendenhall, *Global Assignments: Successfully Expatriating and Repatriating International Managers*; Briscoe, Schuler, and Claus, *International Human Resource Management*; Caligiuri, P. (2000). The big five personality characteristics as predictors of expatriate's desire to terminate the assignment and supervisor-rated performance. *Personnel Psychology*, 53, 67–88; Shaffer, Harrison, Gregersen, Black, and Ferzandi, You can take it with you.

52. Adler and Gundersen, *International Dimensions of Organizational Behavior*; Briscoe, Schuler, and Claus, *International Human Resource Management*; Sanchez, J. I., Spector, P. E., and

Cooper, C. L. (2000). Adapting to a boundaryless world: A developmental expatriate model. *The Academy of Management Executive*, 14, 96–106.

53. Black, Gregersen, and Mendenhall, *Global Assignments: Successfully Expatriating and Repatriating International Managers*; Briscoe, Schuler, and Claus, *International Human Resource Management*; Brislin, R.W., MacNab, B. R., and Nayani, F. (2008). Cross-cultural training. In Smith, Peterson, and Thomas, *Handbook of Cross-Cultural Management Research*, 397–410; Deshpande, S. P., and Viswesvaran, C. (1992). Is cross-cultural training of managers effective? A meta analysis. *International Journal of Intercultural Relations*, 16, 295–310; Fitzgerald-Turner, B. (1997). Myths of expatriate life. *HR Magazine*, June, 1–7.

54. Black, J. S. (1992). Coming home: The relationship of expatriate expectations with repatriation adjustment and job performance. *Human Relations*, 45, 177–192; Black, Gregersen, and Mendenhall, *Global Assignments: Successfully Expatriating and Repatriating International Managers*.

55. Adler and Gundersen, *International Dimensions of Organizational Behavior*; Aryee, S., Chay, Y. W., and Chew, J. (1996). An investigation of the willingness of managerial employees to accept an expatriate assignment. *Journal of Organizational Behavior*, 17, 267–283; Black, Gregersen, and Mendenhall, *Global Assignments: Successfully Expatriating and Repatriating International Managers*; Briscoe, Schuler, and Claus, *International Human Resource Management*; Stroh, L. K., Dennis, L. E., and Cramer, T. C. (1994). Predictors of expatriate adjustment. *International Journal of Organizational Analysis*, 2, 176–192.

56. *The Economist*. (2011). A tale of two expats, January 1, 62–64.

57. Briscoe, Schuler, and Claus, *International Human Resource Management*; Solomon, C. M. (1996). Expats say: Help make us mobile. *Personnel Journal*, July, 43–52.

58. Carpenter, Battling the overseas blues; Hagerty, B. (1993). Trainers help expatriate employees build bridges to different cultures. *The Wall Street Journal*, June 14, B1, B6.

59. Adler and Gundersen, *International Dimensions of Organizational Behavior*; Arthur, W., and Bennett, W. (1995). The international assignee: The relative importance of factors perceived to contribute to success. *Personnel Psychology*, 48, 99–114.

60. Briscoe, Schuler, and Claus, *International Human Resource Management*; Black, J. S., and Gregersen, H. B. (1991). The other half of the picture: Antecedents of spouse cross-cultural adjustment. *Journal of International Business Studies*, 22, 461–477.

61. Carraher, S. M., Sullivan, S. E., and Crocitto, M. M. (2008). Mentoring across global boundaries: An empirical examination of home- and host-country mentors on expatriate career outcomes. *Journal of International Business Studies*, 39, 1310–1326; Reiche, B. S., Harzing, A. W., and Kraimer, M. L. (2009). The role of international assignees' social capital in creating inter-unit intellectual capital: A cross-level model. *Journal of International Business Studies*, 40, 509–526.

62. Carpenter, S., Battling the overseas blues.

63. Tu, H., and Sullivan, S. E. (1994). Preparing yourself for an international assignment. *Business Horizons*, 37, January–February, 67–70; Zaslow, J. (2003). The fourth without fireworks: Americans' quiet patriotism abroad. *The Wall Street Journal*, July 3, D1.

64. Furuya, N., Stevens, M. J., Bird, A., Oddou, G., and Mendenhall, M. (2009). Managing the learning and transfer of global management competence: Antecedents and outcomes of Japanese repatriation effectiveness. *Journal of International Business Studies*, 40, 200–215.

65. Takeuchi, S., Imahori, T., and Matsumoto, D. (2001). Adjustment of criticism styles in Japanese returnees to Japan. *International Journal of Intercultural Relations*, 25, 315–327; Black, J. S. (1992). Coming home: The relationship of expatriate expectations with repatriation adjustment and job performance. *Human Relations*, 45, 177–192; Black, Gregersen, and Mendenhall, *Global Assignments: Successfully Expatriating and Repatriating International Managers*.

66. Briscoe, Schuler, and Claus, *International Human Resource Management*; Solomon, C. M. (1995). Repatriation: Up, down, or out? *Personnel Journal*, January, 28–37; see also www.coherent.com.

chapter 12

evaluating and rewarding employees worldwide

Learning Objectives

After reading this chapter, you should be able to:

■ evaluate employee performance and describe the tradeoffs and challenges associated with appraising the performance of expatriates;

■ understand that providing performance feedback can mean different things to employees with different cultural values and in different locations;

■ recognize that compensation is one of the main reasons to evaluate performance and that this means *more* than just level of pay;

■ explain the different options for compensating expatriates and be able to select an option most likely to be effective in a particular context.

International Challenge

Multinationals Are Making it Harder for Employees to Accept Expatriate Assignments

The cost of sending expatriates abroad has always been a challenge, but maybe more so today than it has ever been. As companies around the world rebuild themselves after a tough recession, they face more international staffing demands than ever—thanks largely to fast-growing countries such as China, Brazil, and India. Today, "lean" is the watchword in most business, but especially when concerning international business and, in turn, the expatriates working for the firms. Compensation packages and perquisites have been cut back significantly—at least compared to "the good old days." Unless you are a very high-level executive, most incentives and allowances have been reduced or eliminated, along with once-common perks such as drivers and maids.

As a result, potential expatriates have increasingly been turning down foreign assignment offers and finding themselves doing more penny-pinching than ever, even when they do agree to an assignment. Multinationals, on the other hand, especially in the U.S. and Western Europe, are finding it difficult to talk employees into going overseas for years at a time, especially with less compensation on the table. Even when compensation is good, savvy employees increasingly factor in the context of the international assignment and the impact that this has on their annual evaluation in the short run, as well as their career path in the longer run.

The reasons for this reluctance are varied, but Americans may be among the most likely to refuse an expatriate assignment: for instance, if you are a 45-year-old mid-level marketing manager earning $140,000 for a Pittsburgh-based company and have a husband and two school-age children. Your company wants to send you to Seoul, South Korea, for three years. Would you want to uproot your children and pull them out of their schools? Likewise, what if your spouse does not want to give up his or her job to move across the world to follow your job?

Another major reason Americans are saying "no" to foreign assignments is that companies are offering less in efforts to control costs, given that traditional expatriates are a huge "money pit." Posting that 45-year-old American marketing manager and her family to South Korea, for example, may cost three times her base salary per year. Consequently, the expatriate package presented to her might not include any bonuses or Foreign Service premiums as incentives to say yes. In the past, these were often worth an additional 10–20 percent of the base salary. Nor will housing or cost-of-living allowances necessarily cover everything. It could be that a portion of housing expenses in Seoul may be out of pocket and frugality in food and clothes shopping will be the byword. All of these expenses would be in addition to the hassle of having to sell or rent out the family home in Pittsburgh before leaving the U.S. This also may be an expense that the company might not help with.

Cost considerations do not stop there. American expatriates often pay twice when it comes to income taxes thanks to U.S. tax regulations. Specifically, U.S. expatriates typically pay income tax to the foreign country in which they are posted, based on their locally earned salaries, as well as U.S. income tax on anything over roughly $97,000 earned abroad (as of 2013). This hits well-paid American expatriates especially hard for those assigned to countries where local income taxes are relatively low (such as Singapore or Russia), but less so in high-tax countries (such as Germany) where amounts paid can be credited against U.S. tax liabilities. Many expatriates end up paying thousands of dollars more a year in income taxes as a result. Moreover, companies are less likely to provide tax equalization benefits to wipe out these extra costs—meaning that while companies save themselves money, expatriates have to pay up instead.

So, here is the big question: if you were that American marketing manager, would you want to be an expatriate under these (complex) circumstances? If not, what kind of compensation and support package would be necessary in order to entice you to sign up for a one-, two-, or three-year posting abroad? Are there other benefits besides money that companies could offer? And on the company side of the ledger, what would you recommend multinationals consider if they want to get more people to say "yes" to expatriate assignments—other than throw lots of money at them (which seems unlikely regardless)? Are there other options for firms, especially U.S.-based multinationals, that are dealing with lots of "no" answers from expatriates, in addition to ever-higher costs of long-term overseas assignments? As you read this chapter, you may come up with some answers or at least some possibilities to consider. Then read the Up to the Challenge? feature at the end of the chapter to learn what some multinationals are doing to address these expatriate compensation issues.[1]

Employee Performance Appraisal: The Global Challenge

Managing employee performance is always challenging and is among the most important functions of a manager or leader. But for multinationals, the difficulty is compounded by having employees scattered all around the world—some of whom embrace different cultural values and welcome the experience of localized practices for performance. Then there is the thorny issue of how to evaluate and manage the performance of expatriates—something that produces yet another major set of headaches.

There is no doubt that employee performance evaluation is more costly and complex for a multinational than for those with single-country operations. It is important to keep in mind the core questions facing multinationals when it comes to managing and appraising employee performance:

- Should the multinational rely on a standardized set of policies, procedures and practices when it comes to managing and appraising employee feedback worldwide?
- Should the multinational rely on a dispersed set of systems that are aligned with local business and management practices in the places where it does business?
- Should the multinational take a blended approach to performance appraisal and management, one that relies on a combination of standardized practices and local latitude aimed at keeping some local practices intact?

The bottom line is that there are no simple answers to these questions. While some multinationals have moved toward a blended approach over the years, this has only made the front-line manager's job more difficult. A key is to keep the global workforce focused on company goals and moving forward to successfully execute firm strategy for international markets—performance appraisal systems are an important mechanism for doing just that. Yet, this all has to be done against a background where employees in different places vary in terms of how they interpret performance, react to feedback, and view their jobs.[2]

Receiving a performance appraisal is not likely to be high on an employee's list of favorite activities. Likewise, conducting performance appraisals is one of the things that many managers dislike most about their jobs. Performance appraisals, after all, are inherently difficult and few managers enjoy providing employees with direct feedback about their performance, especially when the feedback is negative. Anyone who underestimates how hard this is to do has probably not given many evaluations yet.

Imagine you have six employees reporting to you in your firm's London headquarters—your job as a manager is determine how well they performed their jobs and to give them performance appraisal on an annual, semi-annual, or even more frequent basis. But unless you took extensive notes on each employee as the year unfolded, you would need to recall the accomplishments, limitations, and challenges of each person, then somehow sum up these pluses and minuses over the evaluation period accurately, trying not to be overly influenced by recent or overly salient events. Next, you may want to compare these appropriately weighted evaluations across your six employees and rank-order them so that you can distribute your limited pool of rewards and demonstrate to your superiors that you have the fortitude to distinguish between high-performing employees and those deserving of a negative evaluation. Finally comes what is often the hardest part for managers—following the company's procedure to meet with each person to give him or her feedback, outlining rewards that you think his or her service deserves.

Now imagine if one of the subordinates you had to evaluate was an expatriate posted to Mexico City. First, your office is in London, and even if you visited Mexico City during the year it is not likely that you would have had a chance to assess the expatriate's performance in any detailed manner. Moreover, imagine that you have never worked in Mexico and do not know all that much about the environment there, including any differences in culture or business practices. In short, you would probably have great difficulty grasping how you could do a fair job of appraising the expatriate's performance, especially from thousands of miles away.

Consequently, the first half of this chapter details dilemmas just like this—when managers must confront the pitfalls that can occur when conducting performance evaluations of expatriates and foreign nationals. The second half of the chapter reviews the intricacies of making compensation decisions in an international context as well as the challenges of constructing pay and benefits packages for expatriates.

Multinationals and Performance Evaluation for Expatriates

Evaluating expatriates can prove daunting. This is especially the case for large multinationals—firms with expatriates scattered across dozens of countries where they do business. While these firms face considerable diversity in employee attitudes and values across countries, it is also true that multinationals themselves vary—sometimes considerably—in how they approach performance appraisal in the first place.

For instance, in the previous London example, some underlying assumptions are apparent in the description, including that performance appraisal is focused on individual performance, with the best performers getting the biggest share of available rewards. This "winner takes all" orientation is more common among firms based in the U.S. and the U.K. In northern European countries such as Sweden, however, company policies have evolved and adjusted to include greater legal regulation of compensation and associated performance management systems. This most likely emanated from basic egalitarian values that discourage wide compensation differences and "punitive" performance appraisal. Likewise, compared to their American or British counterparts, Japanese multinationals operate in a more collectivistic environment. Consequently, they tend to emphasize loyalty to the company in their performance appraisal procedures, with length of service carrying relatively more weight and individual performance relatively less. It is important to remember that multinationals (in part) are a product of the home environment where they evolved. While they are always changing and evolving, it is not uncommon for those roots to be reflected in the philosophies, policies, and practices of firms, in relation to performance appraisal and compensation.[3]

Regardless of their roots, research shows that when multinationals tailor performance appraisal and other international human resource management (IHRM) practices to the local context, their foreign subsidiaries tend to perform better. This is largely because employees become more motivated and skilled, with their performance improving as a result. Nevertheless, there are experts who argue that multinationals should apply IHRM "best practices" globally, particularly those that help firms execute their international strategies or preserve corporate values deemed important for all employees to embrace— wherever they live and work.[4]

Some multinationals take a blended approach, insisting on certain common practices everywhere while also allowing for considerable tailoring in local units. Interestingly, a number of factors seem to impact how much local tailoring takes place. For instance, as the number of expatriates deployed increases, the amount of local IHRM tailoring tends to decrease. In essence, more expatriates make it easier for multinationals to directly transfer parent company knowledge and practices, including about IHRM, to foreign subsidiaries. The nature of the foreign location itself, however, may also impact how much or how little local IHRM adaptation takes place. For example, consider Western multinationals operating in both China and India. One study found that, compared to their Chinese subsidiaries, Indian subsidiaries were seen as playing a stronger strategic role for the firm while also using more localized IHRM practices. This may reflect India's greater exposure to Western influence, as well as the more common use of English—factors that may make it easier for the parent company and the subsidiary alike to create blended IRHM practices that reflect both the corporation's strategic directions and local preferences.[5]

A company's goals for sending expatriates to foreign locations include the desire for employees to gain additional business skills and to experience a global perspective on the business. These goals are often met. In one study, expatriates reported that their experiences abroad:

- increased their ability to manage cultural differences;
- improved their understanding of international operations;
- made them more open-minded about different problem-solving methods; and
- improved their ability to more flexibly approach human resource issues.[6]

While these growth experiences benefit the employee as well as the company, these are not commonly part of a domestic performance appraisal. If they *are* considered, such experiences are difficult to evaluate, especially without observing the expatriate over a long period of time. Employees from different cultures may have divergent reactions to appraisal feedback as well as a different understanding of how such feedback should be presented. In essence, the challenge of evaluating expatriates is compounded when the evaluations are conducted from a distance—whether that distance is geographical, cultural, or both.

Nevertheless, most multinationals routinely evaluate the performance of their expatriates. Consequently, the remainder of this section will deal with several important questions about performance appraisal for expatriates:

1. *Who* should evaluate their performance?
2. *When* (and how often) should they be evaluated?
3. *What* aspects of performance should be evaluated?

Who Should Evaluate Expatriate Performance?

Multinationals have a variety of options for evaluating expatriates. First, expatriate evaluations can be conducted in the host country, the home country, or both. Moreover, any number of potential evaluators can be involved in this process besides the expatriate's supervisor. This can include peers, subordinates, and HR professionals. In fact, multinationals may use a mix of home- and host-country personnel in the evaluation process. Figure 12.1 shows how frequently different types of personnel are involved in expatriate evaluation. This involvement implies a sophisticated evaluation system, but the reality is that most expatriate evaluations are anything but. Instead, they are often conducted on a relatively informal basis. While expatriate evaluations frequently follow the outlines of domestic performance appraisal processes, an irony is that fewer evaluators may be involved. According to one survey, domestic performance evaluation involved twice as many evaluators than their international counterparts. Nevertheless, evaluating expatriates is actually much more challenging than evaluating domestic employees.[7]

For example, while an American manager assigned to the Netherlands may have a Dutch boss, he or she may still have a boss in the U.S.—and be evaluated by both. Part of the frustration for multinationals is that little hard evidence exists about what the "best practices" are with respect to evaluating expatriates. For instance, there is considerable controversy about which evaluator is better—a host-country manager or a home-country manager.[8]

	Performance Review Conducted in Home Country	Performance Review Conducted in Host Country
% of multinationals conducting review in location	56%—but more common in multinationals with less than 100 expatriates	71%—but more common in multinationals with more than 100 expatriates
% of expatriate appraisals involving a specific evaluator	41%—Immediate supervisor 23%—Corporate HR manager 17%—Regional manager 7%—Assignment sponsor	75%—Immediate supervisor 23%—Expatriate himself or herself 12%—Local HR manager 10%—Peers 7%—Subordinates

Figure 12.1 Who Evaluates Expatriate Performance in Multinationals? A Snapshot.

Source: Adapted from Briscoe, D. R., Schuler, R. S., and Claus, L. (2009). *International Human Resource Management* (3rd ed.), 302–303. New York: Routledge.

Evaluations by Host-Country Professionals

As shown in Figure 12.1, having host-country professionals involved in expatriate evaluation is a popular option, particularly for bigger multinationals with a large number of expatriates to manage. Presumably, the advantages associated with host-country evaluation increase with numbers, making it more difficult for home-country managers to collect the information needed to perform adequate reviews on their far-flung expatriate workforces.

Moreover, host-country professionals are more likely to be familiar with the expatriate's work and performance, particularly given local cultural norms. This is important because the quality of the expatriate's job in large part revolves around how culturally savvy he or she is in the business environment. Consequently, having expatriates evaluated by their host-country supervisors or other local professionals makes a great deal of sense. Indeed, many experts argue that these are the only people who are in a position to closely observe the expatriate's work over a long period of time and who fully understand the local context.[9]

Yet, relying on host-country professionals to evaluate expatriate performance is not without drawbacks. For instance, while local professionals are knowledgeable about their environment, they also bring their own cultural frames of reference to the table in ways that cause problems. One American expatriate working in India pressed his subordinates for their ideas about a project—consistent with participative management techniques that work well in the U.S. But, his host-country supervisor frowned upon this behavior and gave him a negative performance evaluation. The local supervisor's reactions are not surprising given that Indian culture tends to be higher in power distance than the U.S., which makes autocratic forms of leadership more acceptable. But the expatriate nevertheless paid the price—after returning home, this negative evaluation was one of the reasons that he was denied a promotion. One reaction to this incident is that the American expatriate got what he deserved. On the other hand, what if the American parent company wanted the expatriate to instill openness to participative management in its Indian workforce? Regardless of the wisdom of such an approach, should the expatriate be punished for following instructions? Or perhaps the blame could also be placed on the home office, for failing to provide the cultural training necessary for instilling a greater appreciation for business participation in a culturally appropriate manner. Regardless of where the blame lies, this underscores the dangers associated with having host-country professionals evaluate expatriate performance.[10]

Other potential problems associated with a host-country evaluation include language and the fact that the host professional may simply be unable to clearly communicate feedback to the expatriate. Perhaps more important, however, is that dimensions of performance considered important may vary considerably between the local context and the home country. Some of this may stem from cultural differences. But whatever the reason, factors important to the host professionals evaluating expatriates will likely be weighted heavily in the evaluation. The problem occurs, of course, when expatriates do not realize that the evaluation criteria used in the home country and those that are used locally are not aligned. An expatriate in China, for example, may have to learn over time to show considerable restraint in sharing her feelings, even if she is upset with a subordinate. That restraint may count positively in an evaluation by a local manager, while being viewed negatively in the U.S.[11]

Moreover, differences in criteria may be subtle and not directly related to performance per se—instead, reflecting differences in interaction norms. As a result, even if a multinational uses the same performance appraisal system everywhere, the results might be different because of these norms. Naturally, expatriates parachuting into a new environment may not be aware of these norms and make mistakes as a result. For instance, consider Indian expatriates posted to an American subsidiary. Because of common interaction norms in their home country, these Indian expatriates might make an effort to develop a relationship with their bosses because in India, getting a supervisor to like you may positively impact your performance evaluations. American supervisors, often trained to separate personal feelings from performance goals and targets, are unlikely to be swayed by this. Indeed, they may wonder why the Indian expatriates spend so much time on relationship building instead of "doing their jobs." Conversely, American expatriates posted to an Indian subsidiary may not realize the importance of building a positive personal relationship with their immediate supervisor. Failing to do this may be seen as rude and result in supervisory dislike that spills over to the expatriates' evaluation. The evaluations of both the Indian and American expatriates are likely to suffer. Naturally, this is something that could be alleviated by training—for expatriates as well as evaluating professionals in host countries.[12]

Finally, it is important to recognize that host-country professionals may not have the multinational's overall strategy in mind when evaluating expatriates. This can result in negative evaluations when an expatriate is seen as behaving in ways that benefit the corporation as a whole instead of the foreign subsidiary. While one might hope that the home office would recognize and understand what the expatriate has done, this is far from certain. In fact, it may be easier to simply take the evaluation by local professionals in stride.[13]

Overall, the use of host-country professionals to evaluate expatriate performance has both pluses and minuses. Consequently, multinationals may want to use home-office personnel for performance evaluations of expatriates for greater control and continuity.

Evaluations by Home-Country Professionals

Indeed, there are clear advantages to having home-country professionals evaluate expatriates. For one, these managers are typically more familiar with expatriates' experiences, work history, and performance track record. Moreover, in most cases home-country professionals speak the same language and share the same basic cultural roots as the expatriates they are evaluating—a definite advantage over host-country professionals, at least when it comes to communicating performance feedback. These similarities and shared perspectives make it easier for the home-country manager— everything else being equal—to help the expatriate learn and develop from the feedback he or she receives.

On the other hand, home-country professionals also have shortcomings as evaluators of expatriates. One clear disadvantage has to do with distance—both geographic and psychological. Simply put, home-country professionals cannot observe expatriates and their performance in the foreign locations where they work. Moreover, home-country professionals typically receive little feedback or information from the host country about the expatriates that they have to evaluate. Consequently, a major challenge for home-country professionals is gaining access to the information needed to make a quality evaluation of expatriates. Indeed, most expatriates have relatively little "quality" contact with home-office personnel during their overseas assignment, including their direct home-country supervisor. When they do, it is often initiated by expatriates themselves.

Granted, e-mails and video conferencing have made it easier to connect with the home office. But this kind of "lean" contact is no substitute for more extended and "rich" on-the-job observations. Nor does it mean that home-office personnel really understand what is happening in the foreign subsidiary and why. In fact, home-office professionals may not be familiar with, much less grasp, the intricacies of the expatriates' foreign posts or even have any experience in the country whatsoever. As a result, they may not fully understand the pressures that the expatriate faces and the appropriate standards to use when evaluating that person's performance.[14]

Figure 12.2 summarizes the advantages and disadvantages associated with home versus host-country professionals doing performance evaluations of expatriates.

	Performance Evaluation Done by Home-Country Professional	Performance Evaluation Done by Host-Country Professional
Pros	• Typically has a better understanding of overall corporate goals and objectives • Has more background on expatriate's work history • Often shares expatriate's values and language, easier to give performance feedback	• In the best position to observe expatriate's behavior and performance over a long period of time • Has excellent understanding of local context, practices, and values and how they relate to performance
Cons	• May have limited understanding of local context or culture • Little or no direct observation of expatriate performance in foreign location • May have weak grasp of criteria needed to perform well in local context	• Evaluations shaped by local values; may create problems given company objectives • Less familiar with overall company strategies and objectives • More difficulty communicating because of language and cultural differences

Figure 12.2 Pros and Cons of Home-Country versus Host-Country Evaluation of Expatriates.

Sources: Adapted from: Briscoe, D. R., Schuler, R. S., and Claus, L. (2009). *International Human Resource Management* (3rd ed.). New York: Routledge; Oddou, G., and Mendenhall, M. (1991). Expatriate performance appraisal: Problems and solutions. In. M. Mendenhall and G. Oddou (eds) *International Human Resource Management*, 364–374. Boston: PWS-Kent.

Advantages and disadvantages are one thing, but multinationals want to know what approach is the best for evaluating expatriates. The answer, however, is complex. It depends on the multinational's goals, the number of expatriates involved, the location that they are posted to, and the nature of the work required—just to name a few parameters. As you might suspect, some multinationals have tried to capitalize on the respective strengths of home- and host-country professionals by involving both in the evaluation of expatriates. This may translate into home-office professionals playing a supporting rather than leading role in the evaluation of local performance. For example, AT&T and 3M Corporation developed a "career sponsor" program to link expatriates to the corporate office. Sponsors keep the expatriate in touch with what is going on at home and act as mentors. They will also conduct performance evaluations using the cultural perspective of the home office. Assessments of such programs show them to be successful. Likewise, research conducted with a focus on U.S. multinationals has shown that a balanced set of evaluators from both the home and the host country increases the accuracy of performance evaluations.[15]

When Should Expatriate Performance Be Evaluated?

Another important question to address is when to perform the expatriate evaluation. U.S. firms have historically evaluated employees—domestic or international–once or twice a year. Experts, however, have argued that this is too infrequent; it forces evaluators to rely on shaky memories and makes them subject to some well-known errors in judgment. Recent actions and events carry inordinate weight because they are first to mind. Experts suggest that evaluations be done more frequently, depending on the tasks or projects involved, as well as the role of the evaluator.[16]

For example, given the complexities, it may make sense to have local supervisors or professionals conduct evaluations as major projects or task milestones or completed. Home-country professionals, in contrast, might provide less frequent or calendar-based evaluations of performance, such as once every six months, given their distance and inability to make detailed observations. Again, this may vary depending on the expatriate's work role, rank, and experience. Frankly, it may be premature to conduct a formal performance appraisal during the first six months of a foreign assignment in any case. After all, expatriates and their families need time to adjust to their foreign surroundings. On the other hand, if it is obvious that things are not going well, management—in either the host or home country—should let the expatriate know and take steps to help as soon as possible.[17]

This underscores the importance of flexibility in the timing of expatriate evaluations. Early on in their assignments, it might be best to give expatriates informal feedback and wait until after the first six months abroad before conducting anything more formal that is focused on performance. Naturally, the cycle of task or project completion may impact the precise timing of evaluations, particularly those done locally. Still, multinationals would be wise to expect and plan for problems, many of which have already been discussed. For example, obtaining home-office support may be difficult if visits are infrequent or short term in nature, limited to interaction such as brief e-mails, phone calls or video conferences. Sensitive information is typically best conveyed in a personal, face-to-face context, whether individual or group-based—something that is more difficult for home-office professionals to do by definition. Depending on where the expatriate is posted, it may be culturally difficult for local managers or professionals to provide "informal" feedback. Plus, in some cases it may take the expatriate longer than six months to adjust to the point where performance is optimal. Overall, the best time to evaluate expatriates depends on what is "right" given the nature of the overseas assignment and the adjustment of the individual holding it.[18]

Context Variables That Impact Evaluations of Expatriates

In some ways the thorniest question about evaluating expatriates has to do with what areas or criteria should be considered in the evaluation. There are at least three importance features about the context of the assignment that should be kept in mind when evaluating expatriate performance: the *environment* in which the job is done, the *task* or tasks themselves, and the *personal characteristics* of the expatriate.[19]

Environmental Variables

The circumstances under which any job is performed can be more or less demanding. Working in a mine is physically more difficult than working in an office. Consequently, the degree to which the environment presents special challenges should be taken into account when determining performance criteria. Posting expatriates to foreign locations that are full of cultural, legal, and social differences can present unique environmental challenges. For example, an American working for a mining company in Zimbabwe will have more challenges than if they worked for the firm's operations in the state of Montana, which is within the employee's home country. Moreover, given that home-office personnel are not in a position to observe the local context that the expatriate must operate in, it is not likely that the full impact of environmental variables will be appreciated.

For example, imagine that an expatriate running a plant in Mexico has an employee productivity level much lower than a comparable plant running in the U.S. (the firm's home country). Should the expatriate be given a negative evaluation as a result? Experts would say probably not—this outcome could reflect a unique Mexican context. If more detailed data show that this plant's employees were much more productive than their average Mexican counterparts, experts would be even more confident that these results are due not to the expatriate manager's lack of acumen, but perhaps the constraints of working in Mexico.[20]

Task Variables

The nature of the work itself may present special challenges to expatriates in ways that impact their performance, thus close attention should be paid to such challenges when determining performance criteria. For instance, an important job factor in many expatriate roles is how much interaction will be required with locals. Expatriates whose performance relies on effective interactions with locals should have performance evaluations that heavily consider such task criteria. Evaluators may place greater emphasis on displaying cultural savvy in this area than for another assignment. A software engineer is less likely to need the same level of cultural awareness than an expatriate in a marketing role to perform successfully. Likewise, on foreign assignments, American expatriates who are middle-level managers might need to have more interactions with government officials overseas than they would in the comparable roles back in the U.S.[21]

Personal Characteristics

Finally, there are differences among individuals in their ability to handle a foreign assignment—either because of experience, temperament, or other features. For instance, as discussed in Chapter 11, tolerance for ambiguity and flexibility are among the characteristics that help expatriates adjust to their overseas location and to be successful. Consequently, personal characteristics that are known to predict success or failure on expatriate assignments should be taken into consideration, particularly during the process of choosing who to send.

Some Additional Challenges with Cross-Border Performance Evaluations

Even if a firm has considered these three important constraints on performance overseas, measuring an expatriate's performance can still be challenging. For example, while it might seem fairly straightforward to evaluate an expatriate leading a business unit using financial measures, the overseas context complicates matters. First, business laws and tax rules will be different than in the home country, making it harder to calculate things such as profitability. Second, there may be challenges associated with currency conversion and profit repatriation, issues that can prove especially vexing when currency values shift suddenly or nations create hurdles for getting money out of the country.

China is a good example of a country that has loosened currency exchange and profit repatriation rules in recent years. Nevertheless, the regulatory environment in China is burdensome and complex for multinationals, especially when it comes to profit repatriation. Foreign firms must be able to navigate in and around several governing institutions regulating business operations in China. It is easy to see how jumping through all of the bureaucratic hoops required in China could make it more difficult to figure out how well an expatriate leading a multinational's Chinese subsidiary is actually doing from a financial perspective.[22]

Because of tax law and currency differences, multinationals often take a variety of steps to minimize taxes and avoid losses from currency fluctuations. As a result, the true performance of a foreign subsidiary, and the management team running it, is often obscured. Firms may want to use additional yardsticks to evaluate expatriate performance. These measures are designed to tease out and separate tax, currency, and other regulatory hurdles that firms have to deal with when borders are crossed. Granted, companies may not have the time and money to do this. Instead, it may be more practical to follow some general guidelines for effectively evaluating expatriate performance.[23]

General Guidelines for Expatriate Evaluation

Rate the Assignment Difficulty

Doing a thorough assessment of how difficult a specific foreign assignment might be for an expatriate, well in advance of an actual assignment or placement, should pay dividends when the time comes to evaluate his or her performance. Difficulty scores can then be applied to weight the normal process used to evaluate performance. For example, if an expatriate will be posted to a very difficult assignment, his or her usual evaluation could be multiplied by 2.0. If the foreign posting is moderately difficult, then the process could be weighted by 1.5, and so on. Of course, the challenge for human resource personnel is to figure out which assignment is more difficult than others and what specific weighting should be applied.[24]

First, the extent of language adjustment—if any—would certainly add to assignment difficulty. An American expatriate posted to a location such as India, where the primary business language used is English, may have an easier time than if sent to a place where English use is less pervasive, such as Vietnam.

Economic and political stability are factors that would also determine difficulty in posting (see Chapter 2 for more detail). Expatriates who do well in tough places are deserving of excellent evaluations. For example, one American expatriate was instrumental in stopping a strike from occurring in the firm's Chilean plant—this would have shut down the plant and soured relations with the home office. Preventing the strike was a big accomplishment. Clearly, the expatriate demonstrated a good deal of cultural acumen and insight. Unfortunately, while the labor situation was unfolding, volatile exchange rates in Chile caused demand for the plant's product to temporarily drop 30 percent. Rather than recognize the expatriate for averting the strike, the parent company focused on the negative sales figures. As a result, the expatriate received a lackluster performance evaluation.[25]

Additional Suggestions for Expatriate Evaluation

Firms will want to consider features in addition to judging the difficulty of the assignment location. First, while many experts recommend multiple home- and host-country evaluators be involved in expatriate assessment, some place more weight on evaluations performed by host-country managers because they are in a better position to observe an expatriate's actual performance. A related idea, especially if the home office is responsible for expatriate evaluation, is to involve another person who has experience in the same country that an expatriate is posted to. This increases the local knowledge and expertise that can be brought to bear when the home office is evaluating expatriates. Conversely, if host-country personnel have primary responsibility for conducting expatriate evaluations, they should seek input from home-office personnel before conveying any feedback to expatriates. This has the twin benefit of helping local professionals understand how parent company values should shape the performance evaluation, as well as sharing any corporate norms about actual delivery of feedback.

Often overlooked in the evaluation process are expatriates themselves. Regardless of how performance is evaluated, it is important that multinationals:

- communicate up front with expatriates about what performance criteria are important to both host- and home-country managers, as well as what constitutes success relative to those criteria;
- fully explain how the process of performance appraisal will work for expatriates—ideally integrate it into expatriates' assignment plans;
- conduct training for both performance evaluators and expatriates about how their respective frames of reference (including cultural values) can impact both the assessment of performance and how employees react to it;
- emphasize that performance evaluations will be conducted more frequently given the challenges of expatriate assignments while also telling expatriates that their initial evaluation will be delayed somewhat to give them time to adjust.[26]

Evaluating Foreign-Born Employees

Parent-country expatriates are not the only employees that multinationals have to manage successfully. Indeed, they may have to manage foreign nationals in the parent country (such as a Chinese national posted to the headquarters of an American multinational) as well as host-country nationals working for expatriates in a foreign subsidiary. While both scenarios represent just the tip of the personnel iceberg, they nevertheless highlight two common performance evaluation scenarios for multinational firms. Naturally, one of the key challenges in each of these circumstances is how to effectively deliver feedback—regardless of whether the news is good or bad.

As countries develop economically, more seem to be adopting formal performance evaluation processes. This is not to say that economic giants, such as China and India, have large swaths of the business landscape that still embrace local or traditional methods. This may reflect the influence of cultural values. For example, state-owned enterprises in China tend to involve more evaluators, such as peers, and include moral dimensions, such as honesty, compared to private firms operating there. Foreign multinationals operating in China tend to be more frequent users of individual performance evaluations compared to other types of companies—something that Chinese employees appear to generally accept. Overall, like everything else in China, performance evaluation and feedback practices are changing dramatically. In any case, it may be safe to assume that some cultural differences exist that may impact the effectiveness of evaluation and feedback methods used with foreign-born employees.[27]

Compared to the U.S., performance evaluation systems in Middle Eastern countries are usually more informal, with less use of evaluation metrics, forms, and documentation. As a result, feedback can be subjective and informal, with an emphasis on the interpersonal aspects of performance. At a performance appraisal, paper and written evaluations are less likely to change hands or be filed for future reference. This presents an interesting situation because some multinational firms simply export their formal and explicit performance appraisal forms to their foreign subsidiaries. This can create potential for conflict when an implicit and informal culture meets an explicit and formal performance evaluation system.[28]

Likewise, the feedback method itself may be moderated by culture. For example, given the strong emphasis on collective values in Japan, it should come as no surprise that performance evaluations are much more likely to be conducted in a group setting than in Europe or the U.S. While team-based work approaches are popular in many Western countries, performance evaluations are still primarily done at the individual level. Interestingly, over the past 10–15 years, Japanese firms have been slowly shifting toward a greater emphasis on individual performance evaluations—despite the potential disruption to group harmony (a trend Japanese refer to as "performance-ism" or *seikashugi*).[29]

Culture can also shape how foreign employees react to performance feedback and the various types of delivery mechanisms. Consider the U.K., a nation that is culturally similar to the U.S. One study found that British and American employees react somewhat differently to performance feedback. Americans became more productive after receiving either praise or criticism. In general, the more feedback they received, the higher their subsequent performance. This finding was observed for British employees only after they received *praise* for their behavior—they did not respond well to criticism.[30]

Many other differences in reactions to feedback also exist, particularly if we compare Western approaches to the more face-conscious and collective orientations found in some Asian countries. Yet, there are often wide differences in reactions to performance appraisals across Asian countries (e.g., Indonesia, Malaysia, the Philippines, and Thailand). Consequently, it would be a mistake to lump these nations together and assume reactions to feedback will be the same across Asia.[31]

Figure 12.3 summarizes performance appraisal characteristics commonly found in four different countries, particularly in local firms. In the U.S., for example, the emphasis in the appraisal is on evaluation, not on development or improvement per se. Criticism is direct, with relatively lower concern with face-saving of the employee. In other countries, however, the process of providing the feedback is monitored much more carefully for its effect on the recipient. For example, feedback is often more indirect in South Korea, with considerable concern for saving face. The International Insights feature offers some general guidelines for providing feedback to foreign employees that are worth considering.

Characteristic	Country			
	United States	**Saudi Arabia**	**South Korea**	**China**
General purpose	Evaluation of performance	Evaluation, coaching	Coaching	Financial reward, Retention
Feedback from superiors	Considerable amount	Considerable amount	Relatively little	Little, but may receive some from peers
Face-saving concern	Low	High	High	High
Employee involvement	Medium to high	High	Low	Medium self-evaluation expected
Type of feedback	Criticism is direct	Criticism less direct	Criticism mostly indirect	Criticism mostly indirect
Level of formality	Formal; probably written	Informal; not written	Informal; not written, but this is changing	Largely informal
Determinants of positive appraisal	Performance criteria	Seniority, connections	Seniority; ability, performance becoming important	Age, seniority, but becoming more performance oriented

Figure 12.3 Differences in Performance Evaluation Systems: A Four-Country Snapshot.

Sources: Adapted from Cooke, F. L. (2008). Performance management in China. In Varma, A., Budhwar, P. S., and DeNisi, A. (eds) *Performance Management Systems: A Global Perspective*, 193–209. New York: Routledge; Harris, P. R., and Moran, R. T. (1991). *Managing Cultural Differences* (3rd ed.). Houston, TX: Gulf; Yang, H., and Rowley, C. (2008). Performance management in South Korea. In Varma, A., Budhwar, P. S., and DeNisi, A. (eds) *Performance Management Systems: A Global Perspective*, 210–222. New York: Routledge.

International Insights

Some Advice for Providing Performance Feedback to Foreign-Born Employees

In the U.S., the rule of thumb for feedback is to reward in public and criticize in private. This human resources truism, however, may not always be the best for foreign-born employees. The following are some recommendations for crafting feedback that might be delivered as part of performance evaluation. Although these recommendations will not be appropriate for every foreign national, they are very good starting points for U.S. as well as many European managers:

- **Give feedback through a third party.** In many countries, receiving direct feedback from a superior—even if it is positive—can be uncomfortable. That is especially true for employees who embrace collectivistic values and find the prospect of being singled out for feedback disconcerting. Consequently, feedback may often be best delivered through a trusted third party.

- **Communicate to the whole group.** Another way to blunt the effect of direct feedback is to provide feedback on a group basis. A work group can be gathered together and the messages delivered that management thinks reflects their performance. This may be particularly appropriate if tasks are performed in teams or groups—something that can work well even in more individualistic cultures.
- **Change the form of feedback.** In most cases, the same message can be delivered in several different ways. Trying several different approaches, even if employees give the appearance of grasping what they are being told, increases the odds that the core message will be understood.
- **Simplify the feedback.** This recommendation can apply to anyone, but is especially important for foreign-born employees. Messages can almost always be shortened and simplified to improve clarity. For example, the phrase "in spite of the fact that . . ." could be simplified to "although" instead. Other examples include changing "the reason why is that" to "because" and "this is a subject that" to "this subject." Shorter, simpler messages increase comprehension, particularly for foreign employees.
- **Avoid slang.** Phrases such as "the bottom line," "they'll eat this one up," "the home stretch," "I'm all ears," and "let's get rolling" are often very difficult to interpret across cultural, linguistic, or national boundaries. Although these phrases are common and carry obvious meaning for many Western managers, foreign employees may have little or no cultural or experiential context in which to interpret what is really being said.[32]

Compensation of International Employees

Performance evaluations are one of the main inputs into the process of setting and managing compensation for employees around the world, so it is appropriate to discuss this. Compensation includes everything the firm does to recognize and reward employees for their performance, including pay. As employees rise in a firm, compensation may also include additional perquisites, such as extra vacation time and stock options, just to name a few examples.

What is more challenging for multinationals, at least relative to domestic firms, is that their compensation systems need to account for the fact that living costs, attitudes about pay, and laws governing compensation and benefits can vary considerably from country to country. So, multinationals must account for all the diversity that exists across the locations where they do business. On top of that, they must deal with the special compensation challenges associated with their expatriates, a topic addressed later. Overall, compensation systems are typically designed and implemented with several key goals in mind:

- to attract and retain the best people to staff positions worldwide;
- to make it as easy as possible to transfer people to various locations;
- to be consistent and fair toward all employees wherever they are; and
- to set compensation levels that match well with competitors while also holding down costs.[33]

The Meaning of Compensation

The understanding of "compensation" can vary across cultures. Compensation in the U.S. is seen as a swap—employees provide effort and output while receiving wages and benefits in return. While this "exchange" model of compensation is very common in Western cultures, differences in perspective remain. In Germany, the word for compensation also implies achievement, originating among shoemakers who custom-fit shoes to the buyer's feet. Shoes that "measured up" were ones that deserved compensation. In contrast, the Japanese word for compensation suggests protection, consistent with a traditional paternalistic employment system. Other cultures may view compensation as something beyond an exchange-driven process. They may view entitlement and obligation as important components of their compensation. To meet the goals discussed previously, firms need to be aware of these different views and expectations about the employment relationship that comes with doing business across borders.[34]

Pay Levels across Countries

Wage levels themselves can vary considerably across countries—something that multinationals are keenly aware of as they scour the world for the best talent at a cost-effective price. This has, in part, led to the offshoring of jobs and their migration as companies chased low-cost labor around the world. Granted, some companies have reversed their decisions to go to lower-wage locations because of logistical, cultural, and control challenges that acted to increase their costs. But others will doubtless continue to move their facilities abroad because of wage differentials. In 2009, for instance, Whirlpool announced plans to close a plant in Indiana and move the work to a facility in Mexico during 2010. Company representatives cited the need to "reduce excess capacity and improve costs," noting some $275 million that would be saved per year by moving those 1,100 jobs to Mexico. And while the company did not break down individual labor cost savings, it is likely that less expensive Mexican worker salaries played a role in Whirlpool's decision. Mexican manufacturing workers earn, on average, roughly 11 percent of what their American counterparts make.[35]

There are many nations in which workers earn little relative to U.S. workers and others. As of 2008, average wages in Sri Lanka (2 percent) and Poland (19 percent) were only a fraction of those of the average U.S. hourly rate, whereas countries such as Norway (166 percent) and Denmark (150 percent) each have pay rates much higher than the U.S. While these data do not paint the complete cost picture for firms that are interested in foreign relocation, they are instructive. Labor cost differences help explain why American firms sometimes seek lower-priced talent elsewhere and likewise why some foreign firms, such as BMW, have built factories in the U.S. German manufacturing wage rates are 140 percent of comparable American wages. But for American companies, the much lower costs in Mexico for labor—combined with easy access to the U.S. market—are among the reasons why thousands of U.S. firms have established *maquiladoras* (plants) set up in Mexico that are close to the U.S. border.[36]

Average wage data are not very helpful if companies are trying to establish precise compensation patterns in specific industries. Moreover, even within countries, large differences in compensation rates can exist, such as between northern states and southern states within the U.S. Likewise, estimates vary about true wage differences across countries, particularly in certain industries. For example, some estimates place Mexican wage rates closer to their American counterparts (roughly 25–40 percent of U.S. wages) compared to the U.S. Department of Labor estimate of 11 percent. The higher estimates include bonuses commonly distributed in Mexico, such as the custom of providing a Christmas bonus equal to one month's pay. Also, Mexico requires that firms distribute a share of their pretax profits to employees, as well as mandates that workers be paid 365 days a year. Nevertheless, these higher estimates still yield significant wage savings for those moving to Mexico.[37]

Executive Compensation across Countries

Cross-national differences also emerge when we consider the compensation of executives at U.S. firms relative to executives of foreign companies. It was previously discussed that CEO total compensation in the U.S. was twice as high as the next-highest paying country in Europe (Britain). Part of this reflects differences across countries regarding how senior executive compensation is structured. These differences may be closely connected to underlying cultural values in a society (e.g., individualistic and performance-oriented norms in the U.S.) and how "compensation" is viewed as a result.[38]

In U.S. firms, senior executive compensation is often heavily weighted to variable, long-term performance measures connected to stock prices—with performance bonuses and base salary as smaller considerations. According to one survey, roughly 60 percent of a top executive's compensation in the U.S. comes from such long-term incentives, with base salary and performance bonuses splitting the remaining 40 percent. This can produce some mind-boggling results. For instance, one American CEO took home a "small" base salary of $4.6 million while also pocketing over $650 million in long-term compensation in one year.

In contrast, almost 60 percent of the compensation earned by Nordic executives comes from base salary, while in Germany just over 80 percent of compensation comes from base salary and bonuses, with relatively little exposure to long-term incentives. In recent years, there has been a backlash in the U.S. against the heavy reliance on long-term incentives and bonuses for executives, particularly in the wake of a deep recession and financial crisis. Some American firms have even scaled back their compensation packages. But whether this makes a long-term dent in the compensation advantage that American executives have traditionally enjoyed over their foreign counterparts remains to be seen.[39] As we continue to move past the "Great Recession," however, 2012 data shows that executive compensation is again seeing big jumps over the pay of average employees. This is a divergence first observed in the late 1960s and into the 1970s within the U.S.

Perks and Other Forms of Compensation

Although not large enough to make up for the compensation lead enjoyed by American executives, foreign companies often provide a variety of perks to help offset the bite taken by taxes. Perks are typically non-monetary forms of compensation that are given to executives in recognition of their status or performance. Consider a typical signing package received by a Portuguese executive—this may include a maid, a gardener, and a laundress. The executive might also have a company car (with a gas stipend), company-provided housing, a monthly expense allowance, and paid utilities. Likewise, a Mexican executive may receive a company car and chauffeur, along with a certain value of groceries and liquor delivered to his or her home twice a month. In Japan, high tax rates mean that firms sometimes pay up to 50 percent of mortgage interest for all employees, and as they move up within the company they receive much more financial help. Executives may also have access to a car with a chauffeur, a larger expense account, and paid memberships in exclusive golf and social clubs (known in Japan as "castles"). In fact, an American working in Japan said this about one of his Japanese colleagues: "Each time he got promoted, he moved to a better house. And as his expense account grew, the bars he'd visit would get better."[40]

Vacation Time: Less in the U.S., *More in Europe*

Vacation time is another important component of a compensation package. Like all other forms of compensation, vacation time also varies considerably in and across countries. Workers in the U.S. and Canada have among the fewest paid days off of any country in the world. Figure 12.4 shows that many countries offer experienced employees 30–40 paid days off (combining paid vacation days and paid public holidays) compared to the 25 days that their American counterparts enjoy away from their jobs in large American firms. Moreover, in the U.S., companies are not required by law to give workers a minimum number of days off, either paid or unpaid, whereas European firms often must follow legally mandated minimums.

On a regional basis, Figure 12.4 reveals that companies in European, Middle Eastern, and African countries tend to be the most generous with vacation time and companies in North America the least generous. In between are companies in the Asia/Pacific region, although wide variability also exists among nations there, with some (such as Japan) providing more vacation time than the U.S. and others (such as Thailand) less.[41]

Of course, just because the days are provided by firms does not mean that employees actually use those days. Work hours vary dramatically across countries, and sometimes vacation time suffers as a result. The travel website Expedia recently commissioned a survey of over 7,000 employees in 20 countries. U.S. respondents were given an average of 14 days of vacation but took only 12 of those days, whereas the Japanese were given, on average, 15 days of vacation but took only 5. The French and Spanish, on the other hand, each averaged 30 days of paid vacation and most employees took all 30. South Korea provides an interesting perspective on the issue of vacation time. There, firms in partnership with the government have developed some innovative ways to get South Koreans to actually take their vacations. The following International Insights feature explores this further.[42]

Country/Region	Paid Vacation Days (Minimum/Avg.)	Public Holidays (With Pay)	Total Days Off
The Americas			
United States*	15	10	25
Canada*	10	10	20
Asia/Pacific			
Australia	20	11	31
Hong Kong	14	12	26
India	12	19	31
Indonesia	12	13	25
Japan	20	15	35
Philippines	5	14	19
Singapore	14	12	26
South Korea	19	11	30
Taiwan	14	11	25
Thailand	6	13	19
Vietnam	14	8	22
Europe/Scandinavia			
Bulgaria	20	12	32
Czech Republic	20	11	31
Denmark	25	10	35
France	30	10	40
Germany	24	10	34
Greece	25	12	37
Ireland	20	9	29
Italy	20	11	31
Malta	24	14	38
Netherlands	20	8	28
Romania	21	7	28
Slovenia	20	16	36
Spain	22	14	36
Sweden	25	11	36
Middle East/Africa			
Egypt	21	16	37
Israel	24	16	40
Lebanon	15	18	33
Morocco	21	19	40
South Africa	21	12	33
United Arab Emirates	30	9	39

Figure 12.4 Paid Days Off Around the World for Employees with Ten Years on the Job.

*Numbers for the U.S. reflect common practice among big companies—unlike in most countries, U.S. federal law does not require employers to provide a minimum number of vacation days and holidays off, either unpaid or paid. In contrast, countries in the E.U. require paid public holidays plus a minimum of 20 paid days off annually. Several other countries have local rules relating to vacation time.

Source: Adapted from Jeanne Sahadi. (2007). *Who Gets the Most (and Least) Vacation*. CNNMoney.com, June 14, available at: http://money.cnn.com/2007/06/12/pf/vacation_days_worldwide.

International Insights

Taking a Holiday from Vacations: Working Overtime to Change a National Habit

The government of South Korea is cracking down on the amount of vacation time taken by workers. The problem is that people are not taking enough vacation—some not at all! Years of government pleading, combined with the cultural propensity of its people to sacrifice and to work hard for the future, has had an impact that has lasted into today's more prosperous times. It is making Koreans ask, "Should I stay or should I go?"

In fact, according to the Organisation of Economic Co-operation and Development (OECD), South Koreans work more hours in one year than in any other developed country. Workers averaged about 2,300 hours of work per year, down from a historic high of 2,500 hours a decade ago but still well above the 1,768 average found among the 30 OECD countries (and the 1,794 average in the U.S.). If you consider an 8-hour-per-day work period over 52 weeks (with no holidays or vacation days factored in), Koreans work about 45 hours per week. Americans average about 35 hours per week. Koreans work an average of one and a quarter days per week more than do Americans.

Merely working more, however, does not necessarily translate into greater productivity. For example, South Korea's productivity ranks below all but a few of the former Soviet bloc countries among all OECD members. The government is trying to change this situation, and it thinks the solution may be encouraging employees to take time off in order to recharge before returning to work more vigorously and with greater creative juices flowing. The ministry in charge of human resources recently issued a request to the over 1 million government workers—employees were directed to prepare a plan to take 16 days off the coming fiscal year and to submit that plan to their respective boss. This was a real challenge because the average worker was only taking 6 of his or her allotted 23 paid days off.

In addition to previous government efforts to rally workers under the national advancement flag, there are also some cultural drivers of this workaholic attitude among employees. Chapter 2 studied the hierarchical nature of Korean society, and it seems to play a role in the paid time off numbers explained here. In Korean society, superiors are greatly respected and are regularly followed and listened to. Yet, many business and government leaders do not take *any* vacation at all—including a member of South Korean President Lee's cabinet, the very minister who was responsible for issuing the vacation directive. When asked about this by *The Wall Street Journal*, he stated that, "I want them to take more time off . . . but as for me? I don't know." On top of all this, there are some government employees who received pay for their unused vacation days and who view this vacation push by leaders as a money-saving technique. Among the newer Korean companies, however, there is some sign of unfreezing of these attitudes. At LG, the average number of vacation days taken is 10 and, at SK Telecom, workers take between 5 and 15 of their 22 possible days off.[43]

All of this suggests that a complete understanding of a country's laws and customs is needed to fully grasp the compensation costs. We do not, however, wish to overstate the impact of the laws and customs of each individual country. Some evidence suggests that there is increasing similarity in compensation practices among countries with similar cultures. In fact, one study found that cultural grouping (e.g., Asian, Latin, European, etc.) explained compensation practices much better than country-level customs and laws.[44]

Explaining Compensation Differences Across Countries

Cultural values may explain some of the compensation practices seen across countries. These differences persist despite evidence of some ongoing convergence across countries (e.g., toward more performance-based compensation) as well as the desire of multinationals to simplify their systems to better manage them globally. Some studies suggest that while up to half of multinationals manage some aspect of employee performance appraisal on a global basis, 75 percent or more allow base pay, bonuses, sales incentives, and perks to be set locally or regionally. This reflects the strength and longevity of culture-driven nuances and overtones, which are features that have woven their way into compensation practices around the world. Consequently, multinationals that abandon local or regional practices may do so at their peril.[45]

In the U.S., compensation is commonly viewed as an exchange based on deservingness—greater contributions to the company should result in greater compensation of the employee. In essence, this is an equity norm—something strongly embraced in American culture and, hence, by American firms that are more likely to operate on this equity principle than most other countries (see Chapter 10).

In countries where other cultural values are more prominent and equity norms are weaker, compensation approaches have evolved differently. Consider France and its strong norms of equality and the rights of workers to voice opinions. The traditional bonus system used by many French companies is not tied closely to performance. Instead, many French employees receive an extra month's salary before their vacation time in July or August and again before Christmas. This pattern leads many French employees to think in terms of net pay. In fact, when they are offered a monthly salary, new French employees may be quick to ask, "Is it net or gross?" and "How many times a year do I get this salary?" Many French employees have become used to these bonuses and consider them as part of their base pay. This has caused problems for French companies trying to implement performance-based bonuses. For instance, in one company a performance-based bonus was paid for two straight years because the company did well. The third year, however, saw a drop in performance and therefore no bonuses was paid. French workers did not accept this and threatened to close down the plant. Apparently, the "bonus" had become viewed as an entitlement; as a result, the company relented and paid the bonus anyway.[46]

Mexico carries this practice a step further by systematizing worker acquisition of compensation extras. In particular, Mexico has an "acquired rights" law that mandates that if a bonus or benefit is given out at least two years in a row, it becomes the employee's right to receive it in the future. This reflects the paternalistic aspects of Mexican work culture, including the tendency of the government to step in and facilitate disputes between management and unions.[47]

The Japanese view of compensation is traditionally paternalistic as well as egalitarian—one that provides slowly increasing rewards for length of service (which demonstrates loyalty and commitment to a company) and skill acquisition rather than performance, per se. Consequently, wage increases are graduated and a higher percentage of total compensation is fixed (up to 80 percent). One study, for example, examined the pay raise decisions of Japanese and American managers asked to distribute raises to employees, including people described as low and high performers. Not surprisingly, American managers gave much bigger raises to the high performers and much lower raises to the poor performers than did Japanese managers. In particular, the Japanese gave roughly twice as high a raise to low performers and about 80 percent less to the high performers than did the Americans. In essence, there was a stronger link between performance and pay decisions for U.S. than Japanese managers.[48]

While some traditional practices persist in Japan and other Asian countries, such as China, the pressures for change also exist—often due to the rapidly growing economies of these nations. Chinese firms, for example, are under great pressure to find and to secure talent, as are the multinational firms located there. As a result, wage levels continue to dynamically grow in China.[49] Some local and regional practices will persist and perhaps even thrive. Nevertheless, a recent survey of Japanese HR managers shows that the relative impact of seniority to merit in determining pay raises has been dropping. Moreover, top Japanese firms such as Mitsubishi, Toshiba, and Toyota have been offering higher salaries and larger incentive packages to younger employees, including raising the proportion of compensation that is "at risk" and tied to performance.[50]

The Challenges of Expatriate Compensation

This section tackles a complicated and important issue for multinationals—how to construct compensation and benefit packages for expatriates, which are a key group of employees. This presents multinationals with key challenges, especially as their international operations become more complex.

Multinationals have to deal with a multitude of cross-national differences in laws, taxes, and compensation practices. But, they also need to ensure that their employees around the world believe that the various compensation and benefits packages being used are fair. Companies do not want expatriates to somehow feel cheated after agreeing to a post in a foreign country. This is not a trivial or isolated concern. According to one study, nearly 80 percent of the expatriates surveyed were unhappy with their compensation and benefits package.[51]

Nor do multinationals relish the thought of local employees bristling at "overpaid" expatriates who seem to parachute in from the parent company with fat salaries and plenty of special perks. One study found that local employees working for foreign expatriates in China felt that the huge pay gap between the two groups was unfair. Moreover, this had negative effects on Chinese employees' morale and commitment to the firm. To combat this, experts recommend that expatriates work hard to build trust with local employees and to redirect their pay comparisons to other local employees who are often paid less than the salaries offered by multinationals.[52]

Overall, multinationals have to juggle very real location cost issues (for example, Tokyo is a more expensive city than Houston) and fairness comparisons made by employees (inside and outside of the firm). One way that some multinationals are dealing with these issues is by moving away from expatriate packages that are tied to home-country wages and benefits. Some firms now feel that they can offer less in the way of inducements to recruit expatriates in the first place, or simply reduce large pay gaps between expatriates and local employees. But high costs are likely the biggest reasons that multinationals are always looking for new ways to compensate expatriates. For instance, according to one survey, the cumulative net *additional* cost of sending and supporting one expatriate abroad (accompanied by a spouse and children) for three years averages around $750,000. In some expensive locations, the total additional cost for three years may run $1 million or more. Generally speaking, an international relocation costs up to five times as much as a domestic move.[53]

But what exactly accounts for all of these costs? There are the usual things involved in staffing a job, including the interview process and the hiring phase, as well as actual moving costs themselves. Each of these factors is more expensive for an expatriate than for a domestic relocation. A majority of firms, however, go well beyond this by providing a variety of costly benefits, such as housing allowances and tax benefits. These can also include financial allowances, assistance with acclimating to the foreign culture, and costs of an occasional trip home. Figure 12.5 presents examples of additional costs often incurred with expatriates.

In any case, multinationals should first focus on creating a consistent and comprehensive compensation and benefits policy for expatriates that will help educate and

Direct Payments/Reimbursements	Support for Adjustment to Global Assignment
Tax reduction/equalization	Home leave (4–6 weeks)
Housing allowance	Emergency leave
Furnishing allowance	Personal security
Education allowance	Car/driver
Hardship/foreign service premium	Domestic help
Currency protection	Spouse employment
Goods and services differential	Child care provider
Temporary living allowance	Language/translation services
Car/transportation allowance	Cultural training
Assignment completion bonus	Repatriation assistance
Extension bonus	Social club fees
Help renting U.S. home	Imported food and other goods

Figure 12.5 Potential Sources of Costs Associated with Expatriation.

Source: Adapted from Milkovich, G. T., and Newman, J. M. (1999). *Compensation*. Chicago: Irwin.

inform all employees about company goals and what expatriates can expect. This would include how much customization across locations is allowed and would convey the message that expatriates will not profit more by going to one location over another. Regardless, an effective compensation plan for expatriates will often include these features:

- some form of incentive to accept an expatriate assignment (e.g., monetary, benefits, career mobility/advancement);
- maintenance of a reasonable standard of living;
- support for the needs of any trailing family members (spouses, partners, children); and
- provisions to successfully repatriate the employee back into the home country after the foreign assignment concludes.[54]

Methods for Compensating Expatriates

There are a variety of options available that follow from these recommended criteria. Three of the most popular approaches are discussed next, including the ad hoc, localization, and balance sheet methods. Compensation elements overlap among the methods, and firms may also end up using all of them in different situations. But in choosing between these methods, multinationals should think about the answers to the following:

- **How long will the assignment last?** Longer assignments are generally more expensive and may involve more complicated tax issues for both the employee and the company.
- **Who is the expatriate?** Is he or she an inexperienced employee or a seasoned executive? Will he or she be rotated to the next foreign post after the assignment or return home? Answers may determine compensation level and degree of supporting benefits and perks.
- **Why is the expatriate being sent?** Is the assignment a career development move? Or is it need-driven (e.g., for expertise not found locally, to better control the subsidiary, etc.)? The latter may require a more lucrative compensation package to attract needed personnel.
- **What country is the expatriate departing from and going to?** This will help determine relevant wages, living allowances, benefits, and taxes given the laws and regulations of both nations.
- **What will be the benefits of this assignment?** Management should carefully weigh the goals and potential benefits against costs.[55]

The Ad Hoc Method

This method tends to be more frequently used by smaller or still emerging multinationals that have relatively little experience overseas and that must often send an expatriate to address issues abroad. That can mean doing a quick search and then paying whatever is necessary to entice an employee to go. How this actually happens with the ad hoc method is simple—the company and its expatriates negotiate on a case-by-case basis to cover the costs inherent in a foreign assignment.[56]

While the ad hoc method has some merit, the specific drawbacks include:

■ the potential for unequal treatment of expatriates (based on their negotiation skills or lack thereof);
■ an inability to systematically track expatriate compensation packages; and
■ inadequate development of country-specific knowledge (e.g., about taxes, cost of living, etc.) on the parts of both the firm and the employee.

Companies may come out ahead in the short run by successfully negotiating down their costs with expatriates. Yet, having employees find out later that their overseas costs are much higher or that others negotiated a much better deal can have negative effects on morale and overall performance. This method has serious drawbacks and complications, especially for larger multinationals with many expatriates. Some smaller firms, however, cannot afford the price of engaging firms that provide accurate cost-of-living and other data—instead, they do the best they can.[57]

The Localization Method

A more systematic approach to expatriate compensation is the localization method. This method involves paying the expatriate essentially the same as local employees in similar positions. Localization may be especially useful when expatriates want to extend their stay in particular locations or are interested in being permanent expatriates who travel from assignment to assignment. In both cases, the expatriate is less likely to use home-country wage standards to evaluate his or her compensation. Localization is much easier to apply when an expatriate moves to a country with a higher standard of living, such as moving from Mexico to the United States. If, for example, expatriates are moving to Vietnam from Europe or the U.S., it will be more difficult for them to accept a lower level of compensation. Localization is rarely used in its pure form, however; instead, adjustments are often made to base pay, allowances, and retirement packages.[58]

Despite drawbacks, localization is increasingly being used in developing markets such as Indonesia and China—where local talent, especially at senior levels, might be less available. As China's living conditions have improved greatly and the country is often viewed as a launch to career development, expatriates are increasingly interested in extending their stays. These factors, combined with a desire to reduce costs, have led many multinationals to consider localization in China. In a 2009 survey, 57 percent of the Asia-based multinationals responding considered localization for expatriates in China, up from 39 percent in 2007. Likewise, over a quarter of the Western multinationals responding also considered localization in China.

There are complexities associated with localization. For example, foreigners typically cannot participate in local pension plans or the Chinese versions of social security programs found in the U.S. and Europe. Being posted in China may also preclude expatriates from participating in their home-country retirement plans. Consequently, multinationals will sometimes make extra payments to compensate for this, enroll expatriates in third-country pension plans, or, if possible, retain them on the home-country pension system. Of course, this offsets some of the cost advantages of localization, including the savings from paying expatriates at local wage rates. Clearly, multinationals will need to carefully consider whether localization is a good choice or not.[59]

The Balance Sheet Method

By far the most popular approach for expatriate compensation is the balance sheet (or build-up) method. Used by almost 75 percent of the multinationals that participated in a recent worldwide survey, the balance sheet method's core principle is that expatriates should not suffer a loss of income or lifestyle as a result of an international assignment. The idea is to provide them with roughly the same purchasing power in the foreign location as they would enjoy at home. In other words, the objective of the balance sheet method is to "balance out" the cost differences between an expatriate's home country and his or her foreign location. This is particularly important because expatriates often find themselves in places where living costs are higher than at home—or where the costs of duplicating their home lifestyles are very expensive. Indeed, the general goal of "keeping the expatriate whole" is the stated objective of many multinationals.[60]

Traditionally, multinationals not only tried to duplicate the expatriate's home lifestyle and purchasing power as best they could, they also provided additional incentives to entice employees to accept assignments or to recognize them for the hardship of being posted abroad. As costs have escalated in recent years, however, firms have been backing away from duplicating lifestyles and adding on extra incentives. According to one survey, between 25 and 30 percent of multinationals either do not offer expatriates any additional incentive pay or are in the process of phasing such incentives out. Even if they still offer expatriates incentives, many multinationals have been focusing on making "sufficient" living cost adjustments while encouraging expatriates to adapt to local lifestyles and standards when possible. For this reason, it is important to consider how the balance sheet method actually works.[61]

The balance sheet method starts the process of smoothing out cost-of-living and tax differences across countries by dividing expatriate expenses into four basic categories: housing, income taxes, goods and services, and a savings reserve/discretionary component. Typically, expatriates would receive allowances to cover the increased taxes, more expensive housing, and higher living costs (for food, utilities, etc.) encountered abroad. How multinationals calculate these allowances is complex and somewhat controversial—if they calculate them at all. Instead, some rely on consulting firms such as Mercer to do this for them. Indeed, these firms are willing to help multinationals design their specific balance sheet methodology, provide up-to-date information on local compensation practices and living costs, secure housing and relocation support, provide tax services, and even administer the entire program. Monetary incentives are considered next, before examining expatriate expense categories in more detail.[62]

Foreign Service Premiums, Hardship, and Danger Pay

One thing that the balance sheet does not impact is the expatriate's base salary. Using the balance sheet method, salary would be determined in the same way as it would for domestic employees. That is, if domestic employees receive 4 percent (average) pay raises, then so would expatriates. Simply put, the particular economic conditions in the foreign location to which expatriates are assigned do not shape their base salary. Beyond base pay, however, the balance sheet can have a big impact on expatriates' overall compensation abroad if multinationals are offering one of more of the following incentives: foreign service premiums, hardship pay, and danger pay.

Even at today's often reduced incentive levels, their total value can be impressive, especially over several years. Many multinationals still pay a premium or incentive to the expatriate for taking the foreign assignment (often ranging between 10 and 30 percent of base pay). Expatriates may also receive hardship pay if posted to locations where living conditions are significantly harsher or more difficult than in the home country, whether due to extreme weather, limited access to common goods and services, or weak health care, etc. In locations where expatriates may be physically at risk due to civil unrest, war, or violence aimed at foreigners, danger pay may be stacked on top of foreign service premiums and hardship pay.[63]

It is often difficult to make such hardship judgments. Consequently, many multinationals look to available rating schemes, such as the U.S. Department of State's (DOS) *Hardship Post Differentials Guidelines*, which include "allowances and benefits" for personnel being posted abroad in difficult locations. Anyone can look up the specific incentives offered by the DOS based on location or type of benefit. The information is updated every two weeks. The DOS posts thousands of employees overseas and offers danger and hardship pay in 5 percent increments of base pay, starting at 0 percent and going up to 35 percent. For example, being posted to Melbourne, Australia, would yield no extra danger pay or hardship pay, not surprisingly. At the other extreme, however, being posted to Baghdad, Iraq, would provide a 70 percent premium to base pay (35 percent for hardship pay and another 35 percent for danger pay).[64]

Purchasing Power and the Balance Sheet

These challenges aside, the balance sheet method's main goal is to smooth out expenses and to protect the expatriate from incurring significant additional costs in the foreign country. Figure 12.6 lays out this approach. The first column presents the base costs in the home country. Home-country purchasing power changes depending on one's income, family size, and other variables. But for purposes of discussion, consider how purchasing power at home can be translated into purchasing power abroad. Column 2 in Figure 12.6 depicts a common situation—where host-country housing, taxes, and goods and services are all more expensive than at home. Consequently, the balance sheet method makes adjustments (as depicted in Column 3), typically in the form of company-paid allowances, to offset these higher costs and allow the expatriate to maintain his or her home lifestyle overseas without additional out-of-pocket spending (creating what is known as purchasing power parity). This resulting purchasing power equivalence is shown in Column 4 of the figure, along with any premiums or incentive pay the company may provide on top of everything else.[65]

Housing Costs and the Balance Sheet

Housing usually involves considerable expense for companies. According to one survey, over 80 percent of multinationals either provide free housing abroad for their expatriates

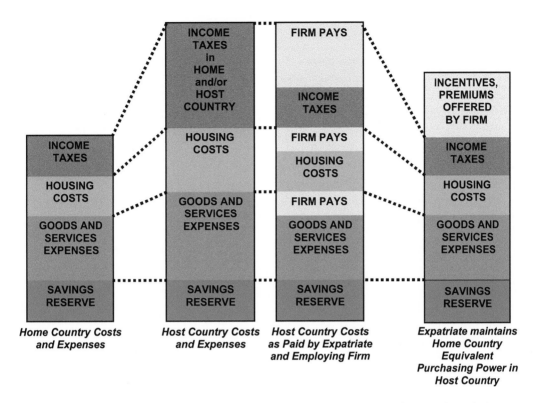

Figure 12.6 The Balance Sheet Approach to Expatriate Compensation: Keeping People "Whole".

Source: Adapted from Reynolds, C. (1994). Compensation basics for North American expatriates: Developing an effective program for employees working abroad. *American Compensation Association.* ACA Building Block #15. Scottsdale, AZ: American Compensation Association.

or a location-specific housing allowance supplemented by the expatriate. That said, there are regional differences among multinationals. Asian, Latin American, and European multinationals are more likely to provide free housing for their expatriates than housing allowances, while the reverse is true for U.S. firms. Either way, housing can be a larger cost than allowances for goods and services or taxes. Indeed, housing alone may account for 50 percent of the total additional compensation package for an expatriate. One reason is that housing is typically rented and often covered by a shorter-term lease due to the nature of the position, as opposed to bought, which drives up prices. Second, expatriates often expect larger and more luxurious residences than their counterparts in a foreign country. That is especially true for U.S. expatriates, who enjoy some of the largest and least expensive housing anywhere in the world while at home, making it difficult and much more expensive to find comparable housing for them in pricey cities such as Tokyo or Hong Kong.[66]

The costs for housing expatriates around the world can vary dramatically. Figure 12.7 presents some estimates of housing costs in selected cities in the world outside of North America. As you can see, housing in many cities is quite expensive, even for Americans coming from more metropolitan U.S. cities such as Chicago or Atlanta. In any case,

Location	Type of Housing Rental	Rental Costs Per Month/Year in U.S. $
Beijing	1 bedroom apartment	$700–1,000/month, $8,400–12,000/year
	3–4 bedroom suburban home	$3,500–8,000/month, $42,000–96,000/year
Dubai, United Arab Emirates	1 bedroom apartment	$2,250/month, $27,000/year
	Multi-bedroom villa	$5,600–$11,300/month, $68,000–136,000/year
Hong Kong	2 bedroom apartment	$2,500–5,000/month, $30,000–60,000/year
	4 bedroom townhouse	$32,000/month, $384,000/year
London	2 bedroom apartment	$4,000–6,400/month, $48,000–76,800/year
	4 bedroom house	$10,000–40,000/month, $120,000–480,000/year
Moscow	2 bedroom apartment	$3,000–10,000/month, $36,000–120,000/year
	3 bedroom house	$10,000/month, $120,000/year
	5 bedroom house	$17,000/month, $204,000/year
Mumbai, India	Multi-bedroom, 2,000-square-foot apartment	$6,400/month, $76,800/year
Sao Paulo, Brazil	2 bedroom apartment	$1,200–2,000/month, $14,400–24,000/year
Tokyo	4 bedroom apartment	$12,000/month, $144,000/year

Figure 12.7 Expatriate Housing Costs in Selected Foreign Cities Outside North America.

Note: These figures are for rentals in areas generally favored by expatriates. Price ranges reflect location-specific or neighborhood differences and/or quality of the housing. Not all locations will have comparable housing types to choose from.

Source: Adapted from Rosman, K. (2007). Expat life gets less cushy. *The Wall Street Journal*, October 26, W1, W10; Tanaka, S. (2013). Big rent increases for expat housing around the world. *The Wall Street Journal*, available at: http://online.wsj.com/ (retrieved 29 September 2013); *The Economist*. (2013). Home truths: Global house prices, January 12, 61–62.

multinationals would typically either pick up the cost of foreign housing for their expatriates, or provide a housing allowance designed to partially or wholly offset the additional housing costs incurring in the foreign location.[67]

The Balance Sheet Approach to Taxes

A second major category of expatriate expenses addressed by the balance sheet method is income taxes. The most common approach for dealing with taxes under the balance sheet method is tax equalization. In essence, the goal is to tie expatriates' tax burdens to their home countries regardless of where they are posted and to simplify their reporting requirements. This makes a good deal of sense because tax laws, regulations, and rates vary considerably from country to country and are constantly in flux. Generally speaking, countries in Western Europe and Scandinavia have the highest personal income tax rates, while at the other end of the spectrum, many oil-rich countries of the Middle East have no income tax.[68] Tax management is probably the most technical and complex aspect of the balance sheet method.[69]

Implementing tax equalization requires that multinationals first determine the total hypothetical income tax burden facing expatriates had they stayed home. Next, companies need to assess what an expatriate's total tax obligation will likely be while posted overseas (which may include higher income taxes in foreign countries). Once that is established, multinationals will deduct an amount equal to what the expatriate's home-country income tax would be from his or her salary while paying off taxes owed to both home-country and host-country tax authorities. In other cases, expatriates may have to pay host-country tax authorities themselves before being reimbursed by the company for this additional cost. Either way, end-of-year reconciliation is often required to see if the firm owes tax equalization money to the expatriate or vice versa once total actual income for the year is available.[70]

Tax agreements that allow for tax equalization or the avoidance of double taxation when citizens are posted to foreign countries can help reduce an expatriate's tax exposure. For instance, the U.S. has tax agreements with over 60 countries that give U.S. citizens tax exemptions or lower rates from foreign tax burdens (with the reverse also true for expatriates posted to the U.S.). In particular, France and Belgium are leaders in making "totalization" agreements. France has included the following items in its laws regarding expatriates:

- an agreement that companies with an office in France can avoid French taxation on expatriates' housing, schooling, and other allowances;
- provisions to eliminate taxes (in France) of expatriate income from sources such as dividends, interest, and capital gains;
- a totalization agreement to eliminate social security taxes in France; and
- a system to greatly reduce French taxes on income from stock options.[71]

Even when foreign tax rates are lower, however, the total tax burden for an expatriate may be higher. Many countries tax not only income but also all allowances, adjustments, and incentives. The U.S. is among the few countries in the world that taxes expatriate income earned abroad (beyond an exempted amount—which was about $97,000 in 2013). As a result, even if an American expatriate is paying relatively low taxes while living in Brazil, he or she will also owe tax in the U.S. Fortunately, the balance sheet method will compensate the expatriate, directly or indirectly, for any additional taxes incurred.[72]

How the Balance Sheet Handles Goods and Services

Besides housing, no other piece of the expatriate compensation package causes more consternation for employees than allowances for goods and services. Multinationals—or the consultants they engage—construct allowances by comparing the cost of a "market basket" of goods and services in the home country with the cost of a similar, if not identical, basket in the assignment country. The ratio of these two cost estimates provides the basis for paying expatriates a cost-of-living allowance to help offset higher living costs expatriates often encountered abroad and giving them the same purchasing power enjoyed at home.[73]

Included in the market basket are goods and services items such as food (consumed at home and in restaurants), alcohol and tobacco, personal care products (such as toothpaste), domestic supplies (such as cleaning products), clothing, home services, transportation, utilities, and entertainment. As you might imagine, coming up with prices for all of these items, particularly across countries, is time-consuming. Moreover, prices are continually fluctuating and vary from outlet to outlet in any case—the price of a loaf of bread may vary considerably depending on where you buy it. You almost need someone to constantly monitor these prices for you, which is something that the firm AIRINC will gladly do for you, for a price. The accompanying Global Innovations feature tells its story. Currency swings can play havoc with goods and services differentials, swelling the value of differentials when local currencies drop significantly and shrinking them when those currencies soar. Consequently, goods and services differentials should be monitored and periodically adjusted up or down as needed to take currency swings into account. Sometimes multinationals pay expatriates in both the home and local currency (referred to as split pay) for this reason—this tends to even out currency fluctuations between two countries.[74]

Global Innovations

What Do Zippers, Prozac, a Dozen Roses, and a Box of Titleists Have in Common? They Are All in a Day's Survey

How do companies determine what they offer in terms of per diems and reimbursements for expatriate expenses? Most companies want to treat employees fairly, but they also are cost-conscious. One solution is provided by the Boston-based Associates for International Research, Inc. (AIRINC). AIRINC is an international survey research company that collects data on the prices of goods and services in countries all around the world. It sells this and other information to clients—including many Fortune 500 companies that in turn use this information to calculate expatriates' cost of living, annual compensation, and other adjustments. Demand for AIRINC's services is on the rise as employers try to keep close accounting of expatriate expenses.

Many firms put their trust in the data provided by AIRINC. One reason is that the firm goes on location to collect its own data rather than using estimates or employee self-reports. These estimates can routinely be way off, either because memories of specific prices are a blur to those traveling across countries in short bursts or because estimates might be inflated in comparison to vague memories of outdated home-country prices (such as the price of gasoline in Dallas).

But getting price data directly from overseas retailers and others can be time-consuming and expensive. Plus, it is just plain hard work. Most of AIRINC's surveyors are in the 22- to 30-year-old age range—young people with fewer roots and more wanderlust, including Megan Lipman, who was a surveyor for seven years with AIRINC. Although she quickly grew to love the job, Lipman had little idea of what it entailed when she first applied. In fact, it never entered her mind that such a job even existed. After graduating from college with dual degrees in Art History and Spanish, and two years of experience as a translator, she responded to a newspaper ad: "job responsibilities include data collection, analysis, and preparation of various statistical data for cost-of-living analysis." It was the last sentence in the ad that made her apply: "Will spend at least one-third of time in international travel." The interviewers fired questions at her such as, "What would you do if you were stranded in a central African nation with three days until the next flight?" Her answer: "If there were no other safe ways to get out, I'd get as much work done on the phone as possible."

Lipman got the job and quickly began flying around the world from city to city for six weeks at a time. She traveled for about half the year, to destinations such as Qatar, the UAE, Bangladesh, New Zealand, Cyprus, Venezuela, to name just a few. Once on site, she spent about three days collecting price data by visiting supermarkets, gas stations, theaters, and beauty salons—among other places. One trip to Malta involved tracking down prices for a 20-centimeter zipper, 20 mg of Prozac, a sleeve of Titleist golf balls, a 14-carat gold wedding ring, Tabasco sauce, a dozen red roses, and the cost of repairing a washing machine. She had a regular schedule of items to price, and the Malta list was not that unusual.

While it may be clear why they collect this data, *how* AIRINC surveyors get the data is another story. Consider Lipman's Malta trip. After settling in, she chose a setting such as a supermarket. She asked for the manager, presented her business card, and asked if she could carry out a pricing survey. She then headed up and down the aisles recording price after price. Most managers were very friendly and helpful. But in some shops, managers resent young foreigners nosing around the store, partly because they think the survey is being done by their competition. While she was in a Malta pharmacy, one manager gruffly pulled Lipman aside and asked to have a word with her. Worried that she would be kicked out of the store and lose hard-earned data, she was relieved when he asked instead if his son could get an internship with AIRINC.

Lipman and other surveyors spend a good deal of time in many (luxury) hotel rooms, collecting even more data. There, hired translators use a phone directory to make calls to physicians, insurance and real estate agents, and repair shops for more prices. When the surveyors return home to Boston, the reams of data must be analyzed, average prices determined, and continued tracking of prices to previous surveys must be prepared. AIRINC then reports to and makes recommendations for clients (e.g., to raise or lower employee cost-of-living allowances).

Lipman and other surveyors often like their jobs. They make a good salary, have very generous expense accounts, and generally enjoy the traveling. But before you search AIRINC to find where to e-mail your application, consider the drawbacks. Travel hassles today abound (e.g., flight delays, cancellations, missed connections, etc.), and it involves a lot of time spent alone. It is also tough to maintain personal relationships, given the demanding travel schedule. But that is all in a day's survey![75]

Despite these challenges, multinationals have many sources for price estimates of goods and services worldwide as well as the differentials that may be necessary when sending expatriates to particular locations. For example, various consulting firms catalog prices on hundreds of goods and services as well as providing cost-of-living indices for virtually every city in the world, based on data that are updated regularly. Using these data, firms can quickly get a sense of which foreign locations are the most or least expensive to send expatriates. Figure 12.8 provides just such an example—it lists the 25 most expensive cities in the world in 2009, taking both housing and goods and services costs into

2009 Cost of Living Index Value	City, Country	2009 Expense Ranking (1= Most Expensive)	2013 Expense Ranking (1= Most Expensive)
143.7	Tokyo, Japan	1	1
119.2	Osaka, Japan	2	3
115.4	Moscow, Russia	3	4
109.2	Geneva, Switzerland	4	5
108.7	Hong Kong	5	9
105.2	Zurich, Switzerland	6	6
105.0	Copenhagen, Denmark	7	21
100.0	New York, U.S.	8	33
99.6	Beijing, China	9	17
98.0	Singapore, Singapore	10	6
96.9	Milan, Italy	11	38
95.2	Shanghai, China	12	16
95.1	Paris, France	13	37
94.2	Oslo, Norway	14	18
93.3	Caracas, Venezuela	15	29
92.7	London, United Kingdom	16	25
91.9	Tel Aviv, Israel	17	31
91.2	Rome, Italy	18	42
90.5	Helsinki, Finland	19	65
90.1	Dubai, UAE	20	94
89.3	Vienna, Austria	21	48
89.0	Shenzhen, China	22	30
87.6	Los Angeles, U.S.	23	68
87.6	Guangzhou, China	24	31
87.4	Dublin, Ireland	25	72

Figure 12.8 Most Expensive Cities in the World: 2009–2013.

Note: The cost of living index sets New York City as the base rating of 100 and is calculated using the average price of over 200 goods and services plus housing costs.

Sources: Adapted from Mercer. (2009). *Mercer's 2009 Cost of Living Survey Highlights—Global*. Updated July 7, 2009, available at: www.mercer.com; Mercer. (2013). *Mercer's 2012 Cost of Living Survey*, available at: www. mercer.com.

account. The figure uses an index value to capture cost of living, with New York City set to 100 (a higher number means that the location is more expensive than New York and a lower number means that the location is less expensive in terms of goods and services, including rental accommodations). We also present the ranking of those cities only three years later in 2012. While there is consistency across years among the top six or so cities, after that values can differ greatly, which is a good selling point for the firms who produce and sell these ratings.[76]

If this list is too hard to swallow, consider the Big Mac "economic index" that is constructed by *The Economist* magazine. The rationale of the index (which is partly tongue in cheek) is to provide a quick and "easily digestible" method that can be used to compare currency valuations across countries. For our purposes, the data can also provide an index of costs of a familiar product in the U.S. (a Big Mac costs $3.54 on average) with prices in other countries. Figure 12.9 presents U.S. dollar equivalent prices,

Country (Exchange Rate to U.S. $)	Cost of Big Mac, Local Currency	Cost of Big Mac, U.S. Dollars	Implied Purchase Power Parity
U.S.	$3.54	$3.54	—
Argentina (3.49)	Peso 11.50	$3.30	3.25 (−7%)
Australia (1.57)	A$3.45	$2.19	0.97 (−38%)
Brazil (2.32)	Real 8.02	$3.45	2.27 (−2%)
Britain (1.44)	£2.29	$3.64	1.55 (−7%)
Canada (1.24)	C$4.16	$3.36	1.18 (−5%)
Chile (617)	Peso 1,550	$2.51	438 (−29%)
China (6.84)	Yuan 12.5	$1.83	3.53 (−48%)
Hong Kong (7.75)	HK$13.3	$1.72	3.76 (−52%)
Indonesia (11,380)	Rupiah 19,800	$1.74	5.59 (−51%)
Japan (89.8)	¥290	$3.23	81.9 (−9%)
Mexico (14.4)	Peso 33.0	$2.30	9.32 (−35%)
Norway (6.91)	Kroner 40.0	$5.79	11.3 (63%)
Philippines (47.4)	Peso 98.0	$2.07	27.7 (−42%)
Russia (35.7)	Ruble 62.0	$1.73	17.5 (−51%)
Saudi Arabia (3.75)	Riyal 10.0	$2.66	3.75 (−25%)
South Africa (10.2)	Rand 16.95	$1.66	4.79 (−53%)
South Korea	Won 3,300	$2.39	932 (−32%)
Switzerland (1.16)	CHF 6.50	$5.60	1.84 (58%)
Thailand (35)	Baht 62.0	$1.77	17.5 (−50%)
Turkey (1.64)	Lire 5.15	$3.13	1.45 (−12%)

Figure 12.9 Do You Want Fries with That Foreign Assignment? The Big Mac in Various Countries.

Note: Prices and currency rates are as of February, 2009; purchasing price parity (ppp) = local price/price in U.S.; comparisons between ppp and actual exchange rate are then reported as a percentage in parentheses; positive values are an indicant of overvaluation and negative percentages undervaluation against the dollar.

Source: Adapted from: Economist.com. (2009). Big Mac Index, February 4, 2009, available at: www.economist.com/markets/indicators/displaystory.cfm?story_id=13055650 (retrieved September 9, 2009).

as well as the cost in local currency, for a Big Mac in selected countries. While a Big Mac in Norway will cost almost $6, South Africa offers a relative bargain in comparison with a $1.66 Big Mac. This is hardly a perfect index of purchasing power parity, but it certainly is food for thought. If your tastes are more highbrow, consider the price of a Starbucks grande latte in New York ($4.30) vs. one in Oslo, Norway ($9.83), Moscow, Russia ($7.27), New Delhi, India ($2.50) or Istanbul, Turkey ($3.75).[77]

Both these values and the costs of goods and services indexes in general that have been released by a number of firms have been criticized. For example, the numbers were calculated for expatriates, a small group of people who seek out similar products and lifestyles wherever they are. This presumes a lot. Plus, currency market fluctuations can render the rankings out of date very quickly. For example, efforts by the Swiss government to drive down the value of the franc have made Zurich and Geneva less expensive worldwide, yet prices locally have not budged. Said differently, currency value drops don't make for a dip in the cost of living for those in Geneva.[78]

Regardless of what index is used, goods and services will inevitably be more expensive in some countries than in others. Yet, even in those countries with relatively low-cost goods and services, some expatriates tend to spend more anyway. Experts believe that some expatriates keep their relatively high-living home-country consumption tastes when posted overseas, even if it costs them more. They may be willing, for instance, to buy expensive imports from their home country, a habit that in turn drives up expenses much higher than locally driven cost-of-living indexes would suggest. In such cases, expatriates might expect to receive an adjustment to their average domestic living expenses while on foreign assignment.

That said, multinationals are increasingly pushing back against these kinds of costs. Indeed, some firms are taking steps to encourage more frugal expatriate behavior. For instance, some multinationals calculate goods and services differentials using an efficient purchaser index (EPI). In essence, the prices used for calculating these allowances are from cheaper or on-sale products that are included in the market basket. The idea is to encourage expatriates to become better and more efficient shoppers over time, finding cheaper places to buy goods, eat out, and more in their foreign location. Naturally, this only works in locations that have plenty of shopping options and sophisticated markets. Nevertheless, it can lead to smaller cost-of-living allowances for expatriates, saving their employers money. Other cost-saving steps that multinationals often take would be to substitute in cheaper transportation options or to exclude pricier items altogether from the market basket (e.g., alcohol).[79]

The Balance Sheet on Balance

All in all, the major goal of the balance sheet method is to treat expatriates fairly. Certainly, the effect of many of the adjustments is to make a foreign posting less of a hardship. This is not to say, however, that the balance sheet approach is without problems. For instance, the approach is complex, expensive, and difficult for multinationals to administer and explain. As we have noted, the balance sheet method requires either collecting or buying sets of data on cost of living and housing. Likewise, the transfer of payments for the various adjustments is also challenging to manage and monitor.[80]

Moreover, some practical problems also emerge when expatriates are sent to places where costs are generally lower than at home. In this case, housing as well as goods and services produce negative differentials. Should the payments to the employee be reduced to reflect a lower cost of living in Mexico? While it would be entirely consistent with the balance sheet method to eliminate "windfalls" to the employee, many multinationals refuse to do this and take no action. Indeed, according to one recent survey, only about 25 percent of firms deduct money or allowances from other parts of the expatriate package (such as from foreign service premiums) to compensate for such negative differentials.[81]

What seems to be more popular among multinationals is to move away from thinking about foreign assignment as something automatically deserving of a special premium. In fact, the number of firms that do not pay any incentive premium at all to work overseas has nearly doubled in recent years. As globalization increases, their rationale is that employees should relish an opportunity to work overseas. If a firm makes the foreign assignment a significant part of its management development track, this may be a reasonable position to take.[82]

Chapter Summary

Few managers enjoy conducting performance evaluations—adding foreign employees into the mix only makes the task more burdensome. There are many problems involved in an appraisal of expatriate performance and they are not easily overcome. These basic questions loom large: *who* will evaluate the expatriate, *how often* will the evaluation be done, and, most importantly, *what* will be evaluated and how? The chapter presents some of the pros and cons associated with each question and presented guidelines for delivering feedback.

Likewise, culture may have an impact on the compensation decisions that evolve from performance evaluation. Multinationals need to be aware of differences, especially ones that persist despite evidence of some convergence toward more performance-based compensation practices. This may explain why performance appraisal and compensation decisions in multinationals take place at multiple levels—with evaluation more likely to be managed on a global basis while pay and perks are more likely to be managed locally.

Finally, the chapter discusses the nuances involved in compensating expatriate employees. Several methods exist and are considered in detail, including the balance sheet method, which remains the most popular. The goal is to maintain the same lifestyle for expatriates overseas as they have at home, without any significant additional expense.

Discussion Questions

1. What are some of the problems encountered in evaluating employee performance, and how are these problems complicated by an international setting?

2. How might cultural beliefs about the basis for compensation affect your approach to rewarding expatriates and host-country nationals in the same firm?

3. What are some of the ways in which employees and executives alike can be compensated for their international service?

4. How should expatriates be compensated? What do you think is the best approach, and why?

Up to the Challenge?

Are American Expatriates Becoming Too Expensive for Multinationals?

At the beginning of this chapter we asked you to take the perspective of a 45-year-old American marketing manager and her family (including school-age kids) in considering an expatriate assignment in Seoul, South Korea. We suggested that this manager might have a tough time accepting the offer given that expatriate packages are not nearly as lucrative as they used to be. Moreover, with a trailing spouse who would have to give up his job, added to concerns about pulling the kids out of their schools in Pittsburgh, the answer might be "no" regardless. But are there circumstances when it might be worth the risk of saying "yes"? And what about multinationals—how can they make expatriate assignments more attractive while still keeping costs down?

If our Pittsburgh manager concluded that a posting to Seoul might prove a life-changing event and would position her well for future promotion, she may go ahead and take the plunge. Indeed, the clearer and more positive the company can be about how this move might impact her career, the better. If, for example, the company says she is being groomed for a senior position and that foreign experience is vital for high-level executives, this might sweeten the offer.

Yet, most of the time, the impact of expatriation on a manager's career will be murky—a job may not even be waiting when the manager returns. It is increasingly likely that some multinationals would get around concerns raised by potential middle-aged expatriates by simply not asking them to travel in the first place. Targeting employees in their 30s (and either childless or single) instead could improve the chances of a "yes" while also cutting expatriate costs. That means smaller home or apartment expenses abroad for the company to pick up, in addition to no worries about expensive schools. At the other end of the spectrum, however, companies are also looking harder at employees in their 50s—a time when kids are grown and trailing spouses or partners are more willing to move.

PricewaterhouseCoopers (PwC), the giant accounting firm, is one of the firms sending some of its expatriates overseas at an earlier age. The company started Life Experience Abroad Program (LEAP) which is aimed at identifying high-potential employees early (only a few years after joining the firm) and then posting them overseas. Upon return, many LEAP employees are promoted. PricewaterhouseCoopers hopes to have 5,000 LEAP expatriates working abroad in a few years.

Other options that also sidestep common objections include sending expatriates on shorter assignments lasting only a few months (thereby preventing the need to uproot an entire family) or using "commuter" expatriates who work in a foreign location, but usually return home every month. The commuter approach is particularly popular within Europe because travel distances are relatively short. An executive posted to Amsterdam could take a quick flight home to Vienna on many weekends.

For American multinationals, another option for cutting costs is to simply not use Americans on expatriate assignments whenever possible. Instead, they can hire locals or rely on nationals from developing countries who often require far less to step into expatriate roles. Indians, Russians, Chinese, and Brazilians can all be posted to developed markets at a fraction of the cost of an American, German, or Italian. Naturally, this has risks—including having your expatriates picked off by competing companies willing to pay more in those developed markets.

Nevertheless, the risks may be worth it simply because sending an American citizen abroad may cost a multinational $30,000–$40,000 more because of tax equalization payments alone in some locations. Plus, annual rent in some expensive locations can run well over $50,000 per year, considerably above the tax exclusion for housing allowances permitted by the U.S. government (although higher limits are now permitted in certain expensive locations). If the company does not pay, then the expatriate has to cough up the difference—something that could easily cause the American to refuse to go. As one executive put it, if American expatriates cost so much more to multinationals, "people who hire will think, 'Am I better off with an Australian or New Zealander who's going to cost me less?'" Indeed, the president of the American Chamber of Commerce office in Korea described U.S. tax laws as a "deterrent for hiring Americans overseas" and noted that U.S. firms in Korea had been "systematically replacing Americans with Australians, Indians, and just about any other nationality to keep a lid on total costs of expatriates."

In the final analysis, perhaps the best strategy for Americans interested in becoming expatriates is to search high and low for a company to work at that still provides generous expatriate packages—one with superb housing allowances, tax equalization payments, and plenty of incentives and other benefits. With the right package, one expatriate consulting expert observed, "you could be saving 70 [percent] to 80 [percent] of your entire salary and that's paying all your taxes and being totally legal."

Of course, this will not be an easy task. At a broader level, what do some of the actions that firms are taking mean for the future, especially for Americans who might want to be expatriates? Are there other actions that these multinationals can take to have their cake on costs and still provide opportunities for Americans abroad? Should both sides be lobbying the U.S. government for tax relief for expatriates? Regardless, in the short run it will behoove everyone to think creatively about how best to structure expatriate assignments.[83]

International Development

Giving Negative Performance Feedback Across Cultures

Purpose

To get a sense of what it is like to provide performance feedback to employees and to develop the skills needed to do this effectively across cultures.

Instructions

Assume that your multinational company has instituted a 360-degree feedback performance evaluation system. Consequently, one of your jobs as a manufacturing division manager is to meet with subordinates individually to go over their results. You are about to meet with a manufacturing supervisor who has been with the company for seven years. A review of his past performance evaluations indicates an employee who has been reliable and has had above-average productivity. Results from his 360, however, have a definitely negative consistency, including comments such as "avoids trying new ideas," "uses coercion with peers and subordinates," "doesn't listen well," "ignores feedback," "often fails to return phone calls or other inquiries," "blames mistakes on others or tries to cover them up," and "is often unavailable when questions arise."

Part A: Evaluation of an American Supervisor

Assume that the manufacturing supervisor described in the instructions is an American based at a company facility outside of Atlanta. Your instructor will put you into groups of three to six students and ask you to prepare an action plan regarding this situation that will help the supervisor improve. Your instructor may ask you to assign someone to speak for the group in summarizing your plan to the class. The instructor may also ask a member of your group to role-play the meeting with the supervisor. Consider some or all of these questions as you work on the plan:

1. How should the manager approach the meeting with the supervisor? What problems might come up? How can the manager ensure that any messages (including ones that are not so positive) will be heard?
2. How can the manager and the supervisor listen to one another without becoming confrontational or defensive?
3. How clear are the goals of the action plan? Why will it be helpful?
4. How should the manager proceed if the goals set with the supervisor are met? What if he fails to meet them?

Part B: Cross-Cultural Evaluation of a Turkish Supervisor

In this section of the exercise, you are being asked to again prepare a plan to communicate performance feedback to the manufacturing supervisor with the same 360 report as described above. Only this time, please assume that the supervisor is a Turkish national who is based at a company plant outside Istanbul. On your visit to the plant, you have the chance to meet with this supervisor. As you prepare your action plan, consider these questions:

1. What might need to be done differently given that the supervisor is Turkish and that Istanbul is the context?
2. What are the key differences between this plan and the one you devised for the American employee? What cultural differences or concerns are reflected in your plan?

Source: Adapted from French, W. (1998). *Human Resources Management* (4th ed.) 362–363. Boston: Houghton Mifflin.

From Theory to International Practice

Assembling an Expatriate Compensation Package

Purpose

To improve your understanding of how salary, tax, and living cost differentials across countries make it challenging to construct an expatriate compensation package.

Instructions

You will write a report summarizing your research on the compensation of expatriates assigned to different countries. Depending on your instructor's directions, this exercise can be completed in small groups or as an individual assignment. Regardless, the scenario is as follows:

An American multinational has plans to send four managers on an expatriate assignment. Below are the pairs of foreign cities under consideration for each manager:

Manager 1: Cape Town, South Africa or Frankfurt, Germany
Manager 2: Moscow, Russia or Jakarta, Indonesia
Manager 3: Cairo, Egypt or Mumbai, India
Manager 4: Santiago, Chile or Shanghai, China.

Assume that you work in human resources for this company and your boss would like your advice on how to structure a compensation package for one of these managers. Your instructor will indicate which pair of cities and countries you will be assigned to research. Unless your instructor specifies otherwise, you can assume that all four potential expatriates are based in Chicago, are married with two school-age children between the ages of 6 and 15, and have a base salary of $150,000. Of this amount, approximately 60 percent is spent on living expenses, about 30 percent goes to cover various taxes, and the remaining 10 percent is allotted to savings.

As noted within the chapter, living expenses are complex and vary dramatically from country to country. Your report will have to account for transportation, clothing, housing, food, school costs, and many other elements that could play a role in this category. Remember that the tax situation for many foreign assignments is complex, and this will have to be factored into your report. All in all, how should the compensation packages differ across the two countries you are assigned to, if at all? In what areas might differences exist and why? What would your recommendations be for handling them and why? Again, be sure to describe why there are differences across countries (or why not) in the specific aspects of the package. In addition to the text and other reference sources, you may find many of the websites below useful for completing your report:

U.S. Department of State Foreign Allowances and Per Diem Pages

• aoprals.state.gov

This main website provides information for living, housing, and education allowances, among other things, by city/country. Detailed quarterly reports produced by the DOS are also available on the allowance page. Other topics of related interest may be found by searching the DOS's subject index page:

• www.state.gov/

STAT-USA/Internet (a service of the U.S. Department of Commerce)

• www.stat-usa.gov/

Here you will find country and market research information as well as detailed summaries of general background information on most countries in the world.

International Tax and Accounting Site Directory

• www.taxsites.com/

This is an international tax site directory, with country-specific data.

OECD (Organisation for Economic Cooperation and Development)

• www.oecd.org

This site presents purchasing power parity data that allows one to compare the cost of a basket of consumer goods and services across a number of countries. A variety of other information is available as well, including on tax treaties and income taxes across countries. This site is easily searchable.

Notes

1. *The Economist*. (2006). Travelling more lightly, June 24, 77–80; Herman, T. (2007). U.S. expats get additional tax relief. *The Wall Street Journal*, September 19, D3; Prystay, C., and Herman, T. (2006). Tax hike hits home for Americans abroad. *The Wall Street Journal*, July 19, D1, D2; Rosman, K. (2007). Expat life gets less cushy. *The Wall Street Journal*, October 26, W1, 10.

2. Briscoe, D. R., Schuler, R. S., and Claus, L. (2009). *International Human Resource Management* (3rd ed.). New York: Routledge.

3. Marin, G. S. (2008). National differences in compensation: The influence of the institutional and cultural context. In L. R. Gomez-Mejia and S. Werner (eds) *Global Compensation: Foundations and Perspectives*, 19–28, New York: Routledge.

4. Fey, C. F., Margulis-Yakushev, S., Park, H. J., and Bjorkman, I. (2009). Opening the black box of the relationship between HRM practices and firm performance: A comparison of MNE subsidiaries in the USA, Finland, and Russia. *Journal of International Business Studies*, 40, 690–712.

5. Bjorkman, I., Budhwar, P., Smale, A., and Sumelius, J. (2009). Human resource management in foreign-owned subsidiaries: China versus India. In Warner, M. (ed.) *Human Resource Management with "Chinese Characteristics": Facing the Challenges of Globalization*, 195–208. New York: Routledge.

6. Aguinis, H., Joo, H., and Gottfredson, R. (2012). Performance management universals: Think globally, act locally. *Business Horizons*, 55, 385–392; Oddou, G., and Mendenhall, M. (1991). Expatriate performance appraisal: Problems and solutions. In M. Mendenhall and G. Oddou (eds) *International Human Resource Management*, 364–374. Boston: PWS-Kent.

7. Briscoe, Schuler, and Claus, *International Human Resource Management*.

8. Tung, R. I. (2008). Expatriate selection and evaluation. In Smith, P. B., Peterson, M. S., and Thomas, D. C. (eds) *Handbook of Cross-Cultural Management Research*, 367–378. Thousand Oaks, CA: Sage.

9. Briscoe, Schuler, and Claus, *International Human Resource Management*.

10. Oddou and Mendenhall, Expatriate performance appraisal: Problems and solutions.

11. Briscoe, Schuler, and Claus, *International Human Resource Management*.

12. Varma, A., Pichler, S., and Srinivas, E. S. (2005). The role of interpersonal affect in performance appraisal: Evidence from two samples—the US and India. *International Journal of Human Resource Management*, 15(11), 2029–2044.

13. Oddou and Mendenhall, Expatriate performance appraisal: Problems and solutions.

14. Briscoe, Schuler, and Claus, *International Human Resource Management*.

15. Cascio, W., and Bailey, E. (1995). International human resource management: The state of research and practice. In O. Shenkar, *Global Perspectives of Human Resource Management*, 15–36. Englewood Cliffs, NJ: Prentice-Hall; Gregersen, H., Hite, J., and Black, J. S. (1996). Expatriate performance appraisal in U.S. multinational firms. *Journal of International Business Studies*, 27, 711–738.

16. Briscoe, Schuler, and Claus, *International Human Resource Management*.

17. Cascio and Bailey, International human resource management: The state of research and practice; Gregersen, Hite, and Black, Expatriate performance appraisal in U.S. multinational firms.

18. Briscoe, Schuler, and Claus, *International Human Resource Management*; Tung, Expatriate selection and evaluation.

19. Dowling, P. J., and Schuler, R. S. (1990). *International Dimensions of Human Resource Management*. Boston: PWS-Kent.

20. Briscoe, Schuler, and Claus, *International Human Resource Management*; Garland, J., and Farmer, R. N. (1986). *International Dimensions of Business Policy and Strategy*. Boston: PWS-Kent.

21. Dowling and Schuler, *International Dimensions of Human Resource Management*.

22. LaSalle Bank. (2006). China Overview—Part 2: Establishing a presence. LaSalle Bank/ABN AMRO publication, available at: www.fpsc.com/RBS/GlobalTradeAdvisor/PDF/China-Establishing_Presence.pdf; www.china-briefing.com; Dowling and Schuler, *International Dimensions of Human Resource Management*; Webb. L. (2003). Corporate dilemma: Profits idle in China. Asia Today Online. January 12, available at: www.asiatoday.com.au/feature_reports.php?id=38.

23. Evans, P., Pucik, V., and Barsoux, J. L. (2002). *The Global Challenge: Frameworks for International Human Resource Management*. New York: McGraw-Hill/Irwin.

24. Oddou and Mendenhall, Expatriate performance appraisal: Problems and solutions.

25. Oddou and Mendenhall, Expatriate performance appraisal: Problems and solutions.

26. Briscoe, Schuler, and Claus, *International Human Resource Management*; Oddou and Mendenhall, Expatriate performance appraisal: Problems and solutions.

27. Cooke, F. L. (2008). Performance management in China. In Varma, A., Budhwar, P. S., and DeNisi, A. (eds) *Performance Management Systems: A Global Perspective*, 193–209. New York: Routledge; DeNisi, A., Varma, A., and Budhwar, P. S. (2008). Performance management around the globe. In Varma, Budhwar, and DeNisi, *Performance Management Systems: A Global Perspective*, 254–261.

28. Ali, A. (1988). A cross-national perspective of managerial work value systems. In R. N. Farmer and E. G. McGowen (eds) *Advances in International Comparative Management*. Greenwich, CT: JAI Press; Arvey, R. D., Bhagat, R. S., and Salas, E. (1991). Cross-cultural and cross-national issues in personnel and human resources management: Where do we go from here? *Research in Personnel and Human Resources Management*, 9, 367–407; DeNisi, Varma, and Budhwar, Performance management around the globe.

29. Morishima, M. (2008). Performance management in Japan. In Varma, Budhwar, and DeNisi, *Performance Management Systems: A Global Perspective*, 223–238.

30. Cheng, K. C., and Cascio, W. (2009). Performance appraisal beliefs of Chinese employees in Hong Kong and the Pearl River Delta. *International Journal of Selection & Assessment*, 17, 329–333; Early, P. C. (1986). Trust, perceived importance of praise and criticism and work performance: An examination of feedback in the U.S. and England. *Journal of Management*, 12, 457–473.

31. Chiang, F. T., and Birtch, T. A. (2010). Appraising performance across borders: An empirical examination of the purposes and practices of performance appraisal in a multi-country context. *Journal of Management Studies*, 47, 1365–1393; Vance, C. M., Paik, Y., Boje, B. M., and Stage, H. D. (1993). A study of the generalizability of performance appraisal design characteristics across four Southeast Asian countries: Assessing the extent of divergence effect. Paper presented at the Academy of Management conference, Atlanta, GA.

32. Stull, J. S. (1988). Giving feedback to foreign-born employees. *Management Solutions*, 33, July, 42–45.

33. Briscoe, Schuler, and Claus, *International Human Resource Management*.

34. Milkovich, G. T., and Newman, J. M. (1996). *Compensation*. Chicago: Irwin.

35. Jelter, J. (2009). Whirlpool to shut Indiana plant, cut 1,100 jobs. MarketWatch, available at: www.marketwatch.com.

36. Kras, E. S. (1989). *Management in Two Cultures: Bridging the Gap between US and Mexican Managers*. Yarmouth, ME: Intercultural Press; wage data from ftp://ftp.bls.gov/pub/special. requests/ForeignLabor/industrynaics.txt.

37. *Fortune*. (1994). Mexican labor's hidden costs. *Fortune*, October 17, 32; Milkovich and Newman, *Compensation*.

38. Tosi, H. L., and Greckhamer, T. (2004). Culture and CEO compensation. *Organization Science*, 15(6), 657–670.

39. *The Economist*. (2009). Attacking the corporate gravy train, May 30, 71–73; *The Economist*. (2008). Executive pay in Europe: Pay attention., June 14, 77–78; Parker-Pope, T. (1996). Executive pay. *The Wall Street Journal*, April, R12; Fryer, B. (2003). In a world of pay. *Harvard Business Review Case & Expert Commentary*, November, 31–40.

40. Mesdag, L. M. (1984). Are you underpaid? *Fortune*, March 19, 22–23.

41. See http://money.cnn.com/2007/06/12/pf/vacation_days_worldwide.

42. Coy, P., and Suddath, C. (2012). The leisure gap. *Bloomberg Businessweek*, July 23–29, 8–9; Expedia. (2011). Expedia vacation deprivation study of 20 countries, available at: http://mediaroom.expedia.com/travel-news/expedia-2011-vacation-deprivation-study-reveals-wide-work-life-disparity-across-five-con (retrieved September 10, 2013).

43. Ramstad, E., and Woo, J. (2010). South Korea works overtime to tackle vacation shortage. *The Wall Street Journal*, March 1, A1, A22.

44. Townsend, A. M., Scott, K. D., and Markham, S. E. (1990). An examination of country and culture-based differences in compensation practices. *Journal of International Business Studies*, 21, 667–678.

45. Fay, C. H.. (2008). The global convergence of compensation practices. In Gomez-Mejia and Werner, *Global Compensation: Foundations and Perspectives*, 131–141.

46. Alis, D., Bournois, F., Croquette, D., and Poulain, P. Y. (2008). HRM in France: Changes in the corpus. In C. Scholz and H. Bohm (eds) *Human Resource Management in Europe: Comparative Analysis and Contextual Understanding*, 113–152, New York: Routledge.

47. Flynn, G. (1994). HR in Mexico: What you should know. *Personnel Journal*, August, 34–44; Ramirez, J., and Zapata-Cantu, L. (2009). HRM systems in Mexico. In Davila, A., and Elvira, M. M. (eds) *Best Human Resource Practices in Latin America*, 97–112. New York: Routledge.

48. Beatty, J. R., McCune, J. T., and Beatty, R. W. (1988). A policy-capturing approach to the study of U.S. and Japanese managers' compensation decisions. *Journal of Management*, 14, 465–474; Marin, National differences in compensation: The influence of the institutional and cultural context.

49. Zhu, C. J., Cooper, B., De Cieri, H., Thomson, S. B., and Zhao, S. (2009). Devolvement of HR practices in transitional economies: Evidence from China. In Warner, *Human Resource Management with "Chinese Characteristics": Facing the Challenges of Globalization*, 71–85; Sovich, N. (2006). Western firms find hiring, retention in China surprisingly tough. *The Wall Street Journal*, August 11, A4.

50. Marin, National differences in compensation: The influence of the institutional and cultural context; Toyama, M., and Frederick, J. (2004). Hiroshi Okuda and Fuji Ocho: Toyota's tenacious twosome. *Time*, April 26, available at: www.time.com/time/magazine.

51. Briscoe, Schuler, and Claus, *International Human Resource Management*.

52. Leung, K., Zhu, Y., and Ge, C. (2009). Compensation disparity between locals and expatriates. *Journal of World Business*, 44, 85–93.

53. Mestre, C., and Traber, Y. (2009). Managing expatriates in unprecedented times. Mercer Human Resource Consulting, February, available at: www.mercer.com.

54. Briscoe, Schuler, and Claus, *International Human Resource Management*.

55. Briscoe, Schuler, and Claus, *International Human Resource Management*.

56. Reynolds, C. (1994). *Compensation Basics for North American Expatriates: Developing an Effective Program for Employees Working Abroad*. Scottsdale, AZ: The American Compensation Association.

57. Briscoe, Schuler, and Claus, *International Human Resource Management*.

58. Reynolds, *Compensation Basics for North American Expatriates*.

59. Feng, S. (2009). Expatriate localization: A Chinese solution. Mercer Human Resource Consulting, available at: www.mercer.com.

60. Cordova, V. (2009). Reducing expatriate program costs under the balance sheet approach. *International HR Journal*, Summer, 10–14; Oemig, D. R. A. (1999). When you say, "we'll keep you whole," do you mean it? *Compensation and Benefits Review*, 31, 40–47.

61. Briscoe, Schuler, and Claus, *International Human Resource Management*; Mestre and Traber, Managing expatriates in unprecedented times: Containing international assignment costs.

62. Reynolds, *Compensation Basics for North American Expatriates*; see also www.mercer.com.

63. Helms, M. (1991). International executive compensation practices. In Mendenhall and Oddou, *International Human Resource Management*, 106–132; Infante, V. D. (2001). Three ways to design international pay: Headquarters, home country, host country. *Workforce*, January, 22–24.

64. For the most recent information about the U.S. Department of State foreign incentives, see: http://aoprals.state.gov/content.asp?content_id=134&menu_id=75; also see U.S. Department of State. (1999). *Indexes of Living Costs Abroad, Quarters Allowances, and Hardship Differentials*. Washington, D.C.: Government Printing Office.

65. Reynolds, *Compensation Basics for North American Expatriates*: see also: www.economist.com/research/Economics/alphabetic.cfm?letter=P.

66. Briscoe, Schuler, and Claus, *International Human Resource Management*; Sepede, M. L. and James, C. (2009). The challenge of expatriate housing—managing costs and expatriates' expectations. Mercer Human Resource Consulting, January 29, available at: www.mercer.com.

67. Cordova, Reducing expatriate program costs under the balance sheet approach; Rosman, Expat life gets less cushy.

68. See: www.kpmg.com/sitecollectiondocuments/individual-income-tax-rates-survey-2009_v2.pdf.

69. Anderson, J. B. (1990). Compensating your overseas executives, Part 2: Europe in 1992. *Compensation and Benefits Review*, 22, 25–35; Briscoe, Schuler, and Claus, *International Human Resource Management*; Klein, R. B. (1992). Compensating your overseas executives, Part 3. *Compensation and Benefits Review*, 23, 27–38.

70. Briscoe, Schuler, and Claus, *International Human Resource Management*; Cordova, Reducing expatriate program costs under the balance sheet approach; Veliotis, S. (2008). The effect of the U.S. stimulus tax rebates on equalization programs. *Compensation and Benefits Review*, 40, 60–65.

71. Anderson, Compensating your overseas executives; for U.S. tax treaties with other nations, see www.irs.gov/businesses/international/article/0,,id=96739,00.html.

72. Cordova, Reducing expatriate program costs under the balance sheet approach; Reynolds, *Compensation Basics for North American Expatriates*; see also www.irs.gov/pub/irs-pdf/i2555.pdf.

73. Cordova, Reducing expatriate program costs under the balance sheet approach.

74. Briscoe, Schuler, and Claus, *International Human Resource Management*; Traber, Y., Gibson, I., and Mestre, C. (2009). Setting and communicating competitive expatriate allowances. Mercer Human Resource Consulting, April, available at: www.mercer.com.

75. Silverman, R. E. (2001). Pricing zippers, Tabasco, Prozac in exotic locales. *The Wall Street Journal*, June 13, B1, B14.

76. Bialik, C. (2013). Useful cost-of-living data don't come cheap. *The Wall Street Journal*, February 9–10, A2; Mercer Human Resource Consulting. (2009). Mercer's 2009 Cost of Living Survey, updated July 7, available at: www.mercer.com.

77. *The Economist*. (2013). Bunfight: the Big Mac index, February 2, 60–61; Iosebashvili, I. (2013). On currencies—what's fair is hard to say. *The Wall Street Journal*, February 22, A12; Vachris, M. A., and Thomas, J. (1999). International price comparisons based on purchasing power parity. *Monthly Labor Review*, October, 3–12; also see: www.economist.com/markets/indicators/displaystory.cfm?story_id=13055650.

78. Bialik, Useful cost-of-living data don't come cheap.

79. Briscoe, Schuler, and Claus, *International Human Resource Management*; Cordova, V. (2009). Reducing expatriate program costs under the balance sheet approach; Wilson, L. E. (2000). The balance sheet approach to expatriate compensation: Still with us after all these years. *Relocation Journal and Real Estate News*, 14, 1–9.

80. Briscoe, Schuler, and Claus, *International Human Resource Management*.

81. Hoak, A. (2012). Thinking about an overseas transfer? First, get the answers to these four questions. *The Wall Street Journal*, September 10, R3; Cordova, Reducing expatriate program costs under the balance sheet approach; Milkovich, G. T., and Bloom, M. (1998). Rethinking international compensation. *Compensation and Benefits Review*, 30, 15–23.

82. Froymovich, R. (2011). Before you get on that plane . . . If you're being transferred outside the U.S. make sure you know the financial implications. *The Wall Street Journal*, June 20, R6; Latta, G. W. (1999). Expatriate policy and practice: A ten-year comparison of trends. *Compensation and Benefits Review*, 31, 35–39; McGowan, R. (2003). The days of the "champagne lifestyle" expatriate assignments are numbered. Mercer Human Resource Consulting, January 29, 1–3; Reynolds, *Compensation Basics for North American Expatriates*.

83. Hoak, Thinking about an overseas transfer? First, get the answers to these four questions; Froymovich, Before you get on that plane; *The Economist*. (2006). Travelling more lightly; Herman, U.S. expats get additional tax relief; Prystay and Herman, Tax hike hits home for Americans abroad; Rosman, Expat life gets less cushy.

chapter 13

managing cultural groups

from small work

Learning Objectives

After reading this chapter, you should be able to:

- recognize the impact of groups in a cross-cultural environment;
- be aware of the promise and pitfalls presented by diversity in and among groups;
- describe the importance of relations between groups of employees and management across countries;
- recognize the various forms and effects of unions across a large number of countries;
- identify various forms of employee decision-making input, beyond unions.

International Challenge

SAP's Plans Hit a Cultural Barrier

Founded in 1972, SAP is Germany's largest software company. The firm grew through the 1980s and 1990s, with most software created by tight-knit groups of developers at company headquarters in Walldorf, Germany. Consequently, SAP's software had a distinctly German flavor. It took more than one year to perfect its programs, with developers trouble-shooting alongside teammates at coffee bars that were strategically placed within SAP's Walldorf facility. Complex and expensive, SAP's software systems often took months to install and debug, but once they were ready for public use they worked well and offered a one-stop shop for corporate customers. At the time, the fact that SAP products did not integrate well with other firms' software was not a big problem.

But in the late 1990s, businesses started focusing more on interconnectedness and integration, thanks to the Internet. This became a problem for SAP's stand-alone software model. Moreover, companies were backing away from buying pricey, complex software suites every five years, turning instead to more flexible web-based software that was offered by SAP's competitors. After tinkering with its business model, SAP decided in 2003 that the answer to these challenges was to become "less German." Implementing this strategy over the next several years produced plenty of change and conflict.

SAP co-CEOs Hasso Plattner and Henning Kagermann felt that their cautious approach to competitive threats had been holding back the firm, especially in the U.S. market. An injection of innovation was needed to shake up the company. This did not come easy because Kagermann (an ex-physics professor) and Plattner (a hot-tempered tech guru) were both known for their cautious management styles. But they acquired a diverse chunk of non-German innovation in one fell swoop by purchasing an Israeli firm that developed web-based applications. This firm was led by Shai Agassi, a young entrepreneur with a brash style that CEOs Kagermann and Plattner took to. They gave Agassi tough management roles and made him responsible for hundreds of SAP programmers. Along the way, Agassi continued to pitch ideas for different and innovative products to his German bosses, despite being repeatedly rebuffed. Finally, one idea caught the eye of Kagermann and Plattner —an idea that became SAP's NetWeaver, a web-based software tool more flexible than traditional SAP software. Agassi was promoted and given more control at SAP.

While SAP was becoming less German thanks to Agassi, it was also becoming more diverse by hiring thousands of programmers from different parts of the world, particularly the United States and India. These programmers were put into development teams to tackle key projects that previously would have been given only to German employees in Walldorf. Agassi also insisted on changing the official language of the company to English, even in SAP's German headquarters. Soon non-Germans occupied 50 percent of top executive positions at SAP. The hope was that this injection of newcomers would increase diversity in SAP and quicken the pace of innovation.

But these moves also created conflict, especially in Walldorf. Most firms start to globalize by building sales or manufacturing units first while keeping research and development (as well as the development of company strategy) close to home. SAP did not follow this model. Instead, it tried to globalize *away* from its German roots from top to bottom—something that came as a big shock to German employees embedded in the insular SAP culture at Walldorf. As you read this chapter, think about some of the effects that these sweeping changes might have brought about, as well as the inter-group challenges that they brought to SAP. At the end of this chapter in the Up to the Challenge? closing feature, we will review some of those problems faced by SAP and the resulting effects on their various teams.[1]

Managing Teams and Smaller Work Groups Across Cultures

Experts define a group as two or more people who interact together in order to pursue common goals. This broad definition is expansive enough to cover small cross-functional teams that disband after solving specific problems all the way to larger groups, such as international offices, divisions, and even international labor unions with hundreds of thousands of members. This wide scope is the purview of this last chapter.

Groups are important to the life of most firms—multinational or not—and they come in many different flavors. There are task forces, cross-functional teams, self-directed work teams, special committees, boards, production crews, and many more. One reason for so many variations is because groups offer extraordinary potential to get things done. Groups provide opportunities to pool knowledge among a set of people, to make more considered decisions, and to leaven any individual tendency to make mistakes. The result *can* be a harder-working, smarter, more productive set of people.

At the same time, this description can be in contradiction with some uniformly lousy group experiences that some students reading this book (and others) may have encountered. How can we reconcile the potential of groups with experience that is contrary? The real challenge for a manager is to set the stage so that the promise of groups can be realized. It is naïve to assume that everyone will work together well and problematic to simply form a group with the hope that somehow you will get a set of people that will not have any conflict. Conflict is not a rare thing that happens only when things go very wrong or when you have the "wrong set of people." Conflict, in fact, is normal and inherent in the social interaction process. To not understand and account for this is not a failure of groups per se, but it is a failure of management to set the stage and to help groups capitalize on differences that will likely emerge. As noted in earlier chapters on communication, training, and performance appraisal, the challenges that management ordinarily faces in these areas is magnified severalfold in multicultural groups. Consequently, the chapter reviews cultural differences in the ways that groups typically operate and then outlines techniques that allow managers to build more effective work teams.

Differences in Group Behavior Across Cultures

If some cultures value groups and accord more importance and attention to those than do other cultures, then right away we might expect some additional sources of conflict to emerge in same-culture teams.

Individuals and Collectivists

As discussed in Chapter 4, one of the most important cultural distinctions is the difference between individualism and collectivism. Examples of countries that tend toward individualistic values include the U.S., Britain, the Netherlands, and Belgium, while collectivistic countries include Taiwan, Mexico, the Philippines, and many South American countries. In more collectivistic countries, people see group goals as more important than individual goals. And, in individualistic countries, people are expected to take care of themselves and the emphasis is on autonomy, individual achievement, and privacy. People in individualistic cultures *tend* to apply the same value standards to everyone, while collectivists take a different approach depending on whether they interact with an in-group or an out-group.[2]

In-groups and Out-groups

Collectivist cultures put great emphasis on the needs of the group and they value cooperation among members—including sometimes over self-interest. But for collectivists, all groups are not the same. Some place their family first (e.g., many Chinese), while others place their organization first (e.g., many Japanese). Regardless of how the in-group is defined, collectivists draw sharper boundaries between their own in-group and an out-group than do most individualists. In general, there is a noticeable distinction between family and neighbors in collectivistic cultures. Of course, family is very important in individualistic cultures too, but not as much as for collectivists. Chapter 5 showed that the self-attitudes of collectivists tend to be more influenced by their standing in groups than is true for individualists. For instance, when asked to describe themselves, collectivists are more likely to use group-based descriptions (e.g., "I am happy when I work with friends") than are individualists ("I am a happy person").

In an individualistic culture, such as the U.S., it is easy to underestimate the pervasive effect of collectivist norms on the lives of people. This does not mean that individualists cannot work well in groups to accomplish tasks—clearly, they can. But when people get together, the process of group interaction differs substantially when individualists and collectivists are involved. This difference in group interaction is learned early in life. To illustrate, one study looked at group interaction patterns of 10- to 12-year-old Chinese and American children who worked on the same task.[3] The Chinese children approached the task in a cooperative, group-enhancing way, while the American children chose strategies that reflected self-enhancing, competitive motives. This pattern underscores both the individualistic and achievement-oriented upbringing that most Americans experience, as well as the traditional Chinese saying, "Friendship first and competition second."[4] Knowing what makes groups tick can help managers learn to function better in a diverse, international setting.[5]

Group Productivity Across Cultures

So, how might groups affect the quality and quantity of work done in various cultures? Let's look at some general answers to this question next.

Social Loafing

In research done within the U.S., people are more productive working alone than when working with others in groups. This phenomenon is known as social loafing and is a very reliable effect observed in study after study. Apparently people "loaf" because they assume that the group will get the job done with or without them and because they can then redirect their efforts toward their *own* goals—even if that just involves relaxing. Similar results have been found in over 50 different studies, encompassing many different types of jobs and organizations but comprising mostly American workers.[6]

But is social loafing a uniquely American (or Western) effect? There is good reason to believe it is because U.S. culture emphasizes individuality, leading Americans to have trouble working and playing well with others, both at home and on the international stage. Other cultures (such as Japanese) tend to be more team-oriented, with the workplace being organized accordingly. At least one study shows that in contrast to Americans, Japanese perform better in groups than when working alone.[7] Likewise, several studies show that social loafing does not occur among Chinese (collectivists) either.[8]

In-groups and Social Loafing

The social loafing research discussed so far only compares people who work alone versus those in groups.[9] But, group effects do not always translate into an advantage for collectivist cultures. For example, there may be surprisingly poor communication among collectivistic employees who work for the same company but who are members of different in-groups.[10] This is what researchers found: collectivists were more competitive than individualists when facing members of out-groups in their company.[11] In general, the type of group matters to collectivists. They are more likely to loaf when they participate in a group that is of no special significance to them (such as an out-group).

In one study examining this issue, managers from China, Israel, and the U.S. were observed when asked to work by themselves vs. when they were placed in two different group situations.[12] An in-group situation was created by leading managers to believe that they shared several characteristics that usually lead to close friendships. An out-group condition was created by telling managers that other group members had different characteristics and that they came from very different backgrounds. In all cases, the managers worked on simulated management tasks such as rating job applications. The Chinese and Israelis were chosen to participate because they came from collectivist cultures, and Americans were chosen to represent an individualistic culture.

People from all three of these countries vary in how collective or individualistic they are, but nevertheless the findings were as the researchers expected. First, the study replicated the common finding that there was a reduction in group performance (loafing) for Americans but not for the more collective Israeli or Chinese managers. The important finding of this study, however, was that the collectivists also loafed, but under special circumstances. They showed evidence of social loafing when they worked with an out-group. The collectivists (from China and Israel) were likely to reduce their effort on a work team project when that group held few ties of any importance to them. When they completed work with an in-group, however, the performance of collectivists was not reduced—they did not show evidence of social loafing.

Implications of Social Loafing Research

What does this all mean for international managers? First, management strategies based on individual performance may be less effective in collectivist cultures. For example, the belief that individual incentives would be uniformly effective in China or Israel fails to recognize the impact and importance of groups to these cultures. Using a traditional American pay-for-performance approach in China, for example, may be counterproductive. That said, this research also suggests that care must be taken when adopting a group incentive plan in a collective culture. The type of group in which collectivists work, not just being in a group per se, may affect their performance. Consequently, forming a group around a natural collection of individuals (i.e., an in-group) may be the best bet for improving performance in a collectivist culture.[13]

Based on this reasoning, a manager might be wise to employ group-based incentive schemes in a location such as China. Nevertheless, workforce diversity appears to be increasing in many rapidly growing economies (such as China) as work and travel patterns change in response to job opportunities. In China, for example, although many people need a work permit to move from the countryside to big cities like Shanghai, there is still remarkable (albeit, illegal) movement of the labor force. As a result, managers will have to be especially clever and insightful when they introduce group performance strategies in such settings, not to mention that traditional values in China might also be undergoing great change.[14]

Conversely, what might be the impact of using group-based management schemes in the highly individualistic U.S.? Team-based approaches have been increasing in the U.S., with about 10 percent of all employees in American firms now organized into self-directed work groups or other team-based approaches.[15] Given the emphasis on individualism in American culture, ensuring that team-based approaches work well in the U.S. can be a challenge. On the other hand, the U.S. is becoming less culturally homogeneous, thanks in part to a steady flow of immigrants. So, another challenge for American managers—as well as foreign expatriate managers—is to understand and to match methods and tasks in an increasingly diverse workforce. One area where this cultural mix has already taken place is among flight crews of commercial airlines. The following International Insights feature illustrates some of the life and death challenges that these groups deal with every day.

International Insights

Team Dynamics at 35,000 Feet

The operation of large commercial jet aircraft is complex, highly technical, and dependent upon a team of experienced professionals. The flight crew of some modern aircraft can exceed 20 people, each playing an important role in operation and safety. The analysis of commercial aviation accidents shows that flight crew behavior, rather than technical failure, has been the cause of nearly 70 percent of all accidents.[16] Consequently, communication, leadership, and decision making have been studied in an attempt to reduce behavioral issues that can lead to accidents. As shown already within this chapter, many of these interpersonal issues are affected by culture.

Following this reasoning, one study looked at the attitudes of flight crews from a variety of countries, including the U.S. and several Asian nations.[17] Commercial aviation is a highly regulated industry, and as a result flight crews perform very similar tasks in very similar environments. Because their job differences are minimized across cultures, any differences in attitudes noted among these workers probably have a cultural base. The researchers asked all crew members, including pilots and flight attendants, to complete a questionnaire about optimal behavior on the flight deck. The results were very interesting. For one, Asian pilots and flight attendants were more similar in their attitudes than were the American crews. This finding might reflect the now familiar need for social harmony among collectivist cultures.

Moreover, the results showed that American flight attendants preferred a captain who encouraged their questions but who also took charge in any emergency. American pilots actually stood out from all the other groups, including American flight attendants. They generally showed highly individualistic attitudes, reflective of the solo flyer of the old days of aviation. In the Asian cultures, however, both the attendants and pilots preferred to see an autocratic but communicative captain in almost all circumstances. These differences present problems for the most common training methods used for today's flight crews. This approach, called crew resource management, or CRM training, emphasizes recognition, acceptance, and the free flow of information among the crew. Accordingly, CRM appears to reflect collectivism and low power distance. As such, the CRM technique may create problems or be an advantage, depending upon the culture of the crew being trained.

Highly individualistic American pilots are asked to forgo their "flyboy" images and work more in teams. Although this may be tough for them, CRM training can also capitalize on the American orientation toward low power distance—via their natural tendency to share flight information. And although Asian crews appear to be more team-oriented and therefore a better fit with CRM training, their high power distance orientation may discourage the open sharing of information. Indeed, CRM training that develops more forceful action by junior officers may be too foreign for a Korean flight crew to adopt. At the same time, the CRM concept of group input may be too much for American pilots to accept. So, in an emergency the groups have both cultural assets and liabilities to fall back on. The challenge for CRM is to make sure all aspects of the training sink into crews from all cultures.

Not only is air travel relatively safe, it has gotten safer over the years, with 2009 being the best in decades. And, CRM (along with many other contributors) has played a role in this increase in safety. The percentage of accidents worldwide due to human error dropped from 70 percent in 1997 to about 54 percent in 2007.[18]

Diversity: Working with Others from Different Groups

Previously, we discussed differences in group behavior across cultures. Yet, often international managers have to deal with more complex diversity as they effectively lead groups of workers, including home-country nationals, third-country nationals, and expatriates. Likewise, staying at home is no escape from diversity issues. Managers in many developed countries, including the U.S., are often faced with leading groups consisting of foreign nationals and members of varying racial and ethnic groups (among other forms of diversity).

Pros and Cons of Diversity

Managers who are responsible for building work groups composed of people from different cultures often have their hands full. Many practical problems need to be overcome in order for groups to run smoothly and effectively (see Chapter 11 for some of these). Some road blocks could be expected simply from the definition of *diversity* itself. Synonyms include "varied," "dissimilar," and "divergent." In general, these three adjectives can mean a heavy lift for managers. Indeed, international executives often have an easier time recalling disadvantages associated with cultural diversity than in pinpointing pluses. As a French executive put it, "I have been involved in many situations over the years, but I can't think of one made easier because it involved more than one culture."[19]

One reason that disadvantages may be easy to recall is that they are so salient. Communication itself is more problematic in multicultural groups, something largely taken for granted (incorrectly) in homogenous groups. Likewise, the potential confusion and conflict that can emerge with cross-cultural groups stands out and is easy to remember because it is distinctive and not like the plain old conflict so often experienced in like-minded groups. In contrast, the benefits associated with diversity take longer to manifest and are more difficult to observe. For example, decisions are likely to be more considered and well rounded and stand the test of time and location better—even if they take longer and are rife with conflict. The many different perspectives brought to the problem offer a kind of built-in brainstorming—the very kind of activity that can lead to creative ideas. The following International Insights feature presents a story of diversity, including pluses and downsides, encountered in an alliance formed by Siemens, Toshiba, and IBM.

International Insights

Cross-Cultural Teams Open in the Catskills

Some years ago, three companies that ordinarily compete with each other formed a strategic alliance to develop a revolutionary computer chip. They called this team the Triad, and it was composed of employees from Siemens AG of Germany, Toshiba of Japan, and IBM of the U.S. The unit would all come together and work on the project in upstate New York at an IBM facility. Nearly 100 scientists were formed into teams that included representatives of the three companies (and continents) in this project. Project managers worried that the diverse cultural backgrounds of the teams might create problems—it turned out that they had reason for concern!

Consider some of the behavior of the Toshiba scientists. The Germans were shocked to find them closing their eyes and apparently sleeping during important meetings. Yet, this is common practice for overburdened Japanese workers when the discussion does not center on them. The Japanese themselves, who ordinarily work in large teams, found it very difficult to sit in small, individual offices and speak English. As a result, they often withdrew whenever possible to the more comfortable confines of all-Japanese groups. Further undercutting the team synergy were the feelings of the American scientists. They felt that the Germans planned way too much and that the Japanese—who typically prefer to review proposals constantly—would not make a specific or clear decision. The Germans and the Japanese complained that their American counterparts didn't spend enough time getting to know them, either at work or at social events.[20] Unfortunately, all this led to a climate of misunderstanding and mistrust. There were even some suspicions that information and progress were being held back from the group by various company cliques.

In theory, the pooling together of a diverse and intelligent group of people to design new advanced technology should pay creative dividends. The reason that this did not work in the Triad project, at least initially, was that people wanted to (and were able to) stay in their separate in-groups. In analyzing the situation, the lack of attention to group interaction and team building was fingered as the culprit. Instead, great efforts were made on the technical and logistical side of things, with only the normal (brief) courses on working and living abroad. One HR executive for Toshiba said, "We should have done more with HR people from Siemens and IBM to develop cooperative training programs." Siemens also briefed their employees on living abroad and on what they called the American "hamburger style of management." Americans, they said, start their criticism gently. They start with "how's the family" small talk; that is the "top of the hamburger bun." Then they go right to the "meat," namely, the criticism, topped off with more "bun" which is words of encouragement. With Germans, in contrast, it is all "meat," and with Japanese you have to learn to find the "meat." Despite all of the obstacles, Triad members said that they learned a lot from their experiences—both about technology and about cooperating with different groups of people from around the world.[21]

Using Diversity to Your Advantage

Research shows that particular diversity composition of a group does impact performance. Across a number of definitions (gender, age, culture), the more varied a group is, the more difficult time they have—at least initially.[22] Diverse groups have more trouble communicating and a tougher time building unit cohesion, and take longer to set up than do more homogenous groups.[23] Nevertheless, once an understanding and structure are put in place, the diverse group becomes as effective as the homogenous group. Because of their ability to bring a variety of perspectives to the table, diverse groups may perform best over the long run, especially on projects requiring creativity and problem solving rather than simple routine tasks. This is exactly what one study of top management teams found—that cultural diversity was responsible for higher team performance and that when conflict did occur, it was also more functional.[24]

Other studies have found that while homogeneous teams (i.e., members who have similar demographic characteristics) outperformed diverse groups at first, over time the performance of highly heterogeneous teams improved and equaled that of the less diverse teams.[25] Teams defined as "moderately" heterogeneous did not perform nearly as well as the other two types of teams. But, getting to that higher productivity is tough going, partially because people have built-in views depending on their background. To illustrate, researchers conducted in-depth interviews of employees in multinational firms in the U.S., France, the Philippines, and Puerto Rico.[26] Coding and analysis of the interviews revealed that different metaphors by country were associated with teams.

People in individualistic countries tend to use sports metaphors to think about and refer to groups. In high power distance countries (such as the Philippines), groups are thought of more as families or referred to with military metaphors. Because of the various meanings of teams, there are different behaviors of members and these are better markers of success. For example, one study found that Mexicans thought that compliments and expressions of support were important for group success, whereas Anglos placed lower emphasis on these and were more likely to see task-type behavior of members as important for sucess.[27]

Given this, how can you cleverly manage diversity to your advantage? Below are guidelines you should consider to get the most out of multicultural teams:[28]

- **Choose appropriate tasks.** It is a mistake to choose a multicultural team based solely on ethnicity. Instead, choose members who have similar high ability levels but diverse perspectives.
- **Explicitly recognize differences.** Instead of minimizing cultural differences, members should be encouraged to describe and recognize differences. This will push team members toward understanding those differences and appreciating what different cultures can contribute. This must be done carefully, however, as it may accentuate existing differences and create "fault lines" within the group.
- **Give team members equal status.** Power differences among team members can be a problem if that stifles creativity. For example, while there are good reasons for international teams to be led by someone from the parent company, that culture may end up dominating the proceedings. This is more likely for high power distance cultures where there is a strong norm to defer to leaders.
- **Provide feedback.** Culturally diverse teams have difficulty agreeing on the benefit of various ideas—perhaps because the methods they use to gauge benefits are different. So, to help develop similar judgment criteria, give frequent feedback to members on their ideas.[29]

It is clear that managing diversity in multicultural teams is difficult. Nevertheless, when correctly set up and managed, diverse teams have much to contribute. That said, these smaller teams are only one part of the equation when it comes to managing groups across cultures.

Labor Relations in and Across Cultures

Working with small multicultural teams is tough enough, but when larger labor forces are involved, the management challenges may cut across entire companies, industries, or countries. The field of labor relations deals with employee–employer relationships and there are wide differences in laws, enforcement, and penalties associated with violations across countries. To address these topics, we will first outline the perspectives of management and workers. We will then discuss agreements or structures that have been devised for soliciting employee input or control. Despite the best intentions of firms, unions, and governments, there are times when conflicts arise and action is taken, either by workers (strikes) or by management (lockouts).

Management and Worker Perspectives on Labor Relations

Worker Control and Input

Workers in all countries are concerned with pay, job security, and working conditions and some join labor unions in order to have input about these work outcomes.[30] Sometimes they wish to extend this power to that of having a say in important decisions facing the firm. Setting aside the possibility of lobbying government for changes in law and/or other indirect tactics, workers often have one main method of getting their way on key issues—by threatening to reduce work output or stop it all together. This threat may be less credible, however, when the employer is a multinational that has many resources at its disposal. These can help the firm outlast a strike by temporarily increasing production elsewhere. The firm may also threaten to permanently move its operations to another country in response to labor strife. Consequently, multinationals typically have considerable power over employees and unions.

Power of the Multinational

An example involving Hyster Corporation of Portland, Oregon, illustrates this power. They operated a 500-person forklift/truck plant in Irvine, Scotland. Thanks to a grant from the British government, Hyster was ready to invest $60 million in that plant, thereby creating another 100 jobs. But, the resulting increase in production would create overcapacity in Hyster's European market. Consequently, enlarging its Scottish plant meant that Hyster would cut back production at its factory in the Netherlands. They determined that this shift of Dutch production capacity to Irvine would mean that Scottish workers had to take a 14-percent pay cut. Hyster gave the workers 48 hours to accept the deal.

As if this were not enough, the next day each Scottish employee got a letter from the company. The letter said, "Hyster is not convinced at this time that Irvine is the best of the many alternatives open to it. It has not made up its mind. The location of the plant to lead Europe is still open." At the bottom of the page, employees were asked to vote for or against consolidation of production (and pay cut) at the Scottish plant. Facing potential job loss, only 11 employees voted no. Employees complained that they had had no warning and no real input into the company's decision process. While Hyster's employees were not unionized, many felt it would not have made a difference. "It was do-or-else," said some employees. In Hyster's defense, they faced incredible competition from the Japanese in the form of lower-cost, higher-efficiency forklifts. Hyster won an anti-dumping case that it filed with the International Trade Commission, resulting in 50-percent import duties on Japanese products. Nevertheless, the company was subsequently bought by another firm.[31]

Tempering the Power of the Multinational

To combat this considerable power of multinationals, unions and other employee groups have tried to use legal means to improve their position. For instance, French unions have begun coordinating lawsuits by members to seek redress for alleged breaches of contract about benefits.[32] Other countries have enacted laws that provide generous protection for workers (such as in France, where 35 hours is the legal weekly work limit for all employees). They also make it very difficult to fire anyone after a probationary period has passed. Even if the required termination conditions are met, the employee may be due a large severance payment.[33] The average American worker who has been laid off receives one week's severance pay for every year of service. German workers, however, get more than four times as much (on average). When you add in other mandated benefits (such as relocation and retraining) that are available in Germany, termination costs in the U.S. seem modest. As one executive recruiter in Germany put it, "U.S. firms are shocked by the termination rules. The possibility of firing someone quickly without cause is impossible."

Legal Constraints

U.S. federal law includes the WARN Act (Worker Adjustment and Retraining Notification). This law requires firms who plan to lay off 50 or more employees to provide those workers a 60-day notice. Yet, during tough economic times, some companies ignored the law, in an effort to stay afloat. Mazer Corporation of Dayton, Ohio, for example, sent an e-mail to their 300 employees at 5 p.m. one day telling them that it was their last day, apologizing for the short notice. Some workers did not receive their last paycheck, let alone the notice and 60 days' pay that is required by WARN. The 20-year-old law has not been enforced all that often, but it provides exemptions to firms (e.g., those having "unforeseeable circumstances), and penalties are not strong.[34]

Enforcement of similar laws elsewhere is stricter and so are the laws. Colgate-Palmolive experienced this after it announced plans to close a factory in Hamburg and eliminate 500 jobs. Colgate initially offered German employees about $40,000 each (over $20 million total). Colgate argued that the plan was similar to, or better than, what other firms in the area had recently provided. German law, however, gives the union an opportunity to approve such decisions, and the union felt that the offer was far too low given that the Hamburg operation was profitable for Colgate. The case involved immense public attention, including stories in local papers about the impact on employees and their families who had worked for Colgate for three generations. Eventually, the mayor of Hamburg publicly condemned the company for its move and the union threatened to drag out the negotiation process. Eventually, Colgate raised its offer and agreed to a settlement.[35]

As this illustrates, managing layoffs can be complex—including navigating the political waters of a country. The laws themselves are very complex and vary markedly from country to country, even in Europe. In France, for example, severance entitlement extends to those with at least one year of employment. The statutory severance payment is approximately 30 days for each year and can be graduated for those with ten years of service or more. So, a 20-year employee making $60,000 a year might be entitled to minimum termination benefits of $100,000 or more.[36] Other European countries are equally as generous (see Figure 13.1).

As a result of this complexity, firms in Europe become very creative in avoiding costs. When Dutch IT firm Pinkroccade NV wanted to shed 700 employees, it terminated

Country	Legal Protections	Common Additions/Summary
Belgium	• Extensive advanced notice • Prorated year-end premium • Holiday pay that's due • Outplacement counseling • Pre-pension payments for workers > 45 years old	Union-negotiated additions (e.g., closure premiums, employment search costs, etc.) can often double the total cost of the severance package
France	• 30 days' pay/each year of service • payments increased if more than 10 years of service • compensation rises if layoff is large-scale • If firm > 1,000 employees, it must offer full pay leave of 4–6 months	Payments often exceed these minimums. If court decides there was no genuine/serious reason for layoffs, damages might be added to payments – amounting to at least 6 months' salary. Employees getting increasingly militant at notice of layoff
Germany	• Notice of up to 7 months • 2 weeks' pay/each year of service • Employer can't choose employees based on individual performance alone, must use social criteria (disability, age)	Payments vary a good deal on specific characteristics of the employee (age, years of service, more)
The Netherlands	• 1 month's salary for 35–45-year-olds; 1.5 months 45–55; and 2 months for those > 55 • Many other social plans provide additional benefits to workers	Must select employees via last-in first-out system (those with less service first). Dutch labor law does not allow unilateral breaking of employment agreement by employer; must consult with works councils
Russia	• 2 months' minimum notice for workers • 1 month's pay + another from layoff until new job • Additional month if employee files for unemployment quickly	Large number of filters used to determine who to lay off (e.g., no women employees with children, single mothers, etc.)

Figure 13.1 Legal Protections for Worker Severance in Several European Countries.

Sources: Adapted from Freshfields Bruckhaus Deringer LLP. (2009). *Managing Mass Redundancies Across Europe* (2nd ed.). Brussels: Freshfields Bruckhaus Deringer LLP; Bush, J., Scott, M., Rowley, L., Lakshman, N., Matlack, C., Ewing, J., and Zhe, H. (2009). The hidden perils of layoffs. *BusinessWeek*, March 2, 52–53.

people in batches of 19—a process that took almost a year. The reason? Dutch law requires firms to enter negotiations with unions to obtain approval for layoffs if more than 20 employees are let go at a time. Other Dutch firms have simply placed unneeded, but perfectly healthy, employees on disability, shifting the cost to the government.[37] While the U.S. increased its spending and assistance to the unemployed as it sought to prop up the economy through 2008–2010, most of Europe already had a strong social safety net. This is illustrated in Figure 13.2, which shows the percentage of government

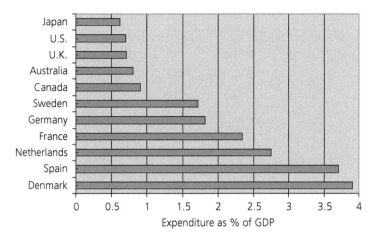

Figure 13.2 Public Expenditures on Labor Market Programs as a Percentage of GDP.

Source: Adapted from OECD. (2013). www.dol.gov.asp/archive/reports/chartbook (based on 2011 data; latest reported).

expenditures as a percentage of GDP in several OECD countries as of 2011. That said, the influence of unions and restrictive laws may be waning across Western Europe, in part due to the ability of multinationals to quickly shift production to lower-wage locations to the east. Volkswagen AG was able to persuade union members at its plant in Spain to accept a 5 percent pay cut by threatening to move jobs to Slovakia where wages are 50 percent less. This power, in combination with governments committed to austerity can render even big strikes ineffective.[38]

Labor Unions Across Countries

We have shown that both unions and multinationals have ways to exert influence over each other. Still, multinationals have the upper hand, with greater overall influence than any employee group or union.[39] This influence varies among countries, so we will review some of the differences in the structure of employee input and control.

As suggested, there are many mechanisms by which employees try to wrest control from management, with unions being the most common approach. Unions in the U.S. were originally established to bring about reform in the workplace before laws existed to protect worker interests and rights. Now, American unions have a relatively high profile, and that profile is not always positive. In fact, national surveys indicate a negative view of unions by Americans and may partly explain why union membership in the U.S. has been steadily declining in recent years. Today, union members make up only about 11 percent of the U.S. workforce.

Other industrialized countries have also seen a general decline in union membership. Figure 13.3 presents data on union "density rates" in a large number of countries. The percentage of workers who are unionized varies greatly across countries, but most have

Country	2011 Density (%)	Change Last Decade (%)
Australia	18.1	−25.2
Belgium	50.4	+2.0
Canada	26.8	−6.0
Denmark	68.5	−7.2
Finland	69.0	−7.4
France	7.8	−2.5
Germany	18.0	−25.0
Ireland	32.6	−13.8
Italy	35.6	+4.1
Japan	18.1	−13.8
Korea	9.9	−17.5
Netherlands	18.2	−13.3
Norway	54.6	+1.1
Spain	15.6	−2.5
Switzerland	17.1	−14.5
United Kingdom	25.6	−15.2
United States	11.3	−12.4

Figure 13.3 Union Density Rates Around the World.

Note: Density reflects estimates of the percentage of wage and salary workers who are union members, with negative numbers reflecting declines.

Source: Adapted from OECD. (2013). *OECD Labor Statistics*, available at: http://stats.oecd.org/ (retrieved October 29, 2013).

seen a decline in union membership over the last decade. The oldest and most well-developed union systems occur in the EU countries, but even there you will note large differences in the percentage of workers covered by unions. France, for example, has only about 8 percent of its workforce covered by unions, while Belgium has a figure over 50 percent. These national differences have been tied to a number of factors, including the political leanings of the government, how wages are determined, and the size of the public employment sector.

These union density rates should not be taken at face value. For one thing, bargaining agreements reached by the union and management often end up covering many more employees than just union members.[40] More importantly, a high union density does *not* necessarily mean that unions are more effective or influential. In fact, in some cases, a relatively low density rate (e.g., France at 8 percent) may belie the true, important degree of union influence (see the section on France that follows). Also, in some countries, labor may be represented by an entire political party, which also increases union influence. Clearly, however, not all unions across borders are structured the same nor are equally influential. Western countries in particular have been in existence longer and/or are well developed.

Unions Among European Union Countries

Because union influence is difficult to index precisely, there is some debate about which unions are influential and why. Nevertheless, it appears that union power, while diminished in recent years, is still a force to be reckoned with.[41]

Unions in France

The French workplace is influenced by five main national unions. And, as in Japan and other countries, most large employers also have a company union. These unions are among the most political in the world. In fact, the chief distinction among these unions is not the industry or the occupations that they cover, but instead their political and social leanings.[42] This can be clearly traced to past ideological issues and conflicts, and the degree to which they reflect the pattern of social division in France. These five major confederations have competed with one another for membership and it is common for all five to be present in any one work setting. Employees may choose to join one depending on their political viewpoint. Presently, this group has expanded to eight notable union federations.

Membership in any of these unions is not large by the standards of other countries. The largest union, the CFDT (Confédération française démocratique du travail), a largely industry/public service union with a communist leaning, has only about 890,000 members. Its 8-percent density rate places France at the low end of OECD countries (see Figure 13.3). Partly, this statistic reflects the fact that unions really do not have to push for new members and workers do not feel a strong need to seek out a union. For much of the time since the mid-1970s until recently, the French government has embraced the idea of protecting, if not enhancing, the rights of employees. In combination with a tradition of extending collective agreements to companies and industries that were not party to the accord, a worker can benefit from the union's influence without having to be a member. As a result, real union influence is much greater than the 8 percent density figure would suggest.

That said, French unions, like their German counterparts, have been under pressure in recent years to cooperate with government efforts to reform onerous labor laws and regulations.[43] When President Nicolas Sarkozy took office in 2007, his government took hard stands against unions through his term, which ended in 2012, those energized unions, including the CGT (Confédération générale du travail), which protested with strikes involving upwards of 1 million people marching in Paris. The CGT also took creative steps in its fight with the giant state-owned power company (EDF). The government wanted to sell a 30 percent stake and the union mobilized in fear of losing its large set of benefits (such as lifetime employment; early retirement for 55 percent of the workforce; pensions of 75 percent of the last year's salary; 32-hour work weeks for a quarter of employees; 90-percent discounts on power bills; free healthcare; subsidized housing, meals, vacations).[44] It is widely believed that the economic tough times have weakened the position of unions in France.

Unions in Germany

Unlike in the U.S., where union contracts are negotiated on a company-by-company basis, Germany relies on a centralized system in which some 60,000 contracts are set using industry-wide bargaining. Unions will typically bargain with a group of employers in an industry. There is only one union for workers in most major industries, and membership is entirely voluntary. As in the U.S., the contract will include most major work issues, including pay, benefits, and conditions of employment. As such, the main goals of the union are economic in form, as opposed to some of the more politically motivated union activity found in countries such as France or Italy. The most important union is the German Confederation of Trade Unions (Deutscher Gewerkschaftsbund [DGB]) which covers more than 6 million workers (about 20 percent of all German employees).

The nature of the relation between unions and management has been fairly cooperative over the last 20 years or so, with just a handful of days lost to strikes every year. One reason is that workers have a number of avenues of input into how the business is run, including representation on the board of directors. Companies in Germany with over 2,000 employees are required to give 50 percent of supervisory board seats to worker representatives. This policy, unique to Germany, is called *codetermination* and was set up by the Allies after World War II. Codetermination was designed to prevent industrial might from working in concert with a potentially threatening government. The system is most predominant in the steel and coal industries, sectors that were critical to pre- and post-war enterprises. There, unions select five board members, shareholders select another five members, and this body then selects an eleventh member. Outside of steel and coal, union membership on boards varies by industry and company size.[45]

In recent years, German unions have been willing to make concessions on working conditions and pay for increased job security. Indeed, in some areas, important German unions, such as the giant IG Metall union (Industrial Union of Metal Workers), have been conciliatory on certain issues, such as fighting for shorter workweeks. Nevertheless, research continues to show that Germans value free time and are willing to trade off money and overtime pay.[46] Overall, attitudes in Germany toward labor unions have hardened, with unions being blamed for higher unemployment rates, expensive wage rates, rigid labor laws, and a (perceived) weakening of German competitiveness. Consequently, union participation rates continue to decline, nearly 25 percent over the last decade (see Figure 13.3).[47]

Unions in the United Kingdom

The union movement in the U.K. has a long history, having been legalized in 1871. British unions are also relatively powerful, although their influence has waned in the last several years. The union movement can be seen as political in Britain, although not as much as some other countries. In fact, the desire for unions to push their political agenda led to the formation of the Labour Party in Britain in 1883. Since then, the trade unions have played a significant role in the party and to this day provide considerable financial support.

Union density in the United Kingdom is over twice that of U.S. union participation but has seen a big dip recently. At the height of its influence in 1979, membership was around 57 percent, dropping to 30 percent in 2001, and to 25 percent in 2011. This drop is due to several factors, but perhaps the biggest has to do with the political environment, with the government passing legislation that reduced union power. Additionally, the economy fared reasonably well in recent years, further reducing the appeal of union membership. Nevertheless, unions still wield considerable power and influence. Because a large firm may negotiate with several unions, the process is complex. Cross-union dealings can be fractionated and this has played into the hands of companies that have successfully pushed collective bargaining down from a national to a business level. Likewise, many new businesses have tried to maintain a nonunion status consistent with the "enterprise culture" of recent governments.[48]

Other Unions in Europe

Because Europe was the first continent to industrialize, there is great complexity and variety of union representation beyond the samples already discussed. In the Netherlands, for example, trade unions were initially formed and developed by religious and political groups. A good case in point is the largest union in Holland, the FNV, which is a merger between a socialist and a Catholic union. These unions, however, are not as ideological as those of the French, and they participate with the government in many initiatives (including the extensive social support mechanisms in Holland). Unions are important in the Netherlands, and several experts have claimed that their influence is much greater than their 18-percent density rate suggests.[49] Likewise, Dutch employees can exert control over the workplace via other unique outlets, as discussed later in the chapter.

Unions in Sweden began as a socialist movement among manual workers. And because of a largely friendly government, they flourished in a mutually cooperative environment. This can perhaps account for why Sweden has such a high density rate (73 percent). Although there has been some hostility between government and the unions in recent years, union membership rates have stayed high. Unions have been in the forefront of recognizing global competitive pressures by embracing management initiatives to improve productivity, such as technological advances.[50] Belgium, too, has a relatively high union density rate (about 50 percent). It might be even higher, however, if there were not as many laws protecting labor. The workplace in Belgium is one of the most highly controlled in the world, covering topics such as compensation, severance pay, and other human resource concerns. The following International Insights feature shows one company's experience in Belgium. Despite the fact that the most important unions are organized around religious or political bases, there is a "culture of compromise" in their interactions.[51]

International Insights

Labor Relations on the Brink in Belgium: A Cautionary Tale for Firms Doing Business in Europe

Brink's, Inc., currently based in Richmond, Virginia, was founded in 1859 in Chicago, Illinois, and is famous for its armored-car delivery business. Now one of the largest providers of logistics solutions and secure transport services, it employs 60,000 people in over 150 countries. About three-quarters of Brink's revenue comes from business outside of North America. In fact, about 17 percent of its 2010 revenue came from France and 40 percent total from

Europe. And, while the EU is one coordinated zone with free movement of goods and services, for businesses on the ground (especially foreign firms like Brink's) features such as taxes, labor costs, and employment laws vary.

The variance can create challenges and hurdles, as it did for Brink's in 2010 in its Belgium business. Since the mid-1970s, the firm had two subsidiaries there: a money-making diamond delivery business (mostly in Antwerp) and Brink's Belgium, a cash delivery unit that provides services to banks. The latter had been losing money (up to $10 million a year), which the firm attributed to high labor costs. Belgium does have the highest labor costs in the EU. The percentage of employer-paid social security is 31 percent, nearly twice that of the United Kingdom (17 percent). About 50 percent of workers were unionized in Belgium (among the highest in Europe at the time). The law also provides for generous and lengthy paid sick leave, severance for a lost job, and full benefits.

Willem Candel, a senior director at Brink's, characterized the problem: "[Sixty-five percent] of our costs was labor. We were no longer competitive." In the first half of 2010, the firm had losses of $7 million on $32 million in sales, making it clear to management that something had to be done. Its analysis showed that one thing was driving many of the problems: the nearly 500 staff members who drove the armored cars and serviced the ATMs were classified as white collar (professional) instead of blue collar (hourly/manual labor). This distinction was the result of a late 1800s law that (at the time) was very favorable to employers and one that made Belgium a low-labor-cost country. Blue-collar workers were to be paid by the hour, less for overtime, and could be laid off more freely than white-collar employees. Brink's claimed that its large number of white-collar employees cost the company $4.5 million more per year than if the drivers and some other workers were correctly classified as blue collar. Brink's also argued that this mistake prevented the company from winning contracts because its bids were too high relative to competition.

While unions continued their efforts to retain the existing job classifications, Brink's developed a strategy. In late 2010, it announced a plan to lay off about 60 workers and to reclassify staff from white collar to blue collar. The unions were stunned and announced a strike. Fearing a prolonged conflict and more losses, Brink's declared bankruptcy in order to escape additional financial problems. Employees of the cash-handling business were laid off, and management moved to the Netherlands. The lucrative diamond delivery business was retained ahead of bankruptcy proceedings.

The union quickly filed suit, contending that changing employees' job status and not providing severance pay was illegal. The union's representative stated that "Brink's acted as if we wouldn't be vigilant, but we have lawyers too." Expert observers say that the company probably erred in not providing severance, but Brink's defended itself, arguing that "we never refused a dialog with the unions . . . they refused to work." Those same experts point out that U.S. firms cannot act the same way about a bankruptcy in Europe, with one suggesting that "U.S. law treats employees as unsecured creditors . . . it's very different in Europe."

A Brussels court rejected the firm's bankruptcy filing. It held that Brink's had no grounds to turn its more profitable diamond transport business into a new firm ahead of the bankruptcy plea. The court suspended Brink's license to operate this business. Court-appointed administrators filed a nearly $29 million claim against Brink's. A settlement was reached in mid-2011, whereby Brink's would pay $10 million to employees in order to drop the suit.[52]

Spain is perhaps on the other end of the regulated spectrum. Recently, there has been more unified union activity, especially in response to the worldwide financial turmoil of the late 2000s. Spain has one of the highest unemployment rates in Europe and concern about this is very high. Worse yet, the government does not expect this problem to abate any time soon (some estimate the rate at 26 percent). The effects have been uneven, with immigrants and the young being the first to be let go by struggling firms. The population of foreign immigrants (about 5 million) has increased by a factor of about ten over the last decade and public spending is at its limit. Offers of lump sum payments to unemployed immigrants to go home didn't work and may have been difficult to finance anyway.[53]

In general, the long history of union organizing has left many full-time, permanent European workers covered by an extensive set of regulations and protections, especially relative to those of the U.S. Many multinationals have long complained about this state of affairs, and there are signs that European countries will slowly roll back many of these expensive protections. In the meantime, however, firms are coping with the current state of affairs by relying on contract, temporary, and part-time workers—in short, workers with fewer legal protections.[54] For instance, in the Netherlands, part-time and short-term workers occupy about one-third of all jobs, compared to less than 15 percent in the U.S.[55]

Unions in Asia

Unions also exert influence in Asia, although this too varies from country to country.

Japanese Unions

As of 2010, there were about 55,000 unions in Japan, a drop of about 18 percent since 1990. Since the 1950s, the vast majority of these have been enterprise unions.[56] This refers to the fact that many different workers in a company, regardless of their profession or vocation, are represented by one omnibus union. While there are some large national unions in the public and private sectors (such as municipal workers, teachers, iron and steel workers, and railway workers) upwards of 90 percent of all unions have followed the tradition of "one company, one union." In other words, these in-house unions represent only the employees of their respective companies and membership is limited to regular and permanent employees of that firm. A large number of workers in any given company are part time or temporary and are not covered by union agreement or by human resource practices that are often associated with Japanese firms (such as lifetime employment). Toyota, for example, has tripled the number of short-term contract workers since 2001.

As might be expected from past discussions of Japanese culture in this book, the relationship between union and management is largely harmonious. Yet, this has not always been the case. After World War II, many Japanese unions were both militant and violent. The labor movement was led by radical and militant union organizers whose agendas frequently included socialist revolution. One of the worst strikes, called the 100-day strike, occurred in 1953 at Nissan where management locked employees out of plants for over three months. Finally, after other strikes similar to that at Nissan, many large Japanese employers basically struck a deal with their unions—they gave lifetime employment and good benefits in exchange for no labor strife.

Both sides have largely kept to the bargain. Indeed, there is relatively little labor strife in Japan. This is partially the case because junior-level managers often occupy union leadership roles. The training received in such union positions is viewed favorably by management and is factored into promotions. Data show that over 15 percent of directors of large enterprises were former union officials.[57] Observers criticize this relationship as being too cozy; they say that Japanese unions function as a management control mechanism rather than a way to represent workers.

Consistent with this view, when Japanese unions go out on strike, they do so for short periods of time—often a half-day or less. For example, a union leader at the Japanese subsidiary of Royal Dutch/Shell claimed that the union was getting "tough" with management over wages: "We went on strike the day before yesterday. We stayed out for 45 minutes. Yesterday we struck again for 15 minutes." The next day, the workers struck briefly again (for higher wages) at lunchtime so that the demonstrators would not have to miss any work. This attitude characterizes most Japanese unions. The average Japanese employee strikes about 4 minutes a year, compared to 9 minutes for the U.S., and 23 minutes for Spain.[58] Strikers often work full shifts after walking a picket line. In addition, productivity often stays steady during a strike. Through all their economic troubles of the last two decades, there is still a high level of consultation among management and employees about company decisions, experts believe, although union density has decreased about 14 percent the last decade.

Unions in China

As in many other aspects of business, China is unlike any other country. One of the traditional hallmarks of China's labor relations approach was full employment. This employment orientation has been referred to as the iron rice bowl, a cradle-to-grave employment system with an egalitarian wage system. In the past, employees could expect that their needs and jobs were taken care of—they were secure and permanent. An employee could not be fired, and pay and housing were guaranteed.

As is widely known, over the last three decades China has been dramatically impacted by its economic reforms, rising to the world's second largest economy (having done so faster than any country in history). While a few vestiges of the old iron rice bowl system persist, for some time now workers can be laid off (made "redundant") and other Western-type managerial prerogatives have become available.

Laws do provide for treatment of laid-off workers and also provide a system for arbitrating any disputes that occur in this process. Employers, for example, must give 30 days' notice or at least one month's wages to affected workers. The number of employees involved in labor disputes handled by arbitration committees is large, nearly 700,000 in 2006 alone, up from 250,000 in 2000.[59]

There are unions in China, including ten national industrial unions in industries such as communications, manufacturing, banking, and construction. There are no independent unions, but instead all are sections under a large national union, the only one allowed by law. The All-China Federation of Trade Unions (ACFTU) is the world's largest national trade union with over 140 million members, at least on paper. The ACFTU recently has been more impactful, playing a role in new legislation to protect women's rights, and other worker issues. But, having said this, the industrial unions have a poor reputation, often playing a supporting role at best and conforming to the ACFTU/party line. Although unions are ostensibly the link between the party and the masses, they are often ridiculed as unnecessary (*pao loong tao*—"a body to fill a temporary vacancy"). The right to strike is still officially unlawful and independent unions are discouraged and suppressed. Even internal union dissent is discouraged, in spite of some leeway offered to the ACFTU. The role of this union—at least in the eyes of the government—is to prevent worker unrest.[60]

From the government perspective, therefore, unions have not done their job because there has been considerable worker unrest over the past decade in China. Some of these have been very high profile, involving thousands of workers, and clashes with authorities. To protest the planned privatization of a state-run steel company in Tonghua, and fearing job losses and pay reductions, nearly 30,000 workers took part in a protest that turned violent. Workers blocked roads and destroyed police cars; more than 100 people were injured and there was one death (a company executive, at the hands of workers).[61] Another example occurred at the HonHai (Foxconn) factory, a major supplier for Apple, where 5,000 police were sent to quell employee unrest and violence over conditions at the plant. These included underage workers, long shifts, improper handling of chemicals, and air quality—among others. Apple had experienced pressure from workers and activists inside and out of China—a market of growing significance to Apple. Indeed, Apple's own annual supplier audit showed that 62 percent were compliant with working-hour limits, 35 percent did not meet standards to prevent injuries, and over 30 percent did not comply with hazardous substance practices. In another recent case, Chinese employees locked the U.S. founder and CEO in his office for days, refusing to let him go until they received severance benefits. In the first third of 2013, 201 cases of labor disputes were officially recorded—eclipsing the total of all 2012. This situation is likely to continue.[62]

Unions in Other Asian Countries

Countries such as India, Indonesia, the Philippines, Thailand, and Vietnam are examples of economies—and labor relations—on the move. Likewise, the so-called "Asian Tigers" (Singapore, South Korea, and Taiwan) have become major influences in the world economy. Although a good deal of government influence is exerted on workplaces in these countries, there are big differences in the state of their labor relations. Labor issues in Singapore and, to a lesser extent, Taiwan have been relatively calm, with emphasis on social partnership and political stability.[63] In contrast, labor relations in South Korea have been more confrontational. A particularly well-publicized strike against Hyundai over a decade ago illustrates this high profile of union activity (yet, only a 10-percent union density rate). The length of the strike and the poor manner in which it was handled by the company was reminiscent of some earlier bad examples in the U.S. Korean workers also violently resisted GM's initial efforts to make a bid for Daewoo, the troubled

Korean car firm. As one Daewoo worker put it, "[s]elling the company to GM would mean handing over a piece of Korea to the U.S." This confrontational style of labor relations has continued through the 2000s, with a fair number of strikes and loss of working days.[64]

Central/South American Unions

Since the passage of the North American Free Trade Agreement (NAFTA), much attention has been focused on Mexico. A variety of federal laws govern labor relations in Mexico, many of which favor labor—including wage and benefits guarantees. Union density rate in Mexico has not declined as have others in North or South America, and remains at about 15 percent, which is roughly where it has been for over a decade.

It takes only 20 employees to form a union in Mexico. As a result, Mexican firms are used to negotiating with many different unions within one unit or factory. If the official union declares a strike, all personnel—including management—must vacate the premises. Flags are stationed at each locked entrance signifying that the plant is under strike. Union members receive pay during the time they are out on a (legal) strike. Unions have won many worker rights, mostly through federal legislation rather than direct union activity. In the *maquiladoras* near the U.S. border, companies are often able to choose submissive, government-affiliated unions for their factories. Other major South American economies (Brazil, Argentina) have varying levels of government control and input into labor relations activity.[65]

African Unionism

Overall, union activity in Africa is relatively underdeveloped. Nevertheless, there are differences across countries, ranging from the relatively compliant approach in Kenya to the more activist unions in South Africa.

In the 1970s, when South African apartheid was at its height, white groups were permitted to form unions and engage in collective bargaining. Blacks, the vast majority of citizens, however, were denied those rights. In 1980, black groups gained limited union rights, and union membership tripled in five years. In the shadow of apartheid, the power of the black unions grew quickly, as did strike activity, some of it violent. Yet, the effects of unions was dramatic: wage increases for black workers approached the percentage gains realized by American workers, which in turn were greater than for Europeans.[66] These occurred mainly among poor, low-skill workers, whose very low wages increased dramatically. So, even while future South African President Nelson Mandela was still in prison, black union workers were winning concessions.

Once he became president, Mandela's challenge was to balance the increasingly strident demands made by both unions and businesses—especially foreign ones. Yet, his priorities were clear. For example, when the national union (COSATU) staged a nationwide strike against a proposed law allowing companies to lock out strikers, Mandela appeared with workers wearing COSATU colors. The provision was quickly deleted. Many businesses and foreign investors felt that this underscored their concern that South

African unions had too much influence. They argued that if South Africa was to be more competitive globally, government needed to adopt more flexible labor rules and perhaps dump some state-run enterprises. The unions countered that such moves would create more unemployment, leaving many of apartheid's inequities unaddressed.

Mandela's successors, Presidents Mbeki and Motlanthe, continued to try to balance competing demands, but challenges remain for current president Jacob Zuma. Months after Zuma was elected in 2009, he faced a strike by the municipal workers union. Police fired rubber bullets at protesters in the townships outside Johannesburg and the strike lingered. Zuma was able to sidestep another problem when the National Union of Mineworkers (NUM) agreed to wage concessions. These problems returned, however, in 2012 after 4,000 miners at the Lonmin platinum mine walked off the job, in violation of labor laws. When miners charged at police with makeshift weapons, police opened fire; 34 miners were shot and another dozen also died during the nearly 50-day strike. A deal was finally reached to increase worker pay, but not before strikes spread elsewhere. Sadly, only a month later, the strike was reinstated to protest the arrest of a striking miner charged in the murder of an NUM officer. This and related effects have been bad for Zuma and the country. Even though he is seen as a workers' president, is from the provinces, and himself spent ten years in notorious Robben Island prison with Mandela (who was prisoner for 27 years), Zuma's hardly been given a pass and is unlikely to get one. His impact has been dramatically lessened by both administration and personal scandals.[67]

International Employee Unions

As noted, unions around the world have had varying degrees of strength and success in recent years. Perhaps the largest challenge to domestic unions, however, is the multinational itself. As explained, one of the main cards multinationals can play is the threat to move some or all of their operations away from the union to another country.[68]

There have been a variety of responses by unions to this challenge. The most noteworthy has been the development of international organizations of workers. As far back as 1919, part of the peace agreement ending World War I was to create the International Labor Organization (ILO). The ILO is composed of groups of employees, employers, and governments, with each having a say in labor policies that are developed.[69] There are now over 170 member countries in this organization. The ILO has mainly been responsible for developing standards for labor conditions and treatment. These guidelines, however, have the same legal status as an international treaty. Accordingly, they must be ratified and agreed to on a nation-by-nation basis. Given the controversial issues that the ILO deals with (such as equal pay, child labor, and discrimination against groups) many countries fail to embrace all the guidelines. Even if a country ratifies a guideline, making sure that it complies with the guideline's stipulations is even tougher. In many ways, the ILO operates like its larger parent organization, the United Nations. Other international organizations have similar goals (such as the Organisation for Economic Cooperation and Development, OECD).

Some unions also maintain international membership, including the International Confederation of Free Trade Unions (ICFTU). Their goal is to help national unions in their dealings with multinationals. Most members come from North America and Europe and it can be a powerful voice for labor. Closely associated with these groups are International Trade Secretariats (ITSs), which often cover major industry types (such as the International Metal Workers Federation). Regardless of the form these organizations take, their general goal is to emulate the organization of a multinational and, in so doing, to develop a transnational bargaining system.

There are some examples of cross-border coordination among unions to meet this goal. For example, the German union IG Metall provided significant financial and other support to striking workers at British Aerospace, and the United Electrical Workers union in the U.S. recently supported a Mexican union's efforts to organize a General Electric plant in Mexico.[70] Likewise, Chiquita signed (and abided by) a global agreement among a consortium of international food unions. That said, most observers believe that international unions have been largely ineffective.[71] There are a number of complex reasons, including the laws of specific countries and multinational opposition. One of the most insidious reasons, however, has been the ability of multinationals to effectively play one country and its unions against another.

Many powerful unions within countries are, in effect, political groups and, as a result, are more concerned with national issues, not necessarily international labor organizations. It is common for a union in one country to gain jobs by dealing with a multinational that is having labor trouble in another country. This competitive attitude is summed up by a Canadian union member: "An American union is not going to fight to protect Canadian jobs at the expense of American jobs."[72] For example, some years ago Hoover Appliances (then owned by Maytag Corporation, now by a Chinese firm, Techtronic) announced plans to close a 600-employee factory in Dijon, France, and to move its operations to Glasgow, Scotland. Hoover's Scottish workers traded changes in work conditions for job security and the 400 new jobs that would result. The French were outraged and took to the streets to protest. They also crossed the channel to take part in a TV debate, during which they accused their Scottish colleagues of taking their jobs. British union leaders were rather quiet about the incident, except to say that "we have nothing to be ashamed of."[73]

Many workers likely see their foreign counterparts as competitors, rather than as allies, and this remains a major obstacle to success for international unions.[74] Nevertheless, several American unions have recently begun to join forces with their European and international counterparts. The AFL-CIO, for example, has made connections with European unions, something it has rarely done, and has also supported immigration amnesty in the U.S. Plus, the Union Network International (UNI) has had some success in obtaining a wide agreement that includes all subsidiaries of several multinationals. The UNI represents nearly 1,000 unions and 15 million members globally and has agreements with multinationals such as Carrefour, Telefonica, and Metro AG.[75]

Other Forms of Employee Input

Unions are not the only means by which employees can obtain desired outcomes. There are a variety of other ways they can have an impact. These methods are known by different terms, including industrial democracy, self-management, and worker participation.

The last term is the most relevant for our purposes because it refers to methods by which workers participate in the management of the firm. Participation can include many different forms of input, ranging from having little to no say, all the way to having the right to veto management action. Although there are many forms, we will discuss three different types of participation: (1) joint consultation committees (JCCs), (2) works councils, and (3) board membership.[76]

Joint Consultation Committees

JCCs are common in many Western countries. These are groups of workers who sit on a committee that deals with topics of mutual interest to employees and management. Their charge can range from concerns about product quality (such as quality circles) to working conditions, plant safety, and even the general quality of work life (as in Sweden). Typically, JCC members make suggestions that may be adopted by management. In turn, management is often expected to keep workers informed about developments via the committee. The effectiveness of these committees depends on the goodwill of a firm and is most likely to be successful in paternalistic companies with relatively good employee relations.[77]

Works Councils

This form of employee participation is more common in Western European countries (e.g., Belgium, France, Germany, the Netherlands). These groups are similar to JCCs in many ways, but works councils often have significant power to block management decisions and actions and to forward solutions to employee concerns. The councils typically originated as a result of national laws that mandated their creation. This step was seen as necessary because of a perceived societal obligation to seek employee input, rather than as a way to necessarily improve competitiveness or the bottom line.[78]

In the Netherlands, for example, Dutch law requires that any firm with 100 or more employees must create a works council (some firms with 35 or more employees must also construct councils, and in even smaller firms the employer is required to hold consultations at least twice a year with employees). The council consists of members who are elected by employees and must be consulted in decisions of importance to the organization. These issues are often related to personnel policy (such as safety and training programs, pay and benefits issues, work relocation, plant closures, etc.). If a firm has 100 or more employees, this consultation could include major financial decisions (such as new capital investments or business acquisitions). Theoretically, the works council should represent the interest of all employees. Members of the council, however, may be managers or production employees. In practice, councils can be co-opted by management via this and other means.[79]

In powerful works councils, such as some in Germany, an employee may effectively hold two jobs—their regular job and a job as council representative. As a result, it is not uncommon to have a second office and perhaps even two staffs, right on company grounds. The council representative may be similar to a shop steward in the U.S. union environment. The difference is that the works council member has more real input in company decisions.[80] Research on the impact of works councils on productivity is mixed, with some studies showing a positive impact and others showing a weak relation.[81]

Board Membership

Board membership is a third, less common mechanism by which workers have input into the business. In this case, input is often extensive. In seven European countries (Austria, Denmark, France, Germany, Luxembourg, Norway, and Sweden) law dictates that workers must have some kind of representation on the board of directors of firms. In most cases, these boards are supervisory boards—the group responsible for selecting a management board that will run day-to-day operations. Codetermination in Germany is an example of a board membership method. Typically, workers have only a minority membership on the board. Employee representatives, however, control half the seats of the advisory boards of firms greater than 2,000 employees. Even though this might seem like a radical idea, research shows that board memberships for workers generally have relatively little effect on the business one way or another. Typically, boards meet very infrequently (often just a few hours a year), and equally often when talk does turn to substantive issues, worker representatives may be at a disadvantage. Some feel they lack the background to fully evaluate the complex information (e.g., financials) discussed in these meetings. Nevertheless, workers can provide valuable input that has changed health, safety, and investment decisions by the firm. At the minimum, boards appear to provide a symbolic function for workers, with some unions (e.g., in Britain, Sweden) viewing them as a valuable source of information rather than as a lever for wielding power.

Finally, several inventive approaches that involve input via a consortium of unions, government, and the private sector seemed to emerge during the height of the Great Recession. The following Global Innovations feature spotlights a Dutch example of such partnerships who worked together to save jobs.

Global Innovations

A New Twist on "Dutch Treat": Government and Private Support Combines to Save Jobs in the Netherlands

Governments around the world are looking for ways to improve the job outlook and reduce joblessness. While many solutions involve a time-honored formula heavily weighted on direct government bailouts, the Netherlands is trying a new twist on the usual formula.

When unemployment rates jumped between 2008 and 2009, in some cases dramatically, governments reacted. Canada, Japan, the U.K., Ireland, Spain, and the U.S. all saw increases in unemployment. In the U.S., for example, the unemployment rate rose from 6.2 percent to 10.2 percent. Many businesses cut back personnel and sought loans and bailouts from the federal government. Those in Germany and the Netherlands, for instance, relied heavily on "short-work programs" to keep people employed. These are a set of actions that combine reduced work hours and/or hiring of temporary workers with government support. These countries were able to keep unemployment down, with the Dutch leading the pack. Unlike the drastic increase in the U.S., France, and Ireland, unemployment in the Netherlands rose from 2.7 percent to only 3.6 percent during the same time.

Short-work programs represent a big change in the general European mind-set. For example, take Theo Witkamp, a 60-year-old machine operator at DAF Trucks in Eindhoven. Although his work hours were cut, he still earned about 85 percent of what his regular wages would have been from his job, through a combination of company and state contributions. Notably, this is also more than he would earn without the job, a reality that might have happened had the firm not undertaken this joint approach to tackling joblessness. As Witkamp said, "it beats being unemployed."

The Netherlands spent nearly $3 billion on this job-saving program in 2010, a pittance relative to the billions provided to financial and other firms in the U.S. The money does seem to be well spent, although some experts also give credit to other measures taken during the height of the worldwide crisis. It is true that the Netherlands has of late trimmed back unemployment and other government-provided benefits in an effort to cut costs and keep people working. With such cuts inevitable in a volatile global economy, there is all the more reason to work to save jobs.

After the global crisis hit, the government, unions, and firms worked to reach an agreement on wage subsidies. Some said this was a harkening back to the Middle Ages for the Dutch, when rival cities and classes grouped to save the dikes when massive floods came. Interestingly, short-work laws were passed in the 1940s, originally during the Nazi occupation, but have been rarely used until now. Regardless, they were not applied haphazardly. Qualifications for subsidies were set up (firms had to show 30 percent drop in revenues over three months), and the subsidies were limited to a six-month period. Firms were responsible for paying a substantial percentage of employees' salaries. Plus, the government set up a network of advisors to work with firms. Nearly 1,500 firms participated in the plan, some even paying a higher portion of their employees' salaries than required by the law.

By many accounts, the program was successful, including the low unemployment figures noted previously. There were, of course, critics—including some economists who slammed the efforts, saying that it was "a form of creeping communism" and that it was "sharing poverty, pure and simple." Perhaps so, said Dutch finance minister Wouter Bos, adding that it makes it tough for markets to assess firm performance. But, even Bos changed his opinion, saying that "you put in some extra money at an early stage, but then you save some money later because people do not have to go for unemployment." Either way, the cost was relatively small compared to some other major bailouts of world economies, including in the U.S. And, perhaps Bos's traditional Dutch optimism will play out with more firms getting back on their feet in the short and long run. It certainly did for DAF trucks, which saved Theo Witkamp's job. DAF was one of the firms that decided to provide more pay than was required by the state. Better yet, because the firm's orders picked up during the second part of the year, it did not seek further government support.[82]

Putting Agreements into Practice

As discussed in the last section, there are many ways that agreements between management and employees can evolve. Unfortunately, there are also a variety of ways that disagreements can come about. The result may be conflict and strife between management and labor.

Relations Between Management and Labor

It is common for multinational firms to consider the general state of relations between management and employees before they choose to invest in a foreign subsidiary. These relations show great variability. Figure 13.4 presents data obtained from a sample of over 12,000 top business executives in 134 countries who were asked to rate how cooperative labor–management relations were across countries. This figure presents a sample of the rankings received by a set of 28 countries, some of which are often referred to in this book. As you will see, Denmark and Japan rank very high—there is a good deal of cooperation between management and labor, a ranking that they have both received for decades now. While there may be good reasons not to locate a plant in

Country	Ranking	Country	Ranking
Denmark	1	India	44
Switzerland	3	Chile	51
Sweden	5	Belgium	55
Japan	6	China	66
Hong Kong	7	Nigeria	67
The Netherlands	9	Mexico	68
Norway	10	Spain	74
Taiwan	12	Russia	82
Malaysia	13	Brazil	84
U.S.	16	Pakistan	88
Indonesia	19	Turkey	116
Germany	27	South Africa	119
Canada	34	France	132
U.K.	35	Venezuela	134

Figure 13.4 Rankings of the Degree of Cooperative Relations between Labor and Employers in 28 Selected Countries.

Note: Rankings are determined by a survey of over 10,000 business executives based on their knowledge of and experience with the country (only 134 countries ranked).

Source: Adapted from: World Economic Forum. (2009). *The Global Competitiveness Report, 2008–2009*. Geneva: The World Economic Forum.

these countries, poor employee relations is not one of them. On the contrary, Venezuela and France rank at the very bottom on this dimension. As you can see, the U.S. comes in at sixteenth place out of the 134 countries ranked in this study—a relatively high showing, and a marked improvement over the previous decade.

Deterioration of Relations

Sometimes labor–management relations can deteriorate to the point at which work slowdowns, sabotage, or even violence occur. These outcomes, however, are difficult to track (slowdowns) and some are not all that common (violence). Strikes, on the other hand, are more common and are easier to observe because they have some easily documented features, such as their frequency, size, and length. But while these variables seem relatively objective, directly comparing strikes across countries isn't that easy.[83] There are many nation-specific definitions of what constitutes a strike or other type of work stoppage. Danish statistics, for example, exclude any disputes that result in fewer than 100 days being lost. Despite this, Denmark regularly ranks among the highest in the world on work days lost because of strikes. Nevertheless, some groups, including the ILO and the OECD, have worked to clarify definitions and make strike data more comparable. For the most part, strike data are usually based on the number of strikes and the number of work days lost because of the strike.

Based on these data, several conclusions can be reached about strikes. First, strike activity has generally been diminishing since the 1970s.[84] The number of days lost to strikes, for example, has declined in recent years, particularly in the European Union, and accelerated by the recession of the late 2000s.[85] Consider the U.K. where about 750,000 working days were lost to strikes in 2008. While this number is large and impacted the British economy, it pales in comparison to the 30 million days lost in 1979. This drop is due to a number of causes, including a decline during economic downturns and increase in times of prosperity.[86] Data also show that there has been a shift in the nature of strikes, which these days are more likely to involve public services (e.g., public transportation systems), and work process issues (e.g., job security, worker participation) rather than workplace *outcomes* per se (e.g., higher pay). Consider Britain again where in 2008, 94 percent of all strikes were by public-sector employees, many concerned with job security.

In Figure 13.5 we present a ranking of a variety of countries on two measures: the number of strikes and lockouts and the number of work days lost from these actions. Note that some countries that are thriving economically have a relatively high number of strikes. Year in and year out, Denmark, Spain, France, and Italy rank high among all countries in strikes. The number of lost work days can be in the millions as a result of these work stoppages. These statistics do not always count shorter, less-than-one-day strikes that seem to be occurring more often. These "just-in-time" strikes inflict a lot of disruption for the lost pay that they cost workers and are not uniformly counted as official strike days. This and other features are affected by cultural and legal structures in place across countries and we turn to this next.

Country	Strikes and Lockouts	Working Days Lost (per 1,000 employees)	Days Not Worked (in millions)
Denmark*	862	21	0.092
Spain	811	62	1.5
France	699	#	1.4
Italy	621	56	0.930
Canada	187	280	0.875
Australia	177	28	0.197
Portugal	174	7	0.045
U.K.	144	6	0.759
Finland	92	322	0.016
Netherlands	20	6	0.026
Japan*	18	#	0.002
U.S.	16	10	1.26
Belgium*	10	#	0.670
Sweden	5	2	0.107
Switzerland	2	1	0.007

Figure 13.5 Strike Activity and Effects in a Variety of Countries.

Note: Number of strikes/lockouts excludes work stoppage involving < 500 workers and lasting < 1 full day or shift. Days lost (in millions) refers to the number of 8-hour days lost due to strikes/lockouts. Most data are for 2008; some (*) are from 2006/7. Working days lost/1,000 workers = 2006; # = no data available.

Source: Adapted from International Labor Organization. (2008). *Statistical Tables*, available at: http://laborsta.ilo.org/STP.

Germany

Despite a long and powerful tradition of union influence, strike activity in Germany is not as common as in other Western European nations (approximately 130,000 work days were lost in 2008). For example, days lost per 1,000 employees was about ten times as much in France as Germany. This is due partly to the many input and control mechanisms of German workers (such as the works councils, codetermination). In addition, however, German labor relations are also covered by many legal regulations, making more extreme steps such as strikes and lockouts less necessary. For example, laws prohibit either strikes or lockouts when a contract is in effect. Consequently, strikes usually occur when contracts have expired and negotiations are ongoing. In the 1980s, German unions struck with an existing contract in place. During this period of high inflation, workers wanted their wages to keep up with this inflation, but these situations are rare in Germany.

Japan

As touched upon previously, union–management relations in Japan are quite good. Figure 13.5 shows that there were only 18 strikes that produced very few lost work days (only about 2,000). Most disagreements are settled amicably. It is rare for relations to get caustic enough to result in a strike. Even when they do, the strike is brief and not bitter—often it is undertaken to either bring issues to the attention of management or to sometimes embarrass them. Lockouts by management are very rare. In fact, although emotional behavior of union members is tolerated, management is expected to always be courteous and civil in their language and behavior.[87]

The U.K.

Strike activity in the U.K. is quite high, as shown in Figure 13.5, with 144 official strikes resulting in nearly 760,000 lost work days. The reason for this high frequency might be the government's traditional "hands-off" approach to labor relations. This approach has resulted in fewer legal constraints on labor action relative to some other EU countries. For example, labor contracts do not prohibit strikes. As a result, they happen more often. Strikes usually occur during a deadlock in negotiations, although no one type of strike (in terms of frequency or style) seems to predominate in Britain.[88] Despite this, strike frequency is tracking down over the last decade in Britain.

The U.S.

The U.S. had 16 official strikes in 2008—a figure that has hovered at about 20 for the last half-decade. But, these resulted in over a million lost work days for the U.S.'s large labor force. American labor contracts typically prohibit strikes during the period of the agreement. So, once a contract is in place, a strike (called a wildcat strike) is rare and usually not authorized by the union. As in Germany, once a contract expires and a new one is not yet approved, a strike becomes a viable option—an option that is sometimes exercised. Employees may choose to continue to work during the negotiation period, while threatening a strike. Lockouts by management do occur on occasion, but they are also relatively rare.

Effect of Unions on Strikes

An important question from management's perspective is the overall effect of having a unionized workforce. Many managers find dealings with unions, regardless of where they are, to be challenging. Nevertheless, there are some benefits from a unionized workforce, including a structured bargaining system and clear contractual obligations that must be fulfilled.

Perhaps a more subtle benefit of union membership, however, is that it may quell more extreme and militant worker action. For instance, the data presented in Figure 13.6 show the relation between overall level of worker militancy and union density in 12 EU countries. Militancy is defined as a combination of variables that are indicative of labor strife and unrest. In general, the figure shows a negative relationship between militancy and union density. In other words, higher union density is generally associated with a lower incidence of violence. For example, the five countries on the right-hand portion of Figure 13.6 (the U.K., France, Greece, Italy, and Spain) all have high levels of militancy and a (relatively) low percentage of workers who are unionized. The left-hand

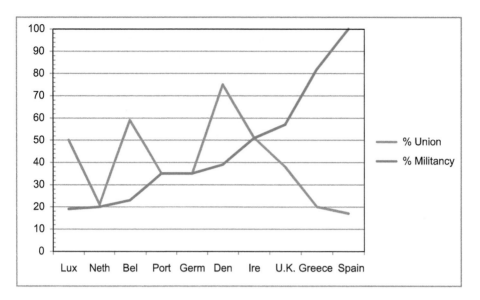

Figure 13.6 The Relationship Between Worker Militancy and Union Density.

Note: Spanish labor relations were considered the most militant and therefore assigned a 100 percent value. Other countries percentages are presented as a fraction of Spain.

Source: Adapted from Sparrow, P., and Hiltrop, J. M. (1994). *European Human Resource Management in Transition*. New York: Prentice-Hall.

side of this graph shows the opposite for several countries (e.g., the Benelux countries). So, despite all the management resistance to unions, there may be a silver lining. Organized employee input—perhaps in many forms—may actually make management–worker relations smoother than would otherwise be the case.

Chapter Summary

Chapter 13 looked at the value and influence of large and small work *groups* across cultures. We reviewed research showing that national and cultural differences have the potential to be both problematic and promising. For example, groups are more important in collectivist countries than they are in individualistic ones. But even in a collectivist culture, in-groups and out-groups vary dramatically in their value. Social loafing, a common effect in individualistic countries, also tends to occur among collectivists but *only* in groups that are unimportant to them.

We then shifted our discussion to larger labor relations issues between management and employees. Employee interests can be represented by unions, although they differ in number and strength across countries. That said, the percentage of union members is on the decline worldwide. One reason is that worker interests can be served by other mechanisms. Various forms of worker input exist, ranging from mild forms—such as having some say or input into work procedures—to having a vote over important firm decisions.

Despite these input methods, sometimes management and employees simply can't agree. Labor strikes are one response to a lack of agreement and management lockouts or plant closures/relocations are another. The nature and prevalence of worker strike activity and/or management prerogatives again can vary across countries due to laws, union power, and more.

Discussion Questions

1. What affects group productivity in various countries? What might increase productivity for U.S., Chinese, or German groups?

2. What might happen when groups of American, Chinese, and German employees get together to complete a project? In other words, what factors could explain why a multicultural group might experience difficulty solving problems in a creative fashion?

3. Why might multinationals have the upper hand in dealing with workers, even if those workers are unionized and spread across a variety of countries?

4. What are some of the differences between how North American, European, and Asian unions operate? Why might those differences exist?

Up to the Challenge?

SAP's Decision to Become Less German

The chapter opening introduced some of the challenges faced by the large German software company SAP. It wanted to change its staid corporate culture in order to more quickly respond to the web-based software of its rivals and to that increasingly preferred by customers. New management, such as Mr. Shai Agassi, made some dramatic changes, including adding thousands of developers from the U.S., India, and other countries. Agassi changed the official company language to English, took key development tasks away from the successful but calcified German teams at corporate headquarters in Walldorf, Germany, and carved up other key tasks. The Palo Alto office handled the look and feel of products, an India office took responsibility for analytical tools, and the Walldorf office worked on hard-core coding.

Veteran German developers at Walldorf complained about being shut out of phases of the development process. Others clashed with Agassi about how SAP units in countries were modifying "their" software. Agassi recalled German developers stating, "they don't tell us what to do—we tell them what to build." Of course, this attitude was exactly what Agassi and his German superiors wanted to change. In response, SAP made Agassi, the non-German, responsible for SAP's traditional software operations in Walldorf as well as all SAP product strategy—moves Agassi later described as "punishment."

Yet, Agassi took his newest assignment to heart and hired hundreds of programmers from Silicon Valley competitors, putting some in senior positions. From California, he created a plan to develop new products in 100 days, later dropping the target to 50 days. He pinpointed German managers whose opposition could threaten these changes and created a list of people to personally win over. To demonstrate that faster development was possible, he created a showcase project, tasking ten developers to produce 100 programs in 12 weeks, much quicker than SAP's traditional approach. The developers pushed back and asked the goal to be set at 30 programs instead. Agassi refused, and they ultimately completed the project.

But the German grousing continued—about the quality of the products SAP was now turning out and that Palo Alto now called the shots. The CEOs supported Agassi's changes and pointed out that employment at Walldorf was higher than ever, yet German veterans were having none of it. They complained about their loss of autonomy and the "American-ization" of SAP. As one German noted, "we used to be kings." They were quick to say that Agassi pushed key product teams into eight centers around the world, all directed from California.

More conflict surfaced at a set of meetings between Agassi and Walldorf developers, called by the CEOs. Agassi was hammered by German employees about goals, jobs at Wall-dorf, and the behavior of foreign managers. At a later set of town hall meetings, the CEOs heard more concerns about Americanization. Things got worse when the German media swooped in with an article entitled "SAP & Globalization: March of the Americans." A German manager noted that "it's clear that Agassi would like to get as many functions to the U.S. as possible." Agassi stated that SAP was simply looking for the best talent it could find.

Eventually, SAP sponsored cultural sensitivity training to mitigate these problems. The training revealed that Indian developers preferred lots of attention and supervision, while Germans would rather be left alone to work. Differences were also uncovered in how feed-back was delivered—ones that were off-putting or sent inconsistent messages. Americans tended to be more effusive with their praise—they would be more likely to compliment a piece of work by saying that it was "excellent," whereas Germans were more likely to describe the same work as "good." Foreign managers hired by SAP were also advised during training about how to interact more effectively with German developers—part of the answer was to work hard and impress them.

But these efforts were apparently too little and too late for Agassi, who had become increasingly frustrated. He decided to resign. During a subsequent interview with reporters, CEO Kagermann stated that he would continue his efforts to persuade and convince employees that SAP could not go back to its old Walldorf-centric ways. When asked about Agassi's departure, Kagermann noted, "it's not easy to manage." It remains to be seen how similar insulated companies, such as Toyota, will fare.[89]

International Development

Understanding Japanese Group Decision-Making

Purpose

To give students the opportunity to work through a meaningful task using the Japanese approach to consensual decision making, as well as to compare the experience that students have making group decisions with the Japanese approach of decision making. This will provide a better understanding of how group processes might differ across cultures.

Instructions

Your instructor will explain the processes of *Ringi* and *Nemawashi* and will set up the structure of the exercise. Group composition includes leaders (*Kacho*) and student managers (*Bucho*). Next, your instructor will divide the class into groups of four to six members. Your group will design a final exam format that is likely to be a valuable learning tool and appropriate basis of evaluation for your class (20 minutes).

Next, your instructor will divide the class into new groups of four to six members (the *Kacho* groups). In your new group, you will continue with the task, using the results of the first group as a starting point. After this meeting, groups can choose their own venue for future meetings. Your instructor will give advice during one or two open-ended class sessions. Outside class meetings will occur at the initiation of the group and student leaders (20 minutes).

Next, the whole class will generate a *Ringi* document that specifies the content of the exam. This document must be signed by all students in the class. Your instructor will discuss what problems, if any, the *Ringi* document might cause. Finally, the whole class will discuss the following questions:

1. How much did your experience resemble the descriptions of *Ringi* and *Nemawashi* provided by your instructor?
2. What difficulties did you encounter?
3. Were those difficulties likely to be present in the Japanese context? If so, how would they probably be managed?

Source: Van Buskirk, B. (1994). Japanese decision making. In D. Marcic and S. Puffer (eds) *Management International: Cases, Exercises, and Readings*. Minneapolis, MN: West Publishing Company. Reprinted by permission.

From Theory to International Practice

Developing Expertise in International Labor Trends

Purpose

To become familiar with features about labor conditions and trends worldwide, which can be valuable knowledge to have, or to know how to get, for an aspiring expatriate.

Instructions

For this exercise, you will examine characteristics about the labor force in four countries, including features about the *quality* (education, attitudes, skill sets) and *quantity* (workforce size overall and in various sectors; number of available employees; age; growth rate; quantity of trained workers, etc.). Your instructor may assign the countries or provide you with options to choose from, although at least one should be a developing country and at least one other from a developed country. Then use the resources below (or additional ones you may find in your research) to summarize the state of labor relations in each country. There are a number of ways to evaluate each country, and some ideas about this are presented below. Regardless of how you conduct your examination, you should be prepared to present your findings to class in a 10-minute report (or in a paper if directed by your professor).

For each country, present a set of labor quantity and quality variables that convey an accurate picture of the situation in your chosen countries. In your report, comment on the data and, importantly, their implications. For example, if you note that over 40 percent of the world's 15- to 20-year-olds live in two developing countries you investigated (China and India), be sure to discuss *why* this might be important.

We also recommend that you assess features about labor conditions in your target countries that may present either opportunities or challenges to firms doing business there. Among other questions to raise about the conditions are the following: (a) Has the labor force been shifting from rural to urban? (b) What is the status of immigrant labor in your target countries and related topics (e.g., brain drain; guest workers)? (c) What about the serious issues of child/forced labor? (d) What is the nature of laws pertaining to various labor groups (e.g., gender, race, etc.)? (e) What are the key employment laws that can impact business functions in your countries (e.g., severance pay, labor force reductions, labor organizing)?

Deliverable

Create a matrix chart that includes your countries as columns and variable comparisons as rows. Include a final row that is your rating on a scale from 1 (tough labor market) to 10 (favorable market) for the multinational you might work for. In your (brief) report, rely on this chart to talk through your rating as well as the key comparison variables that determined your overall rating.

Resources

A number of useful resources are available on the Internet and in your library to help with this assignment. Here are some especially relevant sources to kick-start your research on this project:

- **U.S. Department of Labor, Bureau Labor Statistics (www.bls.gov/).** While this department focuses mainly on the U.S., it also includes a set of international labor comparisons.

- **Michigan State University, Global Edge (http://globaledge.msu.edu/).** This international supersite has many resources and links to those sources that can be of help with this project and that you should bookmark.

- **International Labour Organization (www.ilo.org/).** The ILO has a complete set of data on labor features of many countries and will be very useful for this assignment.

- **Organisation for Economic Co-operation and Development (www.oecd.org).** This provides a wealth of information and comparable statistics on the 34 OECD member states and can be searched easily.

Notes

1. Dvorak, P., and Abboud, L. (2007). Difficult upgrade: SAP's plan to globalize hits cultural barriers; software giant's shift irks German engineers, U.S. star quits effort. *The Wall Street Journal*, May 11, A1.
2. Triandis, H. C. (1988). Collectivism v. individualism: A reconceptualism of a basic concept in cross-cultural social psychology. In G. K. Verma and C. Bagley (eds) *Cross-Cultural Studies of Personality, Attitudes, and Cognition*, 60–95. New York: St Martin's Press.
3. Domino, G. (1992). Cooperation and competition in Chinese and American children. *Journal of Cross-Cultural Psychology*, 23, 456–467.
4. Bond, M. H., and Hwang, K. (1986). The social psychology of the Chinese people. In M. H. Bond (ed.) *The Psychology of the Chinese People*, 213–266. Hong Kong: Oxford University Press.
5. Earley, P. C., and Mosakowski, E. (2004). Cultural intelligence: Knowing what makes groups tick is as important as understanding individuals. *Harvard Business Review*, October, 139–146.
6. Liden, R. C., Wayne, S. J., Jaworski, R. A., and Bennett, N. (2004). Social loafing: A field investigation. *Journal of Management*, 30, 285–304.
7. Matsui, T., Kakuyama, T., and Ongltco, M. L. U. (1987). Effects of goals and feedback on performance in groups. *Journal of Applied Psychology*, 72, 407–415.
8. Earley, P. C. (1989). Social loafing and collectivism. *Administrative Science Quarterly*, 34, 565–581; Gabrenya, W. K., Latane, B., and Wang, Y. (1985). Social loafing on an optimizing task: Cross-cultural differences among Chinese and Americans. *Journal of Cross-Cultural Psychology*, 16, 223–242.
9. Earley, P. C. (1993). East meets West meets Mideast: Further explorations of collectivistic and individualistic work groups. *Academy of Management Journal*, 36, 319–348.
10. Triandis, Collectivism v. individualism: A reconceptualism of a basic concept in cross-cultural social psychology.
11. Espinoza, J. A., and Garza, R. T. (1985). Social group salience and inter-ethnic cooperation. *Journal of Experimental Social Psychology*, 23, 380–392.

12. Earley, East meets West meets Mideast: Further explorations of collectivistic and individualistic work groups.

13. See also Earley, P. C. (1994). Self or group? Cultural effects of training on self-efficacy and performance. *Administrative Science Quarterly*, 39, 89–117.

14. Earley, East meets West meets Mideast: Further explorations of collectivistic and individualistic work groups.

15. Silverman, R. E. (2012). Step into the office-less company—how one firm manages employees scattered across 26 countries and 94 cities. *The Wall Street Journal*, September 5, B6.

16. Boeing Corp. (2009). Statistical summary of commercial jet airplane accidents: Worldwide operations, 1959–2008. Boeing Corp., Seattle, WA, available at: www.boeing.com/news/techissues/pdf/statsum.pdf.

17. Merritt, A. C., and Helmreich, R. L. (1996). Human factors on the flight deck: The influence of national culture. *Journal of Cross-Cultural Psychology*, 27, 5–24.

18. Please see: www.airlinesafety.com/editorials/HumanErrorVsTerrorism.htm (retrieved October 24, 2013).

19. Cramton, C. D., and Hinds, P. L. (2005). Subgroup dynamics in internationally distributed teams: ethnocentrism or cross-national learning? *Research in Organization Behavior*, 26, 231–263; Von Glinow, M., Shapiro, D. L., and Brett, J. M. (2004). Can we talk, and should we? Managing emotional conflict in multicultural teams. *Academy of Management Review*, 29, 578–592.

20. Some of these anecdotal observations have been supported with research findings. See, for example, Salk, J. E., and Brannen, M. Y. (2000). National culture, networks, and individual influence in a multinational management team. *Academy of Management Journal*, 43, 191–202.

21. Browning, E. S. (1994). Computer chip project brings rivals together, but the cultures clash. *The Wall Street Journal*, May 3, A1, A8.

22. Dalton, M., Ernst, C., Deal, J., and Leslie, J. (2002). *Success for the New Global Manager: How to Work Across Distances, Countries, and Cultures.* San Francisco: Jossey-Bass; Earley, P. C., and Mosakowski, E. (2000). Creating hybrid team cultures: An empirical test of transnational team functioning. *Academy of Management Journal*, 43, 26–49; Thomas, D. C. (1999). Cultural diversity and work group effectiveness: An experimental study. *Journal of Cross-Cultural Psychology*, 30, 242–263.

23. Gelfand, M. J., Erez, M., and Aycan, Z. (2007). Cross-cultural organizational behavior. *Annual Review of Psychology*, 58, 479–514; Jehn, K. A., Chadwick, C., and Thatcher, S. M. B. (1997). To agree or not to agree: The effects of value congruence, individual demographic dissimilarity, and conflict on workgroup outcomes. *International Journal of Conflict Management*, 8, 287–305.

24. Earley, P. C., and Mosakowski, E., (2000). Creating hybrid team cultures: An empirical test of transnational team functioning. *Academy of Management Journal*, 43, 26–49; Elron, E. (1997). Top management teams within multinational corporations: Effects of cultural heterogeneity. *Leadership Quarterly*, 8, 393–412; Harrison, D. A., Price, K. H., Gavin, J. H., and Florey, A. (2002). Time, teams and task performance: Changing effects of surface- and deep-level diversity on group functioning. *Academy of Management Journal*, 45, 1029–1045,

25. Ayoko, B. O., Hartel, C. E., and Callan, V. J. (2002). Resolving the puzzle of productive and destructive conflict in culturally heterogeneous workgroups: A communication accommodation theory approach. *International Journal of Conflict Management*, 13, 165–195; Earley and Mosakowski, Creating hybrid team cultures: An empirical test of transnational team functioning.

26. Gibson, C. B., and Zellmer-Bruhn, M. E. (2001). Metaphors and meaning: An intercultural analysis of the concept of teamwork. *Administrative Science Quarterly*, 46, 274–303.

27. Sanchez-Burks, J., Nisbett, R. E., and Ybarra, O. (2000). Cultural styles, relational schemas and prejudice against outgroups. *Journal of Personality & Social Psychology*, 79, 174–189.

28. Adler, *International Dimensions of Organizational Behavior*.

29. Earley, P. C. (1999). Playing follow the leader: Status-determining traits in relations to collective efficacy across cultures. *Organizational Behavior and Human Decision Processes*, 80, 192–212.
30. Tan, H. H., and Aryee, S. (2002). Antecedents and outcomes of union loyalty: A constructive replication and extension. *Journal of Applied Psychology*, 87, 715–722.
31. Newman, B. (1993). Border dispute: Single-country unions of Europe try to cope with multinationals. *The Wall Street Journal*, November 30, A1–A22.
32. Fleming, C. (2004). Europe learns litigious ways. *The Wall Street Journal*, February 24, A16, A17.
33. McCann, D. (2005). *Working Time Laws: A Global Perspective. Findings from the ILO's Conditions of Work and Employment Database*. ILO, available at: www.ilo.org/public.
34. Bush, J., Scott, M., Rowley, I., Lakshman N., Matlack, C., Ewing, J., and Zhe, H. (2009). The hidden perils of layoffs. *BusinessWeek*, March 2, 52–53; Fact Sheet (2009). *The Worker Adjustment and Retaining Notification Act: Fact Sheet*, available at: www.doleta.gov/programs/factsht/warn.htm. Also see: www.dol.gov/compliance/laws/comp-warn.htm; Eder, S. (2008). WARN Act falls short as jobs vanish. *The Toledo Blade*, December 12, B1.
35. Steinmetz, G. (1996). Americans, too, run afoul of rigorous German rules. *The Wall Street Journal*, February 2, A6.
36. Freshfields, Bruckhaus, Deringer (2009). *Managing Mass Redundancies Across Europe*. Freshfields, Bruckhaus, Deringer, Brussels (2nd ed.), available at: www.breshfields.com/publications/pdfs/2009/feb09/25166.pdf; *HR Focus*. (1992). Employee dismissals can prove costly for companies in Europe, August 18. 44.
37. Coy, P. (2012). Cliff ahead. Speed up. *Bloomberg Businessweek*, August 13–26, 8–9; Bilefsky, D. (2003). The Dutch way of firing. *The Wall Street Journal*, July 8, A14; Walker, M., and Thurow, R. (2009). U.S., Europe are ocean apart on human toll of joblessness. *The Wall Street Journal*, May 7, A1, A14.
38. Moffett, M., Brat, I., and Kowsmann, P. (2012). Big Europe strikes have little effect. *The Wall Street Journal*, November 15, A11.
39. Briscoe, D. R., Schuler, R. S., and Claus, L. (2009). *International Human Resource Management* (3rd ed.). New York: Routledge.
40. Ferner, A., and Hyman, R. (1992). *Industrial Relations in the New Europe*. Oxford: Blackwell.
41. Gunnigle, P., Brewster, C., and Morley, M. (1994). European industrial relations: Change and continuity. In C. Brewster and A. Hegewisch (eds) *Policy and Practice in European Human Resource Management: The Price-Waterhouse Cranfield Survey*, Chapter 9, 139–153. London: Routledge.
42. Hollinshead, G., and Leaf, M. (1995). *Human Resource Management: An International and Comparative Perspective*. London: Pitman.
43. Brunstein, I. (ed.) *Human Resource Management in Western Europe*. Berlin: Walter de Gruyter; Matlack, C. (2003). France: Labor disarray is giving reform a chance. *BusinessWeek*, June 16, 48.
44. *The Economist*. (2009). A time of troubles and protest: As European economies sink, fears of social unrest arise, January 24, 55–56; *The Economist*. (2007). The street fights back: Strikes in France, November 24, 55; Carreyrou, J. (2005). At French utility, union wages war to guard its perks. *The Wall Street Journal*, May 10, A1, A10
45. *The Economist*. (2004). German industrial relations: Slowly losing their chains, February 21, 49; Wachter, H. (1997). German co-determination—Quo vadis? A study of the implementation of new management concepts in a German steel company. *Employee Relations*, 19, 27–37.
46. Biehl, J. K. (2003). Germans' love of leisure worries government. SFGate.com, July 3, available at: www.sfgate.com.
47. Sims, G. T., and Rhoads, C. (2003). New era for German labor movement? *The Wall Street Journal*, July 1, A9; Rohwedder, C. (1999). Once the big muscle of German industry, unions see it all sag. *The Wall Street Journal*, November 29, A1; Edmondson, G. (2004). Showdown in the Ruhr Valley. *BusinessWeek*, November 1, 54–55.

48. Hollinshead and Leaf, *Human Resource Management: An International and Comparative Perspective.*
49. Brewster, C., and Hegewisch, A. (1994). *Policy and Practice in European Human Resource Management: The Price-Waterhouse Cranfield Survey.* London: Routledge.
50. Reed, S. (1997). Will Stockholm give away the store? *BusinessWeek*, February 10, 54.
51. Hees, M. (1995). Belgium. In I. Brunstein, *Human Resource Management in Western Europe.*
52. Miller, J. W. (2010). Brink's retreat in Belgium backfires. *The Wall Street Journal,* December 21, B8; Krawitz, A. (2010). Belgium diamond shipments halted as Brink's loses its license: Diamonds worth $200 million being blocked at Zaventem airport, available at: www.diamonds.net/news/NewsItem.aspx?ArticleID=33529.
53. *The Economist.* (2009). Spain's new unemployed: The worrying social fallout from sharply rising unemployment, January 24, 56; *The Economist.* (2001). Spain cuts a Gordian labor knot. March 10, 51.
54. Bush, J. (2007). Russian labor raises its voice: A walkout at a Ford plant near St Petersburg may herald a new era of union activism. *BusinessWeek*, December 10, 34–35.
55. *The Economist.* (2009). A time of troubles and protest: As European economies sink, fears of social unrest arise, January 24, 55–56; *The Economist.* (2003). Part-time workers, November 23, 100.
56. Benson, J. (2008). Trade unions in Japan: Collective justice or managerial compliance? In J. Benson and Y. Zhu (eds) *Trade Unions in Asia: An Economic and Sociological Analysis*, Chapter 3, 24–42. London: Routledge.
57. Benson, Trade unions in Japan: Collective justice or managerial compliance?; Rowley, I., and Hall, K. (2007). Japan's lost generation: Japan Inc. is back, but millions of young workers have been left behind. *BusinessWeek*, May 28, 40–41.
58. Murphy, J. (2009). Joblessness spurs shift in Japan's views on poverty. *The Wall Street Journal*, May 2–3, A5; *BusinessWeek*. (2007). Time lost to strikes: Minutes of lost work per employed person from strikes and lockouts in 2006, December 3, 11.
59. Thornton, E. (2009). The hidden perils of layoffs: Ex-workers are hauling their former companies into court over alleged violations of severance laws. *BusinessWeek*, March 2, 52–53; Roberts, D. (2007). Rumbles over labor reform: Beijing's proposed worker protections are giving multinationals the jitters. *BusinessWeek*, March 12, 57; *The Economist.* (2007). China's new labour law. The party throws a sop to the workers, December 8, 49–50.
60. Warner, M. (2008). Trade unions in China: In search of a new role in the 'harmonious society'. In Benson and Zhu, *Trade Unions in Asia: An Economic and Sociological Analysis*, Chapter 9, 24–42.
61. Canaves, S., and Areddy, J. T. (2009). China killing bares anger over reform. *The Wall Street Journal*, July 31, A1, A14; Canaves, S. (2009). Chinese tell workers fight privatization effort: Right group documents overturned police cars and killing of executive in rally against takeover of government company. *The Wall Street Journal*, July 27, A10.
62. Burkitt, L. (2013). Disgruntled Chinese workers lock U.S. founder in office. *The Wall Street Journal*, June 25, B1, B8; Mozur, P., and Orlik, T. (2012). Chinese factory erupts. *The Wall Street Journal*, September 25, B1, B4; Vascellaro, J. E., and Fletcher, O. (2012). Apple navigates China maze: Company details labor conditions. *The Wall Street Journal*, January 14, B1, B2; Vascellaro, J. E. (2012). Audit faults Apple supplier. *The Wall Street Journal*, March 30, B1, B2; Mozur, P. (2012). New labor attitudes fed into China riot. *The Wall Street Journal*, September 27, B1, B4.
63. Leggett, C. (2008). Trade unions in Singapore: Corporatist paternalism. In Benson and Zhu, *Trade Unions in Asia: An Economic and Sociological Analysis*, Chapter 7, 102–120.
64. Rowley, C., and Yoo, K. S. (2008). Trade unions in South Korea: Transition toward neo-corporatism? In Benson and Zhu, *Trade Unions in Asia: An Economic and Sociological Analysis*, Chapter 4, 43–62; Solomon, J., and Choi, H. W. (2001). For Korea's Daewoo Motors, a hard sale. *The Wall Street Journal*, May 23, A21; *The Economist.* (1997). South Korea: Culture clash, January 11, 35–36.
65. Smith, G. (2000). Mexican workers deserve better than this. *BusinessWeek*, September 11, 127; Briscoe, *International Human Resource Management.*

66. Chege, M. (1988). The state and labor: Industrial relations in independent Kenya. In P. Coughlin and G. Ikiara (eds) *Industrialization in Kenya: In Search of a Strategy.* Nairobi: Heinemann Kenya; Moll, P. G. (1993). Black South African unions: Relative wage effects in international perspective. *Industrial and Labor Relations Review*, 46, 245–261.

67. Maylie, D. (2012). South African mine tensions resume. *The Wall Street Journal*, October 19, A14; Maylie, D. (2012). South African miners end their strike. *The Wall Street Journal*, September 19, A8; McGroarty, P. (2012). South African holds rates steady as strikes bite economy. *The Wall Street Journal*, September 21, A11.

68. Newman, B. (1993). Border dispute: Single-country unions of Europe try to cope with multinationals. *The Wall Street Journal*, November 30, 1, 22.

69. Simpson, W. R. (1994). The ILO and tripartism: Some reflections. *Monthly Labor Review*, September, 40–45.

70. Parry, J., and O'Meara, G. (1990). The struggle for European unions. *International Management*, December, 70–75.

71. *The Economist.* (2012). Going bananas, March 31, 74.

72. Martin, D. (1984). A Canadian split on unions. *The New York Times*, March 12, D12.

73. Forman, C. (1993). France is preparing to battle Britain over flight of jobs across the channel. *The Wall Street Journal*, February 3, A11.

74. *The Economist.* (2009). Unions: In from the cold? March 14, 65–66; Burkins, G. (2000). Labor reaches out to global economy. *The Wall Street Journal*, April 11, A2; Borrus, A. (2000). Workers of the world: welcome. *Business Week*, November 20, 129–133.

75. Cavusgil, S. T., Knight, G., and Riesenberger, J. R. (2008). *International Business.* Upper Saddle River, NJ: Pearson Prentice Hall.

76. Strauss, G. (1982). Worker participation in management: An international perspective. *Research in Organizational Behavior*, 4, 173–265.

77. But please see de Macedo-Soares, T. D. L., and Lucas, D. C. (1996). Key quality management practices of leading firms in Brazil: findings of a pilot-study. *The TQM Magazine*, 8, 55–70.

78. Ramsay, H. (1997). Fool's gold? European works councils and workplace democracy. *Industrial Relations Journal*, December, 119–128; Addison, J., Schabel, C., and Wagner, J. (1997). On the determinants of mandatory works councils in Germany. *Industrial Relations*, 43, 392–420.

79. McFarlin, D., Sweeney, P. D., and Cotton, J. L. (1992). Attitudes toward employee participation in decision-making: A comparison of European and American managers in a US multinational company. *Human Resource Management*, 31, 363–383.

80. Stolz, M. (2009). *Works Councils and Labor Relations in Germany.* American Bar Association, available at: www.bna.com/bnabooks/ababna.

81. Wagner, J. (2005). *German Works Councils and Productivity: First Evidence from a Nonparametric Test.* Bonn: IZA, University of Luneburg Working Paper Series in Economics.

82. Cohen, A. (2010). A Dutch formula holds down joblessness. *The Wall Street Journal*, December 28, A10.

83. Sparrow, P., and Hiltrop, J. M. (1994). *European Human Resource Management in Transition.* New York: Prentice-Hall.

84. *The Economist.* (2001). Labor disputes, May 12, 108.

85. Taylor, A. (2009). Europe's strikers more scare in the recession. Time.com, August 10, available at: www.time.com/time/business.

86. Sparrow and Hiltrop, *European Human Resource Management in Transition.*

87. Inohara, H. (1990). *Human Resource Development in Japanese Companies.* Tokyo: Asian Productivity Organization.

88. Poole, M. (1986). *Industrial Relations: Origins and Patterns of National Diversity.* London: Routledge.

89. Takahashi, Y., and Koh, Y. (2013). Toyota shakes up top ranks: The Japanese automaker intends to add outsiders to board for first time. *The Wall Street Journal*, March, 7, B3; Dvorak and Abboud, Difficult upgrade: SAP's plan to globalize hits cultural barriers; software giant's shift irks German engineers, U.S. star quits effort.

Case 4: The Floundering Expatriate

At exactly 1:40 on a warm, sunny Friday afternoon in July 1995, Frank Waterhouse, CEO of Argos Diesel, Europe, leaves his office on the top floor of the Argos Tower, overlooking the Zürichsee. In the grip of a tension headache, he rides the glass elevator down the outside of the mirrored building.

To quiet his nerves, he studies his watch. In less than half an hour, Waterhouse must look on as Bert Donaldson faces the company's European managers—executives of the parts suppliers that Argos has acquired over the past two years. Donaldson is supposed to give the keynote address at this event, part of the second Argos Management Meeting organized by his training and education department. But late yesterday afternoon he phoned Waterhouse to say he didn't think the address would be very good. Donaldson said he hadn't gotten enough feedback from the various division heads to put together the presentation he had planned. His summary of the company's progress wouldn't be what he had hoped.

It's his meeting! Waterhouse thinks as the elevator moves silently down the second floor. How could he not be prepared? Is this really the man who everyone at corporate headquarters in Detroit thinks is so fantastic?

Waterhouse remembers his introduction to Donaldson just over a year ago. Argos International's CEO and chairman, Bill Loun, had phoned Waterhouse himself to say he was sending the "pick of the litter." He said that Donaldson had a great international background—that

he had been a professor of American studies in Cairo for five years. Then he had returned to the States and joined Argos. Donaldson had helped create the cross-divisional, cross-functional teams that had achieved considerable cost reductions and quality improvements.

Loun had said that Donaldson was just what Argos Europe needed to create a seamless European team—to facilitate communication among the different European parts suppliers that Waterhouse had worked so hard to acquire. Waterhouse had proved his own strategic skills, his own ability to close deals, by successfully building a network of companies in Europe under the Argos umbrella. All the pieces were in place. But for the newly expanded company to meet its financial goals, the units had to work together. The managers had to become an integrated team. Donaldson could help them. Together they would keep the company's share of the diesel engine and turbine market on the rise.

Waterhouse deserved to get the best help, the CEO had said. Bert Donaldson was the best. And later, when the numbers proved the plan successful, Waterhouse could return to the States a hero. (Waterhouse heard Loun's voice clearly in his head: "I've got my eye on you, Frank. You know you're in line.")

Waterhouse had been enthusiastic. Donaldson could help him reach the top. He had met the man several times in Detroit. Donaldson seemed to have a quick mind, and he was very charismatic.

But that wasn't the Donaldson who had arrived in Zürich in August 1994 with his wife and two daughters. This man didn't seem to be a team builder—not in this venue. Here his charisma seemed abrasive.

The elevator comes to a stop. Waterhouse steps into the interior of the building and heads toward the seminar room at the end of the hall.

Waterhouse keeps thinking of his own career. He has spent most of his time since Donaldson's appointment securing three major government contracts in Moscow, Ankara, and Warsaw. He has kept the ball rolling, kept his career on track. It isn't his fault that Donaldson can't handle this assignment. It isn't his fault that the Germans and the French still can't agree on a unified sales plan.

His thoughts turn back to Donaldson. It can't be all Bert's fault either. Donaldson is a smart man, a good man. His successes in the States were genuine. And Donaldson is worried about this assignment; it isn't as though he's just being stubborn. He sounded worried on the phone. He cares. He knows his job is falling apart and he doesn't know what to do. What can he return to at Argos in the States if he doesn't excel in Europe?

Let Donaldson run with the ball—that's what they said in Detroit. It isn't working.

Waterhouse reaches the doorway of the seminar room. Ursula Lindt, his executive assistant, spots him from the other side. Lindt is from a wealthy local family. Most of the local hires go to her to discuss their problems. Waterhouse recalls a few of her comments about Donaldson: staff morale on the fifth floor is lower than ever; there seems to be a general malaise; Herr Direktor Donaldson must be having problems at home—why else would he work until midnight?

Waterhouse takes a seat in the front row and tries to distract himself by studying the meeting schedule. "Managing Change and Creating Vision: Improving Argos with Teamwork" is the title. Donaldson's "vision" for Argos Europe. Waterhouse sighs. Lindt nears him and, catching his eye, begins to complain.

"A few of the managers have been making noises about poor organization," she says. "And Sauras, the Spanish director, called to complain that the meeting schedule was too tight." Her litany of problems continues: "Maurizio, the director in Rome, came up to me this morning and began to lobby for Donaldson's replacement. He feels that we need someone with a better understanding of the European environment." Seeing Waterhouse frown, Lindt backs off. "But he's always stirring up trouble," she says. "Otherwise, the conference appears to be a success." She sits down next to Waterhouse and studies her daily planner.

The room slowly fills with whispers and dark hand-tailored suits. Groups break up and reform. "Grüss Gott, Heinz, wie geht's?" "Jacques, ça va bien?" "Bill, good to see you . . . Great." Waterhouse makes a perfunctory inspection of the crowd. Why isn't Donaldson in here schmoozing? He hears a German accent: "Two-ten. Ja ja. Amerikanische Pünktlichkeit." Punctuality. Unlike Donaldson, he knows enough German to get by.

A signal is given. The chitchat fades with the lights. Waterhouse turns his gaze to the front as Donaldson strides up to the podium.

Donaldson speaks. "As President Eisenhower once said, 'I have two kinds of problems, the urgent and the important. The urgent are not important, and the important are never urgent.'" He laughs, but the rest of the room is silent save for the sound of paper shuffling.

Donaldson pauses to straighten his notes and then delivers a flat ten-minute summary of the European companies' organizational structure. He reviews the basics of the team-building plan he has developed—something with which all the listeners are already familiar. He thanks his secretary for her efforts.

Then he turns the meeting over to Waterhouse, who apologizes for not having been able to give the managers any notice that this season would be shorter than planned. He assures them that the rest of the schedule is intact and asks them to take this time as a break before their 4 p.m. logistics meeting, which will be run by the French division head.

The managers exchange glances, and Waterhouse detects one or two undisguised smiles. Walking out of the seminar room, he hears someone say, "At least the meeting didn't run overtime." Waterhouse fumes. He has put in four years of hard work here in Europe. This is the first year of his second three-year contract. He is being groomed for a top management position back in the States. The last thing he needs is a distraction like this.

He remembers how Detroit reacted when, a little over a month ago, he raised the issue of Donaldson's failure to adjust. He had written a careful letter to Bill Loun suggesting that Donaldson's assignment might be over his head, that the timing wasn't right. The CEO had phoned him right away. "That's rubbish, Frank," his voice had boomed over the line. "You've been asking for someone to help make this plan work, and we've sent you the best we've got. You can't send him back. It's your call—you have the bottom-line responsibility. But I'm hoping he'll be part of your inner circle, Frank. I'd give him more time. Make it work. I'm counting on you."

More time is no longer an option, Waterhouse thinks. But if he fires Donaldson now or sends him back to Detroit, he loses whatever progress has been made toward a unified structure. Donaldson has begun to implement a team-building program; if he leaves, the effort will collapse. And how could he fire Donaldson, anyway? The guy isn't working out here, but firing him would destroy his career. Bert doesn't deserve that.

What's more, the European team program has been touted as a major initiative, and Waterhouse has allowed himself to be thought of as one of its drivers. Turning back would reflect badly on him as well.

On the other hand, the way things are going, if Donaldson stays, he may himself cause the plan to fail. One step forward, two steps back. "I don't have the time to walk Donaldson through remedial cultural adjustment," Waterhouse mumbles under his breath.

Donaldson approaches him in the hall. "I sent a multiple choice survey to every manager. One of them sent back a rambling six-page essay," he says. "I sent them in April. I got back only seven of forty from the Germans. Every time I called, it was 'under review.' One of them told me his people wanted to discuss it—in German. The Portuguese would have responded if I'd brought it personally."

Waterhouse tells Donaldson he wants to meet with him later. "Five o'clock. In my office." He turns away abruptly.

Ursula Lindt follows him toward the elevator. "Herr Direktor, did you hear what Herr Donaldson called Frau Schweri?"

Bettina Schweri, who organizes Donaldson's programs, is essentially his manager. She speaks five languages fluently and writes three with style. Lindt and Schweri have known each other since childhood and eat lunch together every day.

"A secretary," Lindt says, exasperated. "Frau Schweri a secretary? Simply not to believe."

Back in his office, Waterhouse gets himself a glass of water and two aspirin. In his mind, he's sitting across from Donaldson ten months earlier.

"Once I reach a goal," Donaldson says, "I set another one and get back to work. I like to have many things going on at once—especially since I have only two years. I'm going for quick results, Frank. I've even got the first project lined up. We'll bring in a couple of trainers from the Consulting Consortium to run that team-skills workshop we talked about."

Waterhouse comes back to the present. That first workshop hadn't gone too badly—at least he hadn't heard of any problems. But he, Waterhouse, had not

attended. He picks up the phone and places a call to Paul Janssen, vice-president of human resources for Argos Europe. Paul is a good friend, a trusted colleague. The two men often cross paths at the health club.

A few seconds later, Janssen's voice booms over the line. "Frank? Why didn't you just walk down the hall to see me? I haven't seen you at the club in weeks."

Waterhouse doesn't want to chat. "Donaldson's first training weekend, in February," he says. "How'd it go? Really."

"Really. Well, overall, not too bad. A few glitches but nothing out of the ordinary for a first run. Bert had some problems with his assistant. Apparently, Frau Schweri had scheduled the two trainers to arrive in Zürich two days early to prepare everything, recover from jet lag, and have dinner at the Baur au Lac. They came the night before. You can imagine how that upset her. Bert knew about the change but didn't inform Frau Schweri."

Waterhouse has the distinct impression that Janssen has been waiting for a chance to talk about this. "Go on," Waterhouse says.

"Well, there were a few problems with the workshops."

"Problems?"

"Well, yes. One of the managers from Norway—Dr. Godal, I believe—asked many questions during Bert's presentation, and he became rather irascible."

"Bert?" Waterhouse asked.

"Yes. And one of the two trainers wore a Mickey Mouse sweater—"

"Mickey Mouse?" Waterhouse laughs without meaning to.

"A sweater with a depiction of Mickey Mouse on the front."

"What on earth does that have to do with Bert?"

"Well, Bert offered them a two-year contract after Frau Schweri advised him not to. He apparently told her he was satisfied with the trainers, and, so far as he was concerned, questions about their personal habits and clothing weren't worth his time."

"Yes, and—"

"Well, there were complaints—"

"They all went to Frau Schweri?" He is beginning to see.

"One of the managers said the trainers provided too much information; he felt as though they were condescending to him. A bombardment of information, he called it. Other managers complained that Bert didn't provide enough background information. The French managers seemed to think the meeting was worthwhile. But Bert must think that, because his style works with one group, the others will fall into place automatically. And everyone was unhappy with the schedule. The trainers always ran overtime, so everybody was displeased because there weren't any coffee breaks for people from various offices to network. Oh, and the last thing? All the name cards had first names and last names—no titles."

"No titles," Waterhouse says, and lets out a sigh. "Paul, I wish you'd told me all this earlier."

"I didn't think you needed to hear it, Frank. You've been busy with the new contracts." They agree to meet at the club later in the week, and they hang up. Waterhouse stares down at Donaldson's file.

His résumé looks perfect. He has a glowing review from the American University in Cairo. There, Donaldson earned the highest ratings for his effectiveness, his ease among students from forty countries, and his sense of humor. At Argos in the United States, he implemented the cross-divisional team approach in record time. Donaldson is nothing short of a miracle worker.

Waterhouse leans back in his swivel-tilter and lets the scuttlebutt on Donaldson run through his mind. Word is that he's an *Arbeitstier*. "Work animal" is the direct, unflattering translation. He never joins the staff for leisurely lunch in the canteen, preferring a sandwich in his office. Word is he can speak some Arabic from his lecturing days in Cairo but still can't manage a decent "good morning" in Swiss German. Word is he walks around all day—he says it's management walking around—asking for suggestions, ideas, plans, or solutions because he can't think of any himself.

Waterhouse remembers an early conversation with Donaldson in which he seemed frustrated. Should he have paid more attention?

"I met with Jakob Hassler, vice-president of human resources as Schwyz Turbines," Donaldson had said, pacing the office. "I wanted some ideas for the training program. Schwyz is the first company we acquired here; I wanted to show Hassler that I don't bite. When I opened the door, he just stood there. I offered him a chair beside the coffee table, told him to call me Bert. He nodded, so I asked him about his family and the best place to buy ski boots, and he answered but he acted so aloof. I took a chair across from him, listened to ten minutes of one-word answers, and then I finally asked him how things were going in general, to which he said, 'Everything is normal.' Can you beat that, Frank? I told him I was interested in his ideas, so he pushed the chair back and said, 'Please let me know what you expect.' I reminded him that we're all on the same team, have only two years for major change, gave him a week to get back to me with a few ideas, and you know what he said? He said, 'Ja ja.'"

At the time, Donaldson's frustration seemed to stem from normal adjustment problems that expatriates face. But he never did adjust. Why doesn't he just give Hassler what he needs to know and get out? Waterhouse knows this; why hasn't Donaldson figured it out?

His phone rings—the inside line. It's Ursula Lindt. "Frau Direktor Donaldson just called. She said Herr Direktor Donaldson was expected home at 4. I told her you had scheduled a meeting with him for 5." She waits. Waterhouse senses that there is more to her message. "What else did she say, Frau Lindt?"

"I inquired after her health and she said she's near the end of her rope. Bored without her work. She said they thought Zürich would be a breeze after Cairo. Then she went into a tirade. She said that they're having serious problems with their eldest daughter. She'll be in grade 12 at the international school this fall. She's applying to college. Frau Donaldson said her daughter's recommendations from her British teachers are so understated that they'd keep her out of top schools, and she keeps getting Cs because they're using the British grading scale. She reminded me that this is a girl

with a combined SAT score of over 1350."

Lindt is done. Waterhouse thanks her for the information, then hangs up. Julie Ann is usually calm, collected. She has made some friends here. Something must have pushed her over the edge. And their daughter is engaging, bright. Why is this all coming to a head now?

Waterhouse recalls his most recent meeting with Donaldson, a couple of days before Donaldson's vacation in May.

"I've tried everything, Frank. I've delegated, I've let them lead, I've given them pep talks." Waterhouse remembers Donaldson sinking deep into his chair, his voice flat. "No matter what I do—if I change an agenda, if I ask them to have a sandwich with me at my desk—someone's always pissed off. We're talking about streamlining an entire European company and they're constantly looking at their watches. We run ten minutes overtime in a meeting and they're shuffling papers. I tell you, Frank, they're just going to have to join the rest of us in the postindustrial age, learn to do things the Argos way. I worked wonders in Detroit . . ."

The clock in Waterhouse's office reads 4:45. What can he do about Donaldson? Let him blunder along for another year? And take another twelve months of . . . he closes the door on that thought. Send him back and forget? Morale on the fifth floor will improve, the Europeans will be appeased, but with Donaldson will go the training program, such as it is. Corporate will just think that Waterhouse has forgotten how to play the American way. They'll think that he mistreated their star. Can he teach Donaldson cultural awareness? With the Ankara, Moscow, and Warsaw projects chewing up all his time? You can't teach cultural savvy. No way.

He hears Donaldson enter the outer office. A hanger clicks on the coat tree. How can he work this out?

Assignment Questions

1. Assess the mistakes Donaldson has made. Why have these occurred? Whose responsibility are they? What are the implications of not satisfactorily dealing with the Donaldson problem?

2. What should Waterhouse do with Donaldson? Be specific and develop an action plan.

3. What could the company have done to better prepare Donaldson?

4. What does this case suggest about the company's current policy for recruiting and preparing expatriates? Make policy suggestions.

Name Index

Note: Page numbers with *f* indicate figures.

Subject Index